Sunday Mayhem

A Celebration of Pro Football in America

John Walter

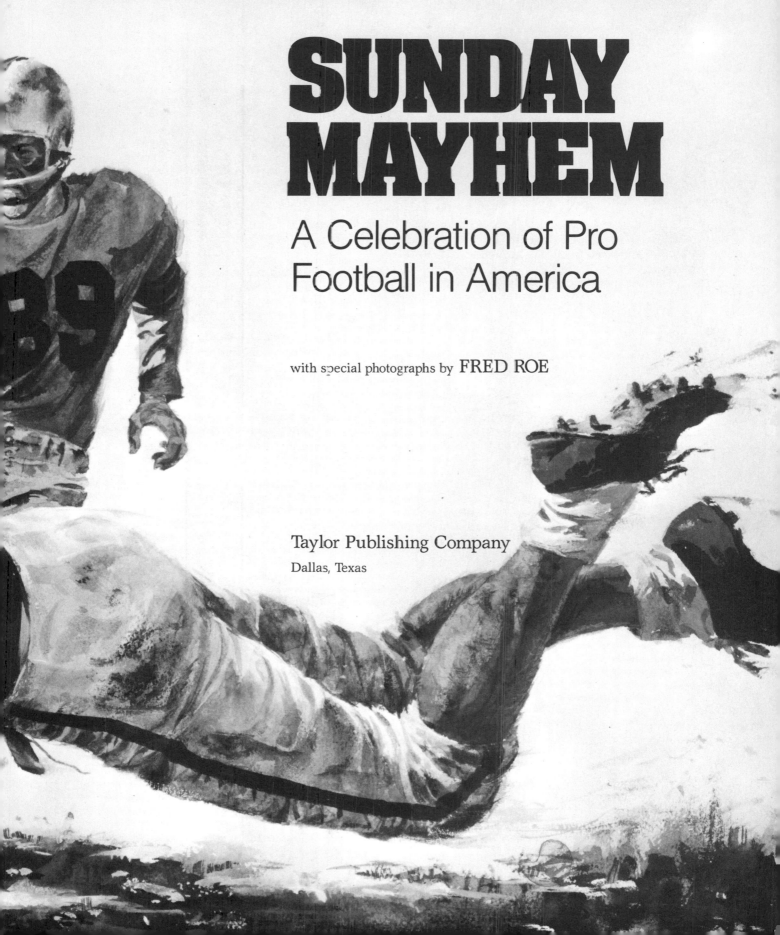

Richard Whittingham

SUNDAY MAYHEM

A Celebration of Pro Football in America

with special photographs by FRED ROE

Taylor Publishing Company

Dallas, Texas

Library of Congress Cataloging-in-Publication Data

Whittingham, Richard.
    Sunday mayhem : a celebration of pro football in America /
Richard Whittingham.
        p.   cm.
    Includes index.
    ISBN 0-87833-548-X : $12.95
    1. Football—United States—History.   I. Title.
GV950.W48 1987
796.332'0973--dc19   87-17902
                                                      CIP

Acknowledgements

The author and publisher would like to express their
grateful appreciation to the National Football League,
Department of Public Relations, especially its director
Jim Heffernan; the Pro Football Hall of Fame in Canton, Ohio, especially curator and archivist Joe Horrigan; and the public relations departments of the 28
NFL teams.

Special thanks are also extended to Fred Roe for
the use of his many exceptional photographs, John
Walter for the use of his painting on the title page
spread, and the late Charles A. Whittingham, Sr., who
penned the illustration on the opening page of this
book back in 1921 when the NFL was but a year old.

Book and Cover Design: Willis Proudfoot, Robert Amft

Cover Photo: Fred Roe

Also by Richard Whittingham

The New York Giants, An Illustrated History
What a Game They Played
LIFE in Sports
Saturday Afternoon
The Chicago Bears, An Illustrated History
The Dallas Cowboys, An Illustrated History
The Los Angeles Dodgers, An Illustrated History
The Final Four
The Rand McNally Almanac of Adventure
Joe D, On the Street with a Chicago Homicide Cop
*Martial Justice, The Last Mass Execution in the United
    States*

Contents

Massillon Morning Gleaner

THE GLEANER RECEIVES THE PUBLISHER'S PRESS WIRE AND CABLE SERVICE OF FROM EIGHT TO TEN THOUS

VOL. V. NO. 139.   MASSILLON, MOHIO, ONDAY MORNING, NOVEMBER 26, 1906.

THE WEATHER.

Washington, Nov. 25—Ohio.—
rain Monday; Tuesday rain or
snow; colder; fresh brisk south
winds.

THEIR HONOR INV

THE FAMOUS MASSILLON TIGERS OF 1906
COULD NOT BE BOUGHT OFF WITH A PRICE

Details of a Plot to Disrupt and Corrupt the Tiger Team and Management Which Failed.----$5,000 In Cash and a "Sure Thing" in a $50,000 Betting Pool Offered But Never Considered.

With the conclusion of the series of games between Canton and Massillon for the world's championship foot ball honors, the time has now arrived to make clear some peculiar and unpleasant conditions which have surrounded the Tigers, coach and management, during the entire season.

Many Massillon fans were surprised at the discharge of Walter R. East, who during the early season, played end on the Tiger team, inasmuch as East had shown wonderful abilities in his position.

The reasons for East's discharge by any of the other players, or players approached, were indignant that East or any one else should make them such a proposition.

They immediately commenced the necessary action to trap East and learn if possible the names of his accomplices and the method by which he proposed to "fix" the games.

East then made his great mistake. He had the nerve and audacity to approach the coach with the same general proposal in an effort to win him

that they tried to bribe the Tigers and failed in their attempt, they can recover their money. Otherwise the Cleveland bank is at liberty to hold it as long as they like.

Second Game.

On the return of the Massillon team to Massillon, after their defeat at the hands of the Canton team, or more properly speaking, Wallace and East, the loyal supporters of the team were discouraged, as they knew that something was wrong. The coach and manager and players were not discouraged. They knew that crooked work had cost them their first defeat in four years.

In the meantime the entire proposition had been opened up to half of a dozen of Massillon's most reputable business men, who agreed, with the coach and management that Wallace and East could not "turn the trick" a second time.

In the first game it was apparent to every spectator, player and official of the game that Maxwell, Shiring and Lamson completely outplayed their opponents, Kerckhoff, Sweet and

WHITE CAPS

Lafayette, La., Nov. 25.—200 white caps, masked, and armed with shot guns and pistols, created a reign of terror, last night, at Maremore near here, brutally murdering Antone Domingue, a peaceable negro, after robbing the man of his horse and buggy. They also held up a second other negroes.

The town was at the mercy of the band throughout the night. Domingue was stopped in the road while going home, and on resisting the white caps was beaten. He defied his team to go home and secure his revolver. On his return he was met with a volley from the whites, his body being riddled with shot. White caps got away before the police this place arrived.

LANDSLIDE

Berne, S
landslides o

BALCONY FELL

KILLING ONE WOMAN AND INJURING MANY MORE WOMEN AND CHILDREN.

Newark, N. J., Nov. 25.—One woman was killed and a score or more women and children injured by the collapse of the lobby of New Century Hall here tonight. Several hundred people congregated at the hall to attend a Yiddish vaudeville benefit performance and the accident was caused by the overcrowding of the vestibule. The balcony was fifteen feet square and about 75 people packed into the small space, while more than 200 were standing on the steps. Mrs. Rebecca Schwartz was killed. The injured were taken to a hospital. Nine of them were fatally hurt.

TROLLEY FATALITL

Pittsfield, Mass., Nov. 25.—One passenger was killed and seven others injured, one fatally, as the result of a trolley car of the Pittsfield street railway company, overturning today. The

Pre-Pro Mayhem

—At Least As We Know It NFL Style

*"Sunday afternoon or Saturday afternoon
in the football season is the only time of year
a man can walk down the street with a blonde
on one arm and a blanket on the other
without encountering raised eyebrows."*

—ANONYMOUS

Football mayhem in the United States got its start back in 1869, on a somewhat organized level anyway. That was the year that Princeton threw down a challenge to Rutgers to a soccer-style game, and the two collegiate squads queued up on a windy November afternoon in New Brunswick, New Jersey and did battle until Rutgers won it 6–4.

The fast-paced game fused over the next few decades with the much more rugged game of rugby and American football emerged, with fatherly figures like Walter Camp, Amos Alonzo Stagg, Pop Warner, and John Heisman shaping and guiding it into a popular sport.

By 1892, money crept in. The Allegheny Athletic Association of Pennsylvania paid William "Pudge" Heffelfinger, an All-American guard from Yale $500 to play for them against the arch-rival Pittsburgh Athletic Club, making him the first known professional football player.

Four years later, the same Allegheny Athletic

The Canton Bulldog and the Massillon Tiger Will Soon be Face to Fac

The first and a foremost pro football rivalry.

Action from a meeting between the Canton Bulldogs and the Columbus Panhandles in 1914. The Canton ballcarrier is identified only as "Schreiner." Ohio was truly the cradle of professional football in America. (Pro Football Hall of Fame)

Association fielded the first team made up entirely of players who were being paid for their services—which were not many because they only played two games that year.

In 1899, a man by the name of Chris O'Brien organized a neighborhood football team on the south side of Chicago, which played under the name of the Morgan Athletic Club. As pro football took shape in the midwest, the club changed its name to the Normals, then the Racine Cardinals (Racine was a street in Chicago near where they played, not the city in Wisconsin), finally the Chicago Cardinals, and eventually the St. Louis Cardinals, making it the oldest continuing pro football organization in history.

In the early 20th Century, pro football prospered most, however, in Ohio. Canton, Massilon, Akron, Columbus, these were the towns that took it seriously. The first truly legitimate pro football rivalry in fact was that staged in the heated football wars between the teams from Canton and Massilon, a prelude of what was to come over the next seven or eight decades.

Interest in professional football spread, gradually and painstakingly, to cities in Pennsylvania, Indiana, Illinois, and a few other nearby states until it became a reality in 1920 at that now famous meeting at Ralph Hay's Hupmobile Agency in Canton, Ohio, which launched what was to become one of America's greatest sports legacies, the National Football League.

(overleaf) ▶
Little Joey Sternaman, only 5'10" and 150 pounds, takes off around end for the Chicago Bears in the 1924 game at Cubs Park against the crosstown rival Chicago Cardinals.

1 THE YOUTHFUL YEARS

Jim Thorpe

The 1920s

The first decade of the National Football League had in its spotlight such luminaries as Jim Thorpe, Red Grange, Ernie Nevers, George Halas, Paddy Driscoll, and Guy Chamberlin. Only four franchises that exist today, however, played in the 1920s: the Cardinals, who were then in Chicago, the Bears, the Packers, and the Giants. Other noteworthy teams that played top-notch football during the decade were the Canton Bulldogs, Frankford Yellow Jackets, Pottsville Maroons, and the Providence Steam Roller.

The football was much rounder in the 1920s than the one used today, the crowds at a game much sparser (5,000 was not a bad draw). The program cost a dime and admission usually not more than two or three dollars for a 50-yard line seat. It was an era when players often eschewed helmets, field goals were frequently drop-kicked, and passing the football was a rarity (except for Benny Friedman, the first truly accomplished passer in the game).

The age of flappers and the Charleston, bootleg whiskey and speakeasies was also the youth of professional football in America.

A begrimed Canton Bulldog models the uniform of the day. The year is 1922 and the player is tackle Link Lyman who would later play for the Frankford Yellow Jackets and the Chicago Bears and earn his way into the Pro Football Hall of Fame.

The Best of the Decade / 1920s

FIRST TEAM

Position	Player	Team
E	Guy Chamberlin	various teams
E	George Halas	Chicago Bears
T	Pete Henry	Canton Bulldogs
T	Ed Healey	Chicago Bears
G	Walt Kiesling	various teams
G	Swede Youngstrom	Buffalo Bisons
C	George Trafton	Chicago Bears
QB	Benny Friedman	Detroit Panthers
RB	Jim Thorpe	various teams
RB	Red Grange	Chicago Bears
RB	Ernie Nevers	Duluth Eskimos/Chicago Cardinals
K	Paddy Driscoll	Chicago Cardinals
P	Pete Henry	Canton Bulldogs
coach	*Guy Chamberlin*	*various teams*

SECOND TEAM

Position	Player	Team
E	Eddie Anderson	Chicago Cardinals
E	Lavie Dilweg	Green Bay Packers
T	Link Lyman	various teams
T	Duke Slater	Chicago Cardinals
G	Al Nesser	Akron Pros/New York Giants
G	Hunk Anderson	Chicago Bears
C	Jug Earpe	Green Bay Packers
QB	Paddy Driscoll	Chicago Cardinals
RB	Jimmy Conzelman	various teams
RB	Verne Lewellen	Green Bay Packers
RB	Joe Guyon	various teams
K	Joey Sternaman	Chicago Bears
P	Jim Thorpe	various teams
coach	*George Halas*	*Chicago Bears*

The toughest of the early Staleys/ Bears, center George Trafton was inducted into the Pro Football Hall of Fame in 1964.

Events and Milestones

The charter New York Giants of 1925. In the backfield (left to right): Dutch Hendrian, Jim Thorpe, Jack McBride, Hinkey Haines; on the line, Lynn Bomar, Century Milstead, Ed McGinley, Doc Alexander, Joe Williams, Art Carney, Paul Jappe.

The American Professional Football Association (APFA), the first professional football league, is formed at a meeting at Ralph Hay's Hupmobile Agency in Canton, Ohio, with representatives of pro teams from 10 cities in attendance (Akron, Canton, Cleveland, and Dayton, Ohio; Chicago, Decatur, and Rock Island, Illinois; Hammond and Muncie, Indiana; Rochester, New York). Jim Thorpe, player/coach of the Canton Bulldogs is named the league's first president. **(1920)**

Joe Carr, manager of the Columbus Panhandles, is named to replace Jim Thorpe as president of the APFA, a position he would hold until his death in 1939. **(1921)**

Joe Carr

An APFA franchise is awarded to John E. Clair of the Acme Packing Company of Green Bay, Wisconsin, for the Packers, a team coached and managed by its star tailback Curly Lambeau. **(1921)**

The Decatur Staleys, under co-owners George Halas and Dutch Sternaman, are moved to Chicago **(1921)**, and change their nickname to Bears. **(1922)**

The APFA formally changes its name to the National Football League (NFL). **(1922)**

Tex Hamer of the Frankford Yellow Jackets sets a single season record with 12 touchdowns rushing. Previously, no player had scored more than 7. **(1924)**

An NFL franchise is purchased by Tim Mara for New York City, and he names his new team the Giants. **(1925)**

On Thanksgiving Day, Red Grange, five days after playing his final college football game, makes his professional debut with the Chicago Bears against their crosstown rivals the Cardinals, a game that ended in a scoreless tie. **(1925)**

Charlie Berry of the Pottsville Maroons sets the standard for PATs, kicking 29 of 34, exceeding the 26 of 31 booted in 1923 by Pete Henry of the Canton Bulldogs. **(1925)**

The Chicago Bears, showcasing Red Grange, stage two postseason barnstorming tours, the first consisting of eight games in seven different cities in an 11-day period, the second involving nine cities ranging from Florida to the west coast over a five-week period. **(1925–26)**

Ernie Nevers

The first American Football League (AFL) is formed as a result of the efforts of C. C. Pyle, agent for Red Grange, who could not come to terms with the Bears in regard to a contract for Grange. Pyle organizes the new league, holds the New York franchise for Grange and himself, and goes into direct competition with the NFL. **(1926)**

Paddy Driscoll of the Chicago Bears establishes two NFL standards: total points scored in a season, 86, 8 more than the previous high he had attained as a Chicago Cardinal in 1923; and most field goals, 12, 2 more than the mark he had set also in 1923. **(1926)**

The AFL folds. **(1927)**

The NFL, experiencing widespread financial difficulties, goes from a 22-team league to one of a mere 12 teams. Leaving the fold are such teams as the Akron Pros, Brooklyn Lions, Canton Bulldogs, Columbus Tigers, Hammond Pros, Hartford Blues, Kansas City Cowboys, Los Angeles Buccaneers, Louisville Colonels, Milwaukee Badgers, and

Racine Tornadoes. The New York Yankees with Red Grange are the only franchise from the AFL to be incorporated into the NFL; and to round out the league the Buffalo Rangers become the Buffalo Bisons. **(1927)**

Benny Friedman of the New York Giants breaks his own record of 13 touchdown passes in a season (1927 as a Cleveland Bulldog) by throwing 19. **(1929)**

Ray Flaherty of the New York Giants sets a new standard of 8 touchdown receptions, eclipsing the mark of 7 registered the year before by Gibby Welch of the New York Yankees. **(1929)**

Ernie Nevers of the Chicago Cardinals ties Tex Hamer's record of 12 touchdowns rushing. **(1929)**

The number of officials for professional football games is increased to four, adding a field judge to the corps that previously fielded only a referee, umpire, and head linesman. **(1929)**

The Packers take on the St. Louis All-Stars in Green Bay in 1923. The ballhandler at far left is tailback coach Curly Lambeau of the Packers. (Pro Football Hall of Fame)

Thorpe's Indians

Jim Thorpe organized, coached and played for an NFL team alternately known as Thorpe's Indians and the Oorang Indians in 1922 and 1923. The team, which played its home games in Marion, Ohio, was owned by a man whose other business pursuit was the Oorang Kennels (oorang is a breed of dog in the terrier family) and who wanted to keep the team name, so to speak, in the family. This was the starting lineup for the Indians in 1923, taken from the program for their game that year with the Chicago Bears.

Other names that were included on the Oorang Indian roster were these:

Baptiste Thunder	**Red Fang**
Bobalash	**Reggie Attache**
Buffalo Newashe	**Stillwell Sanooke**
Deadeye Mason	**Xavier Downwind**
Laughing Gas	

The Oorangians went out of business after the 1923 season, having racked up records of only 2-6 and 1-10, despite having such illustrious football players as Thorpe, Joe Guyon, and Pete Calac.

THORPE'S INDIANS

No.	Name	Position	College	Tribe
5	LITTLE TWIG	L. E.	CARLISLE	Mohawk
18	BUFFALO	L. T.	HASKELL	Chippewa
30	GRAY HORSE	L. G.	CARLISLE	Chippewa
7	LONG TIME SLEEP	C.	CARLISLE	Flat Head
22	LONE WOLF	R. G.	CARLISLE	Chippewa
26	BIG BEAR	R. T.	CARLISLE	Chippewa
16	RUNNING DEER	R. E.	HASKELL	Chippewa
11	RED FOX	Q. B.	HASKELL	Cheerokee
1	JIM THORPE	L. H.	CARLISLE	Sac and Fox
12	TOMAHAWK	R. H.	MIAMI	Wyandotte
6	PETE CALAC	F. B.	CARLISLE	California
—	WOODCHUCK	END	MIAMI	Chippewa
28	JACK THORPE	BACK	CARLISLE	Sac and Fox
11	RED FOX	BACK	HASKELL	Cheerokee
32	EAGLE FEATHER	BACK	CARLISLE	Mohican
8	LU BOUTWELL	GUARD	CARLISLE	Chippewa

	1st	2nd	3rd	4th
CHICAGO				
INDIANS				

CHICAGO VS.
AKRON

SUNDAY, NOV. 11, AT 2:15 P. M.

The Original NFL, 1920

Akron Pros
Buffalo All-Americans
Canton Bulldogs
Chicago Cardinals
Chicago Tigers
Cleveland Tigers
Columbus Panhandles
Dayton Triangles
Decatur Staleys
Detroit Heralds
Hammond Pros
Muncie Flyers
Rock Island Independents
Rochester Jeffersons

The first title went to the Akron Pros, posting a record of 6–0–3, a game better than the 5–1–3 record of George Halas's Decatur Staleys. The title was decided on the last game of the season when Akron, coached by its star tailback Fritz Pollard, played to a 0–0 tie with the Staleys, a team that had, besides Halas, such future Hall of Famers on its roster as Guy Chamberlin, Jimmy Conzelman, and George Trafton. For the Akron game, Decatur also had Hall of Fame bound Paddy Driscoll, whom Halas brought over from the Chicago Cardinals for the occasion—that action going down in history as the first major league rule to be broken in the new NFL.

The Muncie Flyers and the Rochester Jeffersons played and lost only one game each that year, but both would be back for the 1921 season.

Pete "Fats" Henry, ordinarily a lineman, is the ballcarrier for the Canton Bulldogs here. Leaping behind him is helmetless Guy Chamberlin, both destined for enshrinement in the Pro Football Hall of Fame.

Pete Henry

Player / Coaches

In the 1920s and the early 30s it was not uncommon for players to serve as head coaches as well. The most famous to take such dual responsibilities:

PLAYER/COACH	POSITION	TEAM(S)
Guy Chamberlin	End	Canton Bulldogs, Frankford Yellow Jackets, Chicago Cardinals
Jimmy Conzelman	Halfback	Rock Island Independents, Milwaukee Badgers, Detroit Panthers, Providence Steam Roller
Paddy Driscoll	Tailback	Chicago Cardinals
Benny Friedman	Tailback	Brooklyn Dodgers
George Halas	End	Decatur Staleys, Chicago Bears
Pete Henry	Tackle	Canton Bulldogs, Pottsville Maroons
Curly Lambeau	Tailback	Green Bay Packers
Ernie Nevers	Fullback	Duluth Eskimos, Chicago Cardinals
Steve Owen	Tackle	New York Giants
Fritz Pollard	Tailback	Akron Pros, Milwaukee Badgers
Jim Thorpe	Tailback	Canton Bulldogs, Cleveland Indians, Oorang Indians

George Halas

Guy Chamberlin

Curly Lambeau

C. C. Pyle's American Football League

Cash and Carry Pyle, as he was dubbed by a sportswriter of the time, launched the first challenge to the National Football League when he organized a new league after the NFL refused to grant him a franchise to play at Yankee Stadium in New York. His American Football League (AFL) awarded franchises in eight cities. Along with his prize client, Red Grange, Pyle maintained the New York City franchise.

The AFL of 1926:

Boston Bulldogs
Brooklyn Horsemen
Chicago Bulls
Cleveland Panthers
Los Angeles Wildcats
New York Yankees
Newark Bears
Philadelphia Quakers
Rock Island Independents

The teams played different numbers of games, the Yankees the most with 14 and Brooklyn the least with four. The Philadelphia Quakers posted the best record, 7–2, with the Yankees and Red Grange coming in second at 9–5. After its economically disastrous first season the AFL went out of business; but Pyle's Yankees were absorbed into the NFL where they remained for two years before finally going out of business.

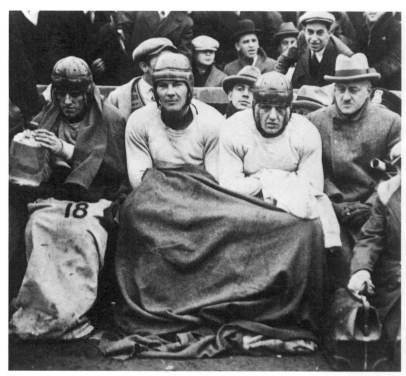

On the sideline for the Chicago Bears, 1925, is Red Grange (second from right) with his agent Cash and Carry Pyle at his left shoulder. At far left, getting ready for a slug of cold water, is Bears' owner/coach/end George Halas.

The Champions / 1920s

1920	Akron Pros	6–0–3
1921	Chicago Staleys	9–1–1
1922	Canton Bulldogs	10–0–2
1923	Canton Bulldogs	11–0–1
1924	Cleveland Bulldogs	7–1–1
1925	Chicago Cardinals	11–2–1
1926	Frankford Yellow Jackets	14–1–1
1927	New York Giants	11–1–1
1928	Providence Steam Roller	8–1–2
1929	Green Bay Packers	12–0–1

The League Leaders / 1920s

1920

Scoring	Frank Bacon, Dayton Triangles, 32 points
Rushing	Pat Smith, Buffalo All Americans, 4 TDs
Passing	Al Manrt, Dayton Triangles, 7 TDs
Receiving	Norb Sacksteder, Dayton Triangles, 3 TDs
	Dave Reese, Dayton Triangles, 3 TDs
Field Goals	Jim Thorpe, Canton Bulldogs, 3
	Jim Laird, Rochester Jeffersons, 3
PATs	Charlie Copley, Akron Pros 12
	George Kinderdine, Dayton Triangles, 12

1921

Scoring	Fritz Pollard, Akron Pros, 42 points
Rushing	Fritz Pollard, Akron Pros, 7 TDs
Passing	Frank Nesser, Columbus Panhandles, 3 TDs
Receiving	George Halas, Chicago Staleys, 3 TDs
Field Goals	Dutch Sternaman, Chicago Staleys, 5
PATs	Elmer Oliphant, Buffalo All Americans, 19

1922

Scoring	Hank Gillo, Racine Legion, 53 points
Rushing	Jimmy Conzelman, Rock Island Independents and Milwaukee Badgers, 7 TDs
Passing	Jimmy Conzelman, Rock Island Independents and Milwaukee Badgers, 3 TDs
	Tommy Hughitt, Buffalo All Americans, 3 TDs
Receiving	several with 2 TDs
Field Goals	Paddy Driscoll, Chicago Cardinals, 8
PATs	Russ Hathaway, Dayton Triangles, 9

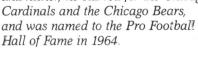

*Paddy Driscoll, one of the first of the
great triple threats. A runner, passer,
and kicker, he starred for the Chicago
Cardinals and the Chicago Bears,
and was named to the Pro Football
Hall of Fame in 1964.*

1923

Scoring	Paddy Driscoll, Chicago Cardinals, 78 points
Rushing	Lou Smythe, Canton Bulldogs, 7 TDs
Passing	Lou Smythe, Canton Bulldogs, 6 TDs
Receiving	Goldie Rapp, Columbus Tigers, 3 TDs
Field Goals	Paddy Driscoll, Chicago Cardinals, 12
PATs	Pete Henry, Canton Bulldogs, 26

1924

Scoring	Joey Sternaman, Chicago Bears, 75 points
Rushing	Tex Hamer, Frankford Yellow Jackets, 12 TDs
Passing	Hoge Workman, Cleveland Bulldogs, 9 TDs
Receiving	Goldie Rapp, Columbus Tigers, 5 TDs
	Tillie Voss, Green Bay Packers, 5 TDs
Field Goals	Joey Sternaman, Chicago Bears, 9
PATs	Jim Welsh, Frankford Yellow Jackets, 17

1925

Scoring	Charlie Berry, Pottsville Maroons, 74 points
Rushing	Tony Latone, Pottsville Maroons, 8 TDs
Passing	Red Dunn, Chicago Cardinals, 9 TDs
Receiving	several with 4 TDs
Field Goals	Paddy Driscoll, Chicago Cardinals, 11
PATs	Charlie Berry, Pottsville Maroons, 29

1926

Scoring	Paddy Driscoll, Chicago Bears, 86 points
Rushing	Barney Wentz, Pottsville Maroons, 10 TDs
Passing	Paddy Driscoll, Chicago Bears, 6 TDs
Receiving	Duke Hanny, Chicago Bears, 3 TDs
Field Goals	Paddy Driscoll, Chicago Bears, 12
PATs	Jack McBride, New York Giants, 15
	Jim Welsh, Pottsville, Maroons, 15

1927

Scoring	Jack McBride, New York Giants, 57 points
Rushing	Jack McBride, New York Giants, 6 TDs
Passing	Benny Friedman, Cleveland Bulldogs, 13 TDs
Receiving	Hinkey Haines, New York Giants, 4 TDs
	Ray Flaherty, New York Yankees, 4 TDs
Field Goals	Ken Mercer, Frankford Yellow Jackets, 5
PATs	Jack McBride, New York Giants, 15

The great Galloping Ghost, Red Grange, put pro football on the proverbial map in 1925 when he and the Chicago Bears barnstormed the country.

Jimmy Conzelman

1928

Scoring	Verne Lewellen, Green Bay Packers, 54 points
Rushing	Verne Lewellen, Green Bay Packers, 7 TDs
Passing	Benny Friedman, Detroit Wolverines, 11 TDs
Receiving	Gibby Welch, New York Yankees, 7 TDs
Field Goals	Harry O'Boyle, Green Bay Packers, 2
PATs	Benny Friedman, Detroit Wolverines, 19

1929

Scoring	Ernie Nevers, Chicago Cardinals, 85 points
Rushing	Ernie Nevers, Chicago Cardinals, 12 TDs
Passing	Benny Friedman, New York Giants, 19 TDs
Receiving	Ray Flaherty, New York Giants, 8 TDs
Field Goals	several with 2
PATs	Benny Friedman, New York Giants, 20

Brooklyn Dodgers' stars: Benny Friedman (right) and Cliff Montgomery

Price **10** cents

N. Y. FOOTBALL GIANTS
• vs •
GREEN BAY PACKERS

HARRY NEWMAN
All-League Quarterback

New York Football Giants

POLO GROUNDS
Sunday, November 11, 1934

The 1930s

The Great Depression shrouded the United States in a grim and glum decade, but professional football managed to muddle through it. The teams and the players were not making much money but they stayed in business and offered the public some very exciting, high-caliber football as a diversion from the nation's collective economic woes.

In the early years of the decade the NFL began keeping records and statistics on a formal basis. All-Pro players were honored and championship games were instituted. The Redskins joined the league but they were up in Boston when they did, and the city of Pittsburgh got a franchise but they called themselves the Pirates then. Detroit, Philadelphia, and Cleveland introduced teams into the NFL. A plethora of new rules were infused into the game. The ball got slimmer, the backs started throwing it much more frequently, the drop kick disappeared. But nonetheless, the players still had to play sixty grueling minutes.

The Green Bay Packers proved to be the *crème de la crème* of the decade, winning titles at each end and turning out marvelous teams throughout it. They had such spectacular players as Johnny Blood McNally and Don Hutson. At the same time, the Bears had Bronko Nagurski, the Lions Dutch Clark, and the Giants Ken Strong.

It was a time of growth and maturation for pro football—before it would have to go to war.

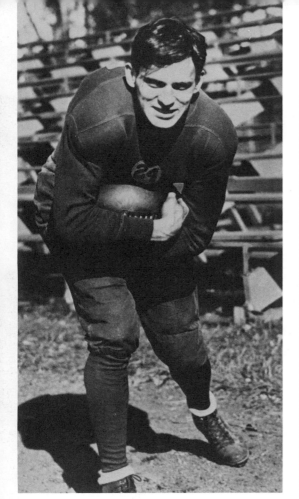

Johnny Blood McNally entered the Pro Football Hall of Fame as a charter member in 1963.

The Best of the Decade / 1930s

FIRST TEAM

Position	Player	Team
E	Don Hutson	Green Bay Packers
E	Bill Hewitt	Chicago Bears
T	Joe Stydahar	Chicago Bears
T	Cal Hubbard	Green Bay Packers
G	Danny Fortmann	Chicago Bears
G	Iron Mike Michalske	Green Bay Packers
C	Mel Hein	New York Giants
QB	Dutch Clark	Detroit Lions
RB	Johnny Blood McNally	Green Bay Packers
RB	Clarke Hinkle	Green Bay Packers
RB	Bronko Nagurski	Chicago Bears
K	Jack Manders	Chicago Bears
P	Ken Strong	New York Giants
coach	*Curly Lambeau*	*Green Bay Packers*

SECOND TEAM

Position	Player	Team
E	Red Badgro	New York Giants
E	Ray Flaherty	New York Giants
T	Turk Edwards	Boston Redskins
T	George Musso	Chicago Bears
G	Ox Emerson	Portsmouth Spartans/Detroit Lions
G	Joe Kopcha	Chicago Bears
C	Nate Barager	Green Bay Packers
QB	Arnie Herber	Green Bay Packers
RB	Tuffy Leemans	New York Giants
RB	Cliff Battles	Boston Redskins
RB	Clarke Hinkle	Green Bay Packers
K	Dutch Clark	Detroit Lions
P	Ralph Kercheval	Brooklyn Dodgers
coach	*Steve Owen*	*New York Giants*

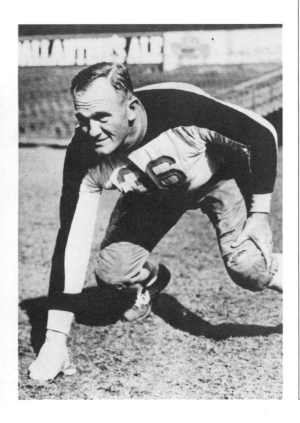

Cal Hubbard, the only man to be inducted into both the Pro Football Hall of Fame and major league baseball's Hall of Fame (as an umpire).

Events and Milestones

The Portsmouth (Ohio) Spartans, who later would evolve into the Detroit Lions, are founded, with Potsy Clark hired as their first head coach. **(1930)**

The Green Bay Packers, coached by Curly Lambeau and paced by future Hall of Famers Johnny Blood McNally, Cal Hubbard, and Iron Mike Michalske, become the first team to win three consecutive NFL titles. **(1931)**

The first All-Pro team is selected. **(1931)**

Boston is granted an NFL franchise, the Braves, owned by a syndicate headed by George Preston Marshall, coached by Lud Wray, and showcasing future Hall of Famers Cliff Battles and Turk Edwards. The name would be changed to Redskins the next year. **(1932)**

The NFL shrinks to eight teams, representing only five cities: Chicago (Bears and Cardinals), New York (Giants, Brooklyn Dodgers, and Staten Island Stapletons), Green Bay (Packers), Portsmouth (Spartans), and Boston (Braves). **(1932)**

Johnny Blood McNally of the Green Bay Packers breaks the record for touchdown receptions in a season, catching 9, one more than Ray Flaherty of the New York Giants caught in 1929. **(1932)**

A franchise is awarded to Bert Bell and Lud Wray for the Philadelphia Eagles. **(1933)**

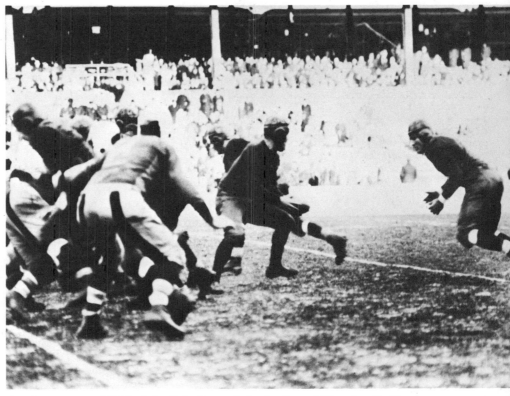

On the ice-coated field of the Polo Grounds in the famed "Sneakers" title tilt of 1934, Bronko Nagurski takes a pitchout, which was called a shuffle pass in those days, from Carl Brumbaugh. But he and the rest of the Bears did not have sneakers that day while the Giants did, at least in the second half, which is why they won 30–13.

Pittsburgh gets an NFL team, named the Pirates by owner Art Rooney. The name would not be changed to Steelers until 1941. **(1933)**

The NFL is reformed into two divisions, the East and the West, each having five teams, the winners of which are slated to meet in a championship game at the end of the season. **(1933)**

Major rules changes are instituted at the prompting of Bears owner George Halas and Redskins owner George Preston Marshall. Among them:
- Goal posts are moved from the end lines to the goal lines.
- Hashmarks are introduced and located 10 yards inbounds from each sideline where the ball would be put in play if it ended up within five yards of a sideline. **(1933)**

Statistics are kept officially for the first time. **(1933)**

The first College All-Star Game is staged at Soldier Field in Chicago, with the Bears and the former collegians playing to a scoreless tie before more than 79,000 spectators. **(1934)**

New rules:
- A forward pass can be thrown from anywhere behind the line of scrimmage.
- A penalty against the defense occurring within 10 yards of its goal line is assessed at half the distance to the goal.
- A runner who falls or is knocked down can get up and advance the ball; he must be held to the ground until the play is whistled dead. **(1934)**

The Portsmouth Spartans are moved to Detroit and renamed the Lions. **(1934)**

Rookie Beattie Feathers of the Chicago Bears gains 1,004 yards rushing to become the first player to rush for more than 1,000 yards in a season, and his average of 9.9 yards per carry remains to this day an NFL record. (**1934**)

Jack Manders of the Bears sets a new PAT standard by booting 31 of 32 extra points. (**1934**)

The hashmarks are moved from 10 to 15 yards in from the sidelines. (**1935**)

The first draft of college players is held. (**1936**)

The player limit for a team is raised from 20 to 25. (**1936**)

Another American Football League (AFL) is formed with franchises in six cities: Boston, Brooklyn, Cleveland, New York, Pittsburgh, and Rochester (NY). (**1936**)

Arnie Herber of the Green Bay Packers becomes the first player to pass for more than 1,000 yards in a single season, gaining a total of 1,239. (**1936**)

Don Hutson of the Packers sets two pass catching records when he snares 34 passes for a total of 526 yards. (**1936**)

George Preston Marshall moves his Redskins from Boston to Washington, D.C. (**1937**)

The Cleveland Rams, owned by Homer Marshman and coached by Hugo Bezdek, join the NFL. (**1937**)

The second AFL goes out of business. (**1937**)

The player limit for a team is increased to 30. (**1938**)

A new penalty is introduced: 15 yards for roughing the passer. (**1938**)

Don Hutson ties the record of 9 touchdown receptions in a season set six years earlier by fellow Packer Johnny Blood McNally. (**1938**)

The first Pro Bowl game is played January 15, 1939, at Wrigley Field in Los Angeles where an estimated crowd of 20,000 watches the New York Giants defeat the Pro All-Stars 13–10. (**1939**)

Carl Storck becomes the new NFL president after the death of Joe Carr. (**1939**)

The game between the Brooklyn Dodgers and the Philadelphia Eagles at Ebbets Field is the first professional football game ever to be televised. The Dodgers win it 23–14. (**1939**)

Parker Hall of the Cleveland Rams sets an NFL standard with 106 pass completions when he becomes the first player to complete more than 100 passes in a season. (**1939**)

Don Hutson of the Packers sets the mark for pass reception yardage, 846, 171 more yards than Gaynell Tinsley racked up for the Chicago Cardinals as an NFL record two years earlier. (**1939**)

For the first time, NFL total regular season attendance exceeds one million. (**1939**)

The Champions / 1930s

1930	Green Bay Packers	10–3–1
1931	Green Bay Packers	12–2–0
1932	Chicago Bears	7–1–6
1933	Chicago Bears (*Bears* 23, *Giants* 21)	10–2–1
1934	New York Giants (*Giants* 30, *Bears* 13)	8–5–0
1935	Detroit Lions (*Lions* 26, *Giants* 7)	7–3–2
1936	Green Bay Packers (*Packers* 21, *Redskins* 6)	10–1–1
1937	Washington Redskins (*Redskins* 28, *Bears* 21)	8–3–0
1938	New York Giants (*Giants* 23, *Packers* 17)	8–2–1
1939	Green Bay Packers (*Packers* 27, *Giants* 0)	9–2–0

The most difficult man to bring to earth in the NFL of the 1930s, the legendary Bronko Nagurski, another charter member of the Pro Football Hall of Fame.

The First NFL Title Game

The very first NFL championship game was played December 17, 1933 at Wrigley Field in Chicago, pitting the Bears, winners of the NFL West with a record of 10–2–1, against the New York Giants, who had triumphed in the East with a record of 11–3–0. The starting lineups:

Bill Hewitt

	BEARS	GIANTS
E	Bill Hewitt	Red Badgro
E	Bill Karr	Ray Flaherty
T	Link Lyman	Len Grant
T	George Musso	Steve Owen
G	Jules Carlson	Butch Gibson
G	Joe Kopcha	Pottsville Jones
C	Ookie Miller	Mel Hein
QB	Carl Brumbaugh	Harry Newman
HB	Keith Molesworth	Ken Strong
HB	Gene Ronzani	Dale Burnett
FB	Bronko Nagurski	Bo Molenda
coach	George Halas	Steve Owen

Bears	3	3	10	7	**23**
Giants	0	7	7	7	**21**

Bill Hewitt's famous lateral in the closing minutes of the first NFL championship game in 1933 to Bill Karr, who carried it in for the touchdown that gave the Bears a 23–21 victory over the Giants.

The Bears took the lead and held it into the second quarter on two field goals from the toe of Automatic Jack Manders, one a 40-yarder. But the Giants went to the locker room at intermission with a 7–6 lead after Harry Newman hit Red Badgro with a 29-yard touchdown pass and Ken Strong's extra point. Manders gave the Bears the lead back with another field goal in the third quarter, but the Giants marched back—all the way to the 1 yard line where Max Krause plunged in for a touchdown. With Strong's PAT the Giants had a 14–9 third quarter lead. Not for long, however, because in the same period of play the Bears drove, icing it with an 8-yard TD toss from Bronko Nagurski to Bill Karr. In the final period, the Giants see-sawed to the lead again with a little razzle-dazzle: Strong took a handoff from Harry Newman, then with a kind of flea-flicker play lateralled the ball back to Newman, who scrambled until he saw Strong alone in the end zone about 10 yards away and threw him the ball. But then in the final minutes, the Bears having moved to New York's 19-yard line, the Chicagoans came up with a little fancy of their own. Nagurski dropped back and hit Bill Hewitt with a short pass. About to be tackled, Hewitt wheeled and pitched the ball to Bill Karr, who had been trailing him, and after a picture-perfect block by Gene Ronzani that took out the two remaining Giant defenders Karr carried it in for the game-winning score.

The League Leaders / 1930s

1930

Scoring	Jack McBride, Brooklyn Dodgers, 57 points
Rushing	Verne Lewellen, Green Bay Packers, 8 TDs
Passing	Benny Friedman, New York Giants, 14 TDs
Receiving	Johnny Blood McNally, Green Bay Packers, 5 TDs
	Rex Thomas, Brooklyn Dodgers, 5 TDs
Field Goals	Frosty Peters, Portsmouth Spartans, 2
PATs	Red Dunn, Green Bay Packers, 14

1931

Scoring	Johnny Blood McNally, Green Bay Packers, 72 points
Rushing	Dutch Clark, Portsmouth Spartans, 9 TDs
Passing	Red Dunn, Green Bay Packers, 7 TDs
Receiving	Johnny Blood McNally, Green Bay Packers, 9 TDs
Field Goals	Ken Strong, Staten Island Stapletons, 2
PATs	Ernie Nevers, Chicago Cardinals, 15

Earl "Dutch" Clark

1932

Scoring	Dutch Clark, Portsmouth Spartans, 55 points
Rushing	Bronko Nagurski, Chicago Bears, 4 TDs
Passing	Arnie Herber, Green Bay Packers, 9 TDs
Receiving	Ray Flaherty, New York Giants, 5 TDs
Field Goals	Dutch Clark, Portsmouth Spartans, 3
PATs	Dutch Clark, Portsmouth Spartans, 10

1933

Scoring	Glenn Presnell, Portsmouth Spartans, 63 points
Rushing	Jim Musick, Boston Redskins, 809 yards
	Glenn Presnell, Portsmouth Spartans, 6 TDs
Passing	Harry Newman, New York Giants, 53 completions
	Harry Newman, New York Giants, 973 yards gained
	Harry Newman, New York Giants, 9 TDs
Receiving	Shipwreck Kelly, Brooklyn Dodgers, 22 receptions
	Paul Moss, Pittsburgh Pirates, 383 yards gained
	many with 3 TDs
Field Goals	Jack Manders, Chicago Bears, 5
	Glenn Presnell, Portsmouth Spartans, 5
	Ken Strong, New York Giants, 5
PATs	Jack Manders, Chicago Bears, 14
	Ken Strong, New York Giants, 14

Morris "Red" Badgro

1934

Scoring	Jack Manders, Chicago Bears, 79 points
Rushing	Beattie Feathers, Chicago Bears, 1,004 yards
	Dutch Clark, Detroit Lions, 8 TDs
Passing	Arnie Herber, Green Bay Packers, 42 completions
	Arnie Herber, Green Bay Packers, 799 yards gained
	Arnie Herber, Green Bay Packers, 8 TDs
Receiving	Joe Carter, Philadelphia Eagles, 16 receptions
	Red Badgro, New York Giants, 16 receptions
	Harry Ebding, Detroit Lions, 257 yards
	Bill Hewitt, Chicago Bears, 5 TDs
Field Goals	Jack Manders, Chicago Bears, 10
PATs	Jack Manders, Chicago Bears, 31

1935

Scoring	Dutch Clark, Detroit Lions, 55 points
Rushing	Doug Russell, Chicago Cardinals, 499 yards
	Ernie Caddel, Detroit Lions, 6 TDs
Passing	Ed Danowski, New York Giants, 57 completions
	Ed Danowski, New York Giants, 795 yards gained
	Ed Danowski, New York Giants, 11 TDs
Receiving	Tod Goodwin, New York Giants, 26 receptions
	Charley Malone, Boston Redskins, 433 yards gained
	Don Hutson, Green Bay Packers, 8 TDs
Field Goals	Armand Niccolai, Pittsburgh Pirates, 6
	Bill Smith, Chicago Cardinals, 6
PATs	Dutch Clark, Detroit Lions, 16
	Jack Manders, Chicago Bears, 16

1936

Scoring	Dutch Clark, Detroit Lions, 73 points
Rushing	Tuffy Leemans, New York Giants, 830 yards
	Dutch Clark, Detroit Lions, 7 TDs
Passing	Arnie Herber, Green Bay Packers, 77 completions
	Arnie Herber, Green Bay Packers, 1,239 yards gained
	Arnie Herber, Green Bay Packers, 11 TDs
Receiving	Don Hutson, Green Bay Packers, 34 receptions
	Don Hutson, Green Bay Packers, 526 yards gained
	Don Hutson, Green Bay Packers, 8 TDs
Field Goals	Jack Manders, Chicago Bears, 7
	Armand Niccolai, Pittsburgh Pirates, 7
PATs	Dutch Clark, Detroit Lions, 19

Clarke Hinkle grimaces here as he totes the ball for the Packers. A fierce competitor and frequent All Pro, Hinkle was elected to the Hall of Fame in 1964.

1937

Scoring	Jack Manders, Chicago Bears, 69 points
Rushing	Cliff Battles, Washington Redskins, 874 yards
	Cliff Battles, Washington Redskins, 5 TDs
	Dutch Clark, Detroit Lions, 5 TDs
	Clarke Hinkle, Green Bay Packers, 5 TDs
Passing	Sammy Baugh, Washington Redskins, 81 completions
	Sammy Baugh, Washington Redskins, 1,127 yards gained
	Bob Monnett, Green Bay Packers, 9 TDs
Receiving	Don Hutson, Green Bay Packers, 41 receptions
	Gaynell Tinsley, Chicago Cardinals, 675 yards gained
	Don Hutson, Green Bay Packers, 7 TDs
Field Goals	Jack Manders, Chicago Bears, 8
PATs	Riley Smith, Washington Redskins, 22

1938

Scoring	Clarke Hinkle, Green Bay Packers, 58 points
Rushing	Whizzer White, Pittsburgh Pirates, 567 yards
	Andy Farkas, Washington Redskins, 6 TDs
Passing	Ed Danowski, New York Giants, 70 completions
	Ace Parker, Brooklyn Dodgers, 865 yards gained
	Bob Monnett, Green Bay Packers, 9 TDs
Receiving	Gaynell Tinsley, Chicago Cardinals, 41 receptions
	Don Hutson, Green Bay Packers, 548 yards gained
	Don Hutson, Green Bay Packers, 9 TDs
Field Goals	Ward Cuff, New York Giants, 5
	Ralph Kercheval, Brooklyn Dodgers, 5
PATs	Ward Cuff, New York Giants, 18

1939

Scoring	Andy Farkas, Washington Redskins, 68 points
Rushing	Bill Osmanski, Chicago Bears, 699 yards
	Johnny Drake, Cleveland Rams, 9 TDs
Passing	Parker Hall, Cleveland Rams, 106 completions
	Davey O'Brien, Philadelphia Eagles, 1,324 yards gained
	Frank Filchock, Washington Redskins, 11 TDs
Receiving	Don Hutson, Green Bay Packers, 34 receptions
	Don Hutson, Green Bay Packers, 846 yards gained
	Jim Benton, Cleveland Rams, 7 TDs
Field Goals	Ward Cuff, New York Giants, 7
PATs	Tiny Engebretsen, Green Bay Packers, 18

Don Hutson, the greatest end of his time, usually did his pass catching for the Packers with more finesse than this. During his 11-year career in Green Bay, he collected just about every record for pass catching and scoring and earned charter membership in the Pro Football Hall of Fame.

First All-Pro Team

The very first official All-Pro team was selected in 1931. The charter members were:

E	Lavie Dilweg	Green Bay Packers
E	Red Badgro	New York Giants
T	Cal Hubbard	Green Bay Packers
T	George Christensen	Portsmouth Spartans
G	Mike Michalske	Green Bay Packers
G	Butch Gibson	New York Giants
C	Frank McNally	Chicago Cardinals
QB	Dutch Clark	Portsmouth Spartans
HB	Red Grange	Chicago Bears
HB	Johnny Blood McNally	Green Bay Packers
FB	Ernie Nevers	Chicago Cardinals

The First Divisions

For the first time, the NFL was restructured into two divisions in 1933. This was the first arrangement:

EAST	WEST
Boston Redskins	Chicago Bears
Brooklyn Dodgers	Chicago Cardinals
New York Giants	Cincinnati Reds
Philadelphia Eagles	Green Bay Packers
Pittsburgh Pirates	Portsmouth Spartans

The Giants conquered the East and the Bears the West and met in the NFL's first official championship game at Wrigley field in Chicago on December 17, 1933. (see Sidebar)

The First College All-Star Game (August 31, 1934)

	CHICAGO BEARS	COLLEGE ALL-STARS
E	Bill Hewitt	Eggs Manske (Northwestern)
E	Luke Johnsos	Joe Skladany (Pittsburgh)
T	Link Lyman	Moose Krause (Notre Dame)
T	George Musso	Abe Schwammel (Oregon State)
G	Zuck Carlson	Frank Walton (Pittsburgh)
G	Joe Zeller	Bob Jones (Indiana)
C	Ookie Miller	Chuck Bernard (Michigan)
QB	Carl Brumbaugh	Homer Griffith (Southern Cal)
HB	Gene Ronzani	Beattie Feathers (Tennessee)
HB	George Corbett	Joe Laws (Iowa)
FB	Bronko Nagurski	Mike Mikulak (Oregon)
coach	George Halas	Nobel Kizer (Purdue)

Bears	0	0	0	0	**0**
All-Stars	0	0	0	0	**0**

The All-Stars had a crack at winning it when Bill Smith (Washington) attempted a 41-yard field goal in the last seconds of the game but the Bears Carl Brumbaugh blocked it.

The First Pro Bowl Game
(January 15, 1939)

	NEW YORK GIANTS	PRO ALL-STARS
E	Jim Lee Howell	Gaynell Tinsley (Chicago Cardinals)
E	Jim Poole	Perry Schwartz (Brooklyn Dodgers)
T	Ed Widseth	Joe Stydahar (Chicago Bears)
T	Ox Parry	Bruiser Kinard (Brooklyn Dodgers)
G	Orville Tuttle	Byron Gentry (Pittsburgh Pirates)
G	Kayo Lunday	Pete Mehringer (Los Angeles Bulldogs)*
C	Mel Hein	John Wiatrak (Detroit Lions)
QB	Nello Falaschi	Ernie Pinckert (Washington Redskins)
HB	Hank Soar	Lloyd Cardwell (Detroit Lions)
HB	Ward Cuff	Sammy Baugh (Washington Redskins)
FB	Ed Danowski	Clarke Hinkle (Green Bay Packers)
coach	Steve Owen	Ray Flaherty (Washington Redskins) Gus Henderson (Detroit Lions)

Giants	0	3	0	10	**13**
Pro All-Stars	0	3	7	0	**10**

Len Barnum kicked a field goal for the Giants and Ernie Smith (Packers) reciprocated with one for the All-Stars in the first half. The All-Stars took the lead in the third quarter when Sammy Baugh connected for a 71-yard touchdown pass play with Lloyd Cardwell, and Joe Stydahar booted the extra point. But the Giants came back in the final period with Ed Danowski tossing a 22-yard TD pass to Chuck Gelatka. Ward Cuff kicked the extra point and a little later an 18-yard field goal to give the New Yorkers a victory.

*Players from the Los Angeles Bulldogs, an independent pro team, were allowed to participate.

The War Years

The Chicago Bears Sid Luckman, first of the great T formation quarterbacks, passes against the Giants. Number 32 of New York is All Pro tackle Al Blozis, killed in Europe in World War II not long after this picture was taken.

The war, at least in America, did not begin with the turn of the decade, but preparations and discomforting anticipations were much a part of the scene as the 1930s became the 1940s. As far as the NFL was concerned, the war years served as a kind of intermission between the old game of football, when running was the name of the offensive game, and the newer form that was personified on the arms of passers from that new breed known as T formation quarterbacks.

In all, a total of 638 NFL players went off to military service in World War II, 21 of whom never returned. The teams for the most part were bereft of talent, but they still managed to play and the fans in uniform on both the European and South Pacific fronts followed their activities on the field with great interest in between the more devastating scrimmages in which they were involved.

Green Bay's Don Hutson was better than ever during the period, teaming up with a passer *extraordinaire* by the name of Cecil Isbell; then there were Sid Luckman of the Bears and Sammy Baugh of the Redskins, running backs like Bullet Bill Dudley and George McAfee, and terrorizing linemen such as Bulldog Turner and Bruiser Kinard.

The short era was a pause before the game of pro football exploded into a festival of offensive pyrotechnics that would come to characterize the game in modern times.

During an early "Pro Bowl" at the Polo Grounds in 1942, Chicago Bear back Ray Nolting follows the interference of fellow back George McAfee. The two "All-Stars" moving in for the tackle are Pug Manders (left) of the Brooklyn Dodgers and Joe Kuharich (88) of the Chicago Cardinals. The Bears beat the All-Stars, incidentally, 35–24.

Events and Milestones

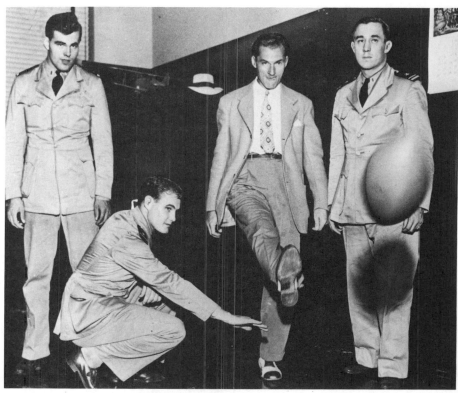

Kicking off a U. S. Navy recruitment drive in the early days of World War II is Don Hutson. The ensign next to him is Heisman Trophy winner Jay Berwanger who had been the first pick in the first NFL draft back in 1936 and the first pro football draftee to choose not to play the game.

A third American Football League (AFL) is launched with franchises in six cities: Boston, Buffalo, Cincinnati, Columbus, Milwaukee, and New York. (1940)

Don Looney of the Philadelphia Eagles sets a new NFL record by catching 58 passes, 17 more than caught by previous record shareholders Don Hutson and Gaynell Tinsley, while his quarterback, Davey O'Brien, chalks up the standard for pass completions with a total of 124. (1940)

Sammy Baugh of the Washington Redskins sets an NFL mark which still stands today by averaging 51.4 yards on his 35 punts during the regular season. No punter before or since has led the league with an average that exceeded 50 yards per punt. (1940)

An NFL championship game is broadcast on network radio for the first time. The announcer is Red Barber and 120 stations carry the Chicago Bear's 73–0 desecration of the Washington Redskins. (1940)

For the chief executive officer of the NFL, the title of president is changed to commissioner, and Elmer Layden, former member of Notre Dame's fabled Four Horsemen who had been serving as coach and athletic director at his alma mater, is appointed to that post. Carl Storck resigns. (1941)

Don Hutson, scoring 12 touchdowns, kicking 20 extra points and 1 field goal, registers a record 95 points, the most since Paddy Driscoll logged 86 for the Bears back in 1926. (1941)

The first divisional playoff game in NFL history is held after the Bears and Packers end the regular season with identical records of 10–1, and the Bears take the NFL West crown by defeating the Pack in Chicago 33–14. (1941)

Packer superstar Don Hutson sets five NFL records in one season. The first breaks his own record set the year before when he scores a total of 138 points (17 TDs, 33 PATs, 1 FG). His 33 (of 34) extra points is another standard, as are his 17 touchdown receptions and his 74 catches for 1,211 yards, the latter enabling Hutson to lay claim to becoming the first receiver ever to go over the millenary mark. (1942)

Hutson's battery mate at Green Bay, Cecil Isbell, not surprisingly sets three NFL standards passing: most yardage gained, 2,021 (the first ever to exceed 2,000 yards passing); most completions, 146; and most touchdown passes, 24. (1942)

For the first time a rule is installed requiring all players to wear helmets. (1943)

Because of the war the NFL loses many of its players to the armed services; as a result the Philadelphia Eagles and Pittsburgh Steelers are allowed to merge for the season, and the Cleveland Rams are permitted to suspend operations for the year without jeopardizing the franchise. (1943)

Sid Luckman of the Chicago Bears breaks two of the passing records set by Cecil Isbell the year before when he throws for a total of 2,194 yards and 28 touchdowns. (1943)

Sammy Baugh, to prove he is not merely a spectacular quarterback and punter for the Redskins, sets the NFL standard for interceptions by picking off 11 opposing team passes. (1943)

The Pittsburgh Steelers merge with the Chicago Cardinals when the Philadelphia Eagles resume play independently. (1944)

The hashmarks are moved from 15 to 20 yards in from the sidelines. (1945)

The Champions / ^EARLY 1940s

1940	Chicago Bears	8–3–0
	(*Bears* 73, *Redskins* 0)	
1941	Chicago Bears	10–1–0
	(*Bears* 37, *Giants* 9)	
1942	Washington Redskins	10–1–0
	(*Redskins* 14, *Bears* 6)	
1943	Chicago Bears	8–1–1
	(*Bears* 41, *Redskins* 21)	
1944	Green Bay Packers	8–2–0
	(*Packers* 14, *Giants* 7)	
1945	Cleveland Rams	9–1–0
	(*Rams* 15, *Redskins* 14)	

George Preston Marshall took his Redskins literally, both in Boston and Washington. His wife, film star Corinne Griffith, here adjusts his headdress before one of Marshall's Indian parades that sometimes preceded Redskins games.

The First Divisional Title Game (December 14, 1941)

Bears	6	24	0	3	**33**
Packers	7	0	7	0	**14**

	CHICAGO BEARS	GREEN BAY PACKERS
E	Dick Plasman	Don Hutson
E	John Siegal	Ray Riddick
T	Ed Kolman	Baby Ray
T	Lee Artoe	Charlie Schultz
G	Danny Fortmann	Buckets Goldenberg
G	Ray Bray	Lee McLaughlin
C	Bulldog Turner	George Svendsen
QB	Sid Luckman	Larry Craig
HB	Ray Nolting	Cecil Isbell
HB	Hugh Gallarneau	Herman Rohrig
FB	Norm Standlee	Clarke Hinkle
coach	George Halas	Curly Lambeau

Clarke Hinkle plunged in for the first score of the game and Don Hutson's extra point gave the Packers their first and only lead of the game. Hugh Gallarneau took a Packer punt and raced 81 yards for a touchdown and at the beginning of the second quarter Bob Snyder added a field goal to give the Bears a 9—6 lead. Then the Bears went on a rampage, scoring three touchdowns before the half ended, two on plunges by Norm Standlee and one on a run by halfback Bobby Swisher. Cecil Isbell hit Hal Van Every with a touchdown pass in the third quarter, but the Pack was never back in the game. Snyder added a field goal in the final quarter to end the Bears scoring for the day.

The League Leaders/ EARLY 1940s

1940

Scoring	Don Hutson, Green Bay Packers, 57 points
Rushing	Whizzer White, Detroit Lions, 514 yards
	Johnny Drake, Cleveland Rams, 9 TDs
Passing	Davey O'Brien, Philadelphia Eagles, 124 completions
	Sammy Baugh, Washington Redskins, 1,367 yards gained
	Sammy Baugh, Washington Redskins, 12 TDs
Receiving	Don Looney, Philadelphia Eagles, 58 receptions
	Don Looney, Philadelphia Eagles, 707 yards gained
	Don Hutson, Green Bay Packers, 7 TDs
Field Goals	Clarke Hinkle, Green Bay Packers, 9
PATs	Ace Parker, Brooklyn Dodgers, 19

Sammy Baugh

Sammy Baugh, the Redskins' great quarterback and punter. Slingin' Sam made the Hall of Fame as a charter enshrinee in 1963.

1941

Scoring	Don Hutson, Green Bay Packers, 95 points
Rushing	Jack Manders, Brooklyn Dodgers, 486 yards
	Hugh Gallarneau, Chicago Bears, 8 TDs
Passing	Cecil Isbell, Green Bay Packers, 117 completions
	Cecil Isbell, Green Bay Packers, 1,479 yards gained
	Cecil Isbell, Green Bay Packers, 15 TDs
Receiving	Don Hutson, Green Bay Packers, 58 receptions
	Don Hutson, Green Bay Packers, 738 yards gained
	Don Hutson, Green Bay Packers, 10 TDs
Field Goals	Clarke Hinkle, Green Bay Packers, 9
PATs	Don Hutson, Green Bay Packers, 20
	Bob Snyder, Chicago Bears, 20

1942

Scoring	Don Hutson, Green Bay Packers, 138 points
Rushing	Bill Dudley, Pittsburgh Steelers, 696 yards
	Gary Famiglietti, Chicago Bears, 8 TDs
Passing	Cecil Isbell, Green Bay Packers, 146 completions
	Cecil Isbell, Green Bay Packers, 2,021 yards gained
	Cecil Isbell, Green Bay Packers, 24 TDs
Receiving	Don Hutson, Green Bay Packers, 74 receptions
	Don Hutson, Green Bay Packers, 1,211 yards gained
	Don Hutson, Green Bay Packers, 17 TDs
Field Goals	Bill Daddio, Chicago Cardinals, 5
PATs	Don Hutson, Green Bay Packers, 33

1943	
Scoring	Don Hutson, Green Bay Packers, 117 points
Rushing	Bill Paschal, New York Giants, 572 yards
	Bill Paschal, New York Giants, 10 TDs
Passing	Sammy Baugh, Washington Redskins, 133 completions
	Sid Luckman, Chicago Bears, 2,194 yards gained
	Sid Luckman, Chicago Bears, 28 TDs
Receiving	Don Hutson, Green Bay Packers, 47 receptions
	Don Hutson, Green Bay Packers, 776 yards gained
	Don Hutson, Green Bay Packers, 11 TDs
Field Goals	Ward Cuff, New York Giants, 3
	Don Hutson, Green Bay Packers, 3
PATs	Bob Snyder, Chicago Bears, 39

1944	
Scoring	Don Hutson, Green Bay Packers, 85 points
Rushing	Bill Paschal, New York Giants, 737 yards
	Bill Paschal, New York Giants, 9 TDs
Passing	Frank Filchock, Washington Redskins, 84 completions
	Irv Comp, Green Bay Packers, 1,159 yards gained
	Frank Filchock, Washington Redskins, 13 TDs
Receiving	Don Hutson, Green Bay Packers, 58 receptions
	Don Hutson, Green Bay Packers, 866 yards gained
	Don Hutson, Green Bay Packers, 9 TDs
Field Goals	Ken Strong, New York Giants, 6
PATs	Pete Gudauskas, Chicago Bears, 36

1945	
Scoring	Steve Van Buren, Philadelphia Eagles, 110 points
Rushing	Steve Van Buren, Philadelphia Eagles, 832 yards
	Steve Van Buren, Philadelphia Eagles, 15 TDs
Passing	Sammy Baugh, Washington Redskins, 128 completions
	Sid Luckman, Chicago Bears, 1,725 yards gained
	Sid Luckman, Chicago Bears, 14 TDs
Receiving	Don Hutson, Green Bay Packers, 47 receptions
	Jim Benton, Cleveland Rams, 1,067 yards gained
	Frank Liebel, New York Giants, 10 TDs
Field Goals	Joe Aguirre, Washington Redskins, 7
PATs	Don Hutson, Green Bay Packers, 31
	Bob Waterfield, Cleveland Rams, 31

The Way It Was...

A Wartime Press Release (1942)

From National Football League... FOR IMMEDIATE RELEASE...

Hugh Gallarneau, Chicago Bear rookie, was called upon to punt against the Chicago Cardinals early in the 1941 season...The kick was blocked and Gallarneau was never asked to punt again....

–0–

Charles Seabright, Cleveland rookie, had a "1.000 per cent" forward passing average in the National Football league last Fall....He threw one pass and it was intercepted ....

–0–

Jim Castiglia, Philadelphia Eagles' full back, has been signed by Connie Mack as the Athletics' batting practice and bullpen catcher....

–0–

Fred Vanzo, veteran National league blocking back released to the Chicago Cardinals by the Detroit Lions in mid-season last year, is stationed at the San Diego, Cal., Naval base as a physical instructor for flying cadets....

–0–

Steve Belichick, the clubhouse boy who wound up playing full back for the Detroit Lions last Fall, handled only one punt but he handled it pretty well....He scampered back 77 yards with it for a touchdown against Green Bay....

–0–

Aldo Forte, Chicago Bear guard stationed at Great Lakes Naval training station, is anxiously awaiting the arrival of teammate George McAfee, who is expected to arrive any day from the Norfolk, Va., station....

EARLY MAYHEM

Fury and a flurry of activity. The Canton Bulldogs of 1920 go after an enemy ballcarrier in the very first year of organized professional football. (Pro Football Hall of Fame)

A panoramic view of the melee. The Green Bay Packers go at it with the Minneapolis Marines in 1924. (Pro Football Hall of Fame)

The immortal Jim Thorpe, a 38-year-old senior citizen of the Canton Bulldogs, tries to maul Chicago Bears back Dutch Sternaman in this 1926 game. Moving in behind Thorpe for a colossal clip is Bear end George Halas. (Pro Football Hall of Fame)

Red Grange, carrying the ball here against a college all-star team, circa 1925, deftly and swiftly avoids the mayhem, as he did so often and so much better than any back before him. (Chicago Bears)

Spread-eagled and upended is Portsmouth Spartan fullback Ace Gutowsky in a 1933 game against the Boston Redskins at Fenway Park. The Redskin tackler is end Ike Frankian. Helmetless number 57 is Father Lumpkin of the Spartans. (Pro Football Hall of Fame)

The greatest pile-driving runner of his time, some say of all time, Bears fullback Bronko Nagurski charges at and over a grounded defender. (Pro Football Hall of Fame)

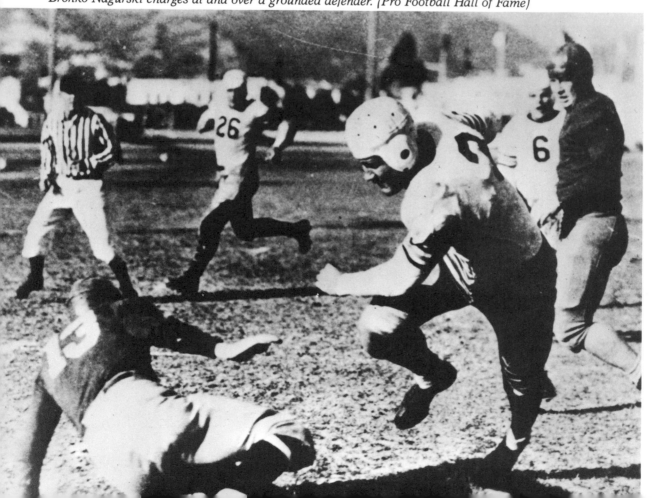

Joining the pile-up is helmetless Hall of Fame end Bill Hewitt of the Bears (coming in from the left). Number 27 is Detroit Lion end Butch Morse. Next to him on the ground is Bear back Gene Ronzani, and at the far right is helmetless Hall of Fame tackle George Musso of Chicago. The Lions, incidentally, won this 1936 brawl in Detroit 14–2. (Pro Football Hall of Fame)

Halfback Ward Cuff, with the ball, of the New York Giants gets a faceful of hand from an overzealous Brooklyn Dodger in this 1939 interborough battle, as the referee appears to either be orchestrating the mayhem or awaiting it with open arms. (Pro Football Hall of Fame) INS

Underwhelmed and overwhelmed is Brooklyn Dodger halfback George Cafego in 1940. Doing the whelming are Washington Redskin defenders Wayne Millner (40), Sammy Baugh (33), Jimmy Johnston (31), Steve Slivinski (16), and Bob Titchenal (18). (Pro Football Hall of Fame)

Airborne in 1943 is Steve Bagarus of the Redskins, trying to garner a few extra yards by high-jumping a Boston Yanks defender. (Pro Football Hall of Fame) Nate Fine Collection)

This high-flying Redskin is defensive halfback Wilbur Moore (35). The object of his attention is Green Bay ballcarrier Ted Fritsch. The cause of his flight is Packer blocker Larry Craig. (Pro Football Hall of Fame / Nate Fine Collection)

In this 1945 face-slapping contest are Chicago Cardinal defender John Knolla (33) and Washington Redskin ballcarrier Joe Carter (29). Number 17 on the Cardinals is guard/linebacker Joe Kuharich. (Pro Football Hall of Fame)

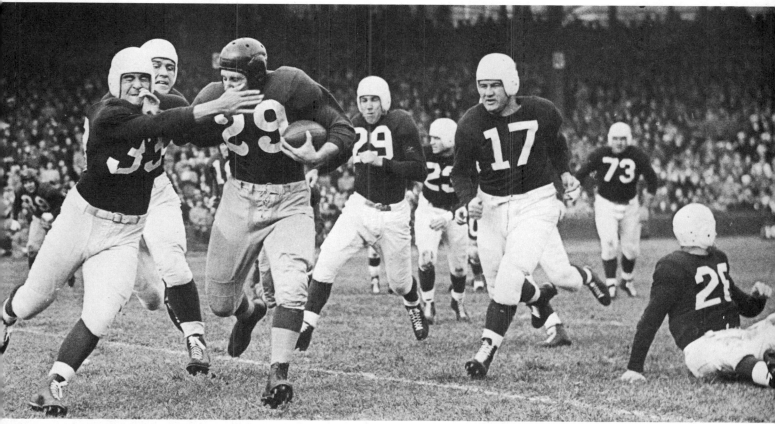

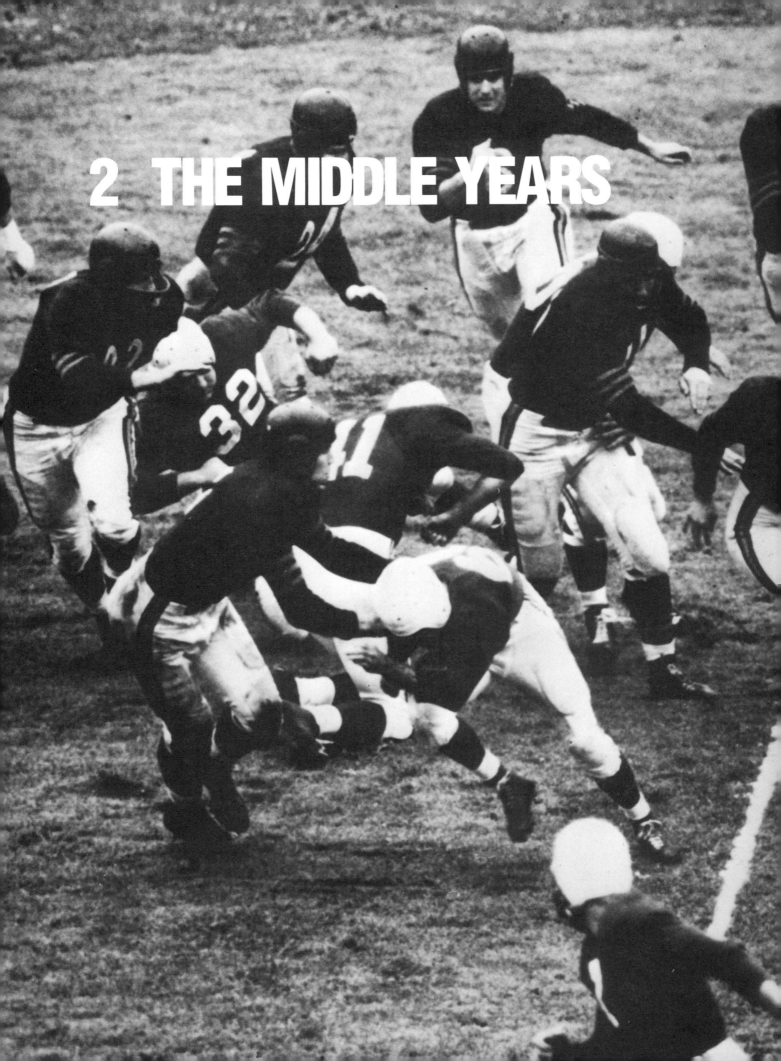

2 THE MIDDLE YEARS

The Late 1940s

Troop ships landing on the east and west coasts of the United States in the mid-1940s were returning many football players to an arena that was unquestionably violent but certainly less deadly than the one they had been involved with in Europe and the Pacific.

Some would not return, like All Pro tackle Al Blozis of the New York Giants, while others would never be able to compete again in the fierce game they had once played. But professional football had survived the war just as it had muddled through the Depression.

The game was now changed noticeably. The T formation had been adopted almost universally, and passing was now the name of the game. Grind-it-out football had given way to a much more diversified offense. Quarterbacks ceased to be simply signal callers and occasional ballhandlers. Sid Luckman and Sammy Baugh had seen to that. Now the influx of quarterbacks with amazing arms overwhelmed the game: Paul Christman of the Cardinals, Bob Waterfield of the Rams, Tommy Thompson of the Eagles, Charlie Conerly of the Giants, Y. A. Tittle of the Colts, Otto Graham of the Browns, and Frankie Albert of the 49ers.

Ends were no longer merely blockers on offense and tacklers on defense. Don Hutson, Gaynell Tinsley, and Jim Benton had seen to that as well. Now came other great pass catchers like Mac Speedie and Dante Lavelli of the Browns, Mal Kutner of the Cardinals, Ken Kavanaugh of the Bears, Pete Pihos of the Eagles, and Tom Fears of the Rams.

And, of course, along came the All-America Football Conference, brainchild of Arch Ward, Chicago Tribune sports columnist, and the first real, true threat to the National Football League. As an entity, the AAFC may not have been able to survive into the 1950s, but it did impart to the NFL the Browns, 49ers, and Colts.

The transition was in full swing in the late 1940s, the game was becoming livelier, scoring was proliferating with each game as quarterback found end or halfback, and fans were flocking to the stadia on Sunday afternoons in numbers they never had before the war.

The Rams played in Cleveland when this picture was taken. But in 1946, they moved to Los Angeles to treat the west coasters to full-time NFL football. Gaylon Smith is the Cleveland Ram ballcarrier here in a game against the Brooklyn Dodgers at Ebbets Field. (Pro Football Hall of Fame) Press Assoc.

The Best of the Decade / 1940s

FIRST TEAM

Position	Player	Team
E	Don Hutson	Green Bay Packers
E	Mac Speedie	Cleveland Browns
T	Al Wistert	Philadelphia Eagles
T	Bruiser Kinard	Brooklyn Dodgers
G	Bill Willis	Cleveland Browns
G	Buster Ramsey	Chicago Cardinals
C	Bulldog Turner	Chicago Bears
QB	Sammy Baugh	Washington Redskins
RB	Charlie Trippi	Chicago Cardinals
RB	Steve Van Buren	Philadelphia Eagles
RB	Marion Motley	Cleveland Browns
K	Lou Groza	Cleveland Browns
P	Sammy Baugh	Washington Redskins
coach	*George Halas*	*Chicago Bears*

SECOND TEAM

Position	Player	Team
E	Ken Kavanaugh	Chicago Bears
E	Mal Kutner	Chicago Cardinals
T	Bucko Kilroy	Philadelphia Eagles
T	Vic Sears	Philadelphia Eagles
G	Bruno Banducci	San Francisco 49ers
G	Len Younce	New York Giants
C	Alex Wojciechowicz	Detroit Lions/Philadelphia Eagles
QB	Sid Luckman	Chicago Bears
RB	Bill Dudley	Pittsburgh Steelers/Detroit Lions
RB	George McAfee	Chicago Bears
RB	Pat Harder	Chicago Cardinals
K	Bob Waterfield	Los Angeles Rams
P	Bob Waterfield	Los Angeles Rams
coach	*Greasy Neale*	*Philadelphia Eagles*

Sid Luckman

Events and Milestones

The Rams move from Cleveland to Los Angeles. **(1946)**

The All-America Football Conference, founded by *Chicago Tribune* sports columnist Arch Ward, begins operation in direct competition with the NFL. Franchises are awarded to eight cities: Brooklyn, Buffalo, Chicago, Cleveland, Los Angeles, Miami, New York, and San Francisco. **(1946)**

Bert Bell, co-owner of the Pittsburgh Steelers, replaces Elmer Layden as commissioner of the NFL. **(1946)**

Both the NFL and AAFC allow black players, who had been unofficially barred from pro football since the early 1930s, to play: the NFL Los Angeles Rams signing back Kenny Washington and end Woody Strode, the AAFC Cleveland Browns contracting with fullback Marion Motley and guard Bill Willis. **(1946)**

Free substitution is withdrawn, the new rule allowing only three players to enter the game at one time. **(1946)**

Steve Van Buren of the Philadelphia Eagles sets an NFL rushing record by gaining 1,008 yards, four more than Beattie Feathers gained for the Bears back in 1934. **(1947)**

The Redskins' Sammy Baugh is the first passer in NFL history to complete more than 200 passes in a single season (210) and to gain more than 2,000 yards passing (2,938). **(1947)**

New rules:
- A fifth official, a back judge, is added.
- Team player limit is increased to 35.
- A bonus draft choice is instituted, one team to get a special selection before the regular draft begins. **(1947)**

Dan Sandifer, a rookie with the Redskins, sets a new mark with 13 interceptions in one season. **(1948)**

Pat Harder of the Chicago Cardinals kicks nine extra points against the New York Giants for an NFL record. **(1948)**

Steve Van Buren gains 1,146 yards rushing for the Eagles to top his previous record. **(1949)**

Tom Fears of the Los Angeles Rams sets the standard for pass catches in a season, snaring 77, three more than Don Hutson grabbed back in 1942. **(1949)**

It often took more than one tackler to stop Steve Van Buren (15). The great Philadelphia Eagles halfback was the premier running back in the NFL during the late 1940s. Against the Redskins here he picks up a few of the 5,860 yards he rushed for during his eight-year NFL career. (Pro Football Hall of Fame / Nate Fine Collection)

Blacks came back to pro football in 1946 after having been purposefully excluded for nearly 15 years in both the NFL and AAFC. One of the first and most famous was Cleveland Brown fullback/linebacker Marion Motley (76) upending halfback Chuck Fenenbock of the Los Angeles Dons in this AAFC game of 1946. (Pro Football Hall of Fame) World Wide Photos

Arch Ward

The Champions/ LATE 1940s

1946	Chicago Bears	8–2–1
	(Bears 24 Giants 14)	
1947	Chicago Cardinals	9–3–0
	(Cardinals 28, Eagles 21)	
1948	Philadelphia Eagles	9–2–1
	(Eagles 7 Cardinals 0)	
1949	Philadelphia Eagles	11–1–0
	(Eagles 14, Rams 0)	

49

The League Leaders/ LATE 1940s

1946

Scoring	Ted Fritsch, Green Bay Packers, 100 points
Rushing	Bill Dudley, Pittsburgh Steelers, 604 yards
	Ted Fritsch, Green Bay Packers, 9 TDs
Passing	Bob Waterfield, Los Angeles Rams, 127 completions
	Sid Luckman, Chicago Bears, 1,826 yards gained
	Bob Waterfield, Los Angeles Rams, 18 TDs
Receiving	Jim Benton, Los Angeles Rams, 63 receptions
	Jim Benton, Los Angeles Rams, 981 yards gained
	Bill Dewell, Chicago Cardinals, 7 TDs
Field Goals	Ted Fritsch, Green Bay Packers, 9
PATs	Bob Waterfield, Los Angeles Rams, 37

1947

Scoring	Pat Harder, Chicago Cardinals, 102 points
Rushing	Steve Van Buren, Philadelphia Eagles, 1,008 yards
	Steve Van Buren, Philadelphia Eagles, 13 TDs
Passing	Sammy Baugh, Washington Redskins, 210 completions
	Sammy Baugh, Washington Redskins, 2,938 yards gained
	Sammy Baugh, Washington Redskins, 25 TDs
Receiving	Jim Keane, Chicago Bears, 64 receptions
	Mal Kutner, Chicago Cardinals, 944 yards gained
	Ken Kavanaugh, Chicago Bears, 13 TDs
Field Goals	Ward Cuff, Green Bay Packers, 7
	Pat Harder, Chicago Cardinals, 7
	Bob Waterfield, Los Angeles Rams, 7
PATs	Scooter McLean, Chicago Bears, 44

1948

Scoring	Pat Harder, Chicago Cardinals, 110 points
Rushing	Steve Van Buren, Philadelphia Eagles, 945 yards
	Steve Van Buren, Philadelphia Eagles, 10 TDs
Passing	Sammy Baugh, Washington Redskins, 185 completions
	Sammy Baugh, Washington Redskins, 2,599 yards gained
	Tommy Thompson, Philadelphia Eagles, 25 TDs
Receiving	Tom Fears, Los Angeles Rams, 51 receptions
	Mal Kutner, Chicago Cardinals, 943 yards gained
	Mal Kutner, Chicago Cardinals, 14 TDs
Field Goals	Cliff Patton, Philadelphia Eagles, 8
PATs	Pat Harder, Chicago Cardinals, 53

Steve Van Buren

1949

Scoring	Pat Harder, Chicago Cardinals, 102 points
Rushing	Steve Van Buren, Philadelphia Eagles, 1,146 yards
	Steve Van Buren, Philadelphia Eagles, 11 TDs
Passing	Johnny Lujack, Chicago Bears, 162 completions
	Johnny Lujack, Chicago Bears, 2,658 yards gained
	Johnny Lujack, Chicago Bears, 23 TDs
Receiving	Tom Fears, Los Angeles Rams, 77 receptions
	Bob Mann, Detroit Lions, 1,014 yards gained
	Tom Fears, Los Angeles Rams, 9 TDs
	Ken Kavanaugh, Chicago Bears, 9 TDs
Field Goals	Cliff Patton, Philadelphia Eagles, 9
	Bob Waterfield, Los Angeles Rams, 9
PATs	Pat Harder, Chicago Cardinals, 45

Green Bay fullback Ted Fritsch gains a few yards for the Packers in this 1947 game. The year before Fritsch led the NFL in scoring. Number 66 on the Chicago Bears is Hall of Famer Clyde 'Bulldog" Turner. (Pro Football Hall of Fame)

The Original AAFC

Otto Graham	QB	Cleveland Browns
Marion Motley	FB	Cleveland Browns
Dante Lavelli	E	Cleveland Browns
Mac Speedie	E	Cleveland Browns
Lou Groza	T	Cleveland Browns
Bill Willis	G	Cleveland Browns
Frank Gatski	C	Cleveland Browns
Ace Parker	TB	New York Yankees
Spec Sanders	HB	New York Yankees
Frank Sinkwich	TB	New York Yankees
Pug Manders	FB	New York Yankees
Bruiser Kinard	T	New York Yankees
Glenn Dobbs	TB	Brooklyn Dodgers
Frankie Albert	QB	San Francisco 49ers
Norm Standlee	FB	San Francisco 49ers
Bruno Banducci	G	San Francisco 49ers
Angelo Bertelli	QB	Los Angeles Dons
Bob Hoernschemeyer	TB	Chicago Rockets
Elroy Hirsch	HB	Chicago Rockets
Wee Willie Wilkin	T	Chicago Rockets

Eastern Division

Brooklyn Dodgers
Buffalo Bisons
Miami Seahawks
New York Yankees

Western Division

Chicago Rockets
Cleveland Browns
Los Angeles Dons
San Francisco 49ers

The Yankees, coached by Ray Flaherty, won the Eastern Division with ease, their record 10–3–1, while the other three teams in the division won only three games apiece. The Cleveland Browns, under the tutelage of Paul Brown, prevailed in the Western Division, posting a record of 12–2–0. The Browns then whipped the Yankees 14–9 in the AAFC's first championship game.

Among the outstanding football players who joined the AAFC in their charter year were:

The Cleveland Browns dominated the AAFC throughout the four years of the league's existence. Here Ed "Special Delivery" Jones falls into the end zone with the Browns first touchdown in the AAFC championship game of 1948. When day was done Cleveland had beaten Buffalo 49–7 to end a perfect 15–0 season and take their third straight AAFC title. (Pro Football Hall of Fame)

Rookie running back Ara Parseghian aims to pick up a few yards for the Cleveland Browns in 1948. About to bring him to earth is San Francisco 49ers' John "Strike" Strzykalski (91). Parseghian, of course, left a much bigger mark on the game as a college coach than as a Browns' running back.

New York, New York . . . a wonderful town
But is the NFL up and the AAFC down?

Civil War with Sandwiches

This article by the great sports columnist Red Smith originally appeared in December 1945 and is reprinted from *Out of Red* (Alfred Knopf Publishing, New York, 1950), with permission.

Tim Mara

CIVIL WAR was declared in New York yesterday, in exquisitely well-bred language and sumptuous surroundings. Small, gooey sandwiches on rye were served, with choice of coffee or milk.

War correspondents observed protocol by devouring the sandwiches, licking their fingertips elegantly, gazing with admiration . . . and taking turns sitting appraisingly on a sample of the new turquois box seats to be installed in Yankee Stadium.

Then Jackie Farrell, America's smallest public relations counselor, announced: "Gentlemen, Major Topping."

"Mister Topping," amended the man about to declare war. His declaration costume was a gray, chalk-striped, double-breasted suit, soft white shirt with button-down collar, wine-and-silver striped tie. Dan Topping fingered his jaw and said he'd just lost two teeth. To a dentist, not to Mr. Tim Mara of the football Giants.

Then he read an announcement of his decision to forsake the National Football League for the All-America Conference and operate a team in Yankee Stadium next year in competition with Mr. Mara's National Leaguers.

This was the formal opening of hostilities, although not notably warlike in tone. The bellicose note crept in during questioning about the cause of the break, the Giants' refusal to yield choice playing dates to Topping.

"If Mara is smart," Topping said, "maybe we can still work out schedules that won't conflict. I'm going to try some more to get along with him. If we can't work it out, the hell with him."

Asked whether he and Mara ever were close to agreement on dates, he replied: "We got closer than we had been, but it never came to an even split on dates. I showed him two schedules that wouldn't conflict and could be alternated from year to year . . . .

"I talked with several National League owners and some gave us their best wishes. I called Mara because I didn't want him to hear about it from other sources, but he didn't seem to want to talk."

Reinforcements for Major Topping arrived. They were led by Lieutenant Commander Jimmy Crowley (retired), commissioner of the All-America Conference, and included John L. Keeshin, owner of the Chicago franchise, and Arch Ward, a dreamy gentleman who sired the new league. Commander Crowley talked about things in general. Mr. Keeshin listed innumerable players he has signed, including the Giants' George Franck.

"But," he said, "I prefer to let Franck stay with the Giants. If he wishes to refund the money we advanced, all right. If not, all right. It's a good experiment, a noble experiment.

"I also have Wee Willie Wilkin, the old Washington lineman. He has two or three good years left. His wife just had twins."

Mr. Keeshin's team will play Friday nights in Chicago. Mr. Keeshin, a hardy gentleman in horn-rimmed glasses, said December nights are not cold in Chicago.

"One thing I guarantee," Major Topping said. "No matter how we do, it won't help the Giants' gate if we play on the same days."

In the Giants' less voluptuous offices, Jack V. Mara, president, smiled and hurled defiance with a sweeping overhand delivery.

"Their franchise wasn't worth five dollars because they destroyed professional ball in Brooklyn," he said amiably. "Coming to us with a five-dollar franchise and asking us to accept his proposed schedule was like asking Tiffany to move to the Bowery.

"We heard about this decision before Topping called us. We were surprised, but not shocked. It was our first information that he was rejecting our offer of dates, so if anyone is acting cheap in this matter, it isn't us. We wish him luck and he'll need it, especially with the same management he had in Brooklyn.

"We love this kind of opposition, because it will let the fans decide what kind of football they prefer."

Mr. Mara's tone was firmly courteous.

Welcome to the NFL, 1940s Style

George Connor often tells the story of his initiation into that street-fighting arena which is more commonly known as the pro football line of scrimmage. As a rookie in 1948, Connor, at least in the pre-season, was used as a back-up tackle for Fred Davis. "When I raise my hand coming out of the huddle," Davis told him before their first exhibition game, "that means I need a rest. You come in on the next play."

Connor watched. When he saw the arm go up, he grabbed his helmet from the bench and when the play was over raced out onto the field. As soon as the ball was snapped on the next play, his face ran smack into the fist of the lineman opposing him. It was an especially unpleasant greeting in those days before face masks were routinely worn. Connor was startled but thought that maybe this was the typical welcome a rookie got to the more brutal game played by the pros.

Later in the same game, Davis raised his hand again, and Connor replaced him on the next play. This time he was lined up opposite a different lineman. But the reaction was the same. When play began, this lineman smashed him square in the face too. It was getting a little out of hand, Connor thought. After the game, he tried again to figure out why it was happening to him; perhaps they resented all the publicity he was getting for a rookie, or maybe it was because he came from Notre Dame—a lot of pro players were less than fond of Fighting Irish alumni in those days. He even asked a few other linemen about this so-called special greeting. They agreed that work in the line was violent as hell, but what was occurring to Connor did seem a little extraordinary.

It went on for several weeks. Then, one Sunday, it all became crystal clear. This time when Davis raised his hand, Connor for some reason kept his eyes on him rather than on the play itself. When the ball was snapped, he saw Davis lunge across the line, punch the opposing lineman in the face, and then trot off toward the Bear bench.

For the rest of that year, Connor announced himself to whoever the opposing lineman was when he lined up after coming into the game: "Connor in, Davis out." It made his life a lot easier the rest of that rookie year.

(From *The Chicago Bears, An Illustrated History* by Richard Whittingham, reprinted with permission)

George Connor, after intercepting a pass, throws a left-jab stiff-arm at an unfortunate L.A. Ram. (Pro Football Hall of Fame)

Bob Waterfield, LA Rams legend.

The 1950s

The decade of the 1950s in pro football began with the NFL prevailing in its battles for fans and players with the AAFC. On the other hand, the NFL learned that a professional football team could be quite good without the aegis of the NFL cloak, the AAFC emigre Cleveland Browns illustrating that all too well from their very first year in the NFL.

That ten-year period in NFL history was somewhat unique in the sense that it began with the absorption of three teams which were relics of a dying league, the All-America Football Conference, and ended with the advent of another interloper, the American Football League, which was destined to try the souls and the pocketbooks of all NFL teams.

In between, the game of professional football took its rightful place as a major sports institution in America, no longer a subordinate to its counterpart on the college level.

Paul Brown's Cleveland Browns were a marvel, a dynasty that would find few equals in the entire history of the sport, fielding a team of which seven of their starting players would eventually be inducted into the Pro

Football Hall of Fame (Otto Graham, Marion Motley, Lou Groza, Dante Lavelli, Bill Willis, Len Ford, and Frank Gatski).

Then there were the spectacular Rams of Los Angeles with Bob Waterfield, Norm Van Brocklin, Crazylegs Hirsch, Tom Fears, and perhaps the most bruising running attack ever with Dan Towler, Dick Hoerner, and Tank Younger.

At the same time, there was Bobby Layne over at Detroit, who, according to fellow Texan and Lions star Doak Walker, "never lost a football game in his life; although once in a while time ran out on him." The savage defense of the New York Giants hung upon the hulks of players like Andy Robustelli, Sam Huff, and Rosey Grier, and was as imposing as China's Great Wall.

Along came the championship Colts with Johnny Unitas and his favorite receiver Raymond Berry. And in the last year of the decade an assistant coach of the Giants by the name of Vince Lombardi took over a Green Bay Packer team which had won only one of 12 games the year before, but a club that had some potential, he thought, with players the caliber of Paul Hornung, Bart Starr, Jim Taylor, and Jerry Kramer among quite a few others.

Sid Luckman of the Bears, pursued by fellow Hall of Famer Tom Fears of the Rams. (Pro Football Hall of Fame)

The Best of the Decade / 1950s

FIRST TEAM—OFFENSE

Position	Player	Team
E	Pete Pihos	Philadelphia Eagles
E	Elroy Hirsch	Los Angeles Rams
T	George Connor	Chicago Bears
T	Roosevelt Brown	New York Giants
G	Dick Stanfel	Detroit Loins
G	Stan Jones	Chicago Bears
C	Chuck Bednarik	Philadelphia Eagles
QB	Otto Graham	Cleveland Browns
RB	Frank Gifford	New York Giants
RB	Hugh McElhenny	San Francisco 49ers
RB	Ollie Matson	Chicago Cardinals

FIRST TEAM—DEFENSE

Position	Player	Team
DE	Gino Marchetti	Baltimore Colts
DE	Len Ford	Cleveland Browns
DT	Leo Nomellini	San Francisco 49ers
DT	Ernie Stautner	Pittsburgh Steelers
LB	Joe Schmidt	Detroit Loins
LB	Chuck Bednarik	Philadelphia Eagles
LB	George Connor	Chicago Bears
DB	Emlen Tunnell	New York Giants
DB	Night Train Lane	Chicago Cardinals/ Detroit Lions
DB	Yale Lary	Detroit Lions
DB	Jack Christiansen	Detroit Lions
K	Lou Groza	Cleveland Browns
P	Horace Gillom	Cleveland Browns
coach	*Paul Brown*	*Cleveland Browns*

SECOND TEAM—OFFENSE

Position	Player	Team
E	Tom Fears	Los Angeles Rams
E	Dante Lavelli	Cleveland Browns
T	Lou Groza	Cleveland Browns
T	Lou Creekmur	Detroit Loins
G	Dick Barwegan	Chicago Bears
G	Abe Gibron	Philadelphia Eagles
C	Frank Gatski	Cleveland Browns
QB	Bobby Layne	Detroit Loins
RB	Joe Perry	San Francisco 49ers
RB	Doak Walker	Detroit Lions
RB	Alan Ameche	Baltimore Colts

SECOND TEAM—DEFENSE

Position	Player	Team
DE	Andy Robustelli	New York Giants
DE	Gene Brito	Washington Redskins
DT	Art Donovan	Baltimore Colts
DT	Arnie Weinmeister	New York Giants
LB	Sam Huff	New York Giants
LB	Bill George	Chicago Bears
LB	Les Richter	Los Angeles Rams
DB	Jack Butler	Pittsburgh Steelers
DB	Bobby Dillon	Green Bay Packers
DB	Tom Landry	New York Giants
DB	Don Paul	Chicago Cardinals/ Cleveland Browns
K	Gordy Soltau	San Francisco 49ers
P	Norm Van Brocklin	Los Angeles Rams
coach	*Buddy Parker*	*Detroit Lions*

Events and Milestones

The AAFC goes out of business, but imparts to the NFL three teams: Baltimore Colts, Cleveland Browns, and San Francisco 49ers. The players from the defunct teams are placed in a pool to be selected by NFL teams. **(1950)**

The NFL changes from two five-team divisions, the East and West, to two conferences, the American (6 teams) and the National (7 teams). **(1950)**

Free substitution is restored. **(1950)**

The Los Angeles Rams become the first NFL team to televise all their games, both at home and away. **(1950)**

Lou Groza of the Browns boots 13 field goals, the most in the NFL since Jack Manders kicked 10 in the 1934 season. **(1950)**

Tom Fears breaks his own record by catching 84 passes for the Rams. He also sets the single game standard with 18 receptions against Green Bay, an NFL mark that still stands today. **(1950)**

Bob Shaw of the Chicago Cardinals bags an NFL record by catching five touchdown passes in a game against the Baltimore Colts. **(1950)**

Spec Sanders of the New York Yanks intercepts 13 passes to tie the season mark set by Dan Sandifer two years earlier. **(1950)**

Night game, white football. And a pair of Hall of Fame bound players of the 1950s, "Bullet" Bill Dudley (35), who played for the Steelers, Lions, and Redskins in his nine-year NFL career and Tom Fears, who was nine years a Los Angeles Ram. (Pro Football Hall of Fame)

Fulcrum of the San Francisco 49ers during its AAFC days and its first few years in the NFL was diminutive quarterback Frankie Albert (13), carrying the ball here against the Packers in the last game of his pro career in 1952. Moving in for the tackle is Green Bay guard Ray Bray (63); number 62 on the 49ers is tackle Bob Toneff. (Pro Football Hall of Fame) AP

Bob Waterfield of the Los Angeles Rams ties the single game mark for points after touchdown by kicking nine against the Colts. **(1950)**

The modern Pro Bowl, pitting all-star teams from the two conferences against each other, is inaugurated. The old Pro Bowl in which an all-star team took on that year's NFL champion had not been played since December 1942. **(1951)**

The Baltimore Colts drop out of competition and the money-losing franchise is returned to the NFL. Players from the Colts are incorporated into that year's collegiate draft. **(1951)**

The Rams cease televising home games after having lost more than $300,000 in gate revenues the year before despite fielding a team that played for the NFL title. **(1951)**

Norm Van Brocklin passes for 554 yards against the New York Yanks, an NFL record that still stands today. **(1951)**

For the first time an NFL championship game is televised coast to coast, and pro football fans throughout the nation are enabled to watch the Rams defeat the Browns 24—17 at the Los Angeles Coliseum. **(1951)**

Elroy "Crazylegs" Hirsch of the Los Angeles Rams sets an NFL record by gaining 1,495 yards on pass receptions. His 17 touchdown catches ties the record set by Don Hutson in 1942. **(1951)**

Dub Jones of the Cleveland Browns ties the single-game mark held by Ernie Nevers when he scores six touchdowns against the Chicago Bears. **(1951)**

The NFL franchise of the New York Yanks is sold back to the NFL and awarded to the Dallas Texans, but the team, averaging less than 15,000 in attendance at the cavernous Cotton Bowl, is returned to the league at midseason. Losing 11 of its 12 games, despite having players the caliber of Frank Tripucka, Buddy Young,

George Taliafero, Dick Hoerner, Zollie Toth, Gino Marchetti, Art Donovan, Barney Poole, Weldon Humble, and Tom Keane, the Texans folded after the season, gaining the distinction of being the last NFL team to go out of business. **(1952)**

Lou Groza boots 19 field goals for the Cleveland Browns, six more than the record he set two years previous. **(1952)**

Dick "Night Train" Lane of the Los Angeles Rams intercepts 14 passes, an NFL record which has yet to be surpassed. **(1952)**

To replace the Dallas Texans, a franchise is returned to Baltimore and the Colts are back in business. **(1953)**

The names American and National Conferences are changed to Eastern and Western Conferences. **(1953)**

Lou Groza of the Browns kicks 23 field goals to break the NFL record of 19. **(1953)**

Charlie Conerly, one of the finest passers of the era, was the New York Giants quarterback from 1948 through 1961. Conerly completed 1,418 passes for 19,488 yards and 173 touchdowns in his 14-year career. (New York Giants)

New rule: It is illegal to grab a player's face mask, except for that of the ball-carrier. **(1956)**

Cleveland Browns coach Paul Brown is the first to install a radio receiver in the helmet of his quarterback in order to transmit plays from the sideline. Shortly thereafter the practice is banned by NFL commissioner Bert Bell. **(1956)**

A single-game NFL attendance record is set when 102,368 fans watch the Rams drub the 49ers 37—24 at the Los Angeles Coliseum. **(1957)**

The bonus draft choice is eliminated. **(1958)**

Jim Brown of the Cleveland Browns breaks two Steve Van Buren rushing records when he gains 1,527 yards and scores 17 touchdowns. **(1958)**

For the first time in history, total paid attendance at NFL regular season games (72 in all) exceeds 3 million (3,006,124) and average paid attendance tops 40,000 (41,752). **(1958)**

The Champions / 1950s

1950	Cleveland Browns (*Browns* 30, *Rams* 28)	10–2–0
1951	Los Angeles Rams (*Rams* 24, *Browns* 17)	8–4–0
1952	Detroit Lions (*Lions* 17, *Browns* 7)	9–3–0
1953	Detroit Loins (*Lions* 17, *Browns* 16)	10–2–0
1954	Cleveland Browns (*Browns* 56, *Lions* 10)	9–3–0
1955	Cleveland Browns (*Browns* 38, *Rams* 14)	9–2–1
1956	New York Giants (*Giants* 47 *Bears* 7)	8–3–1
1957	Detroit Lions (*Lions* 59, *Browns* 14)	8–4–0
1958	Baltimore Colts (*Colts* 23, *Giants* 17)	9–3–0
1959	Baltimore Colts (*Colts* 31, *Giants* 16)	9–3–0

Norm Van Brocklin struggles to let loose a pass for the Rams in the 1952 playoff game against the Lions for the National Conference crown. Thwarting him in the effort is Detroit end Jim Doran. The Lions won it 31-21 and then went on to lick the Cleveland Browns for the NFL title that year. On the ground is 285-pound guard Les Bingaman (65) of the Lions and 214-pound guard Dick Dougherty (67) of the Rams. (Pro Football Hall of Fame) AP

Van Brocklin

Doran

Bingaman

Dougherty

The League Leaders / 1950s

1950

Scoring	Doak Walker, Detroit Lions, 128 points
Rushing	Marion Motley, Cleveland Browns, 810 yards
	Johnny Lujack, Chicago Bears, 11 TDs
Passing	Y. A. Tittle, Baltimore Colts, 161 completions
	Bobby Layne, Detroit Lions, 2,323 yards gained
	George Ratterman, New York Yanks, 22 TDs
Receiving	Tom Fears, Los Angeles Rams, 84 receptions
	Tom Fears, Los Angeles Rams, 1,116 yards gained
	Bob Shaw, Chicago Cardinals, 12 TDs
Field Goals	Lou Groza, Cleveland Browns, 13
PATs	Bob Waterfield, Los Angeles Rams, 54

1951

Scoring	Elroy Hirsch, Los Angeles Rams, 102 points
Rushing	Eddie Price, New York Giants, 971 yards
	Rob Goode, Washington Redskins, 9 TDs
Passing	Bobby Layne, Detroit Lions, 152 completions
	Bobby Layne, Detroit Lions, 2,403 yards gained
	Bobby Layne, Detroit Lions, 26 TDs
Receiving	Elroy Hirsch, Los Angeles Rams, 66 receptions
	Elroy Hirsch, Los Angeles Rams, 1,495 yards gained
	Elroy Hirsch, Los Angeles Rams, 17 TDs
Field Goals	Bob Waterfield, Los Angeles Rams, 13
PATs	Lou Groza, Cleveland Browns, 43
	Doak Walker, Detroit Lions, 43

Elroy "Crazylegs" Hirsch

Hall of Famer Lou "The Toe" Groza boots one of his 234 career field goals. In his 21-year career with the Cleveland Browns, Groza proved to be the first of the truly great place kickers, accounting for a total of 1,349 points, and was also an All Pro offensive tackle. (Cleveland Browns)

Onetime end 6'5", 255-pound Leon Hart, converted to fullback on this occasion, gains 16 yards for the Lions despite the Chicago Bears vaunted defense, which included such stalwarts of the 50s as George Connor (71), Ed Sprinkle (7), Joe Fortunato (31), Bill George (nearest Hart), and Doug Atkins (81). (Pro Football Hall of Fame) Chicago Sun Times

	1952
Scoring	Gordie Soltau, San Francisco 49ers, 94 points
Rushing	Dan Towler, Los Angeles Rams, 894 yards
	Dan Towler, Los Angeles Rams, 10 TDs
Passing	Otto Graham, Cleveland Browns, 181 completions
	Otto Graham, Cleveland Browns, 2,816 yards gained
	Jim Finks, Pittsburgh Steelers, 20 TDs
	Otto Graham, Cleveland Browns, 20 TDs
Receiving	Mac Speedie, Cleveland Browns, 62 receptions
	Billy Howton, Green Bay Packers, 1,231 yards gained
	Cloyce Box, Detroit Lions, 15 TDs
Field Goals	Lou Groza, Cleveland Browns, 19
PATs	Bob Waterfield, Los Angeles Rams, 44

1953

Scoring	Gordie Soltau, San Francisco 49ers, 114 points
Rushing	Joe Perry, San Francisco 49ers, 1,018 yards
	Joe Perry, San Francisco 49ers, 10 TDs
Passing	George Blanda, Chicago Bears, 169 completions
	Otto Graham, Cleveland Browns, 2,722 yards gained
	Bobby Thomason, Philadelphia Eagles, 21 TDs
Receiving	Pete Pihos, Philadelphia Eagles, 63 receptions
	Pete Pihos, Philadelphia Eagles, 1,049 yards gained
	Pete Pihos, Philadelphia Eagles, 10 TDs
	Billy Wilson, San Francisco 49ers, 10 TDs
Field Goals	Lou Groza, Cleveland Browns, 23
PATs	Gordie Soltau, San Francisco 49ers, 48

He could run if he had to, but Johnny Unitas of the Baltimore Colts is remembered principally as a passer, one of the game's all-time greats. On the merits of his accurate arm and astute leadership, he was the NFL's MVP three times and a cinch enshrinee in the Hall of Fame. Unitas completed 2,830 passes for 40,239 yards and 290 touchdowns in his 18-year NFL career. (Indianapolis Colts)

1954

Scoring	Bobby Walston, Philadelphia Eagles, 114 points
Rushing	Joe Perry, San Francisco 49ers, 1,049 yards
	Dan Towler, Los Angeles Rams, 11 TDs
Passing	Tobin Rote, Green Bay Packers, 180 completions
	Norm Van Brocklin, Los Angeles Rams, 2,637 yards gained
	Adrian Burk, Philadelphia Eagles, 23 TDs
Receiving	Pete Pihos, Philadelphia Eagles, 60 receptions
	Billy Wilson, San Francisco 49ers, 60 receptions
	Bob Boyd, Los Angeles Rams, 1,212 yards gained
	Harlon Hill, Chicago Bears, 12 TDs
Field Goals	Lou Groza, Cleveland Browns, 16
PATs	Doak Walker, Detroit Lions, 43

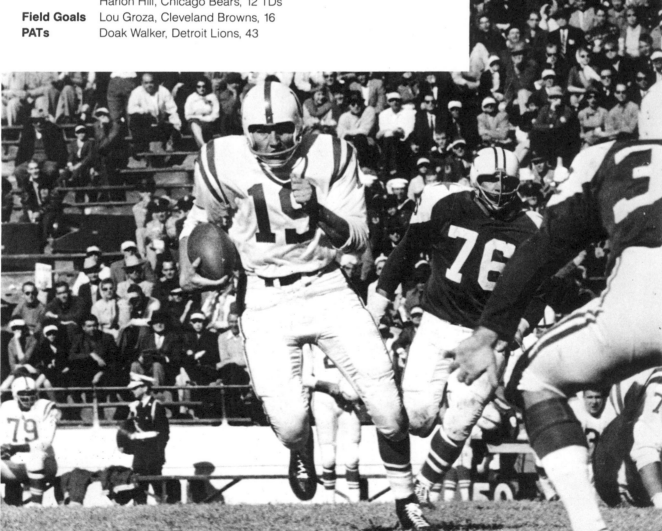

Jumping through the hoop here (hoop courtesy of a publicist of the 50s) is San Francisco's great running back Hugh McElhenny in a game against their arch rival Rams during the 1950s. McElhenny, in his 13 years in the NFL, gained 11,375 combined yards and scored 360 points. (Pro Football Hall of Fame)

A young George Blanda

1955

Scoring	Doak Walker, Detroit Lions. 96 points
Rushing	Alan Ameche, Baltimore Colts, 961 yards
	Alan Ameche, Baltimore Colts. 9 TDs
Passing	Jim Finks, Pittsburgh Steelers, 165 completions
	Jim Finks, Pittsburgh Steelers, 2,270 yards gained
	Tobin Rote, Green Bay Packers, 17 TDs
	Y. A. Tittle, San Francisco 49ers, 17 TDs
Receiving	Pete Pihos, Philadelphia Eagles, 62 receptions
	Pete Pihos, Philadelphia Eagles, 864 yards gained
	Harlon Hill, Chicago Bears, 9 TDs
Field Goals	Fred Cone, Green Bay Packers, 16
PATs	Lou Groza, Cleveland Browns, 44

1956

Scoring	Bobby Layne, Detroit Lions, 99 points
Rushing	Rick Casares, Chicago Bears, 1,126 yards
	Rick Casares, Chicago Bears, 12 TDs
Passing	Tobin Rote, Green Bay Packers, 146 completions
	Tobin Rote, Green Bay Packers, 2,203 yards gained
	Tobin Rote, Green Bay Packers, 18 TDs
Receiving	Billy Wilson, San Francisco 49ers, 60 receptions
	Billy Howton, Green Bay Packers, 1,188 yards gained
	Billy Howton, Green Bay Packers, 12 TDs
Field Goals	Sam Baker, Washington Redskins, 17
PATs	George Blanda, Chicago Bears, 45

Dazzling duo that got its start in the 50s, Paul Hornung (5) and Bart Starr (15) were key figures in Vince Lombardi's Green Bay Packer dynasty. Both made it to the Hall of Fame. Hornung's record of 176 points scored in 1960 is still the NFL standard, no one within 15 points of it as a matter of fact. He scored a total of 760 points, gained 3,711 yards rushing, caught 130 passes, passed well when asked to, and was, in Lombardi's view, "the best when the chips are down, the game on the line." Starr was the MVP in two Super Bowls, passed for a total of 24,718 yards and 152 touchdowns, and was an admired team leader who led Green Bay to five NFL championships. (Fred Roe)

1957

Scoring	Sam Baker, Washington Redskins, 77 points
Rushing	Jim Brown, Cleveland Browns, 942 yards
	Jim Brown, Cleveland Browns, 9 TDs
Passing	Y. A. Tittle, San Francisco 49ers, 176 receptions
	Johnny Unitas, Baltimore Colts, 2,550 yards gained
	Johnny Unitas, Baltimore Colts, 24 TDs
Receiving	Billy Wilson, San Francisco 49ers, 52 receptions
	Raymond Berry, Baltimore Colts, 800 yards gained
	Jim Mutscheller, Baltimore Colts, 8 TDs
Field Goals	Lou Groza, Cleveland Browns, 15
PATs	Paige Cothren, Los Angeles Rams, 38

Frank Gifford, All-American from Southern Cal and the first round draft choice of the Giants in 1952, was the gemstone in the New York backfield as a halfback and flanker through 1964. His combined total yards gained of 9,753 and fine defensive play as well earned him a berth in the Pro Football Hall of Fame. (Pro Football Hall of Fame)

1958

Scoring	Jim Brown, Cleveland Browns, 108 points
Rushing	Jim Brown, Cleveland Browns, 1,527 yards
	Jim Brown, Cleveland Browns, 17 TDs
Passing	Norm Van Brocklin, Philadelphia Eagles, 198 completions
	Bill Wade, Los Angeles Rams, 2,875 yards gained
	Johnny Unitas, Baltimore Colts, 19 TDs
Receiving	Raymond Berry, Baltimore Colts, 56 receptions
	Pete Retzlaff, Philadelphia Eagles, 56 receptions
	Del Shofner, Los Angeles Rams, 1,097 yards gained
	Raymond Berry, Baltimore Colts, 9 TDs
	Tommy McDonald, Philadelphia Eagles, 9 TDs
Field Goals	Paige Cothren, Los Angeles Rams, 14
	Tom Miner, Pittsburgh Steelers, 14
PATs	Steve Myrha, Baltimore Colts, 48

1959

Scoring	Paul Hornung, Green Bay Packers, 94 points
Rushing	Jim Brown, Cleveland Browns, 1,329 yards
	Jim Brown, Cleveland Browns, 14 TDs
Passing	Johnny Unitas, Baltimore Colts, 193 completions
	Johnny Unitas, Baltimore Colts, 2,899 yards gained
	Johnny Unitas, Baltimore Colts, 32 TDs
Receiving	Raymond Berry, Baltimore Colts, 66 receptions
	Raymond Berry, Baltimore Colts, 959 yards gained
	Raymond Berry, Baltimore Colts, 14 TDs
Field Goals	Pat Summerall, New York Giants, 20
PATs	Steve Myrha, Baltimore Colts, 50

A little action under the lights. Alex Webster (29) churns out a few yards for the Giants against the Browns in 1958. New York beat Cleveland three times that season, including a playoff game for Eastern Conference title. Other Giants are center Ray Wietecha (55) and tackle Frank Youso (72); the Browns' defenders are linebackers Vince Costello (50) and Walt Michaels (34) and tackles Henry Jordan (72) and Bob Gain (79). (Pro Football Hall of Fame)

Skeptics Still

In the early days of professional football, college coaches disdained it. Amos Alonzo Stagg, legendary coach at the University of Chicago, wrote: "And now comes along another serious menace, possibly greater than all others, *viz.* Sunday professional football. . . . To cooperate with Sunday professional football games is to cooperate with forces which are destructive of the finest elements of interscholastic and intercollegiate football and to add to the heavy burden of the schools and colleges in preserving it in its ennobling worth."

Bob Zuppke, Red Grange's coach at Illinois, would not speak to his former star halfback for years after the Galloping Ghost became a pro in 1925.

And practically all the big name college coaches of those days held the pro game to be vastly inferior.

By 1950, one would think players like Don Hutson, Sammy Baugh, Otto Graham, and Steve Van Buren and teams like the Chicago Bears of the early 1940s and the Cardinals, Eagles, Rams and Browns of the latter part of the decade might have changed that kind of thinking.

Not so. Stanley Woodward, writing for *Collier's* magazine in 1950, tells of this chat with Earl "Red" Blaik, coach of the great Army teams of that era, after having watched an especially exciting game at Yankee Stadium between the New York Yankees and the Cleveland Browns.

> Going downtown I shared a cab with Colonel Blaik . . . Trying to start a conversation, I said, "Great game, eh?"
> "Yes," said the Colonel, composedly rubbing his chin, "but it wasn't football."
> Not football! . . . .
> "Football is a college game. It calls for these things: youth, condition, spirit, plus continuous hard work by coaches as well as players."
> What's the matter with professional football?
> "Nothing. It's what it aims to be. It's a show. The pros are in the entertainment business. . . . I think a good pro team might get itself up to beat a good college team in a single game. But if the pro team were put into a league with good college teams—like Notre Dame, Michigan, Ohio State, Oklahoma, Southern California, Tennessee, and Texas—it would have to learn to play football the way the colleges do or it wouldn't stand a chance. A fiery team like Tennessee would cripple a pro club. . . .
> "The colleges have the boys in their best years. Few of them ever play as well after they become professionals. As they grow older they acquire responsibilities and perspective, also caution. They lose the reckless abandon that marked their play in college. They get bigger and fatter. They may look imposing to the fans, but they are not the same football players. I know, and other college coaches know, that an active, enthusiastic young fellow of 190 pounds can do everything better than an old pro who weighs 250 or 260. . . . I know for certain that a man who wears a rubber tire can't play football with one who is down to hard condition. . . .
> "I suppose I sound pretty critical."

The New Set-up, 1950

With the admission of three teams from the folded AAFC, the NFL went from two divisions to two new conferences. This was the set-up:

American Conference	National Conference
Chicago Cardinals	Baltimore Colts
Cleveland Browns	Chicago Bears
New York Giants	Detroit Lions
Philadelphia Eagles	Green Bay Packers
Pittsburgh Steelers	Los Angeles Rams
Washington Redskins	New York Yanks
	San Francisco 49ers

The Browns triumphed in the American Conference by defeating the New York Giants in a special playoff game, 8–3 (both teams ended the season with 10–2 records). The Los Angeles Rams won the National Conference in another special playoff contest, beating the Chicago Bears 24–14 (their records were 9–3). Then Cleveland took the title in their maiden year in the NFL, edging the Rams 30–28.

Pay Scales, 1957

The pay for playing professional football in the 1950s was not quite like it is in the 1980s. Witness this list from a report prepared by the National Football League and submitted to the Anti-Trust Subcommittee of the U.S. House of Representatives in July 1957.

Team	Total Players Salaries	Individual Salary Range
Cleveland Browns	$368,031	$6,000–19,000
Los Angeles Ram	$352,958	$5,500–20,000
Chicago Bears	$342,525	$6,500–14,200
San Francisco 49ers	$332,614	$5,600–20,100
Detroit Lions	$330,375	$5,500–20,000
New York Giants	$324,258	$5,200–16,000
Chicago Cardinals	$418,441	$5,500–20,000
Baltimore Colts	$294,392	$6,000–17,500
Philadelphia Eagles	$283,483	$5,750–13,500
Green Bay Packers	$277,642	$5,000–18,500
Pittsburgh Steelers	$276,875	$5,250–12,250
Washington Redskins	$275,942	$5,000–14,000

MIDDLE MAYHEM

Corralled, halfback Steve Bagarus of the Redskins. Number 21 is linebacker Chuck Cherundolo of the Steelers. 1946. (Pro Football Hall of Fame)

Pile-up in the late 1940s. Number 74 is Hall of Fame guard Bill Willis of the Browns, one of the first blacks to break the color barrier back in 1946. (Pro Football Hall of Fame)

Being face-masked, even though he didn't wear a face mask, is quarterback Fred Enke of the Lions. Face-masking him is end Joe Abbey of the Bears. 1948. (Pro Football Hall of Fame)

Battle for the ball. Mal Kutner of the Chicago Cardinals is the intended receiver but he is not alone in his quest for possession; battling him are Ram defenders George Sims (left) and Crazylegs Hirsch (right). 1949. (Pro Football Hall of Fame) Acme Photo

Helmeted, halfback Jim Cason of the 49ers is on his way to the turf. Dehelmeting him is linebacker Ed Sharkey of the New York Yanks. 1950. (Pro Football Hall of Fame) AP

Right cross. Fred Davis of the Bears delivers it to fullback Dick Hoerner of the Rams. The ballcarrier is Los Angeles halfback Paul Barry following the interference of guard Dave Stephenson. Other Bears are Don Kindt (6) and Ed Sprinkle (7). 1950. (Pro Football Hall of Fame) AP

Scrunched, Otto Graham, kept the football and a pained expression but not his helmet. Saying something about the ununiformity of the time are the different helmets worn by Pittsburgh Steeler defenders. Early 50s. (Pro Football Hall of Fame)

Slightly confused, Jim Powers (62) of the 49ers tackles the goalpost. Pinioned against it is Ram halfback Paul Barry. Los Angeles onlookers are Deacon Dan Towler (32), Bob Waterfield (7), and Gil Bouley (66). 1950. (Pro Football Hall of Fame) AP

Going down. Philadelphia's Pete Pihos with the white football of the NFL night games of the day is escorted to the earth by Detroit defensive back Don Doll. 1951. (Pro Football Hall of Fame)

The proverbial priceless expression belongs to Doak Walker of the Lions at the bottom of this pile. The Lion lunging at the Steelers is halfback Bob Hoernschmeyer. 1953. (Pro Football Hall of Fame) AP

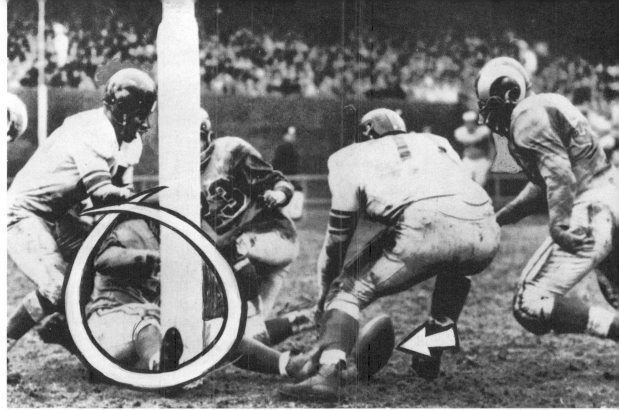

The circle marks the spot where Ram power runner Dan Towler plowed into the goalpost. Stunned, he sits and perhaps foggily contemplates the fact that the immovable object has prevailed over this irresistable force. 1954. (Pro Football Hall of Fame) AP

Goal line mayhem. The Browns and the Lions mingle. Number 54 of Cleveland is linebacker Sam Palumbo; 82 end Carlton Massey. For the Lions, number 66 is guard Harley Sewell and 76 is tackle Lou Creekmur. 1956. (Pro Football Hall of Fame)

3 THE MODERN ERA

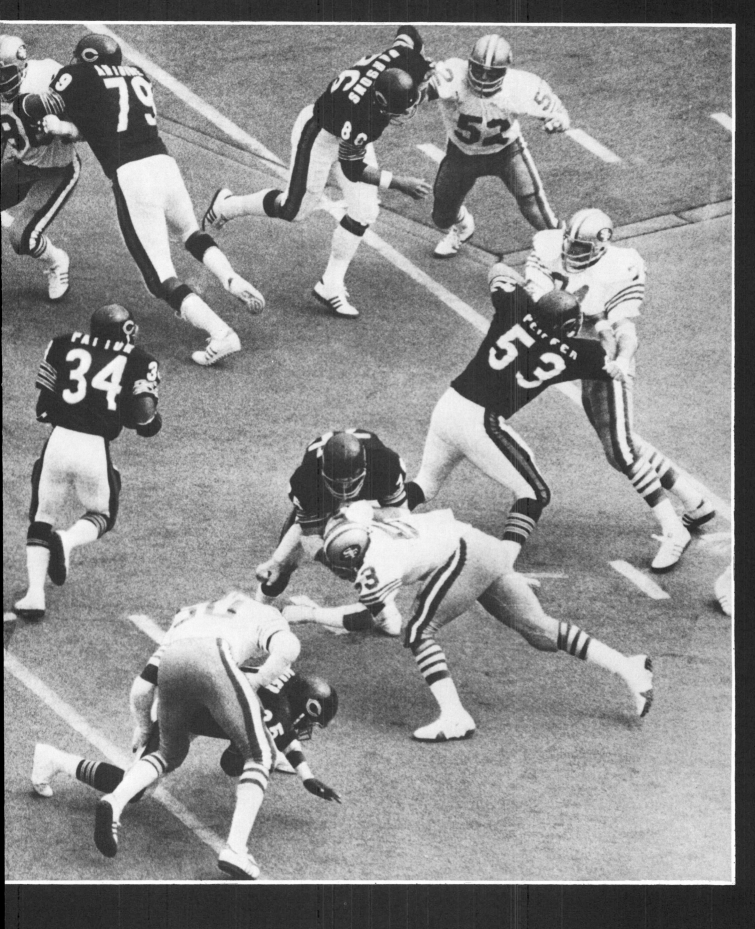

The 1960s

The dawn of the decade of the 60s was truly the beginning of the modern era of professional football. Interest in the sport had increased dramatically, the game had become much more exciting as a result of wide-open offenses, and the value of the franchises soared.

The new interloping American Football League opened its gates and challenged the NFL, and unlike its predecessors it survived and eventually forced a merger. As a result, pro football fans got a slew of new teams to watch and a Super Bowl to climax each season.

In the NFL, the 60s saw the development of Vince Lombardi's dynasty in Green Bay, with greats like Paul Hornung, Bart Starr, Jim Taylor, and so many others; the awesome defense of the New York Giants behind players like Sam Huff, Andy Robustelli, and Rosey Grier; the emergence of Tom Landry's Dallas Cowboys by mid-decade as a consistent powerhouse with the likes of Dandy Don Meredith, Bob Hayes, and Bob Lilly. There was the running of Jim Brown and Gale Sayers, the passing of Y. A. Tittle and Johnny Unitas, the pass catching of Del Shofner and Paul Warfield, and the crushing tackles dealt out by such brutalizers as Dick

Pete Gogolak, the first of the soccer-style kickers, brought his then unorthodox method of booting the football to the AFL in 1964 and the NFL in 1966. (Fred Roe)

83

Butkus, Alex Karras, Gino Marchetti, Merlin Olsen, Deacon Jones, and Ray Nitschke.

Over in the fledgling AFL, George Blanda proved ageless rewriting the pro football record book. In the pass-obsessed AFL along came Len Dawson, Jack Kemp, Joe Namath, and Daryle Lamonica, as well as a host of other players whose names would be tinged with greatness like Lance Alworth, Jim Otto, Ron Mix, Gene Upshaw, Bobby Bell, Don Maynard, and Fred Biletnikoff, among them.

There was competition everywhere in the 60s, on the field and between the leagues, and the fans were royally entertained.

Jim Brown of Cleveland batters his way through a nest of St. Louis Cardinals on his way to setting just about every rushing record during his nine-year NFL career. (Fred Roe)

The Best of the Decade / 1960s

FIRST TEAM–OFFENSE

Position	Player	Team
WR	Raymond Berry	Baltimore Colts
WR	Lance Alworth	San Diego Chargers
TE	Mike Ditka	Chicago Bears
T	Forrest Gregg	Green Bay Packers
T	Jim Parker	Baltimore Colts
G	Billy Shaw	Buffalo Bills
G	Jerry Kramer	Green Bay Packers
C	Jim Ringo	Green Bay Packers
QB	Johnny Unitas	Baltimore Colts
RB	Gale Sayers	Chicago Bears
RB	Jim Brown	Cleveland Browns

FIRST TEAM–DEFENSE

Position	Player	Team
DE	Deacon Jones	Los Angeles Rams
DE	Doug Atkins	Chicago Bears
DT	Bob Lilly	Dallas Cowboys
DT	Merlin Olsen	Los Angeles Rams
LB	Ray Nitschke	Green Bay Packers
LB	Dick Butkus	Chicago Bears
LB	Tommy Nobis	Atlanta Falcons
DB	Herb Adderley	Green Bay Packers
DB	Larry Wilson	St. Louis Cardinals
DB	Ed Meador	Los Angeles Rams
DB	Willie Wood	Green Bay Packers
K	George Blanda	Houston Oilers/ Oakland Raiders
P	Don Chandler	New York Giants/ Green Bay Packers
coach	*Vince Lombardi*	*Green Bay Packers*

SECOND TEAM–OFFENSE

Position	Player	Team
WR	Don Maynard	New York Jets
WR	Del Shofner	New York Giants
TE	John Mackey	Baltimore Colts
T	Ron Mix	San Diego Chargers
T	Ralph Neely	Dallas Cowboys
G	Gene Hickerson	Cleveland Browns
G	Howard Mudd	San Francisco 49ers
C	Jim Otto	Oakland Raiders
QB	Joe Namath	New York Jets
RB	Paul Hornung	Green Bay Packers
RB	Jim Taylor	Green Bay Packers

SECOND TEAM–DEFENSE

Position	Player	Team
DE	Willie Davis	Green Bay Packers
DE	Jim Katcavage	New York Giants
DT	Henry Jordan	Green Bay Packers
DT	Alex Karras	Detroit Lions
LB	Bobby Bell	Kansas City Chiefs
LB	Chuck Howley	Dallas Cowboys
LB	Nick Buoniconti	Boston Patriots/ Miami Dolphins
DB	Bobby Boyd	Baltimore Colts
DB	Johnny Robinson	Kansas City Chiefs
DB	Paul Krause	Washington Redskins
DB	Dave Grayson	Oakland Raiders
K	Jim Bakken	St. Louis Cardinals
P	Jerrell Wilson	Kansas City Chiefs
coach	*Blanton Collier*	*Cleveland Browns*

Gale Sayers, the most dazzling runner the game has yet produced, provided a lot of excitement for Chicago Bear fans during an otherwise lackluster era. (Pro Football Hall of Fame)

Events and Milestones

An NFL franchise is awarded for Dallas to Clint Murchison, Jr., and Bedford Wynne. Taking the name Cowboys, the team is to play in the NFC Western Conference under head coach Tom Landry. **(1960)**

The Chicago Cardinals relocate in St. Louis and remain in the NFC Eastern Conference. **(1960)**

A fourth American Football League begins play. Founded by Lamar Hunt of Dallas, Texas, the new league has franchises in eight cities: Boston, Buffalo, Dallas, Denver, Houston, Los Angeles, New York, and Oakland. **(1960)**

Pete Rozelle, general manager of the Los Angeles Rams, is elected the new commissioner of the National Football League. **(1960)**

Paul Hornung of the Packers sets a new single season scoring record of 176 points (15 TDs, 15 FGs, 41 PATs) eclipsing the mark of 138 set by Don Hutson back in 1942. **(1960)**

Johnny Unitas of the Colts and Jack Kemp of the Chargers become the first pro passers in history to gain more than 3,000 yards; Unitas setting the record with 3,099 and Kemp gaining 3,018. **(1960)**

Frank Tripucka of the AFL Broncos sets a new standard for pass completions with 248, 38 more than Sammy Baugh slung back in 1947. **(1960)**

Lionel Taylor of the Broncos catches more passes than any preceding pro receiver when he gathers in 92. **(1960)**

Bobby Layne, in the twilight of his illustrious career, lines up behind the center for the Steelers in a game against the fledgling Dallas Cowboys in 1960. [Dallas Cowboys]

The Minnesota Vikings, representing the twin cities of Minneapolis/St. Paul join the NFL. Under head coach Norm Van Brocklin, they are to play in the NFL's Western Conference. **(1961)**

The Los Angeles Chargers move to San Diego and remain in the AFL West. **(1961)**

George Blanda of Houston throws more touchdown passes than any player in pro football history, 36. Blanda also sets the record for extra points in a season, booting 64 which was 10 more than Bob Waterfield kicked back in 1950. **(1961)**

Sonny Jurgensen, then playing for the Eagles, takes the record for passing yardage, gaining 3,723 yards. **(1961)**

Denver's Lionel Taylor breaks his own pass catching record with 100 receptions. **(1961)**

Charley Hennigan of the Oilers sets the standard for yards gained on pass receptions with 1,746. **(1961)**

A new rule makes it illegal to grab any player by the face mask (previously it was permissible to take in hand a ballcarrier's face mask). **(1962)**

Green Bay fullback Jim Taylor sets the NFL mark for rushing touchdowns with 19. **(1962)**

Lou Michaels of the NFL Steelers kicks 26 field goals and Gene Mingo of the AFL Broncos boots 27, both breaking the mark of 23 set by Lou Groza in 1953. **(1962)**

The Dallas Texans of the AFL move to Kansas City and change their name to the Chiefs. **(1963)**

The New York Titans change ownership as well as their name, adopting the moniker Jets. **(1963)**

The Pro Football Hall of Fame is dedicated in Canton, Ohio, site of the key meeting at which the National Football League was founded in 1920. Seventeen charter members are inducted. (1963)

Jim Brown of the Cleveland Browns sets an NFL standard by rushing for 1,863 yards, beating his own record by more than 400 yards. (1963)

Y. A. Tittle of the New York Giants, tosses 36 touchdown passes to equal the record set by George Blanda in 1961. (1963)

Houston's George Blanda adds another NFL record to his portfolio when he completes 262 passes. (1964)

Charley Hennigan of the Oilers breaks the single-season pass reception mark by grabbing 101 passes. (1964)

The NFL adds a sixth official, the line judge. (1965)

Rookie Gale Sayers of the Chicago Bears ties the single-game record by scoring six touchdowns against the San Francisco 49ers, and sets an NFL mark by scoring 22 touchdowns in a season. (1965)

The NFL and the AFL agree to merge, although their games will be played within each league during the regular season. A championship game is to be held between the winners of each league. (1966)

The Atlanta Falcons join the NFC, the franchise going to Rankin M. Smith, Jr. The Falcons are slotted in the NFL Eastern Conference along with the Giants, Redskins, Steelers, Cowboys, Eagles, Browns, and Cardinals. (1966)

The AFL accepts the Miami Dolphins into its fold, the franchise awarded to Joe Robbie. The Dolphins are placed in the AFL East, joining the Bills, Jets, Patriots, and Oilers. (1966)

Al Davis, coach and general manager of the Oakland Raiders replaces Joe Foss on an interim basis as AFL commissioner. Milt Woodward, shortly thereafter, takes over the duties of running the AFL and Davis returns to the Raiders. (1966)

Charlie Gogolak of the Redskins kicks nine field goals in one game to tie the NFL record held jointly by Pat Harder and Bob Waterfield. (1966)

Bruce Gossett of the Rams sets a new NFL standard by booting 28 field goals. (1966)

The first Super Bowl, although it would not take on that name until 1968, is played and the NFL Packers defeat the AFL Chiefs 35–10. (1967)

With the NFL and the AFL under one league umbrella, a new alignment is ordered. The AFL keeps two divisions intact, but the NFL's two conferences are divided into two divisions each, four teams per division. (1967)

The New Orleans Saints are admitted to the NFL, the franchise going to John W. Mecom, Jr. The Saints are slated in the NFL Eastern Conference's Capitol Division along with the Eagles, Cowboys, and Redskins. (1967)

Jim Bakken of the St. Louis Cardinals kicks seven field goals in a game against the Steelers, an NFL mark that has never been equalled. (1967)

Joe Namath of the New York Jets becomes the first quarterback in NFL history to pass for more than 4,000 yards in a single season (4,007). At the same time, Sonny Jurgensen of the Redskins sets another NFL passing mark by completing 288 passes. (1967)

The Cincinnati Bengals are added to the AFL, with former Cleveland Browns coach Paul Brown and a group of investors securing the franchise. The Bengals join the AFL West to compete with the Broncos, Chargers, Chiefs, and Raiders. (1968)

Jim Turner of the New York Jets boots 34 field goals, an NFL record that would stand until 1983. (1968)

Lamar Hunt, founder of the American Football League and owner of the Dallas Texans/ Kansas City Chiefs. (Pro Football Hall of Fame)

The Fourth AFL

The charter membership of the American Football League, debuting in 1960, consisted of these eight teams in this divisional alignment:

Eastern Division	Coach
Boston Patriots	Lou Saban
Buffalo Bills	Buster Ramsey
Houston Oilers	Lou Rymkus
New York Titans	Sammy Baugh

Western Division	Coach
Dallas Texans	Hank Stram
Denver Broncos	Frank Filchock
Los Angeles Chargers	Sid Gillman
Oakland Raiders	Eddie Erdelatz

Among the bigger football names who signed to play in the neophyte AFL were:

George Blanda	Oilers
Billy Cannon	Oilers
Charley Hennigan	Oilers
Don Maynard	Titans
Jack Kemp	Chargers
Paul Lowe	Chargers
Ron Mix	Charger
Ben Agajanian	Chargers
Abner Haynes	Texans
Tom Flores	Raiders
Babe Parilli	Raiders
Jim Otto	Raiders
Frank Tripucka	Broncos
Lionel Taylor	Broncos
Gene Mingo	Broncos
Gino Cappelletti	Patriots

In the AFL inaugural season, Houston triumphed in the East with a record of 10-4-0, and the Los Angeles Chargers in the West with an identical record. The Oilers then took the AFL's first championship with a 24–16 victory over the Chargers at Houston behind three touchdown passes thrown by George Blanda, including an 88-yarder to Billy Cannon. Ben Agajanian booted three field goals for the Chargers.

Dan Reeves finds a big hole and a Cowboy touchdown against the Steelers in 1965. Twenty-two years later as a head coach he would take his Denver Broncos to the Super Bowl XXI. (Dallas Cowboys)

Hall of Fame Charter Membership

When the Pro Football Hall of Fame was instituted in 1963, a select group of seventeen pioneers of the sport, some stars on the field and others crucial coaches and/or administrators were selected as charter enshrinees. These, in alphabetical order, were those so honored.

Charter Enshrinee	Principal Affiliation
Sammy Baugh	Washington Redskins
Bert Bell	Owner: Eagles, Steelers/ NFL commissioner
Joe Carr	NFL president
Dutch Clark	Portsmouth Spartans/ Detroit Lions
Red Grange	Chicago Bears
George Halas	Owner/coach/player: Chicago Bears
Mel Hein	New York Giants
Pete Henry	Canton Bulldogs
Cal Hubbard	Green Bay Packers
Don Hutson	Green Bay Packers
Curly Lambeau	Green Bay Packers
Tim Mara	Owner: New York Giants
George Preston Marshall	Owner: Washington Redskins
Johnny Blood McNally	Green Bay Packers
Bronko Nagurski	Chicago Bears
Ernie Nevers	Duluth Eskimos/ Chicago Cardinals
Jim Thorpe	Canton Bulldogs/ Oorang Indians

Cowboy Camp, 1960 Style

The newly enfranchised Dallas Cowboys held their first training camp in the summer of 1960 in Forest Grove, Oregon, far from the plains of Texas. Sam Blair, in his book *Dallas Cowboys, Pro or Con*, tells about one of the first and more eccentric hopefuls, nicknamed Jungle Jamey, who attended it.

Portland was the home of James Bacilerri, which meant it was only a short drive out to the Dallas camp in his battered 1949 Ford, which was covered with autographs and had a hunk of bear meat swinging from the radio aerial. Proximity meant nothing to Jungle Jamey, however. He had traveled the entire country in pursuit of his two greatest pleasures, visiting his favorite teams and gate-crashing. He was capable of turning up anywhere. . . .

You knew right away he wasn't just another guy who dropped by to watch practice. A stocky man in his middle thirties, he wore a white hunter's hat with a snakeskin band, ragged short pants, a football jersey bearing number 22, and he was barefoot. Oh, yes, he had a large white rabbit on a leash. He called the rabbit 'Texas Freeloader.' Jungle Jamey and his rabbit soon were leading the players out of the locker room to the practice field, where he would try a few barefoot field goals and dispense a lot of advice. . . . But it was inevitable that Jamey soon would be at odds with Tex Schramm. Jamey claimed that Schramm shouldn't be there and was disturbed that Tex had so much authority and yet was neither coaching nor playing. Schramm had different ideas about who was out of place. . . .

Intriguing character though he was, Jamey added nothing to the camp in Schramm's opinion. Several nights, Tex was ready to evict him, but couldn't find him. One night, Schramm got down on his hands and knees in the recreation room and looked under a grand piano, where Jamey sometimes slept. But that was one of the nights that Jamey went to the stadium and slept on the 50-yard line. . . .

Landry had no objection to Jamey, and he talked Schramm into letting him stay. He was still there the first weekend in August, when the Cowboys flew to Seattle for their first exhibition game, Jamey was on the plane.

Fritz Hawn had arrived earlier and decided there should be a band to meet the team at the airport. He hired some musicians and gave them a large sign 'Jungle Jamey's Jazz Band.' As the Cowboys left the plane, they played happily and nodded to Jamey.

Eddie LeBaron (14) tosses one for the Cowboys as one lonely fan watches in a game against the Vikings in those embryonic days before the Dallas Cowboys became popular, much less a national institution. (Dallas Cowboys)

The Champions / 1960s

1960	NFL	Philadelphia Eagles	10–2–0
		(*Eagles* 17, *Packers* 13)	
	AFL	Houston Oilers	10–4–0
		(*Oilers* 24, *Chargers* 16)	
1961	NFL	Green Bay Packers	11–3–0
		(*Packers* 37, *Giants* 0)	
	AFL	Houston Oilers	10–3–1
		(*Oilers* 10, *Chargers* 3)	
1962	NFL	Green Bay Packers	13–1–0
		(*Packers* 16, *Giants* 7)	
	AFL	Dallas Texans	11–3–0
		(*Texans* 20, *Oilers* 17)	
1963	NFL	Chicago Bears	11–1–2
		(*Bears* 14, *Giants* 10)	
	AFL	San Diego Chargers	11–3–0
		(*Chargers* 51, *Patriots* 10)	
1964	NFL	Cleveland Browns	10–3–1
		(*Browns* 27, *Colts* 0)	
	AFL	Buffalo Bills	12–2–0
		(*Bills* 20, *Chargers* 7)	
1965	NFL	Green Bay Packers	10–3–1
		(*Packers* 23, *Browns* 12)	
	AFL	Buffalo Bills	10–3–1
		(*Bills* 23, *Chargers* 0)	
1966	NFL	Green Bay Packers	12–2–0
		(*Packers* 34, *Cowboys* 27)	
	AFL	Kansas City Chiefs	11–2–1
		(*Chiefs* 31, *Bills* 7)	

Super Bowl I

Green Bay Packers	35
Kansas City Chiefs	10

1967	NFL	Green Bay Packers	9–4–1
		(*Packers* 21, *Cowboys* 17)	
	AFL	Oakland Raiders	13–1–0
		(*Raiders* 40, *Oilers* 7)	

Super Bowl II

Green Bay Packers	33
Oakland Raiders	14

1968	NFL	Baltimore Colts	13–1–0
		(*Colts* 34, *Browns* 0)	
	AFL	New York Jets	11–3–0
		(*Jets* 27, *Raiders* 23)	

Super Bowl III

New York Jets	16
Baltimore Colts	7

1969	NFL	Minnesota Vikings	12–2–0
		(*Vikings* 27, *Browns* 7)	
	AFL	Kansas City Chiefs	11–2–0
		(*Chiefs* 17, *Raiders* 7)	

Super Bowl IV

Kansas City Chiefs	23
Minnesota Vikings	7

Earl Morrall of the Baltimore Colts flees Giant defender Roger Anderson. (New York Giants)

The League Leaders / 1960s

1960

Scoring

    NFL   Paul Hornung, Green Bay Packers, 176 points

    AFL   Gene Mingo, Denver Broncos, 123 points

Rushing

    NFL   Jim Brown, Cleveland Browns, 1,257 yards

    AFL   Abner Haynes, Dallas Texans, 875 yards

    NFL   Paul Hornung, Green Bay Packers, 13 TDs

    AFL   Abner Haynes, Dallas Texans, 9 TDs

            Paul Lowe, Los Angeles Chargers, 9 TDs

Passing

    NFL   Johnny Unitas, Baltimore Colts, 190 completions

    AFL   Frank Tripucka, Denver Broncos, 248 completions

    NFL   Johnny Unitas, Baltimore Colts, 3,099 yards gained

    AFL   Frank Tripucka, Denver Broncos, 3,038 yards gained

    NFL   Johnny Unitas, Baltimore Colts, 25 TDs

    AFL   Al Dorow, New York Titans, 26 TDs

Receiving

    NFL   Raymond Berry, Baltimore Colts, 74 receptions

    AFL   Lionel Taylor, Denver Broncos, 92 receptions

    NFL   Raymond Berry, Baltimore Colts, 1,298 yards gained

    AFL   Bill Groman, Houston Oilers, 1,473 yards gained

    NFL   Sonny Randle, St. Louis Cardinals, 15 TDs

    AFL   Art Powell, New York Titans, 14 TDs

Field Goals

    NFL   Tommy Davis, San Francisco 49ers, 19

    AFL   Gene Mingo, Denver Broncos, 18

PATs

    NFL   Sam Baker, Cleveland Browns, 44

    AFL   Bill Schockley, New York Titans, 47

Ever-scrambling Fran Tarkenton of the Giants tries to elude a pair of Redskin defenders. (New York Giants)

Broadway Joe Namath made good on his promise to bring the AFL its first Super Bowl championship. (Fred Roe)

1961

Scoring

NFL   Paul Hornung, Green Bay Packers, 146 points
AFL   Gino Cappelletti, Boston Patriots, 147 points

Rushing

NFL   Jim Brown, Cleveland Browns, 1,408 yards
AFL   Billy Cannon, Houston Oilers, 948 yards
NFL   Jim Taylor, Green Bay Packers, 15 TDs
AFL   Abner Haynes, Dallas Texans, 9 TDs
         Paul Lowe, Los Angeles Chargers, 9 TDs

Passing

NFL   Sonny Jurgensen, Philadelphia Eagles, 235 completions
AFL   Al Dorow, New York Titans, 197 completions
NFL   Sonny Jurgensen, Philadelphia Eagles, 3,723 yards gained
AFL   George Blanda, Houston Oilers, 3,330 yards gained
NFL   Sonny Jurgensen, Philadelphia Eagles, 32 TDs
AFL   George Blanda, Houston Oilers, 36 TDs

Receiving

NFL   Jim Phillips, Los Angeles Rams, 78 receptions
AFL   Lionel Taylor, Denver Broncos, 100 receptions
NFL   Tommy McDonald, Philadelphia Eagles, 1,144 yards gained
AFL   Charley Hennigan, Houston Oilers, 1,746 yards gained
NFL   Tommy McDonald, Philadelphia Eagles, 13 TDs
AFL   Bill Groman, Houston Oilers, 17 TDs

Field Goals

NFL   Steve Myrha, Baltimore Colts, 21
AFL   Gino Cappelletti, Boston Patriots, 17

PATs

NFL   Pat Summerall, New York Giants, 46
AFL   George Blanda, Houston Oilers, 64

1962

Scoring

NFL   Jim Taylor, Green Bay Packers, 114 points
AFL   Gene Mingo, Denver Broncos, 137 points

Rushing

NFL   Jim Taylor, Green Bay Packers, 1,474 yards
AFL   Cookie Gilchrist, Buffalo Bills, 1,096 yards
NFL   Jim Taylor, Green Bay Packers, 19 TDs
AFL   Cookie Gilchrist, Buffalo Bills, 13 TDs
         Abner Haynes, Dallas Texans, 13 TDs

Passing

NFL   Bill Wade, Chicago Bears, 225 completions
AFL   Frank Tripucka, Denver Broncos, 240 completions
NFL   Sonny Jurgensen, Philadelphia Eagles, 3,261 yards gained
AFL   Frank Tripucka, Denver Broncos, 2,917 yards gained
NFL   Y. A. Tittle, New York Giants, 33 TDs
AFL   Len Dawson, Dallas Texans, 29 TDs

Receiving

NFL   Bobby Mitchell, Washington Redskins, 72 receptions
AFL   Lionel Taylor, Denver Broncos, 77 receptions
NFL   Bobby Mitchell, Washington Redskins, 1,384 yards gained
AFL   Art Powell, New York Titans, 1,130 yards gained
NFL   Frank Clarke, Dallas Cowboys, 14 TDs
AFL   Chris Burford, Dallas Texans, 12 TDs

Field Goals

NFL   Lou Michaels, Pittsburgh Steelers, 26
AFL   Gene Mingo, Denver Broncos, 27

PATs

NFL   Sam Baker, Dallas Cowboys, 50
AFL   George Blanda, Houston Oilers, 48

1963

Scoring

NFL   Don Chandler, New York Giants, 106 points
AFL   Gino Cappelletti, Boston Patriots, 113 points

Rushing

NFL   Jim Brown, Cleveland Browns, 1,863 yards
AFL   Clem Daniels, Oakland Raiders, 1,099 yards
NFL   Jim Brown, Cleveland Browns, 12 TDs
AFL   Cookie Gilchrist, Buffalo Bills, 12 TDs

Passing

NFL   Johnny Unitas, Baltimore Colts, 237 completions
AFL   George Blanda, Houston Oilers, 224 completions
NFL   Johnny Unitas, Baltimore Colts, 3,481 yards gained
AFL   George Blanda, Houston Oilers, 3,003 yards gained
NFL   Y. A. Tittle, New York Giants, 36 TDs
AFL   Len Dawson, Dallas Texans, 26 TDs

Receiving

NFL   Bobby Joe Conrad, St. Louis Cardinals, 73 receptions
AFL   Lionel Taylor, Denver Broncos, 78 receptions
NFL   Bobby Mitchell, Washington Redskins, 1,436 yards gained
AFL   Art Powell, New York Titans, 1,304 yards gained
NFL   Terry Barr, Detroit Lions, 13 TDs
      Gary Collins, Cleveland Browns, 13 TDs
AFL   Art Powell, New York Titans, 16 TDs

Field Goals

NFL   Jim Martin, Baltimore Colts, 24
AFL   Gino Cappelletti, Boston Patriots, 22

PATs

NFL   Don Chandler, New York Giants, 52
AFL   Mike Mercer, Oakland Raiders, 47

1964

Scoring

NFL   Lenny Moore, Baltimore Colts, 120 points
AFL   Gino Cappelletti, Boston Patriots, 155 points

Intracity faceoff: Alex Webster (left) head coach of the NFL New York Giants and Weeb Ewbank, mentor of the AFL New York Jets before a preseason game at the Yale Bowl. (New York Giants)

In the mud and mire, Jim Taylor of the Packers oozes his way through the Browns defense. (Fred Roe)

Rushing

NFL	Jim Brown, Cleveland Browns,	1,446 yards
AFL	Cookie Gilchrist, Buffalo Bills,	981 yards
NFL	Lenny Moore, Baltimore Colts,	16 TDs
AFL	Sid Blanks, Houston Oilers,	6 TDs
	Cookie Gilchrist, Buffalo Bills,	6 TDs
	Daryle Lamonica, Buffalo Bills,	6 TDs

Passing

NFL	Charley Johnson, St. Louis Cardinals,	223 completions
AFL	George Blanda, Houston Oilers,	262 completions
NFL	Charley Johnson, St. Louis Cardinals,	3,045 yards gained
AFL	Babe Parilli, Boston Patriots,	3,465 yards gained
NFL	Frank Ryan, Cleveland Browns,	25 TDs
AFL	Babe Parilli, Boston Patriots,	31 TDs

Receiving

NFL	Johnny Morris, Chicago Bears,	93 receptions
AFL	Charley Hennigan, Houston Oilers,	101 receptions
NFL	Johnny Morris, Chicago Bears,	1,200 yards gained
AFL	Charley Hennigan, Houston Oilers,	1,546 yards gained
NFL	Bobby Mitchell, Washington Redskins,	10 TDs
	Johnny Morris, Chicago Bears,	10 TDs
	Bucky Pope, Los Angeles Rams,	10 TDs
AFL	Lance Alworth, San Diego Chargers,	13 TDs

Field Goals

NFL	Jim Bakken, St. Louis Cardinals,	25
AFL	Gino Cappelletti, Boston Patriots,	25

PATs

NFL	Lou Michaels, Baltimore Colts,	53
AFL	Tommy Brooker, Kansas City Chiefs,	46

1965

Scoring

NFL Gale Sayers, Chicago Bears, 132 points
AFL Gino Cappelletti, Boston Patriots, 132 points

Rushing

NFL Jim Brown, Cleveland Browns, 1,544 yards
AFL Paul Lowe, San Diego Chargers, 1,121 yards
NFL Jim Brown, Cleveland Browns, 17 TDs
AFL Paul Lowe, San Diego Chargers, 7 TDs

Passing

NFL John Brodie, San Francisco 49ers, 242 completions
AFL George Blanda, Houston Oilers, 186 completions
NFL John Brodie, San Francisco 49ers, 3,112 yards gained
AFL John Hadl, San Diego Chargers, 2,798 yards gained
NFL John Brodie, San Francisco 49ers, 30 TDs
AFL Len Dawson, Kansas City Chiefs, 21 TDs

Receiving

NFL Dave Parks, San Francisco 49ers, 80 receptions
AFL Lionel Taylor, Denver Broncos, 85 receptions
NFL Dave Parks, San Francisco 49ers, 1,344 yards gained
AFL Lance Alworth, San Diego Chargers, 1,602 yards gained
NFL Bob Hayes, Dallas Cowboys, 12 TDs
   Dave Parks, San Francisco 49ers, 12 TDs
AFL Lance Alworth, San Diego Chargers, 14 TDs
   Don Maynard, New York Jets, 14 TDs

Field Goals

NFL Fred Cox, Minnesota Vikings, 23
AFL Pete Gogolak, Buffalo Bills, 28

PATs

NFL Tommy Davis, San Francisco 49ers, 52
   Roger LeClerc, Chicago Bears, 52
AFL Herb Travenio, San Diego Chargers, 40

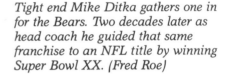

Tight end Mike Ditka gathers one in for the Bears. Two decades later as head coach he guided that same franchise to an NFL title by winning Super Bowl XX. (Fred Roe)

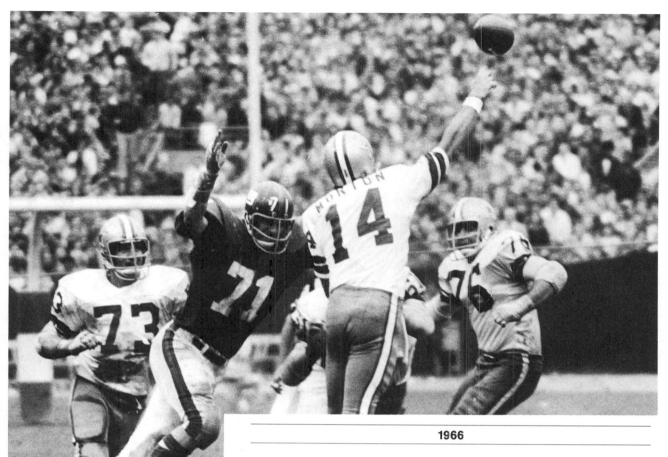

Cowboy Craig Morton lofts one a moment before being engulfed by Giant pass rusher David Tipton. (New York Giants)

1966

Scoring

    NFL   Bruce Gossett, Los Angeles Rams, 113 points

    AFL   Gino Cappelletti, Boston Patriots, 119 points

Rushing

    NFL   Gale Sayers, Chicago Bears, 1,231 yards

    AFL   Jim Nance, Boston Patriots, 1,458 yards

    NFL   Leroy Kelly, Cleveland Browns, 15 TDs

    AFL   Jim Nance, Boston Patriots, 11 TDs

Passing

    NFL   Sonny Jurgensen, Washington Redskins, 254 completions

    AFL   Joe Namath, New York Jets, 232 completions

    NFL   Sonny Jurgensen, Washington Redskins, 3,209 yards gained

    AFL   Joe Namath, New York Jets, 3,379 yards gained

    NFL   Frank Ryan, Cleveland Browns, 29 TDs

    AFL   Len Dawson, Kansas City Chiefs, 26 TDs

Receiving

    NFL   Charley Taylor, Washington Redskins, 72 receptions

    AFL   Lance Alworth, San Diego Chargers, 73 receptions

    NFL   Pat Studstill, Detroit Lions, 1,266 yards gained

    AFL   Lance Alworth, San Diego Chargers, 1,383 yards gained

    NFL   Bob Hayes, Dallas Cowboys, 13 TDs

    AFL   Lance Alworth, San Diego Chargers, 13 TDs

Field Goals

    NFL   Bruce Gossett, Los Angeles Rams, 28

    AFL   Mike Mercer, Oakland/Kansas City, 21

PATs

    NFL   Danny Villanueva, Dallas Cowboys, 56

    AFL   Booth Lusteg, Buffalo Bills, 41

1967

Scoring
    NFL   Jim Bakken, St. Louis Cardinals, 117 points
    AFL   George Blanda, Oakland Raiders, 116 points

Rushing
    NFL   Leroy Kelly, Cleveland Browns, 1,205 yards
    AFL   Jim Nance, Boston Patriots, 1,216 yards
    NFL   Leroy Kelly, Cleveland Browns, 11 TDs
    AFL   Emerson Boozer, New York Jets, 10 TDs

Passing
    NFL   Sonny Jurgensen, Washington Redskins, 288 completions
    AFL   Joe Namath, New York Jets, 258 completions
    NFL   Sonny Jurgensen, Washington Redskins, 3,747 yards
             gained
    AFL   Joe Namath, New York Jets, 4,007 yards gained
    NFL   Sonny Jurgensen, Washington Redskins, 31 TDs
    AFL   Daryle Lamonica, Oakland Raiders, 30 TDs

Receiving
    NFL   Charley Taylor, Washington Redskins, 70 receptions
    AFL   George Sauer, New York Jets, 75 receptions
    NFL   Ben Hawkins, Philadelphia Eagles, 1,265 yards gained
    AFL   Don Maynard, New York Jets, 1,434 yards gained
    NFL   Homer Jones, New York Giants, 13 TDs
    AFL   Al Denson, Denver Broncos, 11 TDs
             Otis Taylor, Kansas City Chiefs, 11 TDs

Field Goals
    NFL   Jim Bakken, St. Louis Cardinals, 27
    AFL   Jan Stenerud, Kansas City Chiefs, 21

PATs
    NFL   Bruce Gossett, Los Angeles Rams, 48
    AFL   George Blanda, Oakland Raiders, 56

1968

Scoring
    NFL   Leroy Kelly, Cleveland Browns, 120 points
    AFL   Jim Turner, New York Jets, 145 points

Rushing
    NFL   Leroy Kelly, Cleveland Browns, 1,239 yards
    AFL   Paul Robinson, Cincinnati Bengals, 1,023 yards
    NFL   Leroy Kelly, Cleveland Browns, 16 TDs
    AFL   Paul Robinson, Cincinnati Bengals, 8 TDs

Passing
    NFL   John Brodie, San Francisco 49ers, 234 completions
    AFL   John Hadl, San Diego Chargers, 208 completions
    NFL   John Brodie, San Francisco 49ers, 3,020 yards gained
    AFL   John Hadl, San Diego Chargers, 3,472 yards gained
    NFL   Earl Morrall, Baltimore Colts, 26 TDs
    AFL   John Hadl, San Diego Chargers, 27 TDs

Receiving
NFL   Clifton McNeil, San Francisco 49ers, 71 receptions
AFL   Lance Alworth, San Diego Chargers, 68 receptions
NFL   Roy Jefferson, Pittsburgh Steelers, 1,074 yards gained
AFL   Lance Alworth, San Diego Chargers, 1,312 yards gained
NFL   Paul Warfield, Cleveland Browns, 12 TDs
AFL   Warren Wells, Oakland Raiders, 11 TDs

Field Goals
NFL   Mac Percival, Chicago Bears, 25
AFL   Jim Turner, New York Jets, 34

PATs
NFL   Mike Clark, Dallas Cowboys, 54
AFL   George Blanda, Oakland Raiders, 54

1969

Scoring
NFL   Fred Cox, Minnesota Vikings, 121 points
AFL   Jim Turner, New York Jets, 129 points

Rushing
NFL   Gale Sayers, Chicago Bears, 1,032 yards
AFL   Dickie Post, San Diego Chargers, 901 yards
NFL   Tom Matte, Baltimore Colts, 11 TDs
AFL   Jim Kiick, Miami Dolphins, 9 TDs

Passing
NFL   Sonny Jurgensen, Washington Redskins, 274 completions
AFL   Daryle Lamonica, Oakland Raiders, 221 completions
NFL   Sonny Jurgensen, Washington Redskins, 3,102 yards gained
AFL   Daryle Lamonica, Oakland Raiders, 3,362 yards gained
NFL   Roman Gabriel, Los Angeles Rams, 24 TDs
AFL   Daryle Lamonica, Oakland Raiders, 34 TDs

Receiving
NFL   Dan Abramowicz, New Orleans Saints, 73 receptions
AFL   Lance Alworth, San Diego Chargers, 64 receptions
NFL   Harold Jackson, Philadelphia Eagles, 1,116 yards gained
AFL   Warren Wells, Oakland Raiders, 1,260 yards gained
NFL   Lance Rentzel, Dallas Cowboys, 12 TDs
AFL   Warren Wells, Oakland Raiders, 14 TDs

Field Goals
NFL   Fred Cox, Minnesota Vikings, 26
AFL   Jim Turner, New York Jets, 32

PATs
NFL   Don Cockcroft, Cleveland Browns, 45
AFL   George Blanda, Oakland Raiders, 45

The 1970s

Ihe age of the 70s was ruled by three dynasties: Don Shula's Miami Dolphins in the first part of the decade, Chuck Noll's Pittsburgh Steelers in the latter half of it, and Tom Landry's Dallas Cowboys competing fiercely throughout the entire ten years. Both Miami and Pittsburgh won back-to-back titles, and Dallas one in each half of that time period.

There were, of course, other very noteworthy teams doing battle in the 70s. Bud Grant's Minnesota Vikings made it to four Super Bowls (counting the January 1970 one), but came up short in each of them. The Oakland Raiders under John Madden were always in contention, one of the winningest teams in the NFL. The Los Angeles Rams, guided by Chuck Knox, consistently posed a threat. Ted Marchibroda's Baltimore Colts were strong, so were George Allen's Washington Redskins and Red Miller's Denver Broncos.

On the field heros abounded: Bob Griese, Roger Staubach, Terry Bradshaw, Fran Tarkenton, Sonny Jurgensen, Ken Stabler, O. J. Simpson, Walter Payton,

Walter Payton, the high-stepping, ground gaining back of the Chicago Bears, eclipsed practically all of Jim Brown's NFL rushing records during a career that began in 1975 and is still going strong. (Chicago Bears)

Lynn Swann, Alan Page, Mean Joe Greene, Jack Youngblood, Drew Pearson, Larry Csonka, Franco Harris, just a few among the many.

During the decade the game took on increased sophistication in the strategies of both offense and defense. The sport itself became an enormous business, and attracted a following on television like no sport before or since. It was a treat not just for the football denizens of Miami, Dallas, and Pittsburgh who became so accustomed to triumph but for all the ever-growing number of fans of the game of professional football.

Roger Staubach, the Dallas Cowboy centerpiece of the 1970s, inventor of the "Hail Mary pass," and a Hall of Famer. (Fred Roe)

The Best of the Decade / 1970s

FIRST TEAM–OFFENSE

Position	Player	Team
WR	Lynn Swann	Pittsburgh Steelers
WR	Fred Biletnikoff	Oakland Raiders
TE	Charlie Sanders	Detroit Lions
T	Ron Yary	Minnesota Vikings
T	Rayfield Wright	Dallas Cowboys
G	Larry Little	Miami Dolphins
G	Gene Upshaw	Oakland Raiders
C	Jim Langer	Miami Dolphins
QB	Roger Staubach	Dallas Cowboys
RB	O. J. Simpson	Buffalo Bills
RB	Walter Payton	Chicago Bears

FIRST TEAM–DEFENSE

Position	Player	Team
DE	Jack Youngblood	Los Angeles Rams
DE	Carl Eller	Minnesota Vikings
DT	Joe Greene	Pittsburgh Steelers
DT	Alan Page	Minnesota Vikings
LB	Willie Lanier	Kansas City Chiefs
LB	Lee Roy Jordan	Dallas Cowboys
LB	Jack Lambert	Pittsburgh Steelers
DB	Roger Wehrli	St. Louis Cardinals
DB	Jimmy Johnson	San Francisco 49ers
DB	Ken Houston	Washington Redskins
DB	Cliff Harris	Dallas Cowboys
K	Jan Stenerud	Kansas City Chiefs
P	Ray Guy	Oakland Raiders
coach	*Chuck Noll*	*Pittsburgh Steelers*

SECOND TEAM–OFFENSE

Position	Player	Team
WR	Paul Warfield	Miami Dolphins/Cleveland Browns
WR	Cliff Branch	Oakland Raiders
TE	Dave Casper	Oakland Raiders
T	Bob Brown	Los Angeles Rams/Oakland Raiders
T	Dan Dierdorf	St. Louis Cardinals
G	Joe DeLamielleure	Buffalo Bills
G	Conrad Dobler	St. Louis Cardinals
C	Forrest Blue	San Francisco 49ers/Baltimore Colts
QB	Fran Tarkenton	Minnesota Vikings
RB	Franco Harris	Pittsburgh Steelers
RB	Larry Csonka	Miami Dolphins

SECOND TEAM–DEFENSE

Position	Player	Team
DE	L. C. Greenwood	Pittsburgh Steelers
DE	Claude Humphrey	Atlanta Falcons
DT	Louie Kelcher	San Diego Chargers
DT	Larry Brooks	Los Angeles Rams
LB	Chris Hanburger	Washington Redskins
LB	Robert Brazile	Houston Oilers
LB	Jack Ham	Pittsburgh Steelers
DB	Louis Wright	Denver Broncos
DB	Monte Jackson	Los Angeles Rams/Oakland Raiders
DB	Charlie Waters	Dallas Cowboys
DB	Dick Anderson	Miami Dolphins
K	Garo Yepremian	Miami Dolphins
P	Dave Jennings	New York Giants
coach	*Tom Landry*	*Dallas Cowboys*
	Don Shula	*Miami Dolphins*

Events and Milestones

The NFL and AFL are formally combined into one league to be known as the National Football League, with two distinct conferences (the NFC and the AFC). the Baltimore Colts, Cleveland Browns, and Pittsburgh Steelers are sent over to the AFC in order to equalize the conferences at 13 teams apiece. A system of playoffs is devised to include a wild card team from each conference. **(1970)**

The phenomenon of Monday Night Football is inaugurated, the first triumverate in the broadcast booth consisting of Howard Cosell, Dandy Don Meredith, and Keith Jackson. **(1970)**

Tom Dempsey of the New Orleans Saints kicks the longest field goal in NFL history, 63 yards to provide a win over the Lions 19–17. **(1970)**

The Boston Patriots move to Foxboro, Massachusetts, and become known as the New England Patriots. **(1971)**

The first modern Pro Bowl, pitting all-stars from the NFC against those from the AFC, is held. Since 1962 the NFL and the AFL had held separate pro bowls with all-stars from the east and west in their respective leagues playing each other. The NFC was victorious in this first clash of conference celebrities, with a decisive 27–6 win. **(1971)**

The hash marks on the field of play are brought in to the goal posts. **(1972)**

For the first time in pro football history, ten backs rushed for 1,000 yards or more in a single season:

O. J. Simpson	Bills	1,251
Larry Brown	Redskins	1,216
Ron Johnson	Giants	1,182
Larry Csonka	Dolphins	1,117
Marv Hubbard	Raiders	1,100
Franco Harris	Steelers	1,055
Calvin Hill	Cowboys	1,036
Mike Garrett	Chargers	1,031
John Brockington	Packers	1,027
Jim Kiick	Dolphins	1,000

(1972)

The NFL adopts a new jersey numbering system:

1–19	Quarterbacks, specialists
20–49	Running backs, defensive backs
50–59	Centers, linebackers
60–79	Defensive linemen, interior offensive linemen (excluding centers)
80–89	Wide receivers, tight ends

(1973)

Fred Dryer, defensive end for the Los Angeles Rams, sets a pro football record when he is credited with two safeties in a game against the Packers. He remains today the only player in pro football history to rack up two safeties in a single game. **(1973)**

Buffalo's O. J. Simpson sets an NFL standard and becomes the first player to rush for more than 2,000 yards in a season, his total of 2,003 gained on 332 carries (an average of 6 yards per carry). **(1973)**

The World Football League is formed to compete with the NFL. A total of 12 franchises are awarded. **(1974)**

The traditional College All-Star game between the prevailing NFL titleholder and a team of selected college all-stars, which had been held annually at Soldier Field in Chicago since 1934, is cancelled. It is never resumed. **(1974)**

New rules:
- The goal posts are moved back to the end lines.
- Kickoffs are moved from the 40 yard line back to the 35.
- A missed field goal from outside the 20 yard line is brought back to the line of scrimmage.
- A sudden death overtime period to last no more than 15 minutes of playing time is instituted for all regular season and preseason games. **(1974)**

The "home field advantage" in the playoffs is introduced, allowing the teams with the best regular season records to host their postseason games. **(1975)**

The WFL collapses after its second season. **(1975)**

An NFL franchise for Seattle is awarded to Seattle Professional Football, Inc. Jack Patera is named the first head coach and the Seahawks are slotted in the NFC Western Division, joining the Rams, 49ers, Falcons, and Saints. **(1976)**

Tampa Bay joins the NFL, the franchise going to Hugh F. Culverhouse. John McKay is signed to coach the Buccaneers who are assigned to the AFC Western Division to compete with the Raiders, Broncos, Chargers, and Chiefs. **(1976)**

The Seattle Seahawks and Tampa Bay Buccaneers switch conferences. The Seahawks replace the Bucs in the AFC West, and Tampa Bay is placed in the NFC Central with the Bears, Packers, Lions, and Vikings. **(1977)**

The head-slap is outlawed. **(1977)**

Walter Payton, in his second year as a Chicago Bear, sets the single-game rushing record when he gains 275 yards against the Vikings, two more than the standard set by O. J. Simpson of the Bills the year before. **(1977)**

The NFL regular season is extended to 16 games, with preseason games set at four. (1978)

A second wild card team is allowed for each conference in the playoffs, the two wild card teams to face each other within their conference in the first postseason game each year. (1978)

A seventh official, the side judge is added. (1978)

Fran Tarkenton of the Vikings throws 345 completions to demolish the NFL mark of 288 held by Sonny Jurgensen. (1978)

A new rule to help protect quarterbacks is instituted: once a quarterback is deemed in the grasp of a defender the play is to be whistled dead. (1979)

Dan Fouts of the San Diego Chargers sets a new NFL record for passing yardage, 4,082, bettering the mark of 4,007 set by Joe Namath 12 years earlier. (1979)

Steve DeBerg of the 49ers eclipses Tarkenton's record for pass completions by two when he logs 347. (1979)

The Champions / 1970s

1970	NFC	Dallas Cowboys	10-4-0
		(Cowboys 17, 49ers 10)	
	AFC	Baltimore Colts	11-2-1
		(Colts 27, Raiders 17)	
	Super Bowl V		
		Baltimore Colts	16
		Dallas Cowboys	13
1971	NFC	Dallas Cowboys	11-3-0
		(Cowboys 14, 49ers 3)	
	AFC	Miami Dolphins	10-3-1
		(Dolphins 21, Colts 0)	
	Super Bowl VI		
		Dallas Cowboys	24
		Miami Dolphins	3
1972	NFC	Washington Redskins	11-3-0
		(Redskins 26, Cowboys 3)	
	AFC	Miami Dolphins	14-0-0
		(Dolphins 21, Steelers 17)	
	Super Bowl VII		
		Miami Dolphins	14
		Washington Redskins	7
1973	NFC	Minnesota Vikings	12-2-0
		(Vikings 27, Cowboys 10)	
	AFC	Miami Dolphins	12-2-0
		(Dolphins 27, Raiders 10)	
	Super Bowl VIII		
		Miami Dolphins	24
		Minnesota Vikings	7
1974	NFC	Minnesota Vikings	10-4-0
		(Vikings 14, Rams 10)	
	AFC	Pittsburgh Steelers	10-3-1
		(Steelers 24, Raiders 13)	
	Super Bowl IX		
		Pittsburgh Steelers	16
		Minnesota Vikings	6

1975	NFC	Dallas Cowboys	10-4-0
		(Cowboys 37, Rams 7)	
	AFC	Pittsburgh Steelers	12-2-0
		(Steelers 16, Raiders 10)	
	Super Bowl X		
		Pittsburgh Steelers	21
		Dallas Cowboys	17
1976	NFC	Minnesota Vikings	11-2-1
		(Vikings 24, Rams 13)	
	AFC	Oakland Raiders	13-1-0
		(Raiders 24, Steelers 7)	
	Super Bowl X		
		Oakand Raiders	32
		Minnesota Vikings	14
1977	NFC	Dallas Cowboys	12-2-0
		(Cowboys 23, Vikings 0)	
	AFC	Denver Broncos	12-2-0
		(Broncos 20, Raiders 17)	
	Super Bowl X I		
		Dallas Cowboys	27
		Denver Broncos	10
1978	NFC	Dallas Cowboys	12-4-0
		(Cowboys 28, Rams 0)	
	AFC	Pittsburgh Steelers	14-2-0
		(Steelers 34, Oilers 5)	
	Super Bowl XIII		
		Pittsburgh Steelers	35
		Dallas Cowboys	31
1979	NFC	Los Angeles Rams	9-7-0
		(Rams 9, Buccaneers 0)	
	AFC	Pittsburgh Steelers	12-4-0
		(Steelers 27, Oilers 13)	
	Super Bowl XIV		
		Pittsburgh Steelers	31
		Los Angeles Rams	19

The Modern NFL

With the institution of the NFC and the AFC as distinct conferences within the NFL in 1970, the basis for the modern National Football League was laid. This was the alignment:

NFC	AFC
Eastern Division	**Eastern Division**
Dallas Cowboys	Baltimore Colts
New York Giants	Boston Patriots
Philadelphia Eagles	Buffalo Bills
St. Louis Cardinals	Miami Dolphins
Washington Redskins	New York Jets
Central Division	**Central Division**
Chicago Bears	Cincinnati Bengals
Detroit Lions	Cleveland Browns
Green Bay Packers	Houston Oilers
Minnesota Vikings	Pittsburgh Steelers
Western Division	**Western Division**
Atlanta Falcons	Denver Broncos
New Orleans Saints	Kansas City Chiefs
Los Angeles Rams	Oakland Raiders
San Francisco 49ers	San Diego Chargers

In that first year of the new NFL, the Cowboys, Vikings, and 49ers triumphed in the NFC, and the Lions secured the wild card playoff berth. The AFC produced divisional winners from Baltimore, Cincinnati, and Oakland, and sent Miami into the postseason as a wild card. Eventually the Cowboys met the Colts to determine the NFL title and Baltimore prevailed 16–13.

Fireplug-sized running back Joe Morris gains a few for the Super Bowl champion Giants of 1986. Number 11 is quarterback Phil Simms, Super Bowl XXI's MVP. (Fred Roe)

The First Modern Pro Bowl

With the new alignment of conferences in the NFL, the Pro Bowl took on a different dimension in January 1971. Now it was a contest between the all-stars of the NFC and those of the AFC. These were the honorees to start in the first modern Pro Bowl game, which was held in Los Angeles.

	NFC			AFC	
Offense		**Team**		**Offense**	**Team**
WR	Gene Washington	49ers		Warren Wells	Raiders
WR	Gene Washington	Vikings		Marlin Briscoe	Bills
TE	Charlie Sanders	Lions		Raymond Chester	Raiders
T	Charlie Cowan	Rams		Jim Tyrer	Chiefs
T	Ernie McMillan	Cardinals		Harry Schuh	Raiders
G	Tom Mack	Rams		Ed Budde	Chiefs
G	Gale Gillingham	Packers		Walt Sweeney	Chargers
C	Ed Flanagan	Lions		Jim Otto	Raiders
QB	John Brodie	49ers		Daryle Lamonica	Raiders
RB	Larry Brown	Redskins		Leroy Kelly	Browns
RB	MacArthur Lane	Cardinals		Hewritt Dixon	Raiders
Defense				**Defense**	
DE	Deacon Jones	Rams		Bubba Smith	Colts
DE	Carl Eller	Vikings		Rich Jackson	Broncos
DT	Alan Page	Vikings		Joe Greene	Steelers
DT	Bob Lilly	Cowboys		Buck Buchanan	Chiefs
LB	Larry Stallings	Cardinals		Bobby Bell	Chiefs
LB	Dick Butkus	Bears		Willie Lanier	Chiefs
LB	Fred Carr	Packers		Andy Russell	Steelers
CB	Jimmy Johnson	49ers		Jim Marsalis	Chiefs
CB	Mel Renfro	Cowboys		Willie Brown	Raiders
S	Willie Wood	Packers		Ken Houston	Oilers
S	Larry Wilson	Cardinals		Johnny Robinson	Chiefs
coach	Dick Nolan	49ers		John Madden	Raiders

The AFC took the lead in the second quarter on a 37-yard field goal from Kansas City's Jan Stenerud, but after that it was total NFC dominance. The most spectacular performance of the day was turned in by Mel Renfro of the Cowboys who returned punts 82 yards and 56 yards for touchdowns. The scoring:

NFC	0	3	10	14	**27**
AFC	0	3	3	0	**6**

The League Leaders / 1970s

1970

Scoring

NFC   Fred Cox, Minnesota Vikings, 125 points
AFC   Jan Stenerud, Kansas City Chiefs, 116 points

Rushing

NFC   Larry Brown, Washington Redskins, 1,125 yards
AFC   Floyd Little, Denver Broncos, 901 yards
NFC   MacArthur Lane, St. Louis Cardinals, 11 TDs
AFC   John Fuqua, Pittsburgh Steelers, 7 TDs
       Jim Nance, Boston Patriots, 7 TDs
       Bo Scott, Cleveland Browns, 7 TDs

Passing

NFC   John Brodie, San Francisco 49ers, 223 completions
AFC   Daryle Lamonica, Oakland Raiders, 179 completions
NFC   John Brodie, San Francisco 49ers, 2,491 yards gained
AFC   Daryle Lamonica, Oakland Raiders, 2,516 yards gained
NFC   John Brodie, San Francisco 49ers, 24 TDs
AFC   John Hadl, San Diego Chargers, 22 TDs
       Daryle Lamonica, Oakland Raiders, 22 TDs

Receiving

NFC   Dick Gordon, Chicago Bears, 71 receptions
AFC   Marlon Briscoe, Buffalo Bills, 57 receptions
NFC   Gene Washington, San Francisco 49ers, 1,100 yards gained
AFC   Marlon Briscoe, Buffalo Bills, 1,036 yards gained
NFC   Dick Gordon, Chicago Bears, 13 TDs
AFC   Gary Garrison, San Diego Chargers, 12 TDs

Field Goals

NFC   Fred Cox, Minnesota Vikings, 30
AFC   Jan Stenerud, Kansas City Chiefs, 30

PATs

NFC   Errol Mann, Detroit Lions, 41
AFC   George Blanda, Oakland Raiders, 36
       Jim O'Brien, Baltimore Colts, 36

Jim Hart of the Cardinals rifles one before Fred Dryer (89) of the Giants can get to him. (New York Giants)

1971

Scoring

NFC   Curt Knight, Washington Redskins, 114 points
AFC   Garo Yepremian, Miami Dolphins, 117 points

Rushing

NFC   John Brockington, Green Bay Packers, 1,105 yards
AFC   Floyd Little, Denver Broncos, 1,133 yards
NFC   Duane Thomas, Dallas Cowboys, 11 TDs
AFC   Leroy Kelly, Cleveland Browns, 11 TDs

Passing

NFC   Fran Tarkenton, New York Giants, 226 completions
AFC   John Hadl, San Diego Chargers, 233 completions
NFC   John Brodie, San Francisco 49ers, 2,642 yards gained
AFC   John Hadl, San Diego Chargers, 3,075 yards gained
NFC   John Brodie, San Francisco 49ers, 18 TDs
AFC   John Hadl, San Diego Chargers, 21 TDs

Receiving
NFC Bob Tucker, New York Giants, 59 receptions
AFC Fred Biletnikoff, Oakland Raiders, 61 receptions
NFC Gene Washington, San Francisco 49ers, 884 yards gained
AFC Otis Taylor, Kansas City Chiefs, 1,110 yards gained
NFC Bob Hayes, Dallas Cowboys, 8 TDs
AFC Paul Warfield, Miami Dolphins, 11 TDs

Field Goals
NFC Curt Knight, Washington Redskins, 29
AFC Garo Yepremian, Miami Dolphins, 28

PATs
NFC Mike Clark, Dallas Cowboys, 47
AFC George Blanda, Oakland Raiders, 41

1972

Scoring
NFC Chester Marcol, Green Bay Packers, 128 points
AFC Bobby Howfield, New York Jets, 121 points

Rushing
NFC Larry Brown, Washington Redskins, 1,216 yards
AFC O. J. Simpson, Buffalo Bills, 1,251 yards
NFC Ron Johnson, New York Giants, 9 TDs
      Greg Landry, Detroit Lions, 9 TDs
AFC Mercury Morris, Miami Dolphins, 12 TDs

Passing
NFC Archie Manning, New Orleans Saints, 230 completions
AFC John Hadl, San Diego Chargers, 190 completions
NFC Archie Manning, New Orleans Saints, 2,781 yards gained
AFC Joe Namath, New York Jets, 2,816 yards gained
NFC Billy Kilmer, Washington Redskins, 19 TDs
AFC Joe Namath, New York Jets, 19 TDs

Receiving
NFC Harold Jackson, Philadelphia Eagles, 62 receptions
AFC Fred Biletnikoff, Oakland Raiders, 58 receptions
NFC Harold Jackson, Philadelphia Eagles, 1,048 yards gained
AFC Rich Caster, New York Jets, 833 yards gained
NFC Gene Washington, San Francisco 49ers, 12 TDs
AFC Rich Caster, New York Jets, 10 TDs

Field Goals
NFC Chester Marcol, Green Bay Packers, 32
AFC Roy Gerela, Pittsburgh Steelers, 28

PATs
NFC Bruce Gossett, San Francisco 49ers, 41
AFC George Blanda, Oakland Raiders, 44

1973

Scoring
NFC David Ray, Los Angeles Rams, 130 points
AFC Roy Gerela, Pittsburgh Steelers, 123 points

Rushing
NFC John Brockington, Green Bay Packers, 1,144 yards
AFC O. J. Simpson, Buffalo Bills, 2,003 yards
NFC Donny Anderson, St. Louis Cardinals, 10 TDs
AFC Floyd Little, Denver Broncos, 12 TDs
O. J. Simpson, Buffalo Bills, 12 TDs

Passing
NFC Roman Gabriel, Philadelphia Eagles, 270 completions
AFC Jim Plunkett, New England Patriots, 193 completions
NFC Roman Gabriel, Philadelphia Eagles, 3,219 yards gained
AFC Jim Plunkett, New England Patriots, 2,550 yards gained
NFC Roman Gabriel, Philadelphia Eagles, 23 TDs
Roger Staubach, Dallas Cowboys, 23 TDs
AFC Charley Johnson, Denver Broncos, 20 TDs

Receiving
NFC Harold Carmichael, Philadelphia Eagles, 67 receptions
AFC Fred Willis, Houston Oilers, 57 receptions
NFC Harold Carmichael, Philadelphia Eagles, 1,116 yards gained
AFC Isaac Curtis, Cincinnati Bengals, 843 yards gained
NFC Harold Jackson, Los Angeles Rams, 13 TDs
AFC Paul Warfield, Miami Dolphins, 11 TDs

Field Goals
NFC David Ray, Los Angeles Rams, 30
AFC Roy Gerela, Pittsburgh Steelers, 29

PATs
NFC Toni Fritsch, Dallas Cowboys, 43
AFC Jim Turner, Denver Broncos, 40

That is running back Norm Bulaich of the Colts who is the subject of so much Cowboy attention. Number 55 on Dallas is linebacker Lee Roy Jordan, and observing the situation for Baltimore is quarterback Earl Morrall (15). (Fred Roe)

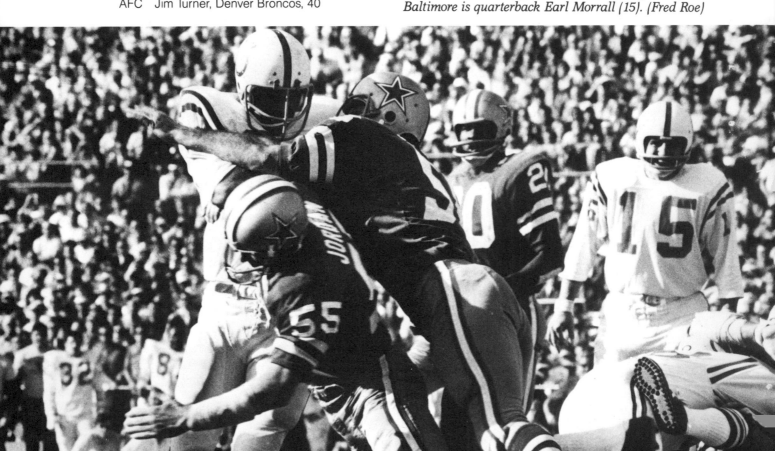

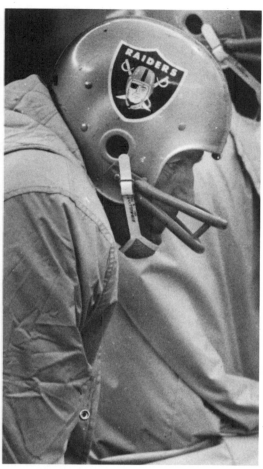

The enduring George Blanda takes a breather in the Raider segment of an NFL career that spanned four decades (1949–75). (Fred Roe)

1974

Scoring
- NFC Chester Marcol, Green Bay Packers, 94 points
- AFC Roy Gerela, Pittsburgh Steelers, 93 points

Rushing
- NFC Lawrence McCutcheon, Los Angeles Rams, 1,109 yards
- AFC Otis Armstrong, Denver Broncos, 1,407 yards
- NFC Tom Sullivan, Philadelphia Eagles, 11 TDs
- AFC Jon Keyworth, Denver Broncos, 10 TDs

Passing
- NFC Jim Hart, St. Louis Cardinals, 200 completions
- AFC Ken Anderson, Cincinnati Bengals, 213 completions
- NFC Fran Tarkenton, Minnesota Vikings, 2,598 yards gained
- AFC Ken Anderson, Cincinnati Bengals, 2,667 yards gained
- NFC Jim Hart, St. Louis Cardinals, 20 TDs
- AFC Ken Stabler, Oakland Raiders, 26 TDs

Receiving
- NFC Charlie Young, Philadelphia Eagles, 63 receptions
- AFC Lydell Mitchell, Baltimore Colts, 72 receptions
- NFC Drew Pearson, Dallas Cowboys, 1,087 yards gained
- AFC Cliff Branch, Oakland Raiders, 1,092 yards gained
- NFC Harold Carmichael, Philadelphia Eagles, 8 TDs
- AFC Cliff Branch, Oakland Raiders, 13 TDs

Field Goals
- NFC Chester Marcol, Green Bay Packers, 25
- AFC Roy Gerela, Pittsburgh Steelers, 20

PATs
- NFC Efren Herrera, Dallas Cowboys, 33
- AFC George Blanda, Oakland Raiders, 44

1975

Scoring
- NFC Chuck Foreman, Minnesota Vikings, 132 points
- AFC O. J. Simpson, Buffalo Bills, 138 points

Rushing
- NFC Jim Otis, St. Louis Cardinals, 1,076 yards
- AFC O. J. Simpson, Buffalo Bills, 1,817 yards
- NFC Chuck Foreman, Minnesota Vikings, 13 TDs
- AFC Pete Banaszak, Oakland Raiders, 16 TDs
-        O. J. Simpson, Buffalo Bills, 16 TDs

Passing
- NFC Fran Tarkenton, Minnesota Vikings, 273 completions
- AFC Ken Anderson, Cincinnati Bengals, 228 completions
- NFC Fran Tarkenton, Minnesota Vikings, 2,994 yards gained
- AFC Ken Anderson, Cincinnati Bengals, 3,169 yards gained
- NFC Fran Tarkenton, Minnesota Vikings, 25 TDs
- AFC Joe Ferguson, Buffalo Bills, 25 TDs

Receiving

NFC Chuck Foreman, Minnesota Vikings, 73 receptions
AFC Lydell Mitchell, Baltimore Colts, 60 receptions
Reggie Rucker, Cleveland Browns, 60 receptions
NFC Mel Gray, St. Louis Cardinals, 1,996 yards gained
AFC Ken Burrough, Houston Oilers, 1,063 yards gained
NFC Mel Gray, St. Louis Cardinals, 11 TDs
AFC Lynn Swann, Pittsburgh Steelers, 11 TDs

Field Goals

NFC Toni Fritsch, Dallas Cowboys, 22
AFC Jan Stenerud, Kansas City Chiefs, 22

PATs

NFC Fred Cox, Minnesota Vikings, 46
AFC John Leypoldt, Buffalo Bills, 51
Toni Linhart, Baltimore Colts, 51

1976

Scoring

NFC Mark Moseley, Washington Redskins, 97 points
AFC Toni Linhart, Baltimore Colts, 109 points

Rushing

NFC Walter Payton, Chicago Bears, 1,390 yards
AFC O. J. Simpson, Buffalo Bills, 1,503 yards
NFC Chuck Foreman, Minnesota Vikings, 13 TDs
Walter Payton, Chicago Bears, 13 TDs
AFC Franco Harris, Pittsburgh Steelers, 14 TDs

Passing

NFC Fran Tarkenton, Minnesota Vikings, 255 completions
AFC Dan Fouts, San Diego Chargers, 208 completions
NFC Fran Tarkenton, Minnesota Vikings, 2,961 yards gained
AFC Bert Jones, Baltimore Colts, 3,014 yards gained
NFC Jim Hart, St. Louis Cardinals, 18 TDs
AFC Ken Stabler, Oakland Raiders, 27 TDs

Receiving

NFC Drew Pearson, Dallas Cowboys, 58 receptions
AFC MacArthur Lane, Kansas City Chiefs, 66 receptions
NFC Sammy White, Minnesota Vikings, 906 yards gained
AFC Roger Carr, Baltimore Colts, 1,112 yards gained
NFC Sammy White, Minnesota Vikings, 10 TDs
AFC Cliff Branch, Oakland Raiders, 12 TDs

Field Goals

NFC Mark Moseley, Washington Redskins, 22
AFC Jan Stenerud, Kansas City Chiefs, 21

PATs

NFC Tom Dempsey, Los Angeles Rams, 36
AFC Toni Linhart, Baltimore Colts, 49

Franco Harris, the battering-ram running back for the four-time NFL champion Pittsburgh Steelers. Behind him is Pitt quarterback Terry Bradshaw (12). (Fred Roe)

1977

Scoring
NFC	Walter Payton, Chicago Bears, 96 points
AFC	Errol Mann, Oakland Raiders, 99 points

Rushing
NFC	Walter Payton, Chicago Bears, 1,852 yards
AFC	Mark van Eeghen, Oakland Raiders, 1,273 yards
NFC	Walter Payton, Chicago Bears, 14 TDs
AFC	Franco Harris, Pittsburgh Steelers, 11 TDs

Passing
NFC	Roger Staubach, Dallas Cowboys, 210 completions
AFC	Bert Jones, Baltimore Colts, 224 completions
NFC	Roger Staubach, Dallas Cowboys, 2,620 yards gained
AFC	Joe Ferguson, Buffalo Bills, 2,803 yards gained
NFC	Ron Jaworski, Philadelphia Eagles, 18 TDs
	Roger Staubach, Dallas Cowboys, 18 TDs
AFC	Bob Griese, Miami Dolphins, 22 TDs

Receiving
NFC	Ahmad Rashad, Minnesota Vikings, 51 receptions
AFC	Lydell Mitchell, Baltimore Colts, 71 receptions
NFC	Drew Pearson, Dallas Cowboys, 870 yards gained
AFC	Ken Burrough, Houston Oilers, 816 yards gained
NFC	Henry Childs, New Orleans Saints, 9 TDs
	Sammy White, Minnesota Vikings, 9 TDs
AFC	Nat Moore, Miami Dolphins, 12 TDs

Field Goals
NFC	Mark Moseley, Washington Redskins, 21
AFC	Errol Mann, Oakland Raiders, 20

PATs
NFC	Efren Herrera, Dallas Cowboys, 39
AFC	Errol Mann, Oakland Raiders, 39

1978

Scoring
NFC	Frank Corral, Los Angeles Rams, 118 points
AFC	Pat Leahy, New York Jets, 107 points

Rushing
NFC	Walter Payton, Chicago Bears, 1,395 yards
AFC	Earl Campbell, Houston Oilers, 1,450 yards
NFC	Terdell Middleton, Green Bay Packers, 11 TDs
	Walter Payton, Chicago Bears, 11 TDs
AFC	David Sims, Seattle Seahawks, 14 TDs

Passing
NFC	Fran Tarkenton, Minnesota Vikings, 345 completions
AFC	Jim Zorn, Seattle Seahawks, 248 completions
NFC	Fran Tarkenton, Minnesota Vikings, 3,468 yards gained
AFC	Jim Zorn, Seattle Seahawks, 3,283 yards gained
NFC	Roger Staubach, Dallas Cowboys, 27 TDs
AFC	Steve Grogan, New England Patriots, 28 TDs
	Brian Sipe, Cleveland Browns, 28 TDs

SUNDAY MAYHEM

Receiving
NFC Rickey Young, Minnesota Vikings, 88 receptions
AFC Steve Largent, Seattle Seahawks, 71 receptions
NFC Harold Carmichael, Philadelphia Eagles, 1,072 yards
      gained
AFC Wesley Walker, New York Jets, 1,169 yards gained
NFC Billy Joe DuPree, Dallas Cowboys, 9 TDs
      Sammy White, Minnesota Vikings, 9 TDs
AFC John Jefferson, San Diego Chargers, 13 TDs

Field Goals
NFC Frank Corral, Los Angeles Rams, 29
AFC Pat Leahy, New York Jets, 22

PATs
NFC Rafael Septien, Dallas Cowboys, 46
AFC Roy Gerela, Pittsburgh Steelers, 44

1979

Scoring
NFC Mark Moseley, Washington Redskins, 114 points
AFC John Smith, New England Patriots, 115 points

Rushing
NFC Walter Payton, Chicago Bears, 1,610 yards
AFC Earl Campbell, Houston Oilers, 1,697 yards
NFC Walter Payton, Chicago Bears, 14 TDs
AFC Earl Campbell, Houston Oilers, 19 TDs

Passing
NFC Steve DeBerg, San Francisco 49ers, 347 completions
AFC Dan Fouts, San Diego Chargers, 332 completions
NFC Steve DeBerg, San Francisco 49ers, 3,652 yards gained
AFC Dan Fouts, San Diego Chargers, 4,082 yards gained
NFC Roger Staubach, Dallas Cowboys, 27 TDs
AFC Steve Grogan, New England Patriots, 28 TDs
      Brian Sipe, Cleveland Browns, 28 TDs

Receiving
NFC Ahmad Rashad, Minnesota Vikings, 80 receptions
AFC Joe Washington, Baltimore Colts, 82 receptions
NFC Ahmad Rashad, Minnesota Vikings, 1,157 yards gained
AFC Steve Largent, Seattle Seahawks, 1,237 yards gained
NFC Harold Carmichael, Philadelphia Eagles, 11 TDs
AFC Stanley Morgan, New England Patriots, 12 TDs

Field Goals
NFC Mark Moseley, Washington Redskins, 25
AFC John Smith, New England Patriots, 23

PATs
NFC Rafael Septien, Dallas Cowboys, 40
AFC Matt Barr, Pittsburgh Steelers, 50

Circle Suite 225 — Chargers Game 1 — Game 1 - Sat., Aug. 6, 1977-8:00 P.M. DALLAS Cowboys vs. SAN DIEGO Chargers — SUITE 225 — SERVICE CREDENTIAL — PRICE $12.00

The 1980s

The one thing about the NFL in the 1980s was that the dynasties, if they could be called that, were on the west coast, unlike the geographic scattering of those of the previous decade. And they were not as concentrated in their dominance.

Bill Walsh's San Francisco 49ers managed to reign victorious in two Super Bowls, but there was a two-year interval between crowns. Tom Flores took one for the Raiders of Oakland at the start of the decade and another for the Raiders of Los Angeles midway through it.

Joe Gibbs and his Washington Redskins paid two visits to the season's-end classic, triumphing once and failing the other time.

Then there were the machines of destruction. Mike Ditka's Chicago Bears of 1985, with its incredible defense, Walter Payton, Jim McMahon, and the 325-pound Refrigerator Perry, mauled everyone in sight during the season, then shut out both their opponents in the playoffs before demolishing the New England Patriots in the most lopsided Super Bowl ever. The next year it was the New York Giants turn. Bill Parcells' team had a defense as niggardly as the Bears the year before with stars like Lawrence Taylor, Jim Burt, and Harry Carson, and he had Joe Morris to run the ball and Phil Simms to throw it. And no team came close to them in the playoffs or Super Bowl XXI.

It was a golden age for running backs. Besides Payton and Morris, there was Earl Campbell, Tony Dorsett, Billy Sims, Wilbert Montgomery, Marcus Allen, Eric Dickerson, and Freeman McNeil, to mention just a few. Passing was dazzling on the arms of such riflers as Joe Montana, Dan Fouts, Ken Anderson, Joe Theismann, and Dan Marino, and in the hands of Kellen Winslow, Steve Largent, James Lofton, Charlie Joiner, Dwight Clark, and Art Monk.

With Super Bowl television audiences counted on a global scale in the hundreds of millions in the 1980s, it can certainly be said that pro football in America has become a spectacle of unequalled proportion. . .a long way from when those soft-helmeted and sometimes helmetless pros took the field back in the 1920s.

A pair of winners in the '80s, perennial All Pro linebacker Lawrence Taylor (56) and defensive tackle Jim Burt of the Giants. (Fred Roe)

The Best of the Decade / 1980s

FIRST TEAM–OFFENSE

Position	Player	Team
WR	James Lofton	Green Bay Packers
WR	Steve Largent	Seattle Seahawks
TE	Kellen Winslow	San Diego Chargers
T	Joe Jacoby	Washington Redskins
T	Anthony Munoz	Cincinnati Bengals
G	John Hannah	New England Patriots
G	Russ Grimm	Washington Redskins
C	Mike Webster	Pittsburgh Steelers
QB	Joe Montana	San Francisco 49ers
RB	Eric Dickerson	Los Angeles Rams
RB	Marcus Allen	Los Angeles Raiders

FIRST TEAM–DEFENSE

Position	Player	Team
DE	Lee Roy Selmon	Tampa Bay Buccaneers
DE	Mark Gastineau	New York Jets
DT	Randy White	Dallas Cowboys
DT	Dan Hampton	Chicago Bears
LB	Lawrence Taylor	New York Giants
LB	Mike Singletary	Chicago Bears
LB	Andre Tippett	New England Patriots
DB	Ronnie Lott	San Francisco 49ers
DB	Mike Haynes	New England Patriots/ Los Angeles Rams
DB	Kenny Easley	Seattle Seahawks
DB	Nolan Cromwell	Los Angeles Rams
K	Mark Moseley	Washington Redskins
P	Rohn Stark	Indianapolis Colts
coach	*Bill Walsh*	*San Francisco 49ers*

SECOND TEAM–OFFENSE

Position	Player	Team
WR	Charlie Joiner	San Diego Chargers
WR	Art Monk	Washington Redskins
TE	Ozzie Newsome	Cleveland Browns
T	Keith Fahnhorst	San Francisco 49ers
T	Jimbo Covert	Chicago Bears
G	Randy Cross	San Francisco 49ers
G	Ed Newman	Miami Dolphins
C	Dwight Stephenson	Miami Dolphins
QB	Dan Marino	Miami Dolphins
RB	Tony Dorsett	Dallas Cowboys
RB	John Riggins	Washington Redskins

SECOND TEAM–DEFENSE

Position	Player	Team
DE	Howie Long	Los Angeles Raiders
DE	Ed Jones	Dallas Cowboys
DT	Doug English	Detroit Lions
DT	Joe Klecko	New York Jets
LB	Karl Mecklenberg	Denver Broncos
LB	E. J. Junior	St. Louis Cardinals
LB	Harry Carson	New York Giants
DB	Mark Haynes	New York Giants
DB	Everson Walls	Dallas Cowboys
DB	Gary Fencik	Chicago Bears
DB	Deron Cherry	Kansas City Chiefs
K	Rafael Septien	Dallas Cowboys
P	Rich Camarillo	New England Patriots
coach	*Joe Gibbs*	*Washington Redskins*

Events and Milestones

The Los Angeles Rams move their home field to Anaheim Stadium in Orange County. **(1980)**

Richard Todd of the Jets sets the NFL record for most passes completed in a game with 42 against the 49ers. **(1980)**

The NFL sets a regular season attendance record of 13.4 million, the average paid attendance for the 224-game regular season is 59,787, another all-time high. **(1980)**

Dan Fouts of the San Diego Chargers sets a pair of NFL marks when he completes 348 passes for 4,715 yards. **(1980)**

The Oakland Raiders become the first wild card entry to win the NFL championship when they defeat the Eagles 27–10 in Super Bowl XV. **(1981)**

LeRoy Irvin of the Los Angeles Rams establishes an NFL mark when he returns punts for a total of 207 yards in a game with the Falcons. **(1981)**

San Diego's Dan Fouts breaks both passing records he set the year before by completing 360 passes for 4,802 yards. **(1981)**

The Oakland Raiders, after a significant court battle, move to Los Angeles and begin playing their games at the L.A. Coliseum. **(1982)**

The NFL players go on strike after two games and the season comes to a halt. After nearly two months the players and management agree to terms and the season resumes on a modified basis. A total of nine games are played and a special playoff tournament is devised, involving the top eight teams from each conference. **(1982)**

NFL team rosters are extended to 49 players. **(1983)**

Tony Dorsett of the Dallas Cowboys makes the longest run from scrimmage in the history of the NFL when he breaks loose on 99-yard sprint against the Vikings. **(1983)**

Defensive end Fred Dean of the 49ers is credited with the most sacks ever in a single game, six against the Saints. **(1983)**

John Riggins of the Washington Redskins sets an NFL record by rushing for 24 touchdowns, five more than the previous record which was shared by Jim Taylor, Earl Campbell, and Chuck Muncie. **(1983)**

Ali Haji-Sheikh, a rookie with the New York Giants, sets the all-time NFL field goal mark by booting 35. **(1983)**

The Baltimore Colts are moved to Indianapolis. **(1984)**

The San Francisco 49ers, coached by Bill Walsh and led by the NFC's top-ranked quarterback Joe Montana and top-scorer Ray Wersching, win 15 of their 16 regular season games, the most victories in a single season in league history. **(1984)**

Dan Marino of the Miami Dolphins rewrites the NFL passing record book, setting three new standards: most completions (362), most yardage gained passing (5,084), and most TD passes (48). **(1984)**

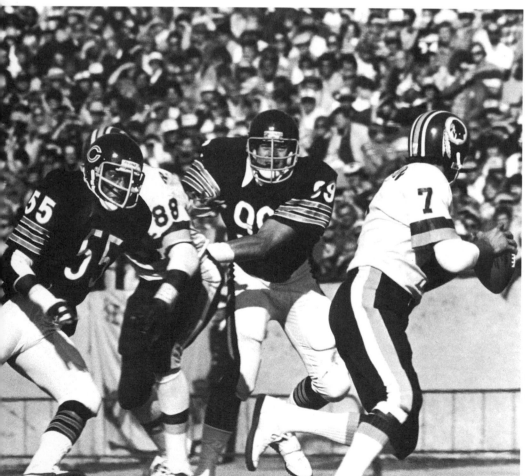

Joe Theismann (7) of the Redskins definitely wants to avoid a sure-to-be painful encounter with the voracious defense of the Bears of the mid-80s, represented here by linebacker Otis Wilson (55) and tackle Dan Hampton (99). (Chicago Bears)

The diver here is Lionel Manuel, gathering one in for the New York Giants. (Fred Roe)

Eric Dickerson of the Rams breaks O. J. Simpson's single season rushing record by gaining a total of 2,105 yards. **(1984)**

Art Monk of the Washington Redskins catches more passes in one season than any player in NFL history, 106, five more than Charley Hennigan caught back in 1964. **(1984)**

Mark Clayton of the Dolphins catches 18 touchdown passes for another NFL mark. **(1984)**

Uwe von Schamann of Miami kicks more extra points than any other player in NFL history, 66. **(1984)**

Defensive end Mark Gastineau of the Jets sets a new standard for sacks in a single season, downing enemy quarterbacks 22 times. **(1984)**

In January pro football racks up the largest television viewing audience for a live event in history with Super Bowl XIX when nearly 116 million people in America watch the 49ers dump the Dolphins 38–16. **(1985)**

Stephone Paige of the Kansas City Chiefs sets a new NFL standard for the most yards on pass receptions in a single game. Paige's 309 yards eclipses the mark of 303 set by Jim Benton of the Cleveland Rams back in 1945. **(1985)**

The Chicago Bears equal San Francisco's record of 15 wins in a regular season. **(1985)**

Two marks are set when the Bears defeat the Patriots in Super Bowl XX. The final score of 46–10 is the largest victory margin in Super Bowl history, and the 127 million television viewers give it the largest audience in television history. **(1986)**

The first NFL game ever to be played in Europe is staged at Wembley Stadium in London when the Chicago Bears and Dallas Cowboys face each other in a preseason contest. **(1986)**

The use of instant replay as an officiating aid is introduced. **(1986)**

Dan Marino of the Dolphins betters his NFL record of pass completions in a season with 378, 16 more than he completed in 1984. His 623 passes are also the most ever thrown by an NFL quarterback in one season. **(1986)**

The Champions / 1980s

1980	NFC	Philadelphia Eagles	12–4–0
		(*Eagles* 20, *Cowboys* 7)	
	AFC	Oakland Raiders	11–5–0
		(*Raiders* 34, *Chargers* 27)	

Super Bowl XV
Oakland Raiders	27
Philadelphia Eagles	10

1981	NFC	San Francisco 49ers	13–3–0
		(*49ers* 28, *Cowboys* 27)	
	AFC	Cincinnati Bengals	12–4–0
		(*Bengals* 27, *Chargers* 7)	

Super Bowl XVI
San Francisco 49ers	26
Cincinnati Bengals	21

1982	NFC	Washington Redskins	8–1–0
		(*Redskins* 31, *Cowboys* 17)	
	AFC	Los Angeles Raiders*	8–1–0
		(*Dolphins* 14, *Jets* 0)	

Super Bowl XVII
Washington Redskins	27
Miami Dolphins	17

*The Raiders lost to the Jets in the semifinals of the playoff tournament.

1983	NFC	Washington Redskins	14–2–0
		(*Redskins* 24, *49ers* 21)	
	AFC	Los Angeles Raiders	12–4–0
		(*Raiders* 30, *Seahawks* 14)	

Super Bowl XVIII
Los Angeles Raiders	38
Washington Redskins	9

1984	NFC	San Francisco 49ers	15–1–0
		(*49ers* 23, *Bears* 0)	
	AFC	Miami Dolphins	14–2–0
		(*Dolphins* 45, *Steelers* 28)	

Super Bowl XIX
San Francisco 49ers	38
Miami Dolphins	16

1985	NFC	Chicago Bears	15–1–0
		(*Bears* 24, *Rams* 0)	
	AFC	New England Patriots	11–5–0
		(*Patriots* 31, *Dolphins* 14)	

Super Bowl XX
Chicago Bears	46
New England Patriots	10

1986	NFC	New York Giants	14–2–0
		(*Giants* 17, *Redskins* 0)	
	AFC	Denver Broncos	11–5–0
		(*Broncos* 23, *Browns* 20)	

Super Bowl XXI
New York Giants	39
Denver Broncos	20

Lefty Jim Zorn of the Packers is about to unleash one against the Bears, oblivious of the pressure applied by pass rusher Steve McMichael (76). (Chicago Bears)

Like a gazelle being downed by Lions, Dallas quarterback Steve Pelluer (16) accepts the inevitable at the hands of defensive end George Martin and linebacker Carl Banks of the Giants. (Fred Roe)

The League Leaders / 1980s

1980

Scoring

NFC	Ed Murray, Detroit Lions, 116 points	
AFC	John Smith, New England Patriots, 129 points	

Rushing

NFC   Walter Payton, Chicago Bears, 1,460 yards
AFC   Earl Campbell, Houston Oilers, 1,934 yards
NFC   Billy Sims, Detroit Lions, 13 TDs
AFC   Earl Campbell, Houston Oilers, 13 TDs

Passing

NFC   Archie Manning, New Orleans Saints, 309 completions
AFC   Dan Fouts, San Diego Chargers, 348 completions
NFC   Archie Manning, New Orleans Saints, 3,716 yards gained
AFC   Dan Fouts, San Diego Chargers, 4,715 yards gained
NFC   Steve Bartkowski, Atlanta Falcons, 31 TDs
AFC   Dan Fouts, San Diego Chargers, 30 TDs
         Brian Sipe, Cleveland Browns, 30 TDs

Receiving

NFC   Earl Cooper, San Francisco 49ers, 83 receptions
AFC   Kellen Winslow, San Diego Chargers, 89 receptions
NFC   James Lofton, Green Bay Packers, 1,226 yards gained
AFC   John Jefferson, San Diego Chargers, 1,340 yards gained
NFC   Earnest Gray, New York Giants, 10 TDs
AFC   John Jefferson, San Diego Chargers, 13 TDs

Field Goals

NFC   Ed Murray, Detroit Lions, 27
AFC   John Smith, New England Patriots, 26
         Frank Steinfort, Denver Broncos, 26

PATs

NFC   Rafael Septien, Dallas Cowboys, 59
AFC   John Smith, New England Patriots, 51

SUNDAY MAYHEM

1981

Scoring

NFC	Ed Murray, Detroit Lions, 121 points	
	Rafael Septien, Dallas Cowboys, 121 points	
AFC	Jim Breech, Cincinnati Bengals, 115 points	
	Nick Lowery, Kansas City Chiefs, 115 points	

Rushing

NFC George Rogers, New Orleans Saints, 1,674 yards
AFC Earl Campbell, Houston Oilers, 1,376 yards
NFC John Riggins, Washington Redskins, 13 TDs
George Rogers, New Orleans Saints, 13 TDs
Billy Sims, Detroit Lions, 13 TDs
AFC Chuck Muncie, San Diego Chargers, 19 TDs

Passing

NFC Tommy Kramer, Minnesota Vikings, 322 completions
AFC Dan Fouts, San Diego Chargers, 360 completions
NFC Tommy Kramer, Minnesota Vikings, 3,912 yards gained
AFC Dan Fouts, San Diego Chargers, 4,802 yards gained
NFC Steve Bartkowski, Atlanta Falcons, 30 TDs
AFC Dan Fouts, San Diego Chargers, 33 TDs

Receiving

NFC Dwight Clark, San Francisco 49ers, 85 receptions
AFC Kellen Winslow, San Diego Chargers, 88 receptions
NFC Alfred Jenkins, Atlanta Falcons, 1,358 yards gained
AFC Frank Lewis, Buffalo Bills, 1,244 yards gained
Steve Watson, Denver Broncos, 1,244 yards gained
NFC Alfred Jenkins, Altanta Falcons, 13 TDs
AFC Steve Watson, Denver Broncos, 13 TDs

Field Goals

NFC Rafael Septien, Dallas Cowboys, 27
AFC Nick Lowery, Kansas City Chiefs, 26

PATs

NFC Mick Luckhurst, Atlanta Falcons, 51
AFC Rolf Benirschke, San Diego Chargers, 55

1982

Scoring

NFC Wendell Tyler, Los Angeles Rams, 78 points
AFC Marcus Allen, Los Angeles Raiders, 84 points

Rushing

NFC Tony Dorsett, Dallas Cowboys, 745 yards
AFC Freeman McNeil, New York Jets, 786 yards
NFC Eddie Lee Ivery, Green Bay Packers, 9 TDs
Wendell Tyler, Los Angeles Rams, 9 TDs
AFC Marcus Allen, Los Angeles Raiders, 11 TDs

Passing

NFC Joe Montana, San Francisco 49ers, 213 completions
AFC Ken Anderson, Cincinnati Bengals, 218 completions
NFC Joe Montana, San Francisco 49ers, 2,613 yards gained
AFC Dan Fouts, San Diego Chargers, 2,883 yards gained
NFC Joe Montana, San Francisco 49ers, 17 TDs
AFC Terry Bradshaw, Pittsburgh Steelers, 17 TDs
Dan Fouts, San Diego Chargers, 17 TDs

Jim McMahon, Chicago Bear quarterback and his infamous Adidas headband. It cost him more than a few dollars in fines from commissioner Pete Rozelle, who frowns on players advertising products during gametime. (Fred Roe)

Receiving
NFC Dwight Clark, San Francisco 49ers, 60 receptions
AFC Kellen Winslow, San Diego Chargers, 54 receptions
NFC Dwight Clark, San Francisco 49ers, 913 yards gained
AFC Wes Chandler, San Diego Chargers, 1,032 yards gained
NFC Charlie Brown, Washington Redskins, 8 TDs
AFC Wes Chandler, San Diego Chargers, 9 TDs

Field Goals
NFC Mark Moseley, Washington Redskins, 20
AFC Nick Lowery, Kansas City Chiefs, 19

PATs
NFC Rafael Septien, Dallas Cowboys, 28
AFC Chris Bahr, Los Angeles Raiders, 32
     Rolf Benirschke, San Diego Chargers, 32

1983

Scoring
NFC Mark Moseley, Washington Redskins, 161 points
AFC Gary Anderson, Pittsburgh Steelers, 119 points

Rushing
NFC Eric Dickerson, Los Angeles Rams, 1,808 yards
AFC Curt Warner, Seattle Seahawks, 1,449 yards
NFC John Riggins, Washington Redskins, 24 TDs
AFC Pete Johnson, Cincinnati Bengals, 14 TDs

Passing
NFC Danny White, Dallas Cowboys, 334 completions
AFC Bill Kenney, Kansas City Chiefs, 346 completions
NFC Lynn Dickey, Green Bay Packers, 4,458 yards gained
AFC Bill Kenney, Kansas City Chiefs, 4,348 yards gained
NFC Lynn Dickey, Green Bay Packers, 32 TDs
AFC Joe Ferguson, Buffalo Bills, 26 TDs
     Brian Sipe, Cleveland Browns, 26 TDs

Receiving
NFC Charlie Brown, Washington Redskins, 78 receptions
     Earnest Gray, New York Giants, 78 receptions
     Roy Green, St. Louis Cardinals, 78 receptions
AFC Todd Christensen, Los Angeles Raiders, 92 receptions
NFC Mike Quick, Philadelphia Eagles, 1,409 yards gained
AFC Carlos Carson, Kansas City Chiefs, 1,351 yards gained
NFC Roy Green, St. Louis Cardinals, 14 TDs
AFC Todd Christensen, Los Angeles Raiders, 12 TDs

Field Goals
NFC Ali Haji-Sheikh, New York Giants, 35
AFC Raul Allegre, Baltimore Colts, 30

PATs
NFC Mark Moseley, Washington Redskins, 62
AFC Chris Bahr, Los Angeles Raiders, 51

Eagle quarterback Ron Jaworski is the victim of the New York Giants' sack-attack, administered here by linebacker Lawrence Taylor (56) and Jim Burt (64). (Fred Roe)

1984

Scoring

    NFC   Ray Wersching, San Francisco 49ers, 131 points

    AFC   Gary Anderson, Pittsburgh Steelers, 117 points

Rushing

    NFC   Eric Dickerson, Los Angeles Rams, 2,105 yards

    AFC   Earnest Jackson, San Diego Chargers, 1,179 yards

    NFC   Eric Dickerson, Los Angeles Rams, 14 TDs

             John Riggins, Washington Redskins, 14 TDs

    AFC   Marcus Allen, Los Angeles Raiders, 13 TDs

Passing

    NFC   Neil Lomax, St. Louis Cardinals, 345 completions

    AFC   Dan Marino, Miami Dolphins, 362 completions

    NFC   Neil Lomax, St. Louis Cardinals, 4,614 yards gained

    AFC   Dan Marino, Miami Dolphins, 5,084 yards gained

    NFC   Neil Lomax, St. Louis Cardinals, 28 TDs

             Joe Montana, San Francisco 49ers, 28 TDs

    AFC   Dan Marino, Miami Dolphins, 48 TDs

Receiving

    NFC   Art Monk, Washington Redskins, 106 receptions

    AFC   Ozzie Newsome, Cleveland Browns, 89 receptions

    NFC   Roy Green, St. Louis Cardinals, 1,555 yards gained

    AFC   John Stallworth, Pittsburgh Steelers, 1,395 yards gained

    NFC   Roy Green, St. Louis Cardinals, 12 TDs

    AFC   Mark Clayton, Miami Dolphins, 18 TDs

Field Goals

    NFC   Paul McFadden, Philadelphia Eagles, 30

    AFC   Gary Anderson, Pittsburgh Steelers, 24

             Matt Bahr, Cleveland Browns, 24

PATs

    NFC   Ray Wersching, San Francisco 49ers, 56

    AFC   Uwe von Schamann, Miami Dolphins, 66

1985

Scoring

    NFC   Kevin Butler, Chicago Bears, 144 points

    AFC   Gary Anderson, Pittsburgh Steelers, 139 points

Rushing

    NFC   Gerald Riggs, Atlanta Falcons, 1,719 yards

    AFC   Marcus Allen, Los Angeles Raiders, 1,759 yards

    NFC   Joe Morris, New York Giants, 21 TDs

    AFC   Marcus Allen, Los Angeles Raiders, 11 TDs

             Ron Davenport, Miami Dolphins, 11 TDs

Passing

    NFC   Joe Montana, San Francisco 49ers, 303 completions

    AFC   Dan Marino, Miami Dolphins, 336 completions

    NFC   Phil Simms, New York Giants, 3,829 yards gained

    AFC   Dan Marino, Miami Dolphins, 4,137 yards gained

    NFC   Joe Montana, San Francisco 49ers, 27 TDs

    AFC   Dan Marino, Miami Dolphins, 30 TDs

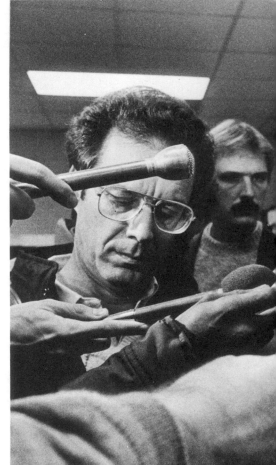

A phenomenon of the 80s, William "Refrigerator" Perry of the Bears, whose gap-toothed smile and 325-pound-plus bulk made him the most talked-about sometime fullback of the decade. (Chicago Bears)

Receiving

NFC Roger Craig, San Francisco 49ers, 92 receptions
AFC Lionel James, San Diego Chargers, 86 receptions
NFC Mike Quick, Philadelphia Eagles, 1,247 yards gained
AFC Steve Largent, Seattle Seahawks, 1,287 yards gained
NFC Mike Quick, Philadelphia Eagles, 11 TDs
AFC Daryl Turner, Seattle Seahawks, 13 TDs

Field Goals

NFC Morten Anderson, New Orleans Saints, 31
     Kevin Butler, Chicago Bears, 31
AFC Gary Anderson, Pittsburgh Steelers, 33

PATs

NFC Ray Wersching, San Francisco 49ers, 52
AFC Bob Thomas, San Diego Chargers, 51

1986

Scoring

NFC Kevin Butler, Chicago Bears, 120 points
AFC Tony Franklin, New England Patriots, 140 points

Rushing

NFC Eric Dickerson, Los Angeles Rams, 1,821 yards
AFC Curt Warner, Seattle Seahawks, 1,481 yards
NFC George Rogers, Washington Redskins, 18 TDs
AFC Curt Warner, Seattle Seahawks, 13 TDs

Passing

NFC Jay Schroeder, Washington Redskins, 276 completions
AFC Dan Marino, Miami Dolphins, 378 completions
NFC Jay Schroeder, Washington Redskins, 4,109 yards gained
AFC Dan Marino, Miami Dolphins, 4,746 yards gained
NFC Tommy Kramer, Minnesota Vikings, 24 TDs
AFC Dan Marino, Miami Dolphins, 44 TDs

Receiving

NFC Jerry Rice, San Francisco 49ers, 86 receptions
AFC Todd Christensen, Los Angeles Raiders, 95 receptions
NFC Jerry Rice, San Francisco 49ers, 1,570 yards gained
AFC Stanley Morgan, New England Patriots, 1,491 yards gained
NFC Jerry Rice, San Francisco 49ers, 15 TDs
AFC Mark Duper, Miami Dolphins, 11 TDs

Field Goals

NFC Kevin Butler, Chicago Bears, 28
AFC Tony Franklin, New England Patriots, 32

PATs

NFC Chuck Nelson, Minnesota Vikings, 44
AFC Fuad Reveiz, Miami Dolphins, 52

MODERN MAYHEM

Captain of the crunch in the 1960s, Chicago Bear linebacker Dick Butkus (51), dispenses a little pain to Green Bay running back Dave Hampton. (Pro Football Hall of Fame)

Earl Morrall (11), quarterbacking for the New York Giants in the mid-60s, is wedged into a fetal position by a pair of Redskin defenders. (Fred Roe)

The Packers and the Colts go at it. Signalling a touchdown is Green Bay flanker Carroll Dale as Paul Hornung is scrunched by a pair of Baltimore defenders. (Fred Roe)

Turfside view of mayhem, defensive back Phil Harris (46) of the Giants pins a Philadelphia Eagle at Yankee Stadium in 1966. (Fred Roe)

129

Officials are not exempt, this one learning the painful way as Calvin Hill of the Cowboys runs over him. (Pro Football Hall of Fame)

In the trench, Roger Brown (76) of the Detroit Lions battles a small herd of Colts.

Aerial encounter: Cowboy safety Cliff Harris soars in to deflect the ball from intended St. Louis Cardinal receiver J. V. Cain. (Dallas Cowboys)

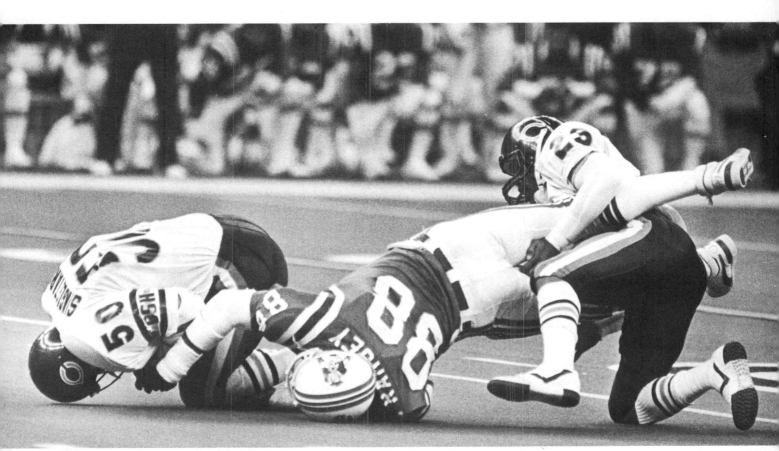

Chicago Bear linebacker Mike Singletary (50) has the ball, a fumble recovery, and is being grabbed at by New England Patriot tight end Derrick Ramsey who is being grabbed at by Bear cornerback Shaun Gayle. (Chicago Bears)

131

The Giants' John Mendenhall manhandles Cowboy quarterback Roger Staubach as George Martin (75) moves in to help with the kill. (New York Giants)

Safety Gary Fencik of the Chicago Bears (45) upends a would-be but couldn't-be Green Bay receiver, couldn't be because the ball is already on the ground. (Chicago Bears)

Upside-down and headed for a sure migraine is Greg Latta (88), tight end for the Chicago Bears, as a pair of Eagles go their way without concern. (Chicago Bears)

TIME OUT

John Madden: Hey, I've Got Some Tips

John Madden, former Raiders' coach, television broadcaster, author, celebrity, and the world's most well-known fear-of-flying personality, offered these tips on handling the pro football season as part of an interview for USA Today.

- On staying in shape for TV football viewing season: Lie around a lot. A mistake some people made in the summer was that they moved around too much. Just practice sitting for six, seven, hey, 10 or 12 hours. Do nothing. Then when you got the sitting part down, it's easy to put the game there in front of you.

- On the importance of pacing yourself: Take it one game at a time, just like the coaches tell their players. Don't try to watch a bunch of games, don't look ahead to the big game, just get through the one you're watching.

- On avoiding Sunday family outings: You say, "Just let me watch the first half." Then you say, "Well, it's a good game, we'll go right after it's over." Before you know it, it's dark and the zoo is closed. You can procrastinate by quarters or by halves. Procrastinating by halves is better.

- On how to reconnect with loved ones at the end of the season: In February, start your recovery. Don't worry about relationships. Just get the blood flowing. You've been in hibernation. Walk around a little. Swing your arms. Stretch. In March or April, you can take care of birthdays, Mother's Day, and all that stuff. But remember: In July the NFL starts training camp. Then you have to start getting in shape to sit around for six or seven hours at a time again. Double-headers are a good place to start.

☆ ☆ ☆ ☆ ☆ ☆ ☆ ☆

POLITICO PROS

☆ ☆ ☆ ☆ ☆ ☆ ☆

The National Football League has yet to field a president of the United States, but it has turned out a number of pros-turned-politicians. The best known:

Byron "Whizzer" White

Pittsburgh Steelers
1938
Detroit Lions
1940–41

Deputy U.S.
Attorney General
1961–62
U.S. Supreme
Court Justice
1962–present

Jack Kemp

Pittsburgh Steelers
1957
New York Giants
1959
Los Angeles/
San Diego Chargers
1960–62
Buffalo Bills
1962–69

U.S. House of
Representatives
1971–present

POLITICO PROS

Ed King

   Buffalo Bills   Governor of
     1948–49   Massachusetts
   Baltimore Colts   1979–83
     1950

Nick Buoniconti

   Boston Patriots   Dade County
     1962–68   Florida Democratic
   Miami Dolphins   Party Chairman
     1969–76   1982–present

Lavie Dilweg

Milwaukee Badgers
1926
Green Bay Packers
1927–34

U.S. House of
Representatives
1943–45

Bill Dudley

Pittsburgh Steelers
1942, 45–46
Detroit Lions
1947–49
Washington Redskins
1950–51, 53

Virginia
General Assembly
1966–74

Yale Lary

Detroit Lions
1952–53, 56–64

Texas State
Legislature
1959–62

The NFL's Most Successful Author

Pete Gent, flanker for the Dallas Cowboys during the 1960s, is the NFL's most successful author. His novel, *North Dallas Forty*, a ribald romp behind the scenes of a fictional professional football team, was also considered a *roman a clef* effort with transparent caricatures of Don Meredith, Tom Landry, and Tex Schramm, among others. It became a national best seller and was made into a successful motion picture.

Gent was also the humorist in residence at Dallas during his playing days. Bob St. John, columnist for the *Dallas Morning News*, often wrote about his escapades, and especially enjoyed this story.

"Once (Bob) Hayes had been injured during a road game and on the return flight, Landry decided he'd move Gent from flanker to the other side, split end, where he'd start against Philadelphia, instead of the injured Hayes. Landry walked to the back of the plane, the players' section, and found Gent.

"'Pete', said Landry, 'you'll be moving to the other side this week. So get ready.'

"'You mean, coach,' said Pete, 'that I'm going to play for Philadelphia?'"

Double Pros

Twelve NFL players who also played professional basketball:

Player, NFL Team	Basketball Team, First Season
Dick Evans, Packers	Sheboygan Redskins, 1941–42
Len Ford, Browns	Dayton Rens, 1949–50
Ted Fritsch, Packers	Oshkosh All-Stars, 1945–46
Otto Graham, Browns	Rochester Royals, 1946–47
Bud Grant, Eagles	Minneapolis Lakers, 1950–51
Vern Huffman, Lions	Indianapolis Kautskys, 1938–39
Connie Mack Berry, Bears	Oshkosh All-Stars, 1940–41
Otto Schnellbacher, Giants	St. Louis Bombers, 1948–49
Bob Shaw, Rams	Youngstown Bears, 1945–46
Clint Wager, Cardinals	Oshkosh All-Stars, 1944–45
Ron Widby, Cowboys	New Orleans Buccaneers, 1967–68
Lonnie Wright, Broncos	Denver Rockets, 1967–68

NFL CELEBRITY QUIZ

1.

This star of the 1926 silent movie *One Minute to Play*, explaining something about football to his leading lady, Mary McAllister, put pro football on the proverbial map in the 1920s.

_____

2.

A cavalryman in *Rio Conchos* here, a member of *The Dirty Dozen* in another motion picture, he seemed to opposing defensive linemen to be riding a fast horse when he led the NFL in rushing seven times.

_____

3.

His legs were as famous in football as Marlene Dietrich's were to the movies. With his leading lady, Joan Vohs, here, he is the only NFL player to star in a movie that was named for him.

_____

4.

He seldom smiled when he was in the defensive line for the NFL champion Pittsburgh Steelers in the 1970s and his arms were much more accustomed to being draped around ballcarriers than a booth, but he imparts a bit of warmth in this scene from the 1974 film *Pop Goes the Weasel*.

5.

He starred in Miami as a Dolphin, not as a member of that city's vice squad, when Don Shula was putting together back-to-back Super Bowl championships. Here he stars in the premiere episode of the television series *Emergency*, in which he plays a chemical worker who goes berserk after he is poisoned by fumes in the plant where he works.

6.

When he was not setting NFL rushing marks or palling around with Arnie Palmer on the television screen, he played a security guard in *The Towering Inferno*.

Without Pictures, the Ultimate Test

1.

He KO'd a horse in Mel Brooks' *Blazing Saddles,* was known as "Tippy Toes" when he played for the Detroit Lions, and was one of the best defensive tackles in the game during the late 1950s and the 60s.

_____

2.

This former quarterback was featured in the movie *Kate Bliss and the Ticker Tape Kid,* and his down-home banter and drawl are familiar to millions of sports-minded television viewers.

_____

3.

Gentle on television, this Hall of Famer, a onetime 270-pound defensive tackle left his mark as a regular on the television series *Little House on the Prairie.*

_____

4.

He played in the original movie version of *M*A*S*H* as well as the ensuing television versions of it, who, when he was a Philadelphia Eagle in the 1960s gained enough yards to rank as the third most productive rusher in team history and once ran a kickoff back 105 yards for a touchdown and a team record.

_____

Answers

1. Red Grange
2. Jim Brown
3. Crazylegs Hirsch
4. Mean Joe Greene
5. Larry Csonka
6. O. J. Simpson

1. Alex Karras
2. Dandy Don Meredith
3. Merlin Olsen
4. Timmy Brown

BILLBOARDS

1. They were all in this one in the late 1940s...
   at least the backs.
2. Only in Hollywood, Crazylegs and
   Lovelylegs.
3. James Caan as Brian Piccolo, Gale Sayers as
   Gale Sayers: *Brian's Song*.
4. The Detroit Lions, cameos of Frank Gifford
   and Vince Lombardi...thanks to George
   Plimpton.

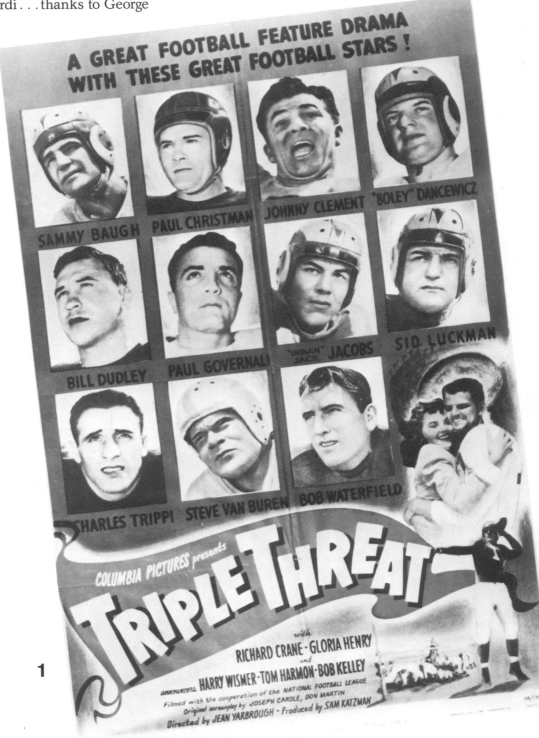

CRAZYLEGS AND LOVELYLEGS ...the Sweethearts of the Campus!

HALL BARTLETT PRODUCTIONS, INC. presents

CRAZYLEGS

starring

ELROY "CRAZYLEGS" HIRSCH · LLOYD NOLAN · JOAN VOHS

featuring JAMES MILLICAN · JAMES BROWN

Written and Produced HALL BARTLETT · Directed by FRANCIS LYON · A REPUBLIC PRESENTATION

RS · DICK "Night Train" LANE · DEACON DAN TOWLER · NORMAN VAN BROCK
BOB WATERFIELD · PAUL "Tank" YOUNGER

2

The tough, ten Story of the ALE SA BRIAN P

3

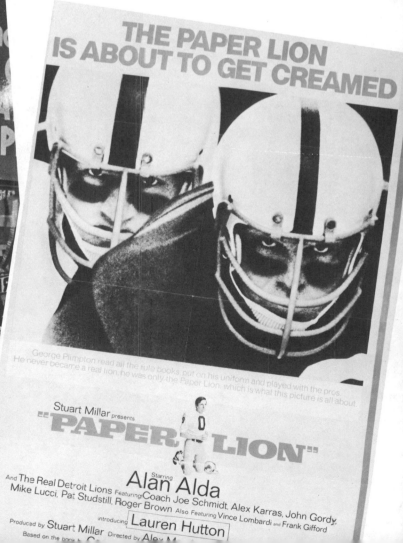

THE PAPER LION IS ABOUT TO GET CREAMED

George Plimpton read all the rule books, put on his uniform and played with the pros. He never became a real lion, he was only the Paper Lion, which is what this picture is all about.

Stuart Millar presents

"PAPER LION"

Starring

Alan Alda

And The Real Detroit Lions Featuring Coach Joe Schmidt, Alex Karras, John Gordy, Mike Lucci, Pat Studstill, Roger Brown Also Featuring Vince Lombardi and Frank Gifford

introducing Lauren Hutton

Produced by Stuart Millar Directed by Alex M

Based on the book

4

4 THE NATIONAL FOOTBALL CONFERENCE

Atlanta Falcons

Suwanee Road I-85
Suwanee, Georgia 30174

Stadium: Atlanta-Fulton County Stadium
(capacity 60,748)

Training camp: Suwanee Road I-85
Suwanee, Georgia 30174

Colors: red, black and silver

Historical Highlights

The 1960s

Rankin Smith, a 41-yr-old businessman, is awarded the NFL franchise for Atlanta for $8.5 million. (1965)

Miss Julia Elliot, a schoolteacher, is notified that her suggested nickname of the "Falcons," has been chosen as the team's nickname. (1965)

Tommy Nobis, All-American linebacker from the University of Texas, and quarterback Randy Johnson of Texas A & I are co-first round choices. (1965)

Norb Hecker, a member of Vince Lombardi's staff at Green Bay, is named head coach. (1966)

Atlanta, after 10 straight losses, defeats the New York Giants 27–16, for its first victory. (1966)

Training camp site is shifted to Johnson City, Tennessee, and the campus of East Tennessee State University. (1967)

The 1970s

For the first time in team history, ticket prices are raised. Most seats increase from $6.00 to $7.50. (1971)

Falcons post first winning season in their history, (7–6–1). (1971)

Falcons defeat Los Angeles 31–3, their first-ever victory over the Rams as running back Dave Hampton scores two touchdowns and rushes for a team record of 161 yards. For the first time in team history, two players, Hampton and Art Malone, gain 100 yards or more rushing in a single game. (1972)

Falcons defeat New Orleans 62–7 in a season opener that smashes 35 team records. (1973)

Atlanta defeats Los Angeles 15–13 as Nick Mike-Mayer kicks five field goals. (1973)

Norm Van Brocklin is fired as head coach/general manager and Marion Campbell, Falcons' defensive coordinator, is named head coach. (1974)

Tommy Nobis came to the Falcons from the University of Texas in 1966 and quickly proved to be one of the finest linebackers in the game, a stalwart until he left the Atlanta lineup after the 1976 season. (Atlanta Falcons)

Marion Campbell is fired as head coach and Pat Pepple is named as interim head coach. (1976)

Rankin M. Smith, Jr., is named president of the club and Eddie LeBaron is named general manager. Leeman Bennett becomes Falcon head coach. (1977)

The construction of a new, year-round training facility begins in Suwanee, Georgia. (1978)

When the Chicago Bears defeat Washington, the Falcons clinch their first playoff berth ever. (1978)

Falcons edge Philadelphia, 14–13, in the NFC wild card playoff game as Steve Bartkowski throws two touchdown passes in the final eight minutes. (1978)

After leading 20–13 at halftime, the Falcons lose a closely-contested playoff game to Dallas, 27–20. (1978)

A new club single-game rushing record is established with William Andrews' 167-yard performance at New Orleans in a 40–34 Atlanta overtime win. (1979)

Falcons lose in overtime to Broncos, 20–17, but Steve Bartkowski establishes a new club single-game passing record of 326 yards gained (20 of 29). (1979)

After he catches two touchdown passes and rushes for another score against Oakland, Lynn Cain becomes the first Falcon player ever to score three touchdowns in a single game. (1979)

William Andrews establishes a new Falcon single-season rushing record of 1,023 yards. (1979)

The 1980s

A new club passing record is established by Steve Bartkowski with 332 yards during a Falcon loss to Miami, 20–17. (1980)

In a dramatic 33–27 Falcon overtime victory at St. Louis, Steve Bartkowski sets a single-game passing record with a 378-yard performance. (1980)

Three Bartkowski touchdown passes and William Andrews' sixth 100-yard rushing performance of the season lead Atlanta to their first NFC Western Division title. (1980)

Falcons lose 30–27 to Dallas in the playoffs before an Atlanta-Fulton County Stadium record crowd of 60,022. (1980)

The Falcons, for the first time, record an opening day shutout, whitewashing New Orleans, 27–0. (1981)

A club record is established by wide receiver Alfred Jenkins when he catches three touchdown passes in a single game against New Orleans. (1981)

Falcons claim their third playoff berth in five seasons after they clip the Super Bowl champs of the previous season, the San Francisco 49ers, 17–7. (1982)

In the first round of the Super Bowl Tournament of the strike-shortened 1982 season, the Falcons lose 30–24 to Minnesota. (1982)

After six years and an overall record of 47–44, Leeman Bennett is dismissed as head coach and Dan Henning, assistant coach of the champion Washington Redskins, replaces him. (1983)

Club marks for single-game carries and yards rushing are set by Gerald Riggs as he rushes 35 times for 202 yards in a 36–22 opening day win at New Orleans. (1984)

Gerald Riggs sets a new club record for career rushing TDs, surpassing William Andrews' 29. (1985)

The Falcons post 16–10 final win over New Orleans as Gerald Riggs rushes for 158 yards, his ninth 100-yard game of the year, a new club record. (1985)

Marion Campbell replaces Dan Henning as head coach. (1987)

Art Malone gains a few yards for the Falcons in a 1972 game against the 49ers. Number 52 is San Francisco linebacker Skip Vanderbundt. (Atlanta Falcons)

Memorable Years

Year	Record	Achievement
1978	9–7–0	Wild card entry
1980	12–4–0	Division champion
1982	5–4–0	Playoff tournament participant

Record Holders

Career

Rushing yards	William Andrews (1979–83)	5,772
Passing yards	Steve Bartkowski (1975–85)	23,468
Passing TD's	Steve Bartkowski (1975–85)	154
Pass receptions	Alfred Jenkins (1975–83)	359
Receiving yards	Alfred Jenkins (1975–83)	6,257
Interceptions	Rolland Lawrence (1973–81)	39
Field Goals	Mick Luckhurst (1981–85)	92
Total TD's	Alfred Jenkins (1975–83)	40
	William Andrews (1979–83)	40
Total points	Mick Luckhurst (1981–85)	451

Season

Rushing yards	Gerald Riggs, 1985	1,719
Passing yards	Steve Bartkowski, 1981	3,830
Passing TD's	Steve Bartkowski, 1980	31
Pass receptions	William Andrews, 1981	81
Receiving yards	Alfred Jenkins, 1981	1,358
Field Goals	Nick Mike-Mayer, 1973	26
Total TD's	Alfred Jenkins, 1981	13
	Gerald Riggs, 1984	13
Total points	Mick Luckhurst, 1981	114

Game

Rushing yards	Gerald Riggs, 9/2/84	202
Passing yards	Steve Bartkowski, 11/15/81	416
Passing TD's	Randy Johnson, 11/16/69	4
	Steve Bartkowski, 10/19/80	4
	Steve Bartkowski, 10/18/81	4
Pass receptions	William Andrews, 11/15/81	15
Receiving yards	Alfred Jackson, 12/2/84	193
Interceptions	many times	2
Field Goals	Nick Mike-Mayer, 11/4/73	5
	Tim Mazzetti, 10/30/78	5
Total TD's	many times	3
Total points	many times	18

Top Coach

	Record	Win Percentage	Years
Leeman Bennett	47–44–0	.516	1977–82

All-Pros

Year	Player	Position
1967	Tommy Nobis	LB
1972	Claude Humphrey	DE
1973	Claude Humphrey	DE
1980	Mike Kenn	T
1981	Alfred Jenkins	WR
1982	R.C. Thielemann	G
1983	Billy Johnson	PR

Chicago Bears

Halas Hall
250 North Washington
Lake Forest, IL 60045

Stadium: Soldier Field (capacity 65,790)

Training camp: Wisconsin-Platteville
                        Platteville, Wisconsin 53818

Colors: navy blue, orange and white

Historical Highlights

The 1920s

A.E. Staley hires George Halas to organize and launch the Decatur Staleys professional football team. (1920)

The Staleys are given to George Halas and Dutch Sternaman, (partners), and are moved to Chicago to play in Wrigley Field. (1921)

The franchise is named the Chicago Bears. (1922)

The first player deal: Bears buy tackle Ed Healey's contract from the Rock Island Independents for $100. (1922)

Red Grange signs with the Bears and they go on a 16-game coast-to-coast tour. (1925)

The 1930s

George Halas replaces himself as head coach with Ralph Jones. (1930)

Bears and Chicago Cardinals play football's first indoor game on an 80-yard field at the Chicago Stadium. (1930)

Bronko Nagurski hits Red Grange with a 2-yard TD pass and the Bears top the Portsmouth Spartans 9-0 for the NFL Championship. The game is played indoors at the Chicago Stadium on an 80-yard field. (1932)

The franchise loses $18,000, prompting Dutch Sternaman to unload his half of the Bears to George Halas. (1932)

George Halas returns as head coach and takes the club out of town for training camp at the University of Notre Dame in South Bend, Indiana. (1933)

The Boston Redskins delight their fans by whitewashing the Bears, 10-0, ending Chicago's 30-game unbeaten streak. (1933)

A pair of Bear legends, Red Grange (left) and Bronko Nagurski. Both are charter members of the Pro Football Hall of Fame. (Chicago Bears)

Bears use rookie Jack Manders' accurate kicking for 11 points and defeat the Giants, 23-11, in the NFL's first official championship game. (1933)

A classic is born as 79,432 watch the NFL Champion Bears held to a scoreless tie by the College All-Star team in a game sponsored by the Chicago Tribune Charities at Soldier Field. (1934)

Rookie Beattie Feathers becomes the first pro back to rush for 1,000 yards, gaining 1,004 to lead the NFL. (1934)

The undefeated Bears slip before the Giants in the NFL Title tilt at the Polo Grounds, 30-13, before 35,059. With Chicago leading 10-3 at the half, New York dons basketball sneakers and scores 27 points. (1934)

Joe Stydahar, tackle, West Virginia, is the Bears first draft choice in the new college player draft. (1936)

Bears win the Western Division title but lose the NFL championship, 28-21, to the Redskins at Wrigley Field. (1937)

The 1940s

Ten Bears tally TDs as Chicago rips Washington 73-0 for the NFL title in Washington, D.C. before 36,034 fans. The Bears receive $873 per man as the winner's share. (1940)

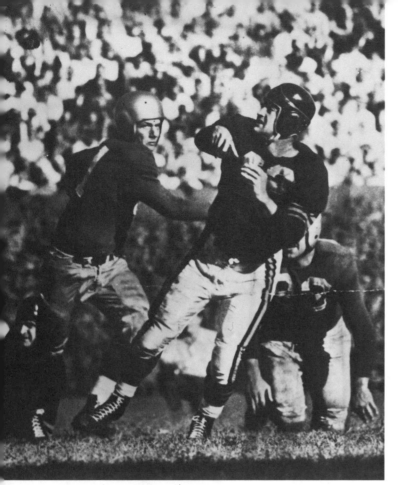

The first of the great T formation quarterbacks, Sid Luckman, a tailback from Columbia's single wing, came to the Bears in 1939 and was weaned to the T by coach George Halas. Luckman, All Pro often during the 40s, is a Hall of Famer. (Pro Football Hall of Fame)

Bears get a new fight song when "Bear Down Chicago Bears" is published. (1941)

George Halas departs for the U.S. Navy prior to the NFL title game, which Chicago loses 14–6 in Washington. (1942)

Hunk Anderson and Luke Johnsos co-coach the wartime Bears for three seasons. (1943–5)

Sid Luckman becomes the first pro to pass for over 400 yards and seven touchdowns in one game, both NFL records. (1943)

The Bears blast Washington 41–21 in Wrigley Field for the NFL title in front of 34,320 fans. Sid Luckman throws five TD passes, two each to Harry Clark and Dante Magnani, and the other to Jim Benton. (1943)

George Halas returns, and the Bears whip the Giants 24–14, before a NFL record crowd of 58,346 at the Polo Grounds for the title. (1946)

Johnny Lujack sets an NFL passing record with 469 yards against the Chicago Cardinals. (1949)

The 1950s

The Bears and the Rams tie for the Western Division Title with 9–3 marks but the Rams trip the Bears in Los Angeles, 24–14, in a playoff game. (1950)

Paddy Driscoll starts a two-year tour as head coach when George Halas retires for a third time. (1956)

Giants, again wearing sneakers, trounce Chicago 47–7 before 56,836 fans in Yankee Stadium for the NFL title. (1956)

Halas returns as head coach. (1958)

Bears and Rams establish an NFL attendance record, drawing 90,833 in the Los Angeles Coliseum to watch a 41–35 Rams victory. (1958)

The 1960s

Bears intercept five Y.A. Tittle passes to capture the NFL title from the Giants, 14–10, in Wrigley Field before a crowd of 45,801. Champs share is $5,899 per man. QB Billy Wade gets both TD's on two short plunges. (1963)

Flanker Johnny Morris catches an NFL record 93 passes. (1964)

The Bears have two first round draft choices and select linebacker Dick Butkus of Illinois and running back Gale Sayers from Kansas. (1965)

Gale Sayers scores six TDs against the 49ers to tie the NFL record. (1965)

Rookie Sayers sets an NFL single-season record with 22 TDs. (1965)

Gale Sayers sets NFL combined yards record with 2,440. (1966)

The all-time winningest coach in football history, George Halas, retires from coaching after 40 seasons, turning the reins over to assistant coach Jim Dooley. (1968)

The 1970s

Bears trounce Green Bay 35–17 in their last game in Wrigley Field. Soldier Field is to become their home in 1971. (1970)

The Bears draft running back Walter Payton from Jackson State. (1975)

En route to leading the NFL in rushing with a Bear record 1,852 yards, Walter Payton dashes through the Vikings defense for an NFL record 275 yards rushing. (1977)

The Bears make the playoffs for the first time since 1963, setting 28 team records and playing before a home field record of 401,513 fans for seven Soldier Field dates. Chicago loses to Dallas in the playoffs, 37–7. (1977)

Neill Armstrong, former defensive coordinator of the Minnesota Vikings becomes head coach. (1978)

Bears occupy Halas Hall, their new $1.6 million headquarters on the Lake Forest College campus. (1979)

The Bears drop 27–17 wild card game to Philadelphia after leading 17–0 at the half. (1979)

The 1980s

Bears equal a club record for points and set new standards for first downs (33) and pass completions percentage (83.3%, 20 of 24), as they whip the Green Bay Packers 61–7 at Soldier Field. Quarterback Vince Evans throws for 316 yards, the most by a Bear in ten years. (1980)

Mike Ditka, assistant offensive coach of the Dallas Cowboys, becomes head coach. (1982)

Bears owner and founder, George Halas, dies at the age of 88. (1983)

Bears clinch a divisional title with their record of 10–6. (1984)

The Bears defeat the Redskins 23–19 in divisional playoffs to advance to the NFC Championship game, but the 49ers defeat the Bears, 23–0, in the NFC final. (1984)

The Bears win the most games ever in team history, 15 victories against one defeat, and easily win their division. Back-to-back shutouts in the playoffs, 21–0, over the Giants, and 24–0, over the Rams, earn the Bears their first trip to the Super Bowl. (1985)

Bears triumph in Super Bowl XX, defeating the New England Patriots, 46–10, in New Orleans. (1986)

Chicago repeats as winner of the NFC Central Division, posting a record of 14–2–0. But, with QB Jim McMahon sidelined by a shoulder injury, the Bears lose in the playoffs to the Redskins 27–13. (1986)

Walter Payton of the Bears shows his famous stutter-step, which has helped gain more yards rushing than any other player in pro football history. From 1975 through the present he has virtually rewritten the NFL's rushing record book. (Chicago Bears)

Memorable Years

Year	Record	Achievement
1921	9–1–1	NFL champion
1932	7–1–6	NFL champion
1933	10–2–1	NFL champion
1934	13–0–0	NFL runner-up
1937	9–1–1	NFL runner-up
1940	8–3–0	NFL champion
1941	10–1–0	NFL champion
1942	11–0–0	NFL runner-up
1943	8–1–1	NFL champion
1946	8–2–1	NFL champion
1950	9–3–0	Conference champ (tie, playoff loss)
1956	9–2–1	NFL runner-up
1963	11–1–2	NFL champion
1977	9–5–0	Playoff participant
1979	10–6–0	Playoff participant
1984	10–6–0	Conference runner-up
1985	15–1–0	NFL champion
1986	14–2–0	Division Champion

Top Coaches

	Record	Win Percentage	Years
George Halas	326–151–31	.683	1920–29, 33–42, 46–55
Mike Ditka	54–25–0	.684	1982–86
Ralph Jones	25–10–7	.706	1930–32
Hunk Anderson/ Luke Johnsos	23–12–2	.657	1942–45
Paddy Driscoll	14–10–1	.583	1956–57

Record Holders

Career

Rushing yards	Walter Payton (1975–86)	16,193
Passing yards	Sid Luckman (1939–50)	14,686
Passing TD's	Sid Luckman (1939–50)	137
Pass receptions	Walter Payton (1975–86)	459
Receiving yards	Walter Payton (1975–86)	5,481
Interceptions	Richie Petitbon (1959–68)	37
Field Goals	Bob Thomas (1975–84)	128
Total TD's	Walter Payton (1975–86)	120
Total points	Walter Payton (1975–86)	720

Season

Rushing yards	Walter Payton, 1977	1,852
Passing yards	Bill Wade, 1962	3,172
Passing TD's	Sid Luckman, 1943	28
Pass receptions	Johnny Morris, 1964	93
Receiving yards	Johnny Morris, 1964	1,200
Interceptions	Roosevelt Taylor, 1963	9
Field Goals	Kevin Butler, 1985	31
Total TD's	Gale Sayers, 1965	22
Total points	Kevin Butler, 1985	144

Game

Rushing yards	Walter Payton, 11/20/77	275
Passing yards	Johnny Lujack, 12/11/49	468
Passing TD's	Sid Luckman, 11/14/43	7
Pass receptions	Jim Keane, 10/23/49	14
Receiving yards	Harlon Hill, 10/31/54	214
Interceptions	many times	3
Field Goals	Roger LeClerc, 12/3/61	5
	Mac Percival, 10/20/68	5
Total TD's	Gale Sayers, 12/12/65	6
Total points	Gale Sayers, 12/12/65	36

All-Pros

Year	Player	Position	Year	Player	Position	Year	Player	Position
1920	Guy Chamberlin	E		Danny Fortmann	G	1958	Bill George	LB
	Hugh Blacklock	T	1941	Sid Luckman	QB	1959	Stan Jones	G
	George Trafton	C		George McAfee	HB		Bill George	LB
1922	Pete Stinchcomb	HB		Danny Fortmann	G	1960	Bill George	LB
	Hugh Blacklock	T		Bulldog Turner	C	1961	Bill George	LB
	Ed Healey	G	1942	Sid Luckman	QB	1963	Mike Ditka	TE
1923	Ed Healey	T		Gary Famiglietti	FB		Doug Atkins	DE
1924	Joey Sternaman	QB		Lee Artoe	T		Bill George	LB
	Ed Healey	T		Danny Fortmann	G		Joe Fortunato	LB
	George Trafton	C		Bulldog Turner	C		Richie Petitbon	DB
1925	Joey Sternaman	QB	1943	Sid Luckman	QB		Roosevelt Taylor	DB
	Ed Healey	T		Harry Clark	HB	1964	Johnny Morris	FL
	Jim McMillen	G		Danny Fortmann	G		Mike Ditka	TE
1926	Paddy Driscoll	HB		Bulldog Turner	C		Joe Fortunato	LB
	Ed Healey	T	1944	Sid Luckman	QB	1965	Gale Sayers	RB
1927	Paddy Driscoll	HB		Bulldog Turner	C		Dick Butkus	LB
1928	Jim McMillen	G	1946	Sid Luckman	HB		Joe Fortunato	LB
1930	Red Grange	HB		Bulldog Turner	C	1966	Gale Sayers	RB
	Luke Johnsos	E	1947	Sid Luckman	QB	1967	Gale Sayers	RB
	Link Lyman	T		Ken Kavanaugh	E	1968	Gale Sayers	RB
1931	Red Grange	HB		Bulldog Turner	C		Dick Butkus	LB
1932	Zuck Carlson	G	1948	Fred Davis	T	1969	Gale Sayers	RB
	Luke Johnsos	E		Chuck Drulis	G		Dick Butkus	LB
	Bronko Nagurski	FB		Bulldog Turner	C	1970	Dick Gordon	WR
1933	Bill Hewitt	E	1949	George Connor	T		Dick Butkus	LB
	Joe Kopcha	G		Ray Bray	G	1972	Dick Butkus	LB
	Bronko Nagurski	FB	1950	Johnny Lujack	QB	1976	Walter Payton	RB
1934	Beattie Feathers	HB		George Connor	T		Wally Chambers	DT
	Bill Hewitt	E		Dick Barwegan	G	1977	Walter Payton	RB
	Joe Kopcha	G	1951	George Connor	T	1978	Walter Payton	RB
	Bronko Nagurski			Dick Barwegan	G	1979	Gary Fencik	DB
1935	Bill Karr	E	1952	George Connor	T	1980	Walter Payton	RB
	George Musso	T	1953	George Connor	T	1981	Gary Fencik	DB
	Joe Kopcha	G	1955	Harlon Hill	E	1982	Dan Hampton	DT
1936	Bill Hewitt	E		Bill Wightkin	T	1984	Walter Payton	RB
1937	Joe Stydahar	T		Stan Jones	G		Dan Hampton	DT
	George Musso	G		Bill George	LB		Mike Singletary	LB
1938	Joe Stydahar	T	1956	Rick Casares	FB	1985	Walter Payton	RB
	Danny Fortmann	G		Harlon Hill	E		Jimbo Covert	T
1939	Bill Osmanski	FB		Stan Jones	G		Richard Dent	DE
	Joe Stydahar	T		Larry Strickland	C		Steve McMichael	DT
	Danny Fortmann	G		Bill George	LB		Mike Singletary	LB
1940	Joe Stydahar	T	1957	Bill George	LB			

Dallas Cowboys

Cowboys Center
One Cowboys Parkway
Irving, Texas 75063

Stadium: Texas Stadium (capacity 63,749)

Training camp: California Lutheran University
              Thousand Oaks, California 91360

Colors: royal blue, metallic blue, silver and white

Vintage Cowboys: Quarterback Dandy Don Meredith with a crewcut and coach Tom Landry with his ubiquitous fedora. (Dallas Cowboys)

Historical Highlights

The 1960s

The NFL awards Clint Murchison, Jr., and Bedford Wynne an expansion franchise. Although listed in the Western Conference, the Cowboys are to play as a swing team their first year, playing every other team once during the season. (1960)

Tom Landry becomes head coach of the Cowboys, hired by newly appointed general manager, Tex Schramm. (1960)

At the league meeting in Los Angeles, a player pool is set up, with each of the 12 NFL teams freezing 25 names on its roster and allowing Dallas to pick three players from each team for a total of 36 veterans. (1960)

The Cowboys get their first league win, defeating Pittsburgh, 27–24, by scoring ten points in the final 56 seconds in the league opener in the Cotton Bowl. A 27-yard field goal by Allen Green on the game's final play wins it before a crowd of 23,500. (1961)

Points are awarded for a penalty for the first time in anyone's memory in an NFL game. The Cowboys are detected holding in the end zone on a 99-yard touchdown pass from Eddie LeBaron to Frank Clarke and Pittsburgh is awarded a safety, aiding the Steelers' 30–28 victory. (1962)

Cowboy Amos Marsh returns a 101-yard kickoff and Mike Gaechter returns a 100-yard pass interception, both for TDs in a fourth quarter win over Philadelphia, 41–19. It is the first time two 100-yard runs are made in the same game by the same team in the same quarter. (1962)

The Cowboys open training at California Lutheran College in Thousand Oaks, California. (1963)

Cowboy Bill Howton breaks Don Hutson's all-time receiving mark with a 14-yard catch against the Red-skins at Washington, giving Howton an even 8,000 career yards. (1963)

Giving Tom Landry possibly the longest contract in pro football history, the Cowboys sign him to a ten-year extension of his original contract. (1964)

The Cotton Bowl is jammed with an overflow crowd of 76,251 for the game against Cleveland, the Cowboys' first sellout. (1965)

The Cowboys defeat New York, 38–20, in their season finale, winning five of their last seven games and earning a trip to the Playoff Bowl in Miami, where they fall to Baltimore, 35–3. (1966)

Clint Murchison, Jr., retains the title of chairman of the board and names Tex Schramm president of the club. (1966)

Capturing the Eastern Conference title with a 10–3–1 record, the Cowboys earn postseason play, but lose the NFL championship game to Green Bay, 34–27. (1966)

The Cowboys easily win the Capitol Division, defeating Cleveland 52–14, in the Cotton Bowl for the Eastern Conference Championship. (1967)

The Packers again stop the Cowboys in their second bid for the NFL title, defeating them 21–17 in 13-degree below zero weather at Green Bay. (1967)

The Cowboys win the Capitol championship for the second straight year but are upset by Cleveland, 31-20, in their third bid for the Eastern championship. (1968)

The Cowboys again take the division championship with an 11-2-1 season but fall to Cleveland, 38-14, in the game for the Eastern Division title at the Cotton Bowl. (1969)

The 1970s

The Cowboys claim the Eastern Division title with a 10-4 season record, making the playoffs for the fifth year in a row, and get a shot at the National Conference title when they defeat Detroit, 5-0. (1970)

The Cowboys triumph over San Francisco 17-10 for the NFC crown and earn the right to meet Baltimore in the Super Bowl. (1970)

Dallas loses to the Colts 16-13 in Super Bowl V. (1971)

The Cowboys open the season at Texas Stadium with a 44-21 victory over the New England Patriots, and the first touchdown in the new stadium is scored by running back Duane Thomas before a crowd of 65,708. (1971)

The Cowboys again win the NFC Eastern Division, then defeat Minnesota in the opening round of the playoffs. (1971)

The NFC showdown again features the Cowboys and the San Francisco 49ers in a victory for Dallas, 14-3, that qualifies the team for their second straight Super Bowl appearance. (1971)

The Cowboys win Super Bowl VI in New Orleans, handing the Miami Dolphins a 24-3 defeat. Roger Staubach is named the Most Valuable Player. (1972)

Calvin Hill becomes the first Dallas player to rush for 100 yards in a game when he gains 111 against the Washington Redskins in Texas Stadium. Hill's season record totals 1,036 yards on a record 245 carries. (1972)

A season record of 10-4 earns the Cowboys a wild card playoff berth, qualifying them for the playoffs the seventh straight year. Roger Staubach passes for two touchdowns in the final minute and a half giving the Cowboys a 30-28 victory in the first round of the playoffs. But Dallas falls 26-3 to the Redskins in their bid for a third straight NFC title. (1972)

With a 10-4 record the Cowboys regain the NFC Eastern Division title and break their own NFL record by reaching the playoffs for the eighth year in a row. The Cowboys defeat Los Angeles in the first round only to bow to Minnesota, 27-10, in the NFC Championship game. (1973)

Roger Staubach, feeling the crunch here, was the Cowboys team leader throughout the 1970s, and was inducted into the Pro Football Hall of Fame in his first year of eligibility. Applying the crunch is Rich Glover of the New York Giants. (Dallas Cowboys)

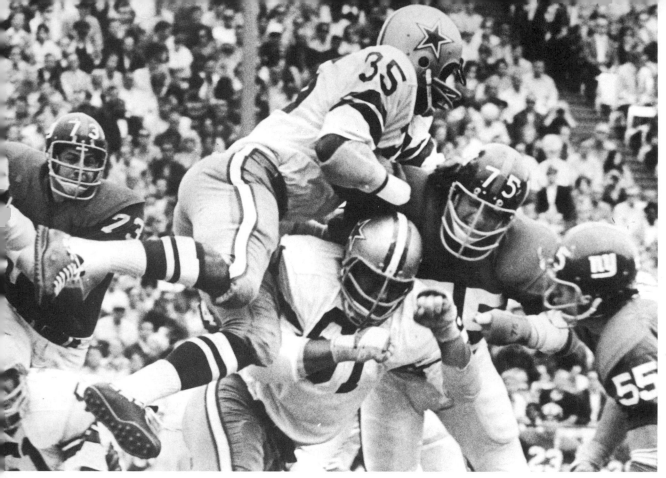

Dallas running back Calvin Hill decides to vault the line of scrimmage in a 1970 game against the Giants. Hill, a product of Yale, ranks behind only Tony Dorsett and Don Perkins in all-time Cowboy rushing yardage. (Dallas Cowboys)

The Cowboys achieve a composite record over ten straight winning seasons of 101–37–2 while their current year's record of 10–4 earns them a wild card play-off spot. (1975)

Roger Staubach's "Hail Mary" pass to Drew Pearson in the first round results in a 17–14 victory over Minnesota and sends the Cowboys to Los Angeles where Staubach shines again, throwing four touchdown passes, three to Drew Pearson to defeat the Rams, 37–7. (1975)

The Cowboys fall to Pittsburgh, 21–17, in Super Bowl X in Miami. (1976)

Dallas wins the Eastern Division title with an 11–3 record, achieving their 10th straight playoff berth. The season ends, however, with a first round loss, 14–12, to Los Angeles. (1976)

The Cowboys win their fourth National Conference crown, defeating the Minnesota Vikings, 23–6, at Texas Stadium and earn the right to meet the Denver Broncos in Super Bowl XII. (1977)

In Super Bowl XII, the Cowboys defeat the Denver Broncos, 27–10, winning their second World Championship and tying Minnesota for most Super Bowl appearances (four) and Green Bay, Miami, and Pittsburgh for most Super Bowl victories (two). Defensive linemen Harvey Martin and Randy White are named co-Most Valuable Players in the game. (1978)

Dallas shuts out the Rams in Los Angeles, 28–0 for the 1978 NFC title. (1978)

The Cowboys lose to Pittsburgh 35–31 in the Super Bowl, the first Super Bowl rematch ever. (1978)

Winning their eleventh division championship after rallying from a mid-season slump, the Cowboys finish the season with an 11–5 record and their 13th trip to the playoffs, but lose there to Los Angeles, 21–19. (1979)

The 1980s

The Cowboys achieve their 15th straight winning season with a 12–4 record with Danny White replacing retired Roger Staubach at quarterback. Entering the playoffs as a wild card bid, they rally past Los Angeles and Atlanta but are defeated 20–7 in the NFC title game. (1980)

When the Cowboys beat Los Angeles 34–13 in the playoffs, Tom Landry joins George Halas and Curly Lambeau as the only coaches with 200 NFL victories in the regular season and playoff games. (1980)

Cowboys win the Eastern Division Championship, their twelfth title since 1966, with a 12–4 record and tie Oakland's record of 16 consecutive winning seasons. They enter the playoffs, advance to the conference title game, but are edged out by San Francisco's last minute touchdown at Candlestick Park, final 28–27. (1981)

Dallas achieves a new NFL record of seventeen consecutive winning seasons, enters the playoffs for the eighth straight year but comes up short in the championship game, losing 31–17 at Washington. (1982)

A season record of 12–4 extends the Cowboys' NFL record to 18 straight winning seasons and a league record is set with their ninth straight appearance in the playoffs. A 24–17 upset victory by the Rams eliminates the Cowboys from the playoffs. (1983)

The Murchison family sells the Cowboys to an 11-member limited partnership headed by Dallas businessman, H.R. "Bum" Bright at the league's annual meeting in Honolulu. (1984)

The Cowboys rack up their 19th straight winning season with a record of 9–7, but for the first time in 10 years do not make the playoffs. (1984)

Dallas loses to the Chicago Bears, 44–0, at Texas Stadium, their worst defeat in team history. (1985)

The Cowboys win their 13th divisional championship, posting a 10–6 record, but are shut out 20–0 by the Rams in their first playoff game. (1985)

Dallas, losing nine of its 16 games, experiences its first losing season since 1964. (1986)

Memorable Years

Year	Record	Achievement
1966	10–3–1	Conference champion
1967	9–5–0	Conference champion
1968	12–2–0	Division champion
1969	11–2–1	Division champion
1970	10–4–0	NFL runner-up
1971	11–3–0	NFL champion
1972	10–4–0	NFC runner-up
1973	10–4–0	NFC runner-up
1975	10–4–0	NFL runner-up
1976	11–3–0	Division champion
1977	12–2–0	NFL champion
1978	12–4–0	NFL runner-up
1979	11–5–0	Division champion
1980	12–4–0	NFC runner-up
1981	12–4–0	NFC runner-up
1982	6–3–0	NFC runner-up
1983	12–4–0	Wild card entry
1985	10–6–0	Division champion

Record Holders

Career		
Rushing yards	Tony Dorsett (1977–86)	11,130
Passing yards	Roger Staubach (1969–79)	22,700
Passing TD's	Roger Staubach (1969–79)	153
Pass receptions	Drew Pearson (1973–83)	489
Receiving yards	Drew Pearson (1973–83)	7,822
Interceptions	Mel Renfro (1964–77)	52
Field Goals	Rafael Septien (1978–86)	162
Total TD's	Tony Dorsett (1977–86)	84
Total points	Rafael Septien (1978–86)	874

Season		
Rushing yards	Tony Dorsett, 1985	1,719
Passing yards	Danny White, 1983	3,980
Passing TD's	Danny White, 1983	29
Pass receptions	Tony Hill, 1985	74
Receiving yards	Bob Hayes, 1966	1,232
Interceptions	Everson Walls, 1981	11
Field Goals	Rafael Septien, 1981	27
Total TD's	Dan Reeves, 1966	16
Total points	Rafael Septien, 1983	123

Game		
Rushing yards	Tony Dorsett, 12/4/77	206
Passing yards	Don Meredith, 11/10/63	460
Passing TD's	many times	5
Pass receptions	Lance Rentzel, 11/19/67	13
Receiving yards	Bob Hayes, 11/13/66	246
Interceptions	Herb Adderley, 9/26/71	3
	Lee Roy Jordan, 11/4/73	3
	Dennis Thurman, 12/13/81	3
Field Goals	many times	4
Total TD's	many times	4
Total points	many times	24

Top Coach

	Record	Win Percentage	Years
Tom Landry	260–157–6	.624	1960–86

All-Pros

Year	Player	Position
1962	Don Perkins	RB
1964	Frank Clarke	WR
	Bob Lilly	DT
1965	Bob Lilly	DT
1966	Bob Hayes	WR
	Bob Lilly	DT
	Chuck Howley	LB
	Cornell Green	CB
1967	Ralph Neely	T
	Bob Lilly	DT
	Chuck Howley	LB
	Cornell Green	CB
1968	Bob Hayes	WR
	Ralph Neely	T
	Bob Lilly	DT
	Chuck Howley	LB
1969	Calvin Hill	RB
	Ralph Neely	T
	John Niland	G
	Bob Lilly	DT
	Chuck Howley	LB
1970	Chuck Howley	LB
1971	Rayfield Wright	T
	John Niland	G
	Bob Lilly	DT
1972	Rayfield Wright	T
1973	Calvin Hill	RB
	Rayfield Wright	T
	Lee Roy Jordan	LB
	Mel Renfro	CB
1974	Drew Pearson	WR
1976	Drew Peason	WR
	Cliff Harris	S
1977	Drew Pearson	WR
	Harvey Martin	DE
	Cliff Harris	S
	Charlie Waters	S
	Efren Herrera	K
1978	Randy White	DT
	Cliff Harris	S
	Charlie Waters	S
1979	Randy White	DT
1980	Herbert Scott	G
	Randy White	DT
1981	Tony Dorsett	RB
	Herbert Scott	G
	Randy White	DT
	Rafael Septien	K
1982	Ed Jones	DE
	Randy White	DT
	Everson Walls	CB
1983	Randy White	DT
	Everson Walls	CB
1984	Randy White	DT
	Michael Downs	S
1985	Randy White	DT
	Everson Walls	CB

Detroit Lions

Pontiac Silverdome
1200 Featherstone Road - Box 4200
Pontiac, Michigan 48057

Stadium: Pontiac Silverdome (capacity 80,638)

Training camp: Oakland University
　　　　　　　　Rochester, Minnesota 48063

Colors: Honolulu blue and silver

Historical Highlights

The 1930s

The Portsmouth (Ohio) Spartans join the NFL. (1930)

Potsy Clark is named the first head coach of the Spartans. (1930)

The team is moved to Detroit and the name is changed to the Lions. (1934)

Before a crowd of 12,000 at the University of Detroit Stadium, the Lions play their first NFL game, beating the New York Giants 9-0. (1934)

The Lions play their first traditional Thanksgiving Day home game before a crowd of 26,000 who see them lose to the Bears 19-16. (1934)

The Lions take the Western Division crown, then win their first championship, defeating the New York Giants 26-7. (1935)

After Potsy Clark quits, Dutch Clark, the Lions' star tailback, takes over the coaching duties as well. (1937)

The Lions open the season in their new home, Briggs Stadium. (1938)

The 1940s

Gus Dorais is named head coach of the Lions. (1943)

Lyle Fife and Edwin J. Anderson head a syndicate which purchases the Detroit franchise for $185,000. Alvin "Bo" McMillin is named general manager and head coach. (1948)

The 1950s

Bobby Layne and Doak Walker join the Lions backfield. (1950)

Buddy Parker succeeds McMillin as Detroit's head coach. (1951)

Dutch Clark, a legend in the 1930s, was a single-wing tailback and a true triple threat who led the NFL in scoring in 1932, 1935, and 1936. He also led the Lions to their first NFL title in 1935. (Pro Football Hall of Fame)

Detroit wins a conference title by defeating Los Angeles, 31-21. (1952)

The Lions defeat the Browns, 17-7, before a Cleveland crowd of 50,934 to win their first NFL championship since 1935. (1952)

A 17-16 decision over Cleveland in Detroit gives the Lions their second straight NFL title before a crowd of 54,577. (1953)

Parker resigns suddenly as head coach and is succeeded by Detroit assistant coach George Wilson the next day. (1957)

Detroit stages a great come-from-behind win in a playoff game for the Western Conference title, scoring 24 points in the second half to beat the 49ers. (1957)

The Lions claim their fourth NFL championship, slaughtering Cleveland, 59-14, in front of 55,263 fans. (1957)

The 1960s

William Clay Ford is elected president of the Lions' organization. (1961)

Ford purchases the franchise for $4.5 million and takes over as the sole owner. (1964)

George Wilson is replaced as head coach by Harry Gilmer. (1965)

Thirteen-season veteran, Joe Schmidt, retires from play to become the Lions linebacker coach. (1966)

Joe Schmidt is named Lions' head coach, replacing Harry Gilmer. (1967)

The 1970s

In their first playoff game since 1957, the Lions, 10–4 for the season, lose to Dallas, 5–0. (1970)

Steve Owens becomes the first Lion to rush for more than 1,000 yards in a season, (1,035 on 246 carries). (1971)

The Lions name Don McCafferty head coach. (1973)

Rick Forzano is named head coach. (1974)

Detroit plays the first game in their new home, the Pontiac Silverdome before a record Lions' crowd of 79,784, but lose to the Cowboys, 26–10. (1975)

Tommy Hudspeth is named interim coach after the resignation of Rick Forzano. (1976)

Monte Clark becomes Detroit's 16th head coach. (1978)

The 1980s

After making it to the special playoff tournament because of the strike-shortened season, Detroit falls to the Redskins, 31–7. (1982)

The Lions win the NFC Central Division, (9–7 record), then, in their second playoff appearance in two years, lose to the San Francisco 49ers, 24–23 when a last second field-goal attempt fails. (1983)

After a successful 20-year college coaching career, Darryl Rogers is named head coach of the Lions. (1985)

Doak Walker, gaining some yardage against the Bears here, joined the Lions in 1950 after a stunning college career at SMU. After six seasons he retired, earning his way into the Hall of Fame by his Detroit deeds. (Detroit Lions)

Memorable Years

Year	Record	Achievement
1935	7–3–2	NFL champion
1952	9–3–0	NFL champion
1953	10–2–0	NFL champion
1954	9–2–1	NFL runner-up
1957	8–4–0	NFL champion
1982	4–5–0	Playoff tournament participant
1983	9–7–0	Division champion

Record Holders

Career		
Rushing yards	Billy Sims (1980–84)	5,106
Passing yards	Bobby Layne (1950–58)	15,710
Passing TD's	Bobby Layne (1950–58)	118
Pass receptions	Charlie Sanders (1968–77)	336
Receiving yards	Gail Cogdill (1960–68)	5,220
Interceptions	Dick LeBeau (1959–72)	62
Field Goals	Errol Mann (1969–76)	141
Total TD's	Billy Sims (1980–84)	47
Total points	Errol Mann (1969–76)	636

Season		
Rushing yards	Billy Sims, 1981	1,437
Passing yards	Gary Danielson, 1980	3,223
Passing TD's	Bobby Layne, 1951	26
Pass receptions	James Jones, 1984	77
Receiving yards	Pat Studstill, 1966	1,266
Interceptions	Don Doll, 1950	12
	Jack Christiansen, 1953	12
Field Goals	Ed Murray, 1980	27
Total TD's	Billy Sims, 1980	16
Total points	Doak Walker, 1950	128

Game		
Rushing yards	Bob Hoernschemeyer, 11/23/50	198
Passing yards	Bobby Layne, 11/5/50	374
Passing TD's	Gary Danielson, 12/9/78	5
Pass receptions	Cloyce Box, 12/3/50	12
Receiving yards	Cloyce Box, 12/3/50	302
Interceptions	Don Doll, 10/23/49	4
Field Goals	Garo Yepremian, 11/13/66	6
Total TD's	Cloyce Box, 12/3/50	4
Total points	Cloyce Box, 12/3/50	24

Top Coaches

	Record	Win Percentage	Years
Potsy Clark	59–31–9	.656	1930–36, 40
George Wilson	55–24–2	.696	1957–64
Buddy Parker	50–24–2	.676	1951–56
Joe Schmidt	43–35–7	.551	1967–72
Dutch Clark	14–8–0	.636	1937–38
Gus Henderson	6–5–0	.545	1939

Defense—not many practitioners any better than Detroit's All Pro tackle Doug English (78) and Ken Fantetti (57) in pursuit here of Bear quarterback Steve Fuller. (Chicago Bears)

All-Pros

Year	Player	Position	Year	Player	Position	Year	Player	Position
1931	Dutch Clark	QB		Lou Creekmur	G	1958	Joe Schmidt	LB
	George Christensen	T		Thurman McGraw	DT		Yale Lary	DB
1932	Dutch Clark	QB		Jack Christiansen	DB	1959	Joe Schmidt	LB
	Father Lumpkin	HB	1953	Doak Walker	HB	1960	Alex Karras	DT
1933	Glenn Presnell	HB		Dick Stanfel	G	1961	Alex Karras	DT
1934	Dutch Clark	QB		Lou Creekmur	G		Joe Schmidt	LB
	George Christensen	T		Les Bingaman	MG		Night Train Lane	DB
1935	Dutch Clark	QB		Jack Christiansen	DB	1962	Roger Brown	DT
	Ernie Caddel	HB	1954	Doak Walker	HB		Joe Schmidt	LB
1936	Dutch Clark	QB		Lou Creekmur	T		Night Train Lane	CB
	Ox Emerson	G		Dick Stanfel	G		Yale Lary	S
1937	Dutch Clark	QB		Les Bingaman	MG	1963	Roger Brown	DT
1938	Lloyd Cardwell	HB		Joe Schmidt	LB	1965	Alex Karras	DT
1940	Whizzer White	HB		Jack Christiansen	DB		Wayne Walker	LB
	John Wiethe	G	1955	Joe Schmidt	LB	1966	Pat Studstill	FL
1944	Frank Sinkwich	HB		Jack Christiansen	DB	1968	Lem Barney	CB
1945	Bob Westfall	FB	1956	Bobby Layne	QB	1969	Lem Barney	CB
	Bill Radovich	G		Lou Creekmur	T	1970	Charlie Sanders	TE
1950	Doak Walker	HB		Joe Schmidt	LB	1971	Charlie Sanders	TE
1951	Doak Walker	HB		Jack Christiansen	DB	1978	Bubba Baker	DE
	Leon Hart	E		Yale Lary	DB	1980	Ed Murray	K
	Lou Creekmur	G	1957	Lou Creekmur	T	1981	Billy Sims	RB
	Les Bingaman	MG		Joe Schmidt	LB	1982	Doug English	DT
1952	Bobby Layne	QB		Jack Christiansen	DB	1983	Doug English	DT
	Cloyce Box	E						

Green Bay Packers

1265 Lombardi Avenue
Green Bay, Wisconsin 54307-0628

Stadium: Lambeau Field (capacity 57,063)
Milwaukee County Stadium
(capacity 55,976)

Training camp: St. Norbert College
DePere, Wisconsin 54115

Colors: dark green, gold and white

Historical Highlights

The 1920s

The American Professional Football Association grants John Clair of the Acme Packing Company a franchise for the Packers, a team organized in Green Bay two years earlier by Curly Lambeau who remains as coach and star player. (1921)

Packers are defeated, 20–0, in the first game of the historic rivalry between Green Bay and the Chicago Bears, then known as the Staleys. (1921)

John Clair turns the Packer franchise back to the league after his team is disciplined for allowing college players to play under assumed names. Curly Lambeau is awarded the franchise. (1922)

Despite bad weather and low attendance, the franchise is saved when local merchants raise $2,500 to fund a non-profit corporation set up under the direction of Andrew Turnbull of the Green Bay Post Gazette and keep Curly Lambeau as coach. (1922)

A new stadium is built for the Packer games, called City Stadium, and has a capacity of 6,000. (1925)

The Packers, comprised of Red Dunn, Johnny Blood McNally, Verne Lewellen, Lavie Dilweg, Cal Hubbard and Iron Mike Michalske, win their first NFL championship with a season record of 13–0–1. (1929)

The 1930s

With a season record of 10–3–1, the Packers win their second NFL title. (1930)

Extending their unbeaten streak to 23 games, the Packers capture their third consecutive NFL title. (1931)

Green Bay loses the NFL crown to the Chicago Bears, whose record, 6–1–6, surpasses the Packers 10–3–1 mark because ties are not counted in the standings. (1932)

The immortal Don Hutson, doing what he did so naturally and frequently for the Packers. Hutson is a charter member of the Pro Football Hall of Fame. (Pro Football Hall of Fame)

A fan falls from the stands in City Stadium, sues the Packers and when the team's insurance company fails, the Packers go into receivership, only to be saved by local businessmen who raise $15,000 in new capital and reorganize the club. (1933)

The Packers sign Alabama end Don Hutson. (1935)

Under the new playoff system, the Packers win their fourth NFL championship, posting an 11–1–1 record to win the Western Division and then defeat the Boston Redskins for the title, 21–6. (1936)

Packers again capture the Western Division, and this time rout the Giants in a title game at Milwaukee, 27–0. (1939)

The 1940s

The Bears and Packers tie for the division title, but the Bears come out on top in the playoff, 33–14. (1941)

Ted Fritsch scores two touchdowns as the Packers beat the Giants 14–7 at New York's Polo Grounds for their sixth NFL title. (1944)

Don Hutson sets an all-time NFL scoring record by scoring 29 points in one quarter of a game after he grabs four touchdown passes and kicks five extra points in the second period of the game against the Detroit Lions leading the Packers to a 57–21 victory. (1945)

Tony Canadeo becomes the first Packer to rush for more than 1,000 yards in a single season, (1,052 on 208 carries). (1949)

The 1950s

Curly Lambeau resigns to become vice-president and head coach of the Chicago Cardinals and is replaced by Gene Ronzani, ex-Chicago Bear star, who becomes head coach. (1950)

Hugh Devore and Scooter McLean are named co-coaches after Ronzani is dismissed. (1953)

Marquette University coach, Lyle Blackburn, is named Packer coach. (1954)

The Packers christen the new Lambeau Field, having a capacity of just over 32,000, with a season opener victory over the Bears, 21-17. (1957)

Vince Lombardi, offensive coach of the New York Giants, is named head coach and general manager of the Packers. (1959)

The 1960s

The Packers, with Bart Starr, Paul Hornung and Jim Taylor in the backfield, win their first division title since 1944, but lose to the Eagles in the NFL title game, 17-13. (1960)

Paul Hornung scores 176 points for the Packers, the most in any season in NFL history. (1960)

In the first championship game ever played in Green Bay, the Packers trounce the Giants, 37-0, and win their seventh NFL crown. (1961)

The Packers defeat the Giants in New York 16-7 for their second straight NFL championship. (1962)

The Cleveland Browns fall to the Packers 23-12 as Green Bay takes its ninth NFL title. (1965)

A spectacular end zone interception by Tom Brown leads the Packers past the Cowboys in Dallas, 34-27, for another NFL title. (1966)

The Packers become the first Super Bowl champs as they defeat Kansas City 35-10 at Los Angeles. (1967)

A one-yard sneak by Bart Starr in 16-below-zero temperature at Lambeau Field pushes the Packers past the Cowboys 21-17 for their third consecutive NFL title. (1967)

The Packers triumph over Oakland 33-14 in Super Bowl II before the first $3 million gate in NFL history. (1968)

Phil Bengston is named Packer general manager after Vince Lombardi resigns to become part owner and head coach of the Washington Redskins. (1969)

The 1970s

Dan Devine, former University of Missouri coach, becomes Packer head coach and general manager. (1971)

The Pack wins its first Central Division title since 1967 but loses to the Redskins in a divisional playoff at Washington 16-3. (1972)

Bart Starr, who quarterbacked the Pack to five NFL titles in seven years in the 1960s, is named head coach and general manager. (1974)

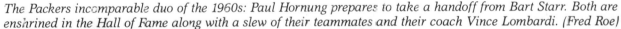

The Packers incomparable duo of the 1960s: Paul Hornung prepares to take a handoff from Bart Starr. Both are enshrined in the Hall of Fame along with a slew of their teammates and their coach Vince Lombardi. (Fred Roe)

The 1980s

Green Bay makes it to the playoffs for the first time since 1972 and defeats St. Louis in the first round, but then loses to Dallas, 37–26. (1982)

Former Packer tackle, Forrest Gregg is named head coach on a five-year contract after Bart Starr is released as head coach. (1983)

James Lofton, All-Pro wide receiver, breaks Don Hutson's record for career receiving yardage. (1985)

Memorable Years

Year	Record	Achievement
1929	13–0–1	NFL champion
1930	10–3–1	NFL champion
1931	12–2–0	NFL champion
1936	10–1–1	NFL champion
1938	8–3–0	Division champion
1939	9–2–0	NFL champion
1944	8–2–0	NFL champion
1960	8–4–0	NFL runner-up
1961	11–3–0	NFL champion
1962	13–1–0	NFL champion
1965	10–3–1	NFL champion
1966	12–2–0	NFL champion
1967	9–4–1	NFL champion
1972	10–4–0	Division champion
1982	5–3–1	Playoff tournament participant

Record Holders

Career		
Rushing yards	Jim Taylor (1958–66)	8,207
Passing yards	Bart Starr (1956–71)	23,718
Passing TD's	Bart Starr (1956–71)	152
Pass receptions	Don Hutson (1935–45)	488
Receiving yards	James Lofton (1978–86)	9,656
Interceptions	Bobby Dillon (1952–59)	52
Field Goals	Chester Marcol (1972–80)	120
Total TD's	Don Hutson (1935–45)	105
Total points	Don Hutson (1935–45)	823

Season		
Rushing yards	Jim Taylor, 1962	1,407
Passing yards	Lynn Dickey, 1983	4,458
Passing TD's	Lynn Dickey, 1983	32
Pass receptions	Don Hutson, 1942	74
Receiving yards	James Lofton, 1984	1,361
Interceptions	Irv Comp, 1943	10
Field Goals	Chester Marcol, 1972	33
Total TD's	Jim Taylor, 1962	19
Total points	Paul Hornung, 1960	176

Game		
Rushing yards	Jim Taylor, 12/3/61	186
Passing yards	Lynn Dickey, 10/12/80	418
Passing TD's	many times	5
Pass receptions	Don Hutson, 11/22/42	14
Receiving yards	Bill Howton, 10/21/56	257
Interceptions	Bobby Dillon, 11/26/53	4
	Willie Buchanon, 9/24/78	4
Field Goals	many times	4
Total TD's	Paul Hornung, 12/12/65	5
Total points	Paul Hornung, 10/8/61	33

Lynn Dickey lets loose with one against the Chicago Bears. The other Packer in the picture is tight end Paul Coffman. (Chicago Bears)

Top Coaches

	Record	Win Percentage	Years
Curly Lambeau	212–106–21	.667	1921–49
Vince Lombardi	98–30–4	.766	1959–67
Gene Ronzani	14–3–1	.824	1950–53

All-Pros

Year	Player	Position	Year	Player	Position	Year	Player	Position
1924	Tillie Voss	E		Don Hutson	E		Jerry Kramer	G
1926	Verne Lewellen	HB	1944	Don Hutson	E		Jim Ringo	C
1927	Verne Lewellen	HB	1945	Don Hutson	E		Henry Jordan	DT
	Lavie Dilweg	E		Charley Brock	C		Herb Adderley	CB
1928	Verne Lewellen	HB	1946	Ted Fritsch	FB	1964	Forrest Gregg	T
	Lavie Dilweg	E	1954	Bobby Dillon	DB		Willie Davis	DE
1929	Verne Lewellen	HB	1955	Roger Zatkoff	LB		Henry Jordan	DT
	Lavie Dilweg	E		Bobby Dillon	DB		Ray Nitschke	LB
	Mike Michalske	G	1956	Billy Howton	E		Willie Wood	S
1930	Lavie Dilweg	E	1957	Billy Howton	E	1965	Forrest Gregg	G
	Mike Michalske	G		Jim Ringo	C		Willie Davis	DE
1931	Johnny Blood McNally	HB		Bobby Dillon	DB		Herb Adderley	CB
	Lavie Dilweg	E	1958	Bobby Dillon	DB		Willie Wood	S
	Cal Hubbard	T	1959	Jim Ringo	C	1966	Bart Starr	QB
	Mike Michalske	G	1960	Paul Hornung	HB		Forrest Gregg	T
1932	Arnie Herber	HB		Forrest Gregg	T		Jerry Kramer	G
	Cal Hubbard	T		Jerry Kramer	G		Willie Davis	DE
	Nate Barager	C		Jim Ringo	C		Ray Nitschke	LB
1933	Cal Hubbard	T		Henry Jordan	DT		Lee Roy Caffey	LB
1935	Mike Michalske	G		Bill Forester	LB		Herb Adderley	CB
1936	Clarke Hinkle	FB	1961	Paul Hornung	HB		Willie Wood	S
	Don Hutson	E		Fuzzy Thurston	G	1967	Forrest Gregg	T
	Ernie Smith	T		Jim Ringo	C		Jerry Kramer	G
	Lon Evans	G		Henry Jordan	DT		Willie Davis	DE
1937	Clarke Hinkle	FB		Bill Forester	LB		Dave Robinson	LB
	Lon Evans	T		Jesse Whittenton	DB		Bob Jeter	CB
1938	Clarke Hinkle	FB	1962	Jim Taylor	RB		Willie Wood	S
	Don Hutson	E		Ron Kramer	TE	1969	Dave Robinson	LB
	Russ Letlow	G		Forrest Gregg	T		Herb Adderley	CB
1939	Don Hutson	E		Jerry Kramer	G	1971	John Brockington	RB
1940	Don Hutson	E		Jim Ringo	C	1972	Chester Marcol	K
1941	Cecil Isbell	HB		Willie Davis	DE	1974	Ted Hendricks	LB
	Clarke Hinkle	FB		Henry Jordan	DT		Chester Marcol	K
	Don Hutson	E		Dan Currie	LB	1978	Willie Buchanon	CB
1942	Cecil Isbell	HB		Bill Forester	LB	1980	James Lofton	WR
	Don Hutson	E		Herb Adderley	CB	1981	James Lofton	WR
1943	Tony Canadeo	FB	1963	Forrest Gregg	T	1983	James Lofton	WR

Los Angeles Rams

2327 West Lincoln Avenue
Anaheim, California 92801

Stadium: Anaheim Stadium (capacity 69,007)

Training camp: California State - Fullerton
Fullerton, California 92634

Colors: royal blue, gold and white

Historical Highlights

The 1930s

The NFL awards a franchise for Cleveland to a syndicate headed by Homer Marshman. (1937)

Hugo Bezdek is named the first head coach of the Cleveland Rams. (1937)

Art Lewis replaces Bezdek as head coach. (1938)

Dutch Clark, future Hall of Famer and former tailback of the Detroit Lions, is signed as head coach. (1939)

The 1940s

The Rams are sold for $100,000 to a partnership of Dan Reeves and Fred Levy. (1941)

Permission is granted by the NFL for the Rams to suspend operations for the 1943 season because the Rams owners are both serving in the military. (1943)

Dan Reeves buys out Fred Levy. (1943)

The Rams return to the NFL with Buff Donelli signed as the new head coach. (1944)

Adam Walsh replaces Donelli as head coach. (1945)

Behind the passing and kicking of rookie quarterback, Bob Waterfield, the Rams win the NFL West with a record of 9-1-0 for their first divisional title. (1945)

With Waterfield throwing touchdown passes to Jim Benton and Jim Gillette and recording a safety, the Cleveland Rams defeat the Washington Redskins to secure their first NFL championship. (1945)

The Rams, having lost money despite their championship season, are allowed to move to Los Angeles. (1946)

Bob Snyder is hired as the new head coach of the L.A. Rams. (1947)

An NFL attendance record is set when 80,899 pay to watch the Rams play the Washington Redskins in a pre-season game at the Los Angeles Coliseum. (1947)

Clark Shaughnessy, famous T formation innovator, is hired to replace Bob Snyder as head coach. (1948)

With a record of 8-2-2, the Rams triumph in the NFL West, but lose the NFL title when they fall 14-0 to the Philadelphia Eagles. (1949)

Joe Stydahar becomes the Rams eighth head coach in the team's then 14-year history after Shaughnessy is fired. (1950)

The 1950s

The Rams set 22 NFL records while turning in a 9-3 record, good enough to end up in a tie for the West Division title with the Chicago Bears. Los Angeles then defeats Chicago to gain the opportunity to play for the NFL title. (1950)

In their former hometown, the Rams lose when Lou Groza, with 20 seconds left in the game, kicks a field goal to give the Cleveland Browns a 30-28 victory and the NFL crown. (1950)

The Rams win their third consecutive divisional title with a record of 8-4-0, then take their second NFL championship by wreaking revenge on the Cleveland Browns 24-17 at the Los Angeles Coliseum. (1951)

Hampton Pool takes over head coaching duties after the departure of Joe Stydahar. (1952)

The Rams decide on Sid Gillman as their new head coach after Hampton Pool resigns. (1955)

The Rams, despite losing to the Chicago Bears twice during the regular season, post a better record (8-3-1 to the Bears 8-4-0), to win the Western Conference title, but are annihilated by the Cleveland Browns 38-14 in the NFL title game. (1955)

Pete Rozelle is named general manager of the Rams. (1957)

An NFL single-game attendance record is set when 102,368 fans buy tickets to watch the Rams overwhelm the San Francisco 49ers 37-24 at the Los Angeles Coliseum. (1957)

The 1960s

Former quarterbacking great Bob Waterfield is hired as head coach of the Rams. (1960)

Harland Svare, former Rams linebacker who was serving as defensive line coach, is moved up to replace Waterfield as head coach. (1962)

Dan Reeves, who had reacquired stock held by others the year before, sells 49 percent of the Rams to a syndicate which includes former cowboy film star, Gene Autry. (1967)

The Fearsome Foursome is formed, a defensive front line consisting of ends Deacon Jones and Lamar Lundy and tackles Merlin Olsen and Rosey Grier. (1963)

George Allen, admired defensive coach of the defending champion Chicago Bears, is signed as head coach. (1966)

The Rams change their training camp to California State University at Fullerton, where it has remained, except for one year in Long Beach, ever since. (1967)

The Rams, boasting a record of 11-1-2, end up in a tie with the Baltimore Colts for the NFL Coastal Division title, but the divisional crown is awarded to the Rams by dint of the fact they had defeated and tied the Colts in their two regular season encounters. The Rams, however, fall to the Super Bowl bound Green Bay Packers in their first playoff game, 28-7. (1967)

Dan Reeves fires coach George Allen, (1968), but, after strong protests from the Los Angeles team members, rehires him. (1969)

With a record of 11-3-0, the Rams easily win the Coastal Division title, but lose 23-20 to the Minnesota Vikings in their first playoff game. (1969)

Jon Arnett, one of the Rams more elusive ballcarriers in the late 1950s and early 60s, tries to free himself from the clutches of a pair of Chicago Bears. Blocking at the left is Leon Clarke. Other Rams include Ollie Matson (33) and quarterback Bill Wade (9). (Los Angeles Rams) Chicago Sun Times

The 1970s

Tommy Prothro is hired as head coach, and William A. Barnes becomes president and general manager after the death of Dan Reeves. (1971)

The Rams are bought by Robert Irsay for $19 million, who then trades the franchise to Carroll Rosenbloom for that of the Baltimore Colts. (1972)

Chuck Knox becomes the Rams' fifteenth head coach. (1973)

Los Angeles wins the Western Division of the NFC, posting a record of 12-2, the most wins for the Rams in any season since they joined the NFL in 1937, but then lose to the Dallas Cowboys 27-16 in the playoffs. (1973)

A single-season attendance record is set when 519,175 pay their way into the Los Angeles Coliseum to watch the Rams. (1973)

The Rams are a repeat winner of the NFC Western Division and defeat the Redskins 19-10 to advance to the NFC championship game at Minnesota where they are edged out by the Vikings 14-10. (1974)

The Rams again reach the NFC title contest by easily conquering the Western Division with 12 victories in their 14 games. After defeating the St. Louis Cardinals in their first conference playoff encounter, however, the Rams are destroyed by the Dallas Cowboys, 37-7. (1975)

Moving in to block this Bear kick is All Pro linebacker Jack Pardee (32) of the Rams. Number 21 is another All Pro Ram, safety Ed Meador. The ill-fated Bear kicker is Roger Leclerc. (Chicago Bears)

For the fourth year in a row, the Rams prevail in the NFC Western Division. They earn their way to the conference championship game by knocking off Dallas but fall to the Vikings out in Minnesota, this time by the score of 24–13. (1976)

Making it five seasons in succession, the Rams take the NFC's Western Division, but again it is the Vikings who destroy their conference title hopes, dishing out a 14–7 defeat on this occasion at the Los Angeles Coliseum. (1977)

George Allen replaces Chuck Knox who resigns in order to take the top job with the Buffalo Bills. Allen is fired in the preseason and replaced by Ray Malavasi. (1978)

The Rams again triumph in the NFC Western Division. After revengefully drubbing the Vikings 34–10 in the division playoff game, Los Angeles succumbs to the Dallas Cowboys 28–0 in the contest for the conference title. (1978)

Georgia Frontiere Rosenbloom inherits ownership of the Rams after the death of her husband, Carroll. (1979)

The Rams win their seventh consecutive divisional title, and earn their first conference championship since 1955 by defeating first the Dallas Cowboys and second the Tampa Bay Buccaneers. (1979)

Los Angeles makes its premiere Super Bowl appearance after the 1979 regular season, taking on the Pittsburgh Steelers who had triumphed in that classic the year before. The Rams, leading 19–17, falter in the fourth quarter of Super Bowl XIV and lose to the Steelers, 31–19. (1980)

The 1980s

The Rams move their home field from the Coliseum in Los Angeles to Aneheim Stadium in Orange County. (1980)

Los Angeles does not win its division for the first time since 1973, but gains the playoffs as a wild card entry. The Rams are demolished by the other wild card team that year, the Dallas Cowboys, by the score of 34–13. (1980)

John Robinson is signed as head coach after the firing of Ray Malavasi. (1983)

Eric Dickerson sets an NFL rookie rushing record and is the NFL's leading ground gainer, credited with 1,808 yards. (1983)

The Rams earn their way into the playoffs as a wild card, defeat the Cowboys 24–17, but then are annihilated by the Super Bowl bound Washington Redskins 51–7. (1983)

Eric Dickerson sets the all-time NFL single-season rushing record by gaining 2,105 yards, 102 more than previous record holder, O.J. Simpson rushed for back in 1973. (1984)

Once again the Rams earn an NFC wild card berth, but they lose to the other wild card entry, the New York Giants, 16–13. (1984)

The Rams win their division with a record of 11–5. (1985)

Eric Dickerson sets an NFL postseason record by rushing for 248 yards in the divisional playoff game in which the Rams rout the Dallas Cowboys 20–0. Los

Angeles bows in the NFC title game to the soon-to-be Super Bowl champion Chicago Bears, 24–0. (1985)

The Rams lose the division title to San Francisco on the last game of the season when they fall to the 49ers 24–14. But Los Angeles gets to the playoffs as a wild card entry only to lose to the Washington Redskins. (1986)

Memorable Years

Year	Record	Achievement
1945	9–1–0	NFL champion
1949	8–2–2	NFL runner-up
1950	9–3–0	NFL runner-up
1951	8–4–0	NFL champion
1955	8–3–1	NFL runner-up
1967	11–1–2	Division champion
1969	11–3–0	Division champion
1973	12–2–0	Division champion
1974	10–4–0	Conference runner-up
1975	12–2–0	Conference runner-up
1976	10–3–1	Conference runner-up
1977	10–4–0	Division champion
1978	12–4–0	Conference runner-up
1979	9–7–0	NFL runner-up
1980	11–5–0	Wild card entry
1983	9–7–0	Wild card entry
1984	10–6–0	Wild card entry
1985	11–5–0	Conference runner-up
1986	10–6–0	Wild card entry

Running back Cullen Bryant (32) struggles for a few Los Angeles yards, although Bear defenders Gary Fencik (45) and Tom Hicks (54) are less than obliging. Number 83 of the Rams is tight end Terry Nelson, 72 guard Kent Hill, and behind Bryant is guard Dennis Harrah. (Chicago Bears)

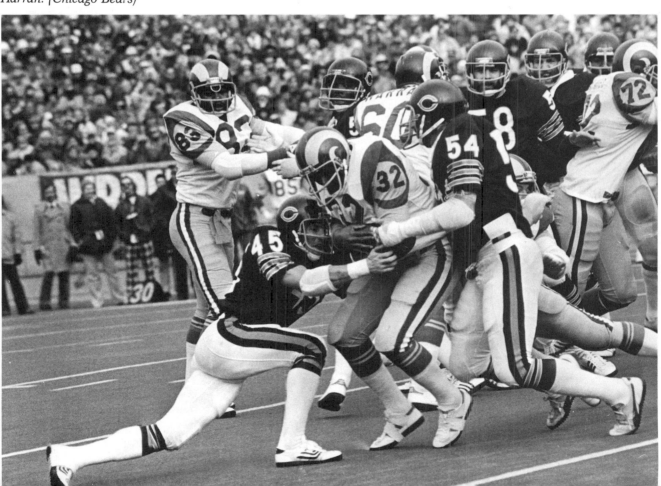

Record Holders

Career

Rushing yards	Eric Dickerson (1983–86)	6,968
Passing yards	Roman Gabriel (1962–72)	22,223
Passing TD's	Roman Gabriel (1962–72)	154
Pass receptions	Tom Fears (1948–56)	400
Receiving yards	Elroy Hirsch (1949–57)	6,289
Interceptions	Ed Meador (1959–70)	46
Field Goals	Bruce Gossett (1964–69)	120
Total TD's	Elroy Hirsch (1949–57)	55
Total points	Bob Waterfield (1946–52)	573

Season

Rushing yards	Eric Dickerson, 1984	2,105
Passing yards	Vince Ferragamo, 1983	3,276
Passing TD's	Vince Ferragamo, 1980	30
Pass receptions	Tom Fears, 1950	84
Receiving yards	Elroy Hirsch, 1951	1,425
Interceptions	Dick (Night Train) Lane, 1952	14
Field Goals	David Ray, 1973	30
Total TD's	Eric Dickerson, 1983	20
Total points	David Ray, 1973	130

Game

Rushing yards	Eric Dickerson, 1/4/86	248
Passing yards	Norm Van Brocklin, 9/28/51	554
Passing TD's	many times	5
Pass receptions	Tom Fears, 12/3/50	18
Receiving yards	Jim Benton, 11/22/45	303
Interceptions	many times	3
Field Goals	Bob Waterfield, 12/9/51	5
Total TD's	Bob Shaw, 12/11/49	4
	Elroy Hirsch, 9/28/51	4
	Harold Jackson, 10/14/73	4
Total points	Bob Shaw, 12/11/49	24
	Elroy Hirsch, 9/28/51	24
	Harold Jackson, 10/14/73	24

Top Coaches

	Record	Win Percentage	Years
Chuck Knox	57–20–1	.588	1973–77
George Allen	49–19–4	.721	1966–70
Ray Malavasi	43–36–0	.544	1978–82
John Robinson	42–28–0	.600	1983–86
Hampton Pool	23–11–2	.676	1952–54
Joe Stydahar	19–9–0	.679	1950–52
Adam Walsh	16–5–1	.762	1945–46
Clark Shaughnessy	14–8–3	.636	1948–49
Tommy Prothro	14–12–2	.538	1971–72
Bob Snyder	6–6–0	.500	1947
Art Lewis	4–4–0	.500	1938

All-Pros

Year	Player	Position	Year	Player	Position	Year	Player	Position
1940	Johnny Drake	FB		Andy Robustelli	DE		Merlin Olsen	DT
1944	Riley Matheson	G		Will Sherman	DB	1973	Harold Jackson	WR
1945	Jim Benton	E	1956	Les Richter	LB		John Hadl	QB
	Riley Matheson	G	1957	Duane Putnam	G		Isiah Robertson	LB
	Bob Waterfield	QB	1958	Del Shofner	E	1974	Tom Mack	G
1946	Bob Waterfield	QB		Duane Putnam	G		Jack Youngblood	DE
1947	Dick Huffman	T		Jon Arnett	HB	1975	Jack Youngblood	DE
	Riley Matheson	G	1959	Del Shofner	E	1976	Jack Youngblood	DE
1948	Dick Huffman	T	1961	Red Phillips	E		Isiah Robertson	LB
1949	Tom Fears	E	1963	Jack Pardee	LB		Monte Jackson	CB
	Dick Huffman	T	1965	Deacon Jones	DE	1978	Jack Youngblood	DE
	Fred Naumetz	C	1966	Deacon Jones	DE	1979	Jack Youngblood	DE
	Bob Waterfield	QB		Merlin Olsen	DT		Larry Brooks	DT
1950	Tom Fears	E	1967	Deacon Jones	DE	1980	Pat Thomas	CB
1951	Elroy Hirsch	E		Merlin Olsen	DT	1981	LeRoy Irvin	KR
	Larry Brink	DE	1968	Deacon Jones	DE		Nolan Cromwell	S
	Tank Younger	LB		Merlin Olsen	DT	1982	Nolan Cromwell	S
1952	Dan Towler	HB		Ed Meador	S	1983	Eric Dickerson	RB
	Stan West	MG	1969	Bob Brown	T	1984	Eric Dickerson	RB
1953	Elroy Hirsch	E		Roman Gabriel	QB		Henry Ellard	KR
	Andy Robustelli	DE		Deacon Jones	DE	1985	Ron Brown	KR
	Don Paul	LB		Merlin Olsen	DT		Dale Hatcher	P
1954	Bob Boyd	E		Ed Meador	S	1986	Eric Dickerson	RB
1955	Duane Putnam	G	1970	Bob Brown	T			

Minnesota Vikings

9520 Viking Drive
Eden Prairie, Minnesota 55344

Stadium: Hubert H. Humphrey Metrodome
(capacity 62,345)
Minneapolis, MN 55415

Training camp: Mankato State University
Mankato, Minnesota 56001

Colors: purple, gold and white

Historical Highlights

The 1960s

The NFL grants a franchise to a group of investors from the twin cities of Minneapolis and St. Paul, to be known simply as Minnesota, the team to begin play in the NFL in 1961. (1960)

The new Minnesota franchise takes the nickname Vikings "due to historical ties believed to exist between the original Vikings and the area as well as the Nordic and Scandanavian ancestry of many in the area." The team adopts Metropolitan Stadium in Bloomington as its home field. (1961)

Former great quarterback for the Rams and Eagles, Norm Van Brocklin, is named the first head coach of the Minnesota Vikings. (1961)

The Vikings receive 36 veterans from the expansion draft, and quarterback Fran Tarkenton from the college draft. (1961)

Wide receiver Paul Flatley is named NFL rookie of the Year. (1963)

Jim Finks is named general manager of the Vikings. (1964)

The Vikings post their first winning season: 8 victories, 5 losses and a tie, good enough for a second-place tie with Vince Lombardi's Green Bay Packers in the NFC's Western Conference. (1964)

A major feud between coach Van Brocklin and quarterback Tarkenton results in the coach's resignation and the quarterback being traded to the New York Giants. (1967)

Bud Grant, coach of Canada's Winnepeg Blue Bombers, takes over the head coaching duties for the Vikings. (1968)

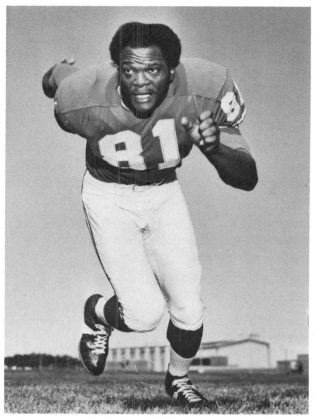

A stalwart at defensive end for Minnesota from 1964 through 1978 was perennial All Pro Carl Eller. (Minnesota Vikings)

The Purple Gang is formed, a front four line consisting of defensive ends Carl Eller and Jim Marshall and tackles Alan Page and Gary Larsen. (1968)

Minnesota wins its first divisional title, taking the Central Division of the NFC's Western Conference with a record of 8–6–0 but loses its first playoff game to the Baltimore Colts 24–14. (1968)

Vikings quarterback Joe Kapp tosses seven touchdown passes in a game against the Colts to tie the NFL mark already shared by Sid Luckman (Bears), Adrian Burk (Eagles), George Blanda (Oilers), and Y.A. Tittle (Giants). (1969)

The Viking defense allows an average of only 9.5 points a game, the least by any team since 1944. The 133 total points allowed is the second lowest ever in the 14-game season, only four points more generous than the 129 given up by Atlanta in 1977. (1969)

Minnesota has little trouble winning its division, then knocks off the Los Angeles Rams and the Cleveland Browns in the playoffs to earn entry to the Super Bowl. (1969)

The 1970s

On a January afternoon at Tulane Stadium, the Vikings, NFC champs of 1969, are routed 23–7 in Super Bowl IV. (1970)

Minnesota wins its third consecutive divisional title but is beaten by the San Francisco 49ers 17–14 in the playoffs. (1970)

The Vikings add another division crown to their trophy rack but disappoint the hometown fans by losing to the Dallas Cowboys 20–12 at Metropolitan Stadium in the playoffs. (1971)

Defensive tackle, Alan Page is named the NFL's most Valuable Player the first (and only) lineman ever accorded that honor. (1971)

Fran Tarkenton returns to the Vikings as a result of a trade with the New York Giants. (1972)

Running back Chuck Foreman wins NFL Rookie of the Year honors. (1973)

Minnesota posts a record of 12–2, equal to its all-time best efforts registered in 1969 and 1970, and easily captures the NFC Central Division. Wins in the playoffs over the Redskins, 27–20, and the Cowboys, 27–10, propel the Vikings into their second Super Bowl appearance. (1973)

The Vikings face the Miami Dolphins, winner of Super Bowl VII, on a mild, overcast January afternoon in Super Bowl VIII at Rice Stadium in Houston, Texas. But the Minnesotans cannot stop Don Shula's Dolphins from becoming the first team to take back-to-back NFL titles since Vince Lombardi's Packers did it in Super Bowls I and II, falling by a score of 24–7. (1974)

Minnesota is again the predominant force in the NFC Central Division. In the playoffs, wins over St. Louis and the Rams give the Vikes the conference crown and a ticket to the Super Bowl. (1974)

The 1974 NFC champion Vikings meet the Pittsburgh Steelers at Tulane Stadium for Super Bowl IX, but again come up short, this time losing 16–6. (1975)

Chalking up another 12–2 record, the Vikings glide essentially uncontested to their seventh divisional title in eight years. With what came to be known as the "Hail Mary pass," Roger Staubach connects with Drew Pearson on a 50-yard touchdown bomb with only 24 seconds remaining in the game to give the Dallas Cowboys a 17–14 victory and eliminate Minnesota from the playoffs. (1975)

Quarterback Fran Tarkenton is named the NFL's Most Valuable Player, and running back Chuck Foreman, gaining 1,070 yards on the ground, becomes the first Viking to rush for more than 1,000 yards in a season. (1975)

The Vikings again dominate the NFC Central Division, winning 11 games, losing 2, and tying another. Minnesota then marches mightily through the playoffs, routing the Redskins 35–20 and the Rams 24–13, enabling the team to participate in its fourth Super Bowl. (1976)

Fran Tarkenton achieves two career milestones that no quarterback before or since has, completing more than 3,000 passes and more than 300 for touchdowns. He also becomes only the second quarterback in NFL history to pass for more than 40,000 yards, joining the Baltimore Colts Johnny Unitas in that select circle. (1976)

Wide receiver Sammy White is named the NFL's Rookie of the Year. (1976)

Before more than 100,000 spectators, the Vikings face John Madden's Oakland Raiders in Super Bowl XI at the Rose Bowl in Pasadena, California. Unfortunately for Minnesota fans on that Sunday afternoon in January, the Vikings run their winless Super Bowl record to four, battered 32–14 by the Raiders. (1977)

The Vikings post a 9–5 record identical to that of the Chicago Bears, but are awarded the divisional crown on the basis of point differential in head-to-head competition (29–26, having defeated them 22–16 and lost to them 10–7). The Minnesotans then eliminate the Rams from the playoffs, winning 14–7, but find themselves out after a 23–6 drubbing by the Dallas Cowboys in the NFC title tilt. (1977)

Minnesota wraps up its sixth consecutive divisional championship, but falls in its first playoff game to the L.A. Rams, 34–10. (1978)

Fran Tarkenton retires, taking with him a bevy of career records which still stand today: most passes attempted, 6,467; most passes completed, 3,686; most yards gained passing, 47,003; most touchdown passes, 342; as well as the dubious honor of being sacked most, 483 times. (1979)

The 1980s

The Vikings return to the top in the NFC Central Division with a 9–7 record after a one-year hiatus. But in the playoff Minnesota is no match for the Philadelphia Eagles, who are on their way to the Super Bowl, and lose decisively, 31–16. (1980)

Minnesota makes it to a playoff tournament specially

devised because the regular season is shortened by a players' strike: their record 5-4. After a win over the Atlanta Falcons 30-24, they succumb to the Redskins 21-7. (1982)

Linebacker Jeff Siemon becomes the first (and only) Viking to be credited with more than 1,000 solo tackles. (1982)

Les Steckel is named head coach after the retirement of Bud Grant, who had been at the Viking helm since 1968. (1984)

Bud Grant returns as head coach, but after an undramatic 7-9 season retires again at season's end. (1985)

Jerry Burns, Minnesota's offensive coordinator and an assistant to Grant since 1968, is signed as the new head coach of the Vikings. The team records its first winning season, with a record of 9-7, since 1982. (1986)

Memorable Years

Year	Record	Achievement
1968	8-6-0	Division champion
1969	12-2-0	NFL champion (but lost to AFL in Super Bowl, NFL and AFL were not merged into conferences until 1970)
1970	12-2-0	Division champion
1971	11-3-0	Division champion
1973	12-2-0	NFL runner-up
1974	10-4-0	NFL runner-up
1975	12-2-0	Division champion
1976	11-2-1	NFL runner-up
1977	9-5-0	Conference runner-up
1978	8-7-1	Division champion
1980	9-7-0	Division champion
1982	5-4-0	Playoff tournament participant

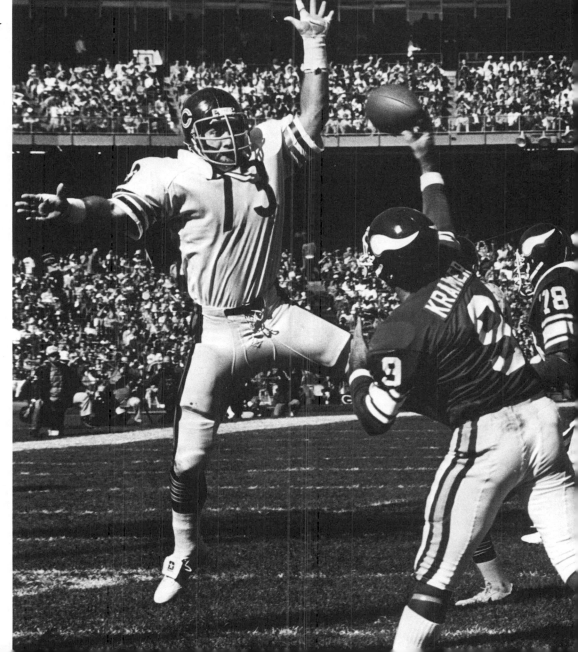

Tommy Kramer tosses one over the outstretched arms of Bear defensive end Mike Hartenstine. Kramer is second only to Fran Tarkenton in career passing stats for Minnesota and holds the team records for passing yardage in a season (3,912 in 1981) and touchdowns passing (26 also in '81). (Minnesota Vikings)

Record Holders

Career

Rushing yards	Chuck Foreman (1973–79)	5,879
Passing yards	Fran Tarkenton (1961–66, 1972–78)	33,098
Passing TD's	Fran Tarkenton (1961–66, 1972–78)	239
Pass receptions	Ahmad Rashad (1976–82)	400
Receiving yards	Sammy White (1976–85)	5,925
Interceptions	Paul Krause (1968–79)	53
Field Goals	Fred Cox (1963–77)	282
Total TD's	Bill Brown (1962–74)	76
Total points	Fred Cox (1963–77)	1,365

Season

Rushing yards	Chuck Foreman, 1976	1,155
Passing yards	Tommy Kramer, 1981	3,912
Passing TD's	Tommy Kramer, 1981	26
Pass receptions	Rickey Young, 1978	88
Receiving yards	Ahmad Rashad, 1979	1,156
Interceptions	Paul Krause, 1975	10
Field Goals	Fred Cox, 1970	30
Total TD's	Chuck Foreman, 1975	22
Total points	Chuck Foreman, 1975	132

Game

Rushing yards	Chuck Foreman, 10/24/76	200
Passing yards	Tommy Kramer, 12/14/80	456
Passing TD's	Joe Kapp, 9/28/69	7
Pass receptions	Rickey Young, 12/16/79	15
Receiving yards	Sammy White, 11/7/76	210
Interceptions	many times	3
Field Goals	Fred Cox, 9/23/73	5
	Jan Stenerud, 9/23/84	5
Total TD's	Chuck Foreman, 12/20/75	4
	Ahmad Rashad, 9/2/79	4
Total points	Chuck Foreman, 12/20/75	24
	Ahmad Rashad, 9/2/79	24

Top Coaches

	Record	Win Percentage	Years
Bud Grant	168–108–5	.609	1967–83, 85
Jerry Burns	9–7–0	.563	1986

All-Pros

Year	Player	Position
1963	Tommy Mason	HB
1964	Mick Tingelhoff	C
1965	Mick Tingelhoff	C
1966	Mick Tingelhoff	C
1968	Carl Eller	DE
	Mick Tingelhoff	C
1969	Carl Eller	DE
	Mick Tingelhoff	C
1970	Carl Eller	DE
	Alan Page	DT
	Mick Tingelhoff	C
1971	Carl Eller	DE
	Alan Page	DT
	Ron Yary	T
1972	Ron Yary	T
1973	Carl Eller	DE
	Alan Page	DT
	Ron Yary	T
1974	Alan Page	DT
	Ron Yary	T
1975	Chuck Foreman	RB
	Paul Krause	S
	Alan Page	DT
	Fran Tarkenton	QB
	Ron Yary	T
1976	Ron Yary	T
1980	Matt Blair	LB

New Orleans Saints

1500 Poydras Street
New Orleans. Louisiana 70112

Stadium: Louisiana Superdome (capacity 69,723)

Training camp: Southeastern Louisiana University
Hammond, Louisiana 70402

Colors: old gold, black and white

Historical Highlights

The 1960s

The National Football League awards the NFL's 16th franchise to New Orleans on All Saints' Day with John W. Mecom, Jr., the majority stockholder. (1966)

Tom Fears is named the first head coach. (1967)

New Orleans' professional football team is named the Saints. (1967)

Seventy-six players, mostly rookies, report for the first training camp at California Western University in San Diego. (1967)

With wide receiver, Walter "The Flea" Roberts scoring three touchdowns, the Saints earn their first NFL victory against Philadelphia, 31–24 at Tulane Stadium after suffering seven straight defeats. (1967)

A record home crowd of 84,728 shows up at Tulane Stadium but the Saints lose to Dallas, 17–3. (1968)

Tom Dempsey sets s Saints record with four field goals against the Giants in New York booting the fourth with only seconds remaining to give New Orleans a 25–24 victory. The Saints begin a three-game winning streak as New Orleans also downs San Francisco 43–38, and Philadelphia, 26–17. (1969)

The 1970s

The National Football Conference is realigned and the Saints join with the Los Angeles Rams, San Francisco 49ers and Atlanta Falcons to form the Western Division. (1970)

J.D. Roberts becomes the second head coach in Saints' history, replacing Tom Fears who was fired. (1970)

Tom Dempsey kicks the longest field goal in NFL history, 63 yards, on the final play of the Saints' 19–17 win over Detroit. (1970)

The Saints draft quarterback Archie Manning of Ole

Archie Manning came to the Saints fresh out of Mississippi in 1971 and went on to set virtually every career club passing record. Manning spent eleven seasons in New Orleans before moving on to the Houston Oilers. (New Orleans Saints)

Miss in the first round after trading quarterback Bill Kilmer to Washington for linebacker Tom Roussel and two 1972 draft choices. (1971)

John North becomes the Saints' third coach, replacing J.D. Roberts. (1973)

The Louisiana Superdome is dedicated and the Saints play Houston in a preseason game before 72,434 fans, their first in the new stadium. The Saints lose 13–7. (1975)

Ernie Hefferle, director of pro-personnel, replaces John North as head coach on an interim basis. (1975)

The Saints hire Hank Stram as their fourth head coach. (1976)

Dick Nolan is appointed head coach to replace Hank Stram. (1978)

Archie Manning becomes the first Saint to pass for more than 3,000 yards in a season, (3,416 on 291 completions). (1978)

The Saints post their first non-losing season with a record of 8-8-0, good enough for second place in the NFC West. (1979)

Chuck Muncie becomes the first Saint to surpass the 1,000-yard milestone, rushing for 1,198 yards on 238 carries. (1979)

The 1980s

O.A. "Bum" Phillips, former head coach of the Houston Oilers, is announced as the new head coach of New Orleans. (1981)

George Rogers, All-American back from South Carolina, is drafted by the Saints. (1981)

In an opening day win over St. Louis at the Super-dome, halfback George Rogers sets a team single-game record by rushing for 206 yards on 24 carries. (1983)

The Saints produce the second .500 season in team history, 8–8–0 and a third place finish in the NFC West. (1983)

Ownership of the Saints is transferred from Mecom to Tom Benson for the sale price of $70.2 million. Benson is to hold the position of managing general partner of the Saints. (1985)

Jim Finks, formerly top administrator with the Minnesota Vikings and Chicago Bears, becomes president and general manager of the Saints. Finks hires Tom Mora as head coach. (1986)

Record Holders

Career		
Rushing yards	George Rogers (1981–84)	4,267
Passing yards	Archie Manning (1971–82)	21,734
Passing TD's	Archie Manning (1971–82)	115
Pass receptions	Dan Abramowicz (1967–73)	309
Receiving yards	Dan Abramowicz (1967–73)	4,875
Interceptions	Tommy Myers (1972–82)	36
Field Goals	Morten Andersen (1982–86)	97
Total TD's	Dan Abramowicz (1967–73)	37
Total points	Morten Andersen (1982–86)	425

Season		
Rushing yards	George Rogers, 1981	1,674
Passing yards	Archie Manning, 1980	3,716
Passing TD's	Archie Manning, 1980	23
Pass receptions	Tony Galbreath, 1978	74
Receiving yards	Wes Chandler, 1979	1,069
Interceptions	Dave Whitsell, 1967	10
Field Goals	Morten Andersen, 1985	31
Total TD's	George Rogers, 1981	13
Total points	Morten Andersen, 1985	120

Game		
Rushing yards	George Rogers, 9/4/83	206
Passing yards	Archie Manning, 12/7/80	377
Passing TD's	Billy Kilmer, 11/2/69	6
Pass receptions	Tony Galbreath, 9/10/78	14
Receiving yards	Wes Chandler, 9/2/79	205
Interceptions	Tommy Myers, 9/3/78	3
Field Goals	Morten Andersen, 12/1/85	5
Total TD's	many times	3
Total points	many times	18

Top Coach

	Record	Win Percentage	Years
Bum Phillips	27–42–0	.391	1981–85

All-Pros

Year	Player	Position
1981	George Rogers	RB

Running back Andrew Jones (36) drags a New York Giant defender far enough for a New Orleans first down in a 1975 encounter. (New Orleans Saints)

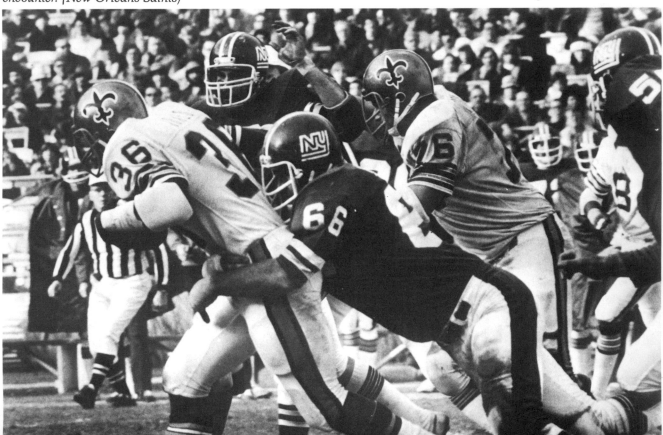

New York Giants

Giants Stadium
East Rutherford, New Jersey 07073

Stadium: Giants Stadium (capacity 76,891)

Training camp: Pace University
　　　　　　　　Pleasantville, New York 10570

Colors: blue, red and white

Historical Highlights

The 1920s

Tim Mara purchases a National League Football franchise for New York, acquires Bob Folwell as head coach, and signs all-time great Jim Thorpe. (1925)

During their first season, more than 70,000 fans jam the Polo Grounds to see the Chicago Bears and Red Grange, enough gate receipts to keep the franchise from bankruptcy. (1925)

Dr. Joe Alexander replaces Folwell as head coach. (1926)

Alexander is replaced by Earl Potteiger and the Giants win their first title with an 11-1-1 record. (1927)

The 1930s

Tim Mara turns club ownership over to his two sons, Jack and Wellington Mara. (1930)

Steve Owen is named head coach. Center Mel Hein joins the Giants. (1931)

With 21 catches, Ray Flaherty becomes the NFL's first officially recognized pass reception leader. (1932)

The Giants easily win the Eastern Division title of the NFL but fall to the Chicago Bears in the league's first championship game 23-21. (1933)

With an 8-5-0 record, New York again conquers the Eastern Division. (1934)

The Giants wear basketball "sneakers" to increase traction on the icy Polo Grounds turf in the second half of the NFL title game and defeat the Chicago Bears, 30-13. (1934)

New York makes it to their third straight NFL championship game but falls to the Detroit Lions 26-7. (1935)

The Giants win their third NFL title, beating Green Bay 23-17. (1938)

Mel Hein, mainstay at center on offense and linebacker on defense for 15 seasons (1931–45) for the Giants, earned All Pro honors an unprecedented and since unequalled eight consecutive seasons. He is also a charter member of the Pro Football Hall of Fame. (Pro Football Hall of Fame)

The Giants, in their fifth NFL championship game in seven years, are trounced by Green Bay 27-0. (1939)

The 1940s

The Giants lose the NFL title to the Chicago Bears, 37-9. (1941)

The Giants rack up five shutouts and outscore their opponents 206-75 to capture the Eastern title, but lose the championship game to Green Bay 14-7. (1944)

The Giants win the Eastern crown for the ninth time in the 14 years the NFL has had two divisions. (1946)

Tailback Frank Filchock, acquired from the Redskins, is suspended indefinitely along with teammate Merle Hapes for alleged gambling involvement. Filchock was allowed to play in the NFL title game (Hapes was not), which the Giants lost to the Bears 24-14. (1946)

The Giants sign quarterback Charlie Conerly. (1948)

The 1950s

In the newly realigned NFL, the Giants are assigned to the American Conference along with the Chicago Cardinals, Eagles, Steelers, Redskins and Browns. (1950)

The Giants sign Kyle Rote (1951) and Frank Gifford. (1952)

Jim Lee Howell is promoted from assistant coach to head coach. (1954)

The Giants switch their home games from the Polo Grounds to Yankee Stadium. (1956)

The Giants win their conference, routing the Chicago Bears 47–7 to produce New York's first NFL title since 1938. (1956)

The Giants defeat the Browns in a playoff game to advance to the NFL championship game with Baltimore. (1958)

New York loses in a sudden death overtime. (1958)

New York takes its conference and again meets Baltimore in the NFL title game. (1959)

The Colts, scoring 24 points in the fourth quarter, win 31–16. (1959)

The 1960s

Allie Sherman replaces the retired Jim Lee Howell as head coach. (1961)

New York, (10–3–1), edges the Eagles, (10–4–0), for the conference title but is annihilated by the Packers 37–0 in the NFL championship game. (1961)

Giants stars Y.A. Tittle, Del Shofner, Alex Webster and Frank Gifford and the NFL's finest defense, (Sam Huff, Andy Robustelli, Rosey Grier, Dick Modzelewski and Jim Katcavage among them), lead the team to the NFL title game only to lose to the Packers 16–7. (1962)

Y.A. Tittle ties George Blanda's NFL record by throwing 36 touchdown passes and kicker Don Chandler leads the league in scoring, (106 points). The Giants win their third straight conference title but their bid for the league championship is lost to the Chicago Bears 14–10. (1963)

The Giants obtain quarterback Fran Tarkenton in a trade with the Minnesota Vikings. (1967)

Alex Webster replaces Allie Sherman as head coach. (1969)

The 1970s

Gaining a total of 1,027 yards, Ron Johnson becomes the Giants' first 1,000 yard rusher. (1970)

The Giants name Bill Arnsparger their new head coach. (1974)

Giants Stadium in the Meadowlands sports complex in East Rutherford, New Jersey, becomes the team's new home. Arnsparger is fired in mid-season and coaching duties are assumed by assistant coach John McVay. (1976)

McVay is fired after the season, followed closely by the resignation of Andy Robustelli, Giants' director of operations since 1974. (1978)

George Young is named general manager and he appoints San Diego Chargers assistant Ray Perkins as head coach. (1979)

The 1980s

The Giants make the playoffs as a wild card entry, their first postseason appearance since 1963. New York defeats the Eagles 38–24 in the divisional playoff game. (1981)

Head coach Ray Perkins resigns to assume coaching duties at the U. of Alabama and is replaced by Giants' defensive coordinator, Bill Parcells. (1982)

Behind the passing of quarterback Phil Simms, the Giants earn an NFC wild card playoff spot, finishing the season with a 9–7 mark. (1984)

One of the Giants all-time greats Frank Gifford (16) moves in to take a handoff, on his way to gaining a few of the 3,609 yards he rushed for as a Giant. The quarterback is George Shaw (15), and moving out to block for Gifford are Daryl Dess (62) and Jack Stroud (66). (Fred Roe)

Phil Simms was the passer of the 1980s for the Giants, following in the illustrious footsteps of Charlie Conerly, Y. A. Tittle, and Fran Tarkenton. Here he is lofting one against the Chicago Bears in the NFL title game of 1985. (Fred Roe)

Simms sets club records by completing 286 passes for 4,044 yards. (1984)

The Giants win over the Rams, 16–13, in the wild card game but lose to the eventual Super Bowl champs San Francisco, 21–10 in the divisional playoff. (1984)

A season record of 10–6 gives the Giants their second consecutive winning season, and another trip to the playoffs as a wild card entry. New York defeats defending Super Bowl champs, San Francisco, 17–3. In the divisional playoffs, the Giants lose to the soon-to-be Super Bowl champion Chicago Bears 21–0. (1985)

Posting a regular season record of 14–2, the Giants win the NFC East for the first time since the NFL was realigned in 1970. New York follows with playoff triumphs over San Francisco, 49–3, and Washington, 17–0, earning their way to their first Super Bowl appearance. (1986)

The Giants decimate the Denver Broncos in Super Bowl XXI 39–20. (1987)

Memorable Years

Year	Record	Achievement
1927	11–1–1	NFL champion
1933	11–3–0	NFL runner-up
1934	8–5–0	NFL champion
1935	9–3–0	NFL runner-up
1938	8–2–1	NFL champion
1939	9–1–1	NFL runner-up
1941	8–3–0	NFL runner-up
1944	8–1–1	NFL runner-up
1946	7–3–1	NFL runner-up
1956	8–3–1	NFL champion
1958	9–3–0	NFL runner-up
1959	10–2–0	NFL runner-up
1961	10–3–1	NFL runner-up
1962	12–2–0	NFL runner-up
1963	11–3–0	NFL runner-up
1981	9–7–0	Playoff participant
1984	9–7–0	Playoff participant
1985	10–6–0	Playoff participant
1986	14–2–0	NFL champion

Record Holders

Career		
Rushing yards	Alex Webster (1955–64)	4,638
Passing yards	Charlie Conerly (1948–61)	19,488
Passing TD's	Charlie Conerly (1948–61)	173
Pass receptions	Joe Morrison (1959–72)	395
Receiving yards	Frank Gifford (1952–60, 1962–64)	5,434
Interceptions	Emlen Tunnell (1948–58)	74
Field Goals	Pete Gogolak (1966–74)	126
Total TD's	Frank Gifford (1952–60, 1962–64)	78
Total points	Pete Gogolak (1966–74)	646

Season		
Rushing yards	Joe Morris, 1986	1,516
Passing yards	Phil Simms, 1984	4,044
Passing TD's	Y.A. Tittle, 1963	36
Pass receptions	Earnest Gray, 1983	78
Receiving yards	Homer Jones, 1967	1,209
Interceptions	Otto Schnellbacher, 1951	11
	Jim Patton, 1958	11
Field Goals	Ali Haji-Sheikh, 1983	35
Total TD's	Joe Morris, 1985	21
Total points	Ali Haji-Sheikh, 1983	127

Game		
Rushing yards	Gene Roberts, 11/12/50	218
Passing yards	Phil Simms, 10/13/85	513
Passing TD's	Y.A. Tittle, 10/28/62	7
Pass receptions	Mark Bavaro, 10/13/85	12
Receiving yards	Del Shofner, 10/28/62	269
Interceptions	many times	3
Field Goals	Joe Danelo, 10/18/81	6
Total TD's	Ron Johnson, 10/2/72	4
	Earnest Gray, 9/7/80	4
Total points	Ron Johnson, 10/2/72	24
	Earnest Gray, 9/7/80	24

Top Coaches

	Record	Win Percentage	Years
Steve Owen	154–108–17	.588	1931–53
Allie Sherman	57–54–4	.514	1961–68
Jim Lee Howell	54–29–4	.651	1954–60
Bill Parcells	41–29–1	.586	1983–86
LeRoy Andrews	26–5–1	.839	1929–30
Earl Potteiger	15–8–3	.652	1927–28
Bob Folwell	8–4–0	.667	1925
Joe Alexander	8–4–1	.667	1926

All-Pros

Year	Player	Position	Year	Player	Position	Year	Player	Position
1925	Jack McBride	FB		Mel Hein	C		Jim Patton	DB
	Art Carney	G	1940	Mel Hein	C	1960	Andy Robustelli	DE
1927	Cal Hubbard	E	1942	Bill Edwards	G		Jim Patton	DB
	Steve Owen	G	1946	Jim White	T	1961	Del Shofner	E
1928	Ray Flaherty	E	1950	Arnie Weinmeister	DT		Roosevelt Brown	T
1929	Benny Friedman	QB	1951	Eddie Price	FB		Jim Katcavage	DE
	Tony Plansky	HB		Arnie Weinmeister	DT		Erich Barnes	DB
	Ray Flaherty	E		Al DeRogatis	DT		Jim Patton	DB
	Joe Westoupal	C		Otto Schnelbacher	DB	1962	Y.A. Tittle	QB
1930	Benny Friedman	QB		Emlen Tunnell	DB		Del Shofner	E
1931	Red Badgro	E	1952	Eddie Price	HB		Roosevelt Brown	T
	Butch Gibson	G		Arnie Weinmeister	DT		Jim Patton	DB
1932	Ray Flaherty	E		Emlen Tunnell	DB	1963	Y.A. Tittle	QB
1933	Harry Newman	QB	1953	Arnie Weinmeister	DT		Del Shofner	E
	Red Badgro	E	1954	Tom Landry	DB		Jim Katcavage	DE
	Mel Hein	C	1955	Frank Gifford	HB		Dick Lynch	CB
1934	Red Badgro	E		Emlen Tunnell	DB	1970	Ron Johnson	RB
	Ken Strong	HB	1956	Frank Gifford	HB	1972	Bob Tucker	TE
	Butch Gibson	G		Roosevelt Brown	T		Jack Gregory	DE
	Mel Hein	C		Andy Robustelli	DE	1979	Dave Jennings	P
	BillMorgan	T		Roosevelt Grier	DT	1980	Dave Jennings	P
1935	Ed Danowski	HB		Emlen Tunnell	DB	1981	Lawrence Taylor	LB
	Mel Hein	C	1957	Frank Gifford	HB	1982	Lawrence Taylor	LB
	Bill Morgan	T		Roosevelt Brown	T		Mark Haynes	CB
1936	Tuffy Leemans	HB	1958	Roosevelt Brown	T		Dave Jennings	P
	Mel Hein	C		Ray Wietecha	C	1983	Lawrence Taylor	LB
1937	Mel Hein	C		Andy Robustelli	DE		Ali Haji-Sheikh	PK
1938	Ed Danowski	HB		Sam Huff	LB	1984	Lawrence Taylor	LB
	Mel Hein	C		Jim Patton	DB		Mark Haynes	CB
	Ed Widseth	T	1959	Frank Gifford	HB	1985	Lawrence Taylor	LB
1939	Tuffy Leemans	HB		Roosevelt Brown	T	1986	Joe Morris	RB
	Jim Poole	E		Andy Robustelli	DE		Lawrence Taylor	LB
	John Dell Isola	G		Sam Huff	LB			

Philadelphia Eagles

Veterans Stadium
Broad Street and Pattison Avenue
Philadelphia, Pennsylvania 19148

Stadium: Veterans Stadium (capacity 69,417)

Training camp: West Chester University
West Chester, Pennsylvania 19380

Colors: kelly green, silver and white

Historical Highlights

The 1930s

The NFL awards the franchise formerly held by the Frankford Yellow Jackets to a syndicate headed by Bert Bell and Lud Wray for $2,500. In honor of the symbol of the New Deal and NRA the club is christened "the Eagles." Philadelphia's first Sunday game at Baker Bowl against the Chicago Bears ends in a 3-3 tie.

The Eagles have first choice in the inaugural college draft and select University of Chicago back Jay Berwanger but fail to sign him. Bert Bell becomes the sole owner of the team with a $4,000 bid, and the playing site for home games is moved from Baker Bowl to Municipal Stadium.

Davey O'Brien, an All-American quarterback from Texas Christian University, signs with the Eagles for a reported $12,000 per year salary and a percentage of the gate. O'Brien plays in every game and sets the NFL passing yardage record with 1,324 yards despite the fact the Eagles win only one of 11 games. (1939)

The 1940s

Art Rooney of Pittsburgh buys half interest in the Eagles after selling the Pittsburgh franchise to Alexis Thompson of New York. The Eagles move from Municipal Stadium to Shibe Park. (1940)

Rooney and Thompson switch franchises, Rooney returning to Pittsburgh and Thompson taking over the Eagles. Bert Bell joins Rooney as a full-time partner in Pittsburgh and Thompson hires Earle, "Greasy," Neale as head coach of the Eagles. (1941)

Because of the war the Eagles are allowed to merge with the Pittsburgh Steelers and are known as "Steagles," and post a record of 5-4-1, their first winning season in the club history. The merger is dissolved at the end of the season. (1943)

The Eagles possessed the most productive runner in pro football in the late 1940s, Steve Van Buren, hurdling a fallen Washington Redskin here. Van Buren set a host of NFL records in his eight-year career at Philadelphia, and is a member of the Pro Football Hall of Fame. (Pro Football Hall of Fame)

Steve Van Buren is drafted by Philadelphia. (1944)

With a 7-3 record the Eagles finish in second place and lead the league in scoring with 272 points. Van Buren leads the NFL with 832 rushing yards and 110 points scored, and sets an NFL record with 15 TDs rushing. (1945)

Rookie end Pete Pihos, Van Buren and Bosh Pritchard combine with an overpowering defense for a divisional title, (8-4-0), and lead the Eagles to the NFL championship game for the first time. The Chicago Cardinals, however, defeat them 28-21 at Comiskey Park. (1947)

Steve Van Buren sets an NFL rushing record by gaining 1,008 yards, four yards better than the mark. (1947)

The Eagles win their first NFL championship, downing the Chicago Cardinals 7-0 in a heavy snowstorm at Shibe Park. (1948)

Alexis Thompson sells the Eagles for $250,000 to a syndicate headed by James P. Clark. The Eagles' first round draft choice is Chuck Bednarik, All-American linebacker and center from the University of Pennsylvania. Philadelphia posts a record of 11-1-0, the best in their entire history and the Eagles win their third straight Eastern Division title. Philadelphia wins its second consecutive NFL championship with a 14-0 victory over the Rams at the Los Angeles Coliseum. (1949)

SUNDAY MAYHEM

The 1950s

After a 6–6 season in 1950, Greasy Neale is replaced as head coach by Alvin "Bo" McMillin. McMillin becomes ill the night before the season opener and is replaced as head coach by Wayne Millner. (1951)

Jim Trimble succeeds Wayne Millner as head coach. (1952)

End Bobby Walston leads the league in scoring with 114 points, as does Pete Pihos in pass receptions with 60, and quarterback Adrian Burk in TD passes with 23. (1954)

Hugh Devore is named to replace Jim Trimble as head coach. (1956)

Quarterback Sonny Jurgensen is drafted by Philadelphia. (1957)

Buck Shaw signs as head coach replacing Hugh Devore. The team moves home games from Connie Mack Stadium to the University of Pennsylvania's Franklin Field and attendance almost doubles. (1958)

The 1960s

The Eagles are led to their first Eastern Division title in 11 years by the passing of 34-year-old Norm Van Brocklin and the 60-minute-a-game play of 35-year-old Chuck Bednarik. Philadelphia then wins its third NFL Championship with a come-from-behind 17–13 victory over Green Bay at Franklin Field. (1960)

Nick Skorich replaces Buck Shaw as head coach. (1961)

Ron Jaworski, about to zing one here against the Giants, came to the Eagles from the Rams in 1977 and has quarterbacked so far through the 1980s. (Fred Roe)

Timmy Brown sets an NFL record for total offense in a single season, 2,428 yards. (1963)

Developer Jerry Wolman purchases the franchise for $5.5 million. (1963)

Former Chicago Cardinals and Washington Redskins coach Joe Kuharich signs as head coach and begins a series of major trades to rebuild the club. (1964)

The Eagles finish 9–5 for their first winning season in five years. (1966)

Leonard Tose purchases the franchise from Jerry Wolman for $16.1 million, at the time a record price for a professional sports team. Tose names former receiving great Pete Retzlaff as general manager and Jerry Williams as head coach. (1969)

The 1970s

The Eagles move to a new home in Veterans Stadium. After three consecutive losses at the beginning of the season, assistant coach Ed Khayat replaces Jerry Williams as head coach. (1971)

Under new coach Mike McCormick and behind new quarterback Roman Gabriel, the Eagles produced an exciting offense but a dismal 5–8–1 record. Harold Carmichael leads the NFL with 67 pass receptions in his first year as a full-time wide receiver. (1973)

Tose appoints 39-year-old Dick Vermeil of UCLA as head coach after a disappointing 4–10 season in 1975. (1976)

The Eagles post a 9–7 record, their first winning season since 1966, and make the NFL playoffs for the first time since 1960. They lose to Atlanta 14–13 on two late touchdowns in the NFC wild card playoff game. Wilbert Montgomery, in his first starting season, rushes for 1,220 yards to become the first Eagle since Steve Van Buren to surpass 1,000 yards in a season. (1978)

With their best season record since 1961, 11–5–0, the Eagles tie Dallas for first place in the NFC East and go to the playoffs as a wild card team. They beat the Chicago Bears, 27–17 in the first round, but then fall to Tampa Bay, 24–17. Montgomery sets a club record with 1,512 rushing yards and Harold Carmichael sets an NFL record against Cleveland by catching a pass in his 106th consecutive game. (1979)

The 1980s

The Eagles win 11 of their first 12 games and go on to a season mark of 12–4, and the NFC East title. Ron Jaworski leads the NFC in passing rating with a mark of

90.9 while throwing for 3,527 yards and 27 touchdowns, and is named NFL player of the year and NFC player of the year. Philadelphia trounces Minnesota in their first playoff game and then upsets Dallas, 20–7, to win the NFC title and a berth in Super Bowl XV. (1980)

At Super Bowl XV the Eagles fall to the Oakland Raiders, 27–10. (1981)

The Eagles post a 10–6 record and appear in the playoffs for the fourth consecutive year. Philadelphia is upset in the NFC wild card game by the New York Giants, 27–21. (1981)

Marion Campbell, after six seasons as the Eagles defensive coordinator, replaces Dick Vermeil as head coach. (1983)

Leonard Tose agrees to sell the Eagles to Norman Braman and Ed Leibowitz, automobile dealers from Florida. (1985)

Buddy Ryan, defensive coordinator of the Super Bowl champion Chicago Bears, is named Philadelphia's new head coach. (1986)

Memorable Years

Year	Record	Achievement
1947	8–4–0	NFL runner-up
1948	9–2–1	NFL champion
1949	11–1–0	NFL champion
1960	10–2–0	NFL champion
1978	9–7–0	Wild card entry
1979	11–5–0	Wild card entry
1980	12–4–0	NFL runner-up
1981	10–6–0	Wild card entry

Record Holders

Career

Rushing yards	Wilbert Montgomery (1977–84)	6,538
Passing yards	Ron Jaworski (1977–86)	26,963
Passing TD's	Ron Jaworski (1977–86)	175
Pass receptions	Harold Carmichael (1971–83)	589
Receiving yards	Harold Carmichael (1971–83)	8,978
Interceptions	Bill Bradley (1969–76)	34
Field Goals	Sam Baker (1964–69)	90
Total TD's	Harold Carmichael (1971–83)	79
Total points	Bobby Walston (1951–62)	881

Season

Rushing yards	Wilbert Montgomery, 1979	1,512
Passing yards	Sonny Jurgensen, 1961	3,723
Passing TD's	Sonny Jurgensen, 1961	32
Pass receptions	Mike Quick, 1985	71
Receiving yards	Mike Quick, 1985	1,409
Interceptions	Bill Bradley, 1971	11
Field Goals	Paul McFadden, 1984	30
Total TD's	Steve Van Buren, 1945	18
Total points	Paul McFadden, 1984	116

Game

Rushing yards	Steve Van Buren, 11/27/49	205
Passing yards	Bobby Thomason, 11/18/53	437
Passing TD's	Adrian Burk, 10/17/54	7
Pass receptions	Don Looney, 11/1/40	14
Receiving yards	Tommy McDonald, 12/10/60	237
Interceptions	Russ Craft, 9/24/50	4
Field Goals	Tom Dempsey, 11/12/72	6
Total TD's	many times	4
Total points	Bobby Walston, 10/17/54	25

Top Coaches

	Record	Win Percentage	Years
Greasy Neale	66–44–5	.600	1941–50
Dick Vermeil	57–51–0	.528	1976–82
Jim Trimble	25–20–3	.556	1952–55
Buck Shaw	20–16–1	.556	1958–60

All-Pros

Year	Player	Position	Year	Player	Position	Year	Player	Position
1936	Bill Hewitt	E	1951	Vic Lindskog	C/LB	1966	Bob Brown	T
1937	Bill Hewitt	E	1952	Pete Pihos	DE	1968	Bob Brown	T
1939	Davey O'Brien	QB		Chuck Bednarik	LB	1971	Bill Bradley	S
1944	Steve Van Buren	HB	1953	Pete Pihos	E	1972	Bill Bradley	S
	Al Wistert	T		Chuck Bednarik	LB	1973	Harold Carmichael	WR
1945	Steve Van Buren	HB	1954	Pete Pihos	E		Charlie Young	TE
	Al Wistert	T		Norm Willey	DE	1974	Bill Bergey	LB
1946	Al Wistert	T		Chuck Bednarik	LB	1975	Charlie Young	TE
1947	Steve Van Buren	HB	1955	Pete Pihos	E	1977	Bill Bergey	LB
	Al Wistert	T	1960	Norm Van Brocklin	QB	1980	Charlie Johnson	DT
1948	Steve Van Buren	HB		Chuck Bednarik	LB	1981	Charlie Johnson	DT
	Tommy Thompson	FB		Tom Brookshier	DB		Jerry Robinson	LB
	Pete Pihos	E	1961	Sonny Jurgensen	QB	1983	Mike Quick	WR
1949	Steve Van Buren	HB	1964	Maxie Baughan	LB	1985	Mike Quick	WR
	Pete Pihos	E	1965	Pete Retzlaff	TE		Wes Hopkins	S
1950	Chuck Bednarik	C		Bob Brown	T			

St. Louis Cardinals

Busch Stadium, Box 888
St. Louis, Missouri 63188

Stadium: Busch Stadium (capacity 51,392)

Training camp: Eastern Illinois University
                     Charleston, Illinois 61920

Colors: cardinal red, black and white

Historical Highlights

The 1920s

The Chicago Cardinals, known as the Racine Cardinals (after a street in Chicago), are a charter member of the American Professional Football Association, which would become the National Football League in 1922. The Cardinals boast football roots that go back to 1899 when the team, founded by Chris O'Brien, played under the name of the Morgan Athletic Club. (1920)

Future Hall of Famer Paddy Driscoll is hired to play halfback and to coach the team. (1920)

The Cardinals begin a rivalry with the Chicago Bears, (known then as the Decatur Staleys), that would last until the Cards left Chicago for St. Louis in 1960. In the first game, played at Normal Park on Racine Avenue in Chicago, the Cardinals triumph 7–6, then fall the following week at the same site, 10–0. (1920)

The Cardinals move their home field to Comiskey Park, also the home of the Chicago White Sox baseball team. (1922)

Norm Barry is signed to handle the Cards head coaching duties. (1925)

The Cardinals are awarded their first NFL title, with a record of 11–2–1, a shade better than the 10–2 Pottsville Maroons. But controversy swirls around the title because the last two wins of the Cardinals are over disbanded teams and owner Chris O'Brien declines to accept the championship. (1925)

Charter Hall of Famer Guy Chamberlin joins the Cardinals as end and head coach. (1927)

Chris O'Brien sells the franchise to David Jones of Chicago. (1929)

The great fullback Ernie Nevers joins the Cardinal backfield. In a game against the Chicago Bears, he scores all the team's 40 points, (six TDs and 4 PATs), which remains today the most points ever scored by a player in an NFL game. (1929)

The 1930s

The Cardinals play in pro football's first indoor game, an exhibition at the Chicago Stadium against the Chicago Bears for the benefit of the local unemployed. (1930)

Ernie Nevers takes on the additional duties of head coach. (1930)

Nevers retires as coach and player. (1932)

Charles W. Bidwill buys the Cardinals franchise from David Jones for $50,000. (1933)

Ernie Nevers comes back as head coach, but then returns to retirement after a 1–10–0 season. (1939)

The 1940s

A great back/coach of the 1920s, Jimmy Conzelman is hired as head coach of the Cardinals. (1940)

When the Cardinals were in Chicago, playing their games at Comiskey Park, no one ran the ball better for them than Charlie Trippi, stepping out here behind the interference of George Petrovich (18) and Knox Ramsey (70). Trippi played for the Cards from 1947 through 1955 and staked a slot in the Hall of Fame as a result of his play there. (Pro Football Hall of Fame)

Ollie Matson (33), brought to the turf here by a slew of Chicago Bears in 1955, was another Chicago Cardinal back destined for the Hall of Fame. Other Cardinals are Harry Thompson (60), Jack Jennings (70), and Lynn Teuws (74). (Chicago Bears)

Phil Handler is named to coach the Cards after Conzelman resigns. (1943)

With World War II depleting the rosters of many teams, the NFL allows the Cardinals to join forces with the Pittsburgh Steelers and compete as a single team. It does not help; they come in last in the NFL West with a record of 0–10–0. (1944)

The first member of the Dream Backfield, quarterback Paul Christman, a rookie out of Missouri, is signed. (1945)

Jimmy Conzelman returns as head coach. Fullback Pat Harder from Wisconsin and halfback Elmer Angsman of Notre Dame are drafted into the Cardinals backfield to join Christman and veteran Marshall Goldberg. (1946)

The Cardinals produce their first winning season since 1935 with a record of 6–5. (1946)

Georgia great Charlie Trippi is signed to round out the Dream Backfield. It is the biggest contract, $100,000 over four years, to be offered since the Red Grange/C.C. Pyle deal with the Chicago Bears back in 1925. (1947)

The Cardinals win the NFL West by defeating their in-tracity rivals, the Bears, in the last game of the season, 30–21. Then they defeat Greasy Neale's Philadelphia Eagles, 28–21, at Comiskey Park to don their first NFL crown since the controversial title of 1925. (1947)

The Cardinals lose only one of 12 games and repeat in the NFL West, the title again clinched when they defeat the Bears in the last game of the regular season, this time by a score of 24–21. But this season the Cards do not fare as well in their encounter with the Eagles for the NFL championship. In a heavy snowstorm in Philadelphia, the Cardinals lose in the final period 7–0 when Steve Van Buren carries it in from the five yard line. (1948)

Buddy Parker and Phil Handler are signed to share the duties of head coach replacing the retired Jimmy Conzelman. (1949)

The 1950s

Charter Hall of Famer and longtime Green Bay Packer legend Curly Lambeau is hired as Cardinals' head coach. (1950)

With the entry of three All-American Football Conference teams into the NFL, the resulting realignment places the Cardinals in the American Conference, along with the Browns, Eagles, Giants, Redskins and Steelers. (1950)

End Bob Shaw sets an NFL record when he catches five touchdown passes from Jim Hardy in a game against the Baltimore Colts, a record that has only been equalled once since, (Kellen Winslow of San Diego grabbed five against Oakland in 1981). (1950)

Curly Lambeau resigns and Phil Handler and Cecil Isbell are assigned the duties of interim co-coaches. (1951)

Joe Kuharich, who played guard for the Cardinals in the 1940's, is named head coach. His first draft choice is running back Ollie Matson from San Francisco. (1952)

Joe Stydahar, a Hall of Fame tackle who played for the Chicago Bears in the 1930s and 1940s, replaces Kuharich as head coach. (1953)

Ray Richards becomes the sixth head coach of the Cardinals in as many years after the firing of Stydahar. (1954)

The Cardinals post their first (and only) winning season, 7–5, of the 1950s and end up in second place in the Eastern Conference trailing only what would prove to be the NFL champion New York Giants. (1956)

Frank "Pop" Ivy is hired to coach the Cardinals after Ray Richards is fired. (1958)

John David Crowe races 83 yards for a touchdown against the Redskins, the longest run from scrimmage in Cardinal history. (1958)

The Cardinals play their last home game in Chicago, not at Comiskey Park but at Soldier Field where they are decimated by their longtime rival Chicago Bears, 31–7. (1959)

The 1960s

The Cardinals relocate in St. Louis, playing their games now in Busch Stadium.

John David Crowe becomes the first (and only) Cardinal runner to rush for more than 200 yards in a game, gaining 203 on 24 carries against the Steelers. He also is the first Cardinal to gain more than 1,000 yards in a season, 1,071 on 183 carries, an average of 5.9 yards per carry. (1960)

Wally Lemm becomes the Cardinals new head coach. (1962)

The Cardinals post a record of 9–5–0, their best effort since 1948. (1963)

Safety Larry Wilson returns an interception 96 yards for a touchdown against the Browns, a club record. (1965)

The Cards hire Charley Winner as head coach after the resignation of Wally Lemm. (1966)

With the NFL reorganization, the Cardinals are slotted in the Century Division of the NFL Eastern Conference, along with the Browns, Giants and Steelers. (1967)

Place kicker Jim Bakken sets an NFL record by kicking seven field goals in a game against the Steelers, a mark that has yet to be equalled. (1967)

The 1970s

The Cardinals replace head coach Charley Winner with Bob Hollway. (1971)

Jim Hart connects with Ahmad Rashad on a 98-yard touchdown pass against the Rams, the longest in club history. (1972)

The Cardinals win the most games in a season since 1948 when they triumph in 10 of 14 contests. It is also their first divisional title since the 40s, (the Redskins had an identical record but the Cards won the crown because they defeated Washington in both encounters that season). (1974)

In their first appearance since 1948, the Cardinals meet the Vikings at Minnesota but fall 30–14. (1974)

The Cardinals repeat as divisional champs with a record of 11–3–0, but succumb to the Los Angeles Rams in their first playoff game 35–23. (1975)

Terry Metcalf sets an NFL standard with 2,462 combined net yards gained (rushing, receiving, and kick, punt, interception and fumble returns), a mark that would stand for more than a decade. (1975)

Bud Wilkinson, once famous Oklahoma University coach and head of the President's Council on Physical Fitness, becomes the 30th regime of Cardinal coaches. (1978)

Ottis Anderson begins his pro football career as the Cardinals first draft choice, and sets two NFL records for a rookie by rushing for 1,605 yards and gaining 100 or more yards in nine different games. (1979)

Roy Green returns a kickoff 106 yards for a touchdown against the Cowboys, the longest ever by a Cardinal. (1979)

The 1980s

Jim Hanifan is named new head coach of the Cardinals. (1980)

In a strike-shortened season, the Cardinals make the special playoff tournament with a record of 5–4, but are annihilated by the Green Bay Packers 41–16 in their first postseason encounter. (1982)

Neil Lomax becomes the first Cardinal ever to complete more than 300 passes and pass for more than 4,000 yards in a single season (4,614 on 345 completions). (1984)

Gene Stallings is hired to coach the Cardinals. (1986)

Before the season, Nick the Greek picks the Cardinals to go to the Super Bowl, but they win only four of 16 games and end up in the cellar of the NFC East. (1986)

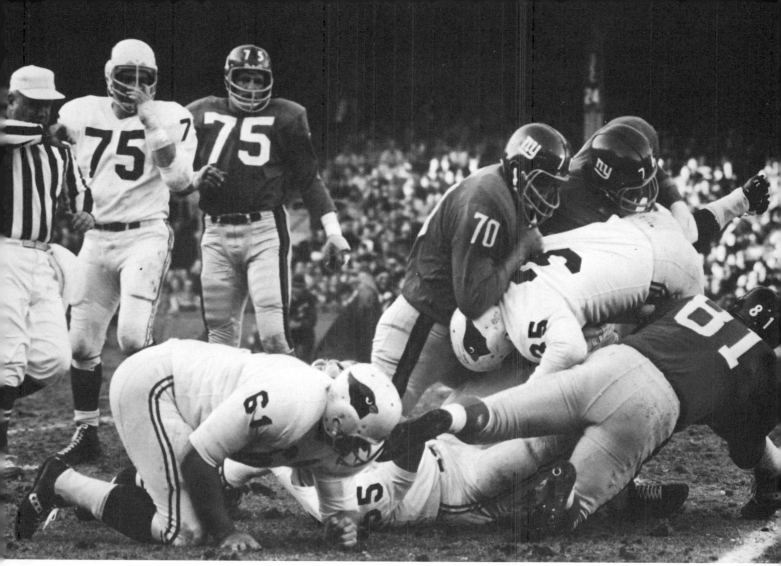

When the Cardinals got to St. Louis, Joe Childress, sandwiched by Giants in this 1963 contest, handled many of the running chores. Other Cardinals are Bob DeMarco (61) and Ed Cook (75). (New York Giants)

Memorable Years

Year	Record	Achievement
1925	11-2-1	NFL champion
1947	9-3-0	NFL champion
1948	11-1-0	NFL runner-up
1974	10-4-0	Division champion
1975	11-3-0	Division champion
1982	5-4-0	Playoff tournament participant

Top Coaches

	Record	Win Percentage	Years
Don Coryell	42-29-1	.592	1973-77
Charley Winner	35-30-5	.538	1966-70
Jimmy Conzelman	35-32-3	.522	1940-42, 1946-48
Wally Lemm	27-26-3	.509	1962-65
Paddy Driscoll	17-8-4	.680	1920-22
Norman Barry	16-8-2	.667	1925-26
Arnold Horween	13-8-1	.619	1923-24
Dewey Scanlon	6-6-1	.500	1929

Record Holders

Career		
Rushing yards	Ottis Anderson (1979–85)	7,845
Passing yards	Jim Hart (1966–83)	34,639
Passing TD's	Jim Hart (1966–83)	209
Pass receptions	Jackie Smith (1963–77)	480
Receiving yards	Jackie Smith (1963–77)	7,918
Interceptions	Larry Wilson (1960–72)	52
Field Goals	Jim Bakken (1962–78)	282
Total TD's	Sonny Randle (1959–66)	60
Total points	Jim Bakken (1962–78)	1,380

Season		
Rushing yards	Ottis Anderson, 1979	1,605
Passing yards	Neil Lomax, 1984	4,614
Passing TD's	Charley Johnson, 1963	28
	Neil Lomax, 1984	28
Pass receptions	Roy Green, 1983, 1984	78
Receiving yards	Roy Green, 1984	1,555
Interceptions	Bob Nussbaumer, 1949	12
Field Goals	Jim Bakken, 1967	27
Total TD's	John David Crowe, 1962	17
Total points	Jim Bakken, 1967	117
	Neil O'Donoghue, 1984	117

Game		
Rushing yards	John David Crowe, 12/18/60	203
Passing yards	Neil Lomax, 12/16/84	468
Passing TD's	Jim Hardy, 10/2/50	6
	Charley Johnson, 9/26/65	6
	Charley Johnson, 11/2/69	6
Pass receptions	Sonny Randle, 11/4/62	16
Receiving yards	Sonny Randle, 11/4/62	256
Interceptions	Bob Nussbaumer, 11/13/49	4
	Jerry Norton, 11/20/60	4
Field Goals	Jim Bakken, 9/24/67	7
Total TD's	Ernie Nevers, 11/28/29	6
Total points	Ernie Nevers, 11/28/29	40

All-Pros

Year	Player	Position
1920	Paddy Driscoll	QB
1922	Eddie Anderson	E
	Paddy Driscoll	HB
1923	Paddy Driscoll	QB
1925	Ralph Claypool	C
	Paddy Driscoll	HB
1926	Walt Ellis	T
1929	Ernie Nevers	FB
1930	Walt Kiesling	G
	Ernie Nevers	FB
1931	Frank McNally	C
	Ernie Nevers	FB
1932	Walk Kiesling	G
1935	Bill Smith	E
	Mike Mikulak	FB
1937	Gaynell Tinsley	E
1938	Gaynell Tinsley	E
1941	Joe Kuharich	G
1943	Ed Rucinzki	E
1947	Mal Kutner	E
	Buster Ramsey	G
	Pat Harder	FB
1948	Mal Kutner	E
	Buster Ramsey	G
	Charlie Trippi	HB
1949	Buster Ramsey	G
	Elmer Angsman	HB
1952	Ollie Matson	DB
1954	Ollie Matson	HB
1955	Ollie Matson	HB
1956	Ollie Matson	HB
	Night Train Lane	DB
1957	Ollie Matson	HB
1960	Sonny Randle	E
	Jerry Norton	S
1963	Bobby Joe Conrad	FL
1964	Ken Gray	G
	Pat Fischer	DB
1966	Larry Wilson	S
1967	Bob DeMarco	C
	Larry Wilson	S
1968	Larry Wilson	S
1969	Larry Wilson	S
1970	Larry Wilson	S
1975	Mel Gray	WR
	Dan Dierdorf	T
	Roger Wehrli	CB
	Jim Bakken	K
1976	Dan Dierdorf	T
	Tom Banks	C
	Roger Wehrli	CB
	Jim Bakken	K
1977	Dan Dierdorf	T
	Roger Wehrli	CB
1978	Dan Dierdorf	T
1979	Ottis Anderson	RB
	Bob Young	G
1983	Roy Green	WR
1984	Roy Green	WR
	E. J. Junior	LB

San Francisco Forty-Niners

711 Nevada Street
Redwood City, California 94061

Stadium: Candlestick Park (capacity 61,499)

Training camp: Sierra Community College
Rocklin, California 95677

Colors: forty-niners gold and scarlet

Historical Highlights

The 1940s

The 49ers are a charter member of the All-American Football Conference, the franchise ownership going to Tony Morabito, and are slated in the AAFC Western Division along with the Cleveland Browns, Chicago Rockets and Los Angeles Dons. (1946)

Buck Shaw is named San Francisco's first head coach, and quarterback Frankie Albert leads the 49ers to a 9–5–0 second place finish behind the Browns with a record of 8–4–2. (1947)

The 49ers score 495 points in 12 games, an average of more than 41 points a game, and 106 more than the Browns, but still end up in second place in the AAFC West with a 12–2–0 record, both losses to the undefeated Browns. (1948)

The 49ers gain 3,663 yards rushing in 14 games, more than any team in the history of professional football (including 16-game seasons) and average a phenomenal 6.1 yards per carry. Biggest ground gainers are Johnny Stryzkalski (925), Joe Perry (562), and Forrest Hall (413), with 10 players in all gaining more than 100 yards rushing. (1948)

San Francisco again outscores Cleveland in total points and even trims them 56–28 at Kezar Stadium in one of their two encounters but still runs second in the AAFC standings.

In a special playoff series at season's end, the 49ers defeat the Brooklyn/New York Yankees but then fall to the Browns in the AAFC title game 21–7, which is also the last AAFC game. (1949)

The 1950s

The 49ers are one of three teams from the defunct AAFC to join the NFL. (1950)

In their NFL debut season, the 49ers win only three

John "Strike" Stryzalski stumbles for several San Francisco yards in 1951. Stryzalski was one of the 49ers top ground gainers in the late 1940s and early 50s. The stumbling block here is the Bears Ed Sprinkle and coming in from behind is George Blanda, who, when he was not quarterbacking or place-kicking, played a little defense. (Chicago Bears)

games and end up in next to last place in the NFL's National Conference behind the Rams, Bears, Yanks, Lions, Packers and ahead of only the 1–11–0 Colts. (1950)

The 49ers post a record of 9–3–0 but run second to the 10–2–0 Detroit Lions. (1953)

Norman P. Strader succeeds Buck Shaw as head coach. (1955)

Former 49er quarterback, Frankie Albert, replaces Strader as head coach. (1956)

The 49ers, with a record of 8–4–0 end up in a tie with the Detroit Lions for the Western Conference title, but lose in a special playoff game 31–27. (1957)

Howard W. "Red" Hickey takes over the coaching chores and keeps the team in contention all year, thanks in part to quarterback John Brodie and J.D. Smith, converted from a defensive back, who becomes only the second 49er to accumulate 1,000 yards rushing. (1959)

189

The 1960s

After Y.A. Tittle is traded to the Giants, quarterbacking is shared by John Brodie and rookie Billy Kilmer. (1961)

Red Hickey quits and Jack Christiansen is appointed to replace him as head coach. (1963)

Dick Nolan, formerly with the Dallas Cowboys, gets his first head coaching assignment, replacing Jack Christiansen at San Francisco. (1968)

The 1970s

Posting a 10-3-0 season record, their best as an NFL club, the 49ers take the NFC Western Division championship and quarterback John Brodie is named the NFL's "Player of the Year." Coach Dick Nolan is the choice as NFC "Coach of the Year." San Francisco gets to the NFC title game by beating the Vikings but is thwarted there by the Dallas Cowboys 17-10. (1970)

In the club's first season in Candlestick Park, the 49ers forge a 9-5-0 record and win their second NFC Western Division title, clinching the crown on the final day by beating Detroit 31-27 (the identical score by which the Lions had knocked the 49ers out of championship play in 1957). San Francisco again faces Dallas in the NFC title tilt after whipping the Redskins, but the Cowboys again vanquish them, this time 14-3. (1971)

Chances for a third straight division title are in doubt when quarterback Brodie is injured. Steve Spurrier steps in for Brodie and keeps things in line. In the final quarter of the final game, Brodie relieves Spurrier and throws two touchdown passes for a 20-17 win over Minnesota that clinches the divisional title. The Cowboys again ride roughshod over the 49ers in the divisional playoff game 30-28. (1972)

After three losing seasons, new coach Monte Clark helps the 49ers post their first winning season, 8-6-0, since 1972. New quarterback Jim Plunkett gets the 49ers off to their best start ever, 6-1, before hitting a mid-season losing streak which keeps the club out of postseason contention. (1976)

The 49ers are bought by Edward J. DeBartolo, Jr., and Joe Thomas is named general manager. The new coach is Ken Meyer. (1977)

The club posts a 2-14 record and two coaches are hired and fired in the same season. Pete McCulley departs after nine games with a 1-8-0 record, Fred O'Connor is let go after the team wins just one of its final seven games. (1978)

Bill Walsh is hired as the new head coach and general manager. (1979)

The 1980s

In his third season as head coach and general manager, Bill Walsh guides the 49ers through a season of firsts and bests. Behind the passing and leadership of Joe Montana, the team posts a 13-3 season record, wins the NFC Western Division title and the NFC championship crown by defeating their previous nemesis, the Dallas Cowboys 28-27. Bill Walsh is named "Coach of the Year." (1981)

On a January afternoon at the Silverdome in Pontiac, Michigan, the 49ers triumph in Super Bowl XVI, defeating the Cincinnati Bengals 26-21. (1982)

For the second time in three seasons, the 49ers play in the NFC championship game. After posting a 10-6 season then squeezing past Detroit 42-23, they lose to Washington 24-21 in the NFC championship contest. (1983)

The 49ers experience the most successful regular season in NFL history by winning an NFL record 15 games, including all eight road contests. The club breaks 14 team records and becomes the first NFC team to sweep all of its conference games and the first NFC West club to win all contests within the division. (1984)

Led by Roger Craig and Joe Montana, San Francisco caps the 1984 season by routing the Miami Dolphins in Super Bowl XIX 38-16. (1985)

With a 10-6 record the 49ers qualify for postseason play after getting off to a slow start during the season. A win over the Los Angeles Rams sends the team on a drive to the playoffs that included seven wins in their last nine games and is climaxed by a come from behind victory over Dallas in the regular season finale. The 49ers lose in the wild card game, however, to the New York Giants 17-3. (1985)

The 49ers post a 10-5-1 record and win the NFC West by beating the (10-6-0) Rams 24-14 in the last game of the season. But San Francisco is no match for the Super Bowl champion-to-be New York Giants, and are annihilated 49-3. (1986)

Memorable Years

Year	Record	Achievement
1970	10-3-1	NFL runner-up
1971	9-5-0	NFL runner-up
1972	8-5-1	Division champion
1981	13-3-0	NFL champion
1983	15-1-0	Division champion
1985	10-6-0	Wild card entry
1986	10-5-1	Division champions

Leaping over a more recent stumbling block is Eric Mullins in this 1986 game against the Giants. (Fred Roe)

Record Holders

Career		
Rushing yards	Joe Perry (1950–60, 1963)	7 344
Passing yards	John Brodie (1957–73)	31 548
Passing TD's	John Brodie (1957–73)	214
Pass receptions	Dwight Clark (1979–86)	482
Receiving yards	Gene Washington (1969–77)	6 664
Interceptions	Jimmy Johnson (1961–76)	47
Field Goals	Ray Wersching (1977–86)	185
Total TD's	Ken Willard (1965–73)	61
Total points	Ray Wersching (1977–86)	896

Season		
Rushing yards	Wendell Tyler, 1984	1,262
Passing yards	Joe Montana, 1983	3,910
Passing TD's	John Brodie, 1965	30
Pass receptions	Roger Craig, 1985	92
Receiving yards	Dave Parks, 1965	1,344
Interceptions	Dave Barker, 1960	10
Field Goals	Bruce Gossett, 1973	26
Total TD's	Roger Craig, 1985	15
Total points	Ray Wersching, 1984	131

Game		
Rushing yards	Delvin Williams, 10/31/76	194
Passing yards	Joe Montana, 10/6/85	429
Passing TD's	John Brodie, 11/23/65	5
	Steve Spurrier, 11/19/72	5
	Joe Montana, 10/6/85	5
Pass receptions	Bernie Casey, 11/13/66	12
	Dwight Clark, 12/11/82	12
	Roger Craig, 10/6/85	12
Receiving yards	Jerry Rice, 12/9/85	241
Interceptions	Dave Baker, 12/4/60	4
Field Goals	Ray Wersching, 10/16/83	6
Total TD's	Billy Kramer, 10/15/61	4
Total points	Gordy Soltau, 10/27/51	26

Top Coaches

	Record	Win Percentage	Years
Bill Walsh	76–54–1	.585	1979–86
Dick Nolan	56–56–5	.500	1968–75
Buck Shaw	33–25–2	.569	1950–54

All-Pros

Year	Player	Position	Year	Player	Position	Year	Player	Position
1946	Alyn Beals	E		Y.A. Tittle	QB		Jimmy Johnson	CB
	Bruno Banducci	G		Billy Wilson	E		Ted Kwalick	TE
1947	Bruno Banducci	G	1959	Leo Nomellini	DT		Gene Washington	WR
1948	Alyn Beals	E		Abe Woodson	CB		Dave Wilcox	OLB
	John Strzykalski	H	1960	Abe Woodson	CB	1973	Forrest Blue	C
1949	Alyn Beals	E	1965	Dave Parks	SE		Dave Wilcox	OLB
	Visco Grigich	G	1968	Clifton McNeil	WR	1976	Tommy Hart	DE
	Joe Perry	B		Howard Mudd	G	1977	Cleveland Elam	DT
	Frank Albert	QB	1970	John Brodie	QB	1981	Randy Cross	G
1951	Leo Nomellini	T		Jimmy Johnson	CB		Fred Dean	DE
1952	Hugh McElhenny	HB		Gene Washington	WR		Ronnie Lott	CB
	Leo Nomellini	DT	1971	Forrest Blue	C	1982	Dwight Clark	WR
	Joe Perry	FB		Jimmy Johnson	CB	1983	Ronnie Lott	CB
1957	Marv Matuszak	LB		Dave Wilcox	OLB	1984	Keith Fahnhorst	T
	Leo Nomellini	DT	1972	Forrest Blue	C	1985	Eric Wright	CB

Tampa Bay Buccaneers

One Buccaneers Place
Tampa, Florida 33607

Stadium: Tampa Stadium (capacity 74,315)

Training camp: One Buccaneer Place
Tampa, Florida 33607

Colors: Florida orange, white and red

Historical Highlights

The 1960s

The Suncoast Pro Football committee is formed to try to obtain an NFL franchise for Tampa Bay. This group functions until 1972 when the Tampa Chamber of Commerce appoints the formal West Coast Task Force headed by J. Leonard Levy. (1968)

The 1970s

The NFL's 27th franchise is awarded to Tampa Bay and it is directed that Tampa Stadium is to be enlarged to 72,000 seats to accommodate the new team and its fans. Ownership is awarded to Hugh F. Culverhouse. Earlier Culverhouse had declined ownership of the Seattle franchise for geographic reasons. (1974)

The club is named the Buccaneers, the choice derived from a local contest. (1975)

A 30-year lease agreement with Buccaneers officials for Tampa Stadium is approved by the Tampa Sports Authority. (1975)

John McKay, who led the University of Southern California to four national championships, is named head coach. (1975)

In the veteran allocation draft, the Buccaneers choose 39 players and select defensive lineman Lee Roy Selmon from the College draft. (1976)

The Bucs welcome their first group of rookies and free agents to training camp at One Buccaneers Place, the newly completed complex of offices and sports facilities; at least 140 players appear, some only briefly, on the Buc's first year roster. (1976)

The Bucs have the unfortunate distinction of becoming the first NFL team to lose all 14 games in one season. (1976)

The Buccaneers are slotted into the NFC's Central Division, joining the Chicago Bears, Green Bay Packers,

Tossing here for Tampa Bay is the team's all-time leading passer Doug Williams, who handled the quarterbacking duties from 1978 through 1982. (New York Giants)

Detroit Lions and Minnesota Vikings. They end in the cellar with a record of 2–12–0. (1977)

Finally turning things in the right direction, the Bucs, with a 17–13 win at Chicago, are the only undefeated team in the NFL with a 5–0 record. Tampa Bay goes on to end the season tied with Chicago in the NFC Central race with records of 10–6. (1979)

Ricky Bell becomes the first Buc to rush for more than 1,000 yards in a season, gaining 1,263 on 283 carries. (1979)

Tampa Bay defeats Philadelphia 24–17 in their first ever postseason game with Ricky Bell rushing for 142 yards and two TDs. But Los Angeles defeats the Bucs 9–0 at Tampa Stadium to leave them one game short of the Super Bowl. (1979)

The 1980s

In their first appearance on national television, the Bucs avenge their NFC title game defeat with a 10–9 victory over the Los Angeles Rams. (1980)

Doug Williams becomes the first Buc to complete more than 200 passes in a season (254) and gain more than 3,000 yards passing, (3,396). (1980)

In a winner-take-all showdown with the Detroit Lions in the last game of the season, Tampa wins the NFC Central Division title by a score of 20–17, but is eliminated from the playoffs two weeks later by the Dallas Cowboys 38–0. (1981)

Kevin House sets a Tampa Bay record and becomes the first Buc to catch passes for more than 1,000 yards, gaining 1,176 on 56 receptions. (1981)

The Buccaneers qualify for postseason play for the third time in four years after a 26–23 win over the Chicago Bears in the last game of a strike-shortened season gives them a record of 5–4. In the playoff tournament, however, Tampa Bay succumbs to Dallas for the second time in two years. (1982)

As the Bucs score a 17–12 victory over Minnesota, James Wilder gains 219 yards rushing, the most in club history and the most by an NFL running back since 1977. Wilder also sets the Tampa Bay season rushing mark by gaining 1,544 yards. His 407 carries is an NFL record which still stands today. (1984)

Leeman Bennett, former coach of the Atlanta Falcons, is named head coach of the Buccaneers, succeeding John McKay who became the club president. (1985)

The Bucs make Auburn running back Bo Jackson the first choice in the NFL draft, but he chooses pro baseball instead of signing with Tampa Bay. (1986)

Ray Perkins replaces Leeman Bennett as head coach. (1987)

Memorable Years

Year	Record	Achievement
1979	10–6–0	NFL runner-up
1981	9–7–0	Division champion
1983	5–4–0	Playoff tournament participant

Top Coach

	Record	Win Percentage	Years
John McKay	45–9⁻–1	.331	1976–84

Record Holders

Career		
Rushing yards	James Wilder (1981–86)	4,882
Passing yards	Doug Williams (1978–82)	12,648
Passing TD's	Doug Williams (1978–82)	73
Pass receptions	James Wilder (1981–86)	296
Receiving yards	Kevin House (1980–85)	4,722
Interceptions	Cedric Brown (1977–84)	29
Field Goals	Bill Capece (1981–83)	43
Total TD's	James Wilder (1981–86)	38
Total points	James Wilder (1981–86)	228

Season		
Rushing yards	James Wilder, 1984	1,544
Passing yards	Doug Williams, 1981	3,563
Passing TD's	Doug Williams, 1980	20
Pass receptions	James Wilder, 1984	85
Receiving yards	Kevin House, 1981	1,176
Interceptions	Cedric Brown, 1981	9
Field Goals	Donald Igwebuike, 1985	22
Total TD's	James Wilder, 1984	13
Total points	Donald Igwebuike, 1985	96

Game		
Rushing yards	James Wilder, 11/6/83	219
Passing yards	Doug Williams, 11/16/80	486
Passing TD's	many times	4
Pass receptions	James Wilder, 9/15/85	13
Receiving yards	Kevin House, 10/18/81	2
Interceptions	many times	2
Field Goals	Bill Capece, 10/30/83	4
	Bill Capece, 1/2/83	4
	Donald Igwebuike, 11/24/85	4
Total TD's	Jimmie Giles, 10/20/85	4
Total points	Jimmie Giles, 10/20/85	24

All-Pros

Year	Player	Position
1979	Lee Roy Selmon	DE
1980	Lee Roy Selmon	DE
1982	Lee Roy Selmon	DE
	Hugh Green	LB
1983	Hugh Green	LB
1984	Lee Roy Selmon	DE
	James Wilder	RB

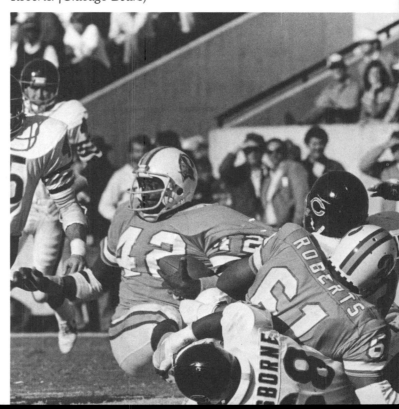

Ricky Bell, second only to James Wilder in Tampa Bay rushing annals is corralled here in a game against the Chicago Bears. Number 61 of the Bucs is guard Greg Roberts. (Chicago Bears)

Washington Redskins

Redskin Park
P.O. Box 17247
Dulles International Airport
Washington, D.C. 20041

Stadium: Robert F. Kennedy Stadium
(capacity 55,750)

Training camp: Dickinson College
Carlisle, Pennsylvania 17013

Colors: burgundy and gold

Historical Highlights

The 1930s

George Preston Marshall heads a syndicate that buys a National Football League franchise for Boston, Massachusetts. Playing in the baseball park of the Boston Braves, the team is called the "Braves." Lud Wray is hired as coach. (1932)

The Boston team moves to Fenway Park, home of the American League Red Sox and the "Braves" become the "Redskins." William "Lone Star" Dietz is the new head coach. (1933)

The Redskins win the Eastern Division with a record of 7-5-0. The NFL title game is moved from Boston to New York at the urging of George Preston Marshall who is disenchanted with the lack of support for his team in his hometown. The Redskins lose the NFL title game to the Packers 21-6. (1936)

Ray Flaherty, Hall of Fame end, is appointed the Redskins new head coach. (1936)

The Washington Redskins are officially born when the National Football league approves the transfer of the Boston Redskins franchise to Washington, D.C. (1937)

"Slingin'" Sammy Baugh of Texas Christian is Washington's first round draft choice. (1937)

The famed Redskins Band is formed, the first of its kind in the league. (1937)

Ten thousand feather-wearing Redskin fans parade up Broadway behind their brass band prior to the Redskin's annihilation of the Giants 49-14 for the Eastern championship. Then Sammy Baugh leads the Redskins past the Bears, completing 17 of 33 for 335 yards and three touchdowns in the NFC championship game. (1937)

One of Jay Schroeder's favorite receivers in the mid-1980's, Gary Clark, goes for the bomb here against the Giants in the NFC title game of 1986. (Fred Roe)

From kick formation Frank Filchock flips a pass to Andy Farkas who goes all the way for a touchdown against the Steelers, setting the NFL record for longest pass play in league history—99 yards. (1939)

The 1940s

The Redskins triumph in the NFL Eastern division with a record of 9-2-0. Washington faces the Chicago Bears in the world championship game at Griffith Stadium and loses 73-0, the most devastating defeat in NFL postseason play ever. (1940)

The Redskins establish training quarters in San Diego at Brown Military Academy, bringing pro football on a large scale to California. (1941)

The Redskins suffer only one loss during the season, to the Giants, who gain only one yard rushing and complete only one pass, good for a touchdown, followed by another touchdown on an interception. The final score: 14-7. (1942)

In the NFL title game the Bears take an early lead, but Sammy Baugh's 85-yard quick kick sets them back and the Redskins clinch the world championship, 14-6. (1942)

After two straight losses, the Redskins bounce back in the Eastern Division title playoff game to defeat the Giants, 29-0. In the championship match, Sammy Baugh suffers a concussion early in the game after

194

tackling Sid Luckman on a punt return, and the Redskins succumb, 41–21. (1943)

The Redskins abandon their double-wing formation and adopt the T formation and Sammy Baugh switches from tailback to T quarterback. (1944)

The Redskins take the Eastern Division title with a record of 8–2–0. (1945)

In sub-zero weather the Redskins lose the world title to the Rams, 15–14 on two freakish plays. Sammy Baugh's pass from the end zone hits the goal post for a safety, and Bob Waterfield's try-for-point hits the crossbar and bounces over for the Rams. (1945)

The first annual Redskins-Rams game for the benefit of the Los Angeles Times Charities, Inc., draws 68,188 to Memorial Coliseum and nets the Times Boys Club $96,711.23. (1946)

The 1950s

Dick Todd is hired as head coach. (1951)

Curly Lambeau replaces Todd at the Washington helm. (1952)

Joe Kuharich becomes the Redskins head coach. (1954)

The Redskins Alumni Association is organized. Twenty-three former players residing in the Washington area adopt a formal constitution and by-laws and invite all non-resident ex-Redskins to join. (1953)

Congress gives a go-ahead to build D.C. Stadium and the Redskins sign a 30-year lease to play there. (1959)

The 1960s

The first game in the new D.C. Stadium draws 37,767 fans but the Redskins fail to hold a 21–0 lead and fall to the Giants 24–21. (1961)

Dick James sets a Redskin single-game record by scoring 4 touchdowns in their win over Dallas 34–24. (1961)

The Redskins sell out all their games in the new D.C. stadium. (1964)

With Washington down, 21–0, Sonny Jurgensen sparks one of the greatest comeback wins in Redskin history. In the 34–31 victory over Dallas, Jurgensen passes for 411 yards and three touchdowns. (1965)

Redskins appoint former Cleveland star quarterback, Otto Graham, as head coach and general manager. (1966)

The Redskins and the Giants score the most points in NFL history in Washington's rout of New York, 72–41. (1966)

Sonny Jurgensen sets new Redskin and NFL passing records for most attempts (508), completions (288), and yards gained (3,747). Receivers Charlie Taylor, Jerry Smith and Bobby Mitchell finish 1, 2 and 4 in the league, highest ever by receivers on the same team. (1967)

Vince Lombardi, fabled Packers coach, becomes head coach of the Washington Redskins. (1969)

The 1970s

On the second offensive play of a game against the Eagles, Larry Brown takes a hand-off from Sonny Jurgensen and gains 12 yards to become the first Redskin in history to become a member of the 1,000 yard club. (1970)

George Allen, winningest coach in the National Football Conference, accepts the head coaching job of the Redskins and is also named general manager. He brings Washington to the playoffs as a wild card entry his first year but they lose there to the 49ers 24–20. (1971)

Allen guides the Redskins to 11 wins, the most in 30 years for Washington. With an 11–3–0 record the Redskins earn their way to the NFL championship game. (1972)

With a convincing 26–3 win over the world champion Dallas Cowboys at RFK Stadium, (formerly D.C. Stadium), the Redskins win the opportunity to meet the Miami Dolphins in Super Bowl VII. (1972)

At the Los Angeles Coliseum, the Redskins lose to the Dolphins 14–7 in Super Bowl VII. (1973)

The Redskins again make the playoffs but lose in a divisional contest to the Vikings 27–20. (1973)

The Redskins have the best record in the NFC East, 10–4–0, and the second best in the NFL, and for the fourth consecutive year under George Allen, the Redskins make the NFL playoffs. (1974)

Redskin wide receiver Charley Taylor becomes the all-time pass receiver in NFL history with his 634th career catch against the Eagles in the season's finale. (1975)

The Redskins make the playoffs for the fifth time in six years by winning their final four games and turning in a record of 10–4–0 but are defeated by the Vikings 35–20. (1976)

Jack Pardee, former Redskin player and coach, is named the 16th head coach of the Redskins. (1978)

Coach Pardee is selected NFL Coach of the Year by the Associated Press, Sports Illustrated, Washington and Seattle touchdown Clubs; NFC Coach of the Year by

United Press International after he guides the Redskins to a 10–6 record. It is the ninth consecutive year the Redskins finish .500 or better. The Redskins lose both the division title as well as a wild card berth with a loss in the final seconds of the last game of the season to Dallas, 35–34. (1979)

The 1980s

Joe Gibbs, offensive coordinator of the San Diego Chargers, becomes the 17th head coach in Redskin history. (1981)

Mark Moseley beats the odds and the New York Giants by kicking his 21st straight field goal in RFK Stadium. Moseley's kick breaks Garo Yepremian's record of 20 and gives the Redskins a 15–14 win in the final seconds of the game. Redskin John Riggins also becomes only the fifth back in NFL history to exceed 2,000 carries. (1982)

For the first time since 1980, the Redskins post a shutout, defeating the Cardinals 28–0. Their 8–1 record is the best in the NFC and gives them the home field advantage in the playoffs. During the strike-shortened season the Redskins give up only 128 points, the fewest in the NFL. (1982)

John Riggins achieves a Redskin playoff record of 185 yards leading the Redskins to a 21–7 win over Minnesota and a spot in the NFC championship game. The Redskins defeat the Cowboys 31–17 to reach their second Super Bowl. (1982)

Washington earns it first world title in 40 years by downing the Dolphins 27–17 in Super Bowl XVII. (1983)

John Riggins breaks an NFL record by scoring 24 touchdowns rushing, and sets a Redskin mark by gaining 1,347 yards rushing. Kicker Mark Moseley scores 161 points, second only in NFL history to Paul Hornung's 176 registered in 1960. (1983)

For the second year in a row, the Redskins finish with the best record in the NFL, 14–2–0. The Redskins also set an NFL record by scoring 541 points. In the most lopsided playoff game in 26 years, the Redskins defeat the LA Rams 51–7 in the NFC title game. The team sets or ties 13 club playoff marks with the 44-point margin of victory, the greatest in the 47-year history of the Redskins. (1983)

After a spectacular 1983 season, the Redskins meet the Los Angeles Raiders at Tampa Stadium in Super Bowl XVIII but suffer a heartbreaking loss 38–9. (1984)

The Redskins finish as Eastern Division champions for the 11th time in the club's history and for the third straight season but lose to the Chicago Bears 23–19 in the playoffs. (1984)

Redskin owner, Jack Kent Cooke, purchases the team's remaining stock interest and becomes 100 percent owner of the Redskins. (1985)

After winning five of their last six games, the Redskins finish in a three-way tie for first in the NFL with the Cowboys and Giants with a 10–6 record. Tie-breakers cost the Redskins the division title as well as the first wild card spot, (to the Giants), and the second wild card spot, (to the 49ers). (1985)

The Redskins win 12 of 16 games and qualify for the playoffs as a wild card entry. After defeating the Rams 19–7, Washington surprises the Super Bowl defending Chicago Bears 27–13. But the Redskins fall to their intra-division rivals, the Giants, who are on their way to an NFL title, 17–0. (1986)

Record Holders

Career		
Rushing yards	John Riggins (1976–79, 1981–85)	7,472
Passing yards	Joe Theismann (1974–85)	25,206
Passing TD's	Sonny Jurgensen (1964–74)	209
Pass receptions	Charley Taylor (1964–77)	649
Receiving yards	Charley Taylor (1964–77)	9,140
Interceptions	Brig Owens (1966–77)	36
Field Goals	Mark Moseley (1974–85)	257
Total TD's	Charley Taylor (1964–77)	90
Total points	Mark Moseley (1974–85)	1,176

Season		
Rushing yards	John Riggins, 1983	1,347
Passing yards	Jay Schroeder, 1986	4,109
Passing TD's	Sonny Jurgensen, 1967	31
Pass receptions	Art Monk, 1984	106
Receiving yards	Bobby Mitchell, 1963	1,436
Interceptions	Dan Sandifer, 1948	13
Field Goals	Mark Moseley, 1983	33
Total TD's	John Riggins, 1983	24
Total points	Mark Moseley, 1983	161

Game		
Rushing yards	George Rogers, 12/21/85	206
Passing yards	Sammy Baugh, 10/31/48	446
Passing TD's	Sammy Baugh, 10/31/43	6
	Sammy Baugh, 11/23/47	6
Pass receptions	Art Monk, 12/15/85	13
Receiving yards	Art Monk, 12/15/85	230
Interceptions	Sammy Baugh, 11/14/43	4
	Dan Sandifer, 10/31/48	4
Field Goals	many times	5
Total TD's	Dick James, 12/17/61	4
	Larry Brown, 12/4/73	4
Total points	Dick James, 12/17/61	24
	Larry Brown, 12/4/73	4

All-Pros

Year	Player	Position
1932	Turk Edwards	T
1933	Cliff Battles	HB
	Turk Edwards	T
1936	Cliff Battles	HB
	Turk Edwards	T
1937	Cliff Battles	HB
	Sammy Baugh	HB
	Turk Edwards	T
1939	Andy Farkas	HB
	Jim Barber	T
1940	Sammy Baugh	HB
1941	Wee Willie Wilkin	T
1942	Bob Masterson	E
	Wee Willie Wilkin	T
1943	Sammy Baugh	HB
	Dick Farman	G
1944	Joe Aguirre	E
1945	Steve Bagarus	HB
1948	Sammy Baugh	QB
1955	Gene Brito	DE
1956	Dick Stanfel	G
	Gene Brito	DE
1957	Dick Stanfel	G
	Gene Brito	DE
1958	Dick Stanfel	G
1962	Bobby Mitchell	FL
1964	Paul Krause	S
1965	Paul Krause	S
1967	Charley Taylor	WR
1969	Jerry Smith	TE
1970	Larry Brown	RB
1972	Larry Brown	RB
	Chris Hanburger	LB
1974	Ken Houston	S
1975	Ken Houston	S
1976	Ken Houston	S
1978	Ken Houston	S
1979	Lemar Parrish	CB
1980	Lemar Parrish	CB
1981	Mike Nelms	PR
1982	Mark Moseley	K
	Mike Nelms	KR
1983	Joe Theismann	QB
	John Riggins	RB
	Joe Jacoby	T
	Russ Grimm	G
	Dave Butz	DT
	Mark Murphy	S
	Mike Nelms	KR
1984	Art Monk	WR
	Joe Jacoby	T
	Russ Grimm	G
1985	Russ Grimm	G

Top Coaches

	Record	Win Percentage	Years
Joe Gibbs	71–29–0	.710	1981–86
George Allen	69–35–1	.663	1971–77
Ray Flaherty	56–23–3	.709	1936–42
Jack Pardee	24–24–0	.500	1978–80
Dudley DeGroot	14–5–1	.700	1944–45
Lone Star Dietz	11–11–2	.500	1933–34
Dutch Bergman	7–4–1	.636	1943
Vince Lombardi	7–5–2	.583	1969
Dick Todd	5–4–0	.556	1951

Joe Theismann, a Redskins institution in the late 1970s and 80s, does here against the Bears what he did so well for Washington, merely throw the football. On the ground is Redskins tackle Terry Hermelling. (Chicago Bears)

Memorable Years

Year	Record	Achievement
1936	7–5–0	NFL runner-up
1937	8–3–0	NFL champion
1940	9–2–0	NFL runner-up
1942	10–1–0	NFL champion
1943	6–3–1	NFL runner-up
1945	8–2–0	NFL runner-up
1971	9–4–1	Wild card entry
1972	11–3–0	NFL runner-up
1973	10–4–0	Wild card entry
1974	10–4–0	Wild card entry
1976	10–4–0	Wild card entry
1982	8–1–0	NFL champion
1983	14–2–0	NFL runner-up
1984	11–5–0	Division champion
1986	12–4–0	NFC runner-up

5 THE AMERICAN FOOTBALL CONFERENCE

Buffalo Bills

One Bills Drive
Orchard Park, New York 14127

Stadium: Rich Stadium (capacity 80,290)

Training camp: Fredonia State University
                    Fredonia, New York 14063

Colors: royal blue, scarlet red and white

Historical Highlights

The 1960s

The American Football League grants a franchise for Buffalo to Ralph C. Wilson who names the teams the Bills. The Bills will play in War Memorial Stadium which the city agrees to enlarge to 36,500 seats. (1960)

Garrard "Buster" Ramsey is named head coach. (1960)

Buster Ramsey exits as head coach and is replaced by Lou Saban. (1962)

Cookie Gilchrist gains 1,099 yards during the season, the AFL's first 1,000 yard runner. (1962)

Gilchrist gains 243 yards rushing and scores five touchdowns in a game against the Jets. (1963)

The Bills' season mark of 7–6–1 lands them in a tie for the Eastern Division title with the Boston Patriots, but Buffalo loses 26–8 in a playoff game. (1963)

The Bills secure the Eastern Division with a record of 12–2–0 (the best in their entire history), then go on to capture the AFL championship, beating San Diego 20–7 before a capacity crowd at War memorial Stadium. Jack Kemp completes 10 passes and scores the Bills' final touchdown. (1964)

Winning 10 of 14 games the Bills take their second straight Eastern Division title. The Bills shut out the Chargers 23–0 to win their second consecutive AFL championship. (1965)

Lou Saban resigns and assistant coach Joe Collier is named head coach. (1966)

The Bills claim their third straight Eastern Division championship posting a record of 9–4–1, but are stopped in the AFL title game by the Kansas City Chiefs 31–7. (1966)

Joe Collier is replaced as head coach by Harry Johnson. (1968)

John Rauch signs on as head coach, and the Bills draft Heisman Trophy winner O.J. Simpson. (1969)

Jack Kemp, Buffalo Bill quarterback in the mid-1960s, before becoming a U.S. Congressman and presidential aspirant. (Fred Roe)

The 1970s

Quarterback Dennis Shaw is named AFC Rookie of the Year after completing 178 of 321 passes for 2,507 yards and 10 touchdowns. Marlin Briscoe is the AFC's top receiver with 57 catches, and is the first Bill to gain more than 1,000 yards on pass receptions (1,036). (1970)

John Rauch resigns and is succeeded as head coach by Lou Saban. (1971)

O.J. Simpson is named AFC Offensive Player of the Year. (1972)

The Bills have their first winning season in six years (9-5-0) as they move into their new playing field in Orchard Park. O.J. Simpson sets an NFL single game rushing record of 250 yards against New England in Foxboro. Then Simpson finishes the season with 2,003 yards, an NFL record that will last until 1984. (1973)

Buffalo claims the AFC East title with a 9-5-0 record. In their first postseason playoff appearance since 1966, the Bills fall to Pittsburgh 32-14 in the first round. (1974)

O.J. Simpson, for the third time earns AFC Offensive Player of the Year honors. (1975)

Former all-pro center for Green Bay, Jim Ringo, signs as head coach after Lou Saban resigns. (1976)

O.J. Simpson breaks his own single-game rushing mark when he gains 273 yards against the Lions He also gains more than 1,000 yards rushing for the fifth season. (1976)

Chuck Knox replaces the fired Jim Ringo as head coach. (1978)

O.J. Simpson is traded to the 49ers (1978)

Joe Ferguson becomes the first Bill to pass for more than 3,000 yards in a season (3,572 on 238 completions). (1979)

Jerry Butler sets a club record by gaining 255 yards on pass receptions in a game against the Jets. (1979)

The 1980s

After four losing seasons Buffalo wins 11 of 16 games and the AFC East title. The Bills, however, cannot get by the San Diego Chargers in the playoffs, losing 20-14. (1980)

Chuck Knox is named AFC Coach of the Year. (1980)

The Bills make it to the playoffs for the second year in a row, their record of 10-6-0 qualifying them for a

One of the greatest ever to carry the ball in the pro ranks, O. J. Simpson sets out on a kickoff for the Bills. (Fred Roe)

wild card entry. They defeat the Jets 31–27, but fall to the Bengals 28–21. (1981)

Frank Lewis sets two club standards by catching 70 passes for 1,244 yards. (1981)

For the first (and only) time in team history, home attendance exceeds 600,000 (601,712). (1981)

Kay Stephenson becomes the new head coach of the Bills. (1983)

Joe Ferguson sets single-game records by completing 38 passes for 419 yards in a game against the Dolphins. (1983)

Hank Bullough replaces Kay Stephenson as head coach. (1985)

Jim Kelly sets a club passing mark when he completes 285 passes in a single season. (1986)

Marv Levy is hired to replace Hank Bullough as head coach. (1987)

Memorable Years

Year	Record	Achievement
1963	7–6–1	Playoff participant
1964	12–2–0	AFL champion
1965	10–3–1	AFL champion
1966	9–4–1	AFL runner-up
1974	9–5–0	Wild card entry
1980	11–5–0	Division champion
1981	10–6–0	Wild card entry

Top Coaches

	Record	Win Percentage	Years
Lou Saban	38–18–3	.678	1962–65
Chuck Knox	38–38–0	.500	1978–82

Record Holders

Career

Rushing yards	O.J. Simpson (1969–77)	10,183
Passing yards	Joe Ferguson (1973–84)	27,590
Passing TD's	Joe Ferguson (1973–84)	181
Pass receptions	Elbert Dubenion (1960–67)	296
Receiving yards	Elbert Dubenion (1960–67)	5,304
Interceptions	George Byrd (1964–70)	40
Field Goals	John Leypoldt (1971–76)	74
Total TD's	O.J. Simpson (1969–77)	70
Total points	O.J. Simpson (1969–77)	420

Season

Rushing yards	O.J. Simpson, 1973	2,003
Passing yards	Joe Ferguson, 1981	3,652
Passing TD's	Joe Ferguson, 1983	26
Pass receptions	Frank Lewis, 1981	70
Receiving yards	Frank Lewis, 1981	1,244
Interceptions	Billy Atkins, 1961	10
	Tom Janik, 1967	10
Field Goals	Pete Gogolak, 1965	28
Total TD's	O.J. Simpson, 1975	23
Total points	O.J. Simpson, 1975	138

Game

Rushing yards	O.J. Simpson, 11/25/76	273
Passing yards	Joe Ferguson, 10/9/83	419
Passing TD's	Joe Ferguson, 9/23/79	5
	Joe Ferguson, 10/9/83	5
Pass receptions	Greg Bell, 9/8/85	13
Receiving yards	Jerry Butler, 9/23/79	255
Interceptions	many times	3
Field Goals	Pete Gogolak, 12/5/65	5
Total TD's	Cookie Gilchrist, 12/8/63	5
Total points	Cookie Cilchrist, 12/8/63	30

All-Pros

Year	Player	Position	Year	Player	Position	Year	Player	Position
1960	Archie Matsos	LB		Billy Shaw	G	1973	Robert James	CB
	Richie McCabe	DB		Mike Stratton	LB		Reggie McKenzie	G
	LaVerne Torczon	DE	1965	George Byrd	CB		O.J. Simpson	RB
1961	Billy Atkins	DB		Jack Kemp	QB	1974	Tony Greene	S
1962	Stew Barber	T		George Saimes	S		Robert James	CB
	Cookie Gilchrist	FB		Tom Sestak	DT		O.J. Simpson	RB
	Harold Olson	T		Billy Shaw	G	1975	Joe DeLamielleure	G
	Billy Shaw	G		Mike Stratton	LB		O.J. Simpson	RB
1963	Stew Barber	T	1966	George Byrd	CB	1976	Joe DeLamielleure	G
	Elbert Dubenion	WR		Jim Dunaway	DT		O.J. Simpson	RB
	Tom Sestak	DT		Ron McDole	DE	1977	Joe DeLamielleure	G
	Billy Shaw	G		Billy Shaw	G	1978	Joe DeLamielleure	G
1964	Stew Barber	T		Mike Stratton	LB	1979	Joe DeLamielleure	G
	Cookie Gilchrist	FB	1967	George Saimes	S	1981	Fred Smerlas	DT
	George Saimes	S	1969	George Byrd	CB	1982	Fred Smerlas	DT
	Tom Sestak	DT	1972	O.J. Simpson	RB			

Cincinnati Bengals

200 Riverfront Stadium
Cincinnati, Ohio 45202

Stadium: Riverfront Stadium (capacity 59,754)

Training camp: Wilmington College
                        Wilmington, Ohio 45177

Colors: black, orange and white

Historical Highlights

The 1960s

Headed by Paul Brown, famed former coach of the Cleveland Browns, a group of investors win a franchise for Cincinnati. Brown names the team the Bengals. (1967)

Cincinnati is booked in the AFC West, joining the Chargers, Chiefs, Broncos, and Raiders. (1968)

Cincinnati wins only 3 of 14 games its first season but running back Paul Robinson leads the AFC in rushing with 1,023 yards and is named the league's Rookie of the year. (1968)

Rookie Greg Cook is the top-rated quaterback in the AFL. Linebacker Bill Bergey is honored as the AFL Defensive Rookie of the Year. Paul Brown is named AFL Coach of the Year. (1969)

The 1970s

In the NFL realignment the Bengals are assigned to the AFC Central Division along with the Steelers, Browns, and Oilers. (1970)

With an 8-6-0 record, the Bengals become the first third-year expansion team to win a division title when they take the AFC Central. Their luck does not follow them to the playoffs, however, where they fall to Baltimore 17-0. (1970)

Paul Brown is honored as AFC Coach of the Year. (1970)

Quarterback Ken Anderson from tiny Augustana College in Rock Island, Illinois, is secured in the NFL draft. (1971)

The Bengals win their second AFC divisional title after splitting their first eight games, and sweeping their last six to finish the year with a 10-4-0 record. The club is again thwarted in the playoffs, losing this time to Miami 24-16. Running back Bobbie Clark is named AFC Rookie of the Year, finishing the season

Ken Anderson (Pro Football Hall of Fame)

with 988 yards rushing and 45 pass receptions, while tandem back Essex Johnson gains 997 yards rushing. Issac Curtis gains more yards receiving (843) and sports the best receiving average, 18.7 yards per reception, in the AFC. (1973)

Despite a mediocre season for the Bengals, quarterback Ken Anderson is the top passer in the NFL completing 213 passes for 2,667 yards and 18 TDs. His 64.9 percentage is also a club record. Lemar Parrish leads the NFL in punt returns, averaging 18.8 yards on 18 returns. (1974)

Cincinnati posts a season record of 11-3-0, its best regular season showing to date and qualifies as the AFC wild card team in the playoffs. The Bengals fall a third time to Oakland 31-28. (1975)

Ken Anderson repeats as the league's top passer, this time gaining 3,169 yards on 228 completions, including 21 touchdown tosses. (1975)

After 41 seasons of coaching, Paul Brown announces his retirement and names Bill Johnson, his line coach, to replace him. Brown continues to serve as general manager and vice president of the Bengals. (1976)

Quarterback Ken Anderson is absent from the first four regular season games and Bill Johnson is replaced as head coach after the Bengals get off to a 0-5 start. Homer Rice is the new head coach. (1978)

For the second straight year the Bengals post a meager 4-12 record. Rice is replaced as head coach by former Cleveland Browns coach, Forrest Gregg. (1979)

The 1980s

Wearing their new tiger-striped helmets, the Bengals triumph in the AFC Central, their 12–4–0 record the best in club history. (1981)

Ken Anderson once again leads the league in passing with a 98.5 rating, his highest career mark, completing 300 passes for 3,754 yards and 29 TDs, and is named AFC Offensive Player of the Year. (1981)

The Bengals snap their postseason losing streak by defeating the Buffalo Bills in the AFC divisional playoff game 28–21. Then, despite a howling wind and sub-zero temperatures at Riverfront Stadium in Cincinnati, the Bengals take the AFC crown, defeating San Diego 27–7, and earn a trip to Super bowl XVI. (1981)

At the Pontiac Silverdome in Super Bowl XVI, a half-time deficit of 20–0 overwhelms the Bengals, and they fall to the San Francisco 49ers 26–21. (1982)

Finishing the strike-shortened season with a 7–2–0 mark, second only to the Raiders, the Bengals again proceed to the playoffs, but lose to the Jets 44–17. (1982)

Ken Anderson again takes passing honors in the AFC with 218 completions for 2,495 yards and 12 TDs. His completion percentage of 70.6 is by far the best in the entire NFL. (1982)

Immediately after the season, Forrest Gregg resigns as head coach to return to Green Bay where he was a perennial All-Pro offensive tackle. He is replaced by Sam Wyche. (1983)

The Bengals miss taking the division by a game, their 8–8–0 just less than the 9–7–0 Steelers. (1984)

Quarterback Boomer Esiason, in his first year as a full-time starter, ranks second in passing in the AFC, completing 251 for 3,443 yards and 12 touchdowns. (1985)

Cincinnati posts its first winning season since 1982 with a record of 10–6–0, but because of qualifiers the team loses out on a wild card entry in the playoffs. (1986)

James Brooks sets a club rushing record by gaining 1,087 yards. (1986)

Wide receiver Cris Collinsworth holds Bengals records for the most yards receiving in a season— 1,130, and in a game—216. (Cincinnati Bengals)

Memorable Years

Year	Record	Achievement
1970	8–6–0	Division champion
1973	10–4–0	Division champion
1975	11–3–0	Wild card entry
1981	12–4–0	NFL runner-up
1974	9–5–0	Wild card entry
1982	7–2–0	Playoff tournament participant

Record Holders

Career		
Rushing yards	Pete Johnson (1977–83)	5,421
Passing yards	Ken Anderson (1973–85)	32,667
Passing TD's	Ken Anderson (1973–85)	196
Pass receptions	Isaac Curtis (1973–84)	420
Receiving yards	Isaac Curtis (1973-84)	7,106
Interceptions	Ken Riley (1969–83)	63
Field Goals	Horst Muhlmann (1969–74)	120
Total TD's	Pete Johnson (1977-83)	70
Total points	Horst Muhlmann (1969–74)	549

Season		
Rushing yards	Pete Johnson, 1981	1,077
Passing yards	Ken Anderson, 1981	3,754
Passing TD's	Dan Ross, 1981	71
Pass receptions	Ken Anderson, 1981	29
Receiving yards	Cris Collinsworth, 1983	1,130
Interceptions	Ken Riley, 1976	9
Field Goals	Horst Muhlmann, 1972	27
Total TD's	Pete Johnson, 1981	16
Total points	Jim Breech, 1985	120

Game		
Rushing yards	Pete Johnson, 12/17/78	160
Passing yards	Ken Anderson, 11/17/75	447
Passing TD's	many times	4
Pass receptions	many times	10
Receiving yards	Cris Collinsworth, 10/2/83	216
Interceptions	many times	3
Field Goals	Horst Muhlmann, 11/8/70, 9/24/72	5
Total TD's	Larry Kinnebrew, 10/28/84	4
Total points	Larry Kinnebrew, 10/28/84	24

Top Coaches

	Record	Win Percentage	Years
Forrest Gregg	34–27–0	.557	1980–83
Sam Wyche	25–23–0	.520	1984–86
Bill Johnson	18–15–0	.545	1976–78

All-Pros

Year	Player	Position
1968	Paul Robinson	RB
1969	Bob Trumpy	TE
1970	Dave Lewis	P
1972	Tommy Casanova	S
1981	Ken Anderson	QB
	Anthony Munoz	T
	Pat McInally	P
1982	Anthony Munoz	T
	Louis Breeden	CB
1983	Anthony Munoz	T
	Ken Riley	CB
1985	Anthony Munoz	T

Cleveland Browns

Tower B
Cleveland Stadium
Cleveland, Ohio 44114

Stadium: Cleveland Stadium (capacity 80,098)

Training camp: Lakeland Community College
Mentor, Ohio 44060

Colors: seal brown, orange and white

Historical Highlights

The 1940s

Cleveland is chosen as one of eight charter cities of the new All-America Football Conference, the franchise to be owned by Arthur "Mickey" McBride. Paul Brown is hired as coach and general manager. Quarterback Otto Graham is the first Cleveland player to be signed. (1946)

The Browns win their first AAFC Western Conference title with a record of 12-2-0, having outscored their opponents 423-137, and meet the New York Yankees for the league championship. The Browns defeat the Yankees 14-9 on a TD pass from Otto Graham to Dante Lavelli in the final period to take the premiere crown. (1946)

Cleveland repeats as Western Conference champs, this time with a record of 12-1-1. In the AAFC title game, the Browns again prevail over the Yankees, their two touchdowns in the 14-3 victory coming on runs by Otto Graham and Special Delivery Jones. (1947)

An undefeated Cleveland Browns, 14-0-0, wins its third consecutive conference championship, and keeps its season's perfect record by demolishing the Buffalo Bills in the title contest 40-7. Marion Motley scores three touchdowns and rushes for 133 yards (a 9.5 yard average) to highlight the Browns attack. (1948)

With the AAFC reduced to a conferenceless seven team league, the Browns end up on top again with a record of 9-1-2. In a special championship game Cleveland defeats the second place San Francisco 49ers (9-3-0) by a score of 21-7 on touchdown runs by Special Delivery Jones, Marion Motley, and Dub Jones. (1949)

The 1950s

The AAFC goes out of business but the Browns are brought into the NFL to play in the American Confer-

Long the guiding force of Cleveland, Paul Brown, with his quarterback Frank Ryan. (Fred Roe)

ence along with the Giants, Eagles, Redskins, Steelers, and Chicago Cardinals. (1950)

With a 10-2-0 season mark, the Browns tie with the New York Giants for the Eastern title and they win the playoff 8-3. Cleveland then defeats the Los Angeles Rams 30-28 and brings home its first NFL championship. Lou Groza kicks the game- and title-winning field goal with 28 seconds to go in the final period. (1950)

The largest crowd ever to watch a Browns game fills Soldier Field in Chicago, 92,180, to watch Cleveland drub the College All-Stars 33-0. (1951)

Dub Jones ties Ernie Nevers' NFL record of six touchdowns in one game when he runs for four and catches passes for two against the Bears. (1951)

Cleveland wins 11 of its 12 games and its second straight conference title. But, for the first time since the team was enfranchised in 1946, the Browns are not the league titleholder, losing the championship to the Rams 24-17. (1951)

Otto Graham, in a game against the Colts, sets a club record by passing for 401 yards, a standard that would remain unequalled until 1981. (1952)

The Browns make it three NFL conference crowns in three years with a record of 8-4-0. They fall to the Lions, however, in the league championship game 17-7. (1952)

Mickey McBride sells the team to a syndicate headed by David Jones for $600,000, then the highest price ever paid for a pro football franchise. (1953)

Cleveland easily takes its fourth consecutive conference title with a record of 11-1-0. But just as they had the year before, the Browns lose out to the Lions in the title game, this time 17-16. (1953)

Making it five conference crowns in a row, Cleveland racks up a record of 9-3-0 and the right to face the Lions once again for the league championship. This time the Browns, with Otto Graham running for three touchdowns and passing for another three, devastate Detroit 56-10. (1954)

The Browns repeat as NFL champs, taking their conference with a record of 9-2-1 and then destroying the Rams 38-14. Playing his last pro football game, Otto Graham runs for two touchdowns and throws two TD passes against the Rams. (1955)

Cleveland drafts future Hall of Famers in back-to-back years: Jim Brown and Bobby Mitchell. (1957-58)

Jim Brown sets a NFL record by rushing for 1,527 yards in a single season and is the first Cleveland rusher ever to gain more than 1,000 yards in a season. (1958)

The 1960s

Art Modell, a former television and advertising executive, buys the Browns. (1961)

Paul Brown is axed and former Browns' assistant coach, Blanton Collier, is named head coach. (1963)

Jim Brown breaks his own NFL rushing record when he gains 1,863 yards (a 6.4 yard average per carry). (1963)

Winning the division title over the New York Giants by a score of 52-40, the Browns move forward to the championship game and capture the NFL crown by defeating the Baltimore Colts 27-0, their first league title since 1955. (1964)

Behind the running of Jim Brown, Cleveland again gets to the NFL title game. The Browns, however, are beaten there by Green Bay 23-12. League MVP Jim Brown retires after the season. (1965)

After the realignment of the NFL, the Browns are placed in the Century Division with the Giants, Steelers, and Cardinals and win it with a record of 9-5-0. Cleveland falls to the Cowboys in the playoffs 52-10. (1967)

The Browns take their division again, posting a season record of 10-4. Although they defeat Dallas in the first playoff game, the Browns are eliminated by Baltimore 34-0 in the NFL title tilt. (1968)

Cleveland wins its third consecutive division crown but the Browns lose to Minnesota 27-7 in the championship game. (1969)

The 1970s

The Browns are shifted into the AFC Central Division, joining the Steelers, Bengals, and Oilers, and finish second with a season mark of 7-7-0. (1970)

Cleveland quarterback and Hall of Famer Otto Graham hurls one of the more than 2,500 career passes he tossed for the Browns, this one against the New York Yankees in 1948. (Pro Football Hall of Fame)

High-stepping Jim Brown gains a few yards for Cleveland before an extraordinarily sparse crowd in Dallas in the early 60s. The teammate he is vaulting over is Ray Renfro and the Cowboy hoping to make the tackle is Tom Franckhauser. (Dallas Cowboys)

Head coaching responsibilities are given to Nick Skorich, a former Browns' assistant. Under Skorich's guidance the team captures its first AFC Central crown with a record of 9–5–0. (1971)

The Browns qualify for postseason play with a mark of 10–4–0, but lose to the eventual NFL champions, the Miami Dolphins, in the playoffs 20–14. (1972)

Browns offensive line coach Forrest Gregg assumes the head coaching job. (1975)

Running back Greg Pruitt racks up his third consecutive 1,000 yard rushing season. (1977)

Sam Rutigliano becomes the first assistant coach from outside the Browns' organization to assume head coaching duties. (1978)

Brian Sipe, in his second year as starting quarterback, sets two club standards by completing 286 passes for 3,793 yards (the first Brown to surpass 3,000 yards). (1979)

The 1980s

Cleveland posts an 11–5–0 season mark to win the AFC Central title, but loses to the eventual Super Bowl champion Oakland Raiders in their first playoff game 14–12. (1980)

Brian Sipe sets three Cleveland standards by completing 337 passes for 4,132 yards and 30 touchdowns and is chosen the league's MVP. (1980)

Cleveland replaces head coach Sam Rutigliano with defensive coordinator Marty Schottenheimer after the Browns post a midseason record of 1–7. They finish the season at only 5–11–0. (1984)

Capturing their third Central Division title, the Browns face Miami in the playoffs and fall 24–21. (1985)

For only the third time in NFL history, teammates rush for over 1,000 yards in a single season when Cleveland's Kevin Mack gains 1,104 and Earnest Byner 1,002. (1985)

Cleveland posts a record of 12–4–0, the best in the entire AFC. (1986)

The Browns, who have not won a playoff game since 1969, come from behind to tie the Jets in the divisional playoff game with just seven seconds left in the game, then win it 23–20 with a field goal from Mark Moseley in the second overtime period. (1987)

In the battle for the 1986 AFC title and the right to go to the Super Bowl, the Browns again go into overtime, but this time they lose out 23–20 to the Denver Broncos. (1987)

Memorable Years

Year	Record	Achievement
1946	12–2–0	AAFC champion
1947	12–1–1	AAFC champion
1948	14–0–0	AAFC champion
1949	9–1–2	AAFC champion
1950	10–2–0	NFL champion
1951	11–1–0	NFL runner-up
1952	8–4–0	NFL runner-up
1953	11–1–0	NFL runner-up
1954	9–3–0	NFL champion
1955	9–2–1	NFL champion
1957	9–2–1	NFL runner-up
1958	9–3–0	Playoff participant
1964	10–3–1	NFL champion
1965	11–3–0	NFL runner-up
1967	9–5–0	Division champion
1968	10–4–0	NFL runner-up
1969	10–3–1	NFL runner-up
1971	9–5–0	Division champion
1972	10–4–0	Wild card entry
1980	11–5–0	Division champion
1982	4–5–0	Playoff tournament participant
1985	8–8–0	Division champion
1986	12–4–0	AFC runner-up

Top Coaches

	Record	Win Percentage	Years
Paul Brown	167–54–8	.756	1946–62
Blanton Collier	79–40–2	.664	1963–70
Sam Rutigliano	47–52–0	.474	1978–84
Nick Skorich	30–26–2	.536	1971–74
Marty Schottenheimer	27–15–0	.643	1984–86

Record Holders

Career		
Rushing yards	Jim Brown (1957–65)	12,312
Passing yards	Brian Sipe (1974–83)	23,713
Passing TD's	Brian Sipe (1974–83)	154
Pass receptions	Ozzie Newsome (1978–85)	502
Receiving yards	Ozzie Newsome (1978–85)	6,281
Interceptions	Thom Darden (1972–74, 76–81)	45
Field Goals	Lou Groza (1950–59, 1961–67)	234
Total TD's	Jim Brown (1957–65)	126
Total points	Lou Groza (1950–59, 1961–67)	1,349

Season		
Rushing yards	Jim Brown, 1963	1,863
Passing yards	Brian Sipe, 1980	4,132
Passing TD's	Brian Sipe, 1980	30
Pass receptions	Ozzie Newsome, 1983, 1984	89
Receiving yards	Paul Warfield, 1968	1,067
Interceptions	Thom Darden, 1978	10
Field Goals	Matt Bahr, 1984	24
Total TD's	Jim Brown, 1965	21
Total points	Jim Brown, 1965	126

Game		
Rushing yards	Jim Brown, 11/24/57	237
	Jim Brown, 11/19/61	237
Passing yards	Brian Sipe, 10/25/81	444
Passing TD's	Frank Ryan, 12/12/64	5
	Bill Nelsen, 11/2/69	5
	Brian Sipe, 10/7/79	5
Pass receptions	Ozzie Newsome, 10/14/84	14
Receiving yards	Ozzie Newsome, 10/14/84	191
Interceptions	many times	3
Field Goals	Don Cockcroft, 10/19/75	5
Total TD's	Dub Jones, 11/25/51	6
Total points	Dub Jones, 11/25/51	36

All-Pros

Year	Player	Position	Year	Player	Position	Year	Player	Position
1950	Marion Motley	RB		Lou Groza	T-K	1966	Leroy Kelly	RB
1951	Otto Graham	QB		Ron McDole	DE	1967	Leroy Kelly	RB
	Dub Jones	RB	1957	Jim Brown	RB		Gene Hickerson	G
1952	Lou Groza	T	1958	Jim Brown	RB	1968	Leroy Kelly	RB
	Bill Willis	MG	1959	Jim Brown	RB		Gene Hickerson	G
	Frank Gatski	C		Jim Ray Smith	G	1969	Gary Collins	WR
	Len Ford	DE	1960	Jim Brown	RB		Gene Hickerson	G
1953	Otto Graham	QB		Jim Ray Smith	G	1970	Gene Hickerson	G
	Frank Gatski	C	1961	Jim Brown	RB	1976	Jerry Sherk	DT
	Lou Groza	T		Jim Ray Smith	G	1978	Thom Darden	S
	Len Ford	DE	1963	Jim Brown	RB	1979	Ozzie Newsome	TE
	Bill Willis	MG		Dick Schafrath	T	1980	Brian Sipe	QB
1954	Otto Graham	QB	1964	Jim Brown	RB		Joe DeLamielleure	G
	Len Ford	DE		Dick Schafrath	G-T		Lyle Alzado	DE
	Lou Groza	T-K	1965	Jim Brown	RB	1983	Chip Banks	LB
1955	Otto Graham	QB		Dick Schafrath	T	1984	Ozzie Newsome	TE

Denver Broncos

5700 Logan Street
Denver, Colorado 80216

Stadium: Denver Mile High Stadium
(capacity 75,100)

Training camp: University of Northern Colorado
Greeley, Colorado 80639

Colors: orange, blue and white

Historical Highlights

The 1960s

Denver is selected as the site for charter membership in the American Football League, the franchise awarded to Bob Howsam and other investors. Frank Filchock is named first head coach of the team. The Broncos are placed in the AFL's Western Division with Dallas, Oakland, and Los Angeles. (1960)

The Broncos defeat Oakland 31–24 at home for their first NFL victory. (1960)

Quarterback Frank Tripucka completes 248 passes, a club record that will stand until John Elway breaks it in 1985. (1960)

A new syndicate headed by Cal Kunz and Gerry Phipps purchases the Broncos. (1961)

Frank Filchock is fired and Jack Faulkner assumes head coaching duties (1962)

After Denver posts its first .500 season (7–7–0), Jack Faulkner is named AFL Coach of the Year. (1962)

Mac Speedie is named head coach after Jack Faulkner is released. (1964)

Ray Malavasi becomes interim head coach of the Broncos during the season after Mac Speedie resigns; and, after Denver's last game, Lou Saban is hired as head coach and general manager. (1966)

The Broncos' home field is officially named Denver Mile High Stadium. (1968)

The 1970s

Lou Saban resigns his position as head coach, remaining as general manager, and appoints offensive line coach Jerry Smith interim head coach. (1971)

John Ralston is named Denver's new head coach and later assumes general manager duties as well. (1972)

John Elway

The Broncos enjoy their first winning season ever, 7–5–2. (1973)

John Ralston wins the honor of AFC Coach of the Year. (1973)

Otis Armstrong takes the NFL rushing title and finishes the season with 1,407 yards, joining only a half dozen players to average more than 100 yards a game in NFL history, and becoming the first Bronco to rush for more than 1,000 yards in a season. (1974)

Broncos kicker Jim Turner becomes only the fifth player in pro football history to surpass 1,200 career points. (1976)

John Ralston resigns as head coach and former Bronco assistant coach, Red Miller, is named Denver's eighth head coach. (1977)

The Broncos clinch a playoff berth and the AFC Western Division championship, both firsts in club history, posting their best season record ever, 12–2–0, and tying the Dallas Cowboys for the best record in the NFL. (1977)

Lyle Alzado is named the AFC's Defensive Player of the Year. (1977)

Red Miller wins AFC Coach of the Year honors and defensive end Lyle Alzado is named the AFC's Defensive Player of the Year. (1977)

The Broncos are victorious over the Pittsburgh Steelers 34–21 in the first round of playoff action, a game in which they draw the largest crowd ever to watch a sporting event in the state of Colorado, 75,011. Then the Broncos take on the NFL's defending champion Oakland Raiders and win 20–17 to earn a trip to the Super Bowl in New Orleans. (1977)

Denver falls to Dallas in Super Bowl XII 27–10. (1978)

The Broncos win 10 of their 16 games and their second straight division championship. But Denver loses to the eventual Super Bowl victors, the Pittsburgh Steelers, 33–10 in the playoffs. (1978)

An all-time high of seven Bronco players are selected for the Pro Bowl: Lyle Alzado, Randy Gradishar, Tom Jackson, Riley Odoms, Bill Thompson, Rick Upchurch, and Louis Wright. (1979)

Setting an NFL record in a game against New England, Bronco Rick Upchurch becomes the all-time pro football top punt returner, surpassing Emlen Tunnell's record of 2,209 yards. (1979)

The Broncos secure a playoff berth for the third year in a row, but lose to Houston 13–7 in the wild card playoff game. (1979)

The 1980s

The Broncos are purchased by Edgar F. Kaiser, Jr., from principal owners Gerald and Allan Phipps. (1981)

Dan Reeves is named head coach of the Broncos. (1981)

The Broncos sport a record of 10–6–0, but lose out on a wild card entry on qualifiers. (1981)

The Broncos acquire quarterback John Elway, the first player taken in the NFL draft, from the Colts, and sign him to a five-year contract. (1983)

Behind the passing of John Elway, the 9–7–0 Broncos clinch a playoff berth. But Denver loses to Seattle 13–7 in the wild card game. (1983)

New Broncos owner, Pat Bowlen, assumes the title of president and chief executive officer of the club. (1984)

The club sets a team record of 10 straight victories and captures the AFC West title with a record of 13–3–0. Denver, however, falls to Pittsburgh 24–17 in the divisional playoff game. (1984)

Dan Reeves is named the AFC's Coach of the Year. (1984)

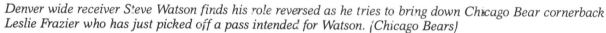

Denver wide receiver Steve Watson finds his role reversed as he tries to bring down Chicago Bear cornerback Leslie Frazier who has just picked off a pass intended for Watson. (Chicago Bears)

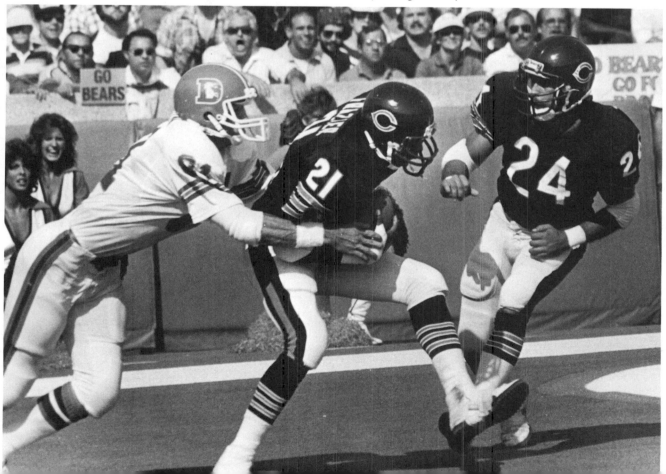

The Broncos post a record of 11–5–0, but still do not qualify for a playoff berth, losing out to the Patriots and Jets who won on tie-breaking factors. (1985)

John Elway sets team records by completing 327 passes for 3,891 yards. (1985)

The Broncos win the AFC West with a record of 11–5–0. (1986)

Running back Sammy Winder leads the AFC in touchdowns scored, 84 points on nine rushing and nine receiving TDs. (1986)

Denver defeats the Patriots, the AFC's representative in the previous Super Bowl 22–17, and then edges the Cleveland Browns in overtime 23–20 to take the AFC crown and earn their second invitation to the Super Bowl. (1986)

The Broncos fall to the New York Giants in Super Bowl XXI at the Rose Bowl in Pasadena, California, by the score of 39–20. (1987)

Memorable Years

Year	Record	Achievement
1977	12–2–0	NFL runner-up
1978	10–6–0	Division champion
1979	10–6–0	Wild card entry
1983	9–7–0	Wild card entry
1984	13–3–0	Division champion
1986	11–5–0	NFL runner-up

Top Coaches

	Record	Win Percentage	Years
Dan Reeves	56–35–0	.615	1981–86
Robert "Red" Miller	42–25–0	.627	1977–80
John Ralston	34–33–3	.507	1972–76

Record Holders

Career

Rushing yards	Floyd Little (1967–75)	6,323
Passing yards	Craig Morton (1977–82)	11,895
Passing TD's	Craig Morton (1977–82)	74
Pass receptions	Lionel Taylor (1960–66)	543
Receiving yards	Lionel Taylor (1960–66)	6,872
Interceptions	Goose Gonsoulin (1960–66)	43
Field Goals	Jim Turner (1971–79)	151
Total TD's	Floyd Little (1967–75)	54
Total points	Jim Turner (1971–79)	742

Season

Rushing yards	Otis Armstrong, 1974	1,407
Passing yards	John Elway, 1985	3,891
Passing TD's	Frank Tripucka, 1960	24
Pass receptions	Lionel Taylor, 1961	100
Receiving yards	Steve Watson, 1981	1,244
Interceptions	Goose Gonsoulin, 1960	11
Field Goals	Gene Mingo, 1962	27
Total TD's	Floyd Little, 1972, 1973	13
	Steve Watson, 1981	13
Total points	Gene Mingo, 1962	137

Game

Rushing yards	Otis Armstrong, 12/8/74	183
Passing yards	Frank Tripucka, 9/15/62	447
Passing TD's	Frank Tripucka, 10/28/62	5
	John Elway, 11/18/84	5
Pass receptions	Lionel Taylor, 11/29/64	13
	Bobby Anderson, 9/30/73	13
Receiving yards	Lionel Taylor, 11/27/60	199
Interceptions	Goose Gonsoulin, 9/18/60	4
	Willie Brown, 11/15/64	4
Field Goals	Gene Mingo, 10/6/63	5
	Rich Karlis, 11/20/83	5
Total TD's	many times	3
Total points	Gene Mingo, 12/10/60	21

All-Pros

Year	Player	Position	Year	Player	Position	Year	Player	Position
1960	Lionel Taylor	E	1965	Cookie Gilchrist	RB		Billy Thompson	S
	Bud McFadin	DT		Lionel Taylor	WR	1978	Randy Gradishar	LB
	Goose Gonsoulin	DB		Eldon Danenhauer	T		Louis Wright	CB
1961	Lionel Taylor	E	1969	Floyd Little	RB		Rick Upchurch	KR
	Bud McFadin	DT		Rich Jackson	DE	1979	Randy Gradishar	LB
1962	Eldon Danenhauer	T	1970	Rich Jackson	DE		Louis Wright	CB
	Bud McFadin	DT	1974	Otis Armstrong	RB		Rick Upchurch	KR
	Goose Gonsoulin	DB		Riley Odoms	TE	1981	Bob Swenson	LB
	Bob Zeman	DB	1977	Lyle Alzado	DE	1982	Rick Upchurch	KR
1963	Goose Gonsoulin	DB		Randy Gradishar	LB		Luke Prestridge	P
1964	Willie Brown	CB		Tom Jackson	LB	1985	Karl Mecklenberg	LB

Houston Oilers

Box 1516
Houston, Texas 77001

Stadium: Astrodome (capacity 50,496)

Training camp: Angelo State University
San Angelo, Texas 76901

Colors: columbia blue, scarlet and white

Historical Highlights

The 1960s

A charter American Football League franchise is awarded to K.S. "Bud" Adams, a Texas oil magnate, for Houston, who names the team the Oilers. (1960)

Louisiana State All-American back and Heisman Trophy winner of 1959, Billy Cannon, is selected by Houston and signed. Veteran pro quarterback and place kicker George Blanda is also signed. (1960)

The Oilers name their first head coach, Lou Rymkus, a former Cleveland Browns tackle. (1960)

The Oilers are victorious over Oakland in their first regular season home game 37-22. The first Oiler touchdown is scored by Charley Hennigan on a 43-yard pass from George Blanda. (1960)

Houston snares the AFL Eastern Division title for the Oilers with a record of 10-4-0. (1960)

The Oilers win the first AFL championship, defeating the Los Angeles Chargers 24-16 at Jeppesen Stadium in Houston. George Blanda completes 16 of 31 passes for 301 yards and three TDs, but Billy Cannon is named the game's MVP. The winning share to each player is $1,016.42. (1961)

Lou Rymkus is replaced as head coach by Wally Lemm. (1961)

George Blanda ties an all-time pro record shared by Sid Luckman of the Bears and Adrian Burk of the Eagles by throwing seven touchdown passes against the New York Titans in a 49-13 Houston win. (1961)

Houston, after winning its last nine games in a row, takes its second straight Eastern Division crown with a record of 10-3-1. The Oilers also become the first pro team in history to score 500 points in one season (513 points in 14 games). (1961)

George Blanda sets an all-time pro record by passing for 36 TDs, and Charley Hennigan gains 1,746 yards

Houston's George Blanda unleashes a pass in the 1962 AFL championship game. Despite passing for 261 yards and a touchdown, Blanda and the Oilers fell to the Dallas Texans 20-17. (Pro Football Hall of Fame)

on pass receptions, the most up to that time in pro football. (1961)

The Oilers defeat San Diego and take their second AFL title, winning 10-3 at San Diego, the winning margin coming on a 35-yard touchdown pass from George Blanda to Billy Cannon. Cannon repeats as MVP, and the winning players take home $1,724. (1961)

Frank "Pop" Ivy is named head coach after Wally Lemm resigns in order to assume head coaching duties for the St. Louis Cardinals. (1962)

The Oilers win their third consecutive Eastern Division title with an 11-3-0 season, but are stopped in the AFL title game by the Dallas Texans 20-17 in double overtime. A touchdown pass and a field goal from George Blanda in the fourth period tied the game for Houston, but it was lost on a 25-yard field goal in the sixth period of play. (1962)

Charles Tolar is the first Oiler to rush for more than 1,000 yards in a season (1,012 on 244 carries). (1962)

Frank Ivy is relieved of his duties as head coach and Bud Adams appoints Sammy Baugh to the position. (1964)

An AFL record is set by Houston rookie Sid Banks

with a 91-yard touchdown run from scrimmage against the New York Jets. (1964)

Sammy Baugh gives up the head coaching duties to Hugh "Bones" Taylor. (1965)

The Oilers sign a five-year lease with Rice University for the use of Rice Stadium after announcing that the team will not play in the Harris County Domed Stadium (Astrodome). (1965)

Clinching the Eastern Division title with a record of 9–4–1 the Oilers become the first team to move from the cellar (3–11–0 the year before) to the title in one season. But the Oilers are annihilated by the Raiders 40–7 in the AFL championship game in Oakland. George Blanda, traded to Oakland that year, kicks four field goals and four PATs for the Raiders in the game. (1967)

The Oilers move to new playing quarters at the Astrodome after settling their contract with Rice University. (1968)

The 1970s

Ed Hughes is hired as head coach. (1971)

An interception against Buffalo in the Oilers' 20–14 victory enables safety Ken Houston to tie the all-time pro record of seven touchdowns on interceptions, then shared by Erich Barnes of the Browns and Herb Adderley of the Packers and Cowboys. (1971)

Bill Peterson, former Florida State and Rice University coach, is named head coach of the Oilers. (1972)

After losing 17 of 18 regular season games in a season and a half, Bill Peterson is fired as head coach. Sid Gillman takes on the task of head coach. (1973)

Sid Gillman is named the AFC Coach of the Year. (1974)

Bum Phillips becomes head coach and general manager (1975)

To secure rights to the NFL number one draft choice, the Oilers trade three draft picks and tight end Jimmy Giles to Tampa Bay. Houston then selects University of Texas All-American running back and Heisman Trophy winner, Earl Campbell. (1978)

Rookie Earl Campbell leads the entire NFL and sets club records in two categories when he gains 1,450 yards and scores 13 touchdowns rushing, and is named AFC Offensive Player of the Year. (1978)

Houston gains entry to the AFC wild card game with a record of 10–6–0 where they defeat the Miami Dolphins 17–9. The Oilers earn their way to the AFC title match by decimating New England 31–14 before 61,297 fans in Foxboro, Massachusetts. But in the championship game the Oilers fall to the soon-to-be Super Bowl champion Pittsburgh Steelers 34–5. (1979)

Houston secures a wild card spot in the playoffs posting a record of 11–5–0, the team's most victories since 1962. The Oilers defeat the Denver Broncos 13–7 in their first playoff game, then edge the San Diego Chargers 17–14 to make it to the AFC title tilt for the second straight year in a row. There, however, they again meet the Steelers, who are on their way to a second straight NFL championship, and the Oilers succumb 27–13. (1979)

Safety Mike Reinfeldt is named AFC Defensive Player of the Year. (1979)

The 1980s

Earl Campbell ties O.J. Simpson for an NFL record by rushing for 200-yards in two consecutive games. (1980)

Houston clinches its third wild card playoff berth in as many years, winning 11 of its 16 games. (1980)

Earl Campbell sets an NFL record by rushing for 200 yards in a single game four times in a season. He finishes the season with 1,934 yards, at the time second in NFL history only to O.J. Simpson's 2,003 of 1973. (1980)

The Oilers lose to the Super Bowl bound Oakland Raiders in the playoffs 27–7. (1980)

Bum Phillips is fired as head coach and general manager, and Ed Biles, former defensive coordinator, is hired as head coach. (1981)

The Oilers open a state-of-the-art $2.5 million dollar training facility two miles from the Astrodome. (1982)

Head coach Ed Biles resigns after 2½ years and is replaced on an interim basis by defensive coordinator Chuck Studley. (1983)

Hugh Campbell is named head coach of the Oilers. (1984)

The Oilers select 1983 Heisman Trophy winner Mike Rozier in the first round of the 1984 supplemental draft. (1985)

Hugh Campbell is relieved of his duties as head coach, and defensive coordinator Jerry Glanville is appointed to the post. (1985)

Memorable Years

Year	Record	Achievement
1960	10–4–0	AFL champion
1961	10–3–1	AFL champion
1962	11–3–0	AFL runner-up
1967	9–4–1	AFL runner-up
1969	6–6–2	Playoff participant
1978	10–6–0	AFC runner-up
1979	11–5–0	AFC runner-up
1980	11–5–0	Wild card entry

Top Coaches

	Record	Win Percentage	Years
Bum Phillips	59–38–0	.608	1975–80
Frank "Pop" Ivy	17–12–0	.586	1962–63
Lou Rymkus	12–7–1	.631	1960–61

Record Holders

Career		
Rushing yards	Earl Campbell (1978–84)	8,574
Passing yards	George Blanda (1960–66)	19,149
Passing TD's	George Blanda (1960–66)	165
Pass receptions	Charley Hennigan (1960–66)	410
Receiving yards	Ken Burrough (1971–82)	6,907
Interceptions	Jim Norton (1960–68)	45
Field Goals	George Blanda (1960–66)	91
Total TD's	Earl Campbell (1978–84)	73
Total points	George Blanda (1960–66)	596

Season		
Rushing yards	Earl Campbell, 1980	1,934
Passing yards	Warren Moon, 1984	3,338
Passing TD's	George Blanda, 1961	36
Pass receptions	Charley Hennigan, 1964	101
Receiving yards	Charley Hennigan, 1961	1,746
Interceptions	Fred Glick, 1963	12
	Mike Reinfeldt, 1979	12
Field Goals	Toni Fritsch, 1979	21
Total TD's	Earl Campbell, 1979	19
Total points	George Blanda, 1960	115

Game		
Rushing yards	Billy Cannon, 12/10/61	216
Passing yards	George Blanda, 10/29/61	464
Passing TD's	George Blanda, 11/19/61	7
Pass receptions	Charley Hennigan, 10/13/61	13
Receiving yards	Charley Hennigan, 10/13/61	272
Interceptions	many times	3
Field Goals	Skip Butler, 10/12/75	6
Total TD's	Billy Cannon, 12/10/61	5
Total points	Billy Cannon, 12/10/61	30

All-Pros

Year	Player	Position	Year	Player	Position
1960	Dave Smith	FB		Pat Holmes	DE
	Bill Groman	WR		George Webster	LB
	Rich Michael	T		Miller Farr	CB
1961	George Blanda	QB	1968	George Webster	LB
	Billy Cannon	HB		Miller Farr	CB
	Charley Hennigan	E	1969	George Webster	LB
	Al Jamison	T	1975	Curley Culp	DT
	Don Floyd	DE	1976	Robert Brazile	LB
	Tony Banfield	CB	1977	Billy Johnson	KR
1962	Charley Hennigan	E	1978	Earl Campbell	RB
	Bob Talamini	G		Robert Brazile	LB
	Don Floyd	DE	1979	Earl Campbell	RB
	Tony Banfield	CB		Leon Gray	T
1963	Bob Talimini	G		Robert Brazile	LB
	Freddy Glick	S		Mike Reinfeldt	S
1964	Willie Frazier	TE		Toni Fritsch	K
	Bob Talamini	G	1980	Earl Campbell	RB
1966	Bob Talamini	G		Leon Gray	T
1967	Bob Talamini	G		Robert Brazile	LB

Earl Campbell

Indianapolis Colts

P.O. Box 24100
Indianapolis, Indiana 46224-0100

Stadium: Hoosier Dome (capacity 60,127)

Training camp: Anderson College
                    Anderson, Indiana 46011

Colors: royal blue, white and silver

Historical Highlights

The 1940s

Bud Rodenburg heads a group that purchases the bankrupt Miami Seahawks franchise in the All-America Football Conference and moves it to Baltimore. A fan contest dubs the club the "Colts." (1946)

Cecil Isbell becomes the Colts first head coach. (1947)

The Colts win their first AAFC game 16-7, defeating the Brooklyn Dodgers, before a home crowd of 27,418. (1947)

The Baltimore Colts are reorganized to include over 200 stockholders; Jake Embry is named president of the club and Walt Driskill becomes its general manager. (1948)

Cecil Isbell is dismissed after the first four games of the season and Walt Driskill succeeds him as head coach. (1949)

After the AAFC goes out of business, the Colts enter the NFL for the 1950 season. (1949)

Abraham Watner is named president of the Baltimore club. (1949)

The 1950s

Clem Crowe becomes head coach. (1950)

Abraham Watner withdraws the Colts franchise from the NFL and is paid $50,000 for the players by the NFL. (1951)

NFL commissioner Bert Bell challenges the Baltimore Colts fans to sell 15,000 season tickets in six weeks in order to re-enter the NFL. The quota of the ticket drive is reached in four weeks, three days. (1952)

Carroll Rosenbloom, with a 52 percent controlling interest, heads the new Colts' ownership group. (1953)

The franchise of the defunct Dallas Texans is given to Baltimore. Don Kellet is named president of the new

Baltimore's immortal Johnny Unitas fades back to pass in the 1958 NFL title game against the Giants. With Unitas throwing for 361 yards and a touchdown, the Colts prevailed 23–17.

franchise and Keith Molesworth becomes head coach. The Colts are slotted in the Western Conference along with the Bears, Packers, Lions, Rams and 49ers. (1953)

Weeb Ewbank is named the new head coach of the Colts. (1954)

Johnny Unitas, Raymond Berry, and Alan Ameche sign with the Colts. (1955)

The Colts annihilate the Green Bay Packers 56–0, setting a club record for the largest margin of victory. (1958)

Before a second straight record home crowd of 57,557, the Colts clinch their first Western Conference title, defeating San Francisco 35–27. (1958)

In a sudden death overtime game the Colts defeat the New York Giants at Yankee Stadium 23-17 for the world championship (1958)

The Colts secure their second Western Conference title by defeating the Los Angeles Rams 45-26 in the last game of the season. (1959)

The Colts defeat the New York Giants for the second time in a row, this time 31-16, to earn their second NFL championship. (1959)

The 1960s

Raymond Berry becomes the first (and only) Colt to gain more than 1,000 yards on pass receptions (1,298). (1960)

Weeb Ewbank, head coach since 1953, is replaced as head coach by Don Shula. (1963)

Jim Martin becomes the first Colt to score more than 100 points in a season, racking up 104 (24 FGs 32 PATs). (1963)

Carroll Rosenbloom purchases the remaining shares of the Colts and secures full ownership of the team. (1964)

Baltimore clinches its third Western Conference title in a season in which they win 11 straight games. (1964)

NFL records are set by the Colts' Raymond Berry, who catches his 506th career pass, and Lenny Moore, who scores 20 touchdowns in one season. (1964)

Baltimore is defeated by the Cleveland Browns 27-0 in the NFL title game. (1964)

Baltimore loses to Green Bay in a sudden death playoff for the Western Conference title, a game in which running back Tom Matte is forced to take over quarterbacking duties because of injuries to Johnny Unitas and Gary Cuozzo. (1965)

The Colts win the Coastal Division and earn the right to play for the Western Conference crown. (1968)

Baltimore defeats Minnesota 24-14 in the conference title game. (1968)

The Colts take their first world title since 1959, shutting out the Cleveland Browns 34-0 in the NFL championship game. (1968)

The NFL is realigned and Baltimore, along with Pitts-

Perennial All Pro and Hall of Fame bound Gino Marchetti of the Colts roars out in pursuit of Cowboy ballcarrier Don McIlhenny. Number 17 of Dallas is Dandy Don Meredith, who had just handed off the ball. (Dallas Cowboys)

burgh and Cleveland, is sent over to the AFC which is composed of the teams from the AFL. (1969)

The 1970s

Don Shula resigns to become head coach of the Miami Dolphins and Don McCafferty is named head coach. (1970)

The Colts take the Eastern Division championship and then win the AFC divisional playoff with the Cincinnati Bengals 17-0. (1970)

Colt linebacker Mike Curtis is named AFC Defensive Player of the Year. (1970)

The Colts great pass catcher Raymond Berry gives a state of the art demonstration on how to keep both feet inbounds when snagging a sideline pass in this game circa 1960. (Fred Roe)

Baltimore wins the first championship of the new AFC by defeating Oakland 27-17. (1971)

Jim O'Brien's 32-yard field goal in the final five seconds wins the NFL title for the Colts by defeating Dallas 16-13 in Super Bowl V. (1971)

The Colts qualify for the playoffs as a wild card entry, then defeat Cleveland 20-3 in the AFC playoff game. But Baltimore falls to Miami 21-0 in the AFC title game at the Orange Bowl. (1971)

Carroll Rosenbloom trades Bob Irsay the Colts for the Los Angeles Rams. (1972)

Don McCafferty is replaced after the fifth game of the season by new head coach John Sandusky. (1972)

Howard Schnellenberger becomes the Colts new head coach. (1973)

Schnellenberger is replaced by Joe Thomas as head coach. (1974)

Baltimore's Bert Jones establishes an NFL record by completing 17 consecutive passes, and Lydell Mitchell sets another with 40 carries in a single game. (1974)

The Colts name Ted Marchibroda head coach. (1975)

Lydell Mitchell, rushing for 1,193 yards, becomes the first Colt running back to gain 1,000 yards in a season. (1975)

Baltimore wins the Eastern Division title, posting a season mark of 10-4-0 in a season that featured a streak of nine straight wins. The Colts fall to the soon-to-be Super Bowl champion Pittsburgh Steelers in the playoffs. (1975)

Ted Marchibroda wins AFC Coach of the Year honors. (1975)

Winning 11 of their 14 games, the Colts again prevail in the AFC East, but again they fall to the Steelers in the playoffs, this time 40-14. Quarterback Bert Jones is named AFC Offensive Player of the Year. (1976)

The Colts clinch their third consecutive AFC East title. In a sudden death overtime game, Baltimore comes up short to the Oakland Raiders 37-31. (1977)

Joe Washington leads the NFL in receptions and sets a team record with 82. (1979)

The 1980s

Mike McCormack is named head coach and the Colts move into their new training facility at Owing Mills, Maryland. (1980)

Frank Kush replaces McCormack as head coach. (1981)

The Colts move to Indianapolis to play in the Hoosier Dome. They are greeted by an overwhelming response for season tickets when 143,000 are requested in only two weeks. (1984)

Hal Hunter replaces Frank Kush as head coach. (1984)

Rod Dowhower is named new head coach of the Indianapolis Colts. (1985)

Rohn Stark leads the entire NFL with a punting average of 45.2 yards. (1986)

Ron Meyer is signed to replace Rod Dowhower as head coach. (1987)

Memorable Years

Year	Record	Achievement
1958	9–3–0	NFL champion
1959	9–3–0	NFL champion
1964	12–2–0	NFL runner-up
1965	10–3–1	Playoff participant
1968	13–1–0	NFL champion (lost in the Super Bowl)
1970	11–2–1	NFL champion
1971	10–4–1	Wild card entry
1975	10–4–0	Division champion
1976	11–3–0	Division champion
1977	10–4–0	Division champion

Top Coaches

	Record	Win Percentage	Years
Don Shula	73–26–4	.737	1963–69
Weeb Ewbank	61–52–1	.540	1954–62
Ted Marchibroda	41–36–0	.532	1975–79
Don McCafferty	26–11–1	.703	1970–72

Record Holders

Career		
Rushing yards	Lydel Mitchell (1972–77)	5,487
Passing yards	Johnny Unitas (1956–72)	39,768
Passing TD's	Johnny Unitas (1956–72)	287
Pass receptions	Raymond Berry (1955–67)	631
Receiving yards	Raymond Berry (1955–67)	9,275
Interceptions	Bob Boyd (1960–68)	57
Field Goals	Lou Michaels (1964–69)	107
Total TD's	Lenny Moore (1956–67)	113
Total points	Lenny Moore (1956–67)	678

Season		
Rushing yards	Lydell Mitchell, 1976	1,200
Passing yards	Johnny Unitas, 1963	3,481
Passing TD's	Johnny Unitas, 1959	32
Pass receptions	Joe Washington, 1979	82
Receiving yards	Raymond Berry, 1960	1,298
Interceptions	Tom Keane, 1953	11
Field Goals	Raul Allegre, 1983	30
Total TD's	Lenny Moore, 1964	20
Total points	Lenny Moore, 1964	120

Game		
Rushing yards	Norm Bulaich, 9/19/71	198
Passing yards	Johnny Unitas, 9/17/67	401
Passing TD's	Gary Cuozzo, 11/14/65	5
Pass receptions	Lydell Mitchell, 12/15/74	13
	Joe Washington, 9/2/79	13
Receiving yards	Raymond Berry, 11/10/57	224
Interceptions	many times	3
Field Goals	many times	5
Total TD's	many times	4
Total points	many times	24

All-Pros

Year	Player	Position	Year	Player	Position	Year	Player	Position
1953	Tom Keane	DB		Jim Parker	T		Gino Marchetti	DE
1954	Art Donovan	DT		Gino Marchetti	DE		Bobby Boyd	CB
1955	Alan Ameche	FB		Big Daddy Lipscomb	DT	1965	Johnny Unitas	QB
	Art Donovan	DT		Andy Nelson	DB		Jimmy Orr	FL
1956	Art Donovan	DT	1960	Lenny Moore	RB		Jim Parker	G
1957	Gino Marchetti	DE		Raymond Berry	E		Bobby Boyd	CB
	Art Donovan	DT		Jim Parker	T	1966	John Mackey	TE
	Milt Davis	DB		Gino Marchetti	DE	1967	Johnny Unitas	QB
1958	Johnny Unitas	QB	1961	Lenny Moore	RB		Willie Richardson	WR
	Lenny Moore	RB		Jim Parker	T		John Mackey	TE
	Raymond Berry	E		Gino Marchetti	DE	1971	Bubba Smith	DE
	Jim Parker	T	1962	O.J. Simpson	RB		Ted Hendricks	LB
	Gino Marchetti	DE		Gino Marchetti	DE		Rick Volk	S
	Big Daddy Lipscomb	DT	1963	Jim Parker	G	1976	Bert Jones	G
1959	Johnny Unitas	QB	1964	Johnny Unitas	QB		John Dutton	DE
	Lenny Moore	RB		Lenny Moore	RB	1983	Rohn Stark	P
	Raymond Berry	E		Jim Parker	G	1985	Rohn Stark	P

Kansas City Chiefs

One Arrowhead Drive
Kansas City, Missouri 64129

Stadium: Arrowhead Stadium (capacity 78,067)

Training camp: William Jewell College
                        Liberty, Missouri 64068

Colors: red, gold and white

Historical Highlights

The 1960s

American Football League founder Lamar Hunt retains the Dallas franchise and names the team the Texans. Hunt hires Hank Stram as coach. (1960)

Quarterback Len Dawson, picked up after he was cut by the Browns, guides the Texans to the Western Division championship with an 11-3 record. Dawson is voted the AFL's Player of the Year and Hank Stram the Coach of the Year. (1962)

Dallas defeats the Houston Oilers in overtime 20-17 to take the AFL title. (1962)

Kansas City Mayor H. Roe Bartle invites Hunt to move the Texans to Missouri and promises to enlarge Municipal Stadium and deliver three times the number of season ticket holders. Hunt moves the team and renames it the Chiefs. (1963)

The Chiefs draft Heisman Trophy running back from USC, Mike Garrett, in an effort to rebuild what has been an injury-plagued team. (1966)

Kansas City finishes the season with an 11-2-1 record earning a playoff bid and trounces Buffalo 31-7 to gain a berth in the first Super Bowl. (1966)

Kansas City's Len Dawson lets one go against the Jets. Dawson let 3,696 passes go for the Chiefs during his 13-year career with them and led the league in passing four times during the 60s. (Fred Roe)

Despite a close first half, the Chiefs fall to Vince Lombardi's Green Bay Packers 35-10 in Super Bowl I. (1967)

The Chiefs tie with Oakland for the Western Division championship after a 12-2 regular season, but they fall in postseason play to the Los Angeles Raiders 41-6. (1968)

The club is forced to go through three quarterbacks in as many weeks but ends the season with an 11-3-0 record, which yields a bid to the postseason playoffs where the Chiefs meet and defeat the defending Super Bowl champion New York Jets 13-6. Then in a face off with the Oakland Raiders, the Chiefs rally from a 7-0 deficit to win the AFC championship and a trip to the Super Bowl. (1969)

The 1970s

Kansas City meets the Minnesota Vikings in Super Bowl IV and defeats them 23-7. (1970)

The Chiefs claim another Western Division title posting a 10-3-1 record, but drop a 27-24 double overtime decision to Eastern Division champion Miami in the playoffs. (1971)

After 15 years as head coach, Hank Stram is axed, and Paul Wiggin, San Francisco 49ers assistant coach, is named head coach for the Chiefs. (1975)

The Chiefs go through two coaches in the same year, first firing Paul Wiggin and then his successor Tom Bettis. (1977)

Marv Levy is hired to coach the Chiefs. (1978)

The 1980s

The Chiefs post a record of 9-7-0, their first above .500 since 1973. (1981)

After the dismissal of Marv Levy, John Mackovic, an assistant to Tom Landry at the Cowboys, is hired. (1983)

Bill Kenney demolishes two club passing marks when he completes 346 passes (previous record of 206 belonged to Len Dawson) for 4,348 yards (previous of 2,879 yards was also a Dawson mark). (1983)

Carlos Carson also sets club records by catching 80 passes for 1,351 yards. (1983)

Wide receiver Stephone Paige breaks the NFL record for yardage on pass receptions in a single game when he gains 309 on eight catches (the previous record of 303 belonging to Jim Benton had stood since 1945). (1985)

Deron Cherry ties an NFL record by intercepting four passes in a game against the Seahawks. (1985)

The Kansas City Chiefs, in a startling turnaround, go from 6-10-0 in 1985 to 10-6-0. (1986)

The Chiefs make the playoffs for the first time since 1971. They meet the Jets at Giants Stadium in the New Jersey Meadowlands in the wild card game and lose 35-15. (1986)

Frank Gansz replaces John Mackovic as head coach. (1987)

Record Holders

Career		
Rushing yards	Ed Fodolak (1969–77)	4,451
Passing yards	Len Dawson (1962–75)	28,507
Passing TD's	Len Dawson (1962–75)	237
Pass receptions	Otis Taylor (1965–75)	410
Receiving yards	Otis Taylor (1965–75)	7,306
Interceptions	Emmitt Thomas (1966–78)	58
Field Goals	Jan Stenerud (1967–79)	279
Total TD's	Otis Taylor (1965–75)	60
Total points	Jan Stenerud (1967–79)	1,231

Season		
Rushing yards	Joe Delaney, 1981	1,121
Passing yards	Bill Kenney, 1983	4,348
Passing TD's	Len Dawson, 1964	30
Pass receptions	Carlos Carson, 1983	80
Receiving yards	Carlos Carson, 1983	1,351
Interceptions	Emmitt Thomas, 1974	12
Field Goals	Jan Stenerud, 1968, 1970	30
Total TDs	Abner Haynes, 1962	19
Total points	Jan Stenerud	129

Game		
Rushing yards	Joe Delaney, 11/15/81	193
Passing yards	Len Dawson, 11/1/64	435
Passing TD's	Len Dawson, 11/1/64	6
Pass receptions	Ed Fodolak, 10/7/73	12
Receiving yards	Stephone Paige, 12/22/85	309
Interceptions	Bobby Ply, 12/16/62	4
	Bobby Ply, 12/4/64	4
Field Goals	Jan Stenerud, 11/2/69	5
	Jan Stenerud, 12/7/69	5
	Jan Stenerud, 12/19/71	5
Total TD's	Abner Haynes, 11/26/61	5
Total points	Abner Haynes, 11/26/61	30

Top Coach

	Record	Win Percentage	Years
Hank Stram	129-79-10	.620	1960–74

Wide receiver Henry Marshall of the Chiefs sprints around a lunging Dan Hampton of the Bears. Marshall maintained his name on the Kansas City roster from 1976 to 1986. (Chicago Bears)

Memorable Years

Year	Record	Achievement
1962	11–3–0	AFL champion
1966	11–2–1	AFL champion (lost in Super Bowl)
1969	11–3–0	AFL champion (won in Super Bowl)
1971	10–3–1	Division champion
1986	10–6–0	Wild card entry

All-Pros

Year	Player	Position	Year	Player	Position	Year	Player	Position
1967	Mike Garrett	RB		Bobby Bell	LB		Emmitt Thomas	CB
	Jim Tyrer	T		Johnny Robinson	S	1972	Jerrel Wilson	P
	Buck Buchanan	DT	1970	Jim Tyrer	T	1973	Jack Rudnay	C
	Bobby Bell	LB		Aaron Brown	DE		Willie Lanier	MLB
	Johnny Robinson	S		Buck Buchanan	DT	1974	Willie Lanier	MLB
1968	Jim Tyrer	T		Bobby Bell	LB		Emmitt Thomas	CB
	Ed Budde	G		Willie Lanier	MLB	1975	Jan Stenerud	K
	Buck Buchanan	DT		Jim Marsalis	CB	1976	Jan Stenerud	K
	Willie Lanier	MLB		Johnny Robinson	S	1979	Bob Grupp	P
	Bobby Bell	LB	1971	Otis Taylor	WR	1980	J.T. Smith	KR
	Johnny Robinson	S		Jim Tyrer	T	1983	Deron Cherry	S
1969	Jim Tyrer	T		Aaron Brown	DE	1984	Nick Lowery	K
	Ed Budde	G		Bobby Bell	LB			
	Buck Buchanan	DT		Willie Lanier	MLB			

Los Angeles Raiders

332 Center Street
El Segundo, California 90245

Stadium: Los Angeles Memorial Coliseum
(capacity 92,516)

Training camp: Hilton Hotel
Oxnard, California 93030

Colors: silver and black

Historical Highlights

The 1960s

The Oakland Raiders are a charter member of the American Football League, the franchise awarded to an Oakland syndicate headed by Chet Soda. Oakland is assigned to the AFC West along with the Chargers, Broncos, and Texans. (1960)

The first head coach of the Raiders is Eddie Erdelatz. (1960)

Al Davis becomes the head coach and general manager of the Raiders. (1963)

The Raiders mark their first winning season with a 10-4-0 record, but it is only good enough for second place behind the 11-3-0 Chargers in the AFC West. (1963)

Al Davis is appointed the second commissioner of the AFL, succeeding Joe Foss, but shortly after he resigns and rejoins the Raiders as managing general partner. (1966)

Johnny Rauch is hired as head coach. (1966)

The Raiders begin play in the new Oakland-Alameda County Coliseum. (1966)

Oakland concludes their best season to date 13-1-0 and the best record yet posted in the AFL. (1967)

With Daryle Lamonica, the AFL's MVP, throwing two touchdown passes and running for another TD, the Raiders win their first AFL championship defeating Houston, 40-7. (1967)

The Raiders participate in Super Bowl II but are defeated by Vince Lombardi's Green Bay Packers 33-14. (1968)

The final minutes of the Raider comeback 43-32 victory over the New York Jets are cut to begin the broadcast of the network special "Heidi" on time, and enraged viewers later learn that the Raiders score two

Hewritt Dixon (35), a key ground gainer for the Raiders in the late 1960s, chalks up a few here for Oakland in a game against the Patriots. (Fred Roe)

quick touchdowns to win the game. (1968)

Oakland decimates Kansas City in a special playoff to win the Western Division title, but the New York Jets defeat the Raiders 27-23 in the AFL championship game. (1968)

John Madden becomes the Raiders head coach, replacing John Rauch who leaves to coach the Buffalo Bills. (1969)

In a 50-21 romp over Buffalo, Raiders' quarterback Daryle Lamonica sets a pro record with six touchdown passes in the first half. (1969)

The Raiders capture their third straight AFL Western Division title when they defeat Kansas City 10-6 in the last game of the season. Oakland then sets a club scoring record in their playoff triumph over Houston 56-7. But before a crowd of 54,544 fans in the Oakland Coliseum, the Raiders are defeated by Kansas City 17-7 in the AFL championship game. (1969)

SUNDAY MAYHEM

Daryle Lamonica is named the AFC Offensive Player of the Year. (1969)

The 1970s

In the newly realigned NFL, the Raiders are slotted in the AFC's Western Division with the Chargers, Chiefs, and Broncos. (1970)

The Raiders become the first AFL club to win four consecutive division titles. (1970)

Oakland defeats the Miami Dolphins 21–14 at the Oakland Coliseum in their first playoff game, but the Baltimore Colts dash the Raiders' title hope in the AFC championship game at Baltimore's Memorial Stadium 27–17. (1970)

George Blanda earns AFC Offensive Player of the Year honors. (1970)

Oakland, winning 10 of its 14 games, captures its fifth AFC Western Division championship in six seasons, and gives the club a collective record of 94–36–10 over the last ten years. (1972)

Capturing their sixth AFC Western Division championship in seven seasons, the Raiders sport a record of 9–4–1. With a 33–14 playoff victory over Pittsburgh, Oakland goes to the AFC championship game. The Raiders, however, go down to defeat, losing to the Miami Dolphins 27–10, a team that wins its third consecutive AFC title. (1973)

Oakland wins its seventh AFC Western Division championship, posting the best won-loss record in the NFL, 12–2–0. Oakland squelches Miami's hopes for a fourth consecutive Super Bowl appearance by defeating the Dolphins 28–26 in the AFC playoffs. But, the Raiders' momentum is stopped by Pittsburgh 24–13 in the AFC championship game. (1974)

Ken Stabler is named AFC Offensive Player of the Year. (1974)

In mid-season the Raiders claim an all-time record 129–77–11, their winning percentage of .626 making them now pro football's winningest team since 1960. (1975)

Oakland gains its eighth AFC Western Division championship in nine years by winning 11 of its 14 games. (1975)

George Blanda becomes the first player in pro football annals to score 2,000 points, the historic point scored on an extra point in a game against Kansas City. (1975)

The Raiders earn their way to another AFC championship game with a 31–28 win over the Cincinnati Bengals in the playoffs. But again Oakland is denied a Super Bowl slating when the Pittsburgh Steelers trim them 16–10 in the AFC championship game. (1975)

The Raiders achieve their ninth Western Division championship in ten years, concluding the regular season with a 13–1–0 record, their best ever, along with that of 1967. (1976)

Oakland defeats New England 24–21 in the AFC playoff game, and then after three straight years as a runner-up, the Raiders win the AFC championship, defeating the Pittsburgh Steelers 24–7 and go to the Super Bowl. (1976)

Before a crowd of 103,424 at the Rose Bowl in Pasadena, California, the Oakland Raiders defeat the Minnesota Vikings 32–14 to win Super Bowl XI, highlighted by Ken Stabler's passes to Fred Biletnikoff and Dave Casper and the rushing of Clarence Davis and Mark van Eeghen. (1977)

John Madden is named Coach of the Year for 1976, and Oakland's managing partner Al Davis is named NFL Executive of the Year. (1977)

The Raiders defeat Kansas City 21–20 to become the first NFL team to win 150 games since 1960. (1977)

The Raiders make it 10 playoff appearances in 11 years by winning 11 of 14 games. (1977)

In a nail-biting double overtime the Raiders defeat the Baltimore Colts 37–31 in the playoffs and advance to

Daryle Lamonica was the Raider quarterback from 1967 to 1974 and led them through four AFL title games and a Super Bowl. (Fred Roe)

the AFC championship game. Denver defeats the Raiders 20-17 in the AFC championship game, the third longest in NFL history (75 minutes, 43 seconds), and the longest in Raider history. (1977)

Tom Flores is named head coach of the Oakland Raiders following John Madden's retirement. (1979)

The Raiders clinch their 15th consecutive winning season with a win over Cleveland, 19-14, tying the NFL record set 35 years earlier by the Chicago Bears, but do not make the playoffs. (1979)

Ken Stabler is the first (and only) Raider to complete more than 300 passes in a season (304 for 3,615 yards, both club records). (1979)

The 1980s

The Oakland Raiders become the first team in NFL history to post 16 consecutive winning seasons with an 11-5 record, ending up in a tie for first place in the AFC West and qualifying for the playoffs for the 11th time since 1967. The Raiders beat Houston 27-7 in the AFC wild card playoff game, and then stop the Cleveland Browns. The Raiders defeat the San Diego Chargers 34-27 to win the AFC title. (1980)

Defensive back Lester Hayes is named the AFC's Defensive Player of the Year. (1980)

The Raiders capture their second Super Bowl crown in five years by defeating the Philadelphia Eagles 27-10 in Super Bowl XV before a crowd of 75,500 and a television audience of 125 million. (1981)

Oakland's first round draft choice is Southern Cal running back and Heisman Trophy winner Marcus Allen. (1982)

A United States Federal District Court of Appeals jury unanimously finds for the Raiders and against the NFL on an anti-trust count which essentially allows the Raiders to move to Los Angeles. (1982)

In their first regular season home game as the Los Angeles Raiders, the team defeats the San Diego Chargers 28-24 at the Coliseum, the stadium with the largest seating capacity in the NFL. (1982)

The Raiders post their 17th winning season in the last 18 years and earn their 200th league victory when they defeat Kansas City 21-6. (1982)

With an 8-1-0 record in a strike-shortened season, the Raiders take their tenth division championship since 1967. The Cleveland Browns fall to the Raiders 27-10 at the Coliseum as Oakland/Los Angeles posts its 16th postseason game victory since 1967. But Los Angeles falls to the New York Jets 17-14 in the playoffs. (1982)

A Federal District Court jury awards the Los Angeles Raiders nearly $35,000,000 in compensatory damages from the NFL for anti-trust and bad faith violations. Los Angeles County Memorial Coliseum receives nearly $15,000,000 in damages in the same decision. (1983)

The California State Superior Court uphold's the Raiders' move to Los Angeles by ruling against the city of Oakland and for the Raiders in an Eminent Domain case heard in Monterey County. The Court rules that Oakland does not have the right to acquire the Raiders through condemnation. (1983)

The Raiders clinch their 18th winning season in 19 years, their record of 12-4-0 once again sending them to the playoffs. (1983)

The Los Angeles Raiders defeat the Pittsburgh Steelers 38-10 in an AFC playoff game before a record crowd of 92,434. Then the Raiders win their 11th conference championship by defeating the Seattle Seahawks 30-12. (1983)

The Raiders are victorious in Super Bowl XVIII, demolishing the Washington Redskins 38-9, and are paced by Marcus Allen who scores two touchdowns and gains 191 yards rushing. (1984)

A Federal Court of Appeals upholds the Raider victory in its anti-trust suit with the NFL on both the anti-trust and bad faith charges. (1984)

The United States Supreme Court upholds the Raider victory in their anti-trust case by refusing to alter favorable previous decisions for the Raiders made by the United States Federal Court of Appeals and a United States Federal District Court jury. (1984)

The Raiders make it to the playoffs as a wild card team but lose to Seattle 13-7. (1984)

The Raiders set an all-time NFL game gate record when 92,487 tickets are issued for their game against San Francisco in the Los Angeles Coliseum. (1985)

The Raiders mark their 20th winning season in 21 years by winning 12 of their 16 games and the division crown. Los Angeles, however, loses to New England 27-20 in the playoffs. (1985)

Marcus Allen, rushing for 1,759 yards, the most in the entire NFL, is named AFC Offensive Player of the Year. (1985)

The Raiders, 8-8-0 for the season, miss the playoffs for the first time since 1981. (1986)

Tight end Todd Christensen leads the entire NFL with 95 pass receptions. (1986)

Memorable Years

Year	Record	Achievement
1967	13–1–0	AFL champion
1968	12–2–0	AFL runner-up
1969	12–1–1	AFL runner-up
1970	8–4–2	AFC runner-up
1972	10–3–1	Division champion
1973	9–4–1	AFC runner-up
1974	12–2–0	AFC runner-up
1975	11–3–0	AFC runner-up
1976	13–1–0	NFL champion
1977	11–3–0	Wild card entry
1980	11–5–0	NFL champion
1982	8–1–0	Playoff tournament participant
1983	12–4–0	NFL champion
1984	11–5–0	Wild card entry
1985	12–4–0	Division champion

Record Holders

Career		
Rushing yards	Mark van Eeghen (1974–81)	5,907
Passing yards	Ken Stabler (1970–79)	19,078
Passing TD's	Ken Stabler (1970–79)	150
Pass receptions	Fred Biletnikoff (1965–78)	589
Receiving yards	Fred Biletnikoff (1965–78)	8,974
Interceptions	Willie Brown (1967–78)	39
Field Goals	George Blanda (1967–75)	156
Total TD's	Fred Biletnikoff (1965–78)	77
Total points	George Blanda (1967–75)	863

Season		
Rushing yards	Marcus Allen, 1985	1,759
Passing yards	Ken Stabler, 1979	3,615
Passing TD's	Daryle Lamonica, 1969	34
Pass receptions	Todd Christensen, 1983	92
Receiving yards	Art Powell, 1964	1,361
Interceptions	Lester Hayes, 1980	13
Field Goals	George Blanda, 1973	23
Total TDs	Marcus Allen, 1984	18
Total points	George Blanda, 1968	117

Game		
Rushing yards	Clem Daniels, 10/20/63	200
Passing yards	Cotton Davidson, 10/25/64	427
Passing TD's	Tom Flores, 12/22/63	6
	Daryle Lamonica, 10/19/69	6
Pass receptions	Dave Casper, 10/3/76	12
Receiving yards	Art Powell, 12/22/63	247
Interceptions	many times	3
Field Goals	many times	4
Total TD's	Art Powell, 12/22/63	4
	Marcus Allen, 9/24/84	4
Total points	Art Powell, 12/22/63	24
	Marcus Allen, 9/24/84	24

Top Coaches

	Record	Win Percentage	Years
John Madden	112–39–7	.742	1969–78
Tom Flores	86–46–0	.652	1979–86
John Rauch	35–10–0	.778	1966–68
Al Davis	23–16–3	.590	1963–65

All-Pros

Year	Player	Position	Year	Player	Position	Year	Player	Position
1960	Jim Otto	C		Dave Grayson	DB		Ray Guy	P
1961	Jim Otto	C	1969	Daryle Lamonica	QB	1977	Dave Casper	TE
1962	Jim Otto	C		Fred Biletnikoff	WR		Art Shell	T
	Fred Williamson	DB		Jim Otto	C		Gene Upshaw	G
1963	Clem Daniels	RB		Harry Schuh	T		Ray Guy	P
	Art Powell	WR		Gene Upshaw	G	1978	Dave Casper	TE
	Jim Otto	C		Willie Brown	DB		Ray Guy	P
	Fred Williamson	DB		Dave Garyson	DB	1980	Ted Hendricks	LB
1964	Jim Otto	C	1970	Gene Upshaw	G		Lester Hayes	CB
1965	Jim Otto	C		Willie Brown	CB	1982	Marcus Allen	RB
	Dave Grayson	DB	1971	Willie Brown	CB		Ted Hendricks	LB
1966	Kent McCloughan	DB	1972	Bob Brown	T	1983	Todd Christensen	TE
1967	Daryle Lamonica	QB		Gene Upshaw	G		Howie Long	DE
	Billy Cannon	TE		Willie Brown	CB	1984	Howie Long	DE
	Jim Otto	C	1973	Willie Brown	CB		Rod Martin	LB
	Ben Davidson	DE		Ray Guy	P		Mike Haynes	CB
	Tom Keating	DT	1974	Ken Stabler	QB		Lester Hayes	CB
	Kent McCloughan	DB		Cliff Branch	WR	1985	Marcus Allen	RB
1968	Hewritt Dixon	RB		Art Shell	T		Todd Christensen	TE
	Gene Upshaw	G		Ray Guy	P		Howie Long	DE
	Jim Otto	C	1975	Ray Guy	P		Mike Haynes	CB
	Dan Birdwell	DT	1976	Cliff Branch	WR			
	Willie Brown	DB		Dave Casper	TE			

Miami Dolphins

4770 Biscayne Boulevard
Suite 1440
Miami, Florida 33137

Stadium: Orange Bowl (capacity 75,206)

Training camp: St. Thomas University
16400-D N.W. 32nd Avenue
Miami, Florida 33054

Colors: aqua, coral and white

Historical Highlights

The 1960s

Joe Robbie and television star Danny Thomas are awarded the AFL's first expansion franchise for $7.5 million. (1965)

Former coach of the Detroit Lions George Wilson assumes head coaching duties for the Miami Dolphins. (1966)

The Dolphins are assigned to the AFC East to compete with the Jets, Oilers, Bills, and Patriots, and end up in the cellar of it that first year with a record of 3-11-0. (1966)

Miami selects quarterback Bob Griese of Purdue in the first round of the league draft. (1967)

The Dolphins take Syracuse fullback Larry Csonka in the first round of the college draft. (1968)

Quarterback Bob Griese sets a team record by completing 186 passes for 2,473 yards and 21 touchdowns. (1968)

Joe Robbie secures majority interest in the club. (1969)

Bob Griese becomes the first Dolphin to pass for 300 yards in a game (327 on 19 completions) against the Bengals. (1969)

The 1970s

The Dolphins are placed in the AFC East in the NFL's conference reorganization and join Boston, Buffalo, the New York Jets, and Baltimore. (1970)

Don Shula, former coach of the Baltimore Colts, becomes head coach and vice president of the Dolphins. (1970)

The Dolphins earn their first playoff berth with a record of 10-4-0. In their premiere postseason appearance the Dolphins lose to the Oakland Raiders. (1970)

Miami can claim the second winningest coach in pro football history, Don Shula, still going strong and in dogged pursuit of George Halas record 326 coaching victories. (Fred Roe)

Miami defeats New England at the Orange Bowl 41-3 in a game in which Bob Griese throws an NFL-record three consecutive touchdown passes in the first quarter. (1971)

Miami wins its first division title with a record of 10-3-1. (1971)

Don Shula is named AFC Coach of the Year. (1971)

Larry Csonka becomes the club's first 1,000 yard rusher with a season mark of 1,051 yards. Wide receiver Paul Warfield sets a club record by gaining 996 yards on pass receptions. Garo Yepremian kicks a season total 117 points to lead the NFL in scoring. (1971)

The Dolphins defeat the Kansas City Chiefs 27-24 when Garo Yepremian kicks a 37-yard field goal in the second overtime of the AFC semifinal game. Then Miami captures its first AFC championship, devastating Baltimore 21-0 before a crowd of 78,939 at the Orange Bowl and earn the right to represent the conference in the Super Bowl. It is also the largest crowd ever to attend a Miami home game. (1971)

SUNDAY MAYHEM

Bob Griese is named the AFC's Offensive Player of the Year. (1971)

The Dolphins fall to Dallas 24–3 in Super Bowl VI at Tulane Stadium in New Orleans. (1972)

The Dolphins run up the largest margin of victory in club history when they demolish the Patriots 52-0. (1972)

Miami posts a season mark of 14-0-0 for the regular season, the first team in the NFL ever to win that many games in a season. (1972)

The undefeated Dolphins also post a slew of team records: Total yards gained (5,036), yards gained rushing (2,960), total points (385), fewest points allowed (171), and attendance at home (551,000). Both Larry Csonka and Mercury Morris rush for more than 1,000 yards, (1,117 and 1,000 respectively). (1972)

Don Shula repeats as AFC coach of the year. (1972)

The Dolphins repeat as AFC champions by defeating Cleveland 20–14 and then Pittsburgh 21–17. (1972)

Miami clinches a perfect season by defeating the Washington Redskins 14–7 at Super Bowl VII in Los Angeles, their two touchdowns coming in the first half on a 28-yard pass from Bob Griese to Howard Twilley and a 1-yard plunge by Jim Kiick. (1973)

Miami's 74,961 season ticket sales set a new NFL record. (1973)

A single 1–1 game Miami rushing record of 197 yards on 15 carries with three touchdowns is set by Mercury Morris in a 44–23 win over New England at the Orange Bowl. (1973)

The Dolphins compile the best two-year record in NFL history, 26-2-0, their 12-2-0 record good enough for another AFC East title. (1973)

Miami beats Cincinnati in the playoffs 34–16 and then clinches its third AFC title at the Orange Bowl by defeating Oakland 27–10. (1973)

The Dolphins win their second consecutive NFL championship by defeating Minnesota 24–7 in Super Bowl VIII at Rice Stadium in Houston. Highlights of that January afternoon include two touchdowns by Larry Csonka, who also rushed for 145 yards, a Super Bowl record, and another TD by Jim Kiick. (1974)

The Dolphins' attempt for a third consecutive NFL championship is thwarted by the Oakland Raiders 28–26 in the AFC semifinal. (1974)

Three Miami Dolphins, fullback Larry Csonka, wide receiver Paul Warfield, and running back Jim Kiick, defect to the World Football League, signing a reported 3.3 million dollar deal with the Toronto franchise. (1975)

Miami's 31-game winning streak at the Orange Bowl ends when Oakland defeats the Dolphins 31–21. (1975)

Mercury Morris, a key member of the Dolphin teams that went to three consecutive Super Bowls in the early 70s and won two in a row, leaps over teammate Bob Kuechenberg in a game against the Jets. (Fred Roe)

In a 20–17 overtime loss to Kansas City at the Orange Bowl, wide-receiver Howard Twilley, an original Dolphin team member, surpasses 3,000 yards gained receiving. (1976)

A 45–27 victory over the Buffalo Bills at the Orange Bowl is highlighted by the spectacular play of wide receiver Freddie Solomon who gains a total 252 yards, many of them coming on three touchdowns that include a 79-yard punt return, 53-yard pass play, and a 59-yard flanker reverse. (1976)

A 10-year lease agreement between the Dolphins and the city of Miami is reached when the Dolphins agree to pay $45,000, double their original rent, and are given a three-year cancellation clause for the use of the Orange Bowl for home games. (1977)

The Dolphins set records of 55 points and 503 yards gained in a Thanksgiving Day annihilation of the Cardinals at St. Louis 55–14, a game in which quarterback Bob Griese throws six touchdown passes, a club record still standing. (1977)

For the second time Bob Griese wins AFC Offensive Player of the Year honors. (1977)

Miami makes it to the playoffs for the first time since 1974 as a wild card (11–5–0), but are eliminated by the Oilers 17–9. (1978)

Miami takes the AFC East title after winning 10 of its 16 games. (1979)

The eventual Super Bowl champs the Pittsburgh Steelers, overwhelm the Dolphins in the playoffs with a 20-point first quarter and 43–14 final score at Pittsburgh. (1979)

The 1980s

Following a 14-year career with Miami, quarterback Bob Griese retires, ranked as the 14th passer in pro football history to gain 25,000 yards passing. Griese is credited with quarterbacking 101 of the Dolphins' 135 victories, completing 1,926 completions in 3,429 attempts, gaining 25,092 career yards passing and possessing a 56.2 percent passing accuracy rating. (1980)

Dolphin linebacker Bob Brudzinski intercepts a pass in overtime to set up Uwe von Schaman for a 30-yard field goal and a 30–27 triumph over New England, giving coach Don Shula his 200th NFL coaching victory. (1981)

Miami prevails in the AFC East with a record of 11–4–1. Then the Dolphins face San Diego in what becomes the highest scoring game in playoff history. Fighting back from a 24–0 deficit, the Dolphins tie in regulation only to fall 41–38 in overtime. Both teams' quar-

terbacks, Miami's Don Strock and San Diego's Dan Fouts, pass for more than 400 yards, an NFL record. (1981)

In a strike-shortened season Miami wins 7 of 9 games and goes to the playoffs. (1982)

In the playoffs which commence in January, Miami is victorious over the New England Patriots, 28–13, winning their first postseason game in nine years. The Dolphins then defeat San Diego 34–13, holding the Chargers to a mere 247 yards, 203 yards below their league-leading average. Next on the agenda is the Jets, and a new AFC playoff record is set by Miami's A.J. Duhe and his three interceptions as the Dolphins win the AFC crown 14–0. (1983)

The Dolphins appear in their fourth NFL championship game, Super Bowl XVII, but despite maintaining a 10-point lead throughout most of the game, they fall in the final minutes to the Washington Redskins 27–17. (1983)

The Dolphins draft University of Pittsburgh All-American quarterback Dan Marino in the first round of the draft. His selection marks the first time ever that Miami has chosen a quarterback with their initial choice. (1983)

Wide receiver Mark Duper becomes the first Dolphin receiver to go over the 1,000 yard mark for pass reception in a single season, and defensive end Doug Betters is named AFC Defensive Player of the Year. (1983)

Miami again wins the AFC East title, the 11th time in 14 years, their record 12–4–0. In the first playoff game, however, they lose to the Seattle Seahawks 27–20. (1983)

Rookie Dan Marino is pegged the AFC's Offensive Player of the Year. (1983)

No team comes close to Miami who win 11 consecutive games and grasp the AFC Eastern division title with a final record of 12–4–0. The victory marks the 12th time in 15 years the club has won the AFC East title. (1984)

Quarterback Dan Marino, the NFL's MVP, breaks the all-time league record for touchdown passes in a season with 48 as well as completions, 362, and yards gained passing, 5,084. Marino also shatters the Dolphins single-game records for most yards passing, 470, and most completions, 35, in a game against the Raiders. (1984)

The Dolphins end the regular season with the best record in the AFC, 14–2–0, and another division crown, the tenth they have won or shared. Dan Marino, for the second year in a row, is named the AFC Offensive Player of the Year. (1984)

Miami defeats the Seattle Seahawks 31–10 in the play-offs and then drubs the Steelers 45–28 for the AFC title and a bid to the Super Bowl. (1984)

In their fifth Super Bowl appearance, Miami succumbs to the San Francisco 49ers 38–16 at Stanford Stadium in Palo Alto, California. (1985)

In his first game back after recovering from a broken leg, wide receiver Mark Duper sets a new Dolphin record by gaining 217 reception yards. (1985)

Ground is broken on the new 73,000 seat Dolphin Stadium by team owner Joe Robbie. (1985)

The Dolphins again conquer the AFC Eastern Division, their 13th title in 16 years with a record of 12–4–0. Then, Miami, led by Tony Nathan's 10 receptions and Ron Davenport's two touchdowns, defeat the Cleveland Browns in the AFC divisional playoff game. But Miami experiences its first loss in the AFC title game in six attempts when the New England Patriots prevail 31–14. (1985)

For the first time since 1980, the Dolphins, with a record of 8–8–0, do not have a winning season nor participate in postseason play. (1986)

Dan Marino is the top quarterback in the AFC with a rating of 92.5 after completing 378 passes for 4,746 yards and 44 touchdowns. (1986)

The Dolphins take up residence in brand new Dolphin Stadium, built at a cost of $100 million. (1987)

Record Holders

Career		
Rushing yards	Larry Csonka (1968–74, 1979)	6,737
Passing yards	Bob Griese (1967–80)	25,092
Passing TD's	Bob Griese (1967–80)	192
Pass receptions	Nat Moore (1974–85)	472
Receiving yards	Nat Moore (1974–85)	7,116
Interceptions	Jake Scott (1970–75)	35
Field Goals	Garo Yepremiam (1970–78)	165
Total TD's	Nat Moore (1974–85)	68
Total points	Garo Yepremiam (1970–78)	830

Season		
Rushing yards	Delvin Williams, 1978	1,258
Passing yards	Dan Marino, 1984	5,084
Passing TD's	Dan Marino, 1984	48
Pass receptions	Mark Clayton, 1984	73
Receiving yards	Mark Clayton, 1984	1,389
Interceptions	Dick Westmoreland, 1967	10
Field Goals	Garo Yepremiam, 1971	28
Total TDs	Mark Clayton, 1984	18
Total points	Garo Yepremiam, 1971	117

Game		
Rushing yards	Mercury Morris, 9/30/73	197
Passing yards	Dan Marino, 12/2/84	470
Passing TD's	Bob Griese, 11/24/77	6
Pass receptions	Duriel Harris, 10/28/79	10
Receiving yards	Mark Duper, 11/10/85	217
Interceptions	Dick Anderson, 12/3/73	4
Field Goals	Garo Yepremiam, 9/26/71	5
Total TD's	Paul Warfield, 12/15/73	4
Total points	Paul Warfield, 12/15/73	24

Memorable Years

Year	Record	Achievement
1970	10–4–2	Wild card entry
1971	10–3–1	NFL runner-up
1972	14–0–0	NFL champion
1973	12–2–0	NFL champion
1974	11–3–0	Division champion
1978	11–5–0	Wild card entry
1979	10–6–0	Division champion
1981	11–4–1	Division champion
1982	7–2–0	NFL runner-up
1983	12–4–0	Division champion
1984	14–2–0	NFL runner-up
1985	12–4–0	Division champion

Top Coach

	Record	Win Percentage	Years
Don Shula	190–81–2	.701	1970–86

All-Pros

Year	Player	Position	Year	Player	Position	Year	Player	Position
1969	Nick Buoniconti	LB	1974	Larry Little	G	1979	Tony Nathan	KR
1971	Bob Griese	QB		Jim Langer	C	1980	Doug Betters	DE
	Larry Csonka	RB	1975	Larry Little	G		Bob Baumhower	DT
	Paul Warfield	WR		Jim Langer	C		Fulton Walker	KR
	Larry Little	G	1976	Jim Langer	C	1984	Dan Marino	QB
	Garo Yepremian	K	1977	Bob Griese	QB		Ed Newman	G
1972	Larry Little	G		Nat Moore	WR		Reggie Roby	P
1973	Larry Little	G		Jim Langer	C		Dwight Stephenson	C
	Jake Scott	S	1978	Delvin Williams	RB	1985	Dan Marino	QB
	Garo Yepremian	K		Bob Kuechenberg	G		Dwight Stephenson	C

New England Patriots

Sullivan Stadium
Route 1
Foxboro, Massachusetts 02035

Stadium: Sullivan Stadium (capacity 61,000)

Training camp: Bryant College
            Smithfield, Rhode Island 02035

Colors: red, white and blue

Historical Highlights

The 1960s

An AFL franchise is awarded to a syndicate headed by William H. Sullivan, Jr., for Boston, the team to be known as the Boston Patriots. (1960)

Lou Saban is appointed first head coach of the Boston franchise. (1960)

The Patriots become the first pro team in history to issue stock to the public. (1960)

Mike Holovak takes over head coaching duties. (1961)

The Patriots win the AFL's Eastern Division title with a 26-8 victory over Buffalo in a special playoff game. (1963)

Babe Parilli becomes the first (and only) Patriot to pass for 400 yards (on 25 completions) in a game against Oakland. (1964)

The Patriots lose the AFL title game to the San Diego Chargers 51-10 at San Diego. (1964)

Jim Nance becomes the first Patriot to gain more than 200 yards rushing in a game (208 on 38 carries). He is also the first to gain 1,000 in a season (1,458, still a New England record). (1966)

The 1970s

John Mazur is hired as head coach. (1970)

The team is moved to Foxboro, Massachusetts and renamed the New England Patriots. (1971)

New England makes financial history by paying its first cash dividend to stockholders of 15 cents per share. (1972)

Chuck Fairbanks is named head coach and general manager. (1973)

After spending the summers of 1969-75 at the University of Massachusetts in Amherst, the Patriots open

Jim Plunkett, quarterback for the New England Patriots in the early 1970s, scrambles for a few yards here, but it was passing for which he is best remembered. (Fred Roe)

their training camp at Bryant College in Smithfield, Rhode Island. (1976)

The Patriots qualify for their first NFL playoff appearance and their first playoff game since 1963 by posting a record of 11-3-0. (1976)

New England loses the AFC wild card playoff game to the Oakland Raiders 24-21 on a field goal in the game's last few seconds of play. (1976)

Chuck Fairbanks is named AFC Coach of the Year. (1976)

Victory over the New York Jets, 51-21, at Foxboro, sets a dozen team and individual records and seven new stadium marks. (1978)

The Patriots capture their first divisional championship with a record of 11-5-0, but lose to Houston 31-14 in the first playoff game ever played in Foxboro. (1978)

The club announces that head coach and general manager Chuck Fairbanks has been allowed to resign to assume new duties as head football coach at the University of Colorado. (1979)

Frank "Bucko" Kilroy is named the new general manager of the Patriots, and former Pats' offensive coordinator Ron "Fargo" Erhardt is named head coach. (1979)

Decimating the New York Jets 56–3, the Patriots set four team and one individual record. (1979)

Harold Jackson and Stanley Morgan become the first Patriots to transcend the 1,000 yard season receiving mark by achieving 1,013 and 1,002 yards respectively. (1979)

The 1980s

Fullback Sam Cunningham surpasses Jim Nance (5,323 yards) as New England's all-time career rushing leader. (1981)

Ron Meyer is hired to coach the Patriots. (1982)

During a 29–21 win over Houston, the Patriots unveil their new $3.7 million DiamondVision scoreboard, the world's largest TV screen. (1982)

Veteran quarterback Steve Grogan betters Babe Parilli's club record for career completions (1,140) and career passing yardage (16,911). (1982)

New England makes the playoff tournament in a strike-shortened season with a record of 5–4–0, but the Patriots are defeated by the eventual AFC champion Miami Dolphins there 28–13. (1982)

Defensive end Julius Adams, a twelve year veteran and oldest active defensive lineman in the NFL, sets the club record for games played in a Patriots uniform. (1983)

Raymond Berry, former great pass receiver of the Colts, replaces Ron Meyer as head coach of the Patriots. Berry had been a Patriots assistant coach and becomes the ninth head coach in club history. (1984)

Steve Grogan, setting up here, came to the Patriots in 1975, took over the starting quarterback job, and kept it through 1983; he holds virtually every career club passing record. (Fred Roe)

Stanley Morgan's single season pass-catching record of 58 set in 1983 is broken by tight end Derrick Ramsey, catching 66 passes in his first full season with New England. (1984)

Stanley Morgan's 43rd career touchdown comes off a 22-yard pass from Tony Eason. The previous team mark had been held by Gino Cappelletti (42). (1985)

Raymond Clayborn starts his 111th straight game, a new club record for consecutive starts. (1985)

New England, winning 11 of its 16 games, gains entry to the playoffs as a wild card. (1985)

The Patriots win their first NFL playoff game when they defeat the New York Jets 26-14, then defeat the Raiders 27-20, and triumph over the Miami Dolphins 31-14 to win the AFC championship. (1985)

Raymond Berry is named AFC Coach of the Year. (1985)

The Chicago Bears decimate the Patriots in Super Bowl XX 46-10 at the Louisiana Superdome in New Orleans. The game was the third rated Super Bowl in TV-viewing history. (1986)

John Hannah, a record nine-time Pro Bowl selection, announces his retirement from the Patriots. (1986)

The Patriots post an 11-5-0 record to win the AFC Eastern Division, but New England falls to the Super Bowl-bound Denver Broncos 22-17 in the divisional playoffs. (1986)

Memorable Years

Year	Record	Achievement
1963	7–6–1	AFL runner-up
1976	11–3–0	Wild card entry
1978	11–5–0	Division champion
1982	5–4–0	Playoff tournament participant
1985	11–5–0	NFL runner-up
1986	11–5–0	Division champion

Record Holders

Career

Rushing yards	Sam Cunningham (1973–79, 1981–82)	5,453
Passing yards	Steve Grogan (1975–85)	21,581
Passing TD's	Steve Grogan (1975–85)	146
Pass receptions	Stanley Morgan (1977–86)	435
Receiving yards	Stanley Morgan (1977–86)	8,692
Interceptions	Ron Hall (1961–67)	29
Field Goals	Gino Cappelletti (1960–70)	176
Total TD's	Sam Cunningham (1973–79, 1981–82)	49
Total points	Gino Cappelletti (1960–70)	1,130

Season

Rushing yards	Jim Nance, 1966	1,458
Passing yards	Babe Parilli, 1964	3,465
Passing TD's	Babe Parilli, 1964	31
Pass receptions	Stanley Morgan, 1986	84
Receiving yards	Stanley Morgan, 1986	1,491
Interceptions	Ron Hall, 1964	11
Field Goals	John Smith, 1980	26
Total TDs	Steve Grogan, 1976	13
	Stanley Morgan, 1979	13
Total points	Gino Cappelletti, 1964	155

Game

Rushing yards	Tony Collins, 9/18/83	212
Passing yards	Babe Parilli, 10/16/64	400
Passing TD's	Babe Parilli, 11/15/64	5
Pass receptions	Art Graham, 11/20/66	11
Receiving yards	Stanley Morgan, 11/8/81	182
Interceptions	many times	3
Field Goals	Gino Cappelletti, 10/4/64	6
Total TD's	many times	3
Total points	Gino Cappelletti, 12/18/65	28

Top Coaches

	Record	Win Percentage	Years
Mike Holovak	53–47–9	.530	1961–68
Chuck Fairbanks	46–41–0	.529	1973–78
Raymond Berry	29–15–0	.853	1984–86
Ron Meyer	18–13–0	.529	1982–84

All-Pros

Year	Player	Position	Year	Player	Position	Year	Player	Position
1960	Tom Addison	LB	1965	Nick Buoniconti	LB	1979	John Hannah	G
	Ross O'Hanley	DB	1966	Jim Nance	RB	1980	John Hannah	G
1961	Chuck Leo	G		Jon Morris	C		Horace Ivory	KR
1963	Larry Eisenhauer	DE		Nick Buoniconti	LB	1981	John Hannah	G
	Houston Antwine	DT	1967	Jim Nance	RB	1982	John Hannah	G
	Tom Addison	LB		Nick Buoniconti	LB	1983	John Hannah	G
1964	Babe Parilli	QB	1968	Jim Whalen	TE		Rich Camarillo	P
	Billy Neighbors	G	1976	John Hannah	G	1984	John Hannah	G
	Larry Eisenhauer	DE	1978	Leon Gray	T	1985	John Hannah	G
	Nick Buoniconti	LB		John Hannah	G			
	Ron Hall	DB		Mike Haynes	CB			

New York Jets

598 Madison Avenue
New York, New York 10022

Stadium: Giants Stadium (capacity 76,891)

Training camp: 1000 Fulton Avenue
Hempstead, New York 11550

Colors: kelly green and white

Historical Highlights

The 1960s

A charter AFL franchise for New York City is awarded to Harry Wismer, former sports broadcaster, and the team is named the Titans. (1960)

The AFL sets up the Eastern Division to include Boston, Buffalo, Houston, and New York. (1960)

Sammy Baugh is hired by Harry Wismer to be the first head coach of the New York Titans. (1960)

Wismer obtains permission to use the Polo Grounds for the Titans home games. (1960)

Don Maynard sets a team receiving record which will stand for eight years when he gains 1,265 yards on pass receptions. (1960)

Clyde "Bulldog" Turner is named the second head coach of the Titans, replacing Sammy Baugh. (1962)

Harry Wismer is unable to meet his financial obligations concerning the team and the AFL steps in to assume the costs of running the club until the end of the season. (1962)

The New York franchise is purchased for $1 million dollars by a five-man syndicate comprised of Sonny Werblin, Townsend Martin, Leon Hess, Donald Lillis and Philip Iselin. (1963)

Weeb Ewbank, former coach of Baltimore, is named head coach of the team. (1963)

The name of the team is changed from the Titans to the Jets. (1963)

The Jets move into Shea Stadium. The first Jet touchdown in Shea is scored by tight end Gene Heeter. (1964)

Rookie Matt Snell rushes for 180 yards, a club record, as the Jets trounce Houston 24–21. (1964)

The Jets use their number one draft choice to select Alabama quarterback Joe Namath. (1964)

Broadway Joe Namath signed for $400,000 in 1965 to do this for the Jets, the most dollars in any NFL or AFL contract up to that time. He earned his money for the Jets and his way into the Hall of Fame.

Matt Snell posts a season mark of 948 yards gained and 56 passes caught, and is named the AFL's Rookie of the Year. (1964)

Joe Namath signs a contract with the Jets for a reported $427,000; Heisman Trophy winner John Huarte from Notre Dame also signs with New York at a reported $200,000. (1965)

With a season mark of 164 of 340 completions for 2,220 yards and 18 TDs with only 15 interceptions, Jet Joe Namath is named AFL Rookie of the Year. (1965)

The Jets defeat Houston 52–13, posting new club records of 52 points and a win margin of 39. (1966)

The Jets mark their first winning season with a record of 8–5–1. (1967)

Joe Namath becomes the first pro to top the 4,000-yard passing mark as he finished the regular season with a total of 4,007 yards. Don Maynard sets a club standard which still stands today by gaining 1,434 yards on his 71 pass receptions. (1967)

The Jets set an AFL attendance record with 437,036 for seven games. (1967)

The last 1:05 of the Jets-Oakland game is cut to allow the children's special, "Heidi," to begin on time, and fans miss the two scores by the Raiders which leave the Jets in defeat, 43–32. (1968)

Joe Namath passes for three TDs to lift the Jets past Oakland 27–23 for their first AFL title. (1968)

Jim Turner sets a club record which still stands by accounting for 145 points (34 FGs, 43 PATs). (1968)

A 16–7 victory over the Baltimore Colts in Miami's Orange Bowl gives the Jets their first (and only) Super Bowl triumph—it is also the first ever won by an AFL team. Joe Namath is named MVP and Weeb Ewbank becomes the first coach to win a world title in both leagues. (1969)

Super Bowl MVP is only the first of the player honors accorded Joe Namath, who also is named AFL MVP and earns the George Halas Award as the Most Courageous Pro Player and Pro Player of the Year. (1969)

The Jets become the first AFL team to play in the Chicago classic against the College All-Stars and defeat them 26–24. (1969)

In the first intracity clash, the Jets beat the Giants 37–14 as Joe Namath throws three touchdown passes. Punt returner Mike Battle's 86-yard return also yields a Jet score. (1969)

The Jets take their second Eastern division title, defeating Houston 34–26. (1969)

Super Bowl bound Kansas City defeats the Jets 13–6 in the interdivisional AFL playoffs. (1969)

The 1970s

Before a record crowd of 63,903 at Shea Stadium the Giants and Jets meet in the first regular season game and the Giants tromp the Jets 22–10. (1970)

In the most outstanding game of his professional career, quarterback Joe Namath throws for 496 yards

All Pro defensive end and in-resident frenetic Mark Gastineau lunges for Chicago's scrambling quarterback Jim McMahon. (Fred Roe)

Freeman McNeil, putting a move on safety Gary Fencik of the Bears, has been the Jets premier running back since 1981. (Chicago Bears)

and six touchdowns as the Jets defeat Baltimore 44–34. Namath and Johnny Unitas set an NFL combined record for passing yardage in the game, totaling 872 yards. (1972)

The Patriots fall to the Jets 41–13 as New York sets a new club rushing record of 333 yards, with John Riggins gaining 168 and Emerson Boozer 150. (1972)

Jet Don Maynard becomes pro football's all-time receiving leader with his 632nd career catch, surpassing the 631 snagged by Raymond Berry during his career. (1972)

Former head coach of the St. Louis Cardinals, Charlie Winner, is hired to replace Weeb Ewbank as head coach. (1974)

The Jets move into their new training center in Hempstead, N.Y., which contains full practice facilities, coaches offices, and players' living quarters. (1974)

Charley Winner is dismissed as head coach, and offensive coordinator Ken Shipp is named interim head coach. (1975)

John Riggins becomes the first back in team history to gain 1,000 yards as he picks up 1,005 on 238 carries. (1975)

Former North Carolina State coach, Lou Holtz, is named new head coach of the Jets. (1976)

Holtz resigns as head coach. Mike Holovak is named as interim coach. (1976)

Walt Michaels is named head coach. (1977)

After a two-month court struggle, the Jets and City of New York arrive at an agreement that allows the team two September games in Shea Stadium, one on either the first or second date of the NFL season, plus two games in October. The agreement covers each of the six years remaining in the Jets' contract with the city, beginning in 1978. State Supreme Court Justice Harold Beer also allows the team to play two pre-season games plus their 1977 home opener at Giants Stadium in the New Jersey Meadowlands. (1977)

The Jets finish the season with an 8–8 mark, the most wins by the team in ten years, their best record since 1974. (1978)

The 1980s

Richard Todd sets an NFL record with 42 pass completions although the Jets lose 37–27 to San Francisco. An AFC record is also set in the game by Clark Gaines with 17 pass receptions. (1980)

The Jets finish the season with a 10–5–1 record and clinch their first playoff spot since 1969. (1981)

Defensive end Joe Klecko is named AFC Defensive Player of the Year. (1981)

New York loses to Buffalo in the wild card contest 31–27. (1981)

The Jets finish the strike-shortened season with a 6–3 record. (1982)

The Jets upset the Cincinnati Bengals 44–17 to mark their first playoff victory since 1968, a game in which Freeman McNeil rushes for 202 yards and Darrol Ray sets a postseason record with a 98–yard interception return for a touchdown. (1982)

The Jets advance to the AFC championship game after defeating the Los Angeles Raiders 17–14. (1982)

The Jets fall to the Miami Dolphins at the Orange Bowl 14–0 in the AFC title game. (1982)

Walt Michaels announces his retirement as head coach after six seasons, and offensive coordinator Joe Walton is named head coach. (1983)

The Jets relocate to Giants Stadium in the New Jersey Meadowlands. (1984)

Defensive end Mark Gastineau sets an NFL record with 22 quarterback sacks. (1984)

The Jets annihilate the Tampa Bay Buccaneers 62–28, scoring the most points in club history and racking up 581 yards on offense. In the game quarterback Ken

O'Brien throws five touchdown passes, three to receiver Mickey Shuler. (1985)

A 96-yard TD pass, the longest in Jet history, is thrown by Ken O'Brien to receiver Wesley Walker in a 27-7 victory over Buffalo. (1985)

The Jets defeat Cleveland 37-10 to finish the season with an 11-5 record and clinch their third playoff berth in five years. (1985)

Season records are set by quarterback Ken O'Brien, who becomes the first Jet to lead the NFL in passer ratings (96.4); receiver Mickey Shuler, who sets a team record for catches with a total 76, and Freeman McNeil who tops the team with 1,331 yards rushing, and most ever in a Jet season. (1985)

The Jets lose 26-14 to the eventual AFC champion New England Patriots in the wild card playoff game. (1985)

The Jets end the season with a 10-6-0 record and a wild card berth in the playoffs. (1986)

New York trounces the Kansas City Chiefs 35-15 to advance to the divisional playoffs. (1986)

The Jets lose a heartbreaker in double overtime to the Cleveland Browns 23-20 and are eliminated from the playoffs. (1987)

Memorable Years

Year	Record	Achievement
1968	11-3-0	NFL champion
1969	10-4-0	Division champion
1981	10-5-1	Wild card entry
1982	6-3-0	AFC runner-up
1985	11-5-0	Wild card entry
1986	10-6-0	Wild card entry

Top Coaches

	Record	Win Percentage	Years
Joe Walton	36-30-0	.545	1983-86
Sammy Baugh	14-14-0	.500	1960-61

Record Holders

Career		
Rushing yards	Emerson Boozer (1966-75)	5,104
Passing yards	Joe Namath (1965-76)	27,057
Passing TD's	Joe Namath (1965-76)	170
Pass receptions	Don Maynard (1960-72)	627
Receiving yards	Don Maynard (1960-72)	11,732
Interceptions	Bill Baird (1963-69)	34
Field Goals	Pat Leahy (1974-86)	200
Total TD's	Don Maynard (1960-72)	88
Total points	Pat Leahy (1974-86)	993

Season		
Rushing yards	Freeman McNeil, 1985	1,331
Passing yards	Joe Namath, 1967	4,007
Passing TD's	Al Dorow, 1960	26
	Joe Namath, 1967	26
Pass receptions	Mickey Shuler, 1985	76
Receiving yards	Don Maynard, 1967	1,434
Interceptions	Dainard Paulson, 1964	12
Field Goals	Jim Turner, 1968	34
Total TDs	Art Powell, 1960	14
	Don Maynard, 1965	14
	Emerson Boozer, 1972	14
Total points	Jim Turner, 1968	145

Game		
Rushing yards	Freeman McNeil, 9/15/85	192
Passing yards	Joe Namath, 9/24/72	496
Passing TD's	Joe Namath, 9/24/72	6
Pass receptions	Clark Gaines, 9/21/80	17
Receiving yards	Don Maynard, 11/17/68	228
Interceptions	Dainard Paulson, 9/28/63	3
	Bill Baird, 10/31/64	3
	Rich Sowells, 9/23/73	3
Field Goals	Jim Turner, 11/3/68	6
	Bobby Howfield, 12/3/72	6
Total TD's	many times	3
Total points	Jim Turner, 11/3/68	19
	Pat Leahy, 9/16/84	19

All-Pros

Year	Player	Position	Year	Player	Position	Year	Player	Position
1960	Bob Mischak	G	1969	Matt Snell	RB		Joe Klecko	DE
1961	Billy Mathis	FB		Don Maynard	WR	1982	Freeman McNeil	RB
	Bob Mischak	G		Gerry Philbin	DE		Marvin Powell	T
1962	Larry Grantham	LB		John Elliott	DT		Joe Fields	C
1964	Larry Grantham	LB	1972	Joe Namath	QB		Mark Gastineau	DE
1967	George Sauer	WR	1978	Wesley Walker	WR	1983	Mark Gastineau	DE
1968	Joe Namath	QB		Pat Leahy	K	1984	Mark Gastineau	DE
	George Sauer	WR	1979	Marvin Powell	T		Bobby Humphrey	KR
	Gerry Philbin	DE	1981	Marvin Powell	T	1985	Joe Klecko	DT

Pittsburgh Steelers

Three Rivers Stadium
300 Stadium Circle
Pittsburgh, Pennsylvania 15212

Stadium: Three Rivers Stadium (capacity 59,000)

Training camp: St. Vincent College
Latrobe, Pennsylvania 15650

Colors: black and gold

Historical Highlights

The 1930s

Art Rooney purchases an NFL franchise for $2,500 and names the team the "Pirates." Forrest Douds is named head coach. (1933)

Luby DiMelio is named coach but his tenure, like Doud's, lasts only one year and he is replaced by Joe Bach. (1934–35)

Johnny Blood McNally becomes the fourth Pirate coach and he plays halfback on the team as well. (1937)

Johnny Blood McNally resigns after the Pirates are decimated by the Chicago Bears 32–0. Walt Kiesling replaces him. (1939)

The 1940s

Art Rooney sells the franchise to Alexis Thompson, then buys an interest in the Philadelphia Eagles, which he later swaps with Thompson to regain control of the Pittsburgh franchise. The team is renamed the Steelers. (1941)

The Steelers merge with the Chicago Cardinals and are known as Card-Pitt, but around the league are called "Carpet" because they lose all 10 of their games. (1944)

Jock Sutherland, former University of Pittsburgh coach, is named head coach of the Steelers. (1946)

Despite a slow start, the Steelers ignite a six-game winning streak and finish the season tied with Philadelphia for first place in the Eastern Division. But the Steelers lose 21–0 to Philadelphia in a playoff game. (1947)

Sutherland is killed in an auto accident and his top assistant, John Michelosen, succeeds him. (1948)

The only quarterback ever to win four Super Bowls, the incomparable Terry Bradshaw, a Steeler from 1970 through 1983. (Fred Roe)

The 1950s

The Steelers produce four lackluster seasons before Michelosen is fired and Joe Bach is rehired as head coach. (1952)

Pittsburgh scores the most points and runs up the widest winning margin in club history when they annihilate the New York Giants 63–7. (1952)

Bach resigns and Walk Kiesling is renamed head coach. (1954)

Buddy Parker, former coach at Detroit, replaces Kiesling as head coach. (1957)

Bobby Layne sets a record by passing for 409 yards in a game, a mark that still stands. (1958)

A strong season finish by the Steelers yields 7–4–1, the Steelers best record since 1947. (1958)

The 1960s

The Steelers finish second in the Eastern Conference and post the finest record thus far in their history, 9–5–0. Led by quarterback Bobby Layne, who had been acquired from the Lions, Pittsburgh wins a spot in the playoffs, but the Steelers are thwarted there by Detroit 17–10. (1962)

Parker resigns and assistant coach Mike Nixon is named interim head coach. (1965)

Bill Austin comes from the Green Bay Packers to assume head coaching duties. (1966)

Austin is fired after the Steelers post a miserable 2–11–1 record for the season. (1968)

Chuck Noll succeeds Austin. (1969)

The 1970s

The Steelers join NFL clubs Baltimore and Cleveland in a move to the AFC following the league merger. Terry Bradshaw, quarterback from Louisiana Tech, is selected by Pittsburgh in the first round of the college draft, after winning a coin toss for that selection from the Chicago Bears, who also wanted him. (1970)

Franco Harris, a fullback from Penn State, joins the Steelers and is named Rookie of the Year after rushing for 1,055 yards, catching 21 passes, and scoring 11 touchdowns in his first season of play. (1972)

The Steelers capture the first division title in the club's history, posting an 11–3–0 record. Then, in their first playoff game since 1947, the Steelers defeat Oakland 13–7 in the final 22 seconds of the game on a touchdown by Franco Harris. Their luck does not hold, though, and the season ends in defeat at the hands of the Miami Dolphins 21–17 in the AFC championship game. (1972)

Pittsburgh, winning 10 of its 14 games, makes it to the playoffs as a wild card entry, but are eliminated by the Oakland Raiders 33–14. (1973)

With their Steel Curtain defense, the passing of Terry Bradshaw, and the rushing of Franco Harris, the Steelers easily take the AFC Central Division crown with a record of 10–3–1. (1974)

Defensive tackle Mean Joe Greene is named AFC Defensive Player of the Year. (1974)

Pittsburgh knocks off the Bills 32–14 to advance to the AFC title game. The underdog Steelers defeat the Raiders at Oakland 24–13 and earn their first invitation to the Super Bowl. (1974)

In Super Bowl IX at Tulane Stadium in New Orleans, the Steelers trounce the Minnesota Vikings 16–6 and bring Pittsburgh its first NFL championship ever. (1975)

Racking up the most wins thus far in their history, 12 against 2 losses, the Steelers repeat as victors of the AFC Central Division. (1975)

Franco Harris sets an all-time record by rushing for 1,246 yards. Cornerback Mel Blount sets another all-time club mark by intercepting 11 passes and is named AFC Defensive Player of the Year. (1975)

The Colts are no match for the Steelers in their playoff opener, Pittsburgh winning decisively 28–10. The Steelers then make it two AFC titles in a row, defeating Oakland 16–10, earning another trip to the Super Bowl. (1975)

Facing the Dallas Cowboys in Super Bowl X, Pittsburgh prevails 21–17 and becomes the third team in history to win back-to-back Super Bowls. (1976)

The Steelers repeat as divisional champs with a record of 10–4–0, then decimate the Colts in the first round of the playoffs by a score of 40–14. In the AFC title tilt, however, Oakland destroy's Pitt's hope for a third straight Super Bowl appearance, 24–7. (1976)

Linebacker Jack Lambert is named the AFC Defensive Player of the Year. (1976)

Dominating their division again, this time with a 9–5–0 record, the Steelers meet the Super Bowl bound Denver Broncos and fall 34–21. (1977)

Pittsburgh wins the most games ever in its history, 14 against 2 losses, to win the divisional title for the fifth consecutive year. (1978)

Handily defeating first the Broncos 33–10 and then the Oilers 34–5, the Steelers earn their way for the third time to a Super Bowl. 1978)

In Super Bowl XIII at the Orange Bowl in Miami, the Steelers again meet the Cowboys and again prevail, this time 35–31. And in what stands as the highest scoring Super Bowl ever, Pittsburgh becomes the first to win three of the postseason classics. (1979)

With 12 wins in its 16 contests, Pittsburgh wins its division title for the sixth year in a row. Another romp through the playoffs, trimming the Dolphins 34–14 and Houston 27–13, the Steelers become the second team ever to appear in four Super Bowls. (1979)

Terry Bradshaw sets two Steeler passing records by throwing 472 completions for 3,724 yards. (1979)

The 1980s

Pittsburgh's opponent in Super Bowl XIV is the Los Angeles Rams and they fare no better than their three predecessors as the Steelers surge to a 31–19 victory. The Steelers become the first and remain the only team to win four Super Bowls. (1980)

After a two-year layoff, the Steelers make it back to postseason play in a strike-shortened season with a record of 6–3–0, but lose in the first round of the playoff tournament to the San Diego Chargers 31–28. (1982)

For the first time since 1979, the Steelers win their division with a record of 10–6–0. But Pitt could not advance in the playoffs, losing this time to the L. A. Raiders 38–10. (1983)

Franco Harris records his eighth 1,000-yard rushing season, at the time an NFL record, one more than Jim Brown's seven, and scores his 100th touchdown, by far the most in Pittsburgh history. (1983)

The Steelers make it two division crowns in a row, winning nine of their 16 games. A 27–14 win over Denver enables Pittsburgh to attend the AFC championship game, but there they are overwhelmed by the Dolphins passing attach and are routed 45–28. (1984)

Wide receiver John Stallworth sets two Steeler standards by catching 80 passes for 1,395 yards. (1984)

Gary Anderson cops a pair of Pittsburgh records when he accounts for 139 points and kicks 33 field goals. (1985)

The only highlight in a 6–10–0 season, the most Pittsburgh losses since 1969, is AFC-leading kickoff returner Lupe Sanchez, who averages 23.6 yards a return. (1986)

Almost obscured by leaping Cowboy George Andre (66) is the Steeler great quarterback Bobby Layne, looking downfield for a receiver. Two are on their way for Pittsburgh, John Powers (88) and Dick Hoak (42); Blocking for Layne is Buzz Nutter (51). (Dallas Cowboys)

Record Holders

Career

Rushing yards	Franco Harris (1972–83)	11,950
Passing yards	Terry Bradshaw (1970–83)	27,989
Passing TD's	Terry Bradshaw (1970–83)	212
Pass receptions	John Stallworth (1974–85)	462
Receiving yards	John Stallworth (1974–85)	7,736
Interceptions	Mel Blount (1971–83)	57
Field Goals	Roy Gerela (1971–78)	146
Total TD's	Franco Harris (1972–83)	100
Total points	Roy Gerela (1971–78)	731

Season

Rushing yards	Franco Harris, 1975	1,246
Passing yards	Terry Bradshaw, 1979	3,724
Passing TD's	Terry Bradshaw, 1978	28
Pass receptions	John Stallworth, 1984	80
Receiving yards	John Stallworth, 1984	1,395
Interceptions	Mel Blount, 1975	11
Field Goals	Gary Anderson, 1985	33
Total TDs	Louis Lipps, 1985	15
Total points	Gary Anderson, 1985	139

Game

Rushing yards	John Fuqua, 12/20/70	218
Passing yards	Bobby Layne, 12/3/58	409
Passing TD's	Terry Bradshaw, 11/15/81	5
	Mark Malone, 9/8/85	5
Pass receptions	J.R. Wilburn, 10/22/67	12
Receiving yards	Buddy Dial, 10/22/61	235
Interceptions	Jack Butler, 12/13/53	4
Field Goals	Gary Anderson, 11/10/85	5
Total TD's	Ray Mathews, 10/17/54	4
	Roy Jefferson, 11/3/68	4
Total points	Ray Mathews, 10/17/54	24
	Roy Jefferson, 11/3/68	24

Memorable Years

Year	Record	Achievement
1972	11–3–0	AFC runner-up
1973	10–4–0	Wild card entry
1974	10–3–1	NFL champion
1975	12–2–0	NFL champion
1976	10–4–0	AFC runner-up
1977	9–5–0	Division champion
1978	14–2–0	NFL champion
1979	12–4–0	NFL champion
1982	6–3–0	Playoff tournament participant
1983	10–6–0	Division champion
1984	9–7–0	AFC runner-up

Top Coaches

	Record	Win Percentage	Years
Chuck Noll	170–114–1	.599	1969–86
Buddy Parker	51–47–6	.520	1957–64
Jock Sutherland	13–10–1	.565	1946–47

All-Pros

Year	Player	Position	Year	Player	Position	Year	Player	Position
1942	Bill Dudley	HB		Jack Ham	LB		Mike Webster	C
1946	Bill Dudley	HB	1975	Lynn Swann	WR		Joe Greene	DT
1947	John Clement	FB		L. C. Greenwood	DE		Jack Lambert	LB
1950	Joe Geri	HB		Jack Lambert	LB		Jack Ham	LB
1951	Jerry Shipkey	DB		Jack Ham	LB		Donnie Shell	S
1952	Jerry Shipkey	LB		Andy Russell	LB	1980	Mike Webster	C
1954	Bill Walsh	C		Mel Blount	CB		Jack Lambert	LB
	Dale Dodrill	MG	1976	Jack Lambert	LB		Donnie Shell	S
1957	Jack Butler	DB		Jack Ham	LB	1981	Mike Webster	C
1958	Ernie Stautner	DT	1977	Franco Harris	RB		Jack Lambert	LB
	Jack Butler	DB		Joe Greene	DT	1982	Mike Webster	C
1959	Jack Butler	DB		Jack Ham	LB		Jack Lambert	LB
1969	Roy Jefferson	WR	1978	Terry Bradshaw	QB		Donnie Shell	S
1972	Joe Greene	DT		Lynn Swann	WR	1983	Mike Webster	C
1973	Joe Greene	DT		Mike Webster	C		Jack Lambert	LB
1974	L. C. Greenwood	DE		Jack Ham	LB	1984	Louis Lipps	PR
	Joe Greene	DT	1979	John Stallworth	WR	1985	Louis Lipps	WR

San Diego Chargers

San Diego Jack Murphy Stadium
P.O. Box 20666
San Diego, California 92120

Training camp: University of California-San Diego
Third College
La Jolla, California 92037

Colors: blue, gold and white

Historical Highlights

The 1960s

Los Angeles gains a charter membership in the AFL, the franchise going to famous hotelier Barron Hilton, and the team is named the Chargers. (1960)

Former Notre Dame University football coach Frank Leahy is named general manager of the Los Angeles team, and former coach of the NFL Los Angeles Rams, Sid Gillman, is named head coach. (1960)

In their first preseason game Paul Lowe returns the opening kickoff 105 yards for a touchdown, and the Chargers beat New York 27–7. (1960)

The Chargers take the AFL Western Division title with a record of 10–4–0. (1960)

Paul Lowe makes the longest run from scrimmage in all Chargers history, 87 yards for a touchdown against Dallas, and Jack Kemp throws a 91-yard touchdown pass to Keith Lincoln, another all-time Charger mark, against Denver. (1961)

Los Angeles falls to Houston 24–16 in the first AFL championship game before a crowd of 32,183 at Jeppesen Stadium in Houston. (1961)

Hilton moves the Chargers to San Diego. (1961)

San Diego wins the AFL West with a record of 12–2–0. (1961)

The Chargers lose in the AFL championship game to Houston 10–3 in San Diego. (1961)

San Diego clinches the AFL West by winning 11 of their 14 games. (1963)

Paul Lowe becomes the first Charger to rush for more than 1,000 yards in a season (1,010). (1963)

On January 5, the Chargers win their first AFL championship, defeating Boston 51–10. Fullback Keith Lincoln rushes for 206 yards and gains 329 yards total offense. (1964)

Lance Alworth (19)

The Chargers take their fourth AFL West title in five years, posting a record of 8–5–1, but they fall to the Bills in the AFL title game in Buffalo 20–7. (1964)

San Diego wins its fifth AFC West title in six years with a record of 9–2–3, but again are deprived of the title by Buffalo, who whip them 23–0 in San Diego. (1965)

Lance Alworth sets a club record which still stands today by gaining 1,602 yards on pass receptions. (1965)

The Chargers are purchased by a syndicate of 21 business executives headed by Eugene V. Klein and Sam Schulman for a record $10 million. (1966)

The Chargers move into the new San Diego Stadium. (1967)

The Chargers defeat Kansas City 45–31 in a game in which both teams combine for 897 yards in total offense and 622 on kick, interception, and fumble returns. Charger Speedy Duncan has 203 yards in returns including 35 on a fumble recovery for a touchdown, 68 on four kickoff returns, and 100 for a touchdown on the longest interception in AFL history. (1967)

Speedy Duncan sets an AFL record with a 95-yard punt return for a touchdown against the Jets. (1968)

Following the resignation of Sid Gillman as head coach, offensive backfield coach Charlie Waller is named head coach. (1969)

Lance Alworth sets a pro football record with pass receptions in 96 consecutive games, bettering the mark held by Don Hutson. (1969)

The 1970s

Club president Gene Klein announces a staff reorganization that includes the return of Sid Gillman as head coach and the naming of Charlie Waller as offensive coach. (1970)

Head coach Sid Gillman resigns and Harland Svare takes over. (1971)

Harland Svare resigns as head coach but stays with the Chargers as general manager. Ron Waller is appointed interim head coach. (1973)

Charger president Gene Klein announces the appointment of Tommy Prothro as head coach. (1974)

Don Woods sets a Chargers rushing record in a single game of 105 yards and a rookie record of 1,162 yards in his first season. Woods is named NFL Rookie of the Year (Offense). (1974)

In an exhibition game in Tokyo's Korakuen Stadium a crowd of 38,000 watches San Diego lose to the St. Louis Cardinals 20–10, the first NFL game ever to be played on a different continent. (1976)

The Chargers round out their international exhibitions with a 17–16 loss to San Francisco in Honolulu. (1976)

Lance Alworth is the first player to be inducted into the San Diego Chargers Hall of Fame. (1977)

Tommy Prothro resigns and Don Coryell is named head coach, the sixth in Charger history. (1978)

Tackle Ron Mix is inducted into the Chargers' Hall of Fame. (1978)

Dan Fouts sets an NFL record of four consecutive 300-yard passing games. (1979)

Paul Lowe becomes a San Diego Chargers' Hall of Famer. (1979)

The Chargers trounce New Orleans 35–0 to secure their first playoff berth in 14 years. All San Diego's points were scored in the first half. (1979)

Before a San Diego Stadium crowd of 51,910 the Chargers defeat Denver to secure their first division title since 1965 with a record of 12–4–0. (1979)

Dan Fouts breaks the record for passing yardage in a season by gaining 4,082. (1979)

In the AFC divisional playoff San Diego loses to Houston 17–14. (1979)

The 1980s

The Chargers wage a one-sided battle against the New York Giants, winning 44–7 as Dan Fouts sets a team record with 444 yards passing. (1980)

Running back Keith Lincoln is inducted into the Chargers Hall of Fame. (1980)

QB Dan Fouts breaks his own passing yardage record netting 4,715. (1980)

With a record of 11–5–0, San Diego again wins the AFC West. After a 20–14 win over Buffalo in the playoffs, however, the Chargers fall to Oakland 34–27. (1980)

San Diego Stadium is renamed San Diego Jack Murphy Stadium after the late sports editor of the San Diego Union. (1980)

For the third straight year, the Chargers clinch the AFC West championship, this time with a record of 10–6–0. For the third straight year as well, Fouts breaks the NFL passing yardage record, this time racking up 4,802 yards. (1981)

The Chargers take a dramatic 41–38 victory over Miami in one of the epic games in NFL playoff history;

San Diego cornerback Terry Lewis chases down New York Giant wide receiver Stacy Robinson in a 1986 encounter. (Fred Roe)

Rolf Benirschke kicking a 27-yard field goal in overtime. But then in what may be the coldest game in NFL history, a wind chill factor of 59 below zero and mercury of 9 below, the Chargers go down to defeat to the Cincinnati Bengals 27-7. (1981)

With a record of 6-3-0 in a strike-shortened season, San Diego earns its way to the playoffs for the fourth straight year. (1982)

The Chargers take the first round playoff game against Pittsburgh, 31-28, as Dan Fouts throws for 333 yards and Chuck Muncie runs for 126 yards on 25 carries, but San Diego is defeated in the second round by Miami, 34-13. (1982)

In a game against Kansas City tight end Kellen Winslow sets a new club record by catching 14 passes. (1983)

The seating capacity of San Diego Jack Murphy Stadium is expanded to 60,100. (1984)

Alex G. Spanos purchases majority interest in the Chargers from Eugene V. Klein. (1984)

Bettering his earlier performance, Kellen Winslow catches 15 passes at Green Bay for a new club record. (1984)

In the fourth quarter of a game against Pittsburgh, wide receiver Charlie Joiner sets a new NFL record with his 650th pass reception. (1984)

Guard Ed White sets the NFL record for playing in the most games as an offensive lineman, 241. (1985)

With the Chargers going 4-12-0, the club's worst record since 1975, and ending up in last place in the AFC West, Don Coryell resigns as head coach. (1986)

Al Saunders, a San Diego assistant coach, is hired to replace Coryell. (1987)

Record Holders

Career

Rushing yards	Paul Lowe (1960–67)	4,963
Passing yards	Dan Fouts (1973–86)	40,523
Passing TD's	Dan Fouts (1973–86)	244
Pass receptions	Charlie Joiner (1976–85)	552
Receiving yards	Lance Alworth (1962–70)	9,585
Interceptions	Dick Harris (1960–65)	29
Field Goals	Rolf Benirschke (1977–85)	130
Total TD's	Lance Alworth (1962–70)	83
Total points	Rolf Benirschke (1977–85)	679

Season

Rushing yards	Earnest Jackson, 1984	1,179
Passing yards	Dan Fouts, 1981	4,802
Passing TD's	Dan Fouts, 1981	33
Pass receptions	Kellen Winslow, 1980	89
Receiving yards	Lance Alworth, 1965	1,602
Interceptions	Charlie McNeil, 1961	9
Field Goals	Rolf Benirschke, 1980	24
Total TDs	Chuck Muncie, 1981	19
Total points	Rolf Benirschke, 1980	118

Game

Rushing yards	Keith Lincoln, 1/5/64	206
Passing yards	Dan Fouts, 10/19/80	444
	Dan Fouts, 12/11/82	444
Passing TD's	Dan Fouts, 11/22/81	6
Pass receptions	Kellen Winslow, 10/7/84	15
Interceptions	many times	3
Field Goals	many times	4
Total TD's	Kellen Winslow, 11/22/81	5
Total points	Kellen Winslow, 11/22/81	30

Top Coaches

	Record	Win Percentage	Years
Sid Gillman	83–51–6	.619	1960–69
Don Coryell	71–53–0	.572	1978–86
Charlie Waller	9–7–3	.562	1969–70

All-Pros

Year	Player	Position	Year	Player	Position	Year	Player	Position
1960	Jack Kemp	QB		Earl Faison	DE		Ron Mix	T
	Paul Lowe	HB	1964	Lance Alworth	WR	1978	Louie Kelcher	DT
	Ron Mix	T		Keith Lincoln	FB		Russ Washington	T
	Volney Peters	DT		Ron Mix	T	1979	Dan Fouts	QB
	Dick Harris	DB		Earl Faison	DE		John Jefferson	WR
1961	Chuck Allen	MLB	1965	Lance Alworth	WR	1980	Kellen Winslow	TE
	Ron Mix	T		Paul Lowe	RB		John Jefferson	WR
	Earl Faison	DE		Earl Faison	DE		Charlie Joiner	WR
	Dick Harris	DB		Ernie Ladd	DT		Gary Johnson	DT
	Charlie McNeil	DB	1966	Lance Alworth	WR		Fred Dean	
1962	Dave Kocurek	TE		Ron Mix	T	1981	Kellen Winslow	TE
	Ron Mix	T	1967	Lance Alworth	WR	1982	Dan Fouts	QB
1963	Tobin Rote	OB		Walt Sweeney	G		Wes Chandler	WR
	Lance Alworth	WR		Ron Mix	T		Doug Wilkerson	G
	Keith Lincoln	FB	1968	Lance Alworth	WR		Kellen Winslow	TE
	Ron Mix	T		Walt Sweeney	G			

Seattle Seahawks

11220 N.E. 53rd Street
Kirkland, Washington 98033

Stadium: Kingdome (capacity 64,984)

Training camp: 11220 N.E. 53rd Street
                Kirkland, Washington 98033

Colors: blue, green and silver

Historical Highlights

The 1970s

The Seattle Seahawks join the NFL as an expansion franchise, ownership going to a syndicate headed by Lloyd W. Nordstrom. The team is slotted in the NFC Western Division along with the Rams, 49ers, Saints, and Falcons, and will play its games at the indoor stadium The Kingdome. (1976)

The first head coach of the Seahawks is Jack Patera, a onetime NFL linebacker, who most recently had served as an assistant to Bud Grant at Minnesota. Despite much promise shown by quarterback Jim Zorn and wide receiver Steve Largent, the Seahawks lose 12 of 14 games in their maiden season. (1976)

The Seahawks are moved to the American Football conference and placed in the Western Division, joining the Raiders, Broncos, Chargers, and Chiefs. (1977)

Seattle runs up the biggest score of its brief history in annihilating the Buffalo Bills 56–17 at the Kingdome, a club high score that has never been equalled. (1977)

The Seahawks post their first winning season, 9–7–0, good enough for a tie with Oakland for second place in the AFC West. Steve Largent leads the AFC in receptions with 71 and in yards gained receiving, 1,168, while running back David Sims leads the entire NFL in touchdowns scored with 15, a club record he still shares today. (1978)

Jack Patera is honored as AFC coach of the year. (1978)

A second consecutive winning season, again 9–7–0, enables Seattle to share third place in the AFC West. (1979)

The 1980s

Defensive back John Harris intercepts 10 passes for Seattle, tops in the AFC, a team standard of which he is still part-owner. (1981)

Jack Patera is fired and Mike McCormack is hired as interim head coach. (1982)

Chuck Knox becomes Seattle's third head coach and Mike McCormack moves to the front office as president and general manager. (1983)

All-American running back Curt Warner from Penn State is Seattle's first round draft choice. (1983)

Behind the rushing of Curt Warner, who led the entire AFC with 1,449 yards on 335 carries, the Seahawks win 9 of 16 games and as a wild card secure their first playoff berth. (1983)

Seattle triumphs over Denver in the AFC wild card game 31–7, highlighted by three touchdown passes from Dave Krieg. Another win over Miami by the score of 27–20 qualifies the Seahawks to confront the Los Angeles Raiders for the AFC championship, but they lose the title 30–14. (1983)

Chuck Knox takes AFC Coach of the Year honors. (1983)

Cornerback Dave Brown ties an NFL record by returning two interceptions for touchdowns in a 45–0 rout of the Kansas City Chiefs, and the Seahawks set a new NFL mark with a total of four interceptions returned for TDs in that game. (1984)

The largest crowd ever to attend a Seattle game, 64,411, fills The Kingdome to watch a game against the Broncos, but the Seahawks disappoint with a 31–14 loss. (1984)

Seattle again earns a place in the playoffs with a record of 12–4–0, the best in its history, but still are a game behind the Broncos in the AFC West. In the wild card match-up, the Seahawks defeat the Raiders 13–7, but then succumb to the Dolphins in the divisional playoff game 31–10. (1984)

Safety Kenny Easley is named AFC Defensive Player of the Year. (1984)

The Seahawks break ground for a new practice and training facility and office complex at Northwest College in Kirkland. (1985)

Steve Largent leads the entire league in pass reception yardage with 1,287, also a club record. (1985)

The Seahawks post an impressive record of 10–6–0, but because of qualifiers are unable to make the playoffs. (1986)

Curt Warner leads the AFC in rushing with 1,481 yards on 319 carries, and his 13 rushing touchdowns are also the conference high. Punt returner Bobby Joe Edmonds leads the NFL with an average return of 12.3 yards. (1986)

*Jim Zorn, southpaw quarterback,
is Seattle's all-time leading
passer, gaining more than
20,000 yards passing between
1976–1984. (Seattle Seahawks)*

*Seattle's all-time top
scorer and pass receiver,
Steve Largent, began his pro
career in Seattle in 1976.
(Seattle Seahawks)*

Memorable Years

Year	Record	Achievement
1983	9-7-0	AFC runner-up
1984	12-4-0	Playoff participant

Record Holders

Career		
Rushing yards	Sherman Smith (1976-82)	3,429
Passing yards	Jim Zorn (1976-84)	20,042
Passing TD's	Jim Zorn (1976-84)	107
Pass receptions	Steve Largent (1976-86)	694
Receiving yards	Steve Largent (1976-86)	11,129
Interceptions	Dave Brown (1976-86)	50
Field Goals	Efren Herrera (1978-81)	64
Total TD's	Steve Largent (1976-86)	88
Total points	Steve Largent (1976-86)	529

Season		
Rushing yards	Curt Warner, 1956	1 481
Passing yards	Dave Krieg, 1984	3 671
Passing TD's	Dave Krieg, 1984	32
Pass receptions	Steve Largent, 1985	79
Receiving yards	Steve Largent, 1985	1,287
Interceptions	John Harris, 1981	10
	Kenny Easley, 1984	10
Field Goals	Efren Herrera, 1980	20
	Norm Johnson, 1984	20
Total TDs	David Sims, 1978	15
	Sherman Smith, 1979	15
Total points	Norm Johnson, 1984	110

Game		
Rushing yards	Curt Warner, 11/27/83	207
Passing yards	Dave Krieg, 11/20/83	418
Passing TD's	Dave Krieg, 12/2/84	5
Pass receptions	David Hughes, 9/27/81	12
	Steve Largent, 11/25/84	12
Receiving yards	Steve Largent, 11/25/84	191
Interceptions	Kenny Easley, 9/3/84	3
Field Goals	Efren Herrera, 10/5/80	4
	Norm Johnson, 9/3/84	4
Total TD's	Daryl Turner, 9/15/85	4
Total points	Daryl Turner, 9/15/85	24

Top Coaches

	Record	Win Percentage	Years
Chuck Knox	42-27-0	.609	1983-86
Mike McCormack	4-3-0	.571	1982

All-Pros

Year	Player	Position
1983	Kenny Easley	S
1984	Joe Nash	DT
	Kenny Easley	S
	Norm Johnson	K
1985	Steve Largent	WR
	Kenny Easley	S

2nd TIME OUT

The Oldest Fight Song

It is often believed that the first pro football fight song came at the urging of the flamboyant, band-conscious George Preston Marshall in the late 1930s. No so.

The very first, at least in traceable history, is credited to the Chicago Bears in their first year in the NFL carrying that team name, 1922. George Halas and Dutch Sternaman, co-owners of the team, adopted this fight song. There was no record of who wrote it or whether that songwriter ever got paid for his or her efforts. There was no band on hand to perform it in those days. There was a great deal of poetic license in the lyrics. But nevertheless it was a fight song, and it is said that others besides the devoted Halas and Sternaman at one time or another in the 1920s sang its lilting lyrics.

From the East and from the West,
They send their very best
To play against the pride of old Chicago.
There is none of them compare with our Chicago Bears.
Through the line they go.
Hold them down Chicago, Hold them down,
Is the cry of everybody in our town.
Just watch the way they meet and tumble their foe,
Out to win Chicago Bears, they will always go.
Cross that line Chicago, cross that line,
That's the way to play, you're doing fine,
And when the season's o'er and you have to play no more'
Chicago Bears will stand out force.

Much more familiar today, at least to Chicago Bears fans, is the team's newer fight song, "Bear Down Chicago Bears," composed by Al Hoffman in 1941. Hoffman's other famous musical hit song was "If I knew you were comin', I'd have baked a cake."

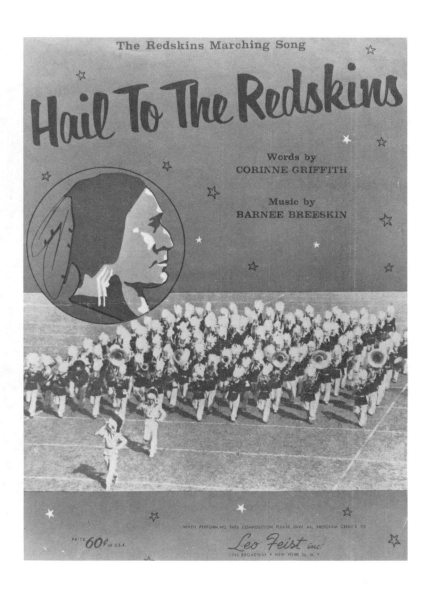

HAIL TO THE REDSKINS

Hail to the Redskins.
Hail Victory!
Braves on the warpath.
Fight for old D.C.
Scalp 'um, swamp 'um, we will
Take 'um big score.
Read 'um,
Weep 'um, touchdown,
We want heap more.
Fight on, fight on, till you have won.
Sons of Wash-ing-ton.
Rah! Rah! Rah!
Hail to the Redskins
Hail Victory!
Braves on the warpath.
Fight for old D.C.

© Copyright, 1938, Leo Feist, Inc.

George Preston Marshall's favored fight song, written in 1937, and his marching band, replete with headdresses, playing it for Washington Redskins fans.

Cheerleaders change

Testament to the fact that cheerleading, like the pro game itself, has changed over the years: the Dallas Cowboys cheerleaders circa 1960, and a representative of the internationally-known Cowboys' cheerleaders of the 1980s.

The Tonawanda Kardex The Forgotten Franchise

By Joe Horrigan

Quick! What is the only National Football League team ever to lose just one league game during its entire existence? Don't look for the answer in the NFL's Official Standings, its not there.

The first year the NFL issued official standings was 1921. According to that list the 10-1-1 Chicago Staleys (renamed the Chicago Bears in 1922) were the league champions, while the 0-8-0 Cincinnati Celts finished last among the 13 listed NFL teams. What the official standings do not list is an additional eight teams that operated in the NFL during that season.

While no official explanation has ever been offered why the teams from Washington, D.C.; Muncie, Hammond and Evansville, Indiana; Louisville, Kentucky; Minneapolis, Minnesota; New York City and Tonawanda, New York are omitted, a generally accepted theory is that they played an insufficient number of league games to be considered in the percentage race for the title. In fact, the Tonawanda team, known as the Kardex, played...and lost...just one league game during its brief existence.

The Tonawanda Kardex (named after and possibly sponsored by the Kardex Company) was granted an NFL franchise on August 27, 1921. However, the *Tonawanda News*, that city's major newspaper, failed to report the event until four days later and after it had already appeared in the neighboring *Buffalo News*. The *Tonawanda News* quoted the Buffalo paper as saying that the team would be "utilized entirely as a road team . . . with some local talent engaged". The paper also reported that there would be "eight or ten such teams to do the touring to the big cities where the dough lies".

The Kardex first game was against an independent pro team from Syracuse. In a rain interrupted game, the two New York State teams sloshed and slopped their way to a scoreless tie.

The next and last team the Tonawandans met was the NFL's charter member Rochester Jeffersons. The Jeffersons, who were by no means a football powerhouse, embarrassed the Kardex team 45-0.

Unable or unwilling to schedule any more league games for the 1921 season, the Tonawanda Kardex packed away their football togs and NFL franchise forever, barely leaving a trace of their existence behind.

(Originally published in the *Coffin Corner*, the official publication of the Professional Football Research Association)

The First NFL Night Game

When was the first National Football League night game played?...Answer: Wednesday night, September 24, 1930, in Portsmouth, Ohio between the Brooklyn Dodgers and the Portsmouth Spartans. Portsmouth, coached by Potsy Clark, won the game 12-0...This bit of NFL history is commemorated by a poster and a set of team rosters recently presented to the Pro Football Hall of Fame in Canton, Ohio, by Earl E. Joseph of Portsmouth, Ohio...Portsmouth, the forerunner of the current Detroit Lions' franchise, went on to finish eighth in the league that year with a 5-6-3 record while Brooklyn, coached by Al Jolley, was fourth with 7-4-1. Research by the Hall of Fame staff discloses that the game touchdowns were scored by Chuck Bennett and Will Glasgow.

Half-Time Dangers

The professional Detroit Lions engaged the Western Army All-Stars in a bruising football battle in Detroit, on September 11, 1942.

Detroit was beaten, 12-0.

Nobody was injured—except a man who never got into the game.

Lloyd Cardwell, a Detroit halfback, while on the bench, decided to get a drink of water between halves. He leaned over to press the faucet and jammed two vertebrae, was carried off the field and taken to a doctor for treatment.

Jimmy Conzelman Says . . .

Yes, sir! Some of these pro fans can tell you off. In one of the Cardinal games a few years back, we were losing by three touchdowns. A plainly disgusted gent wearing a short reefer and a cap sat in one of the front rows. He held his jaws clamped tightly on a bulky cud of tobacco while play was in progress. But, once the ball was dead, his chin quickly resumed its wide, rotary motion. Toward the end of the game, with the score unchanged, a Cardinal player sustained a leg injury. A half dozen of his teammates quickly picked him up, three on each side, and carried him off the field. As they reached a point at the side lines near the tobacco-chewing spectator, one of the players lost his grip on the injured player, dropping him to the ground. The crowd gasped sympathetically; but not so the fan. He opened his mouth, dropped the cud in a waiting hand and stood up.

"Didn't they learn you bums nothing in collich?" he yelled, emphasizing each word with a shake of his head. "Why, you ain't even good pall-bearers!"

Heywood Hale Broun Remembers...

My own first memories of professional football go back to a man I remember as being approximately three feet high, Davey O'Brien, quarterback of the Philadelphia Eagles. To my mind's eye—and the mind is that of a frenzied college freshman now somewhat altered through being stored in the head of a middle-aged man—O'Brien is a tiny creature who has to reach up to take the ball from the center and who then fades desperately back like someone from one of Charles Schulz's Peanuts teams lost in a nightmare of ill-intentioned monsters. Somehow the little O'Brien escapes the huge linesmen and passes the ball 100 yards through the air and we are all cheering...and dealing to each other almost as much punishment as the players are managing on the field.

Some factual researches have revealed to me that O'Brien, though small for a football player, actually weighed 160 pounds at the time, and is a person whom I, at 163 pounds, am not entitled to regard as spectacularly undersized.

John Robertson on the WFL

You could always tell a WFL team when it gathered in a local diner for a pregame meal. The pep talk consisted of three words from the team general manager: "Separate checks, please."

The Philadelphia Bell had announced crowds of 60,000 for each of their first two home games, but enterprising reporters discovered that 90 percent of the house had been papered. Presumably, the owner had let the fans in free—hoping they would pay to get out.

The Blazers were finally beaten in the World Bowl by the Birmingham Americans, coached by former Ottawa Rough Rider mentor Jack Gotta.

"I'll never forget that day," said Gotta. "We were in the dressing room afterward, quaffing some rented champagne, when some guy comes in with a court order to seize our uniforms because the team was bankrupt."

"Well, chuckled Gotta, "they kind of suspected we were in a little financial difficulty when we couldn't pay them for the last few games."

New Officials' Uniforms

The officials will be obliged to appear in the new National league uniforms, sartorially resplendent creations in stripes designed to assist spectators in ascertaining more quickly whether it was the referee or the field judge who made that last decision. Referees will wear black and white stripped shirts. Red and white striped shirts will designate the umpire in all National league games and the field judge will sport green and white. The headlines—men's colors are orange and white. Numbers adorn the back.

For cold or rainy weather, the outfit includes a mackinaw length coat corresponding in design, color scheme and number with the shirts. Those desiring head-pieces must wear the official cap, which is white with the National league shield in front.

Teams That Came and Went

These teams made appearances in the National Football League although most of them left little mark on the league. The majority, like the dinosaur of yore, fell to extinction, while some were merely victims of restlessness and moved to other towns.

Team	Years in NFL
Akron Pros	1920–26
Baltimore Colts	1950–83 (became the Indianapolis Colts in 1984)
Boston Braves	1932
Boston Bulldogs	1929
Boston Redskins	1933–36 (became the Washington Redskins in 1937)
Boston Yanks	1944–48
Brooklyn Dodgers	1930–42
Brooklyn Lions	1926
Brooklyn Tigers	1944
Buffalo All-Americans	1920–23
Buffalo Bisons	1924–25, 27, 29
Buffalo Rangers	1926

Team	Years in NFL
Canton Bulldogs	1920–23, 25–26
Chicago Cardinals	1920–59 (became the St. Louis Cardinals in 1960)
Chicago Tigers	1920
Cincinnati Celts	1921
Cincinnati Reds	1933–34
Cleveland Bulldogs	1924–25, 27
Cleveland Indians	1921, 23, 31
Cleveland Rams	1937–45 (became the Los Angeles Rams in 1946)
Cleveland Tigers	1920
Columbus Panhandles	1920–22
Columbus Tigers	1923–26
Dallas Texans	1952
Dayton Triangles	1920–29
Decatur Staleys	1920 (became the Chicago Staleys in 1921, Chicago Bears in 1922)
Detroit Heralds	1920
Detroit Panthers	1921, 25–26
Detroit Wolverines	1928
Duluth Eskimos	1926–27
Duluth Kelleys	1923–25
Evansville Crimson Giants	1921–22
Frankford Yellow Jackets	1924–31
Hammond Pros	1920–26
Hartford Blues	1926
Kansas City Cowboys	1924–26
Kenosha Maroons	1924
Los Angeles Buccaneers	1926
Louisville Brecks	1921–23
Louisville Colonels	1926
Milwaukee Badgers	1922–26
Minneapolis Marines	1921–24
Minneapolis Redjackets	1929–30
Muncie Flyers	1920–21
New York Bulldogs	1949
New York Yankees	1927–28
New York Yanks	1950–51
Newark Tornadoes	1930
Oorang Indians	1922–23
Orange Tornadoes	1929
Pittsburgh Pirates	1933–40 (became the Pittsburgh Steelers in 1941)
Portsmouth Spartans	1930–33 (became the Detroit Lions in 1934)
Pottsville Maroons	1925–28
Providence Steam Roller	1925–31
Racine Legion	1922–24
Racine Tornadoes	1926
Rochester Jeffersons	1920–25
Rock Island Independents	1920–25
St. Louis All-Stars	1923
St. Louis Gunners	1934
Staten Island Stapletons	1929–32
Toledo Maroons	1922–23

Bull Doehring, one of the more unusual backs in Chicago Bear history. He could throw a pass behind his back as far and as accurately as an average player could overhand. In one game, he threw a 30-yard behind-the-back pass to Luke Johnsos, who was so dazzled by it that he dropped the ball in the end zone. Doehring had an extraordinarily strong passing arm. It was said that he never threw the ball as far as he could because no receiver was fast enough to get that far downfield.

6 LEGENDARY COACHES

George Halas

"He is the nicest rich man I know," said Hall of Fame coach Jimmy Conzelman. "He throws nickels around like manhole covers," Mike Ditka mentioned in regard to him. Economics aside, George Halas was the winningest coach in the history of professional football, and the only man to be associated with the NFL throughout its first six and a half decades.

Halas organized the old Decatur Staleys in 1920, moved them to Chicago the following year with his partner Ed "Dutch" Sternaman, and renamed them the Bears in 1922. Halas and Sternaman co-owned and ran the team until, Papa Bear, as Halas came to be known bought Sternaman out in 1932. Halas served as head coach for 40 seasons, and no other NFL coach comes close to matching his 326 victories.

Halas and his Chicago Bears led the NFL from its rag days to the high-powered, big-money sport of modern times. He was the first with a variety of innovations that shaped the game of professional football in America. The sport was truly his life and his imprint is etched in every facet of the game.

There are no simple secrets to explain the unmatched success of Papa Bear, but an old anecdote may provide one clue. At a Bears practice session, Coach Halas was once approached by a young man who introduced himself as John "Bull" Doehring.

"Do you want the best passer in football?" Doehring asked.

"I want the best of everything," Halas answered. That was his unending pursuit, and often enough he got it.

Another clue to his success was his intensity. He was big enough only to make the "lightweight" football team at Crane High School in Chicago, but in his second year at the University of Illinois he was finally able to attract the attention of the team's legendary coach, Bob Zuppke. During an afternoon scrimmage, the then-halfback Halas repeatedly charged out of the backfield with unbridled fury.

"Who in the world is that?" Zuppke asked one of his assistants.

"George Halas, a kid from Chicago."

"That kid runs so hard he'll get killed," the coach said. "Make an end out of him."

After the 1917 season, Halas's last as an Illini, Bob Zuppke made a speech in which he asked, "Why is it that just as my players begin to know something about football I lose them by graduation?" The words made a permanent impression on the young end.

That very intensity is what helped him to excel at a number of different sports. He was captain of the Illini basketball team in his senior year, and he devel-

George Halas, with his hand in the hair of his favorite T formation quarterback, Sid Luckman

oped his baseball skills sufficiently to earn a tryout with the New York Yankees.

The very next year, however, 1918, Halas was in the Navy, stationed at Great Lakes Naval Training Center north of Chicago. There, he joined a football team that included such stars of the day as Jimmy Conzelman, Paddy Driscoll, Hugh Blacklock, and Harry Eilson. The team was invited to the Rose Bowl to play the Mare Island Marines on New Year's Day 1919, and the Great Lakes' players were offered early discharges from the Navy in exchange for a victory. In one of his finest performances as a player, Halas caught a touchdown pass from Driscoll, and intercepted a Marine pass, returning it 77 yards to the 3-yard line. Great Lakes won the game, 17–0, and Halas, among others, was shortly afterward mustered out of the navy.

Once out of military service, Halas wasted little time signing a contract—as an outfielder with the New York Yankees baseball team. But during the exhibition season, he hit a double off Dodger ace Rube Marquard and seriously injured his hip sliding into third when he tried to stretch it into a triple.

"There goes one of the best outfield prospects I ever saw," said Yankee manager Miller Huggins as he sent Halas off for treatment. Never again would he be the fleet runner that he had been before the injury. The next year, 1920 Huggins found someone to replace Halas in the Yankee outfield, Papa Bear often mentioned later with a glint in his eye, a promising young pitcher recently moved to the outfield named Babe Ruth.

After that Halas joined the Staley Starch Works in Decatur, Illinois, as an employee and athletic director of the firm's sideline sports program. While playing on the company baseball team, Halas also began searching the midwest for football talent to stock the company football team he was directed to organize by owner A.E. Staley. Many young players, recent college graduates, were willing to come to Decatur, lured there, at least partly, by A.E. Staley's offer to provide two hours of each day, with pay, for practice during the football season.

In September of 1920 Halas sat at the organizing meeting, convened in a Hupmobile showroom in Canton, Ohio, of the league that was to become the NFL. With an official league to play in, the Staleys of Decatur in their only year of existence won 10 of 13 games, and came in second to the Akron Pros.

Despite the fine season, A.E. Staley realized that as a result of declining business he could no longer afford to underwrite the expenses of a professional football team. So he suggested that Halas move the team to Chicago, and offered to give him $5,000 to make the transition. "All I ask," he added, "is that you call the team the Staleys for one season." So with Dutch Sternaman as his partner, Halas moved the team to Chicago, where he negotiated a contract with William Veeck, Sr., to lease Wrigley Field in exchange for 15 percent of the gate. The owners of the fledgling team then started from scratch to drum up interest in the sport, traveling to the various newspaper offices in the city with press releases in hand.

"We were always greeted cordially," Halas said. "They listened attentively, or at least politely, then tossed our written releases into the wastebasket. We hopefully looked for just some mention every day— even one of those little one-inchers that come in handy to fill out a column. And, by golly, did we cheer when we found one!"

Filling Wrigley Field with spectators was only a starry-eyed dream in the early days, but the Staleys, renamed the Bears in 1922, continued their winning ways, establishing a championship 9-1-1 record in 1921 and the team's first league title and going 9-3-0

the next season. A highlight of the 1923 season for Coach Halas, still playing end, came when he recovered a Jim Thorpe fumble and scampered 98 yards for the touchdown with the legendary Indian at his heels the entire way, an NFL record that lasted until 1972.

Halas did not encounter his first losing season until 1929, when friction between himself and co-owner Dutch Sternaman became critical. "Here's how bad it was," recalled one of the players. "We had two offenses, one given us by George and the other by Dutch. No one knew what to do on any play. There were times when our own men were bumping heads. You've never seen such a mess."

By the following season, Papa Bear found the radical solution his ailing team needed. He stepped down, both as player and coach, and convinced his partner to agree to hiring a relatively unknown replacement, Ralph Jones, who had recently been in charge of the team at Lake Forest College north of Chicago. To give the new coach a running start, collegiate star Bronko Nagurski was added to the squad that same year, joining Red Grange in a backfield of legendary proportion.

In 1932, calling on help from anywhere he could get it during the height of the Depression, Halas managed to buy out Dutch Sternaman's share of the Bears for $38,000. After three years at the helm, coach Jones quit, and Halas took over, promising that "it will be only temporary, one season at most." In his "temporary" season Coach Halas and his Bears won the first NFL championship playoff between the newly established East and West Conferences. Papa Bear was hooked again. The temporary arrangement lasted 22 years.

One of the great highlights of Papa Bear's career as a coach was the 1940 championship season. After losing a game late in the year to the Washington Redskins, Halas and many of his players complained bitterly that their winning touchdown pass had been prevented by a Washington defender's flagrant interference of the Bears receiver, unnoticed by the officials.

George Halas, on retiring: *"I knew it was time to quit when I was chewing out an official and he walked off the penalty faster than I could keep up with him."*

Redskins owner George Preston Marshall called Halas and the Bears "crybabies." In postgame interviews, Marshall said among other insults, that "the Bears are quitters." Halas, faced with playing the same team for the championship, posted newspaper clippings of the Marshall quotes all over the clubhouse. Soon enough, he had his team worked into a frenzy.

"These guys are so mad," he worried out loud to an assistant, "that they'll be too busy trying to kill the Redskins instead of beating them at football. I've got to calm them down." By the time Halas finished putting his players through days of tough, precision drills, he had shaped their uncontrolled anger to a cool, controlled fury.

Successfully gambling that Washington would not change its hitherto successful defensive patterns, the Chicago offense took total control of the game. At the end of the third quarter, the score was 54–0, Chicago. Later, after the Bears scored their eleventh touchdown of the afternoon, the referee rushed over to Halas.

"George, I'm in a terrible jam," the anxious referee confessed. "The fans have kept every football kicked into the stands after each conversion. This is the last football we have. Would you mind asking your boys not to kick for the extra point but to run or pass for it?"

"My boys are perfect little gentlemen," Halas is said to have replied, and his team passed for the conversion. The final score was 73–0, with 10 different Bear players scoring touchdowns. George Halas and the Chicago Bears, briefly, were a national phenomenon. But after Pearl Harbor Day, many of the Bears, including Lieutenant Commander George Halas, left the football field for Europe and the Far East.

When Halas returned late in November 1945, the once powerful team had lost its first seven games of the season. With Halas taking command, they won their final three games, and won the NFL championship the following year. The 1950s, however, were undistinguished. In 1955, Halas announced that he would retire at season's end, giving way to long-time assistant Paddy Driscoll, two years younger than Halas, who managed to take the Bears to the NFL title game in 1956, but lost there to the Giants. After a losing season in 1957, however, Halas once again took over. In 1963, he commanded his last great Bears team, which compiled an 11–1–2 record and won the NFL crown. That same year, he became a charter member of the Hall of Fame. After four more so-so seasons, Papa Bear retired for good, posting a professional record of 326 wins, 151 defeats, and 30 ties.

Until his death on October 31, 1983, the Bears were not able to win another championship for their founder. But his influence was felt even after his departure, in the championship surge of 1985 and the victory in Super Bowl XX. In his last important decision regarding the Bears, a wheel-chair bound Papa Bear decided on his coaching staff. He signed Buddy Ryan as defensive coordinator and former Bear player and Dallas assistant coach Mike Ditka as head coach. On the field that Super Bowl Sunday Papa Bear was represented there with the monogram GSH on the arm of each of his Chicago Bears.

Downs and Ups

The diversity of the job.

Same team, different times, different coaches.

Jim Dooley, 1969, Chicago Bears, 1–13–0

Mike Ditka, 1985 (season), Chicago Bears, 15–1–0

Earl "Curly" Lambeau

Earl "Curly" Lambeau coached the Green Bay Packers to 212 victories and is credited with founding and nourishing for 31 years the only smalltown team to survive to modern times in the NFL. The onetime playing coach (tailback) pioneered the aggressive use of the forward pass, was one of the first coaches to utilize above-the-ground coaching seats, and is a charter member of the Pro Football Hall of Fame.

But in the years he built his dynasty up in Green Bay, not everyone offered high praise.

"If that buzzard ever died," said Packer Hall of Fame tackle, Cal Hubbard, "they'd have trouble finding six guys to volunteer as pallbearers." Another Hall of Famer, Clarke Hinkle observed, "he was the founder, the creator, the coach. But I never really like him. Not really respected him, either . . . Lambeau learned his football from the players who played for him."

When his team visited other NFL franchises, however, stadium attendance often outnumbered the population of the then tiny Wisconsin city his team represented. And, Curly's performance on the sidelines sometimes matched the excitement on the field. He was often wildly emotional, raising his arms to the sky or pounding his head with his fists. He coached entire games in a rage, once telling a player, "I think better when I'm excited." As one of the harshest taskmasters the game had yet seen, he produced animosity as frequently as he built champions.

Lambeau regarded team discipline as a financial affair. Any player who missed a practice, for example, was automatically fined $500, a particularly stiff levy for the era.

"That will cost you $500 each," he said after four of his players failed to show up one day at the practice field. "Write out the checks." With the kind of sixth sense that seemed to keep him an unhappy step ahead of the players, he added, "And I'm cashing them, too, and I'm doing it before you can stop payment."

After he had written out the check, one lineman said, "If you cash my check I'll kill you."

"It won't do any good," the coach responded. "It would merely cost you another $500."

Like many of the early guiding lights of the sport, Curly Lambeau started his career as a player and eventually mixed coaching with it. As a player, his collegiate credentials were impressive and brief. He played a single season under Knute Rockne at Notre Dame, and was a freshman starter in the backfield along with George Gipp. When complications from a tonsillectomy caused him to miss a semester, Lambeau dropped out of college and returned to Green

Curly Lambeau, with an unidentified Green Bay Packer

Bay, where he began working for the Indian (later Acme) Packing Company of Green Bay.

During the summer of 1919, Curly worked at the packing company for the unusually high salary of $250 a month. But as autumn approached, the urge to play football returned. He talked to one of the company's executives, Frank Peck, about the possibility of backing a team. "We even could call ourselves the Packers," Lambeau suggested.

"I'll let you have $500 for uniforms," Peck said. "From there on its all yours." The words were prophetic. With Lambeau as its coach, captain, and star tailback, the Packers won ten straight games against other midwestern teams. It was not a season of the highest caliber football, but many of the games were tough enough.

"On our first three running plays," Curly recalled about a game with a team from Ishpeming, "we lost three men with broken bones. So we never called for another running play. We just passed them silly and won 33–0. That was the day I realized how valuable the forward pass was."

In 1921, the Packers joined the NFL and finished a respectable fourth. Like many other coaches in the early days of the game, Lambeau stretched the eligibility rules beyond the breaking point by hiring college players under assumed names. But NFL president Joe Carr decided to crack down on the practice, and nailed Curly's team as his first victim. He was forced to return the $50 franchise fee to the Acme Packing Company. In order to save the team, Lambeau used his own savings to buy back the franchise. During the summer of 1922, he attended the NFL meeting in Canton, Ohio, after a friend sold his car to pay for the trip. The Packers and Lambeau were soon back in business.

Under Curly's stringent leadership, the team struggled for years, managing a second place finish in 1927 but slumped the following year. After the 1928 season, Lambeau made the moves that turned his team into champions. He acquired three star players, Cal Hubbard from the Giants, Johnny Blood McNally from Pottsville, and Iron Mike Michalske from the Yankees. The Packers won the NFL championship for the next three years in a row.

During the championship era, Curly played his final game. During a contest when the Packer's vaunted passing attack failed, Curly fell into a rage. "I'll show you fellows how to throw passes," he shouted and put himself into the game as a substitute. The resentment was immediately intense.

"Let's open the gates on Curly," Cal Hubbard told the other players on the field. When the ball was snapped to Lambeau, the Green Bay line opened up and players from the opposing team poured through, hammering the player/coach to the turf. With an angry look at his players, Lambeau hobbled to the sidelines, never to play again.

After the three championship seasons, the Packer's fortunes fell a bit, but revived considerably when Lambeau acquired Don Hutson, the "Alabama Antelope."

Lambeau, Hutson, and the rest of the team traveled to New York and on the way the coach got an idea that transformed the game. "The worst spot on the field for watching a football game is on the bench," he said. "The coach doesn't even see what's going on. The

best spot in the park is the press box. It's high up and the view is unobstructed."

Lambeau announced to his players: "Next Sunday I'll give you your orders from the press box. I'll talk to you before the game and I'll be in the clubhouse at halftime. For the first time in my life, though, I'll know all that's going on."

On that Sunday, Curly coached the first half of the game from the press box, telephoning orders to an assistant coach on the bench. But at halftime, his careful plans went awry. Although he had timed the move from the press box to the clubhouse, he had made the test when the Polo Grounds were empty. Now, thousands of people seemed bent on impeding his progress. He reached his team only in time to see them heading back to the field. "Go get 'em fellows," he shouted weakly.

"Lambeau liked to coach the offense best," one of his guards once said. "He really didn't care if the other team scored 40 points as long as we scored 41." And the Packers scored plenty of points, winning championships five times between 1929 and 1939. Still, as the team grew into a dynasty, there were those who felt Lambeau was too successful for his own good.

He began spending his winters at Malibu Beach in California. No longer suffering through Wisconsin blizzards with the townspeople, one wag labelled him "The Earl of Hollywood." The resentment spread to the players.

In a 1949 game, the Packers were beaten by the NFL champion Chicago Cardinals. Storming into the clubhouse after the game, Curly screamed, "Everyone is fined half his game salary."

"What for?" a player asked.

"Indifferent play," he shot back. They paid, but it was a serious blunder. Although he gave the money back a few months later, Curly Lambeau had lost the respect of his players and was forced to move on. After a few indifferent years as the coach of the Chicago Cardinals and Washington Redskins, he retired from the game. But he left an indelible mark on the formative years of the NFL, and he gave Green Bay fans a sense of dominance they would not experience again until Vince Lombardi came to Wisconsin in 1959.

Earle "Greasy" Neale

The only man ever to play baseball in the World Series, lead a collegiate team to the Rose Bowl, and coach in two NFL championship games actually came to the professional coaching ranks late in his career. But when Greasy Neale finally arrived, he transformed a struggling franchise into a powerhouse.

Greasy Neale, whose nickname went back to his youth when he began calling a childhood friend "Dirty," who returned the compliment with an equally descriptive epithet, got his football coaching career launched early as well. While in high school at Parkersburg, West Virginia, the football coach was forced to resign, and Greasy became both the captain and the coach of his team, which managed to win one game under his leadership.

By 1912, when he arrived on the campus of West Virginia Wesleyan, his confidence as a football player was already well established. Asked what position he wanted to try out for, he answered, "I'm not going to try out for anything. I'm going to play end." In his first game as an end for Wesleyan, Greasy scored the touchdown that gave his team its first win ever over rival West Virginia.

Late in his collegiate career, Neale began playing professional football under the assumed name of Foster for the Canton Bulldogs, whose star player was Jim Thorpe. When the quarterback was hurt, Thorpe told Neale, aka Foster, to play quarterback. Although he had never played the position before, the Bulldogs managed a 3–0 win over Youngstown. But trouble was brewing for Greasy Foster.

Before a game at Akron, he learned that a cleric from Wesleyan was on his way to the Ohio town to look for the player named Foster, as well as another Wesleyan student believed to be playing for the Bulldogs and was prepared to demand both their resignations if caught in the act of playing football for money. "When we heard about this," Neale said, "we backtracked into West Virginia in a hurry and stayed under wraps all day Sunday."

By the next game, Neale was back with the Bulldogs. "All right," Thorpe said to him in the locker room, "you play fullback today."

"Fullback?" Neale protested. "I never backed up a line before."

"Well, you have to today," Thorpe said. "We have nobody else I'd trust."

Following his career at Wesleyan (and secret seasons with the Bulldogs and the Dayton Triangles) he began playing major league baseball with Cincinnati and then Philadelphia. He was with the Reds when they won the world championship in 1919, batting a

Greasy Neale, with his quarterback Tommy Thompson

Series high .357 in that infamous meeting with the Chicago "Black Sox."

"Neale was what I'd call a 'sick cat' player," National League umpire Larry Goetz recalled. "You'd see him at the plate and you wouldn't give a nickel for him, but somehow in the clutch he'd bloop one over the infield or dribble one through for a hit that won the game. Or he'd make an impossible catch to save the day." One impossible catch many people recall was made at the old Polo Grounds in New York. An instant after snaring a line drive, Greasy's head crashed into the fence, knocking him out cold. Although he was completely unconscious, another player had to pry the ball out of his grasp.

During the same years that he played baseball, Neale coached football at the then tiny Washington and Jefferson College (enrollment of 250). "We brought the players in," Neale said. "Didn't make any difference how many people were in the rest of the school." On New Year's Day 1922, his miniscule school played the heavily favored and vastly larger University of California to a scoreless tie in the Rose Bowl. Washington and Jefferson, playing only 11 men the entire game, in fact scored what could have been the winning touchdown, but it was called back on a penalty.

Greasy Neale went on to coach at Virginia and West Virginia and serve as assistant coach at Yale, where, he said, "I had to play with students. But we did all right anyway." Nevertheless, in 1929 he found himself without a job. "I wrote 154 letters," he recalled, "and still didn't get a job."

At the age of 39, he found a job playing and coaching for an independent pro team called the Irontown (Ohio) Tanks. Although the Tanks were not in the NFL, their season included five exhibition games against NFL teams. To the extreme embarrassment of the big-leaguers, Neale's Tanks won four of those contests.

In 1941, a Yale alumnus named Lex Thompson invited Greasy to come to Philadelphia to coach the Eagles, a team Thompson had just recently acquired. The $12,000 a year salary, twice what he had ever made coaching college teams, was "too much to pass up, even though the team was none too strong. All we had," Neale remembered, "was half a football squad that (previous owners) (Bert) Bell and (Art) Rooney didn't want. We didn't even have a number one or number two draft choice, since Bell had traded away the rights to them before Thompson had bought the club."

Setting to work to rebuild the team, Neale poured over college statistics. Without scouting a single player, he drafted 20 and signed 11. He also studied, month after month, game films of the Chicago Bears remarkable 73–0 triumph over Washington in the 1940 championship game. Although he had always promoted the single-wing offense, the Bears' T formation looked impressive enough for him to adopt. When asked if he had borrowed the new style of play from the Bears, he answered: "No, I stole it."

In his first season as an NFL coach, Greasy learned a bitter lesson about life in the big league. In the first quarter of a game against Curly Lambeau's tough Green Bay squad, the Eagles drove to the Packer 5 yard line. Philadelphia's Tommy Thompson, who had sight in only one eye but was still one of the league's finest quarterbacks, passed the ball into the end zone, where it fell incomplete. To Greasy's astonishment, an official brought the ball back to the 20-yard line and awarded it to the Packers. Neale rushed onto the field demanding an explanation.

"The ball touched the ground in the end zone," was the official announcement, "and according to the rules it is a touchback." Although he had little time to study the pro rules, Greasy knew that this was a bonehead call. He demanded that Lambeau be called in for a conference.

"Whatever Lambeau says, goes," Neale said.

The Green Bay coach feigned surprise when he heard the arguments. "Why, Greasy," he said, "everybody knows that's a touchback." Later, Neale confronted Lambeau and shook the rule book in front of him. "Well, what do you know," Curly said with a grin. "It just goes to prove what I always say. A fellow is always learning something new in this pro football business."

During the early 1940s, Greasy Neale learned that it was hard to play good football when most of the young men in the world were at war. But by 1944, his fortunes, like that of the Allied forces, began to rise. Led by rookie halfback Steve Van Buren, the Eagles narrowly missed a divisional title that year, and again in 1945. After a disappointing season in 1946, due in large part to an injury to Van Buren, the Eagle's soared to their first divisional championship in 1947, but lost to the Chicago Cardinals in the NFL title game. Added to the potent offense had been Neale's stunning new Eagle defense with a five-man line and man-to-man pass coverage, innovations which caused considerable confusion among opponents. And in 1948 and 1949 his Eagles won NFL championships, defeating the Cardinals and then the Los Angeles Rams.

In 1949, Lex Thompson sold the team to James P. Clark, the head of a syndicate of 100 businessmen. Although the following season started off well, the defending champions lost their last four games. During the slide, Greasy and new owner James Clark got into a feud, capped by a physical brawl in the Polo Grounds locker room. Neale was fired the next season. Over the next year and a half, the team had three different head coaches.

Greasy Neale was respected by his players not only for his coaching genius but also for his sense of fair play. He is a member of both the Pro Football Hall of Fame and the College Football Hall of Fame.

Steve Owen, after Greasy Neale collapsed at the end of the New York Giant—Philadelphia Eagle game during the 1940s: *"I always knew I would see one of us coaches go that way. I have felt like that myself. But Neale was all right—he was cursing me and my Giants as he crawled into the ambulance."*

Steve Owen

"Football started tough for me," Stout Steve Owen wrote in his popular 1952 book, *My Kind of Football,* "and it stayed tough." The man who led the New York Giants for 23 often glorious seasons started his football career knowing absolutely nothing about the game of which he eventually became a master.

A youngster who grew up in one of the only Caucasian families in Oklahoma's Indian Territory, Owen had never held a football when he went to Phillips University at Enid in 1918. Enrolled in the Student Army Training Corps, he was approached by the school's football coach, Johnny Maulbetsch, who had made a name for himself as the Flying Dutchman halfback at the University of Michigan.

Maulbetsch had noticed that Owen was big and strong, seemingly suited for football. He asked if Steve had ever played the game, and Owen said that he had not but was willing to try to learn. Maulbetsch suggested an immediate tryout and in a few minutes the student was suited up and ready to try blocking against the well-known coach.

For about 15 minutes I felt he was about to beat me to death," Owen wrote. "He put me in position and then blocked me down, and when I got up he put me down again. Only the two of us were there, with him thumping me around, trying to show how to tackle and block. He hit pretty hard, and I began to get a little mad.

"Once I got the hang of it, I hit him as hard as I could. He didn't get mad. He began to grin. After I gave him a few more heavy jolts, he laughed out loud and called it quits. He had found out what he wanted to know, whether I was a battler."

Because he did not understand even the rudimentary rules of football when he became a member of the Phillips team, Steve got a crash course, along with advice on proper eating, early bedtimes, and the avoidance of smoking. By the second game of the season he got into the game as a substitute. His hard play kept him in the lineup for the remainder of his college career, during which he gained a reputation as a superb defensive player.

By 1924, Owen joined the NFL's Kansas City Blues, and played for that city for two years. Following the conclusion of the 1925 season, Owen and Cowboy teammate Dave Nobel stalled their car in a heavy snowstorm in Iowa while en route home following a season-ending game in the East. After a farmer put the pair up for the night and used a team of horses to pull their car out of the snowdrift, Owen continued on to Wichita, Kansas, from where he planned to take a train home. At the station he met Dutch Hill, who was

Stout Steve Owen

rushing to a telegraph office to accept an offer to play some exhibition games in Florida with the brand new New York Giants, which Tim Mara had founded just a few months earlier.

"Tell 'em I'm available, too," Owen told Hill, and within a few days, Steve was in Florida playing with the Giants. The following season Tim Mara purchased Stout Steve's contract for $500 from Kansas City.

At the start of the 1926 season, the New York veterans were happy to give their relatively inexperienced teammate the usual razzing initiation. But before the regular season ever began, Owen was able to return the compliment. At an exhibition game in Trenton, where the temperature was in the 90s, many of the Giants were gasping for breath by halftime. Steve, stout as he was, was in better shape than most of the others. During the intermission, he inquired of each of the exhausted, perspiration-soaked teammates, "Do you fellows up here in New York play football for thirty minutes. Why in Kansas City we always went sixty minutes."

At New York, Owen proved himself an outstanding lineman, big and tough and the equal of any tackle in the game. From that sometimes unenviable position, he also began to learn the finer points of football, especially the defensive game. By the 1927 season, he was named captain of the team.

In 1931 he became head coach, on a handshake agreement with Tim Mara which lasted more than two decades. "The Mara's could not have been kinder to me," he wrote. "I never had a contract from the time I got the job, and there has never been a mention of one. Yet I have heard of coaches who held term contracts and still failed to last a single season."

Owen's first two seasons were less than memorable. The team, completing a 7–6–1 season in 1931, and 4–6–2 the following year.

The year 1933 was Steve Owen's last on the active player's list, but it was the beginning of his Giants dynasty. During a glorious 14-year period, his teams won the Eastern Division championship eight times and the NFL title twice. Among the many innovations he developed during this period was the A-formation offense, in which the line and the backs shifted in opposite directions, and the now-famous umbrella defense, which was particularly effective against the pass.

In 1935, the NFL expanded the team player limit to 24. Seeing that it was possible to field two completely different teams, Owen experimented with playing two different squads, alternating them by quarters in a two-platoon system. "Actually I only sent in 10 new players each quarter; Mel Hein (center and linebacker) was too good on offense and defense to take out and the 60 minutes never bothered him."

Stout Steve always insisted that the basics of football were relatively simple. "The best offense can be built around ten basic plays," he wrote. "Defense can be built on two. All the rest is razzle-dazzle, egomania, and box office." In truth, his basic plays had a fairly lengthy set of variations, and his NFL opponents were often confused by his tightly structured defenses.

Owen was a cagey field general who could think quickly. Several of his most famous coaching moves came when his team was playing against George Halas and the Bears. The 1934 championship game between the Giants and Chicago was played on a frozen field at the Polo Grounds in New York. The Bears jumped out to an early lead, but all the players were sliding on the icy field. Wanting his team to wear gym shoes instead of cleats, Owen dispatched Abe Cohen, his equipment manager, to Manhattan College to expropriate the basketball team's sneakers. In the second half nine Giant players sported sneakers, and the Giants scored 27 points to beat Chicago 30–13. The contest became famous as the "Sneakers Game."

In another contest with Chicago, Owen developed a screen pass featuring big Cal Hubbard, a tackle playing end. Owen admitted that the play was "probably illegal," but he used it effectively against the Bears nevertheless. By the next time the two teams met, Halas was ready, however.

The Bear coach presented a diagram of the suspect play to referee Jim Durfee. "This play is illegal and they can't use it," Halas said. Owen asked the referee to see the diagram, and was dismayed to discover how accurately it had been drawn.

"Jim," he said to Durfee, "Mr. Halas has this drawn out this way. We don't run it exactly that way. We run it legal." But despite his pleas, Owen could tell that the referee was skeptical. So he continued: "Furthermore, Jim, you've officiated enough games to know whether we run a play legal or not, without looking at a diagram." The ego ploy worked perfectly.

"I sure have," Durfee assured both coaches. "Get away from me, Halas."

Despite a couple of excellent seasons with 10–2–0 and 9–2–1 records, the Owen-coached Giants did not win another division championship after 1946. He retired in 1953. But in the glory years of the Giants, and the few lean years they suffered under him, Owen's Giants rarely played a noticeably poor game. In 1952, however, there was an outstanding exception. The Giants, destined to finish with a respectable 7–5 record, were humiliated 63–7 by the Steelers.

"It's a good thing I'm known as a defensive genius," he managed to joke after the game, "or the score might have been 100–7."

Steve Owen, with 153 victories to his credit, the seventh winningest coach in NFL history, was enshrined in the Pro Football Hall of Fame in 1966, two years after his death.

Paul Brown

"They couldn't beat a good junior college team," George Halas said of the Cleveland Browns at the time head coach Paul Brown led the team into the NFL. The Browns had been champions of the old All-America Football Conference for each of the four years of its existence before being absorbed by the NFL in 1950, but most NFL fans felt, like Bear coach Halas, that the Browns would not stand a chance in the stronger league.

"When you get a shot at people making fun of you." Paul Brown said later, "that's when you really go." The Browns answered everyone by winning each of their first three games against NFL teams by three or more touchdowns, including the season opener against the Philadelphia Eagles, defending NFL champions. The fourth game, against Chicago, was another severe test.

"The Bears came to Cleveland by train," Brown recalled. "Just in a fit of being generous, I went down to meet Halas and pay my respects. As they pulled into the station, I got a bit of a jolt. There was Halas and his wife seated at a table in the club car with Bill Downs and his wife. Downs was the referee. It really didn't mean a thing, but for a guy in the National League playing George Halas for the first time, it kind of shook me up."

Still the Browns beat the Bears that weekend, although it was by a mere four points. The Browns went on to take the NFL title in their very first year in the NFL, and won either the division or the league crown for each of their first six years in the league.

For Paul Brown, one of the greatest long-term strategists the pro game has known, Cleveland's success should not have come as much of a surprise. In 1950, he may have been a rookie coach in the NFL, but he was no stranger to football dynasties.

As a 120-pound sophomore, Brown's football career began in earnest at Ohio's Massillon High School when a series of injuries put him in the starting quarterback position. He then enrolled at Ohio State, but quickly realized that his small size would limit if not preclude his playing time in Big Ten football. Transferring to Miami (Ohio) University, he served admirably as the starting quarterback for two years. His first coaching job was at Severn, a U.S. Naval Academy prep school, but in 1932 he returned to Massillon High School, where he coached both football and basketball.

Although he judged his high school's football program a "mess" shortly after he arrived, Brown took a long-term approach to rejuvenating it. Part of his careful planning was to involve in his goals the athletic coaches from the three junior high schools that fed students into Massillon High. It did not take long for

Paul Brown

the record to reflect his work. The Massillon football team went 6–3–1 in 1932, Brown's first year as coach, 8–2 the following year and 9–1 the next. After that, the team went into overdrive, bringing home six Ohio state championships in a row. During that six-year period, the school's overall record was 58–1–1. His 1940 squad outscored its opponents 477–6. The crowds who came to watch the high school team outnumbered those of every college in Ohio except Ohio State.

With those glittering statistics, Paul Brown was a natural to replace Francis Schmidt as head coach of Ohio State in 1941. Although he still took a long-term view of his new position, Brown lost little time building his empire. OSU went 6–1–1 in Brown's first year, and 9–1 his second, good enough for a national championship and Coach of the Year honors for Brown.

But these were also the years of World War II, and by 1944, Brown was in the military, coaching winning teams at Great Lakes Naval Training Center in Illinois for two years (included was a stunning 39–7 drubbing of Notre Dame). At the same time, a group of entrepreneurs were meeting at various locations to discuss the possibility of forming a new professional league, the All-America Football Conference, better known by the acronym, the AAFC.

As the AAFC's Cleveland franchise became firm, owner Arthur McBride offered the head coaching job to Brown. Many people were surprised when he accepted that position with a professional team, but Brown explained that he had always enjoyed watching the pro sport. "In its earliest years, Ohio was a wellspring of professional football talent," he observed. "I think it's going to be again."

In a contest sponsored by McBride, the name "Panthers" for the new Cleveland team was selected. But it was the same name used by a failed NFL team in Cleveland in the 1920s. Brown said, "I won't start out with anything associated with our enterprise that smacks of failure. The old Panther team failed, I want no part of that name." Instead the team took on his name.

In every one of the next 10 years, and 11 out of the next 12, the Paul Brown-coached Cleveland Browns won either a league or division championship. Much of the success is owed to Otto Graham, a tailback from Northwestern, who Brown, doubling as general manager, signed as Cleveland's first AAFC player. Converting Graham to a T formation quarterback, Brown created one of the most fearsome offensive weapons the modern game has seen. "Automatic Otto," with receivers like Dante Lavelli and Mac Speedie, gave the Browns an almost unstoppable aerial attack. But there was really nothing automatic about Graham's remarkable career. Brown made it happen. The coach also breached the color barrier that had existed in pro football for more than a decade in his first year with Cleveland by signing two blacks, fullback Marion Motley and guard Bill Willis, both destined for the Hall of Fame. And Paul Brown was also the man who selected running back Jim Brown in the 1957 draft.

Don Pierson, a sportswriter for the *Chicago Tribune*, summarized some of Paul Brown's remarkable contributions to football: "Brown turned coaching into a science. He was the first to use notebooks and classroom techniques extensively. He was the first to organize film study and player grades, intelligence tests and an elaborate college scouting system.

"Brown invented the face mask. He was the first to send in plays with messenger guards. He tried to put radios into the helmets of his quarterbacks.... Brown was one of the first to split a halfback as a flanker to force the defense to spread. The draw play was his idea to slow the pass rush."

In 1963, following a mediocre 7-6-1 record the previous season, Brown was fired as coach and general manager by Art Modell, who had acquired the team two years earlier. At the time of his firing, his record was 158-48-8.

Just two years later, the aging genius was meeting with the Governor of Ohio to discuss the formation of a new pro team in Cincinnati. The AFL expansion team called the Bengals began its first season in 1968

without much material for Brown to work with, but by 1970 Brown brought an AFC Central Division championship to Cincinnati. After two mediocre seasons, another top finish in the AFC Central came in 1973. Brown retired for good following the 1976 season. His record for his final two years in football was 21-7.

Although he never managed to bring a league championship to Cincinnati, Brown made solid contenders out of an expansion team in three years.

The only other team besides the fledgling Bengals with whom he ever had a losing season was the 1943 Ohio State team, his roster ravaged by the needs of the military. Even during that dismal season, however, he managed to pull off a miracle by winning a game after it was over. The contest with Illinois ended in a 26-26 tie. When the clock expired, Ohio had the ball on the Illinois 28-yard line. In the dressing room, Brown had begun the post-mortem when the referee came in and announced that the game was not over. Illinois had been offsides on the final play and therefore OSU had one more play.

While the team was hastily pulling its uniforms back on, Brown told John Stungis to try for a field goal. If Stungis made it, it would be his first.

"There's nothing to it, John," the coach told his nervous kicker. "I've never missed a field goal in my life." Both teams went back out on the field, and Stungis kicked a wobbly game-winner through the uprights.

"Coach," the joyous kicker screamed, "I'm even with you. I've never missed a field goal either!"

"John," Coach Brown replied, "you're one up on me. I've never even tried one."

On Vince Lombardi:

"When he says sit down, I don't even bother to look for a chair."

—Max McGee

"One night, after a long, cold, difficult day, Lombardi came home late and tumbled into bed. 'God,' his wife said, 'your feet are cold.' And he answered, 'Around the house, dear, you can call me Vince.'"

—Paul Hornung

"He treats us all the same, like dogs."

—Henry Jordan

Vince Lombardi

This is the way the story is told. In 1963, Vince Lombardi was at the acme of his career as a coach. His Green Bay Packers were the defending NFL champions, winners of Super Bowl I as well as Super Bowl II. Also at the top of his game was the Pack's Jim Ringo, a seven-time All Pro center. The coach scheduled a meeting in 1963 to negotiate Ringo's contract.

"This is my lawyer," Ringo said, introducing his uninvited guest when arriving at the meeting. "I brought him since I don't know much about business."

"Excuse me for a second," Lombardi said and walked out of the room. A few minutes later he was back, and said to the attorney, "I am afraid you have come to the wrong city to discuss Mr. James Ringo's contract." He nodded toward his All Pro center. "Mr. James Ringo is now the property of the Philadelphia Eagles."

During the 1960s, Vince Lombardi developed a reputation as the toughest, most fearsome man in football. There are people around Green Bay who still recall how central Wisconsin shook when he hit town following the Pack's pitiful 1–10–1 season in 1958.

There are no survivors from his squads who forget his dominance and power. And there is also no doubt that from 1959 to 1967 he transformed a losing club into one of the greatest dynasties in the history of professional sports, compiling a glittering 98–30–4 record and capturing five NFL titles. Throughout his professional head-coaching career he never had a losing season.

After his first NFL title in 1961, Lombardi passed out diamond "championship" rings to each of his players and mink stoles to each of their wives. After the 1962 title, he gave out more diamond rings and offered the players' wives a choice of a color television set or a stereo console. When the packers won the Super Bowl following the 1967 season, a silver tea set went to each wife, and yet another ring to each player. Lombardi could not help but notice how the letters of thanks from the wives diminished in numbers over the championship seasons, beginning with dozens in 1962 and falling to just a few following Super Bowl I. He knew that success breeds apathy, at least eventually, but he could not help but enjoy the fruits of victory. The Packers, under his leadership, were the first professional football team to have wall-to-wall carpeting installed in their locker room.

Two weeks after Green Bay won Super Bowl II, its third consecutive NFL championship, Lombardi announced that he was retiring from coaching. Throughout the 1968 season, Lombardi served relatively quietly as the Packer's general manager, a position he had also held while coaching. By the time the season

Vince Lombardi

was underway, however, rumors were rampant that Lombardi was looking for another coaching challenge. He allegedly turned down a million dollar package from the Atlanta Falcons, and other lucrative offers from the New Orleans Saints, Boston Patriots, and the Philadelphia Eagles, but was still weighing the situation, according to insiders.

"The prospect of playing for Lombardi frightens me," Washington Redskin tackle Jim Snowden said in reaction to rumors flying that Lombardi was considering a move to the nation's capital. Then, on February 6, 1969, Lombardi held a press conference at the Sheraton-Carlton Hotel in Washington to confirm Snowden's worst fears. Vince Lombardi was the new head coach, general manager, and five percent owner of the Washington Redskins.

"You're supposed to be a real tough guy," a reporter said during the conference. "Are you going to put on a new face here in Washington?"

"I don't know if it's possible," Lombardi answered. "It's the same old face. Actually, I'm a pretty soft guy." The laughter from the press corps filled the room.

During 1969, Vince Lombardi led the Washington Redskins to a 7–5–2 season, its first winning record in 14 years. Less than a year later, Lombardi was dead from cancer at the age of 57. The miracle must have been his that one year with the Redskins because it would be many years later before Washington would enjoy another winning season. His one year in D.C. was a remarkable accomplishment, but his real legacy remains in the small city of Green Bay, Wisconsin, where he remains a revered legend; the name of the street where sits Lambeau Field, the Packers' home stadium, is Lombardi Avenue, a testament that Green Bayans will never forget him.

In his younger years, Lombardi attended Fordham University, and was a member of that football team's front line, which was known with feared respect as the "Seven Blocks of Granite." He also studied law there but left one year short of graduation so that he could get married. "I took a job," he wrote in *Look* magazine, "coaching football and basketball and teaching Latin, chemistry, and physics at St. Cecilia High School in Englewood, N.J."

During his stretch at St. Cecilia's from 1939 to 1946, Lombardi coached some highly successful teams. At one point, he won 36 consecutive games.

After two years as an assistant coach at Fordham, he moved to West Point in 1949 where he coached for six years under the legendary Earl "Red" Blaik.

"Whatever success I have must be attributed to the 'Old Man,' (Blaik)" he wrote. "He molded my methods and my whole approach to the game . . . ." He also wrote that Blaik used to say: "To beat the Navy you have to hate the Navy."

For his part, Blaik noted of his assistant, "Lombardi is a thoroughbred with a vile temper."

Some years later, Lombardi's wife Marie put it this way: "The day of a game, Vince hates everyone connected with that other team, but after the game—win, lose, or draw—it's over."

In 1954, Lombardi signed on with the New York Giants as an assistant coach. In the greatest assistant coach tandem in history, he handled the offense while Tom Landry took care of the defense for head coach Jim Lee Howell. At New York he helped to develop the Giants running attack, and revolutionized offensive line play with his "option" system of blocking, in which linemen could push defenders in either direction, using their own momentum to defeat them. His offensive approach was a radical departure from the old diagrammed plays, and the beginning of a rushing scheme that became famous later as "Run to Daylight."

Lombardi was 45 years old when he got that first head coaching job with the Green Bay Packers in 1959. When the Pack beat their arch-rivals, the Chicago Bears, in the opening game of Coach Lombardi's first season, his players carried him off the field.

The victory came as a result, both figuratively and literally, of a hard-knock training camp. No coach ever worked his players, rookies and veterans alike, harder than Vince Lombardi did during that first Green Bay training camp in 1959. When two of his players disappeared from camp for two days, Lombardi lost control of his temper. When he finally caught up with one of them, wide receiver Max McGee, in a dormitory hallway, he grabbed him by the lapels and started banging his head against the wall. His screaming could be heard throughout the dormitory.

"I'm not gonna play for this son of a bitch," McGee announced afterward and out of Lombardi's presence. "He's a madman!"

An hour later, all was forgiven. Lombardi, on his way to a team meeting, caught up with McGee, slapped him on the back, and said, "C'mon, Max, let's get to the meeting."

"Like my father before me," Lombardi wrote in *Look*, "I have a violent temper with which I have been struggling all my life, and with which I have had to effect a compromise. It is ineradicable, but it must not be irrational. I coach with everything that is within me, and I employ that temper for a purpose."

He used his temper, his keen sense of human psychology, and his football genius to bring to Green Bay a series of big-time championships. In the eight seasons following his first year of rebuilding with the Packers, he only failed to win a division, conference, or league championship twice. Once in 1963 with an 11–2–1 record, and again the following year with a record of 8–5–1. After that came the famous three consecutive NFL titles.

Vince Lombardi's most famous quote has been reprinted countless times: "Winning isn't the most important thing, it's the only thing." To win, Lombardi often treated his players as naughty children, to whom he spoke loudly and still carried a big stick.

"He coached through fear," said former player Bill Curry. "Most of the Packers were afraid of him, of his scoldings and sarcasm." There were few who avoided a Lombardi tongue-lashing for long. But he was not merely feared, Lombardi was respected and his players to a man treasure the memory of the glory trail that he guided them down.

Vince Lombardi: *"If you aren't fired with enthusiasm, you will be fired with enthusiasm."*

Don Shula

Still going strong in the latter half of the 1980s, Don Shula has assured himself an important spot in the annals of the NFL. By the end of the 1986 season, he had won 265 games, tops among active NFL coaches and second only to the legendary George Halas, who can claim 326 victories in his 40 years of coaching. Shula is also the only coach to make six appearances in the Super Bowl, and three of them were made consecutively. His winning percentage of .712 is substantially higher than any of the top 10 all-time winningest coaches in NFL history.

When he took over the then Baltimore Colts in 1963, Shula was the youngest head coach in NFL history. Less than ten years later, with the 1972 Miami Dolphins, he became the youngest coach ever in the NFL to win 100 games. That same year, he led his Dolphins to a record 17-0-0 perfect year, including the postseason victories and capped by the Super Bowl championship, making Miami the first and only team to go undefeated through both the regular season and the playoffs.

Shula's success is hardly relegated to the 1970s, however. During 1983 and 1984, the Dolphins won 16 consecutive games, just missing the NFL record of 17 established by George Halas and his Chicago Bears back in 1933 and 1934.

Despite those stunning statistics, the 1986 season was one of his most disappointing, as the Dolphins managed only an 8-8 record, good for third place in the AFC East. No Shula-coached team has ever finished lower, although three others had also finished third. In 1986, even Dan Marino's near-perfect passing could not consistently save the game that the Dolphins' weak defensive squad often gave away. But even though it was a relatively poor season, it still had its excitement. Shula improved his inconsistent team mid-season, managing six victories in the last nine games. Miami was not eliminated from the playoffs until the final week of the regular season.

"If I'm remembered for anything as a coach," he said, "I hope it's for playing within the rules. I also hope it will be said that my teams showed class and dignity in victory or defeat." During Shula's 17 years in Miami, the Dolphins characteristically have been the least penalized team in the NFL.

Raised in the town of Painesville, Ohio, a few miles from the shore of Lake Erie, Shula attended Cleveland's John Carroll University, where, in his most memorable game as a running back for the Blue Streaks, he gained 125 yards in a 1950 upset of Syracuse.

Until his college roommate joined the Cleveland Browns midway through the 1951 season, Shula was

Don Shula, left, with Redskins coach George Allen

the only rookie on Paul Brown's defending NFL championship team. Two years later, he was involved in the largest trade in NFL history, a 15-player extravaganza that sent him to the Baltimore Colts in 1953. He played four seasons with the Colts and, in 1957, finished his playing career as right cornerback with the Washington Redskins. Although his professional playing career was not dramatic (21 lifetime interceptions for 247 yards), he entered the coaching profession the very next year, where he has indeed inscribed a dramatic mark.

After one-year stints as an assistant collegiate coach at Virginia and Kentucky, he worked for three years as the defensive coordinator of the Detroit Lions. The Lions' head coach at the time was George Wilson, the man Shula would eventually replace at Miami. In 1963, Don Shula got his first pro head coaching spot with the Baltimore Colts.

"I've always tried to learn from all and copy none," Shula once said. "Everyone I played or coached under were different types, and I learned from them while still being myself. I've never gone out and tried to be

Paul Brown or Blanton Collier or George Wilson.... I tried to take all the things I've been exposed to, and if I can't incorporate them into the framework of Don Shula, that's fine."

With the Baltimore Colts, Shula directed some powerhouse teams. In 1964 and again in 1968, the Colts reached the NFL championship game, following 12–2 and 13–1 seasons. Both titles eluded him, however, and a lifetime record of just two victories in seven NFL championship game appearances is one of his less-loved statistics.

In 1969, his final year with Baltimore, the hapless Miami Dolphins had posted a 3–10–1 record, nearly as bad as the 3–11 season they had their first year of existence in 1966. "I'm not a miracle worker," Shula said when he joined the struggling franchise in February 1970. "I have no magic formulas. The only way I know is hard work." But NFL Commissioner Pete Rozelle felt that the Colts had lost something of value to Miami. As compensation for the head coach's move, he ordered the Dolphins to give their first round draft pick to Baltimore in 1971.

In the meantime, Shula proved that hard work was the order of the day in the Dolphins training camp at Biscayne College in North Miami. The workouts began at 7 each morning with a 2-mile run, followed by two often gruelling 90-minute practice sessions. "Walk-throughs" in the evening, gave little time for weary muscles to unwind before the next day's session would begin. But as tough as it was, the hard work paid off, and quickly.

The Dolphins won seven more games in Shula's first year than they had the previous season, clinching the AFC wild card spot. For the first time, the Miami Dolphins made it to the playoffs, although they lost there in the first round. The next season they were AFC champions, and the season after that, 1972, Shula and the undefeated Miami Dolphins struck gold with the Super Bowl VII trophy to ice the unparalleled 1972 perfect season.

Don Shula is a devoted family man, a father of two boys and three girls. But, at least according to his wife Dorothy, the coach has certain priorities on the football field. "I'm fairly confident that if I died tomorrow," she once said, "Don would find a way to preserve me until the season was over and he had the time for a nice funeral."

The ultimate pro football coaching standard still is out there, George Halas's 326 NFL wins, but Don Shula is relentlessly chipping away at it season by season.

Potsy the Poet

Potsy Clark, who began his football coaching career at the University of Kansas in 1916 and ended it at the University of Nebraska in 1948, served in the pro ranks as pilot of the Portsmouth Spartans (1931–33), Detroit Lions (1934–36, 40), and Brooklyn Dodgers (1937–39). He compiled an overall record in the NFL of 64–42–12. And he penned this poem which he distributed regularly to his players.

> *You strive until the goal is gained,*
> *Then look for one still unattained.*
> *Your record points the course you take,*
> *To greater records you can make.*
> *For hope springs not from what you've done,*
> *But from the work you've just begun.*

John Madden

"I'm retiring from football coaching and I'm never going to coach again in my life," Oakland Raider coach John Madden said at a press conference on January 4, 1979. "I gave it everything I had, and I just don't have anything left."

He left the game with a Super Bowl ring, the third highest winning percentage of any NFL coach with 100 or more victories, and a painful bleeding ulcer. At 42, an age when many ex-athletes just begin their head coaching careers, Madden was, in his words, "burned out and washed up." As it turned out, for a man accustomed to doing things early, the end of one career marked the beginning of another one, as a television color commentator for NFL games and the most boisterous of the crowd of ex-Jocks and assorted others who made the TV pitches for LITE beer.

Drafted by the Philadelphia Eagles as a player in 1958, Madden's professional career ended the same day it began in earnest. A knee injury sustained in his first day at training camp made it impossible for him to continue playing. Ten years later, Oakland's general manager Al Davis promoted Madden from an assistant with the team to head coach. At the age of 32, John Madden was the youngest head coach in the NFL. Ten years later he was gone, but far from forgotten.

Just as he was a success as a coach, John Madden manages to work in the same stratum of television broadcasting. On CBS, the hottest game of the week, or of the postseason, is ordinarily covered by the "A-team" of Pat Summerall and John Madden. His "Hey, wait a minute...," became a national catchphrase. His book, *Hey, Wait a Minute, I Wrote a Book*, was at or near the top of the best-seller lists for more than a year. He has been the guest host of NBC's "Saturday Night Live," and once turned down a continuing role in NBC's popular series "Cheers" because, he said, it would have conflicted with his football broadcasting duties. He appears in many industrial training films and is one of the most sought-after speakers on the lecture circuit.

John Madden is clearly the most popular, and most familiar, retired coach in America. He is known to millions as a regular guy with a great sense of humor, a good enough vocabulary to get just about any point across (although he is not unaccustomed to describing a player as "covered with mud and dirt and stuff"). He has a master's degree in physical education, and a deep understanding of the professional game. Few NFL fans have missed his perfect diagrams of plays moments after they were shown on television. After a down, any down, John Madden can take out his electronic chalk board and show where every significant

John Madden

player, on offense and defense, started, ended up, and then demonstrate why the play worked, or didn't work.

His genius for football is one side of him, but he is also remarkably human. It seems ironic that one of the greatest coach's of America's most brutal game is afraid to fly in airplanes, but it is a well-known fact.

"I thought it was an inner ear infection that was aggravated by altitude," Madden said of his fear of flying, "but then I realized that the anxiety would start as soon as the stewardess closed the door. One day I had a flight from Tampa to California with a stop in Houston. I got off there, checked into a hotel and never flew again." And so John Madden has come to know the Amtrak system like few other Americans.

Regardless of his fear of flying, during the decade he coached the Oakland (now Los Angeles) Raiders, John Madden was a most successful coach in professional football. In a field punctuated with unyielding perfectionists and sometime tyrants, Madden had a reputation as a "players coach," exceptionally competent but low-key and friendly. "Of all the coaches I ever played for," George Blanda once said, "John Madden was the kindest and most thoughtful."

Paul Zimmerman, in his book *The New Thinking Man's Guide to Pro Football,* noted that "the Raider's system is different. A head coach can get closer to his player there. He doesn't have to be a fear figure. They've got Al Davis for that." And so to understand the success of John Madden, it is necessary to know a little bit about the Raider's general manager who first gave Madden the reins.

Some years ago, Miami coach Don Shula offered this appraisal of the Raiders' Al Davis: "Someday, it will come down to the Dolphins and the Raiders playing for the American Conference Championship at the Coliseum. There will be six inches of water on the field as the Dolphins drive for the winning touchdown with ten seconds left. We'll be on the three-yard line . . .the clouds will part, and we'll look up to see Al Davis standing on the goal line with a garden hose."

For the majority of his head coaching career, Madden served in the shadow of Al Davis, who took an active part in even the day-to-day activities of the Raiders. Some scribes referred to him as "Davis's coach." In 1975, during his seventh season as Oakland's head man, one reporter inadvertently addressed him as "Al."

"My name is John," Madden said. "That's a helluva thing at this point." The pain at his lack of recognition must have been eased by his stunning successes. That same year Oakland won its fourth consecutive AFC Western Division championship, its sixth in the seven years Madden served as head coach. The next season, at Super Bowl XI, he won it all.

"Al and I had a great relationship," Madden once said. "Nobody will ever believe that, but we did." Many people believed that, while Davis let his head coach run the team during a game, he frequently second-guessed him, especially after postseason losses.

At the 1979 press conference announcing Madden's retirement, Al Davis also spoke, trying to put an end to rumors that he was dissatisfied with the coach's performance during the season just ended. "It's just trash, that's all," Davis said. "John's been fired eight times in 10 years, according to speculation."

"Sure," he added, "John and I had philosophical differences, but I think that's what I most liked about him. I don't think that I'd want a man who just agreed with everything I said."

When Madden left the Raiders after only 10 years as a head coach, he was the last of the active coaches from the old American Football League still coaching in the NFL. And he took with him one of the most glittering records in the history of professional football. His overall record of 106–36–6 was markedly impressive, but the strain had been unbearable. Before his fi-

nal season even began, he was hospitalized because of his ulcer. During at least one game, his players feared that he would collapse on the sideline.

And so he changed careers, where he can now relax a bit, in the low-pressure world of live network broadcasting, best-selling books, multi-million dollar television commercials, and public speaking engagements.

"Hey, wait a minute," he might say, "this stuff really isn't so tough!"

Coaches Quotes

Hank Stram: *"When I got into coaching, I knew I was getting into a high-risk profession. So I adopted the philosophy that yesterday is a cancelled check, today is cash on the line, and tomorrow is a promissory note."*

John Ralston, on leaving the Broncos: *"I left because of illness and fatigue. The fans were sick and tired of me."*

George Allen: *"The future is now!"*

New York Giants' owner Wellington Mara on the profession of coaching in the NFL: *"Few die on the job."*

Bud Grant: *"A good coach needs a patient wife, loyal dog, and a great quarterback—not necessarily in that order."*

Bum Phillips: *"My idea of discipline is not makin' guys do something; it's gettin' 'em to do it. There's a difference in bitchin' and coachin'"*

Bud Grant

The "greatest athlete ever to come out of the state of Minnesota," is how he has been aptly described; in fact he was voted Minnesota's Athlete of the Half Century in 1950 by a panel of sportswriters and sportscasters.

At the University of Minnesota, Grant won nine varsity letters, four in football, three in basketball, and a pair for baseball. As a pro he played simultaneously for the Philadelphia Eagles in the NFL and the Minneapolis Lakers in the NBA. A 6'3" end, Grant was Philadelphia's first round draft choice in 1951, and led the team in all facets of pass receiving the following season. On the hardwood court, he was a member of the 1950 and 1951 NBA champion Lakers.

For all his efforts, he was unable to obtain more than $8,000 a year with the Eagles, and so in 1953 he moved to the Canadian Football League's Winnipeg Blue Bombers, where he led the team in receiving each of his four years as a player.

If the Canadian Football League had been part of the NFL, Bud Grant would be credited as the second winningest coach in the history of the National Football League. He never served a day as an assistant coach, moving directly from player to head coach of the Blue Bombers, where he won 122 games in 10 seasons, including four Canadian championships. That added to the 168 his Minnesota Vikings won gives him a grand total of 290, well ahead of second-ranked Don Shula and 36 short of George Halas.

Grant served as head coach of the Minnesota Vikings for 18 years, where his teams won 11 Central Division championships, four conference titles. The only place where success consistently eluded him was at the Super Bowl, where he brought his Vikings four times without a victory.

To those who watched him direct his championship teams, saw the stolid stare, the emotionless concentration, the blood that seemed to run as cold as the frigid waters of the North country he always called home. He was as coldly analytical as a surgeon. "I don't know if I should interview him or ski him," a writer once quipped.

In a biography of Grant entitled *BUD—The Other Side of the Glacier,* author Bill McGrane told of how the coach's sometimes chilly presence once cooled the hot air of a famous sportscaster. Grant was standing in the lobby of a Detroit Hotel, McGrane explained, waiting for Frank Gifford, who had scheduled an interview preceding a Monday night football game between the Vikings and the Lions to be telecast by ABC.

Suddenly, Bud heard a loud voice from across the lobby calling, "Harry Peter Grant . . ." The voice continued, loudly and never pausing for a breath, and be-

Bud Grant

fore long all the people in the lobby of the Cadillac hotel realized that it belonged to Howard Cosell, at the time the strident analyst of ABC's Monday Night Football. Howard realized that he was attracting considerable attention and continued the non-stop monologue, directing it at Grant but speaking as if he were on a Broadway stage.

"He ended up his sentence," author McGrane explained, "with something like '. . . and what do you think of that, Coach Bud Grant.'

"Gifford was approaching by then, looking vaguely uneasy," McGrane continued.

"What Bud said was nothing . . . for what seemed like about six weeks. He stared at Cosell. After a while, Howard's smile took on a quality to suggest it had been painted into place. Bud just stood there, staring . . . silent.

"Finally, he made a tiny nod and said 'Howard.'

"Then he turned to Gifford and said, 'Let's go up to my room, where we can talk.'

"It was, at least to one witness, a devastating thing to

do . . . Howard was left in their wake, cigar drooping.

"The thing is, Grant doesn't appreciate people who trundle their spotlight around with them.

"He is comfortable around people he knows . . . although the reverse of that theory isn't always true."

As great an athletic performer as Bud Grant proved himself to be, it was truly as a coach that he left his greatest mark. "I don't know that Bud could diagram five plays," Fran Tarkenton once said of his head coach, "but, my goodness, does he know people! He excels at managing people and making people decisions. Everybody who plays for Bud understands him . . . he is where the Buck stops. There is no committee, there's just Bud."

Bud Grant may not have been known as a blackboard man, but he knew how to set up a play, or players perhaps. Once, when he was head coach of the Winnipeg Blue Bombers of the Canadian Football League, he secretly put the mayor of Winnipeg in a Bomber uniform, and had him run back the opening kickoff in an intrasquad game. "We had it blocked beautifully," Grant recalled, "but he ran out of gas at the 20 and fell down."

Like many of the other legendary NFL coaches, Bud Grant was a master of human psychology. "It's possible to make up a rule," he told biographer McGrane, "and learn about people by how they react to it." To prove the point, McGrane related a fascinating anecdote from Grant's early days in training camp with the Vikings. During a team meeting, the new head coach told his players that the field contained an area of newly planted sod and that they should try to avoid it. He pointed out the area to his team, and underscored the need to stay off it.

"After I told the players about staying off the new sod," Grant explained, "I went out on the field and watched.

"There were players who would come running up to the sodded area, recognize it, and go around it.

"There were players who would run onto it and then stop . . . you knew they'd forgotten and then remembered what I said after they started across. Those fellows would back up and go around.

"There were some who could come running out and go across the sodded area without even realizing it.

"Finally, there were fellows who just roared on across the sodded area, in defiance of what I had said.

"It's important to learn things like that about people. You learn who the players are who will forget what you tell them, you learn who will remember what you tell them, and you learn who just won't buy what you tell them. The same thing will happen in a game."

After 35 years in professional sports as a player and a coach, Grant retired in January 1984, but retained as a consultant by the Vikings. Following a disastrous season, however, and with considerable urging by Minnesota's general manager Mike Lynn, Bud returned as head coach for the 1985 season. The team showed drastic improvement that year, including a victory over the defending Super Bowl champion San Francisco 49ers. Feeling that his team was again headed in the right direction, Grant once more announced his retirement, effective January 6, 1986. Offensive coordinator Jerry Burns was promoted to head coach with Grant retained, again, as a consultant.

The Vikings went 7-9 in 1985, his final year as head coach. On paper, it was not one of Coach Grant's better seasons, but he called it one of his most enjoyable. "We had more new people than we'd ever had before," he recalled, "new players and new coaches, young people. I found that very stimulating."

At a December game in Philadelphia, the Eagles led 23-0 with eight minutes remaining in the final period. In a stunning comeback, the Vikings won 28-23. Minnesota's 7-9 record does not indicate how close the team came to making the playoffs. Of their nine losses, five were by 7 points or less. Had they won just two of those games, they would have made the playoffs.

"We went into every game believing we could win," the coach recalled of his final year. "We knew it wouldn't be easy, but we knew we would have an opportunity. A chance is all you can ask. Having a chance made the season exciting."

Chuck Noll

"We regard our Super Bowl XIII trophy as an antique," Steeler head coach Chuck Noll said at the start of the 1979 season. As the first football team in history to win three Super Bowl titles, Noll and the Steelers might have decided to rest on their laurels. Instead there was not even time for the dust to settle on their third Vince Lombardi trophy, symbol of Super Bowl supremacy, before they went out and won another one at Super Bowl XIV. During the 1970s, the Steelers were the premier team in football, winning four Super Bowl crowns in just six years.

Chuck Noll, who has coached the Steelers for more than a decade longer than anyone else in the franchise's more than 50-year history had to struggle to bring his team to a position of pre-eminence. When Steeler owner Art Rooney hired the 36-year-old Noll in 1969, the Pittsburgh franchise was an NFL doormat, boasting of only two winning seasons in the previous nine years, and having won only a total of 18 games in the last five years. In 1968, the year before Noll's arrival, the Steelers' record had been 2-11-1.

The new head coach started out his tenure in Pittsburgh with a season in hell, winning his first game and losing the next 13. It was the second worst record in Steelers' history, overshadowed only by the 0-10-0 record of 1944. The one bright spot, however, was the performance of rookie defensive tackle Mean Joe Greene, who started all 14 games and was named Defensive Rookie of the Year.

"We're going to build a championship team in Pittsburgh," the young head coach prophesied, "and Joe Greene will be the cornerstone." From the beginning, Noll planned to build the Steelers into a championship team through careful selections in the college draft.

"If I could see into the future," he once told interviewer Jim O'Brien, "I'd be at the racetrack today." But Noll's decision to build his club around the draft was flawless. In 1970, he selected Louisiana Tech quarterback Terry Bradshaw in the draft, and the Steelers were headed in the right direction, winning five games during the year. With another good draft in 1971, Pittsburgh and Cleveland ended up tied for first place in the Central Division with a 5-5 record with just four games remaining in the regular season. But in the drive for the playoffs, the young team faltered, losing three of its final four contests while the Browns won all of theirs and the division crown.

"The experience will prove valuable to our younger players," Noll predicted. "I expect us to come back stronger than ever next year." His predictions were as accurate as ever. The year 1972 was a great break-

Chuck Noll

through for Pittsburgh, the Steelers compiling an 11-3-0 record and capturing the AFC East title. From that point on, Noll's team made it to the playoffs eight years in succession.

By 1979, when Pittsburgh was heading toward its fourth NFL championship, every one of its starters had either been selected in the college draft or signed as free agents by Noll. Of the 45 players on the Super Bowl XIII roster, only three had been original Steelers. Noll's method, which he never doubted, of developing fresh talent straight from the college ranks proved to be remarkably sound.

Like his greatest mentors, Paul Brown and Don Shula, Noll is a finesse coach who believes in studious preparation and careful player selection rather than extraordinary motivational efforts to win football games. Not known as a prime motivator, he still admits "motivation is a part of talent. If you don't want to use it, and work at it, you don't have any talent."

More than anything else, Noll considers himself to be a teacher. It is the vocation he would have chosen had he not become a successful coach. Other head coaches have agreed with his self-assessment. Once, while watching Noll lead a Steelers practice session, former Giants' coach Allie Sherman noted: "He's teaching. These guys do it right. They go over all the points, from step one to step ten. Some coaches like to

275

think they're teachers, but they're not. Noll is a teacher."

Instructor Noll has been known to assume his role somewhat sarcastically. He once greeted a group of reporters after a Steelers game by saying, "My, isn't this a well-behaved class? Quiet, attentive, all set to take notes. That's nice." But when he stands in front of a chalkboard diagramming plays for his team, he is all business.

Noll has been in professional football for three and a half decades. After playing at the University of Dayton in Ohio, he was chosen by the Cleveland Browns in the 21st round of the 1953 draft. An offensive guard and later linebacker, he played under the legendary Paul Brown at Cleveland for seven seasons. During his years in Cleveland, the Browns won five Eastern Conference championships and two NFL titles.

His playing career ended in 1959. He hoped to find a job coaching Dayton, his alma mater, but failed to win the head coaching spot. Instead he was hired by Sid Gillman to fill the final open assistant coaching slot with the Los Angeles (later San Diego) Chargers in the new American Football League. Serving for six years as a defensive assistant with the Chargers, his team won five Western Division titles and an AFL championship.

Noll got the opportunity to work with yet another great coach when he became the defensive backfield assistant with Don Shula's Baltimore Colts in 1966. In his three seasons in Baltimore, the Colts lost just seven regular season games.

Chuck Noll was known as a brilliant defensive specialist when Art Rooney hired him as head coach of the Steelers in 1969. It may therefore seem surprising that he has spent the majority of his time in Pittsburgh working with the offense. But as the Steelers' fortunes soared in the 1970s, its defensive unit proved as niggardly in giving up points as the offense was opulent in gaining them. During numerous seasons, the Steelers outscored their opponents by margins of better than two to one.

In 1980, the four-time and current defending NFL champion Steelers finally saw their dynasty come to an end, many of its key players growing a bit too old to remain champions. *Sports Illustrated*'s Paul Zimmerman recalled the end of the era:

"I remember the game in which the Pittsburgh four-Super Bowl dynasty finally ended, a 6–0 loss to Houston in the AstroDome in 1980. I was standing outside the Steelers' locker room as the players walked down the concrete stairway leading from the field. The Houston fans, all those raucous, nasty, Luv Ya Blue maniacs, leaned over the railings and screamed abuse at the Steelers and laughed at them. Not one

player turned around. Not one of them looked up. Eyes straight ahead, heads high, they walked to their dressing room in silence. They looked like kings abdicating the throne. I almost broke down watching that sight."

Noll managed to lead the Steelers into the playoffs in 1982, 1983, and 1984, but it wasn't the same powerhouse team it had been in the 1970s. Each time, Pittsburgh lost in the first or second round. The team finished third in the AFC Central in 1986 with a 6–10 record. The once mighty defense gave up more than 300 points.

Like Tom Landry and Don Shula, the other all-time great NFL coaches who are still active, Chuck Noll faces the prospect of rebuilding his team. He will undoubtedly begin doing it the same way he did years earlier, with inspired draft choices, meticulous planning, and intelligent coaching.

A few years ago, Paul Zimmerman asked a number of NFL coaches to provide capsulized descriptions of themselves. "Just put me down as a teacher," Noll responded. "Don't ever call me a winner. Players win, coaches teach. I was a teacher."

On Tom Landry

"Tom Landry is a perfectionist. If he was married to Raquel Welch, he'd expect her to cook."

—Dandy Don Meredith

"I used to sit by my home telephone the night before every Cowboys game at Texas Stadium, game plan spread at the desk. At 8 p.m. the phone would ring, and it would be Landry. . . . I'd pick up the phone and say, 'Hello.' The next thing I would hear was his voice saying, 'Now you know on that Slant 24, we're going to run it from . . .' He wouldn't say, 'Hello, Roger, this is Coach Landry,' or anything else before starting right in on the game plan."

—Roger Staubach

Tom Landry

Running back and sometime rodeo rider Walt Garrison who played for the Dallas Cowboys in the late 1960s and early 70s, was once asked if Tom Landry ever smiled. "I don't know," Garrison replied. "I only played there nine years."

There is, however, indisputable proof that the only coach the Dallas Cowboys ever had has indeed smiled on at least one occasion. The proof is in the form of an Associated Press photograph, widely reprinted in newspapers throughout the country back in May 1978, clearly showing a slight upward curl in the left corner of Tom Landry's mouth. The occasion for reprinting the photograph was a poll taken that month among the 28 coaches of the National Football League, who were asked to answer the question, "Aside from yourself, who is the best coach in the NFL, and why?"

Only 11 of the head coaches were able to name a single candidate. Of those, Landry received five votes, narrowly defeating Don Shula, who got four. Of the 13 coaches who named multiple possibilities, Landry's name came up on 12 lists, and Shula's on 11. However, on those multiple-name lists, Landry's name was listed first eight times, Shula's twice. In the final analysis at least, Tom Landry was clearly the coaches' coach.

"Landry wins," former Denver head coach Red Miller said. "I think he gets his team ready for the big games consistently better than anybody else."

Chuck Knox, head coach of the Bills, said, "Landry is a great organizer, he is innovative with all his multiple formations in the flex defense. It takes guts to be innovative. And he's also had the longest tenure."

"Longevity," echoed the Cleveland Browns' Sam Rutigliano. "Anybody who survives that long in one place has to be the best coach." That sentiment was uttered a decade ago, when the Dallas Cowboys were the defending Super Bowl champions and in the midst of their glory years.

From 1966 through 1985, the Cowboys missed postseason play only twice during a 20-year stretch, which included five trips to the Super Bowl and two NFL championships.

Landry is still the Cowboys' head coach, but in the 1980s he has had less to smile about. From 1982 through 1986, Dallas managed only a single first-place finish in its tough division. For only the second and third times since 1965, the team missed the playoffs entirely in 1984 and 1986. The Cowboys lost their first playoff game in 1985, and lost the last five games of the disappointing 1986 season.

The future may not be totally bleak for Landry and his team. Although their 7–9 record in 1986 gave

Tom Landry

them their first losing season in 23 years, they are in what is probably the NFL's toughest division, including the Super Bowl champion Giants and the Washington Redskins, who mauled the 1985 NFL champion Chicago Bears in the 1986 playoffs. The problems Landry faces rebuilding his team are certainly not as bad as those he confronted in 1960, when he took over a brand new squad whose core consisted of 36 veteran players cadged in the expansion draft from 12 NFL teams.

Football has always been the focus of Landry's life. As a well-known high school halfback, he played for the Mission, Texas, Eagles, a team so powerful that in Landry's senior year it went not only undefeated but also unscored upon, blowing out its opponents by a cumulative total of 322–0.

His career at the University of Texas was interrupted after a single semester by World War II. As a copilot in a B-17 bomber in the Army Air Force, he flew more than 30 missions over occupied Europe, surviving one crash landing and numerous close calls. When he returned to the University of Texas after the war, he was converted to quarterback. Unfortunately for his own career, Texas also had another quarterback named Bobby Layne. Landry played backup to the immortal Layne, but also proved himself to be an expert defensive back, traveling with his team to the Sugar Bowl in 1948 and the Cotton Bowl the following year.

Turning professional the same year, he played a single season on the doomed New York Yankees of the old All-America Football Conference. But when the Yankees folded, he was picked up by the NFL's New York Giants, where he became an important part of head coach Steve Owen's famed "umbrella defense."

In his initial season under Owen, Landry got his first real taste of coaching. "Steve was a great guy on concepts," Landry said, "but he wasn't much of a detail man. He just drew the thing up on the board and handed me the chalk and left it to me to explain it. I remember it to the day. It's where my coaching started. I was 25 years old."

Defensive back Tom Landry was named All-Pro in 1954, the year after Owen retired. Two years later, Landry himself retired, becoming an assistant to Giants head coach Jim Lee Howell. While Vince Lombardi ran the offense, Landry established the defensive game.

"One day I was walking down the hall," Giants star Kyle Rote recalled, "and I looked on one side and there was Lombardi, looking at films. I looked on the other side and there was Landry, looking at films. I continued on down the hall and saw Jim Lee Howell, the head coach, reading a newspaper."

While Howell worked on other matters, Lombardi and Landry devised counterattacks to pit against one another's strategies. Lombardi began to develop his "run to daylight" scheme, and Landry countered with what would become known as the "flex" defense, in which two linemen were offset to close down the gaps created by the offensive line.

As defensive coach, Landry inherited one of the great defensive squads of all time, including such stars as Sam Huff, Andy Robustelli, Rosey Grier, Dick Modzelewski, and Jim Katcavage. And although Steve Owen's defensive genius was gone, the Giants with defensive coach Tom Landry proved just as tough—or tougher—to score against. In his final two years with the team, the New York Giants defense gave up the fewest points in the NFL.

In 1960, despite a threatened lawsuit on behalf of the AFL Dallas Texans, the NFL awarded a franchise to a team initially called the Texas Rangers. Tex Schramm, who had spent a decade in the Los Angeles Rams front office and was now assistant director of sports for CBS, was named general manager. Schramm was impressed by the Giants' defensive coach and, after a series of meetings in New York, signed him to a 5-year contract as head of the new Texas Rangers, shortly thereafter renamed the Dallas Cowboys.

Because the team was formed too late to participate in the college draft, Schramm and Landry had to make do with veteran players left unprotected by other NFL teams, and a few shrewd trades and acquisitions. Landry immediately set high standards for his questionable recruits at the first training camp. He established the traditional, "Landry Mile," which backs and receivers were expected to complete in under six minutes, linemen in six minutes, thirty seconds. In that first year, not a single player completed the Landry Mile in the allotted time.

Landry and his rookie quarterback, Don Meredith, suffered through a dismal first season. The highlight of the year was a 31–31 tie with New York in week 11 of the schedule. The final Dallas record was 0–11–1.

It took seven years for Landry to build his dynasty, but when he accomplished it by 1966, the Cowboys stayed at or near the top of the NFL for a decade and a half. Of course, there was nothing magical about the Cowboys' gradual rise to prominence. Landry made it happen, calling the plays on both offense and defense. Never showing the slightest emotion from the sidelines, he is respected as one of the most cerebral of all NFL coaches.

After more than a quarter-century as the Cowboys' mentor and guiding force, Tom Landry remains the third winningest coach in NFL history, his 261 victories trailing only George Halas and Don Shula. Landry's record of 20 consecutive winning seasons is an NFL standard that may never be topped.

Perhaps his former quarterback, Hall of Famer Roger Staubach, sums up the Landry mystique best: "In composite I remember him as a towering figure. To me he was, is, and always will be special—a man apart from other men. What made him so, beyond his brilliant technical grasp of football, were two bedrock Landry characteristics: enormous self-discipline and consistency. Landry is the rock against which we all lean, often without realizing it, at some point during our careers."

To a rookie regarding Landry's playbook, *"Don't bother reading it, kid. Everybody gets killed in the end."*

—Pete Gent

William "Lone Star" Dietz, who claimed to be "an artist by recreation and a coach by profession," is ready to preserve in oils here his prize halfback of the Haskell Indians. With a sense of appropriateness, George Preston Marshall hired Dietz, a Sioux Indian who had played alongside Jim Thorpe at Carlisle, to coach his Boston Redskins in 1933 and 1934 after a long career coaching at the college level.

Dietz posted a record of 11–11–2 over two seasons, and is warmly remembered for this incident, often told by his boss Mr. Marshall.

"Dietz had heard that Lambeau and Halas had a coach high up in the stands who radioed instructions down to the bench. So he planned to use it himself. And he also had another strategy that day.

"Just before the start of the game down on the field he instructed his team to kick off no matter whether they won the toss or not. He wanted to bury the Giants deep in their own territory and then get good field position. Then he headed into the stands and back behind them to a ramp that was filled with people but led to the upper deck.

"He had trouble getting through, but when he did he looked down on the field and saw his Redskins lined up to receive the kickoff. He pulled out his walkie-talkie and yelled into it, 'What the hell's going on down there. I said to kick off.'

"There was a pause, then an assistant coach who had the other walkie-talkie said, 'We did kick. Harry Newman ran it back 94 yards for a touchdown.'"

Jimmy Conzelman

A Punch in the Puss

One minute interview with Jimmy Conzelman, coach of Chicago Cardinals football team:

"Football coaches always have been apologists for their profession. For years we've been on the defensive against attacks from reformers who regard us as muscle-bound mentalities exploiting kids for an easy living. Football has been under fire because it involves body contact and it teaches violence. It was considered useless, even dangerous.

"But that's all over now. The bleeding hearts haven't the courtesy to apologize to us, but they're coming around and asking our help in the national emergency. Why?

"Why, because the college commencement classes this month find the customary challenge of life a pale prelude to the demands of a world at war. Instead of job seekers, or home makers, the graduates suddenly have become defenders of a familiar way of life, of an ideology, a religion and of a nation. They have been taught to build. Now they must learn to destroy.

"It may seem reprehensible to inculcate a will to destroy in these amiable young men; but war is reprehensible—and its basic motive is to destroy. The transition will not be an easy one. Democracy makes us a pacific people. The young man must be toughened not only physically, but mentally. He must become accustomed to violence. Football is the No. 1 medium for attuning a man to body-contact and violent physical shock. It teaches that after all there isn't anything so terrifying about a punch in the puss."

Who's Excited?

Jim Conzelman, of the one-time champion Chicago Cardinals professional-football club, is a modest gent when it comes to discussing his own achievements. According to him, winning pro championships wasn't really his style. He thinks that his experience with the Detroit Lions was more typical for him. In 1925, he purchased the Lions' franchise for the bargain price of fifty dollars. After two years, he had worked the team into a startlingly unsuccessful venture, so he returned the franchise to the League and threw away his bottle of aspirin. Approximately fifteen years later, the franchise was bought by Fred Mandel for a cool quarter of a million dollars.

"This," says Jim, "is just a rough idea of the smart way in which I conduct my personal affairs."

The Cardinals in the past few years have developed the habit of pushing the rival Chicago Bears around the field whenever the two teams meet, but there was a time when the conscientious Conzelman had serious difficulties with the Halas-men.

"Don't get the idea," says Jim, "that being beaten by the Bears 42–12 bothered me a bit. Oh, not in the least. I went home after the game, had a good night's rest and a very hearty breakfast. I said good-by to the Missus, and strolled down the hall to the elevator, whistling a light tune. I pushed the elevator bell and took in my profile in the hall mirror. I was a picture of elegance in my Cavenaugh hat, tweed sport jacket, and well-shined tan shoes. Then I went back to my apartment and put on my trousers."

Jimmy Phelan

Jimmy Phelan a protege of Knute Rockne, was basically a college football coach (Missouri, Purdue, Washington, St. Mary's), but he was lured to the pros to tutor the hapless Dallas Texans in their one lonesome year of existence in the NFL, 1952.

The last two scheduled home games (for the Dallas Texans) were against the Chicago Bears and the Detroit Lions. It was decided that the Lions would serve as hosts to the Texans in Detroit, while the Bears would meet the vagabond team in Akron, Ohio.

The Akron game was actually the second half of a football double header with a high school morning game outdrawing the pros. There were so few fans in the stands that in his pre-game remarks Texans' coach Jimmy Phelan suggested that rather than introducing the players on the field, they should "go into the stands and shake hands with each fan." Phelan had not lost his humor and his team had not lost their will to win, as the Texans stunned the George Halas-led Chicago Bears with a 27–23 victory.

"We had a good time in spite of everything," insists Art Donovan, "mostly because of Phelan." He was a likable Irishman and popular with his players. Perhaps part of his popularity was a result

But he left his mark, according to Joe Horrigan, curator of the archives of the Pro Football Hall of Fame, who remembered them in writing this for *Coffin Corner* the official publication of the Pro Football Researchers Association:

of his disdain for practice. "Once," as Donovan recalls, "we ran a couple of plays without fouling up. Phelan stopped practice, loaded everybody on a bus and took us to the racetrack. Jimmy loved the races."

Another popular Phelan story is how he fired Don Klosterman after missing a field goal attempt in the opening game against the Giants. Klosterman, who'd led the nation's passers in 1950 at Loyola, had joined the Texans fully expecting a fair shot at the quarterback spot. When Phelan released him, he was understandably irate. "Hell, I was a quarterback, not a kicking specialist," Klosterman recalled. "The ball hit the upright and bounced back. And the next day I got cut."

Weeks later, while preparing to face the Giants again, the Texans were reviewing the game films. When Klosterman's kick came up, Phelan stopped the film and ran it back a second time. "There," he announced, "who says I didn't give him a second chance?"

The All-Time Winningest Coaches

	Record	Win Pct.	Teams
George Halas	326–151–31	.683	Staleys, Bears
Don Shula	265–107–6	.712	Colts, Dolphins
Tom Landry	261–159–6	.621	Cowboys
Curly Lambeau	229–134–22	.631	Packers, Cardinals, Redskins
Paul Brown	222–113–9	.663	Browns, Bengals
Chuck Noll	170–114–1	.599	Steelers
Bud Grant	168–109–5	.606	Vikings
Steve Owen	153–108–17	.586	Giants
Hank Stram	136–100–10	.576	Texans, Chiefs, Saints
Weeb Ewbank	134–130–7	.508	Colts, Jets

(Note: ties are not counted in calculating winning percentages.)

7 HEROES & CHAMPIONS

The Pro Football Hall of Fame

In 1963, the Pro Football Hall of Fame in Canton, Ohio was officially opened, with seventeen NFL legends as charter enshrinees. The Hall itself is a shrine to the sport. It is open to the public and offers a vast array of exhibits, films, and other memorabilia related to the sport of professional football. An induction into it remains the highest honor a professional football player can achieve.

Hall of Famers

Herb Adderley
Cornerback
Green Bay Packers 1961–69; Dallas Cowboys
   1970–72
College: Michigan State
Inducted: 1980
All Pro 5 times
48 career interceptions, 7 returned for TDs
3,080 yards on kick returns (25.7 yard average,
   2 TDs

Lance Alworth
Flanker
San Diego Chargers 1962–70; Dallas Cowboys
   1971–72
College: Arkansas
Inducted: 1978
All Pro AFL 7 times
542 career receptions for 10,266 yards (fourth
   most in NFL history) and 85 TDs (third most in
   NFL history)
Only receiver ever to gain 200 or more yards on
   receptions five times

Doug Atkins
Defensive End
Cleveland Browns 1953–54; Chicago Bears
   1955–66; New Orleans Saints 1967–69
College: Tennessee
Inducted: 1982
All Pro 3 times
His 17 seasons is the second most for any
   defensive lineman in NFL history

Morris "Red" Badgro
End
New York Yankees 1927; New York Giants
   1930–35; Brooklyn Dodgers 1936
College: Southern California
Inducted: 1981
All Pro 3 times
60-minute man: good receiver, excellent on
   defense

Cliff Battles
Halfback
Boston Braves 1932; Boston Redskins 1933–36;
   Washington Redskins 1937
College: West Virginia Wesleyan
Inducted: 1968
All Pro 3 times
Gained 3,622 yards rushing (4.1 yard average)
First to rush for more than 200 yards in a game

Sammy Baugh
Quarterback, Coach
Washington Redskins 1937–52
College: Texas Christian
Inducted: 1963
All Pro 6 times
Led NFL in passing 6 times, in punting 5 times
Completed 1,693 passes for 21,886 yards and
   187 TDs
Only player ever to lead league in passing,
   punting, and interceptions made in the same
   season (1943)
Only player to average over 50 yards a punt in a
   season

Chuck Bednarik
Center and Linebacker
Philadelphia Eagles 1949–62
College: Pennsylvania
Inducted: 1967
All Pro 7 times (1 as center, 6 as linebacker)
Last of the great 60-minute players

Bert Bell
League Administrator and Owner
College: Pennsylvania
Inducted: 1963
Owner of Eagles (1933–40), Steelers (1941–46)
NFL commissioner (1946–59)

SUNDAY MAYHEM

Bobby Bell
Linebacker and Defensive End
Kansas City Chiefs 1963–74
College: Minnesota
Inducted: 1983
All Pro 9 times
Member Hall of Fame's All-Time AFL team

Raymond Berry
End, Coach
Baltimore Colts 1955–67
College: Southern Methodist
Inducted: 1973
All Pro 3 times
Caught 631 passes for 9,275 yards and 68 TDs
Fumbled only once in 13 seasons

Charles W. Bidwill, Sr.
Owner and Administrator
College: Loyola of Chicago
Inducted: 1967
Owner of Chicago Cardinals (1933–47)

George Blanda
Quarterback and Kicker
Chicago Bears 1949; Baltimore Colts 1950; Chicago
    Bears 1950–58; Houston Oilers 1960–66;
    Oakland Raiders 1967–75
College: Kentucky
Inducted: 1981
All Pro 1 time
Played more seasons (26) and more games (340)
    than anyone in pro football history
Scored more points (2,002) than any player in NFL
    history
Completed 1,911 passes for 26,920 yards and
    236 TDs
Kicked 335 FGs and 943 PATs

On the ground are a pair of Hall of Famers in this 1934 game, the typically helmetless Bill Hewitt (56) of the Chicago Bears and behind him Dutch Clark (7) of the Detroit Lions. Number 3 on Detroit is Glenn Presnell and 16 is Ox Emerson. (Chicago Bears)

Jim Brown
Fullback
Cleveland Browns 1957–65
College: Syracuse
Inducted: 1971
All Pro 8 times
Second leading rusher in NFL history (12,312 yards)
Highest average gain rushing (at least 700 carries) in NFL history (5.22 yards)
Combined yardage total of 15,459 and total points scored of 756

Paul Brown
Coach
Cleveland Browns 1946–62; Cincinnati Bengals 1968–75
College: Miami of Ohio
Inducted: 1967
Won 4 AAFC titles, 3 NFL titles

Roosevelt Brown
Offensive Tackle
New York Giants 1953–65
College: Morgan State
Inducted: 1975
All Pro 8 times
Considered one of game's greatest blockers

Willie Brown
Cornerback
Denver Broncos 1963–66; Oakland Raiders 1967–78
College: Grambling
Inducted: 1984
All Pro 7 times
54 career interceptions, 2 run backs for TDs

Dick Butkus
Middle Linebacker
Chicago Bears 1965–73
College: Illinois
Inducted: 1979
All Pro 7 times
One of the most brutal tacklers in NFL history
Second most opponent fumbles recovered (25) in NFL history

Tony Canadeo
Halfback
Green Bay Packers 1941–44, 1946–52
College: Gonzaga
Inducted: 1974
All Pro 2 times
Gained 4,192 yards on 1,025 rushes
Completed 105 passes for 1,642 yards
Scored 31 TDs, passed for 16

Joe Carr
League Administrator
National Football League 1921–39
No College
Inducted: 1963
One of NFL's original organizers
NFL president 1921–39

Guy Chamberlin
End, Coach
Canton Bulldogs 1919; Decatur Staleys 1920; Chicago Staleys 1921; Canton Bulldogs 1922–23; Cleveland Bulldogs 1924; Frankford Yellow Jackets 1925–26; Chicago Cardinals 1927–28
College: Nebraska
Inducted: 1965
Player/coach of 4 NFL title winners
Has highest win percentage of any coach in NFL history, .784 (58-16-6)

Jack Christiansen
Defensive Back
Detroit Lions 1951–58
College: Colorado State University
Inducted: 1970
All Pro 6 times
Intercepted 46 passes, 3 returned for TDs
Ran back 85 punts for 1,084 yards (12.8 yard average), 8 for TDs

Earl "Dutch" Clark
Quarterback, Coach
Portsmouth Spartans 1931–32; Detroit Lions 1934–38
College: Colorado College
Inducted: 1963
All Pro 6 times
Great triple-threat back
Scored 369 points (42 TDs, 15 FGs, 72 PATs), threw 10 TD passes

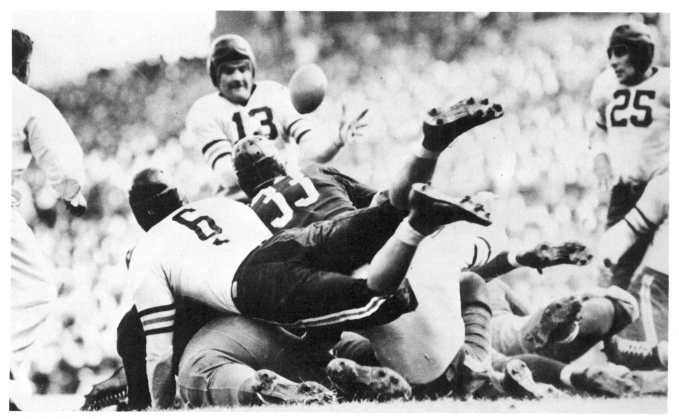

It looks like a lateral, but it is actually a fumble from the hands of one Hall of Famer, Sammy Baugh (33) of the Redskins, to another member of the Hall of Fame, tackle Joe Stydahar (13) of the Bears. It is but one of the hapless moments that beleaguered the Redskins in the 1940 NFL title game which the Bears won 73–0. (Chicago Bears)

George Connor
  Tackle and Linebacker
  Chicago Bears 1948–55
  College: Holy Cross and Notre Dame
  Inducted: 1975
  All Pro 8 times in five years (OT 5 times, LB twice, DT once)
  One of the finest 60-minute linemen ever

Jimmy Conzelman
  Quarterback, Coach, Owner
  Decatur Staleys 1920; Rock Island Independents 1921–22; Milwaukee Badgers 1923–24; Detroit Panthers 1925–26; Providence Steam Roller 1927–30
  College: Washington of St. Louis
  Inducted: 1964
  One of the finest early player-coaches
  Owned Detroit franchise (1925–26)
  Coached Chicago Cardinals (1940–42, 1946–48)

Willie Davis
  Defensive End
  Cleveland Browns 1958–59; Green Bay Packers 1960–69
  College: Grambling
  Inducted: 1981
  All Pro 5 times
  Played in 162 consecutive games, 6 championship games, 2 Super Bowls

Art Donovan
  Defensive Tackle
  Baltimore Colts 1950; New York Yanks 1951; Dallas Texans 1952; Baltimore Colts 1953–61
  College: Boston College
  Inducted: 1968
  All Pro 4 times
  Played in 2 NFL title games

John "Paddy" Driscoll
Quarterback, Coach
Hammond Pros 1919; Decatur Staleys 1920; Chicago Cardinals 1920-25; Chicago Bears 1926-29
College: Northwestern
Inducted: 1965
Top triple-threat back in the first decade of the NFL
Led NFL in scoring twice
Coached Chicago Bears (1956-57)

Bill Dudley
Halfback
Pittsburgh Steelers 1942, 1945-46; Detroit Lions 1947-49; Washington Redskins 1950-51, 1953
College: Virginia
Inducted: 1966
All Pro 2 times
Rushed for 3,057 yards, 19 TDs
Returned punts for 1,515 yards (12.2 average), 3 TDs

Glen "Turk" Edwards
Tackle
Boston Braves 1932; Boston Redskins 1933-36; Washington Redskins 1937-40
College: Washington State
Inducted: 1969
All Pro 4 times
Great 60-minute lineman
Coached Washington Redskins (1946-48)

Weeb Ewbank
Coach
Baltimore Colts 1954-62; New York Jets 1963-69, 1970-73
College: Miami of Ohio
Inducted: 1978
Won three NFL titles
Only coach to win both AFL and NFC championships

Tom Fears
End
Los Angeles Rams 1948-56
College: Santa Clara, UCLA
Inducted: 1970
All Pro 2 times
Caught 400 passes for 5,397 yards, 38 TDs
Holds NFL record for most receptions in a single game, 18

Ray Flaherty
End, Coach
New York Yankees 1927; New York Giants 1928-29, 1931-35; Boston Redskins 1936; Washington Redskins 1937-42; New York Yankees 1946-48; Chicago Hornets 1949
College: Gonzaga
Inducted: 1976
All Pro 2 times
Coached 2 NFL title-winners and two from AAFC

Len Ford
Defensive End
Los Angeles Dons 1948-49; Cleveland Browns 1950-57; Green Bay Packers 1958
College: Morgan State, Michigan
Inducted: 1976
All Pro 5 times
Recovered 20 opponent fumbles

Danny Fortmann
Guard
Chicago Bears 1936-43
College: Colgate
Inducted: 1965
All Pro 6 times
Considered one of the best blockers of the first three decades of NFL football

Frank Gatski
Center
Cleveland Browns 1946-56; Detroit Lions 1957
College: Marshall, Auburn
Inducted: 1985
All Pro 4 times
Played in 11 championship games (4 AAFC, 7 NFL)
Noted pass blocker

Bill George
Linebacker
Chicago Bears 1952-65; Los Angeles Rams 1966
College: Wake Forest
Inducted: 1974
All Pro 8 times
First of the great middle linebackers

Frank Gifford
Halfback and Flanker
New York Giants 1952–60, 1962–64
College: Southern California
Inducted: 1977
All Pro 4 times
Scored 484 points (78 TDs, 2 FGs, 10 PATs)
Rushed for 3,609 yards, 34 TDs
Caught 367 passes for 5,434 yards, 43 TDs
Threw 14 TD passes

Sid Gillman
Coach
Los Angeles Rams 1955–59; Los Angeles Chargers
    1960; San Diego Chargers 1961–69, 1972;
    Houston Oilers 1973–74
College: Ohio State
Inducted: 1983
Great passing-game strategist
Won 1 AFL championship, 5 division titles

Otto Graham
Quarterback
Cleveland Browns 1946–49, 1950–55
College: Northwestern
Inducted: 1965
All Pro 5 times
Played in 10 championship games (4 AAFC,
    6 NFL)
Completed 1,464 passes for 23,584 yards, 88 TDs

Harold "Red" Grange
Halfback
Chicago Bears 1925; New York Yankees 1926–27;
    Chicago Bears 1929–34
College: Illinois
Inducted: 1963
Most famous football player of the 1920s, early 30s
Great running back and considered best defensive
    back of his time

Forrest Gregg
Tackle, Guard, Coach
Green Bay Packers 1956, 1958–70; Dallas Cowboys
    1971
College: Southern Methodist
Inducted: 1977
All Pro 8 times
Was a member of 7 NFL championship teams
Coached Green Bay 1984–87

Lou Groza
Offensive Tackle, Placekicker
Cleveland Browns 1946–59, 1961–67
College: Ohio State
Inducted: 1974
All Pro 6 times
Held practically every place-kicking record when
    he retired after 21 years in pro football
Scored 1,608 points (1 TD, 264 FGs, 810 PATs)

Joe Guyon
Halfback
Canton Bulldogs 1919, 1920; Cleveland Indians
    1921; Oorang Indians 1922–23; Rock Island
    Independents 1924; Kansas City Cowboys
    1924–25; New York Giants 1927
College: Carlisle, Georgia Tech
Inducted: 1966
Triple-threat back
Exceptional defensive player

George Halas
End, Coach, Owner
Decatur Staleys 1920; Chicago Staleys 1921;
    Chicago Bears 1922–83
College: Illinois
Inducted: 1963
One of original organizers of NFL
Winningest coach in NFL history, 326–151–30
Coached 7 NFL championship teams

Ed Healey
Tackle
Rock Island Independents 1920–22; Chicago Bears
    1922–27
College: Dartmouth
Inducted: 1964
Best two-way tackle of the 1920s

Mel Hein
Center, Linebacker
New York Giants 1931–45
College: Washington State
Inducted: 1963
All Pro 8 consecutive times
Played in 172 consecutive games in 15 seasons

Wilbur "Pete" Henry
 Tackle, Kicker
 Canton Bulldogs 1920–23, 1925–26; New York
  Giants 1927; Pottsville Maroons 1927–28
 College: Washington and Jefferson
 Inducted: 1963
 Rugged tackler, exceptional blocker
 One of the best drop-kickers and punters of the
  1920s

Arnie Herber
 Quarterback
 Green Bay Packers 1930–40; New York Giants
  1944–45
 College: Wisconsin, Regis College
 Inducted: 1966
 All Pro once
 Completed 487 passes for 8,033 yards, 79 TDs

Cleveland has two Hall of Famers in this picture, Marion Motley (76) carrying the ball and end Dante Lavelli (86) looking on. The Ram tackler is Tank Younger. (Pro Football Hall of Fame)

Bill Hewitt
  End
  Chicago Bears 1932–36; Philadelphia Eagles
    1937–39; Phil-Pitt 1943
  College: Michigan
  Inducted: 1971
  All Pro 4 times
  One of the best two-way ends of the 30s

Clarke Hinkle
  Fullback
  Green Bay Packers 1932–41
  College: Bucknell
  Inducted: 1964
  All Pro 4 times
  Powerful runner, excellent kicker and punter
  Gained 3,860 yards rushing, 35 TDs
  Scored 370 points (44 TDs, 26 FGs, 28 PATs)

The Los Angeles Rams very versatile quarterback Bob Waterfield—passer, runner, place kicker, punter, defensive back—is about to throw one against the Colts circa 1950. Waterfield was elected to the Hall of Fame in 1965. (Fred Roe)

Elroy "Crazylegs" Hirsch
Halfback, End
Chicago Rockets 1946-48; Los Angeles Rams
  1949-57
College: Wisconsin, Michigan
Inducted: 1968
All Pro 2 times
Caught 343 passes for 7,029 yards, 53 TDs

Paul Hornung
Halfback
Green Bay Packers 1957-62, 1964-66
College: Notre Dame
Inducted: 1986
All Pro 2 times
Holds NFL record for most points scored in a
  season, 176
Led NFL in scoring 3 years in a row, 1959-61
Scored 760 points (62 TDs, 66 FGs, 190 PATs)

Ken Houston
Safety
Houston Oilers 1967-69, 1970-72; Washington
  Redskins 1973-80
College: Prairie View A & M
Inducted: 1986
All Pro 8 times
Intercepted 49 passes, returned 9 for TDs

Cal Hubbard
Tackle
New York Giants 1927-28, 1936; Green Bay
  Packers 1929-33, 1935; Pittsburgh Pirates 1936
College: Centenary, Geneva
Inducted: 1963
All Pro 6 times
Best offensive lineman of his time

Sam Huff
Linebacker
New York Giants 1956-63; Washington Redskins
  1964-67, 1969
College: West Virginia
Inducted: 1982
All Pro 4 times
Played in 6 NFL championship games

Lamar Hunt
AFL Founder, Owner
College: Southern Methodist
Inducted: 1972
Founded American Football League
Owner of Dallas Texans, Kansas City Chiefs

Don Hutson
End
Green Bay Packers 1935-45
College: Alabama
Inducted: 1963
All Pro 9 times
Led NFL in scoring 5 times, in pass receiving
  8 times
Caught 488 passes for 7,991 yards, 99 TDs
Scored 823 points (105 TDs, 7 FGs, 172 PATs)

David "Deacon" Jones
Defensive End
Los Angeles Rams 1961-71; San Diego Chargers
  1972-73; Washington Redskins 1974
College: South Carolina State, Mississippi
  Vocational
Inducted: 1980
All Pro 6 times
Exceptional pass rusher

Sonny Jurgensen
Quarterback
Philadelphia Eagles 1957-63; Washington Redskins
  1964-74
College: Duke
Inducted: 1983
All Pro 2 times
Led NFL in passing 3 times
Completed 2,433 passes for 32,224 yards, 255 TDs

Walt Kiesling
Guard, Coach
Duluth Eskimos 1926-27; Pottsville Maroons 1928;
  Chicago Cardinals 1929-33; Chicago Bears 1934;
  Green Bay Packers 1935-36; Pittsburgh Pirates
  1937-38, 1939; Pittsburgh Steelers 1940-42,
  1954-56
College: St. Thomas of Minnesota
Inducted: 1966
All Pro once
Exceptional blocker

Frank "Bruiser" Kinard
Tackle
Brooklyn Dodgers 1938-44; New York Yankees
  1946-47
College: Mississippi
Inducted: 1971
All Pro 4 times
One of the finest two-way linemen of the 1940s

Earl "Curly" Lambeau
Halfback, Coach
Green Bay Packers 1919–49; Chicago Cardinals
  1950–51; Washington Redskins 1952–53
College: Notre Dame
Inducted: 1963
Founded Green Bay Packers
Fourth winningest coach in NFL history
  (231–133–23)

Dick "Night Train" Lane
Defensive Back
Los Angeles Rams 1952–53; Chicago Cardinals
  1954–59; Detroit Lions 1960–65
College: Scottsbluff Junior College
Inducted: 1974
All Pro 5 times
Holds NFL record for most interceptions in a
  season, 14
Intercepted 68 passes, returned 5 for TDs

Willie Lanier
Linebacker
Kansas City Chiefs 1967–69, 1970-77
College: Morgan State
Inducted: 1986
All Pro 7 times
Exceptionally brutal tackler

Yale Lary
Defensive Back
Detroit Lions 1952–53, 1956–64
College: Texas A & M
Inducted: 1979
All Pro 4 times
Led league in punting 3 times
Averaged 22.5 yards on kickoff returns and 6 on
  punt returns
Averaged 44.3 yards for 503 punts
Intercepted 50 passes, 2 returned for TDs

Dante Lavelli
End
Cleveland Browns 1946–49, 1950–56
College: Ohio State
Inducted: 1975
All Pro 2 times
Caught 386 passes for 6,488 yards, 62 TDs

Bobby Layne
Quarterback
Chicago Bears 1948; New York Bulldogs 1949;
  Detroit Lions 1950–58; Pittsburgh Steelers
  1958–62
College: Texas
Inducted: 1967
All Pro 2 times
Completed 1,814 passes for 26,768 yards, 196 TDs
Gained 2,451 yards rushing, 25 TDs
Scored 372 points (25 TDs, 34 FGs, 120 PATs)

Alphonse "Tuffy" Leemans
Halfback, Fullback
New York Giants 1936–43
College: Oregon, George Washington
Inducted: 1978
All Pro 2 times
Gained 3,142 yards rushing, 17 TDs
Completed 167 passes for 2,324 yards, 25 TDs

Bob Lilly
Defensive Tackle
Dallas Cowboys 1961–74
College: Texas Christian
Inducted: 1980
All Pro 7 times
Played in 5 NFL title games, 2 Super Bowls

Vince Lombardi
Coach
Green Bay Packers 1959–67; Washington Redskins
  1969
College: Fordham
Inducted: 1971
Coached 5 NFL title winners
Second highest win percentage in NFL history,
  .746 (106–36–6)

Sid Luckman
Quarterback
Chicago Bears 1939–50
College: Columbia
Inducted: 1965
All Pro 5 times
First of the great T formation quarterbacks
Set NFL record of 7 TD passes in a game
Completed 904 passes for 14,683 yards, 137 TDs
Punted 230 times, 38.4-yard average

Hall of Famer Norm Van Brocklin (11) flips one to an Eagle receiver on a swing pattern against the Giants in 1958. "The Dutchman," as he was called, excelled at quarterback for both the Rams and Eagles during a 12-year NFL career. (Fred Roe)

Roy "Link" Lyman
Tackle
Canton Bulldogs 1922–23; Cleveland Bulldogs
   1924; Canton Bulldogs 1925; Frankford Yellow
   Jackets 1925; Chicago Bears 1926–28, 1930–31,
   1933–34
College: Nebraska
Inducted: 1964
Played on 4 championship teams
Exceptional defensive lineman

Tim Mara
Administrator
New York Giants
No College
Inducted: 1963
Founded New York Giants

Gino Marchetti
    Defensive End
    Dallas Texans 1952; Baltimore Colts 1953–64, 1966
    College: San Francisco
    Inducted: 1972
    All Pro 7 times
    Played in 10 Pro Bowls

George Preston Marshall
    Administrator
    Boston Braves 1932; Boston Redskins 1933–36;
        Washington Redskins 1937–69
    College: Randolph-Macon
    Inducted: 1963
    Founded Boston Braves, who became Redskins
    Sponsored many rules changes
    Brought in first band and half-time entertainment

Two of the Green Bay Packers in this photo are Hall of Famers; Bart Starr (15) and Jim Taylor (31). Running interference for Taylor is guard Jerry Kramer (64). (Fred Roe)

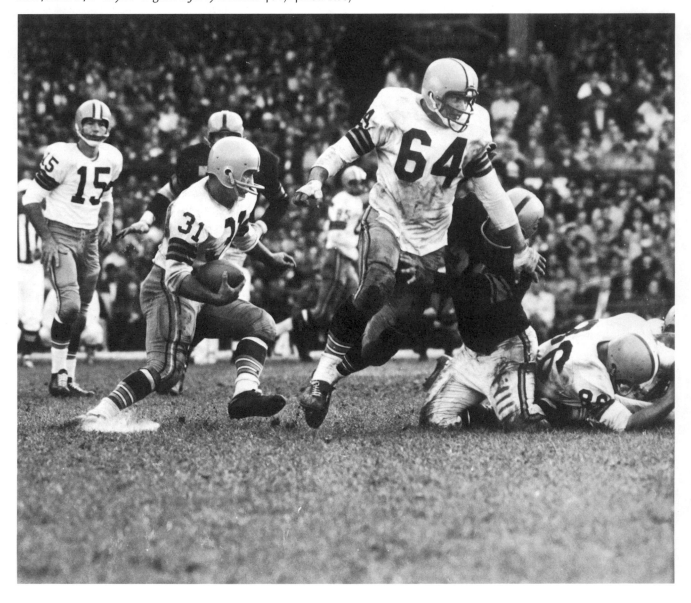

Ollie Matson

Halfback

Chicago Cardinals 1952, 1954-58; Los Angeles
  Rams 1959-62; Detroit Lions 1963; Philadelphia
  Eagles 1964-66

College: San Francisco

Inducted: 1972

All Pro 4 times

Gained 5,173 yards rushing, 3,285 on pass
  receptions, 3,746 on kickoff returns, 595 on punt
  returns

Scored 73 TDs

George McAfee

Halfback

Chicago Bears 1940-41, 1945-50

College: Duke

Inducted: 1966

All Pro once

Has second highest punt return average (12.78) in
  NFL history

Scored 39 TDs

Mike McCormack

Tackle, Coach

New York Yanks 1951; Cleveland Browns 1954-62

College: Kansas

Inducted: 1984

Played in 3 NFL title games

Exceptional blocker

Coached Eagles (1973-75), Colts (1980-81),
  Seahawks (1982)

Hugh McElhenny

Halfback

San Francisco 49ers 1952-60; Minnesota Vikings
  1961-62; New York Giants 1963; Detroit Lions
  1964

College: Washington

Inducted: 1970

All Pro 2 times

Gained 5,281 yards rushing, 3,247 receiving, 1,921
  on kickoff returns, 920 on punt returns

Scored 60 TDs

Johnny Blood McNally

Halfback, Coach

Milwaukee Badgers 1925-26; Duluth Eskimos
  1926-27; Pottsville Maroons 1928; Green Bay
  Packers 1929-33, 1935-36; Pittsburgh Pirates
  1934, 1937-39

College: St. John's of Minnesota

Inducted: 1963

All Pro once

Scored 37 TDs

Coached Steelers (1937-39)

Mike Michalske

Guard

New York Yankees 1926-28; Green Bay Packers
  1929-35, 1937

College: Penn State

Inducted: 1964

All Pro 4 times

Exceptional two-way lineman

Wayne Millner

End

Boston Redskins 1936; Washington Redskins
  1937-41, 1945

College: Notre Dame

Inducted: 1968

Caught 124 passes for 1,578 yards, 12 TDs

Bobby Mitchell

Wide Receiver, Halfback

Cleveland Browns 1958-61; Washington Redskins
  1962-68

College: Illinois

Inducted: 1983

All Pro 2 times

Gained 2,735 yards rushing, 7,954 yards receiving,
  2,690 on kickoff returns, 699 on punt returns

Scored 91 TDs

Ron Mix

Offensive Tackle

Los Angeles Chargers 1960; San Diego Chargers
  1961-69; Oakland Raiders 1971

College: Southern California

Inducted: 1979

All Pro 9 times

Exceptional blocker who had only two holding
  penalties called against him in 10 seasons

Lenny Moore
Flanker, Running Back
Baltimore Colts 1956–67
College: Penn State
Inducted: 1975
All Pro 5 times
Gained 5,174 yards rushing, 6,039 receiving, 1,180 on kickoff returns
Scored 113 TDs

Marion Motley
Fullback
Cleveland Browns 1946–49, 1950–53; Pittsburgh Steelers 1955
College: South Carolina State, Nevada
Inducted: 1968
All Pro once
Leading rusher in AAFC history
Gained 4,720 yards rushing, 5.7-yard average
Scored 38 TDs

George Musso
Tackle, Guard
Chicago Bears 1933–44
College: Millikin
Inducted: 1982
All Pro 2 times
Played in 7 NFL title games

Bronko Nagurski
Fullback
Chicago Bears 1930–37, 1943
College: Minnesota
Inducted: 1963
All Pro 3 times
Brutal runner and tackler
Gained 4,031 yards rushing, 18 TDs

Joe Namath
Quarterback
New York Jets 1965–69, 1970–76; Los Angeles Rams 1977
College: Alabama
Inducted: 1985
All Pro 2 times
Completed 1,886 passes for 27,663 yards, 173 TDs
First QB to pass for more than 4,000 yards in a season

Earle "Greasy" Neale
Coach
Philadelphia Eagles 1941–50
College: West Virginia Wesleyan
Inducted: 1969
Coached Eagles to back-to-back NFL titles (1948–49)

Ernie Nevers
Fullback
Duluth Eskimos 1926–27; Chicago Cardinals 1929–31
College: Stanford
Inducted: 1963
All Pro 5 times
Holds NFL record for most points in a game, 40

Ray Nitschke
Middle Linebacker
Green Bay Packers 1958–72
College: Illinois
Inducted: 1978
All Pro 3 times
Played on 5 NFL championship teams and in two Super Bowls

Leo Nomellini
Defensive Tackle
San Francisco 49ers 1950–63
College: Minnesota
Inducted: 1969
All Pro 6 times
Great two-way lineman

Merlin Olsen
Defensive Tackle
Los Angeles Rams 1962–76
College: Utah State
Inducted: 1982
All Pro 5 times
Played in more Pro Bowl games (14) than any player in NFL history

Jim Otto
Center
Oakland Raiders 1960–69, 1970–74
College: Miami (Fla.)
Inducted: 1980
All Pro AFL 10 straight years
Exceptional blocker

The most dazzling runner perhaps in the history of the game, breakaway back Gale Sayers, who shone for the Bears through the late 1960s and whose touchdown jaunts were truly spectacular, was enshrined in 1977. (Pro Football Hall of Fame)

Steve Owen
Tackle, Coach
Kansas City Cowboys 1924–25; New York Giants 1926–53
College: Phillips University
Inducted: 1966
Exceptional defensive tackle
Coached Giants to 2 NFL titles, 8 division championships

Clarence "Ace" Parker
Quarterback
Brooklyn Dodgers 1937–41; Boston Yanks 1945; New York Yankees 1946
College: Duke
Inducted: 1972
All Pro 2 times
Triple-threat back: rushed for 1,292 yards, passed for 4,701

Jim Parker
Guard, Tackle
Baltimore Colts 1957–67
College: Ohio State
Inducted: 1973
All Pro 8 times
One of the finest blockers in NFL history

Joe Perry
Fullback
San Francisco 49ers 1948–49, 1950–60, 1963; Baltimore Colts 1961–62
College: Compton Junior College
Inducted: 1969
All Pro 2 times
Gained 9,723 yards rushing, 2,021 yards receiving, 758 yards on kickoff returns
Scored 84 TDs

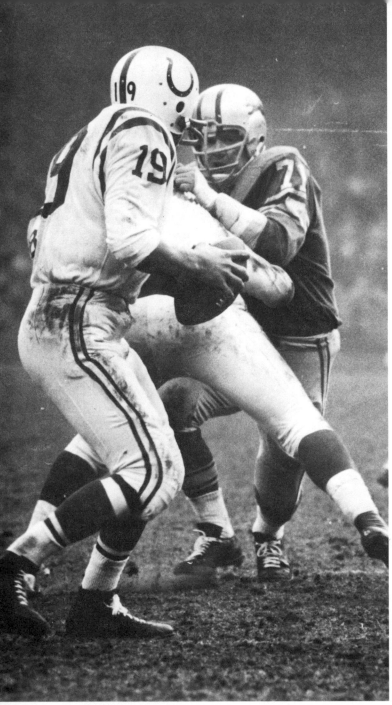

Cinch Hall of Famer Johnny Unitas, high-top shoes and all, gets ready to do what he did so well from 1956 through 1973 for the Colts, pass the football. He gained 40,239 yards passing and threw 290 touchdown passes. The Detroit defender trying to get at him is Alex Karras. (Fred Roe)

Pete Pihos
End
Philadelphia Eagles 1947–55
College: Indiana
Inducted: 1970
All Pro 6 times
Caught 373 passes for 5,619 yards, 61 TDs
Excellent on defense

Hugh "Shorty" Ray
Technical Advisor on Rules, Supervisor of Officials
College: Illinois
Inducted: 1966
Contributions to rules' changes and officiating
    quality

Dan Reeves
Administrator
Cleveland Rams 1941–45; Los Angeles Rams
    1946–71
College: Georgetown
Inducted: 1967
Owner of Cleveland/Los Angeles Rams

Jim Ringo
Center
Green Bay Packers 1953–63; Philadelphia Eagles
    1964–67
College: Syracuse
Inducted: 1981
All Pro 6 times
Played in 3 NFL title games

Andy Robustelli
Defensive End
Los Angeles Rams 1951–55; New York Giants
    1956–64
College: Arnold College
Inducted: 1971
All Pro 7 times
Played in 8 NFL championship games

Art Rooney
Administrator
Pittsburgh Steelers (Pirates) beginning 1933
College: Georgetown, Duquesne
Inducted: 1964
Founded Pittsburgh Steelers

Pete Rozelle
Administrator
College: San Francisco
Inducted: 1985
NFL commissioner, 1960–present

Gale Sayers
Halfback
Chicago Bears 1965–71
College: Kansas
Inducted: 1977
All Pro 5 times
Holds NFL record for TDs in rookie season, 22
Shares NFL record for most TDs in a game, 6
Holds NFL record for career average kickoff
returns, 30.56
Gained 4,956 yards rushing, 1,307 receiving, 2,781
on kickoff returns
Scored 56 TDs

Joe Schmidt
Linebacker
Detroit Lions 1953–65
College: Pittsburgh
Inducted: 1973
All Pro 8 times
Exceptional team leader

O.J. Simpson
Running Back
Buffalo Bills 1969–77; San Francisco 49ers 1978–79
College: Southern California
Inducted: 1985
All Pro 5 times
First player to rush for more than 2,000 yards in a
season
Gained 11,236 yards rushing, 2,142 receiving
Scored 76 TDs

Bart Starr
Quarterback, Coach
Green Bay Packers 1956–71
College: Alabama
Inducted: 1977
All Pro once
Quarterbacked 5 NFL title winners, 2 Super Bowl
champions
Completed 1,808 passes for 24,718 yards, 152 TDs

Roger Staubach
Quarterback
Dallas Cowboys 1969–79
College: Navy
Inducted: 1985
Led NFL in passing 4 times
Quarterbacked 2 Super Bowl champions
Completed 1,685 passes for 22,700 yards, 153 TDs

Ernie Stautner
Defensive Tackle
Pittsburgh Steelers 1950–63
College: Boston College
Inducted: 1969
All Pro 2 times
Recovered 21 opponent fumbles

Ken Strong
Halfback
Staten Island Stapletons 1929–32; New York Giants
1933–35, 1936–37, 1939 and 1944–47
College: New York University
Inducted: 1967
All Pro once
Triple-threat back: scored 496 points (35 TDs,
39 FGs, 169 PATs)

Joe Stydahar
Tackle, Coach
Chicago Bears 1936–42, 1945–46
College: West Virginia
Inducted: 1967
All Pro 4 times
Played in 5 NFL championship games
Exceptional two-way lineman

Fran Tarkenton
Quarterback
Minnesota Vikings 1961–66; New York Giants
1967–71; Minnesota Vikings 1972–78
College: Georgia
Inducted: 1986
All Pro 4 times
Played in 3 Super Bowls
Holds NFL record for pass completions (3,686),
yardage gained passing (47,003), TD passes (342)

Charley Taylor
Wide Receiver
Washington Redskins 1964–75, 1977
College: Arizona State
Inducted: 1984
All Pro 3 times
Caught 649 passes for 9,140 yards, 79 TDs

Jim Taylor
    Fullback
    Green Bay Packers 1958–66; New Orleans Saints
        1967
    College: Louisiana State
    Inducted: 1976
    All Pro 2 times
    Rushed for 8,597 yards, 83 TDs
    Caught 225 passes for 1,756 yards, 10 TDs

Jim Thorpe
    Halfback
    Canton Bulldogs 1915–17, 1919, 1920; Cleveland
        Indians 1921; Oorang Indians 1922–23; Rock
        Island Independents 1924; New York Giants
        1925; Canton Bulldogs 1926; Chicago Cardinals
        1928
    College: Carlisle
    Inducted: 1963
    Considered the greatest football player of his time.
        Great ballcarrier and kicker, brutal defensive
        player

The most menacing, brutalizing defender in an era of carnivorous tacklers, Dick Butkus of the Bears; he was enshrined in the Hall his first year of eligibility, 1979. (Fred Roe)

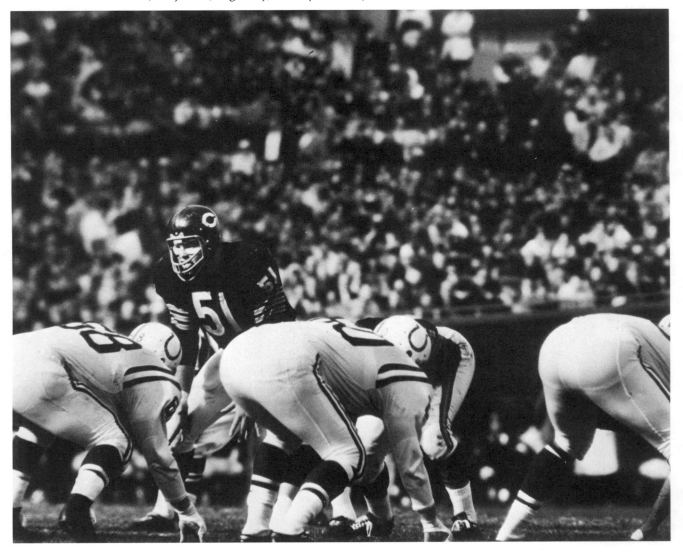

Y.A. Tittle

Quarterback
Baltimore Colts 1948-49, 1950; San Francisco 49ers
    1951-60; New York Giants 1961-64
College: Louisiana State
Inducted: 1971
All Pro 3 times, NFL MVP twice
Completed 2,427 passes for 33,070 yards, 212 TDs
Scored 39 TDs

George Trafton

Center
Decatur Staleys 1920; Chicago Staleys 1921;
    Chicago Bears 1923-32
College: Notre Dame
Inducted: 1964
Exceptional two-way lineman
Best center of the 1920s

Charley Trippi

Halfback and Quarterback
Chicago Cardinals 1947-55
College: Georgia
Inducted: 1968
All Pro once
Rushed for 3,506 yards, 23 TDs
Gained 1,321 yards on receptions, 1,457 on kickoff
    returns, 864 on punt returns
Passed for 2,547 yards, 16 TDs
Scored 37 TDs

Emlen Tunnell

Defensive Back
New York Giants 1948-58; Green Bay Packers
    1959-61
College: Toledo, Iowa
Inducted: 1967
All Pro 4 times
Holds NFL record for yardage gained on pass
    interceptions during a career, 1,282
Holds NFL record for most punt returns, 258
Intercepted 79 passes, returned 4 for TDs
Gained 2,209 yards on punt returns (8.6-yard
    average), 5 TDs

Clyde "Bulldog" Turner

Center, Linebacker
Chicago Bears 1940-52
College: Hardin-Simmons
Inducted: 1966
All Pro 6 times
Exceptional two-way player
Played on 4 NFL title teams

Johnny Unitas

Quarterback
Baltimore Colts 1956-72; San Diego Chargers 1973
College: Louisville
Inducted: 1979
All Pro 5 times
Ranked second in passing yardage in NFL history,
    40,239, and TD passes, 290
Completed 2,830 passes

Norm Van Brocklin

Quarterback
Los Angeles Rams 1949-57; Philadelphia Eagles
    1958-60
College: Oregon
Inducted: 1971
All Pro once
Completed 1,553 passes for 23,611 yards, 173 TDs
Averaged 42.9 yards on 523 punts

Steve Van Buren

Halfback
Philadelphia Eagles 1944-51
College: Louisiana State
Inducted: 1965
All Pro 4 times
Set new NFL rushing records twice, gaining 1,008
    yards in 1947 and 1,146 in 1949
Rushed for 5,860 yards, 69 TDs

Doak Walker

Halfback
Detroit Lions 1950-55
College: Southern Methodist University
Inducted: 1986
All Pro 4 times
Scored 534 points (34 TDs, 49 FGs, 183 PATs)

Paul Warfield

Wide Receiver
Cleveland Browns 1964-69, 1976-77; Miami
    Dolphins 1970-74
College: Ohio State
Inducted: 1983
All Pro 5 times
Caught 452 passes for 8,987 yards, 88 TDs

Bob Waterfield
  Quarterback
  Cleveland Rams 1945; Los Angeles Rams 1946–52
  College: UCLA
  Inducted: 1965
  All Pro 3 times
  Completed 814 passes for 11,849 yards, 97 TDs
  Scored 573 points (13 TDs, 60 FGs, 315 PATs)
  Averaged 42.4 yards on 314 punts

Arnie Weinmeister
  Defensive Tackle
  New York Yankees 1948–49; New York Giants
    1950–53
  College: Washington
  Inducted: 1984
  All Pro 4 times
  Considered the finest defensive lineman of the
    early 1950s

Sonny Jurgensen (9) was an Eagle when this photo was taken, a seven-year stint there before spending 11 years with the Redskins. Throwing 2,433 completions and 255 TD passes, he joined the Hall's illustrious fraternity in 1983. (Fred Roe)

Bill Willis
Guard
Cleveland Browns 1946–53
College: Ohio State
Inducted: 1977
All Pro 4 times
Best middle guard on defense in the early 1950s

Larry Wilson
Free Safety
St. Louis Cardinals 1960–72
College: Utah
Inducted: 1978
All Pro 6 times
Intercepted 52 passes, returned 5 for TDs

Alex Wojciechowicz
Center, Linebacker
Detroit Lions 1938–46; Philadelphia Eagles
    1946–50
College: Fordham
Inducted: 1968
Exceptional two-way player

Super Bowls Revisited

The NFL championship each season since 1966 has been determined at the Super Bowl, the annual ultimate conflict between the National Football Conference and the American Football Conference. It has grown to be the most observed sports event in the world, attracting hundreds of millions of television viewers and radio listeners each year. And, of course, its outcome determines who will possess the coveted NFL crown and sport the Vince Lombardi Trophy in its showcase.

Super Bowls Revisited

Super Bowl I

Green Bay Packers   35
Kansas City Chiefs   10
The Coliseum, Los Angeles, CA
January 15, 1967

Vince Lombardi's dynastic Packers, 12-2-0 in the regular season, had no trouble defeating Hank Stram's Chiefs in the premiere Super Bowl. Bart Starr connected with Max McGee on a 37-yard touchdown pass in the first period to give Green Bay a 7-0 lead. Kansas City's Len Dawson came back and hit Curtis McClinton on a 7-yarder to tie the score in the second quarter. Jim Taylor broke through on a 14-yard run for a TD. The Chiefs added a field goal, but the Pack had a 14-10 halftime lead.

After that it was totally Green Bay: Elijah Pitts ran 5 yards for a TD, Max McGee caught another Starr TD-pass, and Pitts ran still another in to give Green Bay a decisive 35-10 victory.

	Green Bay	**Kansas City**
Passing	Bart Starr 16/23, 53 yds, 1 TD	Len Dawson 16/27, 211 yds, 1 TD
	Zeke Bratkowski 0/1	Pete Beathard 1/5, 17 yds
Rushing	Jim Taylor 16/53 yds, 1 TD	Len Dawson 3/24 yds
	Elijah Pitts 45 yds, 2 TDs	Mike Garrett 6/17 yds
	Donny Anderson 30 yds	Curtis McClinton 6/16 yds
	Jim Grabowski 2 yds	Pete Beathard 1/14 yds
		Bert Coan 3/1 yd
Receiving	Max McGee 7/138 yds, 2 TDs	Chris Burford 4/67 yds
	Carroll Dale 4/59 yds	Otis Taylor 4/57 yds
	Elijah Pitts 2/32 yds	Mike Garrett 3/28 yds
	Marv Fleming 2/22 yds	Curtis McClinton 2/34 yds, 1 TD
	Jim Taylor 1/−1	Fred Arbanas 2/30 yds
		Reg Carolan 1/7 yds
		Bert Coan 1/5 yds
MVP	Bart Starr, Packers QB	

Super Bowl II

Green Bay Packers   33
Oakland Raiders   14
Orange Bowl, Miami, FL
January 14, 1968

Again Vince Lombardi's Packers proved invincible, and the AFL appeared definitely inferior to the senior NFL with John Rauch's Raiders never in the game. Two field goals from Don Chandler and a 62-yard pass play from Bart Starr to Boyd Dowler gave the Pack a 13-0 lead in the first half. Daryle Lamonica connected with Bill Miller for a Raider TD, but Chandler added another field goal to give Green Bay a 16-7 halftime edge.

Donny Anderson scored from the two in the second half, Chandler booted his fourth field goal of the day, and Herb Adderley picked off a Lamonica pass intended for Fred Biletnikoff and ran it 60 yards for a touchdown. A touchdown pass from Lamonica to Miller late in the fourth quarter was of no consequence in the Packer 33-14 triumph.

	Green Bay	**Oakland**
Passing	Bart Starr 13/24, 202 yds, 1 TD	Daryle Lamonica 15/34, 208 yds, 2 TDs
Rushing	Ben Wilson 17/62 yds	Hewritt Dixon 12/54 yds
	Donny Anderson 14/48 yds, 1 TD	Larry Todd 2/37 yds
	Travis Williams 8/36 yds	Pete Banaczak 6/16 yds
	Bart Starr 1/14 yds	
	Chuck Mercein 1/0	
Receiving	Carroll Dale 4/43 yds	Bill Miller 5/84 yds, 2 TDs
	Marv Fleming 4/35 yds	Pete Banaszak 4/69 yds
	Boyd Dowler 2/71 yds, 1 TD	Billy Cannon 2/45 yds
	Donny Anderson 2/18 yds	Fred Biletnikoff 2/10 yds
	Max McGee 1/35 yds	Warren Wells 1/17 yds
		Hewritt Dixon 1/3 yds
MVP	Bart Starr, Packers QB	

Jim Taylor (31) grinds out a few for the Pack in Super Bowl I. Trying to derail him is Kansas City linebacker E. J. Holub. Number 63 on Green Bay is Fuzzy Thurston, number 75 on the Chiefs is Jerry Mays. (Fred Roe)

In Super Bowl II, Boyd Dowler is about to gather in a Bart Starr pass for the Packers. Oakland defenders, a bit out of position, are linebacker Dan Conners (55) and cornerback Howie Williams (29). (Fred Roe)

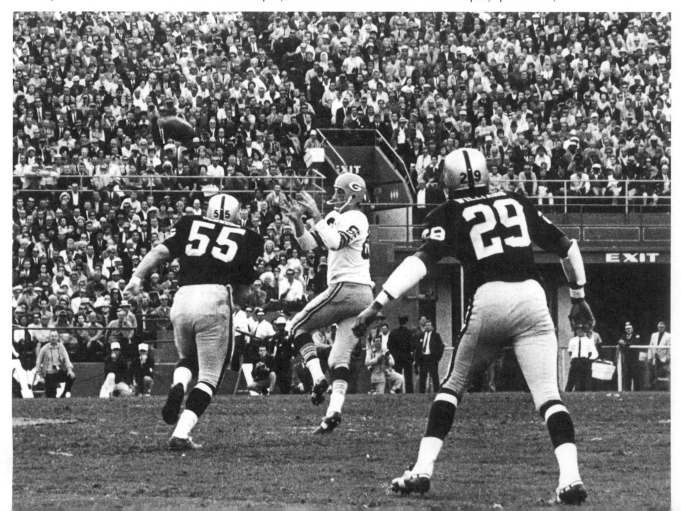

Super Bowl III

New York Jets   16
Baltimore Colts   7
Orange Bowl, Miami, FL
January 12, 1969

The AFL came of age. Weeb Ewbank's New York Jets surprised Don Shula's Colts and astonished a nation of football fans. After Joe Namath pretensiously predicted a win, the Jets he guided on the field completely dominated the game. Matt Snell gave New York its first score with a touchdown on a 4-yard run in the second quarter. That was followed by three straight Jet field goals in the second half by Jim Turner. A 1-yard plunge in the fourth quarter by Jerry Hill kept the Colts from being shutout, the final 16–7, Jets, just as Broadway Joe prognosticated.

	New York	**Baltimore**
Passing	Joe Namath 17/28, 206 yds	Johnny Unitas 11/24, 110 yds
	Babe Parilli 0/1	Earl Morrall 6/17, 71 yds
Rushing	Matt Snell 30/121 yds, 1 TD	Tom Matte 11/116 yds
	Emerson Boozer 10/19 yds	Jerry Hill 9/29 yds, 1 TD
	Bill Mathis 3/2 yds	Johnny Unitas 1/0 yds
		Earl Morrall 2/–2 yds
Receiving	George Sauer 8/133 yds	Willie Richardson 6/58 yds
	Matt Snell 4/40 yds	Jimmy Orr 3/42 yds
	Bill Mathis 3/20 yds	John Mackey 3/35 yds
	Pete Lammons 2/13 yds	Tom Matte 2/30 yds
		Jerry Hill 2/1 yd
		Tom Mitchel 1/15 yds
MVP	Joe Namath, Jets QB	

Super Bowl IV

Kansas City Chiefs   23
Minnesota Vikings   7
Tulane Stadium, New Orleans, LA
January 11, 1970

The AFL win the year before was not a fluke, Hank Stram's Chiefs proved that by methodically destroying Bud Grant's Minnesota Vikings to even the Super Bowl at two triumphs each for the AFL and NFL. And it was one-sided. Three Jan Stenerud field goals and a 5-yard TD run by Mike Garrett gave Kansas City a 16–0 halftime lead.

Minnesota forged a score in the third period when Dave Osborn bulled in for a touchdown, but Kansas City countered that with a 46-yard pass play when Len Dawson found Otis Taylor to round out a 23–7 victory.

	Chiefs	**Vikings**
Passing	Len Dawson 12/17, 142 yds, 1 TD	Joe Kapp 16/25, 183 yds
		Gary Cuozzo 1/3, 16 yds
Rushing	Mike Garrett 11/39 yds, 1 TD	Bill Brown 6/26 yds
	Frank Pitts 3/37 yds	Oscar Reed 4/17 yds
	Wendell Hayes 8/31 yds	Dave Osborn 7/15 yds, 1 TD
	Warren McVea 12/26 yds	Joe Kapp 2/9 yds
	Len Dawson 3/11 yds	
	Robert Holmes 5/7 yds	
Receiving	Otis Taylor 6/81 yds	John Henderson 7/111 yds
	Frank Pitts 3/33 yds	Bill Brown 3/11 yds
	Mike Garrett 2/25 yds	John Beasley 2/41 yds
	Wendell Hayes 1/3 yds	Oscar Reed 2/16 yds
		Dave Osborn 2/11 yds
		Gene Washington 1/9 yds
MVP	Len Dawson, Chiefs QB	

Super Bowl V

Baltimore Colts 16
Dallas Cowboys 13
Orange Bowl, Miami, FL
January 17, 1971

In certainly the most exciting Super Bowl to date, Don McCafferty's Colts made it three in a row for the AFL as Tom Landry's Cowboys lost out in the last five seconds of the game. The only score in the first period came on a 14-yard field goal from the toe of Cowboy Mike Clark. He added another, a 30-yarder, in the second quarter.

Baltimore tied it shortly after when Johnny Unitas tossed a pass that bounced off several hands before falling into those of John Mackey who carried it in for a 75-yard touchdown pass play. The try for extra point, however, was blocked. Dallas responded with a TD pass of its own, albeit quite a bit shorter, a 7-yarder from Craig Morton to Duane Thomas. At the half, the Cowboys led 13–7.

The score remained the same until midway through the fourth quarter when, after Baltimore's Rick Volk intercepted a Morton pass and returned it to the Dallas three, Tom Nowatzke banged in for the touchdown and the successful PAT tied the game. Another interception of a Morton pass with about a minute remaining enabled the Colts to move to the Dallas 25 yard line where, with just five seconds on the clock Jim O'Brien booted a field goal to win the game for Baltimore, 16–13.

	Baltimore	Dallas
Passing	Earl Morrall 7/15, 147 yds Johnny Unitas 3/9, 88 yds, 1 TD	Craig Morton 12/26, 127 yds, 1 TD
Rushing	Tom Nowatzke 10/33 yds, 1 TD Norm Bulaich 18/28 yds Johnny Unitas 1/4 yds Sam Havrilak 1/3 yds Earl Morrall 1/1 yd	Walt Garrison 12/65 yds Duane Thomas 18/35 yds Craig Morton 1/2 yds
Receiving	Roy Jefferson 3/52 yds John Mackey 2/80 yds, 1 TD Eddie Hinton 2/51 yds Sam Havrilak 2/27 yds Tom Nowatzke 1/45 yds Norm Bulaich 1/5 yds	Dan Reeves 5/46 yds Duane Thomas 4/21 yds Walt Garrison 2/19 yds Bob Hayes 1/41 yds
MVP	Chuck Howley, Cowboys LB	

A menacing Colt linebacker, Mike Curtis, glowers over the line in Super Bowl V. It worked, Baltimore won 16–13. (Fred Roe)

Craig Morton throws one out to the side for Dallas in Super Bowl V. But it was not his day, three interceptions and a loss. (Fred Roe)

Super Bowl VI

Dallas Cowboys 24
Miami Dolphins 3
Tulane Stadium, New Orleans, LA
January 16, 1972

Hot for revenge for the heartbreaker they lost in the previous Super Bowl, Tom Landry's Cowboys were primed for this one with Don Shula's Dolphins. As he had the year before, Mike Clark got the scoring going for Dallas in the first quarter with a 9-yard field goal. In the next period Roger Staubach drilled one to Lance Alworth in the end zone. Miami managed to score as the half was about to expire when Garo Yepremian booted a 34-yard field goal.

That was it for Miami, skunked in the second half. Dallas added a touchdown in each period, Duane Thomas lugging one in from the three and Mike Ditka scoring on a pass from Staubach, giving the Cowboys a 24–3 victory.

	Cowboys	Dolphins
Passing	Roger Staubach 12/19, 119 yds, 2 TDs	Bob Griese 12/23, 134 yds
Rushing	Duane Thomas 19/95 yds, 1 TD	Larry Csonka 9/40 yds
	Walt Garrison 14/74 yds	Jim Kiick 10/40 yds
	Calvin Hill 7/25 yds	Bob Griese 1/0 yds
	Roger Staubach 5/18 yds	
	Mike Ditka 1/17 yds	
	Bob Hayes 1/16 yds	
	Dan Reeves 1/7 yds	
Receiving	Duane Thomas 3/17 yds	Paul Warfield 4/39 yds
	Lance Alworth 2/28 yds, 1 TD	Jim Kiick 3/21 yds
	Mike Ditka 2/28 yds, 1 TD	Larry Csonka 2/18 yds
	Bob Hayes 2/23 yds	Marv Fleming 1/27 yds
	Walt Garrison 2/11 yds	Howard Twilley 1/20 yds
	Calvin Hill 1/12 yds	Jim Mandich 1/9 yds
MVP	Roger Staubach, Cowboys QB	

Duane Thomas (33) of the Cowboys struggles out of the grasp of a Miami defender in Super Bowl VI, which Dallas won 24–3. Thomas may be best remembered for his remark that "If it (the Super Bowl) is the ultimate game, how come they play it every year."

Super Bowl VII

Miami Dolphins   14
Washington Redskins   7
The Coliseum, Los Angeles, CA
January 14, 1973

It was Don Shula's turn for revenge and his Miami team, which had gone undefeated in the regular season, had little trouble with George Allen's Redskins, who were making their debut appearance in the post-season spectacle. The Dolphins scored in the first period when Bob Griese hit Howard Twilley with a 28-yard TD pass. Jim Kiick bulled in from the one in the ensuing period and Miami took a 14-0 lead into the intermission.

Those two scores were all the Dolphins needed. Washington was blanked again in the third quarter, and were only able to score once in the fourth quarter on a freakish play. Garo Yepremian's field goal attempt for Miami was blocked and, when he picked up the ball and tried to pass, it floated into the hands of Redskin Mike Bass who ran with it 49 yards for a touchdown. That was all for Washington, and Miami ended its perfect season with a 14-7 triumph.

	Dolphins	Redskins
Passing	Bob Griese	Billy Kilmer
	8/11, 88 yds, 1 TD	14/28, 104 yds
Rushing	Larry Csonka	Larry Brown
	15/112 yds	22/72 yds
	Jim Kiick	Charley Harraway
	12/38 yds, 1 TD	10/37 yds
	Mercury Morris	Billy Kilmer
	10/34 yds	2/18 yds
		Charley Taylor
		1/8 yds
		Jerry Smith
		1/6 yds
Receiving	Paul Warfield	Roy Jefferson
	3/36 yds	5/50 yds
	Jim Kiick	Larry Brown
	2/6 yds	5/26 yds
	Howard Twilley	Charley Taylor
	1/28 yds, 1 TD	2/20 yds
	Jim Mandich	Jerry Smith
	1/19 yds	1/11 yds
	Larry Csonka	Charley Harraway
	1/−1 yds	1/−3 yds
MVP	Jake Scott, Dolphins S	

Super Bowl VIII

Miami Dolphins   24
Minnesota Vikings   7
Rice Stadium, Houston, TX
January 13, 1974

Don Shula's Miami Dolphins keep coming back like a song to the Super Bowl, and in this one had even less trouble with Bud Grant's Minnesota Vikings. Miami totally dominated the game. Two drives in the first quarter resulted in touchdowns by Larry Csonka and Jim Kiick. Garo Yepremian added a field goal in the second period, and the score at half was 17-0. In the third quarter the Dolphins marched again, and again Csonka carried it in for the score. Minnesota got a token TD in the last period when Fran Tarkenton ran four yards into the end zone. The final was 24-7, and Miami became the first team since Green Bay in Super Bowls I and II to win the classic two years straight.

	Dolphins	Vikings
Passing	Bob Griese	Fran Tarkenton
	6/7, 73 yds	18/28, 182 yds
Rushing	Larry Csonka	Oscar Reed
	33/145 yds, 2 TDs	11/32 yds
	Mercury Morris	Chuck Foreman
	11/34 yds	7/18 yds
	Jim Kiick	Fran Tarkenton
	7/10 yds	4/17 yds, 1 TD
	Bob Griese	Ed Marinaro
	2/7 yds	1/3 yds
		Bill Brown
		1/2 yds
Receiving	Paul Warfield	Chuck Foreman
	2/33 yds	5/27 yds
	Jim Mandich	John Gilliam
	2/21 yds	4/44 yds
	Marlin Briscoe	Stu Voight
	2/19 yds	3/46 yds
		Ed Marinaro
		2/39 yds
		Bill Brown
		1/9 yds
		Doug Kingsriter
		1/9 yds
		Jim Lash
		1/9 yds
		Oscar Reed
		1/−1 yds
MVP	Larry Csonka, Dolphins RB	

Super Bowl IX

Pittsburgh Steelers   16
Minnesota Vikings   6
Tulane Stadium, New Orleans, LA
January 12, 1975

Chuck Noll brought his mean black and gold Steelers to their first Super Bowl and set a brutal precedent as they blitzed and bludgeoned Bud Grant's Vikings. It was a game of awesome defenses and that is how the scoring began. In the second quarter Pittsburgh defensive end Dwight White nabbed Fran Tarkenton in the end zone for a safety. And that was the extent of the scoring in the first half.

Pitt capitalized on a fumble turnover in the third quarter and turned it into a touchdown when Franco Harris carried it in from the nine. Then, in the fourth quarter, Minnesota got on the scoreboard, the result of another defensive coup, when Terry Brown recovered a blocked punt in the Steeler end zone. Pittsburgh then staged one of the best drives of the game, capping it with a rifle shot from Terry Bradshaw to Larry Brown for a touchdown. Pitt's Steel Curtain then held the Vikes and the final was 16-6, the Steelers.

	Steelers	Vikings
Passing	Terry Bradshaw 9/14, 96 yds, 1 TD	Fran Tarkenton 11/26, 102 yds
Rushing	Franco Harris 34/158 yds, 1 TD Rocky Bleier 17/65 yds Terry Bradshaw 5/33 yds Lynn Swann 1/ − 7 yds	Chuck Foreman 12/18 yds Fran Tarkenton 1/0 Dave Osborn 8/ − 1 yd
Receiving	Larry Brown 3/49 yds, 1 TD John Stallworth 3/24 yds Rocky Bleier 2/11 yds Frank Lewis 1/12 yds	Chuck Foreman 5/50 yds Stu Voight 2/31 yds Dave Osborn 2/7 yds John Gilliam 1/16 yds Oscar Reed 1/ − 2 yds
MVP	Franco Harris, Steelers RB	

Super Bowl X

Pittsburgh Steelers   21
Dallas Cowboys   17
Orange Bowl, Miami, FL
January 18, 1976

Chuck Noll gave testimony on the field that his Steelers had an offense as well as a defense when he escaped Tom Landry's determined but deterred Cowboys. Dallas took the lead in the first quarter with Roger Staubach tossing a 28-yard touchdown pass to Drew Pearson. Terry Bradshaw countered it with his own TD throw to Randy Grossman in the second quarter, but the Cowboys took a 10-7 lead to the locker room at the half after Toni Fritsch booted a 36-yard field goal.

Both teams posted goose eggs in the third period, but then the game was determined on four consecutive Steeler scores in the fourth quarter. First Reggie Harrison batted a Dallas punt out of the end zone for a safety, then Roy Gerella kicked two field goals, and finally Bradshaw unloaded a bomb to Lynn Swann for a 64-yard touchdown. Down 21-10, Staubach brought the Cowboys back with a lengthy march and a touchdown toss to Percy Howard. He drove them again in the waning seconds but this time the drive ended with an interception and Pitt held on to win 21-17.

	Steelers	Cowboys
Passing	Terry Bradshaw 9/19, 209 yds, 1 TD	Roger Staubach 15/24, 204 yds, 2 TDs
Rushing	Franco Harris 27/82 yds Rocky Bleier 15/51 yds Terry Bradshaw 4/16 yds	Robert Newhouse 16/56 yds Roger Staubach 5/22 yds Doug Dennison 5/16 yds Preston Pearson 5/14 yds
Receiving	Lynn Swann 4/161 yds, 1 TD John Stallworth 2/8 yds Franco Harris 1/26 yds Randy Grossman 1/7 yds, 1 TD Larry Brown 1/7 yds	Preston Pearson 5/23 yds Charles Young 3/31 yds Drew Pearson 2/59 yds Robert Newhouse 2/12 yds Percy Howard 1/34 yds, 1 TD Jean Fugett 1/9 yds Doug Dennison 1/6 yds
MVP	Lynn Swann, Steelers WR	

Super Bowl XI

Oakland Raiders 32
Minnesota Vikings 14
Rose Bowl, Pasadena, CA
January 9, 1977

Many thought it was about time for Bud Grant and his Vikings to win the title, after all this was Minnesota's fourth trip to the Super Bowl, but John Madden and his Raiders hardly concurred. After a scoreless first period, Oakland took control of the game and never let loose of it. A field goal by Errol Mann, a short TD pass from Ken Stabler to Dave Casper, and a plunge into the end zone by Pete Banaszak gave Oakland a 16–0 halftime lead.

Mann booted another field goal in the third period before Minnesota could post a score, but the Vikings finally did when Fran Tarkenton threw an 8-yarder to Sammy White. But Banaszak again bucked in for a score after a Raider drive, and then cornerback Willie Brown picked off a Tarkenton pass and raced 75 yards with it for another score. An inconsequential TD pass from Minnesota's Bob Lee to Stu Voight ended the day's scoring, and the Vikes had lost once again, this time 32–14.

	Raiders	Vikings
Passing	Ken Stabler 12/19, 180 yds, 1 TD	Fran Tarkenton 17/35, 205 yds, 1 TD
		Bob Lee 7/9, 81 yds, 1 TD
Rushing	Clarence Davis 16/137 yds	Carl Foreman 17/44 yds
	Mark van Eeghen 18/73 yds	Sammy Johnson 2/9 yds
	Carl Garrett 4/19 yds	Sammy White 1/7 yds
	Pete Banaszak 10/19 yds, 2 TDs	Bob Lee 1/4 yds
	Hubert Ginn 2/9 yds	Robert Miller 2/4 yds
	Mike Rae 2/9 yds	Brent McClanahan 3/3 yds
Receiving	Fred Biletnikoff 4/79 yds	Sammy White 5/77 yds, 1 TD
	Dave Casper 4/70 yds, 1 TD	Chuck Foreman 5/62 yds
	Cliff Branch 3/20 yds	Stu Voight 4/49 yds, 1 TD
	Carl Garrett 1/11 yds	Robert Miller 4/19 yds
		Ahmad Rashad 3/53 yds
		Sammy Johnson 3/26 yds
MVP	Fred Biletnikoff, Raiders WR	

Super Bowl XII

Dallas Cowboys 27
Denver Broncos 10
The Superdome, New Orleans, LA
January 15, 1978

Tom Landry had brought his Cowboys to three previous Super Bowls, won one, and was thirsting to even his record, and Red Miller's Broncos were obliging. Too obliging most spectators thought, Denver was never really in the game. Tony Dorsett ran one in from the three to start the Dallas surge in the first quarter. Efren Herrera booted a pair of long field goals, and the Cowboys were up 13–0 at intermission.

Jim Turner kicked a field goal for Denver to start the second half, but Dallas responded with a 45-yard touchdown pass from Roger Staubach to Butch Johnson. Denver then got its lone touchdown of the game on a 1-yard plunge by Rob Lytle. A little bit of trickery insured the final score of 27–10 when Cowboy running back Robert Newhouse headed out around end, pulled up, and lofted a 29-yard touchdown pass to Golden Richards.

	Cowboys	Broncos
Passing	Roger Staubach 17/25, 183 yds, 1 TD	Craig Morton 4/15, 39 yds
	Robert Newhouse 1/1, 29 yds, 1 TD	Norris Weese 4/10, 22 yds
	Danny White 1/2, 5 yds	
Rushing	Tony Dorsett 15/66 yds, 1 TD	Rob Lytle 10/35 yds, 1 TD
	Robert Newhouse 14/55 yds	Otis Armstrong 7/27 yds
	Danny White 1/13 yds	Norris Weese 3/26 yds
	Preston Pearson 3/11 yds	Jim Jensen 1/16 yds
	Roger Staubach 3/6 yds	Jon Keyworth 5/9 yds
	Scott Laidlaw 1/–1 yd	Lonnie Perrin 3/9 yds
	Butch Johnson 1/–9 yds	
Receiving	Preston Pearson 5/37 yds	Jack Dolbin 2/24 yds
	Billy Joe DuPree 4/66 yds	Riley Odoms 2/9 yds
	Robert Newhouse 3/–1 yd	Haven Moses 1/21 yds
	Butch Johnson 2/53 yds, 1 TD	Rick Upchurch 1/9 yds
	Golden Richards 2/38 yds, 1 TD	Jim Jensen 1/5 yds
	Tony Dorsett 2/11 yds	Lonnie Perrin 1/–7 yds
	Drew Pearson 1/13 yds	
MVP	Harvey Martin, Cowboys DE; Randy White, Cowboys DT	

Super Bowl XIII

Pittsburgh Steelers   35
Dallas Cowboys   31
Orange Bowl, Miami, FL
January 21, 1979

Back again for both, both two-time takers of Super Bowl honors; Chuck Noll's Steelers, however, were destined to become the first team to win three Super Bowl trophies, and Tom Landry's Cowboys would have to settle for the consolation of being the first team to appear in five Super Bowls. But it was an absolutely super Super Bowl, the highest scoring in all history.

It was Terry Bradshaw's day, beginning with a 28-yard TD pass to John Stallworth in the first quarter to give the Steelers an early lead. But it also was Roger Staubach's day. He came back with a 39-yard touchdown strike to Tony Hill. Then linebacker Larry Hegman collided with Terry Bradshaw, ended up with the football, and brought it 37 yards for a Dallas touchdown, and that would prove to be their only lead of the game. Bradshaw responded with vitriol, first a 75-yard TD toss to John Stallworth, then a 7-yarder to Rocky Bleier. Pitt led 21–14 at the half.

Rafael Septien contributed the only score in the third period, a 27-yard Dallas field goal. Then Pittsburgh took hold. Franco Harris scored on a 22-yard run, and Lynn Swann took an 18-yard TD pass from Bradshaw. The score seemed a prohibitive 35–17 with just over two minutes remaining in the fourth quarter. Not to Dallas, however. Staubach came out flinging: a touchdown pass to Billy Joe DuPree, then another to Butch Johnson after recovering an onsides kick. Another onsides kick, and maybe, but it did not work, and Pitt prevailed 35–31.

	Steelers	Cowboys
Passing	Terry Bradshaw 17/30, 318 yds, 4 TDs	Roger Staubach 17/30, 228 yds, 3 TDs
Rushing	Franco Harris 20/68 yds, 1 TD	Tony Dorsett 16/96 yds
	Rocky Bleier 2/3 yds	Roger Staubach 4/37 yds
	Terry Bradshaw 2/−5 yds	Scott Laidlaw 3/12 yds
		Preston Pearson 1/6 yds
		Robert Newhouse 8/3 yds
Receiving	Lynn Swann 7/124 yds, 1 TD	Tony Dorsett 5/44 yds
	John Stallworth 3/115 yds, 2 TDs	Drew Pearson 4/73 yds
	Randy Grossman 3/29 yds	Tony Hill 2/49 yds, 1 TD
	Theo Bell 2/21 yds	Butch Johnson 2/30 yds, 1 TD
	Franco Harris 1/22 yds	Billy Joe DePree 2/17 yds, 1 TD
	Rocky Bleier 1/7 yds, 1 TD	Preston Pearson 2/15 yds
MVP	Terry Bradshaw, Steelers QB	

Super Bowl XIV

Pittsburgh Steelers   31
Los Angeles Rams   19
Rose Bowl, Pasadena, CA
January 20, 1980

Four for four is what Steeler fans wanted, Chuck Noll raised his eyebrows at the mention of it, but Pittsburgh got just that as no team had before and none has since. To the chagrin, it should be added, of Ray Malavasi and his L. A. Rams. And the Steelers had to stage a dramatic comeback to do it. Matt Bahr kicked a field goal to give Pitt an early lead, but it disappeared in the same first quarter when Cullen Bryant bucked in from the one for a Ram touchdown. Harris contributed the same thing for the Steelers, but then Frank Corral kicked a pair of field goals for L. A. before the half ended, and the score at intermission was Rams 13, Steelers 10.

Terry Bradshaw connected with Lynn Swann, a 47-yard TD toss, to give Pitt the lead in the third quarter, but the Rams rescued it when running back Lawrence McCutcheon opted on an end run to throw a bomb to Ron Smith. Going into the fourth quarter, it was now the Rams 19, the Steelers 17. The tide turned, however, with Bradshaw's passing and the Steel Curtain's defense. In the last period Bradshaw teamed with John Stallworth on a 73-yard touchdown spectacular, then passed the Steelers into a position where Franco Harris could bull it in from the one. The Curtain contained the Rams, and the final was Pitt 31, L. A. 19

	Steelers	Rams
Passing	Terry Bradshaw 14/21, 309 yds, 2 TDs	Vince Ferragamo 15/25, 212 yds
		Lawrence McCutcheon 1/1, 24 yds, 1 TD
Rushing	Franco Harris 20/46 yds, 2 TDs	Wendell Tyler 17/60 yds
	Rocky Bleier 10/25 yds	Cullen Bryant 6/30 yds, 1 TD
	Terry Bradshaw 3/9 yds	Lawrence McCutcheon 5/10 yds
	Sidney Thornton 4/4 yds	Vince Ferragamo 1/7 yds
Receiving	Lynn Swann 5/79 yds, 1 TD	Billy Waddy 3/75 yds
	John Stallworth 3/121 yds, 1 TD	Cullen Bryant 3/21 yds
	Franco Harris 3/66 yds	Wendell Tyler 3/20 yds
	Bennie Cunningham 2/21 yds	Preston Dennard 2/32 yds
	Sidney Thornton 1/22 yds	Terry Nelson 2/20 yds
		Drew Hill 1/28 yds
		Ron Smith 1/24 yds, 1 TD
		Lawrence McCutcheon 1/16 yds
MVP	Terry Bradshaw, Steelers QB	

Super Bowl XV

Oakland Raiders   27
Philadelphia Eagles   10
The Superdome, New Orleans, LA
January 25, 1981

Tom Flores was now in charge of the Raiders when they squared off against Dick Vermeil's Eagles, and the Oaklanders were ready, offense and defense alike. They surged to a 14–0 lead in the first quarter on a 2-yard Jim Plunkett to Cliff Branch touchdown pass, which Plunkett followed with a sideline pass to Kenny King who broke free and scored on an 80-yard TD pass play. Philadelphia managed a field goal in the second quarter from the toe of Tony Franklin, but that was it.

Plunkett was back in the third quarter, getting the ball to Branch for another touchdown and moving the game out of reach. Ron Jaworski got the Eagles a touchdown when he hit Keith Krepfle with an 8-yarder. A field goal from Chris Bahr iced it, however, for the Raiders 27–10.

	Raiders	**Eagles**
Passing	Jim Plunkett 13/21, 261 yds, 3 TDs	Ron Jaworsk 18/38, 291 yds, 1 TD
Rushing	Mark van Eeghen 19/80 yds	Wilbert Montgomery 16/44 yds
	Kenny King 6/18 yds	Leroy Harris 7/14 yds
	Derrick Jensen 3/12 yds	Louie Giammona 1/7 yds
	Jim Plunkett 3/9 yds	Perry Harrington 1/4 yds
	Arthur Whittington 3/–2	Ron Jaworsk 1/0 yds
Receiving	Cliff Branch 5/67 yds, 2 TDs	Wilbert Montgomery 6/91 yds
	Bob Chandler 4/77 yds	Harold Carmichael 5/83 yds
	Kenny King 2/93 yds, 1 TD	Charles Smith 2/59 yds
	Raymond Chester 2/24 yds	Keith Krepfle 1/16 yds, 1 TD
		John Spagnola 1/22 yds
		Rodney Parker 1/19 yds
		Leroy Harris 1/1 yd
MVP	Jim Plunkett, Raiders QB	

Super Bowl XVI

San Francisco 49ers   26
Cincinnati Bengals   21
The Silverdome, Pontiac, MI
January 24, 1982

Bill Walsh's 49ers were known for their explosive offense, but it was the defense that made the day for them when they met the Cincinnati Bengals, coached by former Packer Forrest Gregg, who had played in Super Bowls I and II. Joe Montana guided a drive for San Francisco in the first quarter, finalizing it by sneaking it in himself for a touchdown. In the second period, Montana hit Earl Cooper for another touchdown, and Ray Wersching added a pair of field goals; the score at the half standing at 20–0, San Francisco.

The Bengals came back, however, QB Ken Anderson running it in for Cincinnati's first score. In the fourth period, Anderson drilled one to Dan Ross for another touchdown and the Bengals were back in the game. But the 49er defense shut them down when they had to, and another pair of Wershing field goals was enough to offset another Anderson to Ross TD pass, giving San Francisco its first Super Bowl victory 26–21.

	49ers	**Bengals**
Passing	Joe Montana 14/22, 157 yds, 1 TD	Ken Anderson 25/34, 300 yds, 2 TDs
Rushing	Ricky Patton 17/55 yds	Pete Johnson 14/36 yds
	Earl Cooper 9/34 yds	Charles Alexander 5/17 yds
	Joe Montana 6/18 yds 1 TD	Ken Anderson 4/15 yds, 1 TD
	Bill Ring 5/17 yds	Archie Griffin 1/4 yds
	Johnny Davis 2/5 yds	
	Dwight Clark 1/–2	
Receiving	Freddie Solomon 4/52 yds	Dan Ross 11/104 yds, 2 TDs
	Dwight Clark 4/45 yds	Cris Collinsworth 5/107 yds
	Earl Cooper 2/15 yds 1 TD	Isaac Curtis 3/42 yds
	Mike Wilson 1/22 yds	Steve Kreider 2/36 yds
	Charley Young 1/14 yds	Pete Johnson 2/8 yds
	Ricky Patton 1/6 yds	Charles Alexander 2/3 yds
	Bill King 1/3 yds	
MVP	Joe Montana, 49ers QB	

Super Bowl XVII

Washington Redskins   27
Miami Dolphins   17
Rose Bowl, Pasadena, CA
January 30, 1983

Don Shula was back with his Dolphins, dreams of the back-to-back Super Bowl championships dancing in his head, but this was the 1980s, and the Washington Redskins under Joe Gibbs were a team unimpressed with past credentials. In the beginning, however, it appeared Miami might give Shula his third Super Bowl trophy. They got on the board with a spectacular David Woodley to Jimmy Cefalo 76-yard touchdown pass in the first quarter. Mark Moseley kicked a field goal for the Redskins, but it was matched by one from Miami's Uwe von Schamann. Washington came back to tie the game when Joe Theismann connected with Alvin Garrett for a TD. Moments later, however, a crowd-dazzler was provided by Fulton Walker who ran the kickoff back 98 yards for a touchdown to give the Dolphins a 17–10 halftime lead.

Whatever Joe Gibbs did in the locker room at half-time worked. The Redskins came back out, totally shut down Miami, scored on a field goal by Moseley, a 43-yard run by John Riggins, and a short pass from Theismann to Charlie Brown, an easy Washington win 27–17.

	Redskins	Dolphins
Passing	Joe Theismann 15/23, 143 yds, 2 TDs	David Woodley 4/14, 97 yds, 1 TD
		Don Strock 0/3, 0 yds
Rushing	John Riggins 38/166 yds, 1 TD	Andra Franklin 16/49 yds
	Alvin Garrett 1/44 yds	Tony Nathan 7/26 yds
	Clarence Harmon 9/40 yds	David Woodley 4/16 yds
	Joe Theismann 3/20 yds	Tom Vigorito 1/4 yds
	Rick Walker 1/6 yds	Duriel Harris 1/1 yd
Receiving	Charlie Brown 6/20 yds, 1 TD	Jimmy Cefalo 2/82 yds, 1 TD
	Don Warren 5/28 yds	Duriel Harris 2/15 yds
	Alvin Garrett 2/13 yds, 1 TD	
	Rick Walker 1/27 yds	
	John Riggins 1/15 yds	
MVP	John Riggins, Redskins RB	

Super Bowl XVIII

Los Angeles Raiders   38
Washington Redskins   9
Tampa Stadium, Tampa, FL
January 22, 1984

The Raiders and Tom Flores had moved south to L. A. The Redskins, under Joe Gibbs, were thinking dynasty, but the Redskins were very wrong as the Raiders mercilessly showed them. Everything went wrong for Washington from the very beginning. Derrick Jensen grabbed a blocked Redskin punt in the end zone to give L. A. a 7–0 lead. Then Jim Plunkett found Cliff Branch on a 12-yard TD pass. Mark Moseley kicked a 3-pointer for Washington, but Jack Squirek of the Raiders regained the momentum by picking off a pass for another Raider TD and a 21–3 halftime lead.

Riggins scored for the Redskins in the second half, but from that point on it was all Los Angeles, *nee* Oakland. First a 5-yard TD jaunt by Marcus Allen, then he took off around end and went 74 yards for another touchdown. Chris Bahr's final field goal merely gilded the 38–9 triumph for the Raiders.

	Raiders	Redskins
Passing	Jim Plunkett 16/25, 172 yds, 1 TD	Joe Theismann 16/35, 243 yds
Rushing	Marcus Allen 22/191 yds, 2 TDs	John Riggins 26/64 yds, 1 TD
	Greg Pruitt 5/17 yds	Joe Theismann 3/18 yds
	Kenny King 3/12 yds	Joe Washington 3/8 yds
	Chester Willis 1/7 yds	
	Frank Hawkins 3/6 yds	
	Jim Plunkett 1/–2 yds	
Receiving	Cliff Branch 6/94 yds, 1 TD	Clint Didier 5/65 yds
	Todd Christensen 4/32 yds	Charlie Brown 3/93 yds
	Frank Hawkins 2/20 yds	Joe Washington 3/20 yds
	Marcus Allen 2/18 yds	Nick Giaquinto 2/21 yds
	Kenny King 2/8 yds	Art Monk 1/26 yds
		Alvin Garrett 1/17 yds
		John Riggins 1/1 yd
MVP	Marcus Allen, Raiders RB	

Super Bowl XIX

San Francisco 49ers 38
Miami Dolphins 16
Stanford Stadium, Palo Alto, CA
January 20, 1985

This game was touted as the battle of the quarterbacks, a free-throwing contest between San Francisco's Joe Montana and Miami's Dan Marino. The Bill Walsh-tutored Montana came out on top, as the 49ers virtually devoured Don Shula's Dolphins. Miami was in it for the first quarter, even held the lead twice. Uwe von Schamann kicked a field goal for the Dolphins early, then, after Montana threw a TD strike to Carl Monroe for the 49ers, Marino came right back and zinged one to Dan Johnson to regain the lead.

After that, however, it was San Francisco demonstrating a destruction machine. Montana hit Roger Craig for a touchdown, then each of those two in turn ran the ball in for touchdowns. For Miami, von Schamann booted a pair of field goals, and the score at half was San Francisco 23, the Dolphins 16. The Frisco defense did it all in the second half, shutting out Miami while Ray Wersching kicked a field goal, and Montana and Craig again teamed up on a TD pass, the final 38–16, 49ers.

	49ers	Dolphins
Passing	Joe Montana 24/35, 331 yds, 3 TDs	Dan Marino 29/50, 318 yds, 1 TD
Rushing	Wendell Tyler 13/65 yds	Tony Nathan 5/18 yds
	Joe Montana 5/59 yds, 1 TD	Woody Bennett 3/7 yds
	Roger Craig 15/58 yds, 1 TD	Dan Marino 1/0 yds
	Derrick Harmon 5/20 yds	
	Freddie Solomon 1/5 yds	
	Earl Cooper 1/4 yds	
Receiving	Roger Craig 7/77 yds, 2 TDs	Tony Nathan 10/83 yds
	Dwight Clark 6/77 yds	Mark Clayton 6/92 yds
	Russ Francis 5/60 yds	Joe Rose 6/73 yds
	Wendell Tyler 4/70 yds	Dan Johnson 3/28 yds, 1 TD
	Carl Monroe 1/33 yds, 1 TD	Nat Moore 2/17 yds
	Freddie Solomon 1/14 yds	Jimmy Cefalo 1/14 yds
		Mark Duper 1/11 yds
MVP	Joe Montana, 49ers QB	

Super Bowl XX

Chicago Bears 46
New England Patroits 10
The Superdome, New Orleans, LA
January 26, 1986

The Chicago Bears, under Mike Ditka who had played in a Super Bowl for Dallas, were on the prowl and rapacious after shutting out both teams they faced in the playoffs. They were unable to skunk Raymond Berry's Patriots but they did ring up the widest winning margin in Super Bowl history. New England had a short-lived lead when Tony Franklin kicked a field goal in the first period, but Kevin Butler countered that with two in a row for the Bears. Matt Suhey added a touchdown on an 11-yard run before the period elapsed. Jim McMahon carried another in and Butler added another field goal before the half, and it was indeed a blowout.

McMahon snuck another TD in the third quarter, then Reggie Phillips intercepted a Steve Grogan pass and ran it back 28 yards for a touchdown, and 325-pound William "Refrigerator" Perry, ordinarily a defensive tackle but a sometime bulking fullback, plunged in from the one for Chicago's fifth touchdown of the day. Adding a cherry to the sundae, Bear Henry Waechter tackled Grogan in the end zone for a safety, and the Chicagoans won 46–10.

	Bears	Patriots
Passing	Jim McMahon 12/20, 256 yds	Steve Grogan 17/30, 177 yds, 1 TD
	Steve Fuller 0/4, 0 yds	Tony Eason 0/6, 0 yds
Rushing	Walter Payton 22/61 yds	Tony Collins 3/4 yds
	Matt Suhey 11/52 yds, 1 TD	Robert Weathers 1/3 yds
	Dennis Gentry 3/15 yds	Steve Grogan 1/3 yds
	Thomas Sanders 4/15 yds	Craig James 5/1 yd
	Jim McMahon 5/14 yds, 2 TDs	Greg Hawthorne 1/−4 yds
	Calvin Thomas 2/8 yds	
	William Perry 1/1 yd, 1 TD	
	Steve Fuller 1/1 yd	
Receiving	Willie Gault 4/129 yds	Stanley Morgan 7/70 yds
	Dennis Gentry 2/41 yds	Stephen Starring 2/39 yds
	Ken Margerum 2/36 yds	Irving Fryar 2/24 yds, 1 TD
	Emery Moorehead 2/22 yds	Tony Collins 2/19 yds
	Matt Suhey 1/24 yds	Tom Ramsey 2/16 yds
	Calvin Thomas 1/4 yds	Craig James 1/6 yds
		Robert Weathers 1/3 yds
MVP	Richard Dent, Bears DE	

The Super Bowl's biggest back ever, William "Refrigerator" Perry, 325-pound-plus, bulls in for a touchdown for the Bears in Super Bowl XX. (Chicago Bears)

Willie Gault gathers in a pass against the Patriots, contributing in part to the widest victory margin in Super Bowl history, 46–10. Number 42 on New England is cornerback Ronnie Lippitt. (Chicago Bears)

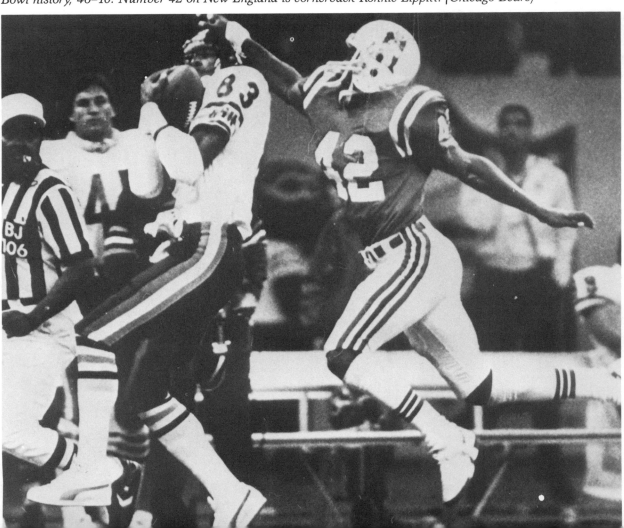

Super Bowl XXI

New York Giants 39
Denver Broncos 20
Rose Bowl, Pasadena, CA
January 25, 1987

The Giants, coached by Bill Parcells, were as forbidding in the playoffs as the Bears had been the year before and were a 9-point favorite in taking on Dan Reeves' Broncos. They lived up to the pregame predictions. Denver got the lead in the game on a Bill Karlis field goal on their first possession, but New York took it away on their first possession when Phil Simms hit Zeke Mowatt with a 6-yard TD pass. The Broncos came right back and marched to the New York four yard line where John Elway fooled everybody with a quarterback draw up the middle. Nobody could tally an offensive score in the second quarter but the Giants' vaunted defense came up with two points when defensive end George Martin tackled Elway in the end zone. Denver led at the half 10–9.

The momentum, however, was all in the Giants camp during the second half. It began when Phil Simms connected with tight end Mark Bavaro on a 13-yard touchdown pass. Raul Allegre added a field goal for New York. Then, after a 44-yard pass from Simms to Phil McConkey, Joe Morris burst in from the one, the score now Giants 26, Denver 10. In the fourth quarter, New York moved again and when a Simms pass bounced off Bavaro's hands, McConkey made a diving save of it in the end zone for another six points. Karlis booted another field goal for Denver, but the margin was still a large 20 points. Two minutes later it was 26 points when New York's Ottis Anderson bulled one in from the two. The Broncos got a touchdown with about three minutes left when John Elway tossed a 53-yarder to Vance Johnson, but the game was well out of reach and it ended 39–20, Giants.

	Giants	Broncos
Passing	Phil Simms 22/25, 268 yds, 3 TDs	John Elway 22/37, 304 yds, 1 TD
		Gary Kubiak 4/4, 48 yds
Rushing	Joe Morris 20/67 yds, 1 TD	John Elway 6/27 yds, 1 TD
	Phil Simms 2/25 yds	Gerald Willhite 4/19 yds
	Lee Rouson 3/22 yds	Steve Sewell 3/4 yds
	Tony Galbreath 4/17 yds	Gene Lang 2/2 yds
	Maurice Carthon 3/4 yds	Sammy Winder 4/0 yds
	Ottis Anderson 2/1 yd, 1 TD	
	Jeff Rutledge 3/0 yds	
Receiving	Mark Bavaro 4/51 yds, 1 TD	Vance Johnson 5/121 yds, 1 TD
	Joe Morris 4/20 yds	Gerald Willhite 5/39 yds
	Maurice Carthon 4/13 yds	Sammy Winder 4/34 yds
	Stacy Robinson 3/62 yds	Mark Jackson 3/51 yds
	Lionel Manuel 3/43 yds	Steve Watson 2/54 yds
	Phil McConkey 2/50 yds, 1 TD	Clint Sampson 2/20 yds
	Lee Rouson 1/23 yds	Orson Mobley 2/17 yds
	Zeke Mowatt 1/6 yds, 1 TD	Steve Sewell 2/12 yds
		Gene Lang 1/4 yds
MVP	Phil Simms, Giants QB	

RECORDS

All-Time Records

Outstanding Performers

Yearly Statistical Leaders

The following individual and team records and
statistics, compiled by Elias Sports Bureau, are
reprinted from the *Official National Football
League Record and Fact Book*, the single authority
on the subject. They are reproduced with
permission of the National Football League,
to whom grateful appreciation is extended.

Compiled by Elias Sports Bureau

The following records reflect all available official information on the National Football League from its formation in 1920 to date. Also included are all applicable records from the American Football League, 1960-69. Rookie records are limited to those players who had never played in a professional game in the United States in any previous season.

INDIVIDUAL RECORDS

SERVICE

Most Seasons
- 26 George Blanda, Chi. Bears, 1949, 1950-58; Baltimore, 1950; Houston, 1960-66; Oakland, 1967-75
- 21 Earl Morrall, San Francisco, 1956; Pittsburgh, 1957-58; Detroit, 1958-64; N.Y. Giants, 1965-67; Baltimore, 1968-71; Miami, 1972-76
- 20 Jim Marshall, Cleveland, 1960; Minnesota, 1961-79

Most Seasons, One Club
- 19 Jim Marshall, Minnesota, 1961-79
- 18 Jim Hart, St. Louis, 1966-83
- 17 Lou Groza, Cleveland, 1950-59, 1961-67
  - Johnny Unitas, Baltimore, 1956-72
  - John Brodie, San Francisco, 1957-73
  - Jim Bakken, St. Louis, 1962-78
  - Mick Tingelhoff, Minnesota, 1962-78
  - Jeff Van Note, Atlanta, 1969-85

Most Games Played, Career
- 340 George Blanda, Chi. Bears, 1949, 1950-58; Baltimore, 1950; Houston, 1960-66; Oakland, 1967-75
- 282 Jim Marshall, Cleveland, 1960; Minnesota, 1961-79
- 263 Jan Stenerud, Kansas City, 1967-79; Green Bay, 1980-83; Minnesota, 1984-85

Most Consecutive Games Played, Career
- 282 Jim Marshall, Cleveland, 1960; Minnesota, 1961-79
- 240 Mick Tingelhoff, Minnesota, 1962-78
- 234 Jim Bakken, St. Louis, 1962-78

Most Seasons, Coach
- 40 George Halas, Chi. Bears, 1920-29, 1933-42, 1946-55, 1958-67
- 33 Earl (Curly) Lambeau, Green Bay, 1921-49; Chi. Cardinals, 1950-51; Washington, 1952-53
- 26 Tom Landry, Dallas, 1960-85

SCORING

Most Seasons Leading League
- 5 Don Hutson, Green Bay, 1940-44
  - Gino Cappelletti, Boston, 1961, 1963-66
- 3 Earl (Dutch) Clark, Portsmouth, 1932; Detroit, 1935-36
  - Pat Harder, Chi. Cardinals, 1947-49
  - Paul Hornung, Green Bay, 1959-61
- 2 Jack Manders, Chi. Bears, 1934, 1937
  - Gordy Soltau, San Francisco, 1952-53
  - Doak Walker, Detroit, 1950, 1955
  - Gene Mingo, Denver, 1960, 1962
  - Jim Turner, N.Y. Jets, 1968-69
  - Fred Cox, Minnesota, 1969-70
  - Chester Marcol, Green Bay, 1972, 1974
  - John Smith, New England, 1979-80

Most Consecutive Seasons Leading League
- 5 Don Hutson, Green Bay, 1940-44
- 4 Gino Cappelletti, Boston, 1963-66
- 3 Pat Harder, Chi. Cardinals, 1947-49
  - Paul Hornung, Green Bay, 1959-61

POINTS

Most Points, Career
- 2,002 George Blanda, Chi. Bears, 1949, 1950-58; Baltimore, 1950; Houston, 1960-66; Oakland, 1967-75 (9-td, 943-pat, 335-fg)
- 1,699 Jan Stenerud, Kansas City, 1967-79; Green Bay, 1980-83; Minnesota, 1984-85 (580-pat, 373-fg)
- 1,439 Jim Turner, N.Y. Jets, 1964-70; Denver, 1971-79 (1-td, 521-pat, 304-fg)

Most Points, Season
- 176 Paul Hornung, Green Bay, 1960 (15-td, 41-pat, 15-fg)
- 161 Mark Moseley, Washington, 1983 (62-pat, 33-fg)
- 155 Gino Cappelletti, Boston, 1964 (7-td, 38-pat, 25-fg)

Most Points, No Touchdowns, Season
- 161 Mark Moseley, Washington, 1983 (62-pat, 33-fg)
- 145 Jim Turner, N.Y. Jets, 1968 (43-pat, 34-fg)
- 144 Kevin Butler, Chicago, 1985 (51-pat, 31-fg)

Most Seasons, 100 or More Points
- 7 Jan Stenerud, Kansas City, 1967-71; Green Bay, 1981, 1983
- 6 Gino Cappelletti, Boston, 1961-66
  - George Blanda, Houston, 1960-61; Oakland, 1967-69, 1973
  - Bruce Gossett, Los Angeles, 1966-67, 1969; San Francisco, 1970-71, 1973
- 5 Lou Michaels, Pittsburgh, 1962; Baltimore, 1964-65, 1967-68

Most Points, Rookie, Season
- 144 Kevin Butler, Chicago, 1985 (51-pat, 31-fg)
- 132 Gale Sayers, Chicago, 1965 (22-td)
- 128 Doak Walker, Detroit, 1950 (11-td, 38-pat, 8-fg)
  - Cookie Gilchrist, Buffalo, 1962 (15-td, 14-pat, 8-fg)
  - Chester Marcol, Green Bay, 1972 (29-pat, 33-fg)

Most Points, Game
- 40 Ernie Nevers, Chi. Cardinals vs. Chi. Bears, Nov. 28, 1929 (6-td, 4-pat)
- 36 Dub Jones, Cleveland vs. Chi. Bears, Nov. 25, 1951 (6-td)
  - Gale Sayers, Chicago vs. San Francisco, Dec. 12, 1965 (6-td)
- 33 Paul Hornung, Green Bay vs. Baltimore, Oct. 8, 1961 (4-td, 6-pat, 1-fg)

Most Consecutive Games Scoring
- 151 Fred Cox, Minnesota, 1963-73
- 133 Garo Yepremian, Miami, 1970-78; New Orleans, 1979
- 128 Rafael Septien, Los Angeles, 1977; Dallas, 1978-85

TOUCHDOWNS

Most Seasons Leading League
- 8 Don Hutson, Green Bay, 1935-38, 1941-44
- 3 Jim Brown, Cleveland, 1958-59, 1963
  - Lance Alworth, San Diego, 1964-66
- 2 By many players

Most Consecutive Seasons Leading League
- 4 Don Hutson, Green Bay, 1935-38, 1941-44
- 3 Lance Alworth, San Diego, 1964-66
- 2 By many players

Most Touchdowns, Career
- 126 Jim Brown, Cleveland, 1957-65 (106-r, 20-p)
- 116 John Riggins, N.Y. Jets, 1971-75; Washington, 1976-79, 1981-85 (104-r, 12-p)
- 113 Lenny Moore, Baltimore, 1956-67 (63-r, 48-p, 2-ret)

Most Touchdowns, Season
- 24 John Riggins, Washington, 1983 (24-r)
- 23 O.J. Simpson, Buffalo, 1975 (16-r, 7-p)
- 22 Gale Sayers, Chicago, 1965 (14-r, 6-p, 2-ret)
  - Chuck Foreman, Minnesota, 1975 (13-r, 9-p)

Most Touchdowns, Rookie, Season
- 22 Gale Sayers, Chicago, 1965 (14-r, 6-p, 2-ret)
- 20 Eric Dickerson, L.A. Rams, 1983 (18-r, 2-p)
- 16 Billy Sims, Detroit, 1980 (13-r, 3-p)

Most Touchdowns, Game
- 6 Ernie Nevers, Chi. Cardinals vs. Chi. Bears, Nov. 28, 1929 (6-r)
  - Dub Jones, Cleveland vs. Chi. Bears, Nov. 25, 1951 (4-r, 2-p)
  - Gale Sayers, Chicago vs. San Francisco, Dec. 12, 1965 (4-r, 1-p, 1-ret)
- 5 Bob Shaw, Chi. Cardinals vs. Baltimore, Oct. 2, 1950 (5-p)
  - Jim Brown, Cleveland vs. Baltimore, Nov. 1, 1959 (5-r)
  - Abner Haynes, Dall. Texans vs. Oakland, Nov. 26, 1961 (4-r, 1-p)
  - Billy Cannon, Houston vs. N.Y. Titans, Dec. 10, 1961 (3-r, 2-p)
  - Cookie Gilchrist, Buffalo vs. N.Y. Jets, Dec. 8, 1963 (5-r)
  - Paul Hornung, Green Bay vs. Baltimore, Dec. 12, 1965 (3-r, 2-p)
  - Kellen Winslow, San Diego vs. Oakland, Nov. 22, 1981 (5-p)
- 4 By many players

Most Consecutive Games Scoring Touchdowns
- 18 Lenny Moore, Baltimore, 1963-65
- 14 O.J. Simpson, Buffalo, 1975
- 13 John Riggins, Washington, 1982-83

POINTS AFTER TOUCHDOWN

Most Seasons Leading League
- 8 George Blanda, Chi. Bears, 1956; Houston, 1961-62; Oakland, 1967-69, 1972, 1974
- 4 Bob Waterfield, Cleveland, 1945; Los Angeles, 1946, 1950, 1952
- 3 Earl (Dutch) Clark, Portsmouth, 1932; Detroit, 1935-36
  - Jack Manders, Chi. Bears, 1933-35
  - Don Hutson, Green Bay, 1941-42, 1945

Most Points After Touchdown Attempted, Career
- 959 George Blanda, Chi. Bears, 1949, 1950-58; Baltimore, 1950; Houston, 1960-66; Oakland, 1967-75
- 657 Lou Groza, Cleveland, 1950-59, 1961-67
- 601 Jan Stenerud, Kansas City, 1967-79; Green Bay, 1980-83; Minnesota, 1984-85

Most Points After Touchdown Attempted, Season
- 70 Uwe von Schamann, Miami, 1984
- 65 George Blanda, Houston, 1961
- 63 Mark Moseley, Washington, 1983

Most Points After Touchdown Attempted, Game
- 10 Charlie Gogolak, Washington vs. N.Y. Giants, Nov. 27, 1966
- 9 Pat Harder, Chi. Cardinals vs. N.Y. Giants, Oct. 17, 1948; vs. N.Y. Bulldogs, Nov. 13, 1949
  - Bob Waterfield, Los Angeles vs. Baltimore, Oct. 22, 1950
  - Bob Thomas, Chicago vs. Green Bay, Dec. 7, 1980
- 8 By many players

Most Points After Touchdown, Career
- 943 George Blanda, Chi. Bears, 1949, 1950-58; Baltimore, 1950; Houston, 1960-66; Oakland, 1967-75
- 641 Lou Groza, Cleveland, 1950-59, 1961-67
- 580 Jan Stenerud, Kansas City, 1967-79; Green Bay, 1980-83; Minnesota, 1984-85

Most Points After Touchdown, Season
- 66 Uwe von Schamann, Miami, 1984
- 64 George Blanda, Houston, 1961
- 62 Mark Moseley, Washington, 1983

Most Points After Touchdown, Game
- 9 Pat Harder, Chi. Cardinals vs. N.Y. Giants, Oct. 17, 1948
  - Bob Waterfield, Los Angeles vs. Baltimore, Oct. 22, 1950
  - Charlie Gogolak, Washington vs. N.Y. Giants, Nov. 27, 1966
- 8 By many players

Most Consecutive Points After Touchdown
- 234 Tommy Davis, San Francisco, 1959-65
- 221 Jim Turner, N.Y. Jets, 1967-70; Denver, 1971-74
- 201 George Blanda, Oakland, 1967-71

Highest Points After Touchdown Percentage, Career (200 points after touchdown)
- 99.43 Tommy Davis, San Francisco, 1959-69 (350-348)
- 99.07 Nick Lowery, New England, 1978; Kansas City, 1980-85 (214-212)
- 98.33 George Blanda, Chi. Bears, 1949, 1950-58; Baltimore, 1950; Houston, 1960-66; Oakland, 1967-75 (959-943)

Most Points After Touchdown, No Misses, Season
- 56 Danny Villanueva, Dallas, 1966
  - Ray Wersching, San Francisco, 1984
- 54 Mike Clark, Dallas, 1968
  - George Blanda, Oakland, 1968
- 53 Pat Harder, Chi. Cardinals, 1948

Most Points After Touchdown, No Misses, Game
- 9 Pat Harder, Chi. Cardinals vs. N.Y. Giants, Oct. 17, 1948
  - Bob Waterfield, Los Angeles vs. Baltimore, Oct. 22, 1950
- 8 By many players

FIELD GOALS

Most Seasons Leading League
- 5 Lou Groza, Cleveland, 1950, 1952-54, 1957
- 4 Jack Manders, Chi. Bears, 1933-34, 1936-37
  - Ward Cuff, N.Y. Giants, 1938-39, 1943; Green Bay, 1947
  - Mark Moseley, Washington, 1976-77, 1979, 1982
- 3 Bob Waterfield, Los Angeles, 1947, 1949, 1951
  - Gino Cappelletti, Boston, 1961, 1963-64
  - Fred Cox, Minnesota, 1965, 1969-70
  - Jan Stenerud, Kansas City, 1967, 1970, 1975

Most Consecutive Seasons Leading League
- 3 Lou Groza, Cleveland, 1952-54
- 2 By many players

Most Field Goals Attempted, Career
- 638 George Blanda, Ch. Bears, 1949, 1950-58; Baltimore, 1950; Houston, 1960-66; Oakland, 1967-75
- 558 Jan Stenerud, Kansas City, 1967-79; Green Bay, 1980-83; Minnesota, 1984-85
- 488 Jim Turner, N.Y. Jets, 1964-70; Denver, 1971-79

Most Field Goals Attempted, Season
- 49 Bruce Gossett, Los Angeles, 1966
  - Curt Knight, Washington, 1971
- 48 Chester Marcol, Green Bay, 1972
- 47 Jim Turner, N.Y. Jets, 1969
  - David Ray, Los Angeles, 1973
  - Mark Moseley, Washington, 1983

Most Field Goals Attempted, Game
- 9 Jim Bakken, St. Louis vs. Pittsburgh, Sept. 24, 1967
- 8 Lou Michaels, Pittsburgh vs. St. Louis, Dec. 2, 1962
  - Garo Yepremian, Detroit vs. Minnesota, Nov. 13, 1966
  - Jim Turner, N.Y. Jets vs. Buffalo, Nov. 3, 1968
- 7 By many players

Most Field Goals, Career
- 373 Jan Stenerud, Kansas City, 1967-79; Green Bay, 1980-83; Minnesota, 1984-85
- 335 George Blanda, Ch. Bears, 1949, 1950-58; Baltimore, 1950; Houston, 1960-66; Oakland, 1967-75
- 304 Jim Turner, N.Y. Jets, 1964-70; Denver, 1971-79

Most Field Goals, Season
- 35 Ali Haji-Sheikh, N.Y. Giants, 1983
- 34 Jim Turner, N.Y. Jets, 1968
- 33 Chester Marcol, Green Bay, 1972
  - Mark Moseley, Washington, 1983
  - Gary Anderson, Pittsburgh, 1985

Most Field Goals, Rookie, Season
- 35 Ali Haji-Sheikh, N.Y. Giants, 1983
- 33 Chester Marcol, Green Bay, 1972
- 31 Kevin Butler, Chicago, 1985

Most Field Goals, Game
- 7 Jim Bakken, St. Louis vs. Pittsburgh, Sept. 24, 1967
- 6 Gino Cappelletti, Boston vs. Denver, Oct. 4, 1964
  - Garo Yepremian, Detroit vs. Minnesota, Nov. 13, 1966
  - Jim Turner, N.Y. Jets vs. Buffalo, Nov. 3, 1968
  - Tom Dempsey, Philadelphia vs. Houston, Nov. 12, 1972
  - Bobby Howfield, N.Y. Jets vs. New Orleans, Dec. 3, 1972
  - Jim Bakken, St. Louis vs. Atlanta, Dec. 9, 1973
  - Joe Danelo, N.Y. Giants vs. Seattle, Oct. 18, 1981
  - Ray Wersching, San Francisco vs. New Orleans, Oct. 16, 1983
- 5 By many players

Most Field Goals, One Quarter
- 4 Garo Yepremian, Detroit vs. Minnesota, Nov. 13, 1966 (second quarter)
  - Curt Knight, Washington vs. N.Y. Giants, Nov. 15, 1970 (second quarter)
- 3 By many players

Most Consecutive Games Scoring Field Goals
- 31 Fred Cox, Minnesota, 1968-70
- 28 Jim Turner, N.Y. Jets, 1970; Denver, 1971-72
- 21 Bruce Gossett, San Francisco, 1970-72

Most Consecutive Field Goals
- 23 Mark Moseley, Washington, 1981-82
- 20 Garo Yepremian, Miami, 1978; New Orleans, 1979
- 18 Gary Anderson, Pittsburgh, 1985

Longest Field Goal
- 63 Tom Dempsey, New Orleans vs. Detroit, Nov. 8, 1970
- 60 Steve Cox, Cleveland vs. Cincinnati, Oct. 21, 1984
- 59 Tony Franklin, Philadelphia vs. Dallas, Nov. 12, 1979

Highest Field Goal Percentage, Career (100 field goals)
- 76.84 Nick Lowery, New England, 1978; Kansas City, 1980-85 (177-136)
- 74.86 Ed Murray, Detroit, 1980-85 (179-134)
- 71.04 Rolf Benirschke, San Diego, 1977-85 (183-130)

Highest Field Goal Percentage, Season (Qualifiers)
- 95.24 Mark Moseley, Washington, 1982 (21-20)
- 91.67 Jan Stenerud, Green Bay, 1981 (24-22)
- 88.89 Nick Lowery, Kansas City, 1985 (27-24)

Most Field Goals, No Misses, Game
- 6 Gino Cappelletti, Boston vs. Denver, Oct. 4, 1964
  - Joe Danelo, N.Y. Giants vs. Seattle, Oct. 18, 1981
  - Ray Wersching, San Francisco vs. New Orleans, Oct. 16, 1983
- 5 Roger LeClerc, Chicago vs. Detroit, Dec. 3, 1961
  - Lou Michaels, Baltimore vs. San Francisco, Sept. 25, 1966
  - Mac Percival, Chicago vs. Philadelphia, Oct. 20, 1968
  - Roy Gerela, Houston vs. Miami, Sept. 28, 1969
  - Jan Stenerud, Kansas City vs. Buffalo, Nov. 2, 1969; vs. Buffalo, Dec. 7, 1969; Minnesota vs. Detroit, Sept. 23, 1984
  - Horst Muhlmann, Cincinnati vs. Buffalo, Nov. 8, 1970; vs. Pittsburgh, Sept. 24, 1972
  - Bruce Gossett, San Francisco vs. Denver, Sept. 23, 1973
  - Nick Mike-Mayer, Atlanta vs. Los Angeles, Nov. 4, 1973
  - Curt Knight, Washington vs. Baltimore, Nov. 18, 1973
  - Tim Mazzetti, Atlanta vs. Los Angeles, Oct. 30, 1978
  - Ed Murray, Detroit vs. Green Bay, Sept. 14, 1980
  - Rich Karlis, Denver vs. Seattle, Nov. 20, 1983
  - Pat Leahy, N.Y. Jets vs. Cincinnati, Sept. 16, 1984
  - Nick Lowery, Kansas City vs. L.A. Raiders, Sept. 12, 1985
  - Eric Schubert, N.Y. Giants vs. Tampa Bay, Nov. 3, 1985
  - Gary Anderson, Pittsburgh vs. Kansas City, Nov. 10, 1985
  - Morten Andersen, New Orleans vs. L.A. Rams, Dec. 1, 1985

Most Field Goals, 50 or More Yards, Career
- 17 Jan Stenerud, Kansas City, 1967-79; Green Bay, 1980-83; Minnesota, 1984-85
- 12 Tom Dempsey, New Orleans, 1969-70; Philadelphia, 1971-74; Los Angeles, 1975-76; Houston, 1977; Buffalo, 1978-79
  - Mark Moseley, Philadelphia, 1970; Houston, 1971-72; Washington, 1974-85
  - Nick Lowery, New England, 1978; Kansas City, 1980-85
- 10 Joe Danelo, Green Bay, 1975; N.Y. Giants, 1976-82; Buffalo, 1983-84
  - Ed Murray, Detroit, 1980-85

Most Field Goals, 50 or More Yards, Season
- 5 Fred Steinfort, Denver, 1980
- 4 Horst Muhlmann, Cincinnati, 1970
  - Mark Moseley, Washington, 1977
  - Nick Lowery, Kansas City, 1980
  - Raul Allegre, Baltimore, 1983
- 3 By many players

Most Field Goals, 50 or More Yards, Game
- 2 Jim Martin, Detroit vs. Baltimore, Oct. 23, 1960
  - Tom Dempsey, New Orleans vs. Los Angeles, Dec. 6, 1970
  - Chris Bahr, Cincinnati vs. Houston, Sept. 23, 1979
  - Nick Lowery, Kansas City vs. Seattle, Sept. 14, 1980; vs. New Orleans, Sept. 8, 1985
  - Mark Moseley, Washington vs. New Orleans, Oct. 26, 1980
  - Fred Steinfort, Denver vs. Seattle, Dec. 21, 1980
  - Mick Luckhurst, Atlanta vs. Denver, Dec. 5, 1982; vs. L.A. Rams, Oct. 7, 1984
  - Morten Andersen, New Orleans vs. Philadelphia, Dec. 11, 1983
  - Paul McFadden, Philadelphia vs. Detroit, Nov. 4, 1984
  - Pat Leahy, N.Y. Jets vs. New England, Oct. 20, 1985
  - Tony Zendejas, Houston vs. San Diego, Nov. 24, 1985

SAFETIES

Most Safeties, Career
- 4 Ted Hendricks, Baltimore, 1969-73; Green Bay, 1974; Oakland, 1975-81; L.A. Raiders, 1982-83
  - Doug English, Detroit, 1975-79, 1981-85
- 3 Bill McPeak, Pittsburgh, 1949-57
  - Charlie Krueger, San Francisco, 1959-73
  - Ernie Stautner, Pittsburgh, 1950-63
  - Jim Katcavage, N.Y. Giants, 1956-68
  - Roger Brown, Detroit, 1960-66; Los Angeles, 1967-69
  - Bruce Maher, Detroit, 1960-67; N.Y. Giants, 1968-69
  - Ron McDole, St. Louis, 1961; Houston, 1962; Buffalo, 1963-70; Washington, 1971-78
  - Alan Page, Minnesota, 1967-78; Chicago, 1979-81
- 2 By many players

Most Safeties, Season
- 2 Tom Nash, Green Bay, 1932
  - Roger Brown, Detroit, 1962
  - Ron McDole, Buffalo, 1964
  - Alan Page, Minnesota, 1971
  - Fred Dryer, Los Angeles, 1973
  - Benny Barnes, Dallas, 1973
  - James Young, Houston, 1977
  - Tom Hannon, Minnesota, 1981
  - Doug English, Detroit, 1983
  - Don Blackmon, New England, 1985

Most Safeties, Game
- 2 Fred Dryer, Los Angeles vs. Green Bay, Oct. 21, 1973

RUSHING

Most Seasons Leading League
- 8 Jim Brown, Cleveland, 1957-61, 1963-65
- 4 Steve Van Buren, Philadelphia, 1945, 1947-49
  - O.J. Simpson, Buffalo, 1972-73, 1975-76
- 3 Earl Campbell, Houston, 1978-80

Most Consecutive Seasons Leading League
- 5 Jim Brown, Cleveland, 1957-61
- 3 Steve Van Buren, Philadelphia, 1947-49
  - Jim Brown, Cleveland, 1963-65
  - Earl Campbell, Houston, 1978-80
- 2 Bill Paschal, N.Y. Giants, 1943-44
  - Joe Perry, San Francisco, 1953-54
  - Jim Nance, Boston, 1966-67
  - Leroy Kelly, Cleveland, 1967-68
  - O.J. Simpson, Buffalo, 1972-73, 1975-76
  - Eric Dickerson, L.A. Rams, 1983-84

ATTEMPTS

Most Seasons Leading League
- 6 Jim Brown, Cleveland, 1958-59, 1961, 1963-65
- 4 Steve Van Buren, Philadelphia, 1947-50
  - Walter Payton, Chicago, 1976-79
- 3 Cookie Gilchrist, Buffalo, 1963-64; Denver, 1965
  - Jim Nance, Boston, 1966-67, 1969
  - O.J. Simpson, Buffalo, 1973-75

Most Consecutive Seasons Leading League
- 4 Steve Van Buren, Philadelphia, 1947-50
  - Walter Payton, Chicago, 1976-79
- 3 Jim Brown, Cleveland, 1963-65
  - Cookie Gilchrist, Buffalo, 1963-64; Denver, 1965
  - O.J. Simpson, Buffalo, 1973-75
- 2 By many players

Most Attempts, Career
- 3,371 Walter Payton, Chicago, 1975-85
- 2,949 Franco Harris, Pittsburgh, 1972-83; Seattle, 1984
- 2,916 John Riggins, N.Y. Jets, 1971-75; Washington, 1976-79, 1981-85

Most Attempts, Season
- 407 James Wilder, Tampa Bay, 1984
- 397 Gerald Riggs, Atlanta, 1985
- 390 Eric Dickerson, L.A. Rams, 1983

Most Attempts, Rookie, Season
- 390 Eric Dickerson, L.A. Rams, 1983
- 378 George Rogers, New Orleans, 1981
- 335 Curt Warner, Seattle, 1983

325

Most Attempts, Game
43 Butch Woolfolk, N.Y. Giants vs. Philadelphia, Nov. 20, 1983
   James Wilder, Tampa Bay vs. Green Bay, Sept. 30, 1984 (OT)
42 James Wilder, Tampa Bay vs. Pittsburgh, Oct. 30, 1983
41 Franco Harris, Pittsburgh vs. Cincinnati, Oct. 17, 1976
   Gerald Riggs, Atlanta vs. L.A. Rams, Nov. 17, 1985

YARDS GAINED
Most Yards Gained, Career
14,860 Walter Payton, Chicago, 1975-85
12,312 Jim Brown, Cleveland, 1957-65
12,120 Franco Harris, Pittsburgh, 1972-83; Seattle, 1984
Most Seasons, 1,000 or More Yards Rushing
9 Walter Payton, Chicago, 1976-81, 1983-85
8 Franco Harris, Pittsburgh, 1972, 1974-79, 1983
   Tony Dorsett, Dallas, 1977-81, 1983-85
7 Jim Brown, Cleveland, 1958-61, 1963-65
Most Consecutive Seasons, 1,000 or More Yards Rushing
6 Franco Harris, Pittsburgh, 1974-79
   Walter Payton, Chicago, 1976-81
5 Jim Taylor, Green Bay, 1960-64
   O. J. Simpson, Buffalo, 1972-76
   Tony Dorsett, Dallas, 1977-81
4 Jim Brown, Cleveland, 1958-61
   Earl Campbell, Houston, 1978-81
Most Yards Gained, Season
2,105 Eric Dickerson, L.A. Rams, 1984
2,003 O.J. Simpson, Buffalo, 1973
1,934 Earl Campbell, Houston, 1980
Most Yards Gained, Rookie, Season
1,808 Eric Dickerson, L.A. Rams, 1983
1,674 George Rogers, New Orleans, 1981
1,605 Ottis Anderson, St. Louis, 1979
Most Yards Gained, Game
275 Walter Payton, Chicago vs. Minnesota, Nov. 20, 1977
273 O.J. Simpson, Buffalo vs. Detroit, Nov. 25, 1976
250 O.J. Simpson, Buffalo vs. New England, Sept. 16, 1973
Most Games, 200 or More Yards Rushing, Career
6 O.J. Simpson, Buffalo, 1969-77; San Francisco, 1978-79
4 Jim Brown, Cleveland, 1957-65
   Earl Campbell, Houston, 1978-84; New Orleans, 1984-85
2 Walter Payton, Chicago, 1975-85
   Eric Dickerson, L.A. Rams, 1983-85
   George Rogers, New Orleans, 1981-84; Washington, 1985
Most Games, 200 or More Yards Rushing, Season
4 Earl Campbell, Houston, 1980
3 O.J. Simpson, Buffalo, 1973
2 Jim Brown, Cleveland, 1963
   O.J. Simpson, Buffalo, 1976
   Walter Payton, Chicago, 1977
   Eric Dickerson, L.A. Rams, 1984
Most Consecutive Games, 200 or More Yards Rushing
2 O.J. Simpson, Buffalo, 1973, 1976
   Earl Campbell, Houston, 1980
Most Games, 100 or More Yards Rushing, Career
73 Walter Payton, Chicago, 1975-85
58 Jim Brown, Cleveland, 1957-65
47 Franco Harris, Pittsburgh, 1972-83; Seattle, 1984
Most Games, 100 or More Yards Rushing, Season
12 Eric Dickerson, L.A. Rams, 1984
11 O.J. Simpson, Buffalo, 1973
   Earl Campbell, Houston, 1979
   Marcus Allen, L.A. Raiders, 1985
10 Walter Payton, Chicago, 1977, 1985
   Earl Campbell, Houston, 1980
Most Consecutive Games, 100 or More Yards Rushing
9 Walter Payton, Chicago, 1985
   Marcus Allen, L.A. Raiders, 1985 (current)
7 O.J. Simpson, Buffalo, 1972-73
   Earl Campbell, Houston, 1979
6 Jim Brown, Cleveland, 1958
   Franco Harris, Pittsburgh, 1972
   Earl Campbell, Houston, 1980
   Walter Payton, Chicago, 1984
   Eric Dickerson, L.A. Rams, 1984
   James Wilder, Tampa Bay, 1984-85
Longest Run From Scrimmage
99 Tony Dorsett, Dallas vs. Minnesota, Jan. 3, 1983 (TD)
97 Andy Uram, Green Bay vs. Chi. Cardinals, Oct. 8, 1939 (TD)
   Bob Gage, Pittsburgh vs. Chi. Bears, Dec. 4, 1949 (TD)
96 Jim Spavital, Baltimore vs. Green Bay, Nov. 5, 1950 (TD)
   Bob Hoernschemeyer, Detroit vs. N.Y. Yanks, Nov. 23, 1950 (TD)

AVERAGE GAIN
Highest Average Gain, Career (700 attempts)
5.22 Jim Brown, Cleveland, 1957-65 (2,359-12,312)
5.14 Eugene (Mercury) Morris, Miami, 1969-75; San Diego, 1976 (804-4,133)
5.00 Gale Sayers, Chicago, 1965-71 (991-4,956)
Highest Average Gain, Season (Qualifiers)
9.94 Beattie Feathers, Chi. Bears, 1934 (101-1,004)
6.87 Bobby Douglass, Chicago, 1972 (141-968)
6.78 Dan Towler, Los Angeles, 1951 (126-854)
Highest Average Gain, Game (10 attempts)
17.09 Marion Motley, Cleveland vs. Pittsburgh, Oct. 29, 1950 (11-188)
16.70 Bill Grimes, Green Bay vs. N.Y. Yanks, Oct. 8, 1950 (10-167)
16.57 Bobby Mitchell, Cleveland vs. Washington, Nov. 15, 1959 (14-232)

TOUCHDOWNS
Most Seasons Leading League
5 Jim Brown, Cleveland, 1957-59, 1963, 1965
4 Steve Van Buren, Philadelphia, 1945, 1947-49
3 Abner Haynes, Dall. Texans, 1960-62
   Cookie Gilchrist, Buffalo, 1962-64

Paul Lowe, L.A. Chargers, 1960; San Diego, 1961, 1965
   Leroy Kelly, Cleveland, 1966-68
Most Consecutive Seasons Leading League
3 Steve Van Buren, Philadelphia, 1947-49
   Jim Brown, Cleveland, 1957-59
   Abner Haynes, Dall. Texans, 1960-62
   Cookie Gilchrist, Buffalo, 1962-64
   Leroy Kelly, Cleveland, 1966-68
Most Touchdowns, Career
106 Jim Brown, Cleveland, 1957-65
104 John Riggins, N.Y. Jets, 1971-75; Washington, 1976-79, 1981-85
98 Walter Payton, Chicago, 1975-85
Most Touchdowns, Season
24 John Riggins, Washington, 1983
21 Joe Morris, N.Y. Giants, 1985
19 Jim Taylor, Green Bay, 1962
   Earl Campbell, Houston, 1979
   Chuck Muncie, San Diego, 1981
Most Touchdowns, Rookie, Season
18 Eric Dickerson, L.A. Rams, 1983
14 Gale Sayers, Chicago, 1965
13 Cookie Gilchrist, Buffalo, 1962
   Earl Campbell, Houston, 1978
   Billy Sims, Detroit, 1980
   George Rogers, New Orleans, 1981
   Curt Warner, Seattle, 1983
Most Touchdowns, Game
6 Ernie Nevers, Chi. Cardinals vs. Chi. Bears, Nov. 28, 1929
5 Jim Brown, Cleveland vs. Baltimore, Nov. 1, 1959
   Cookie Gilchrist, Buffalo vs. N.Y. Jets, Dec. 8, 1963
4 By many players
Most Consecutive Games Rushing for Touchdowns
13 John Riggins, Washington, 1982-83
11 Lenny Moore, Baltimore, 1963-64
9 Leroy Kelly, Cleveland, 1968

PASSING
Most Seasons Leading League
6 Sammy Baugh, Washington, 1937, 1940, 1943, 1945, 1947, 1949
4 Len Dawson, Dall. Texans; 1962; Kansas City, 1964, 1966, 1968
   Roger Staubach, Dallas, 1971, 1973, 1978-79
   Ken Anderson, Cincinnati, 1974-75, 1981-82
3 Arnie Herber, Green Bay, 1932, 1934, 1936
   Norm Van Brocklin, Los Angeles, 1950, 1952, 1954
   Bart Starr, Green Bay, 1962, 1964, 1966
Most Consecutive Seasons Leading League
2 Cecil Isbell, Green Bay, 1941-42
   Milt Plum, Cleveland, 1960-61
   Ken Anderson, Cincinnati, 1974-75, 1981-82
   Roger Staubach, Dallas, 1978-79

PASS RATING
Highest Pass Rating, Career (1,500 attempts)
92.4 Joe Montana, San Francisco, 1979-85
83.4 Roger Staubach, Dallas, 1969-79
82.6 Sonny Jurgensen, Philadelphia, 1957-63; Washington, 1964-74
Highest Pass Rating, Season (Qualifiers)
110.4 Milt Plum, Cleveland, 1960
109.9 Sammy Baugh, Washington, 1945
108.9 Dan Marino, Miami, 1984
Highest Pass Rating, Rookie, Season (Qualifiers)
96.0 Dan Marino, Miami, 1983
88.2 Greg Cook, Cincinnati, 1969
84.0 Charlie Conerly, N.Y. Giants, 1948

ATTEMPTS
Most Seasons Leading League
4 Sammy Baugh, Washington, 1937, 1943, 1947-48
   Johnny Unitas, Baltimore, 1957, 1959-61
   George Blanda, Chi. Bears, 1953; Houston, 1963-65
3 Arnie Herber, Green Bay, 1932, 1934, 1936
   Sonny Jurgensen, Washington, 1966-67, 1969
2 By many players
Most Consecutive Seasons Leading League
3 Johnny Unitas, Baltimore, 1959-61
   George Blanda, Houston, 1963-65
2 By many players
Most Passes Attempted, Career
6,467 Fran Tarkenton, Minnesota, 1961-66, 1972-78; N.Y. Giants, 1967-71
5,186 Johnny Unitas, Baltimore, 1956-72; San Diego, 1973
5,076 Jim Hart, St. Louis, 1966-83; Washington, 1984
Most Passes Attempted, Season
609 Dan Fouts, San Diego, 1981
605 John Elway, Denver, 1985
603 Bill Kenney, Kansas City, 1983
Most Passes Attempted, Rookie, Season
450 Warren Moon, Houston, 1984
439 Jim Zorn, Seattle, 1976
392 Butch Songin, Boston, 1960
Most Passes Attempted, Game
68 George Blanda, Houston vs. Buffalo, Nov. 1, 1964
62 Joe Namath, N.Y. Jets vs. Baltimore, Oct. 18, 1970
   Steve Dils, Minnesota vs. Tampa Bay, Sept. 5, 1981
   Phil Simms, N.Y. Giants vs. Cincinnati, Oct. 13, 1985
61 Tommy Kramer, Minnesota vs. Buffalo, Dec. 16, 1979

COMPLETIONS
Most Seasons Leading League
5 Sammy Baugh, Washington, 1937, 1943, 1945, 1947-48
4 George Blanda, Chi. Bears, 1953; Houston, 1963-65
   Sonny Jurgensen, Philadelphia, 1961; Washington, 1966-67, 1969
3 Arnie Herber, Green Bay, 1932, 1934, 1936
   Johnny Unitas, Baltimore, 1959-60, 1963

John Brodie, San Francisco, 1965, 1968, 1970
Fran Tarkenton, Minnesota, 1975-76, 1978
Most Consecutive Seasons Leading League
- 3 George Blanda, Houston, 1963-65
- 2 By many players

Most Passes Completed, Career
- 3,686 Fran Tarkenton, Minnesota, 1961-66, 1972-78; N.Y. Giants, 1967-71
- 2,839 Dan Fouts, San Diego, 1973-85
- 2,830 Johnny Unitas, Baltimore, 1956-72; San Diego, 1973

Most Passes Completed, Season
- 362 Dan Marino, Miami, 1984
- 360 Dan Fouts, San Diego, 1981
- 348 Dan Fouts, San Diego, 1980

Most Passes Completed, Rookie, Season
- 259 Warren Moon, Houston, 1984
- 218 Dieter Brock, L.A. Rams, 1985
- 208 Jim Zorn, Seattle, 1976

Most Passes Completed, Game
- 42 Richard Todd, N.Y. Jets vs. San Francisco, Sept. 21, 1980
- 40 Ken Anderson, Cincinnati vs. San Diego, Dec. 20, 1982
  - Phil Simms, N.Y. Giants vs. Cincinnati, Oct. 13, 1985
- 38 Tommy Kramer, Minnesota vs. Cleveland, Dec. 14, 1980
  - Tommy Kramer, Minnesota vs. Green Bay, Nov. 29, 1981
  - Joe Ferguson, Buffalo vs. Miami, Oct. 9, 1983 (OT)

Most Consecutive Passes Completed
- 20 Ken Anderson, Cincinnati vs. Houston, Jan. 2, 1983
- 18 Steve DeBerg, Denver vs. L.A. Rams (17), Dec. 12, 1982; vs. Kansas City (1), Dec. 19, 1982
  - Lynn Dickey, Green Bay vs. Houston, Sept. 4, 1983
  - Joe Montana, San Francisco vs. L.A. Rams (13), Oct. 28, 1984; vs. Cincinnati (5), Nov. 4, 1984
- 17 Bert Jones, Baltimore vs. N.Y. Jets, Dec. 15, 1974

COMPLETION PERCENTAGE
Most Seasons Leading League
- 8 Len Dawson, Dall. Texans, 1962; Kansas City, 1964-69, 1975
- 7 Sammy Baugh, Washington, 1940, 1942-43, 1945, 1947-49
- 4 Bart Starr, Green Bay 1962, 1966, 1968-69

Most Consecutive Seasons Leading League
- 6 Len Dawson, Kansas City, 1964-69
- 3 Sammy Baugh, Washington, 1947-49
  - Otto Graham, Cleveland, 1953-55
  - Milt Plum, Cleveland, 1959-61
- 2 By many players

Highest Completion Percentage, Career (1,500 attempts)
- 63.28 Joe Montana, San Francisco, 1979-85 (2,571-1,627)
- 59.85 Ken Stabler, Oakland, 1970-79; Houston 1980-81; New Orleans 1982-84 (3,793-2,270)
- 59.42 Danny White, Dallas, 1976-85 (2,393-1,422)

Highest Completion Percentage, Season (Qualifiers)
- 70.55 Ken Anderson, Cincinnati, 1982 (309-218)
- 70.33 Sammy Baugh, Washington, 1945 (182-128)
- 67.29 Steve Bartkowski, Atlanta, 1984 (269-181)

Highest Completion Percentage, Rookie, Season (Qualifiers)
- 59.73 Dieter Brock, L.A. Rams, 1985 (365-218)
- 58.45 Dan Marino, Miami, 1983 (296-173)
- 57.56 Warren Moon, Houston, 1984 (450-259)

Highest Completion Percentage, Game (20 attempts)
- 90.91 Ken Anderson, Cincinnati vs. Pittsburgh, Nov. 10, 1974 (22-20)
- 90.48 Lynn Dickey, Green Bay vs. New Orleans, Dec. 13, 1981 (21-19)
- 87.50 Danny White, Dallas vs. Philadelphia, Nov. 6, 1983 (24-21)

YARDS GAINED
Most Seasons Leading League
- 5 Sonny Jurgensen, Philadelphia, 1961-62; Washington, 1966-67, 1969
- 4 Sammy Baugh, Washington, 1937, 1940, 1947-48
  - Johnny Unitas, Baltimore, 1957, 1959-60, 1963
  - Dan Fouts, San Diego, 1979-82
- 3 Arnie Herber, Green Bay, 1932, 1934, 1936
  - Sid Luckman, Chi. Bears, 1943, 1945-46
  - John Brodie, San Francisco, 1965, 1968 1970
  - John Hadl, San Diego, 1965, 1968, 1971
  - Joe Namath, N.Y. Jets, 1966-67, 1972

Most Consecutive Seasons Leading League
- 4 Dan Fouts, San Diego, 1979-82
- 2 By many players

Most Yards Gained, Career
- 47,003 Fran Tarkenton, Minnesota, 1961-66, 1972-78; N.Y. Giants, 1967-71
- 40,239 Johnny Unitas, Baltimore, 1956-72; San Diego, 1973
- 37,492 Dan Fouts, San Diego, 1973-85

Most Seasons, 3,000 or More Yards Passing
- 5 Sonny Jurgensen, Philadelphia, 1961-62; Washington, 1966-67, 1969
  - Dan Fouts, San Diego, 1979-81, 1984-85
- 4 Brian Sipe, Cleveland, 1979-81, 1983
  - Ron Jaworski, Philadelphia, 1980-81, 1983, 1985
  - Tommy Kramer, Minnesota, 1979-81, 1985
  - Joe Montana, San Francisco, 1981, 1983-85
  - Danny White, Dallas, 1980-81, 1983, 1985
- 3 By many players

Most Yards Gained, Season
- 5,084 Dan Marino, Miami, 1984
- 4,802 Dan Fouts, San Diego, 1981
- 4,715 Dan Fouts, San Diego, 1980

Most Yards Gained, Rookie, Season
- 3,338 Warren Moon, Houston, 1984
- 2,658 Dieter Brock, L.A. Rams, 1985
- 2,571 Jim Zorn, Seattle, 1976

Most Yards Gained, Game
- 554 Norm Van Brocklin, Los Angeles vs. N.Y. Yanks, Sept. 28, 1951
- 513 Phil Simms, N.Y. Giants vs. Cincinnati, Oct. 13, 1985
- 509 Vince Ferragamo, L.A. Rams vs. Chicago, Dec. 26, 1982

Most Games, 400 or More Yards Passing, Career
- 6 Dan Fouts, San Diego, 1973-85

- 5 Sonny Jurgensen, Philadelphia, 1957-63; Washington, 1964-74
- 4 Dan Marino, Miami, 1983-85

Most Games, 400 or More Yards Passing, Season
- 4 Dan Marino, Miami, 1984
- 2 George Blanda, Houston, 1961
  - Sonny Jurgensen, Philadelphia, 1961
  - Joe Namath, N.Y. Jets, 1972
  - Dan Fouts, San Diego, 1982, 1985
  - Phil Simms, N.Y. Giants, 1985

Most Consecutive Games, 400 or More Yards Passing
- 2 Dan Fouts, San Diego, 1982
  - Dan Marino, Miami, 1984
  - Phil Simms, N.Y. Giants, 1985

Most Games, 300 or More Yards Passing, Career
- 47 Dan Fouts, San Diego, 1973-85
- 26 Johnny Unitas, Baltimore, 1956-72; San Diego, 1973
- 25 Sonny Jurgensen, Philadelphia 1957-63; Washington, 1964-74

Most Games, 300 or More Yards Passing, Season
- 9 Dan Marino, Miami, 1984
- 8 Dan Fouts, San Diego, 1980
- 7 Dan Fouts, San Diego, 1981, 1985
  - Bill Kenney, Kansas City, 1983
  - Neil Lomax, St. Louis, 1984

Most Consecutive Games, 300 or More Yards Passing, Season
- 5 Joe Montana, San Francisco, 1982
- 4 Dan Fouts, San Diego, 1979
  - Bill Kenney, Kansas City, 1983
- 3 By many players

Longest Pass Completion (All TDs except as noted)
- 99 Frank Filchock (to Farkas) Washington vs. Pittsburgh, Oct. 15, 1939
  - George Izo (to Mitchell), Washington vs. Cleveland, Sept. 15, 1963
  - Karl Sweetan (to Studstill) Detroit vs. Baltimore, Oct. 16, 1966
  - Sonny Jurgensen (to Allen), Washington vs. Chicago, Sept. 15, 1968
  - Jim Plunkett (to Branch), L.A. Raiders vs. Washington, Oct. 2, 1983
  - Ron Jaworski (to Quick), Philadelphia vs. Atlanta, Nov. 10, 1985
- 98 Doug Russell (to Tinsley), Chi. Cardinals vs. Cleveland, Nov. 27, 1938
  - Ogden Compton (to Lane), Chi. Cardinals vs. Green Bay, Nov. 13, 1955
  - Bill Wade (to Farrington), Chicago Bears vs. Detroit, Oct. 8, 1961
  - Jacky Lee (to Dewveall), Houston vs. San Diego, Nov. 25, 1962
  - Earl Morrall (to Jones), N.Y. Giants vs. Pittsburgh, Sept. 11, 1966
  - Jim Hart (to Moore), St. Louis vs. Los Angeles, Dec. 10, 1972 (no TD)
- 97 Pat Coffee (to Tinsley), Chi. Cardinals vs. Chi. Bears, Dec. 5, 1937
  - Bobby Layne (to Box), Detroit vs. Green Bay, Nov. 26, 1953
  - George Shaw (to Tarr), Denver vs. Boston, Sept. 21, 1962

AVERAGE GAIN
Most Seasons Leading League
- 7 Sid Luckman, Chi. Bears, 1939-43, 1946-47
- 3 Arnie Herber, Green Bay, 1932, 1934, 1936
  - Norm Van Brocklin, Los Angeles, 1950, 1952, 1954
  - Len Dawson, Dall. Texans, 1962; Kansas City, 1966, 1968
  - Bart Starr, Green Bay, 1966-68

Most Consecutive Seasons Leading League
- 5 Sid Luckman, Chi. Bears, 1939-43
- 3 Bart Starr, Green Bay, 1966-68
- 2 Bernie Masterson, Chi. Bears, 1937-38
  - Sid Luckman, Chi. Bears, 1946-47
  - Johnny Unitas, Baltimore 1964-65
  - Terry Bradshaw, Pittsburgh, 1977-78
  - Steve Grogan, New England, 1980-81

Highest Average Gain, Career (1,500 attempts)
- 8.63 Otto Graham, Cleveland, 1950-55 (1,565-13,499)
- 8.42 Sid Luckman, Chi. Bears, 1939-50 (1,744-14,686)
- 8.16 Norm Van Brocklin, Los Angeles, 1949-57; Philadelphia, 1958-60 (2,895-23,611)

Highest Average Gain, Season (Qualifiers)
- 11.17 Tommy O'Connell, Cleveland, 1957 (110-1,229)
- 10.86 Sid Luckman, Chi. Bears 1943 (202-2,194)
- 10.55 Otto Graham, Cleveland, 1953 (258-2,722)

Highest Average Gain, Rookie, Season (Qualifiers)
- 9.411 Greg Cook, Cincinnati, 1969 (197-1,854)
- 9.409 Bob Waterfield, Cleveland, 1945 (171-1,609)
- 8.36 Zeke Bratkowski, Chi. Bears, 1954 (130-1,087)

Highest Average Gain, Game (20 attempts)
- 13.58 Sammy Baugh, Washington vs. Boston, Oct. 31, 1948 (24-446)
- 13.50 Johnny Unitas, Baltimore vs. Atlanta, Nov. 12, 1967 (20-370)
- 17.71 Joe Namath, N.Y. Jets vs. Baltimore, Sept. 24, 1972 (28-496)

TOUCHDOWNS
Most Seasons Leading League
- 4 Johnny Unitas, Baltimore, 1957-60
  - Len Dawson, Dall. Texans, 1962; Kansas City, 1963, 1965-66
- 3 Arnie Herber, Green Bay, 1932, 1934, 1936
  - Sid Luckman, Chi. Bears, 1943, 1945-46
  - Y.A. Tittle, San Francisco, 1955; N.Y. Giants, 1962-63
- 2 By many players

Most Consecutive Seasons Leading League
- 4 Johnny Unitas, Baltimore, 1957-60
- 2 By many players

Most Touchdown Passes, Career
- 342 Fran Tarkenton, Minnesota, 1961-66, 1972-78; N.Y. Giants, 1967-71
- 290 Johnny Unitas, Baltimore, 1956-72; San Diego, 1973
- 255 Sonny Jurgensen, Philadelphia, 1957-63; Washington, 1964-74

Most Touchdown Passes, Season
- 48 Dan Marino, Miami, 1984
- 36 George Blanda, Houston, 1961
  - Y.A. Tittle, N.Y. Giants, 1963
- 34 Daryle Lamonica, Oakland, 1969

Most Touchdown Passes, Rookie Season
- 22 Charlie Conerly, N.Y. Giants, 1948
  - Butch Songin, Boston, 1960
- 20 Dan Marino, Miami, 1983
- 19 Jim Plunkett, New England, 1971

Most Touchdown Passes, Game
- 7 Sid Luckman, Chi. Bears vs. N.Y. Giants, Nov. 14, 1943
  Adrian Burk, Philadelphia vs. Washington, Oct. 17, 1954
  George Blanda, Houston vs. N.Y. Titans, Nov. 19, 1961
  Y.A. Tittle, N.Y. Giants vs. Washington, Oct. 28, 1962
  Joe Kapp, Minnesota vs. Baltimore, Sept. 28, 1969
- 6 By many players. Last time: Dan Fouts, San Diego vs. Oakland, Nov. 22, 1981

Most Games, Four or More Touchdown Passes, Career
- 17 Johnny Unitas, Baltimore, 1956-72; San Diego, 1973
- 13 George Blanda, Chi. Bears, 1949, 1950-58; Baltimore, 1950; Houston, 1960-66; Oakland, 1967-75
- 12 Sonny Jurgensen, Philadelphia, 1957-63; Washington, 1964-74
  Fran Tarkenton, Minnesota, 1961-66, 1972-78; N.Y. Giants, 1967-71
  Dan Fouts, San Diego, 1973-85

Most Games, Four or More Touchdown Passes, Season
- 6 Dan Marino, Miami, 1984
- 4 George Blanda, Houston, 1961
  Vince Ferragamo, Los Angeles, 1980
- 3 By many players

Most Consecutive Games, Four or More Touchdown Passes
- 4 Dan Marino, Miami, 1984
- 2 By many players

Most Consecutive Games, Touchdown Passes
- 47 Johnny Unitas, Baltimore, 1956-60
- 28 Dave Krieg, Seattle, 1983-85
- 25 Daryle Lamonica, Oakland, 1968-70

HAD INTERCEPTED
Most Consecutive Passes Attempted, None Intercepted
- 294 Bart Starr, Green Bay, 1964-65
- 208 Milt Plum, Cleveland, 1959-60
- 206 Roman Gabriel, Los Angeles, 1968-69

Most Passes Had Intercepted, Career
- 277 George Blanda, Chi. Bears, 1949, 1950-58; Baltimore, 1950; Houston, 1960-66; Oakland, 1967-75
- 268 John Hadl, San Diego, 1962-72; Los Angeles, 1973-74; Green Bay, 1974-75; Houston, 1976-77
- 266 Fran Tarkenton, Minnesota, 1961-66, 1972-78; N.Y. Giants, 1967-71

Most Passes Had Intercepted, Season
- 42 George Blanda, Houston, 1962
- 34 Frank Tripucka, Denver, 1960
- 32 John Hadl, San Diego, 1968
  Fran Tarkenton, Minnesota, 1978

Most Passes Had Intercepted, Game
- 8 Jim Hardy, Chi. Cardinals vs. Philadelphia, Sept. 24, 1950
- 7 Parker Hall, Cleveland vs. Green Bay, Nov. 8, 1942
  Frank Sinkwich, Detroit vs. Green Bay, Oct. 24, 1943
  Bob Waterfield, Los Angeles vs. Green Bay, Oct. 17, 1948
  Zeke Bratkowski, Chicago vs. Baltimore, Oct. 2, 1960
  Tommy Wade, Pittsburgh vs. Philadelphia, Dec. 12, 1965
  Ken Stabler, Oakland vs. Denver, Oct. 16, 1977
- 6 By many players

Most Attempts, No Interceptions, Game
- 57 Joe Montana, San Francisco vs. Atlanta, Oct. 6, 1985
- 51 Scott Brunner, N.Y. Giants vs. St. Louis, Dec. 26, 1982
- 50 Dan Fouts, San Diego vs. Green Bay, Oct. 7, 1984

LOWEST PERCENTAGE, PASSES HAD INTERCEPTED
Most Seasons Leading League, Lowest Percentage, Passes Had Intercepted
- 5 Sammy Baugh, Washington, 1940, 1942, 1944-45, 1947
- 3 Charlie Conerly, N.Y. Giants, 1950, 1956, 1959
  Bart Starr, Green Bay, 1962, 1964, 1966
  Roger Staubach, Dallas, 1971, 1977, 1979
  Ken Anderson, Cincinnati, 1972, 1981-82
- 2 By many players

Lowest Percentage, Passes Had Intercepted, Career (1,500 attempts)
- 2.61 Joe Montana, San Francisco, 1979-85 (2,571-67)
- 3.31 Roman Gabriel, Los Angeles, 1962-72; Philadelphia, 1973-77 (4,498-149)
- 3.52 Bill Kenney, Kansas City, 1980-85 (1,735-61)

Lowest Percentage, Passes Had Intercepted, Season (Qualifiers)
- 0.66 Joe Ferguson, Buffalo, 1976 (151-1)
- 1.16 Steve Bartkowski, Atlanta, 1983 (432-5)
- 1.20 Bart Starr, Green Bay, 1966 (251-3)

Lowest Percentage, Passes Had Intercepted, Rookie, Season (Qualifiers)
- 2.03 Dan Marino, Miami, 1983 (296-6)
- 2.10 Gary Wood, N.Y. Giants, 1964 (143-3)
- 2.82 Bernie Kosar, Cleveland, 1985 (248-7)

TIMES SACKED
Times Sacked has been compiled since 1963.

Most Times Sacked, Career
- 483 Fran Tarkenton, Minnesota, 1961-66, 1972-78; N.Y. Giants, 1967-71
- 405 Craig Morton, Dallas, 1965-74; N.Y. Giants, 1974-76; Denver, 1977-82
- 397 Ken Anderson, Cincinnati, 1971-85

Most Times Sacked, Season
- 62 Ken O'Brien, N.Y. Jets, 1985
- 61 Neil Lomax, St. Louis, 1985
- 59 Tony Eason, New England, 1984

Most Times Sacked, Game
- 12 Bert Jones, Baltimore vs. St. Louis, Oct. 26, 1980
  Warren Moon, Houston vs. Dallas, Sept. 29, 1985
- 11 Charley Johnson, St. Louis vs. N.Y. Giants, Nov. 1, 1964
  Bart Starr, Green Bay vs. Detroit, Nov. 7, 1965
  Jack Kemp, Buffalo vs. Oakland, Oct. 15, 1967
  Bob Berry, Atlanta vs. St. Louis, Nov. 24, 1968
  Greg Landry, Detroit vs. Dallas, Oct. 6, 1975
  Ron Jaworski, Philadelphia vs. St. Louis, Dec. 18, 1983
  Paul McDonald, Cleveland vs. Kansas City, Sept. 30, 1984
  Archie Manning, Minnesota vs. Chicago, Oct. 28, 1984
- 10 By many players

PASS RECEIVING
Most Seasons Leading League
- 8 Don Hutson, Green Bay, 1936-37, 1939, 1941-45
- 5 Lionel Taylor, Denver, 1960-63, 1965
- 3 Tom Fears, Los Angeles, 1948-50
  Pete Pihos, Philadelphia, 1953-55
  Billy Wilson, San Francisco, 1954, 1956-57
  Raymond Berry, Baltimore, 1958-60
  Lance Alworth, San Diego, 1966, 1968-69

Most Consecutive Seasons Leading League
- 5 Don Hutson, Green Bay, 1941-45
- 4 Lionel Taylor, Denver, 1960-63
- 3 Tom Fears, Los Angeles, 1948-50
  Pete Pihos, Philadelphia, 1953-55
  Raymond Berry, Baltimore, 1958-60

Most Pass Receptions, Career
- 716 Charlie Joiner, Houston, 1969-72; Cincinnati, 1972-75; San Diego, 1976-85
- 649 Charley Taylor, Washington, 1964-75, 1977
- 633 Don Maynard, N.Y. Giants, 1958; N.Y. Jets, 1960-72; St. Louis, 1973

Most Seasons, 50 or More Pass Receptions
- 8 Steve Largent, Seattle, 1976, 1978-81, 1983-85
- 7 Raymond Berry, Baltimore, 1958-62, 1965-66
  Art Powell, N.Y. Titans, 1960-62; Oakland, 1963-66
  Lance Alworth, San Diego, 1963-69
  Charley Taylor, Washington, 1964, 1966-67, 1969, 1973-75
  Charlie Joiner, San Diego, 1976, 1979-81, 1983-85
- 6 Lionel Taylor, Denver, 1960-65
  Bobby Mitchell, Washington, 1962-67
  Ahmad Rashad, Minnesota, 1976-81
  Wes Chandler, New Orleans, 1979-80; New Orleans-San Diego, 1981; San Diego, 1983-85
  Dwight Clark, San Francisco, 1980-85
  James Lofton, Green Bay, 1979-81, 1983-85
  Ozzie Newsome, Cleveland, 1979-81, 1983-85

Most Pass Receptions, Season
- 106 Art Monk, Washington, 1984
- 101 Charley Hennigan, Houston, 1964
- 100 Lionel Taylor, Denver, 1961

Most Pass Receptions, Rookie, Season
- 83 Earl Cooper, San Francisco, 1980
- 72 Bill Groman, Houston, 1960
- 67 Jack Clancy, Miami, 1967
  Cris Collinsworth, Cincinnati, 1981

Most Pass Receptions, Game
- 18 Tom Fears, Los Angeles vs. Green Bay, Dec. 3, 1950
- 17 Clark Gaines, N.Y. Jets vs. San Francisco, Sept. 21, 1980
- 16 Sonny Randle, St. Louis vs. N.Y. Giants, Nov. 4, 1962

Most Consecutive Games, Pass Receptions
- 127 Harold Carmichael, Philadelphia, 1972-80
- 123 Steve Largent, Seattle, 1977-85 (current)
- 121 Mel Gray, St. Louis, 1973-82

YARDS GAINED
Most Seasons Leading League
- 7 Don Hutson, Green Bay, 1936, 1938-39, 1941-44
- 3 Raymond Berry, Baltimore, 1957, 1959-60
  Lance Alworth, San Diego, 1965-66, 1968
- 2 By many players

Most Consecutive Seasons Leading League
- 4 Don Hutson, Green Bay, 1941-44
- 2 By many players

Most Yards Gained, Career
- 11,834 Don Maynard, N.Y. Giants, 1958; N.Y. Jets, 1960-72; St. Louis, 1973
- 11,706 Charlie Joiner, Houston, 1969-72; Cincinnati, 1972-75; San Diego, 1976-85
- 10,372 Harold Jackson, Los Angeles, 1968, 1973-77; Philadelphia, 1969-72; New England, 1978-81; Minnesota, 1982; Seattle, 1983

Most Seasons, 1,000 or More Yards, Pass Receiving
- 7 Lance Alworth, San Diego, 1963-69
  Steve Largent, Seattle, 1978-81, 1983-85
- 5 Art Powell, N.Y. Titans, 1960, 1962; Oakland, 1963-64, 1966
  Don Maynard, N.Y. Jets, 1960, 1962, 1965, 1967-68
  James Lofton, Green Bay, 1980-81, 1983-85
- 4 Del Shofner, Los Angeles, 1958; N.Y. Giants, 1961-63
  Lionel Taylor, Denver, 1960-61, 1963, 1965
  Charlie Joiner, San Diego, 1976, 1979-81
  Wes Chandler, New Orleans, 1979; New Orleans-San Diego, 1981; San Diego, 1982, 1985

Most Yards Gained, Season
- 1,746 Charley Hennigan, Houston, 1961
- 1,602 Lance Alworth, San Diego, 1965
- 1,555 Roy Green, St. Louis, 1984

Most Yards Gained, Rookie, Season
- 1,473 Bill Groman, Houston, 1960
- 1,231 Bill Howton, Green Bay, 1952
- 1,124 Harlon Hill, Chi. Bears, 1954

Most Yards Gained, Game
- 309 Stephone Paige, Kansas City vs. San Diego, Dec. 22, 1985
- 303 Jim Benton, Cleveland vs. Detroit, Nov. 22, 1945
- 302 Cloyce Box, Detroit vs. Baltimore, Dec. 3, 1950

Most Games, 200 or More Yards Pass Receiving, Career
- 5 Lance Alworth, San Diego 1962-70; Dallas, 1971-72
- 4 Don Hutson, Green Bay, 1935-45
  Charley Hennigan, Houston, 1960-66
- 3 Don Maynard, N.Y. Giants, 1958; N.Y. Jets, 1960-72; St. Louis, 1973
  Wes Chandler, New Orleans, 1978-81; San Diego, 1981-85

Most Games, 200 or More Yards Pass Receiving, Season
- 3 Charley Hennigan, Houston, 1961
- 2 Don Hutson, Green Bay, 1942
  Gene Roberts, N.Y. Giants, 1949
  Lance Alworth, San Diego, 1963
  Don Maynard, N.Y. Jets, 1968

Most Games, 100 or More Yards Pass Receiving, Career
50 Don Maynard, N.Y. Giants, 1958; N.Y. Jets, 1960-72; St. Louis, 1973
41 Lance Alworth, San Diego, 1962-70; Dallas, 1971-72
36 Steve Largent, Seattle, 1976-85

Most Games, 100 or More Yards Pass Receiving, Season
10 Charley Hennigan, Houston, 1961
9 Elroy (Crazylegs) Hirsch, Los Angeles, 1951
  Bill Groman, Houston, 1960
  Lance Alworth, San Diego, 1965
  Don Maynard, N.Y. Jets, 1967
8 Charley Hennigan, Houston, 1964
  Lance Alworth, San Diego, 1967

Most Consecutive Games, 100 or More Yards Pass Receiving
7 Charley Hennigan, Houston, 1961
  Bill Groman, Houston, 1961
6 Raymond Berry, Baltimore, 1960
  Pat Studstill, Detroit, 1966
5 Elroy (Crazylegs) Hirsch, Los Angeles, 1951
  Bob Boyd, Los Angeles, 1954
  Terry Barr, Detroit, 1963
  Lance Alworth, San Diego, 1966

Longest Pass Reception (All TDs except as noted)
99 Andy Farkas (from Filchock), Washington vs. Pittsburgh, Oct. 15, 1939
  Bobby Mitchell (from Izo), Washington vs. Cleveland, Sept. 15, 1963
  Pat Studstill (from Sweetan), Detroit vs. Baltimore, Oct. 16, 1966
  Gerry Allen (from Jurgensen), Washington vs. Chicago, Sept. 15, 1968
  Cliff Branch (from Plunkett), L.A. Raiders vs. Washington, Oct. 2, 1983
  Mike Quick (from Jaworski), Philadelphia vs. Atlanta, Nov. 10, 1985
98 Gaynell Tinsley (from Russell), Chi. Cardinals vs. Cleveland, Nov. 17, 1938 •
  Dick (Night Train) Lane (from Compton), Chi. Cardinals vs. Green Bay, Nov. 13, 1955
  John Farrington (from Wade), Chicago vs. Detroit, Oct. 8, 1961
  Willard Dewveall (from Lee), Houston vs. San Diego, Nov. 25, 1962
  Homer Jones (from Morrall), N.Y. Giants vs. Pittsburgh, Sept. 11, 1966
  Bobby Moore (from Hart), St. Louis vs. Los Angeles, Dec. 10, 1972 (no TD)
97 Gaynell Tinsley (from Coffee), Chi. Cardinals vs. Chi. Bears, Dec. 5, 1937
  Cloyce Box (from Layne), Detroit vs. Green Bay, Nov. 26, 1953
  Jerry Tarr (from Shaw), Denver vs. Boston, Sept. 21, 1962

AVERAGE GAIN

Highest Average Gain, Career (200 receptions)
22.26 Homer Jones, N.Y. Giants, 1964-69; Cleveland, 1970 (224-4,986)
20.82 Buddy Dial, Pittsburgh, 1959-63; Dallas, 1964-66 (261-5,436)
20.52 Stanley Morgan, New England, 1977-85 (351-7,201)

Highest Average Gain, Season (24 receptions)
32.58 Don Currivan, Boston, 1947 (24-782)
31.44 Bucky Pope, Los Angeles, 1964 (25-786)
27.58 Jimmy Orr, Pittsburgh, 1958 (33-910)

Highest Average Gain, Game (3 receptions)
60.67 Bill Groman, Houston vs. Denver, Nov. 20, 1960 (3-182)
  Homer Jones, N.Y. Giants vs. Washington, Dec. 12, 1965 (3-182)
60.33 Don Currivan, Boston vs. Washington, Nov. 30, 1947 (3-181)
59.67 Bobby Duckworth, San Diego vs. Chicago, Dec. 3, 1984 (3-179)

TOUCHDOWNS

Most Seasons Leading League
9 Don Hutson, Green Bay, 1935-38, 1940-44
3 Lance Alworth, San Diego, 1964-66
2 By many players

Most Consecutive Seasons Leading League
5 Don Hutson, Green Bay, 1940-44
4 Don Hutson, Green Bay, 1935-38
3 Lance Alworth, San Diego, 1964-66

Most Touchdowns, Career
99 Don Hutson, Green Bay, 1935-45
88 Don Maynard, N.Y. Giants, 1958; N.Y. Jets, 1960-72; St. Louis, 1973
85 Lance Alworth, San Diego, 1962-70; Dallas, 1971-72
  Paul Warfield, Cleveland, 1964-69, 1976-77; Miami, 1970-74

Most Touchdowns, Season
18 Mark Clayton, Miami, 1984
17 Don Hutson, Green Bay, 1942
  Elroy (Crazylegs) Hirsch, Los Angeles, 1951
  Bill Groman, Houston, 1961
16 Art Powell, Oakland, 1963

Most Touchdowns, Rookie, Season
13 Bill Howton, Green Bay, 1952
  John Jefferson, San Diego, 1979
12 Harlon Hill, Chi. Bears, 1954
  Bill Groman, Houston, 1960
  Mike Ditka, Chicago, 1961
  Bob Hayes, Dallas, 1965
10 Bill Swiacki, N.Y. Giants, 1948
  Bucky Pope, Los Angeles, 1964
  Sammy White, Minnesota, 1976
  Daryl Turner, Seattle, 1984

Most Touchdowns, Game
5 Bob Shaw, Chi. Cardinals vs. Baltimore, Oct. 2, 1950
  Kellen Winslow, San Diego vs. Oakland, Nov. 22, 1981
4 By many players

Most Consecutive Games, Touchdowns
11 Elroy (Crazylegs) Hirsch, Los Angeles, 1950-51
  Buddy Dial, Pittsburgh, 1959-60
9 Lance Alworth, San Diego, 1963
8 Bill Groman, Houston, 1961
  Dave Parks, San Francisco, 1965

INTERCEPTIONS BY

Most Seasons Leading League
3 Everson Walls, Dallas, 1981-82, 1985
2 Dick (Night Train) Lane, Los Angeles, 1952; Chi. Cardinals, 1954
  Jack Christiansen, Detroit, 1953, 1957
  Milt Davis, Baltimore, 1957, 1959
  Dick Lynch, N.Y. Giants, 1961, 1963

Johnny Robinson, Kansas City, 1966, 1970
Bill Bradley, Philadelphia, 1971-72
Emmitt Thomas, Kansas City, 1969, 1974

Most Interceptions By, Career
81 Paul Krause, Washington, 1964-67; Minnesota, 1968-79
79 Emlen Tunnell, N.Y. Giants, 1948-58; Green Bay, 1959-61
68 Dick (Night Train) Lane, Los Angeles, 1952-53; Chi. Cardinals, 1954-59; Detroit, 1960-65

Most Interceptions By, Season
14 Dick (Night Train) Lane, Los Angeles, 1952
13 Dan Sandifer, Washington, 1948
  Orban (Spec) Sanders, N.Y. Yanks, 1950
  Lester Hayes, Oakland, 1980
12 By nine players

Most Interceptions By, Rookie, Season
14 Dick (Night Train) Lane, Los Angeles, 1952
13 Dan Sandifer, Washington, 1948
12 Woodley Lewis, Los Angeles, 1950
  Paul Krause, Washington, 1964

Most Interceptions By, Game
4 Sammy Baugh, Washington vs. Detroit, Nov. 14, 1943
  Dan Sandifer, Washington vs. Boston, Oct. 31, 1948
  Don Doll, Detroit vs. Chi. Cardinals, Oct. 23, 1949
  Bob Nussbaumer, Chi. Cardinals vs. N.Y. Bulldogs, Nov. 13, 1949
  Russ Craft, Philadelphia vs. Chi. Cardinals, Sept. 24, 1950
  Bobby Dillon, Green Bay vs. Detroit, Nov. 26, 1953
  Jack Butler, Pittsburgh vs. Washington, Dec. 13, 1953
  Austin (Goose) Gonsoulin, Denver vs. Buffalo, Sept. 18, 1960
  Jerry Norton, St. Louis vs. Washington, Nov. 20, 1960; vs. Pittsburgh, Nov. 26, 1961
  Dave Baker, San Francisco vs. L.A. Rams, Dec. 4, 1960
  Bobby Ply, Dall. Texans vs. San Diego, Dec. 16, 1962
  Bobby Hunt, Kansas City vs. Houston, Oct. 4, 1964
  Willie Brown, Denver vs. N.Y. Jets, Nov. 15, 1964
  Dick Anderson, Miami vs. Pittsburgh, Dec. 3, 1973
  Willie Buchanon, Green Bay vs. San Diego, Sept. 24, 1978
  Deron Cherry, Kansas City vs. Seattle, Sept. 29, 1985

Most Consecutive Games, Passes Intercepted By
8 Tom Morrow, Oakland, 1962-63
7 Paul Krause, Washington, 1964
  Larry Wilson, St. Louis, 1966
  Ben Davis, Cleveland, 1968
6 Dick (Night Train) Lane, Chi. Cardinals, 1954-55
  Will Sherman, Los Angeles, 1954-55
  Jim Shofner, Cleveland, 1960
  Paul Krause, Minnesota, 1968
  Willie Williams, N.Y. Giants, 1968
  Kermit Alexander, San Francisco, 1968-69
  Mel Blount, Pittsburgh, 1975
  Eric Harris, Kansas City, 1980
  Lester Hayes, Oakland, 1980

YARDS GAINED

Most Seasons Leading League
2 Dick (Night Train) Lane, Los Angeles, 1952; Chi. Cardinals, 1954
  Herb Adderley, Green Bay, 1965, 1969
  Dick Anderson, Miami, 1968, 1970

Most Yards Gained, Career
1,282 Emlen Tunnell, N.Y. Giants, 1948-58; Green Bay, 1959-61
1,207 Dick (Night Train) Lane, Los Angeles, 1952-53; Chi. Cardinals, 1954-59; Detroit, 1960-65
1,185 Paul Krause, Washington, 1964-67; Minnesota, 1968-79

Most Yards Gained, Season
349 Charlie McNeil, San Diego, 1961
301 Don Doll, Detroit, 1949
298 Dick (Night Train) Lane, Los Angeles, 1952

Most Yards Gained, Rookie, Season
301 Don Doll, Detroit, 1949
298 Dick (Night Train) Lane, Los Angeles, 1952
275 Woodley Lewis, Los Angeles, 1950

Most Yards Gained, Game
177 Charlie McNeil, San Diego vs. Houston, Sept. 24, 1961
167 Dick Jauron, Detroit vs. Chicago, Nov. 18, 1973
151 Tom Myers, New Orleans vs. Minnesota, Sept. 3, 1978
  Mike Haynes, L.A. Raiders vs. Miami, Dec. 2, 1984

Longest Return (All TDs)
102 Bob Smith, Detroit vs. Chi. Bears, Nov. 24, 1949
  Erich Barnes, N.Y. Giants vs. Dall. Cowboys, Oct. 22, 1961
  Gary Barbaro, Kansas City vs. Seattle, Dec. 11, 1977
  Louis Breeden, Cincinnati vs. San Diego, Nov. 8, 1981
101 Richie Petitbon, Chicago vs. Los Angeles, Dec. 9, 1962
  Henry Carr, N.Y. Giants vs. Los Angeles, Nov. 13, 1966
  Tony Greene, Buffalo vs. Kansas City, Oct. 3, 1976
  Tom Pridemore, Atlanta vs. San Francisco, Sept. 20, 1981
100 Vern Huffman, Detroit vs. Brooklyn, Oct. 17, 1937
  Mike Gaechter, Dall. Cowboys vs. Philadelphia, Oct. 14, 1962
  Les (Speedy) Duncan, San Diego vs. Kansas City, Oct. 15, 1967
  Tom Janik, Buffalo vs. N.Y. Jets, Sept. 29, 1968
  Tim Collier, Kansas City vs. Oakland, Dec. 18, 1977

TOUCHDOWNS

Most Touchdowns, Career
9 Ken Houston, Houston, 1967-72; Washington, 1973-80
7 Herb Adderley, Green Bay, 1961-69; Dallas, 1970-72
  Erich Barnes, Chi. Bears, 1958-60; N.Y. Giants, 1961-64; Cleveland, 1965-70
  Lem Barney, Detroit, 1967-77
6 Tom Janik, Denver, 1963-64; Buffalo, 1965-68; Boston, 1969-70; New England, 1971
  Miller Farr, Denver, 1965; San Diego, 1965-66; Houston, 1967-69; St. Louis, 1970-72; Detroit, 1973
  Bobby Bell, Kansas City, 1963-74

Most Touchdowns, Season
4 Ken Houston, Houston, 1971

Jim Kearney, Kansas City, 1972
3   Dick Harris, San Diego, 1961
    Dick Lynch, N.Y. Giants, 1963
    Herb Adderley, Green Bay, 1965
    Lem Barney, Detroit, 1967
    Miller Farr, Houston, 1967
    Monte Jackson, Los Angeles, 1976
    Rod Perry, Los Angeles, 1978
    Ronnie Lott, San Francisco, 1981
2   By many players

Most Touchdowns, Rookie, Season
3   Lem Barney, Detroit, 1967
    Ronnie Lott, San Francisco, 1981
2   By many players

Most Touchdowns, Game
2   Bill Blackburn, Chi. Cardinals vs. Boston, Oct. 24, 1948
    Dan Sandifer, Washington vs. Boston, Oct. 31, 1948
    Bob Franklin, Cleveland vs. Chicago, Dec. 11, 1960
    Bill Stacy, St. Louis vs. Dall. Cowboys, Nov. 5, 1961
    Jerry Norton, St. Louis vs. Pittsburgh, Nov. 26, 1961
    Miller Farr, Houston vs. Buffalo, Dec. 7, 1968
    Ken Houston, Houston vs. San Diego, Dec. 19, 1971
    Jim Kearney, Kansas City vs. Denver, Oct. 1, 1972
    Lemar Parrish, Cincinnati vs. Houston, Dec. 17, 1972
    Dick Anderson, Miami vs. Pittsburgh, Dec. 3, 1973
    Prentice McCray, New England vs. N.Y. Jets, Nov. 21, 1976
    Kenny Johnson, Atlanta vs. Green Bay, Nov. 27, 1983 (OT)
    Mike Kozlowski, Miami vs. N.Y. Jets, Dec. 16, 1983
    Dave Brown, Seattle vs. Kansas City, Nov. 4, 1984

PUNTING

Most Seasons Leading League
4   Sammy Baugh, Washington, 1940-43
    Jerrel Wilson, Kansas City, 1965, 1968, 1972-73
3   Yale Lary, Detroit, 1959, 1961, 1963
    Jim Fraser, Denver, 1962-64
    Ray Guy, Oakland, 1974-75, 1977
2   By many players

Most Consecutive Seasons Leading League
4   Sammy Baugh, Washington, 1940-43
3   Jim Fraser, Denver, 1962-64
2   By many players

PUNTS
Most Punts, Career
1,083   John James, Atlanta, 1972-81; Detroit, 1982, Houston, 1982-84
1,072   Jerrel Wilson, Kansas City, 1963-77; New England, 1978
1,005   Dave Jennings, N.Y. Giants, 1974-84; N.Y. Jets, 1985

Most Punts, Season
114   Bob Parsons, Chicago, 1981
109   John James, Atlanta, 1978
106   David Beverly, Green Bay, 1978

Most Punts, Rookie, Season
96   Mike Connell, San Francisco, 1978
     Chris Norman, Denver, 1984
93   Wilbur Summers, Detroit, 1977
     Ken Clark, Los Angeles, 1979
     Jim Arnold, Kansas City, 1983
92   Mike Horan, Philadelphia, 1984

Most Punts, Game
14   Dick Nesbitt, Chi. Cardinals vs. Chi. Bears, Nov. 30, 1933
     Keith Molesworth, Chi. Bears vs. Green Bay, Dec. 10, 1933
     Sammy Baugh, Washington vs. Philadelphia, Nov. 5, 1939
     Carl Kinscherf, N.Y. Giants vs. Detroit, Nov. 7, 1943
     George Taliaferro, N.Y. Yanks vs. Los Angeles, Sept. 28, 1951
12   Parker Hall, Cleveland vs. Green Bay, Nov. 26, 1939
     Beryl Clark, Chi. Cardinals vs. Detroit, Sept. 15, 1940
     Len Barnum, Philadelphia vs. Washington, Oct. 4, 1942
     Horace Gillom, Cleveland vs. Philadelphia, Dec. 3, 1950
     Adrian Burk, Philadelphia vs. Green Bay, Nov. 2, 1952; vs. N.Y. Giants, Dec. 12, 1954
     Bob Scarpitto, Denver vs. Oakland, Sept. 10, 1967
     Bill Van Heusen, Denver vs. Cincinnati, Oct. 6, 1968
     Tom Blanchard, New Orleans vs. Minnesota, Nov. 16, 1975
     Rusty Jackson, Los Angeles vs. San Francisco, Nov. 21, 1976
     Wilbur Summers, Detroit vs. San Francisco, Oct. 23, 1977
     John James, Atlanta vs. Washington, Dec. 10, 1978
     Luke Prestridge, Denver vs. Buffalo, Oct. 25, 1981
     Greg Coleman, Minnesota vs. Green Bay, Nov. 21, 1982
11   By many players

Longest Punt
98   Steve O'Neal, N.Y. Jets vs. Denver, Sept. 21, 1969
94   Joe Lintzenich, Chi. Bears vs. N.Y. Giants, Nov. 16, 1931
90   Don Chandler, Green Bay vs. San Francisco, Oct. 10, 1965

AVERAGE YARDAGE
Highest Average, Punting, Career (300 punts)
45.16   Rohn Stark, Baltimore, 1982-83; Indianapolis, 1984-85 (313-14,135)
45.10   Sammy Baugh, Washington, 1937-52 (338-15,245)
44.68   Tommy Davis, San Francisco, 1959-69 (511-22,833)

Highest Average, Punting, Season (Qualifiers)
51.40   Sammy Baugh, Washington, 1940 (35-1,799)
48.94   Yale Lary, Detroit, 1963 (35-1,713)
48.73   Sammy Baugh, Washington, 1941 (30-1,462)

Highest Average, Punting, Rookie, Season (Qualifiers)
46.40   Bobby Walden, Minnesota, 1964 (72-3,341)
46.22   Dave Lewis, Cincinnati, 1970 (79-3,651)
45.92   Frank Sinkwich, Detroit, 1943 (12-551)

Highest Average, Punting, Game (4 punts)
61.75   Bob Cifers, Detroit vs. Chi. Bears, Nov. 24, 1946 (4-247)
61.60   Roy McKay, Green Bay vs. Chi. Cardinals, Oct. 28, 1945 (5-308)
59.40   Sammy Baugh, Washington vs. Detroit, Oct. 27, 1940 (5-297)

PUNTS HAD BLOCKED
Most Consecutive Punts, None Blocked
623   Dave Jennings, N.Y. Giants, 1976-83
578   Bobby Walden, Minnesota, 1964-67; Pittsburgh, 1968-72
533   Bobby Joe Green, Pittsburgh, 1960-61; Chicago, 1962-68

Most Punts Had Blocked, Career
14   Herman Weaver, Detroit, 1970-76, Seattle, 1977-80
12   Jerrel Wilson, Kansas City, 1963-77; New England, 1978
     Tom Blanchard, N.Y. Giants, 1971-73; New Orleans, 1974-78; Tampa Bay, 1979-81
11   David Lee, Baltimore, 1966-78

PUNT RETURNS

Most Seasons Leading League
3   Les (Speedy) Duncan, San Diego, 1965-66; Washington, 1971
    Rick Upchurch, Denver, 1976, 1978, 1982
2   Dick Christy, N.Y. Titans, 1961-62
    Claude Gibson, Oakland, 1963-64
    Billy Johnson, Houston, 1975, 1977

PUNT RETURNS
Most Punt Returns, Career
258   Emlen Tunnell, N.Y. Giants, 1948-58; Green Bay, 1959-61
253   Alvin Haymond, Baltimore, 1964-67; Philadelphia, 1968; Los Angeles, 1969-71; Washington, 1972; Houston, 1973
252   Mike Fuller, San Diego, 1975-80; Cincinnati, 1981-82

Most Punt Returns, Season
70   Danny Reece, Tampa Bay, 1979
62   Fulton Walker, Miami-L.A. Raiders, 1985
58   J.T. Smith, Kansas City, 1979
     Greg Pruitt, L.A. Raiders, 1983

Most Punt Returns, Rookie, Season
54   James Jones, Dallas, 1980
53   Louis Lipps, Pittsburgh, 1984
52   Leon Bright, N.Y. Giants, 1981
     Robbie Martin, Detroit, 1981

Most Punt Returns, Game
11   Eddie Brown, Washington vs. Tampa Bay, Oct. 9, 1977
10   Theo Bell, Pittsburgh vs. Buffalo, Dec. 16, 1979
     Mike Nelms, Washington vs. New Orleans, Dec. 26, 1982
9   Rodger Bird, Oakland vs. Denver, Sept. 10, 1967
     Ralph McGill, San Francisco vs. Atlanta, Oct. 29, 1972
     Ed Podolak, Kansas City vs. San Diego, Nov. 10, 1974
     Anthony Leonard, San Francisco vs. New Orleans, Oct. 17, 1976
     Butch Johnson, Dallas vs. Buffalo, Nov. 15, 1976
     Larry Marshall, Philadelphia vs. Tampa Bay, Sept. 18, 1977
     Nesby Glasgow, Baltimore vs. Kansas City, Sept. 2, 1979
     Mike Nelms, Washington vs. St. Louis, Dec. 21, 1980
     Leon Bright, N.Y. Giants vs. Philadelphia, Dec. 11, 1982
     Pete Shaw, N.Y. Giants vs. Philadelphia, Nov. 20, 1983
     Cleotha Montgomery, L.A. Raiders vs. Detroit, Dec. 10, 1984

FAIR CATCHES
Most Fair Catches, Season
24   Ken Graham, San Diego, 1969
22   Lem Barney, Detroit, 1976
21   Ed Podolak, Kansas City, 1970
     Steve Schubert, Chicago, 1978
     Stanley Morgan, New England, 1979

Most Fair Catches, Game
7   Lem Barney, Detroit vs. Chicago, Nov. 21, 1976
6   Jake Scott, Miami vs. Buffalo, Dec. 20, 1970
    Greg Pruitt, L.A. Raiders vs. Seattle, Oct. 7, 1984
5   By many players

YARDS GAINED
Most Seasons Leading League
3   Alvin Haymond, Baltimore, 1965-66; Los Angeles, 1969
2   Bill Dudley, Pittsburgh, 1942, 1946
    Emlen Tunnell, N.Y. Giants, 1951-52
    Dick Christy, N.Y. Titans, 1961-62
    Claude Gibson, Oakland, 1963-64
    Rodger Bird, Oakland, 1966-67
    J.T. Smith, Kansas City, 1979-80

Most Yards Gained, Career
3,036   Billy Johnson, Houston, 1974-80; Atlanta, 1982-85
3,008   Rick Upchurch, Denver, 1975-83
2,660   Mike Fuller, San Diego, 1975-80; Cincinnati, 1981-82

Most Yards Gained, Season
692   Fulton Walker, Miami-L.A. Raiders, 1985
666   Greg Pruitt, L.A. Raiders, 1983
656   Louis Lipps, Pittsburgh, 1984

Most Yards Gained, Rookie, Season
656   Louis Lipps, Pittsburgh, 1984
655   Neal Colzie, Oakland, 1975
608   Mike Haynes, New England, 1976

Most Yards Gained, Game
207   LeRoy Irvin, Los Angeles vs. Atlanta, Oct. 11, 1981
205   George Atkinson, Oakland vs. Buffalo, Sept. 15, 1968
184   Tom Watkins, Detroit vs. San Francisco, Oct. 6, 1963

Longest Punt Return (All TDs)
98   Gil LeFebvre, Cincinnati vs. Brooklyn, Dec. 3, 1933
     Charlie West, Minnesota vs. Washington, Nov. 3, 1968
     Dennis Morgan, Dallas vs. St. Louis, Oct. 13, 1974
97   Greg Pruitt, L.A. Raiders vs. Washington, Oct. 2, 1983
96   Bill Dudley, Washington vs. Pittsburgh, Dec. 3, 1950

AVERAGE YARDAGE
Highest Average, Career (75 returns)
13.51   Henry Ellard, L.A. Rams, 1983-85 (83-1,121)
12.78   George McAfee, Chi. Bears, 1940-41, 1945-50 (112-1,431)
12.75   Jack Christiansen, Detroit, 1951-58 (85-1,084)

Highest Average, Season (Qualifiers)
```
23.00   Herb Rich, Baltimore, 1950 (12-276)
21.47   Jack Christiansen, Detroit, 1952 (15-322)
21.28   Dick Christy, N.Y. Titans, 1961 (18-383)
```
Highest Average, Rookie, Season (Qualifiers)
```
23.00   Herb Rich, Baltimore, 1950 (12-276)
20.88   Jerry Davis, Chi. Cardinals, 1948 (16-334)
20.73   Frank Sinkwich, Detroit, 1943 (11-228)
```
Highest Average, Game (3 returns)
```
47.67   Chuck Latourette, St. Louis vs. New Orleans, Sept. 29, 1968 (3-143)
47.33   Johnny Roland, St. Louis vs. Philadelphia, Oct. 2, 1966 (3-142)
45.67   Dick Christy, N.Y. Titans vs. Denver, Sept. 24, 1961 (3-137)
```

TOUCHDOWNS

Most Touchdowns, Career
```
8   Jack Christiansen, Detroit, 1951-58
    Rick Upchurch, Denver, 1975-83
6   Billy Johnson, Houston, 1974-80; Atlanta, 1982-85
5   Emlen Tunnell, N.Y. Giants, 1948-58; Green Bay, 1959-61
```
Most Touchdowns, Season
```
4   Jack Christiansen, Detroit, 1951
    Rick Upchurch, Denver, 1976
3   Emlen Tunnell, N.Y. Giants, 1951
    Billy Johnson, Houston, 1975
    LeRoy Irvin, Los Angeles, 1981
2   By many players
```
Most Touchdowns, Rookie, Season
```
4   Jack Christiansen, Detroit, 1951
2   By five players
```
Most Touchdowns, Game
```
2   Jack Christiansen, Detroit vs. Los Angeles, Oct. 14, 1951; vs. Green Bay,
       Nov. 22, 1951
    Dick Christy, N.Y. Titans vs. Denver, Sept. 24, 1961
    Rick Upchurch, Denver vs. Cleveland, Sept. 26, 1976
    LeRoy Irvin, Los Angeles vs. Atlanta, Oct. 11, 1981
```

KICKOFF RETURNS

Most Seasons Leading League
```
3   Abe Woodson, San Francisco, 1959, 1962-63
2   Lynn Chandnois, Pittsburgh, 1951-52
    Bobby Jancik, Houston, 1962-63
    Travis Williams, Green Bay, 1967; Los Angeles, 1971
```

KICKOFF RETURNS

Most Kickoff Returns, Career
```
275   Ron Smith, Chicago, 1965, 1970-72; Atlanta, 1966-67; Los Angeles, 1968-69;
         San Diego, 1973; Oakland, 1974
243   Bruce Harper, N.Y. Jets, 1977-84
193   Abe Woodson, San Francisco, 1958-64; St. Louis, 1965-66
```
Most Kickoff Returns, Season
```
60   Drew Hill, Los Angeles, 1981
55   Bruce Harper, N.Y. Jets, 1978, 1979
     David Turner, Cincinnati, 1979
     Stump Mitchell, St. Louis, 1981
53   Eddie Payton, Minnesota, 1980
     Buster Rhymes, Minnesota, 1985
```
Most Kickoff Returns, Rookie, Season
```
55   Stump Mitchell, St. Louis, 1981
53   Buster Rhymes, Minnesota, 1985
50   Nesby Glasgow, Baltimore, 1979
     Dino Hall, Cleveland, 1979
```
Most Kickoff Returns, Game
```
9   Noland Smith, Kansas City vs. Oakland, Nov. 23, 1967
    Dino Hall, Cleveland vs. Pittsburgh, Oct. 7, 1979
8   George Taliaferro, N.Y. Yanks vs. N.Y. Giants, Dec. 3, 1950
    Bobby Jancik, Houston vs. Boston, Dec. 8, 1963; vs. Oakland, Dec. 22, 1963
    Mel Renfro, Dallas vs. Green Bay, Nov. 29, 1964
    Willie Porter, Boston vs. N.Y. Jets, Sept. 22, 1968
    Keith Moody, Buffalo vs. Seattle, Oct. 30, 1977
    Brian Baschnagel, Chicago vs. Houston, Nov. 6, 1977
    Bruce Harper, N.Y. Jets vs. New England, Oct. 29, 1978; vs. New England,
       Sept. 9, 1979
    Dino Hall, Cleveland vs. Pittsburgh, Nov. 25, 1979
    Terry Metcalf, Washington vs. St. Louis, Sept. 20, 1981
    Harlan Huckleby, Green Bay vs. Washington, Oct. 17, 1983
    Gary Ellerson, Green Bay vs. St. Louis, Sept. 29, 1985
7   By many players
```

YARDS GAINED

Most Seasons Leading League
```
3   Bruce Harper, N.Y. Jets, 1977-79
2   Marshall Goldberg, Chi. Cardinals, 1941-42
    Woodley Lewis, Los Angeles, 1953-54
    Al Carmichael, Green Bay, 1956-57
    Timmy Brown, Philadelphia, 1961, 1963
    Bobby Jancik, Houston, 1963, 1966
    Ron Smith, Atlanta, 1966-67
```
Most Yards Gained, Career
```
6,922   Ron Smith, Chicago, 1965, 1970-72; Atlanta, 1966-67; Los Angeles, 1968-69;
           San Diego, 1973; Oakland, 1974
5,538   Abe Woodson, San Francisco, 1958-64; St. Louis, 1965-66
5,407   Bruce Harper, N.Y. Jets, 1977-84
```
Most Yards Gained, Season
```
1,345   Buster Rhymes, Minnesota, 1985
1,317   Bobby Jancik, Houston, 1963
1,314   Dave Hampton, Green Bay, 1971
```
Most Yards Gained, Rookie, Season
```
1,345   Buster Rhymes, Minnesota, 1985
1,292   Stump Mitchell, St. Louis, 1981
1,245   Odell Barry, Denver, 1964
```
Most Yards Gained, Game
```
294   Wally Triplett, Detroit vs. Los Angeles, Oct. 29, 1950
247   Timmy Brown, Philadelphia vs. Dallas, Nov. 6, 1966
```

```
244   Noland Smith, Kansas City vs. San Diego, Oct. 15, 1967
```
Longest Kickoff Return (All TDs)
```
106   Al Carmichael, Green Bay vs. Chi. Bears, Oct. 7, 1956
      Noland Smith, Kansas City vs. Denver, Dec. 17, 1967
      Roy Green, St. Louis vs. Dallas, Oct. 21, 1979
105   Frank Seno, Chi. Cardinals vs. N.Y. Giants, Oct. 20, 1946
      Ollie Matson, Chi. Cardinals vs. Washington, Oct. 14, 1956
      Abe Woodson, San Francisco vs. Los Angeles, Nov. 8, 1959
      Timmy Brown, Philadelphia vs. Cleveland, Sept. 17, 1961
      Jon Arnett, Los Angeles vs. Detroit, Oct. 29, 1961
      Eugene (Mercury) Morris, Miami vs. Cincinnati, Sept. 14, 1969
      Travis Williams, Los Angeles vs. New Orleans, Dec. 5, 1971
104   By many players
```

AVERAGE YARDAGE

Highest Average, Career (75 returns)
```
30.56   Gale Sayers, Chicago, 1965-71 (91-2,781)
29.57   Lynn Chandnois, Pittsburgh, 1950-56 (92-2,720)
28.69   Abe Woodson, San Francisco, 1958-64; St. Louis, 1965-66 (193-5,538)
```
Highest Average, Season (Qualifiers)
```
41.06   Travis Williams, Green Bay, 1967 (18-739)
37.69   Gale Sayers, Chicago, 1967 (16-603)
35.50   Ollie Matson, Chi. Cardinals, 1958 (14-497)
```
Highest Average, Rookie, Season (Qualifiers)
```
41.06   Travis Williams, Green Bay, 1967 (18-739)
33.08   Tom Moore, Green Bay, 1960 (12-397)
32.88   Duriel Harris, Miami, 1976 (17-559)
```
Highest Average, Game (3 returns)
```
73.50   Wally Triplett, Detroit vs. Los Angeles, Oct. 29, 1950 (4-294)
67.33   Lenny Lyles, San Francisco vs. Baltimore, Dec. 18, 1960 (3-202)
65.33   Ken Hall, Houston vs. N.Y. Titans, Oct. 23, 1960 (3-196)
```

TOUCHDOWNS

Most Touchdowns, Career
```
6   Ollie Matson, Chi. Cardinals, 1952, 1954-58; L.A. Rams, 1959-62; Detroit, 1963;
       Philadelphia, 1964
    Gale Sayers, Chicago, 1965-71
    Travis Williams, Green Bay, 1967-70; Los Angeles, 1971
5   Bobby Mitchell, Cleveland, 1958-61; Washington, 1962-68
    Abe Woodson, San Francisco, 1958-64; St. Louis, 1965-66
    Timmy Brown, Green Bay, 1959; Philadelphia, 1960-67; Baltimore, 1968
4   Cecil Turner, Chicago, 1968-73
```
Most Touchdowns, Season
```
4   Travis Williams, Green Bay, 1967
    Cecil Turner, Chicago, 1970
3   Verda (Vitamin T) Smith, Los Angeles, 1950
    Abe Woodson, San Francisco, 1963
    Gale Sayers, Chicago, 1967
    Raymond Clayborn, New England, 1977
    Ron Brown, L.A. Rams, 1985
2   By many players
```
Most Touchdowns, Rookie, Season
```
4   Travis Williams, Green Bay, 1967
3   Raymond Clayborn, New England, 1977
2   By six players
```
Most Touchdowns, Game
```
2   Timmy Brown, Philadelphia vs. Dallas, Nov. 6, 1966
    Travis Williams, Green Bay vs. Cleveland, Nov. 12, 1967
    Ron Brown, L.A. Rams vs. Green Bay, Nov. 24, 1985
```

COMBINED KICK RETURNS

Most Combined Kick Returns, Career
```
510   Ron Smith, Chicago, 1965, 1970-72; Atlanta, 1966-67; Los Angeles, 1968-69;
         San Diego, 1973; Oakland, 1974 (p-235, k-275)
426   Bruce Harper, N.Y. Jets, 1977-84 (p-183, k-243)
423   Alvin Haymond, Baltimore, 1964-67; Philadelphia, 1968; Los Angeles, 1969-71;
         Washington, 1972; Houston, 1973 (p-253, k-170)
```
Most Combined Kick Returns, Season
```
100   Larry Jones, Washington, 1975 (p-53, k-47)
97    Stump Mitchell, St. Louis, 1981 (p-42, k-55)
94    Nesby Glasgow, Baltimore, 1979 (p-44, k-50)
```
Most Combined Kick Returns, Game
```
13   Stump Mitchell, St. Louis vs. Atlanta, Oct. 18, 1981 (p-6, k-7)
12   Mel Renfro, Dallas vs. Green Bay, Nov. 29, 1964 (p-4, k-8)
     Larry Jones, Washington vs. Dallas, Dec. 13, 1975 (p-6, k-6)
     Eddie Brown, Washington vs. Tampa Bay, Oct. 9, 1977 (p-11, k-1)
     Nesby Glasgow, Baltimore vs. Denver, Sept. 2, 1979 (p-9, k-3)
11   By many players
```

YARDS GAINED

Most Yards Returned, Career
```
8,710   Ron Smith, Chicago, 1965, 1970-72; Atlanta, 1966-67; Los Angeles, 1968-69;
           San Diego, 1973; Oakland, 1974 (p-1,788, k-6,922)
7,191   Bruce Harper, N.Y. Jets, 1977-84 (p-1,784, k-5,407)
6,740   Les (Speedy) Duncan, San Diego, 1964-70; Washington, 1971-74
           (p-2,201, k-4,539)
```
Most Yards Returned, Season
```
1,737   Stump Mitchell, St. Louis, 1981 (p-445, k-1,292)
1,658   Bruce Harper, N.Y. Jets, 1978 (p-378, k-1,280)
1,591   Mike Nelms, Washington, 1981 (p-492, k-1,099)
```
Most Yards Returned, Game
```
294   Wally Triplett, Detroit vs. Los Angeles, Oct. 29, 1950 (k-294)
      Woodley Lewis, Los Angeles vs. Detroit, Oct. 18, 1953 (p-120, k-174)
289   Eddie Payton, Detroit vs. Minnesota, Dec. 17, 1977 (p-105, k-184)
282   Les (Speedy) Duncan, San Diego vs. N.Y. Jets, Nov. 24, 1968 (p-102, k-180)
```

TOUCHDOWNS

Most Touchdowns, Career
```
9   Ollie Matson, Chi. Cardinals, 1952, 1954-58; Los Angeles, 1959-62;
       Detroit, 1963; Philadelphia, 1964-66 (p-3, k-6)
8   Jack Christiansen, Detroit, 1951-58 (p-8)
    Bobby Mitchell, Cleveland, 1958-61; Washington, 1962-68 (p-3, k-5)
    Gale Sayers, Chicago, 1965-71 (p-2, k-6)
```

331

Rick Upchurch, Denver, 1975-83 (p-8)
Billy Johnson, Houston, 1974-80; Atlanta, 1982-85 (p-6, k-2)
7 Abe Woodson, San Francisco, 1958-64; St. Louis, 1965-66 (p-2, k-5)

Most Touchdowns, Season
4 Jack Christiansen, Detroit, 1951 (p-4)
    Emlen Tunnell, N.Y. Giants, 1951 (p-3, k-1)
    Gale Sayers, Chicago, 1967 (k-4)
    Travis Williams, Green Bay, 1967 (k-4)
    Cecil Turner, Chicago, 1970 (k-4)
    Billy Johnson, Houston, 1975 (p-3, k-1)
    Rick Upchurch, Denver, 1976 (p-4)
3 Verda (Vitamin T) Smith, Los Angeles, 1950 (k-3)
    Abe Woodson, San Francisco, 1963 (k-3)
    Raymond Clayborn, New England, 1977 (k-3)
    Billy Johnson, Houston, 1977 (p-2, k-1)
    LeRoy Irvin, Los Angeles, 1981 (p-3)
    Ron Brown, L.A. Rams, 1985 (k-3)
2 By many players

Most Touchdowns, Game
2 Jack Christiansen, Detroit vs. Los Angeles, Oct. 14, 1951 (p-2); vs. Green Bay, Nov. 22, 1951 (p-2)
    Jim Patton, N.Y. Giants vs. Washington, Oct. 30, 1955 (p-1, k-1)
    Bobby Mitchell, Cleveland vs. Philadelphia, Nov. 23, 1958 (p-1, k-1)
    Dick Christy, N.Y. Titans vs. Denver, Sept. 24, 1961 (p-2)
    Al Frazier, Denver vs. Boston, Dec. 3, 1961 (k-2)
    Timmy Brown, Philadelphia vs. Dallas, Nov. 6, 1966 (k-2)
    Travis Williams, Green Bay vs. Cleveland, Nov. 12, 1967 (k-2); vs. Pittsburgh, Nov. 2, 1969 (p-1, k-1)
    Gale Sayers, Chicago vs. San Francisco, Dec. 3, 1967 (p-1, k-1)
    Rick Upchurch, Denver vs. Cleveland, Sept. 26, 1976 (p-2)
    Eddie Payton, Detroit vs. Minnesota, Dec. 17, 1977 (p-1, k-1)
    LeRoy Irvin, Los Angeles vs. Atlanta, Oct. 11, 1981 (p-2)
    Ron Brown, L.A. Rams vs. Green Bay, Nov. 24, 1985 (k-2)

FUMBLES

Most Fumbles, Career
105 Roman Gabriel, Los Angeles, 1962-72; Philadelphia, 1973-77
95 Johnny Unitas, Baltimore, 1956-72; San Diego, 1973
92 Dan Fouts, San Diego, 1973-85

Most Fumbles, Season
17 Dan Pastorini, Houston, 1973
    Warren Moon, Houston, 1984
16 Don Meredith, Dallas, 1964
    Joe Cribbs, Buffalo, 1980
    Steve Fuller, Kansas City, 1980
    Paul McDonald, Cleveland, 1984
    Phil Simms, N.Y. Giants, 1985
15 Paul Christman, Chi. Cardinals, 1946
    Sammy Baugh, Washington, 1947
    Sam Etcheverry, St. Louis, 1961
    Len Dawson, Kansas City, 1964
    Terry Metcalf, St. Louis, 1976
    Steve DeBerg, Tampa Bay, 1984

Most Fumbles, Game
7 Len Dawson, Kansas City vs. San Diego, Nov. 15, 1964
6 Sam Etcheverry, St. Louis vs. N.Y. Giants, Sept. 17, 1961
5 Paul Christman, Chi. Cardinals vs. Green Bay, Nov. 10, 1946
    Charlie Conerly, N.Y. Giants vs. San Francisco, Dec. 1, 1957
    Jack Kemp, Buffalo vs. Houston, Oct. 29, 1967
    Roman Gabriel, Philadelphia vs. Oakland, Nov. 21, 1976

FUMBLES RECOVERED
Most Fumbles Recovered, Career, Own and Opponents'
43 Fran Tarkenton, Minnesota, 1961-66, 1972-78; N.Y. Giants, 1967-71 (43 own)
38 Jack Kemp, Pittsburgh, 1957; L.A. Chargers, 1960; San Diego, 1961-62; Buffalo, 1962-67, 1969 (38 own)
37 Roman Gabriel, Los Angeles, 1962-72; Philadelphia, 1973-77 (37 own)

Most Fumbles Recovered, Season, Own and Opponents'
9 Don Hultz, Minnesota, 1963 (9 opp)
8 Paul Christman, Chi. Cardinals, 1945 (8 own)
    Joe Schmidt, Detroit, 1955 (8 opp)
    Bill Butler, Minnesota, 1963 (8 own)
    Kermit Alexander, San Francisco, 1965 (4 own, 4 opp)
    Jack Lambert, Pittsburgh, 1976 (1 own, 7 opp)
    Danny White, Dallas, 1981 (8 own)
7 By many players

Most Fumbles Recovered, Game, Own and Opponents'
4 Otto Graham, Cleveland vs. N.Y. Giants, Oct. 25, 1953 (4 own)
    Sam Etcheverry, St. Louis vs. N.Y. Giants, Sept. 17, 1961 (4 own)
    Roman Gabriel, Los Angeles vs. San Francisco, Oct. 12, 1969 (4 own)
    Joe Ferguson, Buffalo vs. Miami, Sept. 18, 1977 (4 own)
3 By many players

OWN FUMBLES RECOVERED
Most Own Fumbles Recovered, Career
43 Fran Tarkenton, Minnesota, 1961-66, 1972-78; N.Y. Giants, 1967-71
38 Jack Kemp, Pittsburgh, 1957; L.A. Chargers, 1960; San Diego, 1961-62; Buffalo, 1962-67, 1969
37 Roman Gabriel, Los Angeles, 1962-72; Philadelphia, 1973-77

Most Own Fumbles Recovered, Season
8 Paul Christman, Chi. Cardinals, 1945
    Bill Butler, Minnesota, 1963
    Danny White, Dallas, 1981
7 Sammy Baugh, Washington, 1947
    Tommy Thompson, Philadelphia, 1947
    John Roach, St. Louis, 1960
    Jack Larscheid, Oakland, 1960
    Gary Huff, Chicago, 1974
    Terry Metcalf, St. Louis, 1974
    Joe Ferguson, Buffalo, 1977
    Fran Tarkenton, Minnesota, 1978
    Greg Pruitt, L.A. Raiders, 1983
    Warren Moon, Houston, 1984

6 By many players

Most Own Fumbles Recovered, Game
4 Otto Graham, Cleveland vs. N.Y. Giants, Oct. 25, 1953
    Sam Etcheverry, St. Louis vs. N.Y. Giants, Sept. 17, 1961
    Roman Gabriel, Los Angeles vs. San Francisco, Oct. 12, 1969
    Joe Ferguson, Buffalo vs. Miami, Sept. 18, 1977
3 By many players

OPPONENTS' FUMBLES RECOVERED
Most Opponents' Fumbles Recovered, Career
29 Jim Marshall, Cleveland, 1960; Minnesota, 1961-79
25 Dick Butkus, Chicago, 1965-73
23 Carl Eller, Minnesota, 1964-78; Seattle, 1979

Most Opponents' Fumbles Recovered, Season
9 Don Hultz, Minnesota, 1963
8 Joe Schmidt, Detroit, 1955
7 Alan Page, Minnesota, 1970
    Jack Lambert, Pittsburgh, 1976

Most Opponents' Fumbles Recovered, Game
3 Corwin Clatt, Chi. Cardinals vs. Detroit, Nov. 6, 1949
    Vic Sears, Philadelphia vs. Green Bay, Nov. 2, 1952
    Ed Beatty, San Francisco vs. Los Angeles, Oct. 7, 1956
    Ron Carroll, Houston vs. Cincinnati, Oct. 27, 1974
    Maurice Spencer, New Orleans vs. Atlanta, Oct. 10, 1976
    Steve Nelson, New England vs. Philadelphia, Oct. 8, 1978
    Charles Jackson, Kansas City vs. Pittsburgh, Sept. 6, 1981
    Willie Buchanon, San Diego vs. Denver, Sept. 27, 1981
    Joey Browner, Minnesota vs. San Francisco, Sept. 8, 1985
2 By many players

YARDS RETURNING FUMBLES
Longest Fumble Run (All TDs)
104 Jack Tatum, Oakland vs. Green Bay, Sept. 24, 1972 (opp)
98 George Halas, Chi. Bears vs. Oorang Indians, Marion, Ohio, Nov. 4, 1923 (opp)
97 Chuck Howley, Dallas vs. Atlanta, Oct. 2, 1966 (opp)

TOUCHDOWNS
Most Touchdowns, Career (Total)
4 Bill Thompson, Denver, 1969-81
3 Ralph Heywood, Detroit, 1947-48; Boston, 1948; N.Y. Bulldogs, 1949
    Leo Sugar, Chi. Cardinals, 1954-59; St. Louis, 1960; Philadelphia, 1961; Detroit, 1962
    Bud McFadin, Los Angeles, 1952-56; Denver, 1960-63; Houston, 1964-65
    Doug Cline, Houston, 1960-66; San Diego, 1966
    Bob Lilly, Dall. Cowboys, 1961-74
    Chris Hanburger, Washington, 1965-78
    Lemar Parrish, Cincinnati, 1970-77; Washington, 1978-81; Buffalo, 1982
    Paul Krause, Washington, 1964-67; Minnesota, 1968-79
    Brad Dusek, Washington, 1974-81
    David Logan, Tampa Bay, 1979-85
    Thomas Howard, Kansas City, 1977-83; St. Louis, 1984-85
2 By many players

Most Touchdowns, Season (Total)
2 Harold McPhail, Boston, 1934
    Harry Ebding, Detroit, 1937
    John Morelli, Boston, 1944
    Frank Maznicki, Boston, 1947
    Fred (Dippy) Evans, Chi. Bears, 1948
    Ralph Heywood, Boston, 1948
    Art Tait, N.Y. Yanks, 1951
    John Dwyer, Los Angeles, 1952
    Leo Sugar, Chi. Cardinals, 1957
    Doug Cline, Houston, 1961
    Jim Bradshaw, Pittsburgh, 1964
    Royce Berry, Cincinnati, 1970
    Ahmad Rashad, Buffalo, 1974
    Tim Gray, Kansas City, 1977
    Charles Phillips, Oakland, 1978
    Kenny Johnson, Atlanta, 1981
    George Martin, N.Y. Giants, 1981
    Del Rodgers, Green Bay, 1982
    Mike Douglass, Green Bay, 1983
    Shelton Robinson, Seattle, 1983

Most Touchdowns, Career (Own recovered)
2 Ken Kavanaugh, Chi. Bears, 1940-41, 1945-50
    Mike Ditka, Chicago, 1961-66; Philadelphia, 1967-68; Dallas, 1969-72
    Gail Cogdill, Detroit, 1960-68; Baltimore, 1968; Atlanta, 1969-70
    Ahmad Rashad, St. Louis, 1972-73; Buffalo, 1974; Minnesota, 1976-82
    Jim Mitchell, Atlanta, 1969-79
    Drew Pearson, Dallas, 1973-83
    Del Rodgers, Green Bay, 1982, 1984

Most Touchdowns, Season (Own recovered)
2 Ahmad Rashad, Buffalo, 1974
    Del Rodgers, Green Bay, 1982
1 By many players

Most Touchdowns, Career (Opponents' recovered)
3 Leo Sugar, Chi. Cardinals, 1954-59; St. Louis, 1960; Philadelphia, 1961; Detroit, 1962
    Doug Cline, Houston, 1960-66; San Diego, 1966
    Bud McFadin, Los Angeles, 1952-56; Denver, 1960-63; Houston, 1964-65
    Bob Lilly, Dall. Cowboys, 1961-74
    Chris Hanburger, Washington, 1965-78
    Paul Krause, Washington, 1964-67; Minnesota, 1968-79
    Lemar Parrish, Cincinnati, 1970-77; Washington, 1978-81; Buffalo, 1982
    Bill Thompson, Denver, 1969-81
    Brad Dusek, Washington, 1974-81
    David Logan, Tampa Bay, 1979-85
    Thomas Howard, Kansas City, 1977-83; St. Louis, 1984-85
2 By many players

Most Touchdowns, Season (Opponents' recovered)
2 Harold McPhail, Boston, 1934
    Harry Ebding, Detroit, 1937

John Morelli, Boston, 1944
Frank Maznicki, Boston, 1947
Fred (Dippy) Evans, Chi. Bears, 1948
Ralph Heywood, Boston, 1948
Art Tait, N.Y. Yanks, 1951
John Dwyer, Los Angeles, 1952
Leo Sugar, Chi. Cardinals, 1957
Doug Cline, Houston, 1961
Jim Bradshaw, Pittsburgh, 1964
Royce Berry, Cincinnati, 1970
Tim Gray, Kansas City, 1977
Charles Phillips, Oakland, 1978
Kenny Johnson, Atlanta, 1981
George Martin, N.Y. Giants, 1981
Mike Douglass, Green Bay, 1983
Shelton Robinson, Seattle, 1983

Most Touchdowns, Game (Opponents' recovered)
2 Fred (Dippy) Evans, Chi. Bears vs. Washington, Nov. 28, 1948

COMBINED NET YARDS GAINED

Rushing, receiving, interception returns, punt returns, kickoff returns, and fumble returns

Most Seasons Leading League
5 Jim Brown, Cleveland, 1958-61, 1964
3 Cliff Battles, Boston, 1932-33; Washington, 1937
Gale Sayers, Chicago, 1965-67
2 By many players

Most Consecutive Seasons Leading League
4 Jim Brown, Cleveland, 1958-61
3 Gale Sayers, Chicago, 1965-67
2 Cliff Battles, Boston, 1932-33
Charley Trippi, Chi. Cardinals, 1948-49
Timmy Brown, Philadelphia, 1962-63
Floyd Little, Denver, 1967-68
James Brooks, San Diego, 1981-82
Eric Dickerson, L.A. Rams, 1983-84

ATTEMPTS

Most Attempts, Career
3,831 Walter Payton, Chicago, 1975-85
3,281 Franco Harris, Pittsburgh, 1972-83; Seattle, 1984
3,174 John Riggins, N.Y. Jets, 1971-75; Washington, 1976-79, 1981-85

Most Attempts, Season
496 James Wilder, Tampa Bay, 1984
449 Marcus Allen, L.A. Raiders, 1985
442 Eric Dickerson, L.A. Rams, 1983

Most Attempts, Rookie, Season
442 Eric Dickerson, L.A. Rams, 1983
395 George Rogers, New Orleans, 1981
390 Joe Cribbs, Buffalo, 1980

Most Attempts, Game
48 James Wilder, Tampa Bay vs. Pittsburgh, Oct. 30, 1983
47 James Wilder, Tampa Bay vs. Green Bay, Sept. 30, 1984 (OT)
46 Gerald Riggs, Atlanta vs. L.A. Rams, Nov. 17, 1985

YARDS GAINED

Most Yards Gained, Career
19,338 Walter Payton, Chicago, 1975-85
15,459 Jim Brown, Cleveland, 1957-65
14,622 Franco Harris, Pittsburgh, 1972-83; Seattle, 1984

Most Yards Gained, Season
2,535 Lionel James, San Diego, 1985
2,462 Terry Metcalf, St. Louis, 1975
2,444 Mack Herron, New England, 1974

Most Yards Gained, Rookie, Season
2,272 Gale Sayers, Chicago, 1965
2,212 Eric Dickerson, L.A. Rams, 1983
2,100 Abner Haynes, Dall. Texans, 1960

Most Yards Gained, Game
373 Billy Cannon, Houston vs. N.Y. Titans, Dec. 10, 1961
345 Lionel James, San Diego vs. L.A. Raiders, Nov. 10, 1985 (OT)
341 Timmy Brown, Philadelphia vs. St. Louis, Dec. 16, 1962

SACKS

Sacks have been compiled since 1982.

Most Sacks, Career
60.5 Mark Gastineau, N.Y. Jets, 1982-85
46 Dexter Manley, Washington, 1982-85
45.5 Jacob Green, Seattle, 1982-85

Most Sacks, Season
22 Mark Gastineau, N.Y. Jets, 1984
19 Mark Gastineau, N.Y. Jets, 1983
18.5 Andre Tippett, New England, 1984

Most Sacks, Game
6 Fred Dean, San Francisco vs. New Orleans, Nov. 13, 1983
5.5 William Gay, Detroit vs. Tampa Bay, Sept. 4, 1983
5 Howie Long, L.A. Raiders vs. Washington, Oct. 2, 1983
Jim Jeffcoat, Dallas vs. Washington, Nov. 10, 1985

MISCELLANEOUS

Longest Return of Missed Field Goal (All TDs)
101 Al Nelson, Philadelphia vs. Dallas, Sept. 26, 1971
100 Al Nelson, Philadelphia vs. Cleveland, Dec. 11, 1966
Ken Ellis, Green Bay vs. N.Y. Giants, Sept. 19, 1971
99 Jerry Williams, Los Angeles vs. Green Bay, Dec. 16, 1951
Carl Taseff, Baltimore vs. Los Angeles, Dec. 12, 1959
Timmy Brown, Philadelphia vs. St. Louis, Sept. 16, 1962

TEAM RECORDS

CHAMPIONSHIPS

Most Seasons League Champion
11 Green Bay, 1929-31, 1936, 1939, 1944, 1961-62, 1965-67

9 Chi. Bears, 1921, 1932-33, 1940-41, 1943, 1946, 1963, 1985
4 N.Y. Giants, 1927, 1934, 1938, 1956
Detroit, 1935, 1952-53, 1957
Clev. Browns, 1950, 1954-55, 1964
Baltimore, 1958-59, 1968, 1970
Pittsburgh, 1974-75, 1978-79
Oakland/L.A. Raiders, 1967, 1976, 1980, 1983

Most Consecutive Seasons League Champion
3 Green Bay, 1929-31, 1965-67
2 Canton, 1922-23
Chi. Bears, 1932-33, 1940-41
Philadelphia, 1948-49
Detroit, 1952-53
Cleveland, 1954-55
Baltimore, 1958-59
Houston, 1960-61
Green Bay, 1961-62
Buffalo, 1964-65
Miami, 1972-73
Pittsburgh, 1974-75, 1978-79

Most Times Finishing First, Regular Season (Since 1933)
15 Clev./L.A. Rams, 1945, 1949-51, 1955, 1967, 1969, 1973-79, 1985
Clev. Browns, 1950-55, 1957, 1964-65, 1967-69, 1971, 1980, 1985
14 N.Y. Giants, 1933-35, 1938-39, 1941, 1944, 1946, 1956, 1958-59, 1961-63
13 Dall. Cowboys, 1966-71, 1973, 1976-79, 1981, 1985

Most Consecutive Times Finishing First, Regular Season (Since 1933)
7 Los Angeles, 1973-79
6 Cleveland, 1950-55
Dallas, 1966-71
Minnesota, 1973-78
Pittsburgh, 1974-79
5 Oakland, 1972-76

GAMES WON

Most Consecutive Games Won (Incl. postseason games)
18 Chi. Bears, 1933-34, 1941-42
Miami, 1972-73
17 Oakland, 1976-77
14 Washington, 1942-43

Most Consecutive Games Won (Regular season)
17 Chi. Bears, 1933-34
16 Chi. Bears, 1941-42
Miami, 1971-73, 1983-84
15 L.A. Chargers, San Diego, 1960-61

Most Consecutive Games Without Defeat (Incl. postseason games)
24 Canton, 1922-23 (won 21, tied 3)
23 Green Bay, 1928-30 (won 21, tied 2)
18 Chi. Bears, 1933-34 (won 18), 1941-42 (won 18)
Miami, 1972-73 (won 18)

Most Consecutive Games Without Defeat (Regular season)
24 Canton, 1922-23 (won 21, tied 3)
Chi. Bears, 1941-43 (won 23, tied 1)
23 Green Bay, 1928-30 (won 21, tied 2)
17 Chi. Bears, 1933-34 (won 17)

Most Games Won, One Season (Incl. postseason games)
18 San Francisco, 1984
Chicago, 1985
17 Miami, 1972
Pittsburgh, 1978
16 Oakland, 1976
San Francisco, 1981
Washington, 1983
Miami, 1984

Most Games Won, Season (Since 1932)
15 San Francisco, 1984
Chicago, 1985
14 Miami, 1972, 1984
Pittsburgh, 1978
Washington, 1983
13 Chi. Bears, 1934
Green Bay, 1962
Oakland, 1967, 1976
Baltimore, 1968
San Francisco, 1981
Denver, 1984

Most Consecutive Games Won, One Season (Incl. postseason games)
17 Miami, 1972
13 Chi. Bears, 1934
Oakland, 1976
12 Minnesota, 1969
San Francisco, 1984
Chicago, 1985

Most Consecutive Games Won, One Season
14 Miami, 1972
13 Chi. Bears, 1934
12 Minnesota, 1969
Chicago, 1985

Most Consecutive Games Won, Start of Season
14 Miami, 1972, entire season
13 Chi. Bears, 1934, entire season
12 Chicago, 1985

Most Consecutive Games Won, End of Season
14 Miami, 1972, entire season
13 Chi. Bears, 1934, entire season
11 Chi. Bears, 1942, entire season
Cleveland, 1951

Most Consecutive Games Without Defeat, One Season (Incl. postseason games)
17 Miami, 1972
13 Chi. Bears, 1926, 1934
Green Bay, 1929
Baltimore, 1967
Oakland, 1976
12 Canton, 1922, 1923

333

Minnesota, 1969
San Francisco, 1984
Chicago, 1985

Most Consecutive Games Without Defeat, One Season
14 Miami, 1972
13 Chi. Bears, 1926, 1934
Green Bay, 1929
Baltimore, 1967
12 Canton, 1922, 1923
Minnesota, 1969
Chicago, 1985

Most Consecutive Games Without Defeat, Start of Season
14 Miami, 1972, entire season
13 Chi. Bears, 1926, 1934, entire seasons
Green Bay, 1929, entire season
Baltimore, 1967
12 Canton, 1922, 1923, entire seasons
Chicago, 1985

Most Consecutive Games Without Defeat, End of Season
14 Miami, 1972, entire season
13 Green Bay, 1929, entire season
Chi. Bears, 1934, entire season
12 Canton, 1922, 1923, entire seasons

Most Consecutive Home Games Won
27 Miami, 1971-74
20 Green Bay, 1929-32
18 Oakland, 1968-70
Dallas, 1979-81

Most Consecutive Home Games Without Defeat
30 Green Bay, 1928-33 (won 27, tied 3)
27 Miami, 1971-74 (won 27)
18 Chi. Bears, 1932-35 (won 17, tied 1); 1941-44 (won 17, tied 1)
Oakland, 1968-70 (won 18)
Dallas, 1979-81 (won 18)

Most Consecutive Road Games Won
11 L.A. Chargers/San Diego, 1960-61
10 Chi. Bears, 1941-42
Dallas, 1968-69
9 Chi. Bears, 1933-34
Kansas City, 1966-67
Oakland, 1967-68, 1974-75, 1976-77
Pittsburgh, 1974-75
Washington, 1981-83
San Francisco, 1983-84

Most Consecutive Road Games Without Defeat
13 Chi. Bears, 1941-43 (won 12, tied 1)
12 Green Bay, 1928-30 (won 10, tied 2)
11 L.A. Chargers/San Diego, 1960-61 (won 11)
Los Angeles, 1966-68 (won 10, tied 1)

Most Shutout Games Won or Tied, Season (Since 1932)
7 Chi. Bears, 1932 (won 4, tied 3)
Green Bay, 1932 (won 6, tied 1)
Detroit, 1934 (won 7)
5 Chi. Cardinals, 1934 (won 5)
N.Y. Giants, 1944 (won 5)
Pittsburgh, 1976 (won 5)
4 By many teams

Most Consecutive Shutout Games Won or Tied (Since 1932)
7 Detroit, 1934 (won 7)
3 Chi. Bears, 1932 (tied 3)
Green Bay, 1932 (won 3)
New York, 1935 (won 3)
St. Louis, 1970 (won 3)
Pittsburgh, 1976 (won 3)
2 By many teams

GAMES LOST

Most Consecutive Games Lost
26 Tampa Bay, 1976-77
19 Chi. Cardinals, 1942-43, 1945
Oakland, 1961-62
18 Houston, 1972-73

Most Consecutive Games Without Victory
26 Tampa Bay, 1976-77 (lost 26)
23 Washington, 1960-61 (lost 20, tied 3)

Most Games Lost, Season (Since 1932)
15 New Orleans, 1980
14 Tampa Bay, 1976, 1983, 1985
San Francisco, 1978, 1979
Detroit, 1979
Baltimore, 1981
New England, 1981
Houston, 1983
Buffalo, 1984, 1985
13 Oakland, 1962
Chicago, 1969
Pittsburgh, 1969
Buffalo, 1971
Houston, 1972, 1973, 1984
Minnesota, 1984

Most Consecutive Games Lost, One Season
14 Tampa Bay, 1976
New Orleans, 1980
Baltimore, 1981
13 Oakland, 1962
12 Tampa Bay, 1977

Most Consecutive Games Lost, Start of Season
14 Tampa Bay, 1976, entire season
New Orleans, 1980
13 Oakland, 1962
12 Tampa Bay, 1977

Most Consecutive Games Lost, End of Season
14 Tampa Bay, 1976, entire season

---

13 Pittsburgh, 1969
11 Philadelphia, 1936
Detroit, 1942, entire season
Houston, 1972

Most Consecutive Games Without Victory, One Season
14 Tampa Bay, 1976, entire season
New Orleans, 1980
Baltimore, 1981
13 Washington, 1961
Oakland, 1962
12 Dall. Cowboys, 1960, entire season
Tampa Bay, 1977

Most Consecutive Games Without Victory, Start of Season
14 Tampa Bay, 1976, entire season
New Orleans, 1980
13 Washington, 1961
Oakland, 1962
12 Dall. Cowboys, 1960, entire season
Tampa Bay, 1977

Most Consecutive Games Without Victory, End of Season
14 Tampa Bay, 1976, entire season
13 Pittsburgh, 1969
12 Dall. Cowboys, 1960, entire season

Most Consecutive Home Games Lost
13 Houston, 1972-73
Tampa Bay, 1976-77
11 Oakland, 1961-62
Los Angeles, 1961-63
10 Pittsburgh, 1937-39, 1943-45
Washington, 1960-61
N.Y. Giants, 1973-75
New Orleans, 1979-80

Most Consecutive Home Games Without Victory
13 Houston, 1972-73 (lost 13)
Tampa Bay, 1976-77 (lost 13)
12 Philadelphia, 1936-38 (lost 11, tied 1)
11 Washington, 1960-61 (lost 10, tied 1)
Oakland, 1961-62 (lost 11)
Los Angeles, 1961-63 (lost 11)

Most Consecutive Road Games Lost
23 Houston, 1981-84
19 Tampa Bay, 1983-85 (current)
18 San Francisco, 1977-79

Most Consecutive Road Games Without Victory
23 Houston, 1981-84 (lost 23)
19 Tampa Bay, 1983-85 (lost 19; current)
18 Washington, 1959-62 (lost 15, tied 3)
New Orleans, 1971-74 (lost 17, tied 1)
San Francisco, 1977-79 (lost 18)

Most Shutout Games Lost or Tied, Season (Since 1932)
6 Cincinnati, 1934 (lost 6)
Pittsburgh, 1934 (lost 6)
Philadelphia, 1936 (lost 6)
Tampa Bay, 1977 (lost 6)
5 Boston, 1932 (lost 4, tied 1), 1933 (lost 4, tied 1)
N.Y. Giants, 1932 (lost 4, tied 1)
Cincinnati, 1933 (lost 4, tied 1)
Brooklyn, 1934 (lost 5), 1942 (lost 5)
Detroit, 1942 (lost 5)
Tampa Bay, 1976 (lost 5)
4 By many teams

Most Consecutive Shutout Games Lost or Tied (Since 1932)
6 Brooklyn, 1942-43 (lost 6)
4 Chi. Bears, 1932 (lost 1, tied 3)
Philadelphia, 1936 (lost 4)
3 Chi. Cardinals, 1934 (lost 3), 1938 (lost 3)
Brooklyn, 1935 (lost 3), 1937 (lost 3)
Oakland, 1981 (lost 3)

TIE GAMES

Most Tie Games, Season
6 Chi. Bears, 1932
5 Frankford, 1929
4 Chi. Bears, 1924
Orange, 1929
Portsmouth, 1929

Most Consecutive Tie Games
3 Chi. Bears, 1932
2 By many teams

SCORING

Most Seasons Leading League
9 Chi. Bears, 1934-35, 1939, 1941-43, 1946-47, 1956
6 Green Bay, 1932, 1936-38, 1961-62
L.A. Rams, 1950-52, 1957, 1967, 1973
5 Oakland, 1967-69, 1974, 1977
Dall. Cowboys, 1966, 1968, 1971, 1978, 1980
San Diego, 1963, 1965, 1981-82, 1985

Most Consecutive Seasons Leading League
3 Green Bay, 1936-38
Chi. Bears, 1941-43
Los Angeles, 1950-52
Oakland, 1967-69

POINTS
Most Points, Season
541 Washington, 1983
513 Houston, 1961
Miami, 1984
479 Dallas, 1983

Fewest Points, Season (Since 1932)
37 Cincinnati/St. Louis, 1934

38 Cincinnati, 1933
   Detroit, 1942
51 Pittsburgh, 1934
   Philadelphia, 1936

Most Points, Game
72 Washington vs. N.Y. Giants, Nov. 27, 1966
70 Los Angeles vs. Baltimore, Oct. 22, 1950
65 Chi. Cardinals vs. N.Y. Bulldogs, Nov. 13, 1949
   Los Angeles vs. Detroit, Oct. 29, 1950

Most Points, Both Teams, Game
113 Washington (72) vs. N.Y. Giants (41), Nov. 27, 1966
101 Oakland (52) vs. Houston (49), Dec. 22, 1963
99 Seattle (51) vs. Kansas City (48), Nov. 27, 1983 (OT)

Fewest Points, Both Teams, Game
0 In many games. Last time: N.Y. Giants vs. Detroit, Nov. 7, 1943

Most Points, Shutout Victory, Game
64 Philadelphia vs. Cincinnati, Nov. 6, 1934
59 Los Angeles vs. Atlanta, Dec. 4, 1976
57 Chicago vs. Baltimore, Nov. 25, 1962

Fewest Points, Shutout Victory, Game
2 Green Bay vs. Chi. Bears, Oct. 16, 1932
   Chi. Bears vs. Green Bay, Sept. 18, 1938

Most Points Overcome to Win Game
28 San Francisco vs. New Orleans, Dec. 7, 1980 (OT) (trailed 7-35, won 38-35)
24 Philadelphia vs. Washington, Oct. 27, 1946 (trailed 0-24, won 28-24)
   Detroit vs. Baltimore, Oct. 20, 1957 (trailed 3-27, won 31-27)
   Philadelphia vs. Chi. Cardinals, Oct. 25, 1959 (trailed 0-24, won 28-24)
   Denver vs. Boston, Oct. 23, 1960 (trailed 0-24, won 31-24)
   Miami vs. New England, Dec. 15, 1974 (trailed 0-24, won 34-27)
   Minnesota vs. San Francisco, Dec. 4, 1977 (trailed 0-24, won 28-27)
   Denver vs. Seattle, Sept. 23, 1979 (trailed 10-34, won 37-34)
   Houston vs. Cincinnati, Sept. 23, 1979 (OT) (trailed 0-24, won 30-27)
   L.A. Raiders vs. San Diego, Nov. 22, 1982 (trailed 0-24, won 28-24)

Most Points Overcome to Tie Game
31 Denver vs. Buffalo, Nov. 27, 1960 (trailed 7-38, tied 38-38)
28 Los Angeles vs. Philadelphia, Oct. 3, 1948 (trailed 0-28, tied 28-28)

Most Points, Each Half
1st: 49 Green Bay vs. Tampa Bay, Oct. 2, 1983
     45 Green Bay vs. Cleveland, Nov. 12, 1967
2nd: 49 Chi. Bears vs. Philadelphia, Nov. 30, 1941
     48 Chi. Cardinals vs. Baltimore, Oct. 2, 1950
        N.Y. Giants vs. Baltimore, Nov. 19, 1950

Most Points, Both Teams, Each Half
1st: 70 Houston (35) vs. Oakland (35), Dec. 22, 1963
2nd: 65 Washington (38) vs. N.Y. Giants (27), Nov. 27, 1966

Most Points, One Quarter
41 Green Bay vs. Detroit, Oct. 7, 1945 (second quarter)
   Los Angeles vs. Detroit, Oct. 29, 1950 (third quarter)
37 Los Angeles vs. Green Bay, Sept. 21, 1980 (second quarter)
35 Chi. Cardinals vs. Boston, Oct. 24, 1948 (third quarter)
   Green Bay vs. Cleveland, Nov. 12, 1967 (first quarter); vs. Tampa Bay, Oct. 2, 1983 (second quarter)

Most Points, Both Teams, One Quarter
49 Oakland (28) vs. Houston (21), Dec. 22, 1963 (second quarter)
48 Green Bay (41) vs. Detroit (7), Oct. 7, 1945 (second quarter)
   Los Angeles (41) vs. Detroit (7), Oct. 29, 1950 (third quarter)
47 St. Louis (27) vs. Philadelphia (20), Dec. 13, 1964 (second quarter)

Most Points, Each Quarter
1st: 35 Green Bay vs. Cleveland, Nov. 12, 1967
2nd: 41 Green Bay vs. Detroit, Oct. 7, 1945
3rd: 41 Los Angeles vs. Detroit, Oct. 29, 1950
4th: 31 Oakland vs. Denver, Dec. 17, 1960; vs. San Diego, Dec. 8, 1963
        Atlanta vs. Green Bay, Sept. 13, 1981

Most Points, Both Teams, Each Quarter
1st: 42 Green Bay (35) vs. Cleveland (7), Nov. 12, 1967
2nd: 49 Oakland (28) vs. Houston (21), Dec. 22, 1963
3rd: 48 Los Angeles (41) vs. Detroit (7), Oct. 29, 1950
4th: 42 Chi. Cardinals (28) vs. Philadelphia (14), Dec. 7, 1947
        Green Bay (28) vs. Chi. Bears (14), Nov. 6, 1955
        N.Y. Jets (28) vs. Boston (14), Oct. 27, 1968
        Pittsburgh (21) vs. Cleveland (21), Oct. 18, 1969

GAMES
Most Consecutive Games Scoring
274 Cleveland, 1950-71
218 Dallas, 1970-85
217 Oakland, 1966-81

TOUCHDOWNS
Most Seasons Leading League, Touchdowns
13 Chi. Bears, 1932, 1934-35, 1939, 1941-44, 1946-48, 1956, 1965
7 Dall. Cowboys, 1966, 1968, 1971, 1973, 1977-78, 1980
6 Oakland, 1967-69, 1972, 1974, 1977
   San Diego, 1963, 1965, 1979, 1981-82, 1985

Most Consecutive Seasons Leading League, Touchdowns
4 Chi. Bears, 1941-44
   Los Angeles, 1949-52
3 Chi. Bears, 1946-48
   Baltimore, 1957-59
   Oakland, 1967-69
2 By many teams

Most Touchdowns, Season
70 Miami, 1984
66 Houston, 1961
64 Los Angeles, 1950

Fewest Touchdowns, Season (Since 1932)
3 Cincinnati, 1933
4 Cincinnati/St. Louis, 1934
5 Detroit, 1942

Most Touchdowns, Game
10 Philadelphia vs. Cincinnati, Nov. 6, 1934
   Los Angeles vs. Baltimore, Oct. 22, 1950
   Washington vs. N.Y. Giants, Nov. 27, 1966

9 Chi. Cardinals vs. Rochester, Oct. 7, 1923; vs. N.Y. Giants, Oct. 17, 1948; vs. N.Y. Bulldogs, Nov. 13, 1949
   Los Angeles vs. Detroit, Oct. 29, 1950
   Pittsburgh vs. N.Y. Giants, Nov. 30, 1952
   Chicago vs. San Francisco, Dec. 12, 1965; vs. Green Bay, Dec. 7, 1980
8 By many teams

Most Touchdowns, Both Teams, Game
16 Washington (10) vs. N.Y. Giants (6), Nov. 27, 1966
14 Chi. Cardinals (9) vs. N.Y. Giants (5), Oct. 17, 1948
   Los Angeles (10) vs. Baltimore (4), Oct. 22, 1950
   Houston (7) vs. Oakland (7), Dec. 22, 1963
13 New Orleans (7) vs. St. Louis (6), Nov. 2, 1969
   Kansas City (7) vs. Seattle (6), Nov. 27, 1983 (OT)
   San Diego (8) vs. Pittsburgh (5), Dec. 8, 1985

Most Consecutive Games Scoring Touchdowns
166 Cleveland, 1957-69
97 Oakland, 1966-73
96 Kansas City, 1963-70

POINTS AFTER TOUCHDOWN
Most Points After Touchdown, Season
66 Miami, 1984
65 Houston, 1961
62 Washington, 1983

Fewest Points After Touchdown, Season
2 Chi. Cardinals, 1933
3 Cincinnati, 1933
   Pittsburgh, 1934
4 Cincinnati/St. Louis, 1934

Most Points After Touchdown, Game
10 Los Angeles vs. Baltimore, Oct. 22, 1950
9 Chi. Cardinals vs. N.Y. Giants, Oct. 17, 1948
   Pittsburgh vs. N.Y. Giants, Nov. 30, 1952
   Washington vs. N.Y. Giants, Nov. 27, 1966
8 By many teams

Most Points After Touchdown, Both Teams, Game
14 Chi. Cardinals (9) vs. N.Y. Giants (5), Oct. 17, 1948
   Houston (7) vs. Oakland (7), Dec. 22, 1963
   Washington (9) vs. N.Y. Giants (5), Nov. 27, 1966
13 Los Angeles (10) vs. Baltimore (3), Oct. 22, 1950
12 In many games

FIELD GOALS
Most Seasons Leading League, Field Goals
11 Green Bay, 1935-36, 1940-43, 1946-47, 1955, 1972, 1974
7 Washington, 1945, 1956, 1971, 1976-77, 1979, 1982
   N.Y. Giants, 1933, 1937, 1939, 1941, 1944, 1959, 1983
5 Portsmouth/Detroit, 1932-33, 1937-38, 1980

Most Consecutive Seasons Leading League, Field Goals
4 Green Bay, 1940-43
3 Cleveland, 1952-54
2 By many teams

Most Field Goals Attempted, Season
49 Los Angeles, 1966
   Washington, 1971
48 Green Bay, 1972
47 N.Y. Jets, 1969
   Los Angeles, 1973
   Washington, 1983

Fewest Field Goals Attempted, Season (Since 1938)
0 Chi. Bears, 1944
2 Cleveland, 1939
   Card-Pitt, 1944
   Boston, 1946
   Chi. Bears, 1947
3 Chi. Bears, 1945
   Cleveland, 1945

Most Field Goals Attempted, Game
9 St. Louis vs. Pittsburgh, Sept. 24, 1967
8 Pittsburgh vs. St. Louis, Dec. 2, 1962
   Detroit vs. Minnesota, Nov. 13, 1966
   N.Y. Jets vs. Buffalo, Nov. 3, 1968
7 By many teams

Most Field Goals Attempted, Both Teams, Game
11 St. Louis (6) vs. Pittsburgh (5), Nov. 13, 1966
   Washington (6) vs. Chicago (5), Nov. 14, 1971
   Green Bay (6) vs. Detroit (5), Sept. 29, 1974
   Washington (6) vs. N.Y. Giants (5), Nov. 14, 1976
10 Denver (5) vs. Boston (5), Nov. 11, 1962
   Boston (7) vs. San Diego (3), Sept. 20, 1964
   Buffalo (7) vs. Houston (3), Dec. 5, 1965
   St. Louis (7) vs. Atlanta (3), Dec. 11, 1966
   Boston (7) vs. Buffalo (3), Sept. 24, 1967
   Detroit (7) vs. Minnesota (3), Sept. 20, 1971
   Washington (7) vs. Houston (3), Oct. 10, 1971
   Green Bay (5) vs. St. Louis (5), Dec. 5, 1971
   Kansas City (7) vs. Buffalo (3), Dec. 19, 1971
   Kansas City (5) vs. San Diego (5), Oct. 29, 1972
   Minnesota (6) vs. Chicago (4), Sept. 23, 1973
   Cleveland (7) vs. Denver (3), Oct. 19, 1975
   Cleveland (5) vs. Denver (5), Oct. 5, 1980
9 In many games

Most Field Goals, Season
35 N.Y. Giants, 1983
34 N.Y. Jets, 1968
33 Green Bay, 1972
   Washington, 1983
   Pittsburgh, 1985

Fewest Field Goals, Season (Since 1932)
0 Boston, 1932, 1935
   Chi. Cardinals, 1932, 1945
   Green Bay, 1932, 1944
   New York, 1932

335

Brooklyn, 1944
Card-Pitt, 1944
Chi. Bears, 1944, 1947
Boston, 1946
Baltimore, 1950
Dallas, 1952

Most Field Goals, Game
- 7 St. Louis vs. Pittsburgh, Sept. 24, 1967
- 6 Boston vs. Denver, Oct. 4, 1964
  Detroit vs. Minnesota, Nov. 13, 1966
  N.Y. Jets vs. Buffalo, Nov. 3, 1968; vs. New Orleans, Dec. 3, 1972
  Philadelphia vs. Houston, Nov. 12, 1972
  St. Louis vs. Atlanta, Dec. 9, 1973
  N.Y. Giants vs. Seattle, Oct. 18, 1981
  San Francisco vs. New Orleans, Oct. 16, 1983
- 5 By many teams

Most Field Goals, Both Teams, Game
- 8 Cleveland (4) vs. St. Louis (4), Sept. 20, 1964
  Chicago (5) vs. Philadelphia (3), Oct. 20, 1968
  Washington (5) vs. Chicago (3), Nov. 14, 1971
  Kansas City (5) vs. Buffalo (3), Dec. 19, 1971
  Detroit (4) vs. Green Bay (4), Sept. 29, 1974
  Cleveland (5) vs. Denver (3), Oct. 19, 1975
  New England (4) vs. San Diego (4), Nov. 9, 1975
  San Francisco (6) vs. New Orleans (2), Oct. 16, 1983
- 7 In many games

Most Consecutive Games Scoring Field Goals
- 31 Minnesota, 1968-70
- 21 San Francisco, 1970-72
- 20 Los Angeles, 1970-71
  Miami, 1970-72

SAFETIES
Most Safeties, Season
- 4 Detroit, 1962
- 3 Green Bay, 1932, 1975
  Pittsburgh, 1947
  N.Y. Yanks, 1950
  Detroit, 1960
  St. Louis, 1960
  Buffalo, 1964
  Minnesota, 1965, 1981
  Cleveland, 1970
  L.A. Rams, 1973, 1984
  Houston, 1977
  Dallas, 1981
  Oakland, 1981
  Chicago, 1985
- 2 By many teams

Most Safeties, Game
- 3 L.A. Rams vs. N.Y. Giants, Sept. 30, 1984
- 2 Cincinnati vs. Chi. Cardinals, Nov. 19, 1933
  Detroit vs. Brooklyn, Dec. 1, 1935
  N.Y. Giants vs. Pittsburgh, Sept. 17, 1950; vs. Washington, Nov. 5, 1961
  Chicago vs. Pittsburgh, Nov. 9, 1969
  Dallas vs. Philadelphia, Nov. 19, 1972
  Los Angeles vs. Green Bay, Oct. 21, 1973
  Oakland vs. San Diego, Oct. 26, 1975
  Denver vs. Seattle, Jan. 2, 1983

Most Safeties, Both Teams, Game
- 3 L.A. Rams (3) vs. N.Y. Giants (0), Sept. 30, 1984
- 2 Chi. Bears (1) vs. San Francisco (1), Oct. 19, 1952
  Cincinnati (1) vs. Los Angeles (1), Oct. 22, 1972
  Atlanta (1) vs. Detroit (1), Oct. 5, 1980
  (Also see previous record)

FIRST DOWNS

Most Seasons Leading League
- 9 Chi. Bears, 1935, 1939, 1941, 1943, 1945, 1947-49, 1955
- 7 San Diego, 1965, 1969, 1980-83, 1985
- 6 L.A. Rams, 1946, 1950-51, 1954, 1957, 1973

Most Consecutive Seasons Leading League
- 4 San Diego, 1980-83
- 3 Chi. Bears, 1947-49
- 2 By many teams

Most First Downs, Season
- 387 Miami, 1984
- 380 San Diego, 1985
- 379 San Diego, 1981

Fewest First Downs, Season
- 51 Cincinnati, 1933
- 64 Pittsburgh, 1935
- 67 Philadelphia, 1937

Most First Downs, Game
- 38 Los Angeles vs. N.Y. Giants, Nov. 13, 1966
- 37 Green Bay vs. Philadelphia, Nov. 11, 1962
- 36 Pittsburgh vs. Cleveland, Nov. 25, 1979 (OT)

Fewest First Downs, Game
- 0 N.Y. Giants vs. Green Bay, Oct. 1, 1933; vs. Washington, Sept. 27, 1942
  Pittsburgh vs. Boston, Oct. 29, 1933
  Philadelphia vs. Detroit, Sept. 20, 1935
  Denver vs. Houston, Sept. 3, 1966

Most First Downs, Both Teams, Game
- 62 San Diego (32) vs. Seattle (30), Sept. 15, 1985
- 59 Miami (31) vs. Buffalo (28), Oct. 9, 1983 (OT)
  Seattle (33) vs. Kansas City (26), Nov. 27, 1983 (OT)
- 58 Los Angeles (30) vs. Chi. Bears (28), Oct. 24, 1954
  Denver (34) vs. Kansas City (24), Nov. 18, 1974
  Atlanta (35) vs. New Orleans (23), Sept. 2, 1979 (OT)
  Pittsburgh (36) vs. Cleveland (22), Nov. 25, 1979 (OT)
  San Diego (34) vs. Miami (24), Nov. 18, 1984 (OT)
  Cincinnati (32) vs. San Diego (26), Sept. 22, 1985

Fewest First Downs, Both Teams, Game
- 5 N.Y. Giants (0) vs. Green Bay (5), Oct. 1, 1933

Most First Downs, Rushing, Season
- 181 New England, 1978
- 177 Los Angeles, 1973
- 176 Chicago, 1985

Fewest First Downs, Rushing, Season
- 36 Cleveland, 1942
  Boston, 1944
- 39 Brooklyn, 1943
- 40 Philadelphia, 1940
  Detroit, 1945

Most First Downs, Rushing, Game
- 25 Philadelphia vs. Washington, Dec. 2, 1951
- 21 Cleveland vs. Philadelphia, Dec. 13, 1959
  Los Angeles vs. New Orleans, Nov. 25, 1973
  Pittsburgh vs. Kansas City, Nov. 7, 1976
  New England vs. Denver, Nov. 28, 1976
  Oakland vs. Green Bay, Sept. 17, 1978
- 20 By eight teams

Fewest First Downs, Rushing, Game
- 0 By many teams

Most First Downs, Passing, Season
- 259 San Diego, 1985
- 244 San Diego, 1980
- 243 Miami, 1984

Fewest First Downs, Passing, Season
- 18 Pittsburgh, 1941
- 23 Brooklyn, 1942
  N.Y. Giants, 1944
- 24 N.Y. Giants, 1943

Most First Downs, Passing, Game
- 29 N.Y. Giants vs. Cincinnati, Oct. 13, 1985
- 27 San Diego vs. Seattle, Sept. 15, 1985
- 25 Denver vs. Kansas City, Nov. 18, 1974
  N.Y. Jets vs. San Francisco, Sept. 21, 1980

Fewest First Downs, Passing, Game
- 0 By many teams

Most First Downs, Penalty, Season
- 39 Seattle, 1978
- 38 Buffalo, 1983
  Denver, 1983
- 37 Cleveland, 1981

Fewest First Downs, Penalty, Season
- 2 Brooklyn, 1940
- 4 Chi. Cardinals, 1940
  N.Y. Giants, 1942, 1944
  Washington, 1944
  Cleveland, 1952
  Kansas City, 1969
- 5 Brooklyn, 1939
  Chi. Bears, 1939
  Detroit, 1953
  Los Angeles, 1953
  Houston, 1982

Most First Downs, Penalty, Game
- 11 Denver vs. Houston, Oct. 6, 1985
- 9 Chi. Bears vs. Cleveland, Nov. 25, 1951
  Baltimore vs. Pittsburgh, Oct. 30, 1977
- 8 Philadelphia vs. Detroit, Dec. 2, 1979
  Cincinnati vs. N.Y. Jets, Oct. 6, 1985

Fewest First Downs, Penalty, Game
- 0 By many teams

NET YARDS GAINED RUSHING AND PASSING

Most Seasons Leading League
- 12 Chi. Bears, 1932, 1934-35, 1939, 1941-44, 1947, 1949, 1955-56
- 7 San Diego, 1963, 1965, 1980-83, 1985
- 6 L.A. Rams, 1946, 1950-51, 1954, 1957, 1973
  Baltimore, 1958-60, 1964, 1967, 1976
  Dall. Cowboys, 1966, 1968-69, 1971, 1974, 1977

Most Consecutive Seasons Leading League
- 4 Chi. Bears, 1941-44
  San Diego, 1980-83
- 3 Baltimore, 1958-60
  Houston, 1960-62
  Oakland, 1968-70
- 2 By many teams

Most Yards Gained, Season
- 6,936 Miami, 1984
- 6,744 San Diego, 1981
- 6,535 San Diego, 1985

Fewest Yards Gained, Season
- 1,150 Cincinnati, 1933
- 1,443 Chi. Cardinals, 1934
- 1,486 Chi. Cardinals, 1933

Most Yards Gained, Game
- 735 Los Angeles vs. N.Y. Yanks, Sept. 28, 1951
- 683 Pittsburgh vs. Chi. Cardinals, Dec. 13, 1958
- 682 Chi. Bears vs. N.Y. Giants, Nov. 14, 1943

Fewest Yards Gained, Game
- -7 Seattle vs. Los Angeles, Nov. 4, 1979
- -5 Denver vs. Oakland, Sept. 10, 1967
- 14 Chi. Cardinals vs. Detroit, Sept. 15, 1940

Most Yards Gained, Both Teams, Game
- 1,133 Los Angeles (636) vs. N.Y. Yanks (497), Nov. 19, 1950
- 1,102 San Diego (661) vs. Cincinnati (441), Dec. 20, 1982
- 1,087 St. Louis (589) vs. Philadelphia (498), Dec. 16, 1962

Fewest Yards Gained, Both Teams, Game
- 30 Chi. Cardinals (14) vs. Detroit (16), Sept. 15, 1940

Most Consecutive Games, 400 or More Yards Gained
- 11 San Diego, 1982-83
- 6 Houston, 1961-62

San Diego, 1981
    5   Chi. Bears, 1947, 1955
        Los Angeles, 1950
        Philadelphia, 1953
        Oakland, 1968
        New England, 1981
Most Consecutive Games, 300 or More Yards Gained
    29   Los Angeles, 1949-51
    26   Miami, 1983-85
    20   Chi. Bears, 1948-50

RUSHING

Most Seasons Leading League
    15   Chi. Bears, 1932, 1934-35, 1939-42, 1951, 1955-56, 1968, 1977, 1983-85
    6   Cleveland, 1958-59, 1963, 1965-67
    5   Buffalo, 1962, 1964, 1973, 1975, 1982
Most Consecutive Seasons Leading League
    4   Chi. Bears, 1939-42
    3   Detroit, 1936-38
         San Francisco, 1952-54
         Cleveland, 1965-67
         Chicago, 1983-85
    2   By many teams
Most Rushing Attempts, Season
    681 Oakland, 1977
    674 Chicago, 1984
    671 New England, 1978
Fewest Rushing Attempts, Season
    211 Philadelphia, 1982
    219 San Francisco, 1982
    225 Houston, 1982
Most Rushing Attempts, Game
    72   Chi. Bears vs. Brooklyn, Oct. 20, 1935
    70   Chi. Cardinals vs. Green Bay, Dec. 5, 1948
    69   Chi. Cardinals vs. Green Bay, Dec. 6, 1936
         Kansas City vs. Cincinnati, Sept. 3, 1978
Fewest Rushing Attempts, Game
    6   Chi. Cardinals vs. Boston, Oct. 29, 1933
    7   Oakland vs. Buffalo, Oct. 15, 1963
         Houston vs. N.Y. Giants, Dec. 8, 1985
    8   Denver vs. Oakland, Dec. 17, 1960
         Buffalo vs. St. Louis, Sept. 9, 1984
Most Rushing Attempts, Both Teams, Game
    108 Chi. Cardinals (70) vs. Green Bay (38), Dec. 5, 1948
    105 Oakland (62) vs. Atlanta (43), Nov. 30, 1975 (OT)
    103 Kansas City (53) vs. San Diego (50), Nov. 12, 1978 (OT)
Fewest Rushing Attempts, Both Teams, Game
    36   Cincinnati (16) vs. Chi. Bears (20), Sept. 30, 1934
    37   Atlanta (18) vs. San Francisco (19), Oct. 6, 1985
    38   N.Y. Jets (13) vs. Buffalo (25), Nov. 8, 1964

YARDS GAINED
Most Yards Gained Rushing, Season
    3,165   New England, 1978
    3,088   Buffalo, 1973
    2,986   Kansas City, 1978
Fewest Yards Gained Rushing, Season
    298   Philadelphia, 1940
    467   Detroit, 1946
    471   Boston, 1944
Most Yards Gained Rushing, Game
    426   Detroit vs. Pittsburgh, Nov. 4, 1934
    423   N.Y. Giants vs. Baltimore, Nov. 19, 1950
    420   Boston vs. N.Y. Giants, Oct. 8, 1933
Fewest Yards Gained Rushing, Game
    −53   Detroit vs. Chi. Cardinals, Oct. 17, 1943
    −36   Philadelphia vs. Chi. Bears, Nov. 19, 1939
    −33   Phil-Pitt vs. Brooklyn, Oct. 2, 1943
Most Yards Gained Rushing, Both Teams, Game
    595   Los Angeles (371) vs. N.Y. Yanks (224), Nov. 18, 1951
    574   Chi. Bears (396) vs. Pittsburgh (178), Oct. 10, 1934
    557   Chi. Bears (406) vs. Green Bay (151), Nov. 6, 1955
Fewest Yards Gained Rushing, Both Teams, Game
    −15   Detroit (−53) vs. Chi. Cardinals (38), Oct. 17, 1943
    4   Detroit (−10) vs. Chi. Cardinals (14), Sept. 15, 1940
    63   Chi. Cardinals (−1) vs. N.Y. Giants (64), Oct. 18, 1953

AVERAGE GAIN
Highest Average Gain, Rushing, Season
    5.74   Cleveland, 1963
    5.65   San Francisco, 1954
    5.56   San Diego, 1963
Lowest Average Gain, Rushing, Season
    0.94   Philadelphia, 1940
    1.45   Boston, 1944
    1.55   Pittsburgh, 1935

TOUCHDOWNS
Most Touchdowns, Rushing, Season
    36   Green Bay, 1962
    33   Pittsburgh, 1976
    30   Chi. Bears, 1941
         New England, 1978
         Washington, 1983
Fewest Touchdowns, Rushing, Season
    1   Brooklyn, 1934
    2   Chi. Cardinals, 1933
         Cincinnati, 1933
         Pittsburgh, 1934, 1940
         Philadelphia, 1935, 1936, 1937, 1938, 1972
    3   By many teams
Most Touchdowns, Rushing, Game
    7   Los Angeles vs. Atlanta, Dec. 4, 1976

    6   By many teams
Most Touchdowns, Rushing, Both Teams, Game
    8   Los Angeles (6) vs. N.Y. Yanks (2), Nov. 18, 1951
         Cleveland (6) vs. Los Angeles (2), Nov. 24, 1957
    7   In many games

PASSING

ATTEMPTS
Most Passes Attempted, Season
    709 Minnesota, 1981
    662 San Diego, 1984
    641 Kansas City, 1983
Fewest Passes Attempted, Season
    102 Cincinnati, 1933
    106 Boston, 1933
    120 Detroit, 1937
Most Passes Attempted, Game
    68   Houston vs. Buffalo, Nov. 1, 1964
    63   Minnesota vs. Tampa Bay, Sept. 5, 1981
    62   N.Y. Jets vs. Denver, Dec. 3, 1967; vs. Baltimore, Oct. 18, 1970
         Dallas vs. Detroit, Sept. 15, 1985
         N.Y. Giants vs. Cincinnati, Oct. 13, 1985
Fewest Passes Attempted, Game
    0   Green Bay vs. Portsmouth, Oct. 8, 1933; vs. Chi. Bears, Sept. 25, 1949
         Detroit vs. Cleveland, Sept. 10, 1937
         Pittsburgh vs. Brooklyn, Nov. 16, 1941; vs. Los Angeles, Nov. 13, 1949
         Cleveland vs. Philadelphia, Dec. 3, 1950
Most Passes Attempted, Both Teams, Game
    102 San Francisco (57) vs. Atlanta (45), Oct. 6, 1985
    100 Tampa Bay (54) vs. Kansas City (46), Oct. 28, 1984
    98   Minnesota (56) vs. Baltimore (42), Sept. 28, 1969
Fewest Passes Attempted, Both Teams, Game
    4   Chi. Cardinals (1) vs. Detroit (3), Nov. 3, 1935
         Detroit (0) vs. Cleveland (4), Sept. 10, 1937
    6   Chi. Cardinals (2) vs. Detroit (4), Sept. 15, 1940
    8   Brooklyn (2) vs. Philadelphia (6), Oct. 1, 1939

COMPLETIONS
Most Passes Completed, Season
    401 San Diego, 1984
    386 San Diego, 1985
    382 Minnesota, 1981
Fewest Passes Completed, Season
    25   Cincinnati, 1933
    33   Boston, 1933
    34   Chi. Cardinals, 1934
         Detroit, 1934
Most Passes Completed, Game
    42   N.Y. Jets vs. San Francisco, Sept. 21, 1980
    40   Cincinnati vs. San Diego, Dec. 20, 1982
         Dallas vs. Detroit, Sept. 15, 1985
         N.Y. Giants vs. Cincinnati, Oct. 13, 1985
    38   Minnesota vs. Cleveland, Dec. 14, 1980; vs. Green Bay, Nov. 29, 1981
         Buffalo vs. Miami, Oct. 9, 1983 (OT)
Fewest Passes Completed, Game
    0   By many teams. Last time: Buffalo vs. N.Y. Jets, Sept. 29, 1974
Most Passes Completed, Both Teams, Game
    68   San Francisco (37) vs. Atlanta (31), Oct. 6, 1985
    66   Cincinnati (40) vs. San Diego (26), Dec. 20, 1982
    65   San Diego (33) vs. San Francisco (32), Dec. 11, 1982
         San Diego (37) vs. Miami (28), Nov. 18, 1984 (OT)
Fewest Passes Completed, Both Teams, Game
    1   Chi. Cardinals (0) vs. Philadelphia (1), Nov. 8, 1936
         Detroit (0) vs. Cleveland (1), Sept. 10, 1937
         Chi. Cardinals (0) vs. Detroit (1), Sept. 15, 1940
         Brooklyn (0) vs. Pittsburgh (1), Nov. 29, 1942
    2   Chi. Cardinals (0) vs. Detroit (2), Nov. 3, 1935
         Buffalo (0) vs. N.Y. Jets (2), Sept. 29, 1974
    3   Brooklyn (1) vs. Philadelphia (2), Oct. 1, 1939

YARDS GAINED
Most Seasons Leading League, Passing Yardage
    10   San Diego, 1965, 1968, 1971, 1978-83, 1985
    8   Chi. Bears, 1932, 1939, 1941, 1943, 1945, 1949, 1954, 1964
    7   Washington, 1938, 1940, 1944, 1947-48, 1967, 1974
Most Consecutive Seasons Leading League, Passing Yardage
    6   San Diego, 1978-83
    4   Green Bay, 1934-37
    2   By many teams
Most Yards Gained, Passing, Season
    5,018   Miami, 1984
    4,870   San Diego, 1985
    4,739   San Diego, 1981
Fewest Yards Gained, Passing, Season
    302   Chi. Cardinals, 1934
    357   Cincinnati, 1933
    459   Boston, 1934
Most Yards Gained, Passing, Game
    554   Los Angeles vs. N.Y. Yanks, Sept. 28, 1951
    530   Minnesota vs. Baltimore, Sept. 28, 1969
    506   L.A. Rams vs. Chicago, Dec. 26, 1982
Fewest Yards Gained, Passing, Game
    −53   Denver vs. Oakland, Sept. 10, 1967
    −52   Cincinnati vs. Houston, Oct. 31, 1971
    −39   Atlanta vs. San Francisco, Oct. 23, 1976
Most Yards Gained, Passing, Both Teams, Game
    883   San Diego (486) vs. Cincinnati (397), Dec. 20, 1982
    834   Philadelphia (419) vs. St. Louis (415), Dec. 16, 1962
    822   N.Y. Jets (490) vs. Baltimore (332), Sept. 24, 1972
Fewest Yards Gained, Passing, Both Teams, Game
    −11   Green Bay (−10) vs. Dallas (−1), Oct. 24, 1965
    1   Chi. Cardinals (0) vs. Philadelphia (1), Nov. 8, 1936
    7   Brooklyn (0) vs. Pittsburgh (7), Nov. 29, 1942

TIMES SACKED
Most Seasons Leading League, Fewest Times Sacked
- 5 Miami, 1973, 1982-85
- 4 San Diego, 1963-64, 1967-68
   San Francisco, 1964-65, 1970-71
- 3 N.Y. Jets, 1965-66, 1968
   Houston, 1961-62, 1978
   St. Louis, 1974-76

Most Consecutive Seasons Leading League, Fewest Times Sacked
- 4 Miami, 1982-85
- 3 St. Louis, 1974-76
- 2 By many teams

Most Times Sacked, Season
- 70 Atlanta, 1968
- 69 Atlanta, 1985
- 68 Dallas, 1964

Fewest Times Sacked, Season
- 8 San Francisco, 1970
   St. Louis, 1975
- 9 N.Y. Jets, 1966
- 10 N.Y. Giants, 1972

Most Times Sacked, Game
- 12 Pittsburgh vs. Dallas, Nov. 20, 1966
   Baltimore vs. St. Louis, Oct. 26, 1980
   Detroit vs. Chicago, Dec. 16, 1984
   Houston vs. Dallas, Sept. 29, 1985
- 11 St. Louis vs. N.Y. Giants, Nov. 1, 1964
   Los Angeles vs. Baltimore, Nov. 22, 1964
   Denver vs. Buffalo, Dec. 13, 1964; vs. Oakland, Nov. 5, 1967
   Green Bay vs. Detroit, Nov. 7, 1965
   Buffalo vs. Oakland, Oct. 15, 1967
   Atlanta vs. St. Louis, Nov. 24, 1968; vs. Cleveland, Nov. 18, 1984
   Detroit vs. Dallas, Oct. 6, 1975
   Philadelphia vs. St. Louis, Dec. 18, 1983
   Cleveland vs. Kansas City, Sept. 30, 1984
   Minnesota vs. Chicago, Oct. 28, 1984
- 10 By many teams

Most Times Sacked, Both Teams, Game
- 18 Green Bay (10) vs. San Diego (8), Sept. 24, 1978
- 17 Buffalo (10) vs. N.Y. Titans (7), Nov. 23, 1961
   Pittsburgh (12) vs. Dallas (5), Nov. 20, 1966
   Atlanta (9) vs. Philadelphia (8), Dec. 16, 1984
- 16 Los Angeles (11) vs. Baltimore (5), Nov. 22, 1964
   Buffalo (11) vs. Oakland (5), Oct. 15, 1967

COMPLETION PERCENTAGE
Most Seasons Leading League, Completion Percentage
- 11 Washington, 1937, 1939-40, 1942-45, 1947-48, 1969-70
- 7 Green Bay, 1936, 1941, 1961-62, 1964, 1966, 1968
- 6 Cleveland, 1951, 1953-55, 1959-60
   Dall. Texans/Kansas City, 1962, 1964, 1966-69
   San Francisco, 1952, 1957-58, 1965, 1981, 1983

Most Consecutive Seasons Leading League, Completion Percentage
- 4 Washington, 1942-45
   Kansas City, 1966-69
- 3 Cleveland, 1953-55
- 2 By many teams

Highest Completion Percentage, Season
- 70.6 Cincinnati, 1982 (310-219)
- 64.3 Oakland, 1976 (361-232)
- 64.2 San Francisco, 1983 (528-339)

Lowest Completion Percentage, Season
- 22.9 Philadelphia, 1936 (170-39)
- 24.5 Cincinnati, 1933 (102-25)
- 25.0 Pittsburgh, 1941 (168-42)

TOUCHDOWNS
Most Touchdowns, Passing, Season
- 49 Miami, 1984
- 48 Houston, 1961
- 39 N.Y. Giants, 1963

Fewest Touchdowns, Passing, Season
- 0 Cincinnati, 1933
   Pittsburgh, 1945
- 1 Boston, 1932, 1933
   Chi. Cardinals, 1934
   Cincinnati/St. Louis, 1934
   Detroit, 1942
- 2 Chi. Cardinals, 1932, 1935
   Stapleton, 1932
   Brooklyn, 1936
   Pittsburgh, 1942

Most Touchdowns, Passing, Game
- 7 Chi. Bears vs. N.Y. Giants, Nov. 14, 1943
   Philadelphia vs. Washington, Oct. 17, 1954
   Houston vs. N.Y. Titans, Nov. 19, 1961; vs. N.Y. Titans, Oct. 14, 1962
   N.Y. Giants vs. Washington, Oct. 28, 1962
   Minnesota vs. Baltimore, Sept. 28, 1969
   San Diego vs. Oakland, Nov. 22, 1981
- 6 By many teams

Most Touchdowns, Passing, Both Teams, Game
- 12 New Orleans (6) vs. St. Louis (6), Nov. 2, 1969
- 11 N.Y. Giants (7) vs. Washington (4), Oct. 28, 1962
   Oakland (6) vs. Houston (5), Dec. 22, 1963
- 9 In many games

PASSES HAD INTERCEPTED
Most Passes Had Intercepted, Season
- 48 Houston, 1962
- 45 Denver, 1961
- 41 Card-Pitt, 1944

Fewest Passes Had Intercepted, Season
- 5 Cleveland, 1960

- 5 Green Bay, 1966
- 6 Green Bay, 1964
   St. Louis, 1982
- 7 Los Angeles, 1969

Most Passes Had Intercepted, Game
- 9 Detroit vs. Green Bay, Oct. 24, 1943
   Pittsburgh vs. Philadelphia, Dec. 12, 1965
- 8 Green Bay vs. N.Y. Giants, Nov. 21, 1948
   Chi. Cardinals vs. Philadelphia, Sept. 24, 1950
   N.Y. Yanks vs. N.Y. Giants, Dec. 16, 1951
   Denver vs. Houston, Dec. 2, 1962
   Chi. Bears vs. Detroit, Sept. 22, 1968
   Baltimore vs. N.Y. Jets, Sept. 23, 1973
- 7 By many teams. Last time: Detroit vs. Denver, Oct. 7, 1984

Most Passes Had Intercepted, Both Teams, Game
- 13 Denver (8) vs. Houston (5), Dec. 2, 1962
- 11 Philadelphia (7) vs. Boston (4), Nov. 3, 1935
   Boston (6) vs. Pittsburgh (5), Dec. 1, 1935
   Cleveland (7) vs. Green Bay (4), Oct. 30, 1938
   Green Bay (7) vs. Detroit (4), Oct. 20, 1940
   Detroit (7) vs. Chi. Bears (4), Nov. 22, 1942
   Detroit (7) vs. Cleveland (4), Nov. 26, 1944
   Chi. Cardinals (8) vs. Philadelphia (3), Sept. 24, 1950
   Washington (7) vs. N.Y. Giants (4), Dec. 8, 1963
   Pittsburgh (9) vs. Philadelphia (2), Dec. 12, 1965
- 10 In many games

PUNTING

Most Seasons Leading League (Average Distance)
- 6 Washington, 1940-43, 1945, 1958
   Denver, 1962-64, 1966-67, 1982
   Kansas City, 1968, 1971-73, 1979, 1984
- 4 L.A. Rams, 1946, 1949, 1955-56
   Baltimore/Indianapolis, 1966, 1969, 1983, 1985
- 3 Cleveland, 1950-52
   San Francisco, 1957, 1962, 1965
   Oakland, 1974, 1975, 1977
   Cincinnati, 1970, 1978, 1981

Most Consecutive Seasons Leading League (Average Distance)
- 4 Washington, 1940-43
- 3 Cleveland, 1950-52
   Denver, 1962-64
   Kansas City, 1971-73

Most Punts, Season
- 114 Chicago, 1981
- 113 Boston, 1934
   Brooklyn, 1934
- 112 Boston, 1935

Fewest Punts, Season
- 23 San Diego, 1982
- 31 Cincinnati, 1982
- 32 Chi. Bears, 1941

Most Punts, Game
- 17 Chi. Bears vs. Green Bay, Oct. 22, 1933
   Cincinnati vs. Pittsburgh, Oct. 22, 1933
- 16 Cincinnati vs. Portsmouth, Sept. 17, 1933
   Chi. Cardinals vs. Chi. Bears, Nov. 30, 1933; vs. Detroit, Sept. 15, 1940

Fewest Punts, Game
- 0 By many teams. Last time: Minnesota vs. Detroit, Nov. 3, 1985

Most Punts, Both Teams, Game
- 31 Chi. Bears (17) vs. Green Bay (14), Oct. 22, 1933
   Cincinnati (17), vs. Pittsburgh (14), Oct. 22, 1933
- 29 Chi. Cardinals (15) vs. Cincinnati (14), Nov. 12, 1933
   Chi. Cardinals (16) vs. Chi. Bears (13), Nov. 30, 1933
   Chi. Cardinals (16) vs. Detroit (13), Sept. 15, 1940

Fewest Punts, Both Teams, Game
- 1 Dall. Cowboys (0) vs. Cleveland (1), Dec. 3, 1961
   Chicago (0) vs. Detroit (1), Oct. 1, 1972
   San Francisco (0) vs. N.Y. Giants (1), Oct. 15, 1972
   Green Bay (0) vs. Buffalo (1), Dec. 5, 1982
- 2 In many games

AVERAGE YARDAGE
Highest Average Distance, Punting, Season
- 47.6 Detroit, 1961 (56-2,664)
- 47.0 Pittsburgh, 1961 (73-3,431)
- 46.9 Pittsburgh, 1953 (80-3,752)

Lowest Average Distance, Punting, Season
- 32.7 Card-Pitt, 1944 (60-1,964)
- 33.9 Detroit, 1969 (74-2,510)
- 34.4 Phil-Pitt, 1943 (62-2,132)

PUNT RETURNS

Most Seasons Leading League (Average Return)
- 8 Detroit, 1943-45, 1951-52, 1962, 1966, 1969
- 5 Chi. Cardinals, 1948-49, 1955-56, 1959
   Cleveland, 1958, 1960, 1964-65, 1967
   Green Bay, 1950, 1953-54, 1961, 1972
   Dall. Texans/Kansas City, 1960, 1968, 1970, 1979-80
- 4 Denver, 1963, 1967, 1969, 1982

Most Consecutive Seasons Leading League (Average Return)
- 3 Detroit, 1943-45
- 2 By many teams

Most Punt Returns, Season
- 71 Pittsburgh, 1976
   Tampa Bay, 1979
   L.A. Raiders, 1985
- 67 Pittsburgh, 1974
   Los Angeles, 1978
   L.A. Raiders, 1984
- 65 San Francisco, 1976

Fewest Punt Returns, Season
- 12 Baltimore, 1981

San Diego, 1982
14 Los Angeles, 1961
Philadelphia, 1962
Baltimore, 1982
15 Houston, 1960
Washington, 1960
Oakland, 1961
N.Y. Giants, 1969
Philadelphia, 1973
Kansas City, 1982

Most Punt Returns, Game
12 Philadelphia vs. Cleveland, Dec. 3, 1950
11 Chi. Bears vs. Chi. Cardinals, Oct. 8 1950
Washington vs. Tampa Bay, Oct. 9, 1977
10 Philadelphia vs. N.Y. Giants, Nov. 26, 1950
Philadelphia vs. Tampa Bay, Sept. 18, 1977
Pittsburgh vs. Buffalo, Dec. 16, 1979
Washington vs. New Orleans, Dec. 26, 1982

Most Punt Returns, Both Teams, Game
17 Philadelphia (12) vs. Cleveland (5), Dec. 3, 1950
16 N.Y. Giants (9) vs. Philadelphia (7), Dec. 12, 1954
Washington (11) vs. Tampa Bay (5), Oct. 9, 1977
15 Detroit (8) vs. Cleveland (7), Sept. 27, 1942
Los Angeles (8) vs. Baltimore (7), Nov. 27, 1966
Pittsburgh (3) vs. Houston (12), Dec. 1, 1974
Philadelphia (10) vs. Tampa Bay (5), Sept. 18, 1977
Baltimore (9) vs. Kansas City (6), Sept. 2, 1979
Washington (10) vs. New Orleans (5), Dec. 26, 1982

FAIR CATCHES
Most Fair Catches, Season
34 Baltimore, 1971
32 San Diego, 1969
30 St. Louis, 1967
Minnesota, 1971

Fewest Fair Catches, Season
0 San Diego, 1975
New England, 1976
Tampa Bay, 1976
Pittsburgh, 1977
Dallas, 1982
1 Cleveland, 1974
San Francisco, 1975
Kansas City, 1976
St. Louis, 1976, 1982
San Diego, 1976
L.A. Rams, 1982
Tampa Bay, 1982
2 By many teams

Most Fair Catches, Game
7 Minnesota vs. Dallas, Sept. 25, 1966
Detroit vs. Chicago, Nov. 21, 1976
6 By many teams

YARDS GAINED
Most Yards, Punt Returns, Season
785 L.A. Raiders, 1985
781 Chi. Bears, 1948
774 Pittsburgh, 1974

Fewest Yards, Punt Returns, Season
27 St. Louis, 1965
35 N.Y. Giants, 1965
37 New England, 1972

Most Yards, Punt Returns, Game
231 Detroit vs. San Francisco, Oct. 6, 1963
225 Oakland vs. Buffalo, Sept. 15, 1968
219 Los Angeles vs. Atlanta, Oct. 11, 1981

Most Yards, Punt Returns, Both Teams, Game
282 Los Angeles (219) vs. Atlanta (63), Oct. 11, 1981
245 Detroit (231) vs. San Francisco (14), Oct. 6, 1963
244 Oakland (225) vs. Buffalo (19), Sept. 15, 1968

AVERAGE YARDS RETURNING PUNTS
Highest Average, Punt Returns, Season
20.2 Chi. Bears, 1941 (27-546)
19.1 Chi. Cardinals, 1948 (35-669)
18.2 Chi. Cardinals, 1949 (30-546)

Lowest Average, Punt Returns, Season
1.2 St. Louis, 1965 (23-27)
1.5 N.Y. Giants, 1965 (24-35)
1.7 Washington, 1970 (27-45)

TOUCHDOWNS RETURNING PUNTS
Most Touchdowns, Punt Returns, Season
5 Chi. Cardinals, 1959
4 Chi. Cardinals, 1948
Detroit, 1951
N.Y. Giants, 1951
Denver, 1976
3 Washington, 1941
Detroit, 1952
Pittsburgh, 1952
Houston, 1975
Los Angeles, 1981

Most Touchdowns, Punt Returns, Game
2 Detroit vs. Los Angeles, Oct. 14, 1951; vs. Green Bay, Nov. 22, 1951
Chi. Cardinals vs. Pittsburgh, Nov. 1, 1959; vs. N.Y. Giants, Nov. 22, 1959
N.Y. Titans vs. Denver, Sept. 24, 1961
Denver vs. Cleveland, Sept. 26, 1976
Los Angeles vs. Atlanta, Oct. 11, 1981

Most Touchdowns, Punt Returns, Both Teams, Game
2 Philadelphia (1) vs. Washington (1), Nov. 9, 1952
Kansas City (1) vs. Buffalo (1), Sept. 11, 1966

Baltimore (1) vs. New England (1), Nov. 18, 1979
(Also see previous record)

KICKOFF RETURNS
Most Seasons Leading League (Average Return)
7 Washington, 1942, 1947, 1962-63, 1973-74, 1981
6 Chicago Bears, 1943, 1948, 1958, 1966, 1972, 1985
5 N.Y. Giants, 1944, 1946, 1949, 1951, 1953

Most Consecutive Seasons Leading League (Average Return)
3 Denver, 1965-67
2 By many teams

Most Kickoff Returns, Season
88 New Orleans, 1980
86 Minnesota, 1984
84 Baltimore, 1981

Fewest Kickoff Returns, Season
17 N.Y. Giants, 1944
20 N.Y. Giants, 1941, 1943
Chi. Bears, 1942
23 Washington, 1942

Most Kickoff Returns, Game
12 N.Y. Giants vs. Washington, Nov. 27, 1966
10 By many teams

Most Kickoff Returns, Both Teams, Game
19 N.Y. Giants (12) vs. Washington (7), Nov. 27, 1966
18 Houston (10) vs. Oakland (8), Dec. 22, 1963
17 Washington (9) vs. Green Bay (8), Oct. 17, 1983
San Diego (9) vs. Pittsburgh (8), Dec. 8, 1985

YARDS GAINED
Most Yards, Kickoff Returns, Season
1,973 New Orleans, 1980
1,824 Houston, 1963
1,801 Denver, 1963

Fewest Yards, Kickoff Returns, Season
282 N.Y. Giants, 1940
381 Green Bay, 1940
424 Chicago, 1963

Most Yards, Kickoff Returns, Game
362 Detroit vs. Los Angeles, Oct. 29, 1950
304 Chi. Bears vs. Green Bay, Nov. 9, 1952
295 Denver vs. Boston, Oct. 4, 1964

Most Yards, Kickoff Returns, Both Teams, Game
560 Detroit (362) vs. Los Angeles (198), Oct. 29, 1950
453 Washington (236) vs. Philadelphia (217), Sept. 28, 1947
447 N.Y. Giants (236) vs. Cleveland (211), Dec. 4, 1966

AVERAGE YARDAGE
Highest Average, Kickoff Returns, Season
29.4 Chicago, 1972 (52-1,528)
28.9 Pittsburgh, 1952 (39-1,128)
28.2 Washington, 1962 (61-1,720)

Lowest Average, Kickoff Returns, Season
16.3 Chicago, 1963 (26-424)
16.4 Chicago, 1983 (58-953)
16.5 San Diego, 1961 (51-842)

TOUCHDOWNS
Most Touchdowns, Kickoff Returns, Season
4 Green Bay, 1967
Chicago, 1970
3 L.A. Rams, 1950, 1985
Chi. Cardinals, 1954
San Francisco, 1963
Denver, 1966
Chicago, 1967
New England, 1977
2 By many teams

Most Touchdowns, Kickoff Returns, Game
2 Chi. Bears vs. Green Bay, Sept. 22, 1940; vs. Green Bay, Nov. 9, 1952
Philadelphia vs. Dallas, Nov. 6, 1966
Green Bay vs. Cleveland, Nov. 12, 1967
L.A. Rams vs. Green Bay, Nov. 24, 1985

Most Touchdowns, Kickoff Returns, Both Teams, Game
2 Washington (1) vs. Philadelphia (1), Nov. 1, 1942
Washington (1) vs. Philadelphia (1), Sept. 28, 1947
Los Angeles (1) vs. Detroit (1), Oct. 29, 1950
N.Y. Yanks (1) vs. N.Y. Giants (1), Nov. 4, 1951 (consecutive)
Baltimore (1) vs. Chi. Bears (1), Oct. 4, 1958
Buffalo (1) vs. Boston (1), Nov. 3, 1962
Pittsburgh (1) vs. Dallas (1), Oct. 30, 1966
St. Louis (1) vs. Washington (1), Sept. 23, 1973 (consecutive)
(Also see previous record)

FUMBLES
Most Fumbles, Season
56 Chi. Bears, 1938
San Francisco, 1978
54 Philadelphia, 1946
51 New England, 1973

Fewest Fumbles, Season
8 Cleveland, 1959
11 Green Bay, 1944
12 Brooklyn, 1934
Detroit, 1943
Cincinnati, 1982
Minnesota, 1982

Most Fumbles, Game
10 Phil-Pitt vs. New York, Oct. 9, 1943
Detroit vs. Minnesota, Nov. 12, 1967
Kansas City vs. Houston, Oct. 12, 1969
San Francisco vs. Detroit, Dec. 17, 1978

9 Philadelphia vs. Green Bay, Oct. 13, 1946
   Kansas City vs. San Diego, Nov. 15, 1964
   N.Y. Giants vs. Buffalo, Oct. 20, 1975
   St. Louis vs. Washington, Oct. 25, 1976
   San Diego vs. Green Bay, Sept. 24, 1978
   Pittsburgh vs. Cincinnati, Oct. 14, 1979
   Cleveland vs. Seattle, Dec. 20, 1981
8 By many teams. Last time: Tampa Bay vs. New York Jets, Dec. 12, 1982

Most Fumbles, Both Teams, Game

14 Chi. Bears (7) vs. Cleveland (7), Nov. 24, 1940
    St. Louis (8) vs. N.Y. Giants (6), Sept. 17, 1961
    Kansas City (10) vs. Houston (4), Oct. 12, 1969
13 Washington (8) vs. Pittsburgh (5), Nov. 14, 1937
    Philadelphia (7) vs. Boston (6), Dec. 8, 1946
    N.Y. Giants (7) vs. Washington (6), Nov. 5, 1950
    Kansas City (9) vs. San Diego (4), Nov. 15, 1964
    Buffalo (7) vs. Denver (6), Dec. 13, 1964
    N.Y. Jets (7) vs. Houston (6), Sept. 12, 1965
    Houston (8) vs. Pittsburgh (5), Dec. 9, 1973
    St. Louis (9) vs. Washington (4), Oct. 25, 1976
    Cleveland (9) vs. Seattle (4), Dec. 20, 1981
    Green Bay (7) vs. Detroit (6), Oct. 6, 1985
12 In many games

FUMBLES LOST

Most Fumbles Lost, Season

36 Chi. Cardinals, 1959
31 Green Bay, 1952
29 Chi. Cardinals, 1946
    Pittsburgh, 1950

Fewest Fumbles Lost, Season

3 Philadelphia, 1938
   Minnesota, 1980
4 San Francisco, 1960
   Kansas City, 1982
5 Chi. Cardinals, 1943
   Detroit, 1943
   N.Y. Giants, 1943
   Cleveland, 1959
   Minnesota, 1982

Most Fumbles Lost, Game

8 St. Louis vs. Washington, Oct. 25, 1976
7 Cincinnati vs. Buffalo, Nov. 30, 1969
   Cleveland vs. Seattle, Dec. 20, 1981
.6 By many teams. Last time: L.A. Rams vs. New England, Dec. 11, 1983

FUMBLES RECOVERED

Most Fumbles Recovered, Season, Own and Opponents'

58 Minnesota, 1963 (27 own, 31 opp)
51 Chi. Bears, 1938 (37 own, 14 opp)
    San Francisco, 1978 (24 own, 27 opp)
47 Atlanta, 1978 (22 own, 25 opp)

Fewest Fumbles Recovered, Season, Own and Opponents'

9 San Francisco, 1982 (5 own, 4 opp)
11 Cincinnati, 1982 (5 own, 6 opp)
13 Baltimore, 1967 (5 own, 8 opp)
   N.Y. Jets, 1967 (7 own, 6 opp)
   Philadelphia, 1968 (6 own, 7 opp)
   Miami, 1973 (5 own, 8 opp)
   Chicago, 1982 (6 own, 7 opp)
   Denver, 1982 (6 own, 7 opp)
   Miami, 1982 (5 own, 8 opp)
   N.Y. Giants, 1982 (7 own, 6 opp)

Most Fumbles Recovered, Game, Own and Opponents'

10 Denver vs. Buffalo, Dec. 13, 1964 (5 own, 5 opp)
    Pittsburgh vs. Houston, Dec. 9, 1973 (5 own, 5 opp)
    Washington vs. St. Louis, Oct. 25, 1976 (2 own, 8 opp)
9   St. Louis vs. N.Y. Giants, Sept. 17, 1961 (6 own, 3 opp)
    Houston vs. Cincinnati, Oct. 27, 1974 (4 own, 5 opp)
    Kansas City vs. Dallas, Nov. 10, 1975 (4 own, 5 opp)
    Green Bay vs. Detroit, Oct. 6, 1985 (5 own, 4 opp)
8   By many teams

Most Own Fumbles Recovered, Season

37 Chi. Bears, 1938
27 Philadelphia, 1946
    Minnesota, 1963
26 Washington, 1940
    Pittsburgh, 1948

Fewest Own Fumbles Recovered, Season

2 Washington, 1958
3 Detroit, 1956
   Cleveland, 1959
   Houston, 1982
4 By many teams

Most Opponents' Fumbles Recovered, Season

31 Minnesota, 1963
29 Cleveland, 1951
28 Green Bay, 1946
    Houston, 1977
    Seattle, 1983

Fewest Opponents' Fumbles Recovered, Season

3 Los Angeles, 1974
4 Philadelphia, 1944
   San Francisco, 1982
5 Baltimore, 1982

Most Opponents' Fumbles Recovered, Game

8 Washington vs. St. Louis, Oct. 25, 1976
7 Buffalo vs. Cincinnati, Nov. 30, 1969
   Seattle vs. Cleveland, Dec. 20, 1981
6 By many teams. Last time: New England vs. L.A. Rams, Dec. 11, 1983

TOUCHDOWNS

Most Touchdowns, Fumbles Recovered, Season, Own and Opponents'

5 Chi. Bears, 1942 (1 own, 4 opp)
   Los Angeles, 1952 (1 own, 4 opp)
   San Francisco, 1965 (1 own, 4 opp)
   Oakland, 1978 (2 own, 3 opp)
4 Chi. Bears, 1948 (1 own, 3 opp)
   Boston, 1948 (4 opp)
   Denver, 1979 (1 own, 3 opp), 1984 (4 opp)
   Atlanta, 1981 (1 own, 3 opp)
3 By many teams

Most Touchdowns, Own Fumbles Recovered, Season

2 Chi. Bears, 1953
   New England, 1973
   Buffalo, 1974
   Denver, 1975
   Oakland, 1978
   Green Bay, 1982
   New Orleans, 1983

Most Touchdowns, Opponents' Fumbles Recovered, Season

4 Detroit, 1937
   Chi. Bears, 1942
   Boston, 1948
   Los Angeles, 1952
   San Francisco, 1965
   Denver, 1984
3 By many teams

Most Touchdowns, Fumbles Recovered, Game, Own and Opponents'

2 Detroit vs. Cleveland, Nov. 7, 1937 (2 opp); vs. Green Bay, Sept. 17, 1950
   (1 own, 1 opp); vs. Chi. Cardinals, Dec. 6, 1959 (1 own, 1 opp);
   vs. Minnesota, Dec. 9, 1962 (1 own, 1 opp)
   Philadelphia vs. New York, Sept. 25, 1938 (2 opp); vs. St. Louis, Nov. 21, 1971
   (1 own, 1 opp)
   Chi. Bears vs. Washington, Nov. 28, 1948 (2 opp)
   N.Y. Giants vs. Pittsburgh, Sept. 17, 1950 (2 opp); vs. Green Bay, Sept. 19,
   1971 (2 opp)
   Cleveland vs. Dall. Cowboys, Dec. 3, 1961 (2 opp); vs. N.Y. Giants, Oct. 25,
   1964 (2 opp)
   Green Bay vs. Dallas, Nov. 26, 1964 (2 opp)
   San Francisco vs. Detroit, Nov. 14, 1965 (2 opp)
   Oakland vs. Buffalo, Dec. 24, 1967 (2 opp)
   Washington vs. San Diego, Sept. 16, 1973 (2 opp); vs. Minnesota, Nov. 29,
   1984 (1 own, 1 opp)
   New Orleans vs. San Francisco, Oct. 19, 1975 (2 opp)
   Cincinnati vs. Pittsburgh, Oct. 14, 1979 (2 opp)
   Atlanta vs. Detroit, Oct. 5, 1980 (2 opp)
   Kansas City vs. Oakland, Oct. 5, 1980 (2 opp)
   New England vs. Baltimore, Nov. 23, 1980 (2 opp)
   Denver vs. Green Bay, Oct. 15, 1984 (2 opp)

Most Touchdowns, Own Fumbles Recovered, Game

1 By many teams

Most Touchdowns, Opponents' Fumbles Recovered, Game

2 Detroit vs. Cleveland, Nov. 7, 1937
   Philadelphia vs. N.Y. Giants, Sept. 25, 1938
   Chi. Bears vs. Washington, Nov. 28, 1948
   N.Y. Giants vs. Pittsburgh, Sept. 17, 1950; vs. Green Bay, Sept. 19, 1971
   Cleveland vs. Dall. Cowboys, Dec. 3, 1961; vs. N.Y. Giants, Oct. 25, 1964
   Green Bay vs. Dallas, Nov. 26, 1964
   San Francisco vs. Detroit, Nov. 14, 1965
   Oakland vs. Buffalo, Dec. 24, 1967
   Washington vs. San Diego, Sept. 16, 1973
   New Orleans vs. San Francisco, Oct. 19, 1975
   Cincinnati vs. Pittsburgh, Oct. 14, 1979
   Atlanta vs. Detroit, Oct. 5, 1980
   Kansas City vs. Oakland, Oct. 5, 1980
   New England vs. Baltimore, Nov. 23, 1980
   Denver vs. Green Bay, Oct. 15, 1984

TURNOVERS

(Number of times losing the ball on interceptions and fumbles.)

Most Turnovers, Season

63 San Francisco, 1978
58 Chi. Bears, 1947
    Pittsburgh, 1950
    N.Y. Giants, 1983
57 Green Bay, 1950
    Houston, 1962, 1963
    Pittsburgh, 1965

Fewest Turnovers, Season

12 Kansas City, 1982
14 N.Y. Giants, 1943
    Cleveland, 1959
16 San Francisco, 1960
    Cincinnati, 1982
    St. Louis, 1982
    Washington, 1982

Most Turnovers, Game

12 Detroit vs. Chi. Bears, Nov. 22, 1942
    Chi. Cardinals vs. Philadelphia, Sept. 24, 1950
    Pittsburgh vs. Philadelphia, Dec. 12, 1965
11 San Diego vs. Green Bay, Sept. 24, 1978
10 Washington vs. N.Y. Giants, Dec. 4, 1938; vs. N.Y. Giants, Dec. 8, 1963
    Pittsburgh vs. Green Bay, Nov. 23, 1941
    Detroit vs. Green Bay, Oct. 24, 1943; vs. Denver, Oct. 7, 1984
    Chi. Cardinals vs. Green Bay, Nov. 10, 1946; vs. N.Y. Giants, Nov. 2, 1952
    Minnesota vs. Detroit, Dec. 9, 1962
    Houston vs. Oakland, Sept. 7, 1963
    Chicago vs. Detroit, Sept. 22, 1968
    St. Louis vs. Washington, Oct. 25, 1976
    N.Y. Jets vs. New England, Nov. 21, 1976
    San Francisco vs. Dallas, Oct. 12, 1980
    Cleveland vs. Seattle, Dec. 20, 1981

Most Turnovers, Both Teams, Game
  17 Detroit (12) vs. Chi. Bears (5), Nov. 22, 1942
      Boston (9) vs. Philadelphia (8), Dec. 8, 1946
  16 Chi. Cardinals (12) vs. Philadelphia (4), Sept. 24, 1950
      Chi. Cardinals (8) vs. Chi. Bears (8), Dec. 7, 1958
      Minnesota (10) vs. Detroit (6), Dec. 9, 1962
      Houston (9) vs. Kansas City (7), Oct. 12, 1969
  15 Philadelphia (8) vs. Chi. Cardinals (7), Oct. 3, 1954
      Denver (9) vs. Houston (6), Dec. 2, 1962
      Washington (10) vs. N.Y. Giants (5), Dec. 8, 1963
      St. Louis (9) vs. Kansas City (6), Oct. 2, 1933

PENALTIES

Most Seasons Leading League, Fewest Penalties
  10 Miami, 1968, 1976-84
   9 Pittsburgh, 1946-47, 1950-52, 1954, 1963, 1965, 1968
   5 Green Bay, 1955-56, 1966-67, 1974
Most Consecutive Seasons Leading League, Fewest Penalties
   9 Miami, 1976-84
   3 Pittsburgh, 1950-52
   2 By many teams
Most Seasons Leading League, Most Penalties
  16 Chi. Bears, 1941-44, 1946-49, 1951, 1959-61, 1963, 1965, 1968, 1976
   7 Oakland/L.A. Raiders, 1963, 1966, 1968-69, 1975, 1982, 1984
   6 L.A. Rams, 1950, 1952, 1962, 1969, 1978, 1980
Most Consecutive Seasons Leading League, Most Penalties
   4 Chi. Bears, 1941-44, 1946-49
   3 Chi. Cardinals, 1954-56
      Chi. Bears, 1959-61
Fewest Penalties, Season
  19 Detroit, 1937
  21 Boston, 1935
  24 Philadelphia, 1936
Most Penalties, Season
 144 Buffalo, 1983
 143 L.A. Raiders, 1984
 138 Detroit, 1984
Fewest Penalties, Game
   0 By many teams. Last time: New Orleans vs. Seattle, Nov. 10, 1985
Most Penalties, Game
  22 Brooklyn vs. Green Bay, Sept. 17, 1944
      Chi. Bears vs. Philadelphia, Nov. 26, 1944
  21 Cleveland vs. Chi. Bears, Nov. 25, 1951
  20 Tampa Bay vs. Seattle, Oct. 17, 1976
Fewest Penalties, Both Teams, Game
   0 Brooklyn vs. Pittsburgh, Oct. 28, 1934
      Brooklyn vs. Boston, Sept. 28, 1936
      Cleveland vs. Chi. Bears, Oct. 9, 1938
      Pittsburgh vs. Philadelphia, Nov. 10, 1940
Most Penalties, Both Teams, Game
  37 Cleveland (21) vs. Chi. Bears (16), Nov. 25, 1951
  35 Tampa Bay (20) vs. Seattle (15), Oct. 17, 1976
  33 Brooklyn (22) vs. Green Bay (11), Sept. 17, 1944

YARDS PENALIZED
Most Seasons Leading League, Fewest Yards Penalized
  11 Miami, 1967-68, 1973, 1977-84
   8 Boston/Washington 1935, 1953-54, 1956-58, 1970, 1985
   7 Pittsburgh, 1946-47, 1950, 1952, 1962, 1965, 1968
Most Consecutive Seasons Leading League, Fewest Yards Penalized
   8 Miami 1977-84
   3 Washington, 1956-58
      Boston, 1964-66
   2 By many teams
Most Seasons Leading League, Most Yards Penalized
  15 Chi. Bears, 1935, 1937, 1939-44, 1946-47, 1949, 1951, 1961-62, 1968
   7 Oakland/L.A. Raiders, 1963-64, 1968-69, 1975, 1982, 1984
   6 Buffalo, 1962, 1967, 1970, 1972, 1981, 1983
Most Consecutive Seasons Leading League, Most Yards Penalized
   6 Chi. Bears, 1939-44
   3 Cleveland, 1976-78
   2 By many teams
Fewest Yards Penalized, Season
 139 Detroit, 1937
 146 Philadelphia, 1937
 159 Philadelphia, 1936
Most Yards Penalized, Season
1,274 Oakland, 1969
1,239 Baltimore, 1979
1,209 L.A. Raiders, 1984
Fewest Yards Penalized, Game
   0 By many teams. Last time: New Orleans vs. Seattle, Nov. 10, 1985
Most Yards Penalized, Game
 209 Cleveland vs. Chi. Bears, Nov. 25, 1951
 190 Tampa Bay vs. Seattle, Oct. 17, 1976
 189 Houston vs. Buffalo, Oct. 31, 1965
Fewest Yards Penalized, Both Teams, Game
   0 Brooklyn vs. Pittsburgh, Oct. 28, 1934
      Brooklyn vs. Boston, Sept. 28, 1936
      Cleveland vs. Chi. Bears, Oct. 9, 1938
      Pittsburgh vs. Philadelphia, Nov. 10, 1940
Most Yards Penalized, Both Teams, Game
 374 Cleveland (209) vs. Chi. Bears (165), Nov. 25, 1951
 310 Tampa Bay (190) vs. Seattle (120), Oct. 17, 1976
 309 Green Bay (184) vs. Boston (125), Oct. 21, 1945

DEFENSE

SCORING

Most Seasons Leading League, Fewest Points Allowed
   8 N.Y. Giants, 1935, 1938-39, 1941, 1944 1958-59, 1961
   7 Chi. Bears, 1932, 1936-37, 1942, 1948, 1963, 1985
   6 Clev. Browns, 1951, 1953-57

Most Consecutive Seasons Leading League, Fewest Points Allowed
   5 Cleveland, 1953-57
   3 Buffalo, 1964-66
      Minnesota, 1969-71
   2 By many teams
Fewest Points Allowed, Season (Since 1932)
  44 Chi. Bears, 1932
  54 Brooklyn, 1933
  59 Detroit, 1934
Most Points Allowed, Season
 533 Baltimore, 1981
 501 N.Y. Giants, 1966
 487 New Orleans, 1980
Fewest Touchdowns Allowed, Season (Since 1932)
   6 Chi. Bears, 1932
      Brooklyn, 1933
   7 Detroit, 1934
   8 Green Bay, 1932
Most Touchdowns Allowed, Season
  68 Baltimore, 1981
  66 N.Y. Giants, 1966
  63 Baltimore, 1950

FIRST DOWNS

Fewest First Downs Allowed Season
  77 Detroit, 1935
  79 Boston, 1935
  82 Washington, 1937
Most First Downs Allowed, Season
 406 Baltimore, 1981
 371 Seattle, 1981
 366 Green Bay, 1983
Fewest First Downs Allowed, Rushing, Season
  35 Chi. Bears, 1942
  40 Green Bay, 1939
  41 Brooklyn, 1944
Most First Downs Allowed, Rushing, Season
 179 Detroit, 1985
 178 New Orleans 1980
 175 Seattle, 1981
Fewest First Downs Allowed, Passing, Season
  33 Chi. Bears, 1943
  34 Pittsburgh, 1941
      Washington, 1943
  35 Detroit, 1940
      Philadelphia, 1940, 1944
Most First Downs Allowed, Passing, Season
 218 San Diego, 1985
 216 San Diego, 1981
 214 Baltimore, 1981
Fewest First Downs Allowed, Penalty, Season
   1 Boston, 1944
   3 Philadelphia 1940
      Pittsburgh, 1945
      Washington, 1957
   4 Cleveland, 1940
      Green Bay, 1943
      N.Y. Giants, 1943
Most First Downs Allowed, Penalty, Season
  48 Houston, 1985
  43 L.A. Raiders, 1984
  41 Detroit, 1979

NET YARDS ALLOWED RUSHING AND PASSING

Most Seasons Leading League, Fewest Yards Allowed
   7 Chi. Bears, 1942-43, 1948, 1958, 1963, 1984-85
   6 N.Y. Giants, 1938, 1940-41, 1951, 1956, 1959
   5 Boston/Washington, 1935-37, 1939, 1946
      Philadelphia, 1944-45, 1949, 1953, 1981
Most Consecutive Seasons Leading League, Fewest Yards Allowed
   3 Boston/Washington, 1935-37
   2 By many teams
Fewest Yards Allowed, Season
1,539 Chi. Cardinals, 1934
1,703 Chi. Bears, 1942
1,789 Brooklyn, 1933
Most Yards Allowed, Season
6,793 Baltimore, 1981
6,403 Green Bay, 1983
6,352 Minnesota, 1984

RUSHING

Most Seasons Leading League, Fewest Yards Allowed
   8 Chi. Bears, 1937, 1939, 1942, 1946, 1949, 1963, 1984-85
   7 Detroit, 1938, 1950, 1952, 1962, 1970, 1980-81
   6 Dallas, 1966-69, 1972, 1978
Most Consecutive Seasons Leading League, Fewest Yards Allowed
   4 Dallas, 1966-69
   2 By many teams
Fewest Yards Allowed, Rushing Season
 519 Chi. Bears, 1942
 558 Philadelphia, 1944
 762 Pittsburgh, 1982
Most Yards Allowed, Rushing, Season
3,228 Buffalo, 1978
3,106 New Orleans, 1980
3,010 Baltimore, 1978
Fewest Touchdowns Allowed, Rushing, Season
   2 Detroit, 1934
      Dallas, 1968
      Minnesota 1971
   3 By many teams

Most Touchdowns Allowed, Rushing, Season
    36 Oakland, 1961
    31 N.Y. Giants, 1980
    30 Baltimore, 1981

PASSING
Most Seasons Leading League, Fewest Yards Allowed
    8 Green Bay, 1947-48, 1962, 1964-68
    7 Washington, 1939, 1942, 1945, 1952-53, 1980, 1985
    6 Chi. Bears, 1938, 1943-44, 1958, 1960, 1963
Most Consecutive Seasons Leading League, Fewest Yards Allowed
    5 Green Bay, 1964-68
    2 By many teams
Fewest Yards Allowed, Passing, Season
    545 Philadelphia, 1934
    558 Portsmouth, 1933
    585 Chi. Cardinals, 1934
Most Yards Allowed, Passing, Season
    4,311 San Diego, 1981
    4,293 San Diego, 1985
    4,128 Baltimore, 1981
Fewest Touchdowns Allowed, Passing, Season
    1 Portsmouth, 1932
        Philadelphia, 1934
    2 Brooklyn, 1933
        Chi. Bears, 1934
    3 Chi. Bears, 1932, 1936
        Green Bay, 1932, 1934
        N.Y. Giants, 1939, 1944
Most Touchdowns Allowed, Passing, Season
    40 Denver, 1963
    38 St. Louis, 1969
    37 Washington, 1961
        Baltimore, 1981

SACKS
Most Seasons Leading League
    4 Boston/New England, 1961, 1963, 1977, 1979
        Dallas, 1966, 1968-69, 1978
        Oakland/L.A. Raiders, 1966-68, 1982
    3 Dallas/Kansas City, 1960, 1965, 1969
        San Francisco, 1967, 1972, 1976
    2 Baltimore, 1964, 1975
        San Diego, 1962, 1980
        N.Y. Giants, 1963, 1985
Most Consecutive Seasons Leading League
    3 Oakland, 1966-68
    2 Dallas, 1968-69
Most Sacks, Season
    72 Chicago, 1984
    68 N.Y. Giants, 1985
    67 Oakland, 1967
Fewest Sacks, Season
    11 Baltimore, 1982
    12 Buffalo, 1982
    13 Baltimore, 1981
Most Sacks, Game
    12 Dallas vs. Pittsburgh, Nov. 20, 1966; vs. Houston, Sept. 29, 1985
        St. Louis vs. Baltimore, Oct. 26, 1980
        Chicago vs. Detroit, Dec. 16, 1984
    11 N.Y. Giants vs. St. Louis, Nov. 1, 1964
        Baltimore vs. Los Angeles, Nov. 22, 1964
        Buffalo vs. Denver, Dec. 13, 1964
        Detroit vs. Green Bay, Nov. 7, 1965
        Oakland vs. Buffalo, Oct. 15, 1967; vs. Denver, Nov. 5, 1967
        St. Louis vs. Atlanta, Nov. 24, 1968; vs. Philadelphia, Dec. 18, 1983
        Dallas vs. Detroit, Oct. 6, 1975
        Kansas City vs. Cleveland, Sept. 30, 1984
        Chicago vs. Minnesota, Oct. 28, 1984
        Cleveland vs. Atlanta, Nov. 18, 1984
    10 By many teams
Most Opponents Yards Lost Attempting to Pass, Season
    666 Oakland, 1967
    583 Chicago, 1984
    573 San Francisco, 1976
Fewest Opponents Yards Lost Attempting to Pass, Season
    75 Green Bay, 1956
    77 N.Y. Bulldogs, 1949
    78 Green Bay, 1958

INTERCEPTIONS BY
Most Seasons Leading League
    9 N.Y. Giants, 1933, 1937-39, 1944, 1948, 1951, 1954, 1961
    8 Green Bay, 1940, 1942-43, 1947, 1955, 1957, 1962, 1965
    7 Chi. Bears, 1935-36, 1941-42, 1946, 1963, 1985
Most Consecutive Seasons Leading League
    5 Kansas City, 1966-70
    3 N.Y. Giants, 1937-39
    2 By many teams
Most Passes Intercepted By, Season
    49 San Diego, 1961
    42 Green Bay, 1943
    41 N.Y. Giants, 1951
Fewest Passes Intercepted By, Season
    3 Houston, 1982
    5 Baltimore, 1982
    6 Houston, 1972
        St. Louis, 1982
Most Passes Intercepted By, Game
    9 Green Bay vs. Detroit, Oct. 24, 1943
        Philadelphia vs. Pittsburgh, Dec. 12, 1965
    8 N.Y. Giants vs. Green Bay, Nov. 21, 1948; vs. N.Y. Yanks, Dec. 16, 1951
        Philadelphia vs. Chi. Cardinals, Sept. 24, 1950

342

Houston vs. Denver, Dec. 2, 1962
        Detroit vs. Chicago, Sept. 22, 1968
        N.Y. Jets vs. Baltimore, Sept. 23, 1973
    7 By many teams. Last time: Denver vs. Detroit, Oct. 7, 1984
Most Consecutive Games, One or More Interceptions By
    46 L.A. Chargers/San Diego, 1960-63
    37 Detroit, 1960-63
    36 Boston, 1944-47
        Washington, 1962-65
Most Yards Returning Interceptions, Season
    929 San Diego, 1961
    712 Los Angeles, 1952
    697 Seattle, 1984
Fewest Yards Returning Interceptions, Season
    5 Los Angeles, 1959
    42 Philadelphia, 1982
    47 Houston, 1982
Most Yards Returning Interceptions, Game
    325 Seattle vs. Kansas City, Nov. 4, 1984
    314 Los Angeles vs. San Francisco, Oct. 18, 1964
    245 Houston vs. N.Y. Jets, Oct. 15, 1967
Most Touchdowns, Returning Interceptions, Season
    9 San Diego, 1961
    7 Seattle, 1984
    6 Cleveland, 1960
        Green Bay, 1966
        Detroit, 1967
        Houston, 1967
Most Touchdowns Returning Interceptions, Game
    4 Seattle vs. Kansas City, Nov. 4, 1984
    3 Baltimore vs. Green Bay, Nov. 5, 1950
        Cleveland vs. Chicago, Dec. 11, 1960
        Philadelphia vs. Pittsburgh, Dec. 12, 1965
        Baltimore vs. Pittsburgh, Sept. 29, 1968
        Buffalo vs. N.Y. Jets, Sept. 29, 1968
        Houston vs. San Diego, Dec. 19, 1971
        Cincinnati vs. Houston, Dec. 17, 1972
        Tampa Bay vs. New Orleans, Dec. 11, 1977
    2 By many teams
Most Touchdowns Returning Interceptions, Both Teams, Game
    4 Philadelphia (3) vs. Pittsburgh (1), Dec. 12, 1965
        Seattle (4) vs. Kansas City (0), Nov. 4, 1984
    3 Los Angeles (2) vs. Detroit (1), Nov. 1, 1953
        Cleveland (2) vs. N.Y. Giants (1), Dec. 18, 1960
        Pittsburgh (2) vs. Cincinnati (1), Oct. 10, 1983
        (Also see previous record)

PUNT RETURNS
Fewest Opponents Punt Returns, Season
    7 Washington, 1962
        San Diego, 1982
    10 Buffalo, 1982
    11 Boston, 1962
Most Opponents Punt Returns, Season
    71 Tampa Bay, 1976, 1977
    69 N.Y. Giants, 1953
    68 Cleveland, 1974
Fewest Yards Allowed, Punt Returns, Season
    22 Green Bay, 1967
    34 Washington, 1962
    39 Cleveland, 1959
        Washington, 1972
Most Yards Allowed, Punt Returns, Season
    932 Green Bay, 1949
    913 Boston, 1947
    906 New Orleans, 1974
Lowest Average Allowed, Punt Returns, Season
    1.20 Chi. Cardinals, 1954 (46-55)
    1.22 Cleveland, 1959 (32-39)
    1.55 Chi. Cardinals, 1953 (44-68)
Highest Average Allowed, Punt Returns, Season
    18.6 Green Bay, 1949 (50-932)
    18.0 Cleveland, 1977 (31-558)
    17.9 Boston, 1960 (20-357)
Most Touchdowns Allowed, Punt Returns, Season
    4 New York, 1959
    3 Green Bay, 1949
        Chi. Cardinals, 1951
        Los Angeles, 1951
        Washington, 1952
        Dallas, 1952
        Pittsburgh, 1959
        N.Y. Jets, 1968
        Cleveland, 1977
    2 By many teams

KICKOFF RETURNS
Fewest Opponents Kickoff Returns, Season
    10 Brooklyn, 1943
    15 Detroit, 1942
        Brooklyn, 1944
    18 Cleveland, 1941
        Boston, 1944
Most Opponents Kickoff Returns, Season
    91 Washington, 1983
    89 New England, 1980
    88 San Diego, 1981
Fewest Yards Allowed, Kickoff Returns, Season
    225 Brooklyn, 1943
    293 Brooklyn, 1944
    361 Seattle, 1982
Most Yards Allowed, Kickoff Returns, Season
    2,045 Kansas City, 1966

1,827 Chicago, 1935
1,816 N.Y. Giants, 1963
Lowest Average Allowed, Kickoff Returns, Season
14.3 Cleveland, 1980 (71-1,018)
15.0 Seattle, 1982 (24-361)
15.8 Oakland, 1977 (63-997)
Highest Average Allowed, Kickoff Returns, Season
29.5 N.Y. Jets, 1972 (47-1,386)
29.4 Los Angeles, 1950 (48-1,411)
29.1 New England, 1971 (49-1,427)
Most Touchdowns Allowed, Kickoff Returns, Season
3 Minnesota, 1963, 1970
   Dallas, 1966
   Detroit, 1980
2 By many teams

FUMBLES

Fewest Opponents Fumbles, Season
11 Cleveland, 1956
    Baltimore, 1982
13 Los Angeles, 1956
    Chicago, 1960
    Cleveland, 1963, 1965
    Detroit, 1967
    San Diego, 1969
14 Baltimore, 1970
    Oakland, 1975
    Buffalo, 1982
    St. Louis, 1982
    San Francisco, 1982
Most Opponents Fumbles, Season
50 Minnesota, 1963
    San Francisco, 1978
48 N.Y. Giants, 1980
47 N.Y. Giants, 1977
    Seattle, 1984

TURNOVERS
(Number of times losing the ball on interceptions and fumbles.)
Fewest Opponents Turnovers, Season
11 Baltimore, 1982
13 San Francisco, 1982
15 St. Louis, 1982
Most Opponents Turnovers, Season
66 San Diego, 1961
63 Seattle, 1984
61 Washington, 1983
Most Opponents Turnovers, Game
12 Chi. Bears vs. Detroit, Nov. 22, 1942
    Philadelphia vs. Chi. Cardinals, Sept. 24, 1950; vs. Pittsburgh, Dec. 12, 1965
11 Green Bay vs. San Diego, Sept. 24, 1978
10 N.Y. Giants vs. Washington, Dec. 4, 1938; vs. Chi. Cardinals, Nov. 2, 1952;
        vs. Washington, Dec. 8, 1963
    Green Bay vs. Pittsburgh, Nov. 23, 1941; vs. Detroit, Oct. 24, 1943;
        vs. Chi. Cardinals, Nov. 10, 1946
    Detroit vs. Minnesota, Dec. 9, 1962; vs. Chicago, Sept. 22, 1968
    Oakland vs. Houston, Sept. 7, 1963
    Washington vs. St. Louis, Oct. 25, 1976
    New England vs. N.Y. Jets, Nov. 21, 1976
    Dallas vs. San Francisco, Oct. 12, 1980
    Seattle vs. Cleveland, Dec. 20, 1981
    Denver vs. Detroit, Oct. 7, 1984

1,000 YARDS RUSHING IN A SEASON

Year	Player, Team	Att.	Yards	Avg.	Long	TD
1985	Marcus Allen, L.A. Raiders[3]	390	1,759	4.6	61	11
	Gerald Riggs, Atlanta[2]	397	1,719	4.3	50	10
	Walter Payton, Chicago[9]	324	1,551	4.8	40	9
	Joe Morris, N.Y. Giants	294	1,336	4.5	65	21
	Freeman McNeil, N.Y. Jets[2]	294	1,331	4.5	69	3
	Tony Dorsett, Dallas[8]	305	1,307	4.3	60	7
	James Wilder, Tampa Bay[2]	365	1,300	3.6	28	10
	Eric Dickerson, L.A. Rams[3]	292	1,234	4.2	43	12
	Craig James, New England	263	1,227	4.7	65	5
	*Kevin Mack, Cleveland	222	1,104	5.0	61	7
	Curt Warner, Seattle[2]	291	1,094	3.8	38	8
	George Rogers, Washington[3]	231	1,093	4.7	35	7
	Roger Craig, San Francisco	214	1,050	4.9	62	9
	Earnest Jackson, Philadelphia[2]	282	1,028	3.6	59	5
	Stump Mitchell, St. Louis	183	1,006	5.5	64	7
	Earnest Byner, Cleveland	244	1,002	4.1	36	8
1984	Eric Dickerson, L.A. Rams[2]	379	2,105	5.6	66	14
	Walter Payton, Chicago[8]	381	1,684	4.4	72	11
	James Wilder, Tampa Bay	407	1,544	3.8	37	13
	Gerald Riggs, Atlanta	353	1,486	4.2	57	13
	Wendell Tyler, San Francisco[3]	246	1,262	5.1	40	7
	John Riggins, Washington[5]	327	1,239	3.8	24	14
	Tony Dorsett, Dallas[7]	302	1,189	3.9	31	6
	Earnest Jackson, San Diego	296	1,179	4.0	32	8
	Ottis Anderson, St. Louis[5]	289	1,174	4.1	24	6
	Marcus Allen, L.A. Raiders[2]	275	1,168	4.2	52	13
	Sammy Winder, Denver	296	1,153	3.9	24	4
	*Greg Bell, Buffalo	262	1,100	4.2	85	7
	Freeman McNeil, N.Y. Jets	229	1,070	4.7	53	5
1983	*Eric Dickerson, L.A. Rams	390	1,808	4.6	85	18
	William Andrews, Atlanta[4]	331	1,567	4.7	27	7
	*Curt Warner, Seattle	335	1,449	4.3	60	13
	Walter Payton, Chicago[7]	314	1,421	4.5	49	6
	John Riggins, Washington[4]	375	1,347	3.6	44	24
	Tony Dorsett, Dallas[6]	289	1,321	4.6	77	8
	Earl Campbell, Houston[5]	322	1,301	4.0	42	12
	Ottis Anderson, St. Louis[4]	296	1,270	4.3	43	5
	Mike Pruitt, Cleveland[4]	293	1,184	4.0	27	10
	George Rogers, New Orleans[2]	256	1,144	4.5	76	5
	Joe Cribbs, Buffalo[3]	263	1,131	4.3	45	3
	Curtis Dickey, Baltimore	254	1,122	4.4	56	4
	Tony Collins, New England	219	1,049	4.8	50	10
	Billy Sims, Detroit[3]	220	1,040	4.7	41	7
	Marcus Allen, L.A. Raiders	266	1,014	3.8	19	9
	Franco Harris, Pittsburgh[8]	279	1,007	3.6	19	5
1981	*George Rogers, New Orleans	378	1,674	4.4	79	13
	Tony Dorsett, Dallas[5]	342	1,646	4.8	75	4
	Billy Sims, Detroit[2]	296	1,437	4.9	51	13
	Wilbert Montgomery, Philadelphia[3]	286	1,402	4.9	41	8
	Ottis Anderson, St. Louis[3]	328	1,376	4.2	28	9
	Earl Campbell, Houston[4]	361	1,376	3.8	43	10
	William Andrews, Atlanta[3]	289	1,301	4.5	29	10
	Walter Payton, Chicago[6]	339	1,222	3.6	39	6
	Chuck Muncie, San Diego[2]	251	1,144	4.6	73	19
	*Joe Delaney, Kansas City	234	1,121	4.8	82	3
	Mike Pruitt, Cleveland[3]	247	1,103	4.5	21	7
	Joe Cribbs, Buffalo[2]	257	1,097	4.3	35	3
	Pete Johnson, Cincinnati	274	1,077	3.9	39	12
	Wendell Tyler, Los Angeles[2]	260	1,074	4.1	69	12
	Ted Brown, Minnesota	274	1,063	3.9	34	6
1980	Earl Campbell, Houston[3]	373	1,934	5.2	55	13
	Walter Payton, Chicago[5]	317	1,460	4.6	69	6
	Ottis Anderson, St. Louis[2]	301	1,352	4.5	52	9
	William Andrews, Atlanta[2]	265	1,308	4.9	33	4
	*Billy Sims, Detroit	313	1,303	4.2	52	13
	Tony Dorsett, Dallas[4]	278	1,185	4.3	56	11
	*Joe Cribbs, Buffalo	306	1,185	3.9	48	11
	Mike Pruitt, Cleveland[2]	249	1,034	4.2	56	6
1979	Earl Campbell, Houston[2]	368	1,697	4.6	61	19
	Walter Payton, Chicago[4]	369	1,610	4.4	43	14
	*Ottis Anderson, St. Louis	331	1,605	4.8	76	8
	Wilbert Montgomery, Philadelphia[2]	338	1,512	4.5	62	9
	Mike Pruitt, Cleveland	264	1,294	4.9	77	9
	Ricky Bell, Tampa Bay	283	1,263	4.5	49	7
	Chuck Muncie, New Orleans	238	1,198	5.0	69	11
	Franco Harris, Pittsburgh[7]	267	1,186	4.4	71	11
	John Riggins, Washington[3]	260	1,153	4.4	66	9
	Wendell Tyler, Los Angeles	218	1,109	5.1	63	9
	Tony Dorsett, Dallas[3]	250	1,107	4.4	41	6
	*William Andrews, Atlanta	239	1,023	4.3	23	3
1978	*Earl Campbell, Houston	302	1,450	4.8	81	13
	Walter Payton, Chicago[3]	333	1,395	4.2	76	11
	Tony Dorsett, Dallas[2]	290	1,325	4.6	63	7
	Delvin Williams, Miami[2]	272	1,258	4.6	58	8
	Wilbert Montgomery, Philadelphia	259	1,220	4.7	47	9
	Terdell Middleton, Green Bay	284	1,116	3.9	76	11
	Franco Harris, Pittsburgh[6]	310	1,082	3.5	37	8
	Mark van Eeghen, Oakland[3]	270	1,080	4.0	34	9
	*Terry Miller, Buffalo	238	1,060	4.5	60	7
	Tony Reed, Kansas City	206	1,053	5.1	62	5
	John Riggins, Washington[2]	248	1,014	4.1	31	5
1977	Walter Payton, Chicago[2]	339	1,852	5.5	73	14
	Mark van Eeghen, Oakland[2]	324	1,273	3.9	27	7
	Lawrence McCutcheon, Los Angeles[4]	294	1,238	4.2	48	7
	Franco Harris, Pittsburgh[5]	300	1,162	3.9	61	11
	Lydell Mitchell, Baltimore[3]	301	1,159	3.9	64	3
	Chuck Foreman, Minnesota[3]	270	1,112	4.1	51	6
	Greg Pruitt, Cleveland[3]	236	1,086	4.6	78	3
	Sam Cunningham, New England	270	1,015	3.8	31	4
	Tony Dorsett, Dallas	208	1,007	4.8	84	12
1976	O.J. Simpson, Buffalo[5]	290	1,503	5.2	75	8
	Walter Payton, Chicago	311	1,390	4.5	60	13
	Delvin Williams, San Francisco	248	1,203	4.9	80	7
	Lydell Mitchell, Baltimore[2]	289	1,200	4.2	43	5
	Lawrence McCutcheon, Los Angeles[3]	291	1,168	4.0	40	9
	Chuck Foreman, Minnesota[2]	278	1,155	4.2	46	13
	Franco Harris, Pittsburgh[4]	289	1,128	3.9	30	14
	Mike Thomas, Washington	254	1,101	4.3	28	5
	Rocky Bleier, Pittsburgh	220	1,036	4.7	28	5
	Mark van Eeghen, Oakland	233	1,012	4.3	21	3
	Otis Armstrong, Denver[2]	247	1,008	4.1	31	5
	Greg Pruitt, Cleveland[2]	209	1,000	4.8	64	4
1975	O.J. Simpson, Buffalo[4]	329	1,817	5.5	88	16
	Franco Harris, Pittsburgh[3]	262	1,246	4.8	36	10
	Lydell Mitchell, Baltimore	289	1,193	4.1	70	11
	Jim Otis, St. Louis	269	1,076	4.0	30	5
	Chuck Foreman, Minnesota	280	1,070	3.8	31	13
	Greg Pruitt, Cleveland	217	1,067	4.9	50	8
	John Riggins, N.Y. Jets	238	1,005	4.2	42	8
	Dave Hampton, Atlanta	250	1,002	4.0	22	5
1974	Otis Armstrong, Denver	263	1,407	5.3	43	9
	*Don Woods, San Diego	227	1,162	5.1	56	7
	O.J. Simpson, Buffalo[3]	270	1,125	4.2	41	3
	Lawrence McCutcheon, Los Angeles[2]	236	1,109	4.7	23	3
	Franco Harris, Pittsburgh[2]	208	1,006	4.8	54	5
1973	O.J. Simpson, Buffalo[2]	332	2,003	6.0	80	12
	John Brockington, Green Bay[3]	265	1,144	4.3	53	3
	Calvin Hill, Dallas[2]	273	1,142	4.2	21	6
	Lawrence McCutcheon, Los Angeles	210	1,097	5.2	37	2
	Larry Csonka, Miami[3]	219	1,003	4.6	25	5
1972	O.J. Simpson, Buffalo	292	1,251	4.3	94	6
	Larry Brown, Washington[2]	285	1,216	4.3	38	8
	Ron Johnson, N.Y. Giants[2]	298	1,182	4.0	35	9
	Larry Csonka, Miami[2]	213	1,117	5.2	45	6
	Marv Hubbard, Oakland	219	1,100	5.0	39	4
	*Franco Harris, Pittsburgh	188	1,055	5.6	75	10
	Calvin Hill, Dallas	245	1,036	4.2	26	6
	Mike Garrett, San Diego[2]	272	1,031	3.8	41	6
	John Brockington, Green Bay[2]	274	1,027	3.7	30	8
	Eugene (Mercury) Morris, Miami	190	1,000	5.3	33	12
1971	Floyd Little, Denver	284	1,133	4.0	40	6
	*John Brockington, Green Bay	216	1,105	5.1	52	4
	Larry Csonka, Miami	195	1,051	5.4	28	7
	Steve Owens, Detroit	246	1,035	4.2	23	8
	Willie Ellison, Los Angeles	211	1,000	4.7	80	4
1970	Larry Brown, Washington	237	1,125	4.7	75	5
	Ron Johnson, N.Y. Giants	263	1,027	3.9	68	8
1969	Gale Sayers, Chicago[2]	236	1,032	4.4	28	8
1968	Leroy Kelly, Cleveland[3]	248	1,239	5.0	65	16
	*Paul Robinson, Cincinnati	238	1,023	4.3	87	8
1967	Jim Nance, Boston[2]	269	1,216	4.5	53	7
	Leroy Kelly, Cleveland[2]	235	1,205	5.1	42	11
	Hoyle Granger, Houston	236	1,194	5.1	67	6
	Mike Garrett, Kansas City	236	1,087	4.6	58	9
1966	Jim Nance, Boston	299	1,458	4.9	65	11
	Gale Sayers, Chicago	229	1,231	5.4	58	8
	Leroy Kelly, Cleveland	209	1,141	5.5	70	15
	Dick Bass, Los Angeles[2]	248	1,090	4.4	50	8
1965	Jim Brown, Cleveland[7]	289	1,544	5.3	67	17
	Paul Lowe, San Diego[2]	222	1,121	5.0	59	7
1964	Jim Brown, Cleveland[6]	280	1,446	5.2	71	7
	Jim Taylor, Green Bay[5]	235	1,169	5.0	84	12
	John Henry Johnson, Pittsburgh[2]	235	1,048	4.5	45	7
1963	Jim Brown, Cleveland[5]	291	1,863	6.4	80	12
	Clem Daniels, Oakland	215	1,099	5.1	74	3
	Jim Taylor, Green Bay[4]	248	1,018	4.1	40	9
	Paul Lowe, San Diego	177	1,010	5.7	66	8
1962	Jim Taylor, Green Bay[3]	272	1,474	5.4	51	19
	John Henry Johnson, Pittsburgh	251	1,141	4.5	40	7
	*Cookie Gilchrist, Buffalo	214	1,096	5.1	44	13
	Abner Haynes, Dall. Texans	221	1,049	4.7	71	13
	Dick Bass, Los Angeles	196	1,033	5.3	57	6
	Charlie Tolar, Houston	244	1,012	4.1	25	7
1961	Jim Brown, Cleveland[4]	305	1,408	4.6	38	8
	Jim Taylor, Green Bay[2]	243	1,307	5.4	53	15
1960	Jim Brown, Cleveland[3]	215	1,257	5.8	71	9
	Jim Taylor, Green Bay	230	1,101	4.8	32	11
	John David Crow, St. Louis	183	1,071	5.9	57	6
1959	Jim Brown, Cleveland[2]	290	1,329	4.6	70	14
	J.D. Smith, San Francisco	207	1,036	5.0	73	10
1958	Jim Brown, Cleveland	257	1,527	5.9	65	17
1956	Rick Casares, Chi. Bears	234	1,126	4.8	68	12
1954	Joe Perry, San Francisco[2]	173	1,049	6.1	58	8
1953	Joe Perry, San Francisco	192	1,018	5.3	51	10
1949	Steve Van Buren, Philadelphia[2]	263	1,146	4.4	41	11
	Tony Canadeo, Green Bay	208	1,052	5.1	54	4
1947	Steve Van Buren, Philadelphia	217	1,008	4.6	45	13
1934	*Beattie Feathers, Chi. Bears	101	1,004	9.9	82	8

**First year in the league.*

200 YARDS RUSHING IN A GAME

Date	Player, Team, Opponent	Att.	Yards	TD
Dec. 21, 1985	George Rogers, Washington vs. St. Louis	34	206	1
Dec. 21, 1985	Joe Morris, N.Y. Giants vs. Pittsburgh	36	202	3

Dec. 9, 1984	Eric Dickerson, L.A. Rams vs. Houston	27	215	2
Nov. 18, 1984	*Greg Bell, Buffalo vs. Dallas	27	206	1
Nov. 4, 1984	Eric Dickerson, L.A. Rams vs. St. Louis	21	208	0
Sept. 2, 1984	Gerald Riggs, Atlanta vs. New Orleans	35	202	2
Nov. 27, 1983	*Curt Warner, Seattle vs. Kansas City (OT)	32	207	3
Nov. 6, 1983	James Wilder, Tampa Bay vs. Minnesota	31	219	1
Sept. 18, 1983	Tony Collins, New England vs. N.Y. Jets	23	212	3
Sept. 4, 1983	George Rogers, New Orleans vs. St. Louis	24	206	2
Dec. 21, 1980	Earl Campbell, Houston vs. Minnesota	29	203	1
Nov. 16, 1980	Earl Campbell, Houston vs. Chicago	31	206	0
Oct. 26, 1980	Earl Campbell, Houston vs. Cincinnati	27	202	2
Oct. 19, 1980	Earl Campbell, Houston vs. Tampa Bay	33	203	0
Nov. 26, 1978	*Terry Miller, Buffalo vs. N.Y. Giants	21	208	2
Dec. 4, 1977	*Tony Dorsett, Dallas vs. Philadelphia	23	206	2
Nov. 20, 1977	Walter Payton, Chicago vs. Minnesota	40	275	1
Oct. 30, 1977	Walter Payton, Chicago vs. Green Bay	23	205	2
Dec. 5, 1976	O.J. Simpson, Buffalo vs. Miami	24	203	1
Nov. 25, 1976	O.J. Simpson, Buffalo vs. Detroit	29	273	2
Oct. 24, 1976	Chuck Foreman, Minnesota vs. Philadelphia	28	200	2
Dec. 14, 1975	Greg Pruitt, Cleveland vs. Kansas City	26	214	3
Sept. 28, 1975	O.J. Simpson, Buffalo vs. Pittsburgh	28	227	1
Dec. 16, 1973	O.J. Simpson, Buffalo vs. N.Y. Jets	34	200	1
Dec. 9, 1973	O.J. Simpson, Buffalo vs. New England	22	219	1
Sept. 16, 1973	O.J. Simpson, Buffalo vs. New England	29	250	2
Dec. 5, 1971	Willie Ellison, Los Angeles vs. New Orleans	26	247	1
Dec. 20, 1970	John (Frenchy) Fuqua, Pittsburgh vs. Philadelphia	20	218	2
Nov. 3, 1968	Gale Sayers, Chicago vs. Green Bay	24	205	0
Oct. 30, 1966	Jim Nance, Boston vs. Oakland	38	208	2
Oct. 10, 1964	John Henry Johnson, Pittsburgh vs. Cleveland	30	200	3
Dec. 8, 1963	Cookie Gilchrist, Buffalo vs. N.Y. Jets	36	243	5
Nov. 3, 1963	Jim Brown, Cleveland vs. Philadelphia	28	223	1
Oct. 20, 1963	Clem Daniels, Oakland vs. N.Y. Jets	27	200	2
Sept. 22, 1963	Jim Brown, Cleveland vs. Dallas	20	232	2
Dec. 10, 1961	Billy Cannon, Houston vs. N.Y. Titans	25	216	3
Nov. 19, 1961	Jim Brown, Cleveland vs. Philadelphia	34	237	4
Dec. 18, 1960	John David Crow, St. Louis vs. Pittsburgh	24	203	0
Nov. 15, 1959	Bobby Mitchell, Cleveland vs. Washington	14	232	3
Nov. 24, 1957	*Jim Brown, Cleveland vs. Los Angeles	31	237	4
Dec. 16, 1956	*Tom Wilson, Los Angeles vs. Green Bay	23	223	0
Nov. 22, 1953	Dan Towler, Los Angeles vs. Baltimore	14	205	1
Nov. 12, 1950	Gene Roberts, N.Y. Giants vs. Chi. Cardinals	26	218	2
Nov. 27, 1949	Steve Van Buren, Philadelphia vs. Pittsburgh	27	205	0
Oct. 8, 1933	Cliff Battles, Boston vs. N.Y. Giants	16	215	1

*First year in the league.

Times 200 or More
43 times by 30 players . . . Simpson 6; Brown, Campbell 4; Dickerson, Payton, Rogers 2.

400 YARDS PASSING IN A GAME

Date	Player, Team, Opponent	Att.	Comp.	Yards	TD
Dec. 20, 1985	John Elway, Denver vs. Seattle	42	24	432	1
Nov. 10, 1985	Dan Fouts, San Diego vs. L.A. Raiders (OT)	41	26	436	4
Oct. 13, 1985	Phil Simms, N.Y. Giants vs. Cincinnati	62	40	513	1
Oct. 13, 1985	Dave Krieg, Seattle vs. Atlanta	51	33	405	4
Oct. 6, 1985	Phil Simms, N.Y. Giants vs. Dallas	36	18	432	3
Oct. 6, 1985	Joe Montana, San Francisco vs. Atlanta	57	37	429	5
Sept. 19, 1985	Tommy Kramer, Minnesota vs. Chicago	55	28	436	3
Sept. 15, 1985	Dan Fouts, San Diego vs. Seattle	43	29	440	4
Dec. 16, 1984	Neil Lomax, St. Louis vs. Washington	46	37	468	2
Dec. 9, 1984	Dan Marino, Miami vs. Indianapolis	41	29	404	4
Dec. 2, 1984	Dan Marino, Miami vs. L.A. Raiders	57	35	470	4
Nov. 25, 1984	Dave Krieg, Seattle vs. Denver	44	30	406	3
Nov. 4, 1984	Dan Marino, Miami vs. N.Y. Jets	42	23	422	2
Oct. 21, 1984	Dan Fouts, San Diego vs. L.A. Raiders	45	24	410	3
Sept. 30, 1984	Dan Marino, Miami vs. St. Louis	36	24	429	3
Sept. 2, 1984	Phil Simms, N.Y. Giants vs. Philadelphia	30	23	409	4
Dec. 11, 1983	Bill Kenney, Kansas City vs. San Diego	41	31	411	4
Nov. 20, 1983	Dave Krieg, Seattle vs. Denver	42	31	418	3
Oct. 9, 1983	Joe Ferguson, Buffalo vs. Miami (OT)	55	38	419	5
Oct. 2, 1983	Joe Theismann, Washington vs. L.A. Raiders	39	23	417	3
Sept. 25, 1983	Richard Todd, N.Y. Jets vs. L.A. Rams (OT)	50	37	446	2
Dec. 26, 1982	Vince Ferragamo, L.A. Rams vs. Chicago	46	30	509	3
Dec. 20, 1982	Dan Fouts, San Diego vs. Cincinnati	40	25	435	1
Dec. 20, 1982	Ken Anderson, Cincinnati vs. San Diego	56	40	416	2
Dec. 11, 1982	Dan Fouts, San Diego vs. San Francisco	48	33	444	5
Nov. 21, 1982	Joe Montana, San Francisco vs. St. Louis	39	26	408	3
Nov. 15, 1981	Steve Bartkowski, Atlanta vs. Pittsburgh	50	33	416	2
Oct. 25, 1981	Brian Sipe, Cleveland vs. Baltimore	41	30	444	4
Oct. 25, 1981	David Woodley, Miami vs. Dallas	37	21	408	3
Oct. 11, 1981	Tommy Kramer, Minnesota vs. San Diego	43	27	444	4
Dec. 14, 1980	Tommy Kramer, Minnesota vs. Cleveland	49	38	456	4
Nov. 16, 1980	Doug Williams, Tampa Bay vs. Minnesota	55	30	486	4
Oct. 19, 1980	Dan Fouts, San Diego vs. N.Y. Giants	41	26	444	3
Oct. 12, 1980	Lynn Dickey, Green Bay vs. Tampa Bay (OT)	51	35	418	1
Sept. 21, 1980	Richard Todd, N.Y. Jets vs. San Francisco	60	42	447	3
Oct. 3, 1976	James Harris, Los Angeles vs. Miami	29	17	436	2
Nov. 17, 1975	Ken Anderson, Cincinnati vs. Buffalo	46	30	447	2
Nov. 18, 1974	Charley Johnson, Denver vs. Kansas City	42	28	445	2
Dec. 11, 1972	Joe Namath, N.Y. Jets vs. Oakland	46	25	403	1
Sept. 24, 1972	Joe Namath, N.Y. Jets vs. Baltimore	28	15	496	6
Dec. 21, 1969	Don Horn, Green Bay vs. St. Louis	31	22	410	5
Sept. 28, 1969	Joe Kapp, Minnesota vs. Baltimore	43	28	449	7
Sept. 9, 1968	Pete Beathard, Houston vs. Kansas City	48	23	413	2
Nov. 26, 1967	Sonny Jurgensen, Washington vs. Cleveland	50	32	418	3
Oct. 1, 1967	Joe Namath, N.Y. Jets vs. Miami	39	23	415	3
Sept. 17, 1967	Johnny Unitas, Baltimore vs. Atlanta	32	22	401	2
Nov. 13, 1966	Don Meredith, Dallas vs. Washington	29	21	406	2
Nov. 28, 1965	Sonny Jurgensen, Washington vs. Dallas	43	26	411	3
Oct. 24, 1965	Fran Tarkenton, Minnesota vs. San Francisco	35	21	407	3
Nov. 1, 1964	Len Dawson, Kansas City vs. Denver	38	23	435	6
Oct. 25, 1964	Cotton Davidson, Oakland vs. Denver	36	23	427	5
Oct. 16, 1964	Babe Parilli, Boston vs. Oakland	47	25	422	4
Dec. 22, 1963	Tom Flores, Oakland vs. Houston	29	17	407	6
Nov. 17, 1963	Norm Snead, Washington vs. Pittsburgh	40	23	424	2
Nov. 10, 1963	Don Meredith, Dallas vs. San Francisco	48	30	460	3
Oct. 13, 1963	Charley Johnson, St. Louis vs. Pittsburgh	41	20	428	2
Dec. 16, 1962	Sonny Jurgensen, Philadelphia vs. St. Louis	34	15	419	5
Nov. 18, 1962	Bill Wade, Chicago vs. Dall. Cowboys	46	28	466	2
Oct. 28, 1962	Y.A. Tittle, N.Y. Giants vs. Washington	39	27	505	7
Sept. 15, 1962	Frank Tripucka, Denver vs. Buffalo	56	29	447	2
Dec. 17, 1961	Sonny Jurgensen, Philadelphia vs. Detroit	42	27	403	3
Nov. 19, 1961	George Blanda, Houston vs. N.Y. Titans	32	20	418	7
Oct. 29, 1961	George Blanda, Houston vs. Buffalo	32	18	464	4
Oct. 29, 1961	Sonny Jurgensen, Philadelphia vs. Washington	41	27	436	3
Oct. 13, 1961	Jacky Lee, Houston vs. Boston	41	27	457	2
Dec. 13, 1958	Bobby Layne, Pittsburgh vs. Chi. Cardinals	49	23	409	2
Nov. 8, 1953	Bobby Thomason, Philadelphia vs. N.Y. Giants	44	22	437	4
Oct. 4, 1952	Otto Graham, Cleveland vs. Pittsburgh	49	21	401	3
Sept. 28, 1951	Norm Van Brocklin, Los Angeles vs. N.Y. Yanks	41	27	554	5
Dec. 11, 1949	Johnny Lujack, Chi. Bears vs. Chi. Cardinals	39	24	468	6
Oct. 31, 1948	Sammy Baugh, Washington vs. Boston	24	17	446	4
Oct. 31, 1948	Jim Hardy, Los Angeles vs. Chi. Cardinals	53	28	406	3
Nov. 14, 1943	Sid Luckman, Chi. Bears vs. N.Y. Giants	32	21	433	7

Times 400 or More
73 times by 47 players . . . Fouts 6; Jurgensen 5; Marino 4; Kramer, Krieg, Namath, Simms 3; Anderson, Blanda, Johnson, Meredith, Todd 2.

1,000 YARDS PASS RECEIVING IN A SEASON

Year	Player, Team	No.	Yards	Avg.	Long	TD
1985	Steve Largent, Seattle[7]	79	1,287	16.3	43	6
	Mike Quick, Philadelphia[3]	73	1,247	17.1	99	11
	Art Monk, Washington[2]	91	1,226	13.5	53	2
	Wes Chandler, San Diego[4]	67	1,199	17.9	75	10
	Drew Hill, Houston	64	1,169	18.3	57	9
	James Lofton, Green Bay[5]	69	1,153	16.7	56	4
	Louis Lipps, Pittsburgh	59	1,134	19.2	51	12
	Cris Collinsworth, Cincinnati[3]	65	1,125	17.3	71	5
	Tony Hill, Dallas[3]	74	1,113	15.0	53	7
	Lionel James, San Diego	86	1,027	11.9	67	6
	Roger Craig, San Francisco	92	1,016	11.0	73	6
1984	Roy Green, St. Louis[2]	78	1,555	19.9	83	12
	John Stallworth, Pittsburgh[3]	80	1,395	17.4	51	11
	Mark Clayton, Miami	73	1,389	19.0	65	18
	Art Monk, Washington	106	1,372	12.9	72	7
	James Lofton, Green Bay[4]	62	1,361	22.0	79	7
	Mark Duper, Miami[2]	71	1,306	18.4	80	8
	Steve Watson, Denver[3]	69	1,170	17.0	73	7
	Steve Largent, Seattle[6]	74	1,164	15.7	65	12
	Tim Smith, Houston[2]	69	1,141	16.5	75	4
	Stacey Bailey, Atlanta	67	1,138	17.0	61	6
	Carlos Carson, Kansas City[2]	57	1,078	18.9	57	4
	Mike Quick, Philadelphia[2]	61	1,052	17.2	90	9
	Todd Christensen, L.A. Raiders[2]	80	1,007	12.6	38	7
	Kevin House, Tampa Bay[2]	76	1,005	13.2	55	5
	Ozzie Newsome, Cleveland[2]	89	1,001	11.2	52	5
1983	Mike Quick, Philadelphia	69	1,409	20.4	83	13
	Carlos Carson, Kansas City	80	1,351	16.9	50	7
	James Lofton, Green Bay[3]	58	1,300	22.4	74	8
	Todd Christensen, L.A. Raiders	92	1,247	13.6	45	12
	Roy Green, St. Louis	78	1,227	15.7	71	14
	Charlie Brown, Washington	78	1,225	15.7	75	8
	Tim Smith, Houston	83	1,176	14.2	47	6
	Kellen Winslow, San Diego[3]	88	1,172	13.3	46	8
	Earnest Gray, N.Y. Giants	78	1,139	14.6	62	5
	Steve Watson, Denver[2]	59	1,133	19.2	78	5
	Cris Collinsworth, Cincinnati[2]	66	1,130	17.1	63	5
	Steve Largent, Seattle[5]	72	1,074	14.9	46	11
	Mark Duper, Miami	51	1,003	19.7	85	10
1982	Wes Chandler, San Diego[3]	49	1,032	21.1	66	9
1981	Alfred Jenkins, Atlanta[2]	70	1,358	19.4	67	13
	James Lofton, Green Bay[2]	71	1,294	18.2	75	8
	Frank Lewis, Buffalo[2]	70	1,244	17.8	33	4
	Steve Watson, Denver	60	1,244	20.7	95	13
	Steve Largent, Seattle[4]	75	1,224	16.3	57	9
	Charlie Joiner, San Diego[4]	70	1,188	17.0	57	7
	Kevin House, Tampa Bay	56	1,176	21.0	84	9
	Wes Chandler, N.O.-San Diego[2]	69	1,142	16.6	51	6
	Dwight Clark, San Francisco	85	1,105	13.0	78	4
	John Stallworth, Pittsburgh[2]	63	1,098	17.4	55	5
	Kellen Winslow, San Diego[2]	88	1,075	12.2	67	10
	Pat Tilley, St. Louis	66	1,040	15.8	75	3
	Stanley Morgan, New England[2]	44	1,029	23.4	76	6
	Harold Carmichael, Philadelphia[3]	61	1,028	16.9	85	6
	Freddie Scott, Detroit	53	1,022	19.3	48	5
	*Cris Collinsworth, Cincinnati	67	1,009	15.1	74	8
	Joe Senser, Minnesota	79	1,004	12.7	53	8
	Ozzie Newsome, Cleveland	69	1,002	14.5	62	6
	Sammy White, Minnesota	66	1,001	15.2	53	3
1980	John Jefferson, San Diego[2]	82	1,340	16.3	58	13
	Kellen Winslow, San Diego	89	1,290	14.5	65	9
	James Lofton, Green Bay	71	1,226	17.3	47	4
	Charlie Joiner, San Diego[3]	71	1,132	15.9	51	4
	Ahmad Rashad, Minnesota[2]	69	1,095	15.9	76	5

	Steve Largent, Seattle[3]	66	1,064	16.1	67	6
	Tony Hill, Dallas[2]	60	1,055	17.6	58	8
	Alfred Jenkins, Atlanta	57	1,026	18.0	57	6
1979	Steve Largent, Seattle[2]	66	1,237	18.7	55	9
	John Stallworth, Pittsburgh	70	1,183	16.9	65	8
	Ahmad Rashad, Minnesota	80	1,156	14.5	52	9
	John Jefferson, San Diego[2]	61	1,090	17.9	65	10
	Frank Lewis, Buffalo	54	1,082	20.0	55	2
	Wes Chandler, New Orleans	65	1,069	16.4	85	6
	Tony Hill, Dallas	60	1,062	17.7	75	10
	Drew Pearson, Dallas[2]	55	1,026	18.7	56	8
	Wallace Francis, Atlanta	74	1,013	13.7	42	8
	Harold Jackson, New England[3]	45	1,013	22.5	59	7
	Charlie Joiner, San Diego[2]	72	1,008	14.0	39	4
	Stanley Morgan, New England	44	1,002	22.8	63	12
1978	Wesley Walker, N.Y. Jets	48	1,169	24.4	77	8
	Steve Largent, Seattle	71	1,168	16.5	57	8
	Harold Carmichael, Philadelphia[2]	55	1,072	19.5	56	8
	John Jefferson, San Diego	56	1,001	17.9	46	13
1976	Roger Carr, Baltimore	43	1,112	25.9	79	11
	Cliff Branch, Oakland[2]	46	1,111	24.2	88	12
	Charlie Joiner, San Diego	50	1,056	21.1	81	7
1975	Ken Burrough, Houston	53	1,063	20.1	77	8
1974	Cliff Branch, Oakland	60	1,092	18.2	67	13
	Drew Pearson, Dallas	62	1,087	17.5	50	2
1973	Harold Carmichael, Philadelphia	67	1,116	16.7	73	9
1972	Harold Jackson, Philadelphia[2]	62	1,048	16.9	77	4
	John Gilliam, Minnesota	47	1,035	22.0	66	7
1971	Otis Taylor, Kansas City[2]	57	1,110	19.5	82	7
1970	Gene Washington, San Francisco	53	1,100	20.8	79	12
	Marlin Briscoe, Buffalo	57	1,036	18.2	48	8
	Dick Gordon, Chicago	71	1,026	14.5	69	13
	Gary Garrison, San Diego[2]	44	1,006	22.9	67	12
1969	Warren Wells, Oakland[2]	47	1,260	26.8	80	14
	Harold Jackson, Philadelphia	65	1,116	17.2	65	9
	Roy Jefferson, Pittsburgh[2]	67	1,079	16.1	63	9
	Dan Abramowicz, New Orleans	73	1,015	13.9	49	7
	Lance Alworth, San Diego[7]	64	1,003	15.7	76	4
1968	Lance Alworth, San Diego[6]	68	1,312	19.3	80	10
	Don Maynard, N.Y. Jets[5]	57	1,297	22.8	87	10
	George Sauer, N.Y. Jets[3]	66	1,141	17.3	43	3
	Warren Wells, Oakland	53	1,137	21.5	94	11
	Gary Garrison, San Diego	52	1,103	21.2	84	10
	Roy Jefferson, Pittsburgh	58	1,074	18.5	62	11
	Paul Warfield, Cleveland	50	1,067	21.3	65	12
	Homer Jones, N.Y. Giants[3]	45	1,057	23.5	84	7
	Fred Biletnikoff, Oakland	61	1,037	17.0	82	6
	Lance Rentzel, Dallas	54	1,009	18.7	65	6
1967	Don Maynard, N.Y. Jets[4]	71	1,434	20.2	75	10
	Ben Hawkins, Philadelphia	59	1,265	21.4	87	10
	Homer Jones, N.Y. Giants[2]	49	1,209	24.7	70	13
	Jackie Smith, St. Louis	56	1,205	21.5	76	9
	George Sauer, N.Y. Jets[2]	75	1,189	15.9	61	6
	Lance Alworth, San Diego[5]	52	1,010	19.4	71	9
1966	Lance Alworth, San Diego[4]	73	1,383	18.9	78	13
	Otis Taylor, Kansas City	58	1,297	22.4	89	8
	Pat Studstill, Detroit	67	1,266	18.9	99	5
	Bob Hayes, Dallas[2]	64	1,232	19.3	95	13
	Charlie Frazier, Houston	57	1,129	19.8	79	12
	Charley Taylor, Washington	72	1,119	15.5	86	12
	George Sauer, N.Y. Jets	63	1,081	17.2	77	5
	Homer Jones, N.Y. Giants	48	1,044	21.8	98	8
	Art Powell, Oakland[5]	53	1,026	19.4	46	11
1965	Lance Alworth, San Diego[3]	69	1,602	23.2	85	14
	Dave Parks, San Francisco	80	1,344	16.8	53	12
	Don Maynard, N.Y. Jets[3]	68	1,218	17.9	56	14
	Pete Retzlaff, Philadelphia	66	1,190	18.0	78	10
	Lionel Taylor, Denver[4]	85	1,131	13.3	63	6
	Tommy McDonald, Los Angeles[3]	67	1,036	15.5	51	9
	*Bob Hayes, Dallas	46	1,003	21.8	82	12
1964	Charley Hennigan, Houston[3]	101	1,546	15.3	53	8
	Art Powell, Oakland[4]	76	1,361	17.9	77	11
	Lance Alworth, San Diego[2]	61	1,235	20.2	82	13
	Johnny Morris, Chicago	93	1,200	12.9	63	10
	Elbert Dubenion, Buffalo	42	1,139	27.1	72	10
	Terry Barr, Detroit[2]	57	1,030	18.1	58	9
1963	Bobby Mitchell, Washington[2]	69	1,436	20.8	99	7
	Art Powell, Oakland[3]	73	1,304	17.9	85	16
	Buddy Dial, Pittsburgh[2]	60	1,295	21.6	83	9
	Lance Alworth, San Diego	61	1,205	19.8	85	11
	Del Shofner, N.Y. Giants[4]	64	1,181	18.5	70	9
	Lionel Taylor, Denver[3]	78	1,101	14.1	72	10
	Terry Barr, Detroit	66	1,086	16.5	75	13
	Charley Hennigan, Houston[2]	61	1,051	17.2	83	10
	Sonny Randle, St. Louis[2]	51	1,014	19.9	68	12
	Bake Turner, N.Y. Jets	71	1,009	14.2	53	6
1962	Bobby Mitchell, Washington	72	1,384	19.2	81	11
	Sonny Randle, St. Louis	63	1,158	18.4	86	7
	Tommy McDonald, Philadelphia[2]	58	1,146	19.8	60	10
	Del Shofner, N.Y. Giants[3]	53	1,133	21.4	69	12
	Art Powell, N.Y. Titans[2]	64	1,130	17.7	80	8
	Frank Clarke, Dall. Cowboys	47	1,043	22.2	66	14
	Don Maynard, N.Y. Titans[2]	56	1,041	18.6	86	8
1961	Charley Hennigan, Houston	82	1,746	21.3	80	12
	Lionel Taylor, Denver[2]	100	1,176	11.8	52	4
	Bill Groman, Houston[2]	50	1,175	23.5	80	17
	Tommy McDonald, Philadelphia	64	1,144	17.9	66	13
	Del Shofner, N.Y. Giants[2]	68	1,125	16.5	46	11
	Jim Phillips, Los Angeles	78	1,092	14.0	69	5
	*Mike Ditka, Chicago	56	1,076	19.2	76	12
	Dave Kocourek, San Diego	55	1,055	19.2	76	4
	Buddy Dial, Pittsburgh	53	1,047	19.8	88	12
	R.C. Owens, San Francisco	55	1,032	18.8	54	5
1960	*Bill Groman, Houston	72	1,473	20.5	92	12
	Raymond Berry, Baltimore	74	1,298	17.5	70	10
	Don Maynard, N.Y. Titans	72	1,265	17.6	65	6
	Lionel Taylor, Denver	92	1,235	13.4	80	12
	Art Powell, N.Y. Titans	69	1,167	16.9	76	14
1958	Del Shofner, Los Angeles	51	1,097	21.5	92	8
1956	Bill Howton, Green Bay[2]	55	1,188	21.6	66	12
	Harlon Hill, Chi. Bears[2]	47	1,128	24.0	79	11
1954	Bob Boyd, Los Angeles	53	1,212	22.9	80	6
	*Harlon Hill, Chi. Bears	45	1,124	25.0	76	12
1953	Pete Pihos, Philadelphia	63	1,049	16.7	59	10
1952	*Bill Howton, Green Bay	53	1,231	23.2	90	13
1951	Elroy (Crazylegs) Hirsch, Los Angeles	66	1,495	22.7	91	17
1950	Tom Fears, Los Angeles[2]	84	1,116	13.3	53	7
	Cloyce Box, Detroit	50	1,009	20.2	82	11
1949	Bob Mann, Detroit	66	1,014	15.4	64	4
	Tom Fears, Los Angeles	77	1,013	13.2	51	9
1945	Jim Benton, Cleveland	45	1,067	23.7	84	8
1942	Don Hutson, Green Bay	74	1,211	16.4	73	17

**First year in the league.*

250 YARDS PASS RECEIVING IN A GAME

Date	Player, Team, Opponent	No.	Yards	TD
Dec. 22, 1985	Stephone Paige, Kansas City vs. San Diego	8	309	2
Dec. 20, 1982	Wes Chandler, San Diego vs. Cincinnati	10	260	2
Sept. 23, 1979	*Jerry Butler, Buffalo vs. N.Y. Jets	10	255	4
Nov. 4, 1962	Sonny Randle, St. Louis vs. N.Y. Giants	16	256	1
Oct. 28, 1962	Del Shofner, N.Y. Giants vs. Washington	11	269	1
Oct. 13, 1961	Charley Hennigan, Houston vs. Boston	13	272	1
Oct. 21, 1956	Billy Howton, Green Bay vs. Los Angeles	7	257	2
Dec. 3, 1950	Cloyce Box, Detroit vs. Baltimore	12	302	4
Nov. 22, 1945	Jim Benton, Cleveland vs. Detroit	10	303	1

**First year in the league.*

2,000 COMBINED NET YARDS GAINED IN A SEASON

Year	Player, Team	Rushing Att.-Yds.	Pass Rec.	Punt Ret.	Kickoff Ret.	Fum. Runs	Total Yds.
1985	Lionel James, San Diego	105-516	86-1,027	25-213	36-779	1-0	253-2,535
	Marcus Allen, L.A. Raiders	380-1,759	67-555	0-0	0-0	2-(−6)	449-2,308
	Roger Craig, San Fran.	214-1,050	92-1,016	0-0	0-0	0-0	306-2,066
	Walter Payton, Chicago	324-1,551	49-483	0-0	0-0	1-0	374-2,034
1984	Eric Dickerson, L.A. Rams	379-2,105	21-139	0-0	0-0	4-15	404-2,259
	James Wilder, Tampa Bay	407-1,544	85-685	0-0	0-0	4-0	496-2,229
	Walter Payton, Chicago	381-1,684	45-368	0-0	0-0	1-0	427-2,052
1983	*Eric Dickerson, L.A. Rams	390-1,808	51-404	0-0	0-0	1-0	442-2,212
	William Andrews, Atlanta	331-1,567	59-609	0-0	0-0	2-0	392-2,176
	Walter Payton, Chicago	314-1,421	53-607	0-0	0-0	2-0	369-2,028
1981	*James Brooks, San Diego	109-525	46-329	22-290	40-949	2-0	219-2,093
	William Andrews, Atlanta	289-1,301	81-735	0-0	0-0	0-0	370-2,036
1980	Bruce Harper, N.Y. Jets	45-126	50-634	28-242	49-1,070	3-0	175-2,072
1979	Wilbert Montgomery, Phil.	338-1,512	41-494	0-0	1-6	2-0	382-2,012
1978	Bruce Harper, N.Y. Jets	58-303	13-196	30-378	55-1,280	1-0	157-2,157
1977	Walter Payton, Chicago	339-1,852	27-269	0-0	2-95	5-0	373-2,216
	Terry Metcalf, St. Louis	149-739	34-403	14-108	32-772	1-0	230-2,022
1975	Terry Metcalf, St. Louis	165-816	43-378	23-285	35-960	2-23	268-2,462
	O.J. Simpson, Buffalo	329-1,817	28-426	0-0	0-0	1-0	358-2,243
1974	Mack Herron, New England	231-824	38-474	35-517	28-629	3-0	335-2,444
	Otis Armstrong, Denver	263-1,407	38-405	0-0	16-386	1-0	318-2,198
	Terry Metcalf, St. Louis	152-718	50-377	26-340	20-623	7-0	255-2,058
1973	O.J. Simpson, Buffalo	332-2,003	6-70	0-0	0-0	0-0	338-2,073
1966	Gale Sayers, Chicago	229-1,231	34-447	6-44	23-718	3-0	295-2,440
	Leroy Kelly, Cleveland	209-1,141	32-366	13-104	19-403	0-0	273-2,014
1965	*Gale Sayers, Chicago	166-867	29-507	16-238	21-660	4-0	236-2,272
1963	Timmy Brown, Philadelphia	192-841	36-487	16-152	33-945	2-3	279-2,428
	Jim Brown, Cleveland	291-1,863	24-268	0-0	0-0	0-0	315-2,131
1962	Timmy Brown, Philadelphia	137-545	52-849	6-81	30-831	4-0	229-2,306
	Dick Christy, N.Y. Titans	114-535	62-538	15-250	38-824	2-0	231-2,147
1961	Billy Cannon, Houston	200-948	43-586	9-70	18-439	2-0	272-2,043
1960	*Abner Haynes, Dall. Texans	156-875	55-576	14-215	19-434	4-0	248-2,100

**First year in the league.*

300 COMBINED NET YARDS GAINED IN A GAME

Date	Player, Team, Opponent	No.	Yards	TD
Dec. 22, 1985	Stephone Paige, Kansas City vs. San Diego	8	309	2
Nov. 10, 1985	Lionel James, San Diego vs. L.A. Raiders (OT)	23	345	0
Sept. 22, 1985	Lionel James, San Diego vs. Cincinnati	20	316	2
Dec. 21, 1975	Walter Payton, Chicago vs. New Orleans	32	300	1
Nov. 23, 1975	Greg Pruitt, Cleveland vs. Cincinnati	28	304	2
Nov. 1, 1970	Eugene (Mercury) Morris, Miami vs. Baltimore	17	302	0
Oct. 4, 1970	O. J. Simpson, Buffalo vs. N.Y. Jets	26	303	2
Dec. 6, 1969	Jerry LeVias, Houston vs. N.Y. Jets	18	329	1
Nov. 2, 1969	Travis Williams, Green Bay vs. Pittsburgh	11	314	3
Dec. 18, 1966	Gale Sayers, Chicago vs. Minnesota	20	339	2
Dec. 12, 1965	Gale Sayers, Chicago vs. San Francisco	17	336	6
Nov. 17, 1963	Gary Ballman, Pittsburgh vs. Washington	12	320	2
Dec. 16, 1962	Timmy Brown, Philadelphia vs. St. Louis	19	341	2
Dec. 10, 1961	Billy Cannon, Houston vs. N.Y. Titans	32	373	5
Nov. 19, 1961	Jim Brown, Cleveland vs. Philadelphia	38	313	4
Dec. 3, 1950	Cloyce Box, Detroit vs. Baltimore	13	302	4
Oct. 29, 1950	Wally Triplett, Detroit vs. Los Angeles	11	331	1
Nov. 22, 1945	Jim Benton, Cleveland vs. Detroit	10	303	1

TOP 10 SCORERS

Player	Years	TD	FG	PAT	TP
George Blanda	26	9	335	943	2,002
Jan Stenerud	19	0	373	580	1,699
Jim Turner	16	1	304	521	1,439
Jim Bakken	17	0	282	534	1,380
Fred Cox	15	0	282	519	1,365
Lou Groza	17	1	234	641	1,349
Mark Moseley	15	0	288	457	1,321
Gino Cappelletti	11	42	176	350	1,130
Don Cockroft	13	0	216	432	1,080
Garo Yepremian	14	0	210	444	1,074

Cappelletti's total includes four two-point conversions.

TOP 10 TOUCHDOWN SCORERS

Player	Years	Rush	Pass Rec.	Returns	Total TD
Jim Brown	9	106	20	0	126
John Riggins	14	104	12	0	116
Lenny Moore	12	63	48	2	113
Walter Payton	11	98	11	0	109
Don Hutson	11	3	99	3	105
Franco Harris	13	91	9	0	100
Jim Taylor	10	83	10	0	93
Bobby Mitchell	11	18	65	8	91
Leroy Kelly	10	74	13	3	90
Charley Taylor	13	11	79	0	90

TOP 10 RUSHERS

Player	Years	Att.	Yards	Avg.	Long	TD
Walter Payton	11	3,371	14,860	4.4	76	98
Jim Brown	9	2,359	12,312	5.2	80	106
Franco Harris	13	2,949	12,120	4.1	75	91
John Riggins	14	2,916	11,352	3.9	66	104
O. J. Simpson	11	2,404	11,236	4.7	94	61
Tony Dorsett	9	2,441	10,832	4.4	99	66
Earl Campbell	8	2,187	9,407	4.3	81	74
Jim Taylor	10	1,941	8,597	4.4	84	83
Joe Perry	14	1,737	8,378	4.8	78	53
Larry Csonka	11	1,891	8,081	4.3	54	64

TOP 10 PASSERS

Player	Years	Att.	Comp.	Pct. Comp.	Yards	TD	Pct. TD	Int.	Pct. Int.	Avg. Gain	Rating
Joe Montana	7	2,571	1,627	63.3	19,262	133	5.2	67	2.6	7.49	92.4
Roger Staubach	11	2,958	1,685	57.0	22,700	153	5.2	109	3.7	7.67	83.4
Sonny Jurgensen	18	4,262	2,433	57.1	32,224	255	6.0	189	4.4	7.56	82.6
Len Dawson	19	3,741	2,136	57.1	28,711	239	6.4	183	4.9	7.67	82.6
Neil Lomax	5	1,826	1,047	57.3	13,406	79	4.3	55	3.0	7.34	82.3
Danny White	10	2,393	1,422	59.4	17,911	130	5.4	107	4.5	7.48	82.3
Ken Anderson	15	4,452	2,643	59.4	32,667	196	4.4	158	3.5	7.34	82.0
Dan Fouts	13	4,810	2,839	59.0	37,492	228	4.7	205	4.3	7.79	81.8
Bart Starr	16	3,149	1,808	57.4	24,718	152	4.8	138	4.4	7.85	80.5
Fran Tarkenton	18	6,467	3,686	57.0	47,003	342	5.3	266	4.1	7.27	80.4

1,500 or more attempts. The passing ratings are based on performance standards established for completion percentage, interception percentage, touchdown percentage, and average gain. Passers are allocated points according to how their marks compare with those standards.

TOP 10 PASS RECEIVERS

Player	Years	No.	Yards	Avg.	Long	TD
Charlie Joiner	17	716	11,706	16.3	87	63
Charley Taylor	13	649	9,110	14.0	88	79
Don Maynard	15	633	11,834	18.7	87	88
Raymond Berry	13	631	9,275	14.7	70	68
Steve Largent	10	624	10,059	16.1	74	78
Harold Carmichael	14	590	8,985	15.2	85	79
Fred Biletnikoff	14	589	8,974	15.2	82	76
Harold Jackson	16	579	10,372	17.9	79	76
Lionel Taylor	10	567	7,195	12.7	80	45
Lance Alworth	11	542	10,266	18.9	85	85

TOP 10 INTERCEPTORS

Player	Years	No.	Yards	Avg.	Long	TD
Paul Krause	16	81	1,185	14.6	81	3
Emlen Tunnell	14	79	1,282	16.2	55	4
Dick (Night Train) Lane	14	68	1,207	17.8	80	5
Ken Riley	15	65	596	9.2	66	5
Dick LeBeau	13	62	762	12.3	70	3
Emmitt Thomas	13	58	937	16.2	73	5
Bobby Boyd	9	57	994	17.4	74	4
Johnny Robinson	12	57	741	13.0	57	1
Mel Blount	14	57	736	12.9	52	2
Lem Barney	11	56	1,077	19.2	71	7
Pat Fischer	17	56	941	16.8	69	4

TOP 10 PUNTERS

Player	Years	No.	Yards	Avg.	Long	Blk.
Rohn Stark	4	313	14,135	45.2	72	2
Sammy Baugh	16	338	15,245	45.1	85	9
Tommy Davis	11	511	22,833	44.7	82	2
Yale Lary	11	503	22,279	44.3	74	4
Horace Gillom	7	385	16,872	43.8	85	5
Jerry Norton	11	358	15,671	43.8	78	2
Don Chandler	12	660	28,678	43.5	90	4
Rich Camarillo	5	317	13,687	43.2	76	0
Jerrel Wilson	16	1,072	46,139	43.0	72	12
Norm Van Brocklin	12	523	22,413	42.9	72	3

300 or more punts.

TOP 10 PUNT RETURNERS

Player	Years	No.	Yards	Avg.	Long	TD
Henry Ellard	3	83	1,121	13.5	83	4
George McAfee	8	112	1,431	12.8	74	2
Jack Christiansen	8	85	1,084	12.8	89	8
Claude Gibson	5	110	1,381	12.6	85	3
Louis Lipps	2	89	1,093	12.3	76	3
Bill Dudley	9	124	1,515	12.2	96	3
Billy Johnson	11	250	3,036	12.1	87	6
Rick Upchurch	9	248	3,008	12.1	92	8
Mack Herron	3	84	982	11.7	66	0
Bill Thompson	13	157	1,814	11.6	60	0

75 or more returns.

TOP 10 KICKOFF RETURNERS

Player	Years	No.	Yards	Avg.	Long	TD
Gale Sayers	7	91	2,781	30.6	103	6
Lynn Chandnois	7	92	2,720	29.6	93	3
Abe Woodson	9	193	5,538	28.7	105	5
Claude (Buddy) Young	6	90	2,514	27.9	104	2
Travis Williams	5	102	2,801	27.5	105	6
Joe Arenas	7	139	3,798	27.3	96	1
Clarence Davis	8	79	2,140	27.1	76	0
Lenny Lyles	12	81	2,161	26.7	103	3
Steve Van Buren	8	76	2,030	26.7	98	3
Eugene (Mercury) Morris	8	111	2,947	26.5	105	3

75 or more returns.

TOP 10 COMBINED YARDS GAINED

Player	Tot.	Rush.	Rec.	Int. Ret.	Punt Ret.	Kickoff Ret.	Fumble
Walter Payton	19,338	14,860	3,939	0	0	539	0
Jim Brown	15,459	12,312	2,499	0	0	648	0
Franco Harris	14,622	12,120	2,287	0	0	233	-18
O. J. Simpson	14,368	11,236	2,142	0	0	990	0
Bobby Mitchell	14,078	2,735	7,954	0	699	2,690	0
Tony Dorsett	13,853	10,832	2,988	0	0	0	33
John Riggins	13,435	11,352	2,090	0	0	0	-7
Greg Pruitt	13,262	5,672	3,069	0	2,007	2,514	0
Ollie Matson	12,884	5,173	3,285	51	595	3,746	34
Tim Brown	12,684	3,862	3,399	0	639	4,781	3

YEARLY STATISTICAL LEADERS

ANNUAL SCORING LEADERS

Year	Player, Team	TD	FG	PAT	TP
1985	*Kevin Butler, Chicago, NFC	0	31	51	144
	Gary Anderson, Pittsburgh, AFC	0	33	40	139
1984	Ray Wersching, San Francisco, NFC	0	25	56	131
	Gary Anderson, Pittsburgh, AFC	0	24	45	117
1983	Mark Moseley, Washington, NFC	0	33	62	161
	Gary Anderson, Pittsburgh, AFC	0	27	38	119
1982	*Marcus Allen, L.A. Raiders, AFC	14	0	0	84
	Wendell Tyler, L.A. Rams, NFC	13	0	0	78
1981	Ed Murray, Detroit, NFC	0	25	46	121
	Rafael Septien, Dallas, NFC	0	27	40	121
	Jim Breech, Cincinnati, AFC	0	22	49	115
	Nick Lowery, Kansas City, AFC	0	26	37	115
1980	John Smith, New England, AFC	0	26	51	129
	*Ed Murray, Detroit, NFC	0	27	35	116
1979	John Smith, New England, AFC	0	23	46	115
	Mark Moseley, Washington, NFC	0	25	39	114
1978	*Frank Corral, Los Angeles, NFC	0	29	31	118
	Pat Leahy, N.Y. Jets, AFC	0	22	41	107
1977	Errol Mann, Oakland, AFC	0	20	39	99
	Walter Payton, Chicago, NFC	16	0	0	96
1976	Toni Linhart, Baltimore, AFC	0	20	49	109
	Mark Moseley, Washington, NFC	0	22	31	97
1975	O.J. Simpson, Buffalo, AFC	23	0	0	138
	Chuck Foreman, Minnesota, NFC	22	0	0	132
1974	Chester Marcol, Green Bay, NFC	0	25	19	94
	Roy Gerela, Pittsburgh, AFC	0	20	33	93
1973	David Ray, Los Angeles, NFC	0	30	40	130
	Roy Gerela, Pittsburgh, AFC	0	29	36	123
1972	*Chester Marcol, Green Bay, NFC	0	33	29	128
	Bobby Howfield, N.Y. Jets, AFC	0	27	40	121
1971	Garo Yepremian, Miami, AFC	0	28	33	117
	Curt Knight, Washington, NFC	0	29	27	114
1970	Fred Cox, Minnesota, NFC	0	30	35	125
	Jan Stenerud, Kansas City, AFC	0	30	26	116
1969	Jim Turner, N.Y. Jets, AFL	0	32	33	129
	Fred Cox, Minnesota, NFL	0	26	43	121
1968	Jim Turner, N.Y. Jets, AFL	0	34	43	145
	Leroy Kelly, Cleveland, NFL	20	0	0	120
1967	Jim Bakken, St. Louis, NFL	0	27	36	117
	George Blanda, Oakland, AFL	0	20	56	116
1966	Gino Cappelletti, Boston, AFL	6	16	35	119
	Bruce Gossett, Los Angeles, NFL	0	28	29	113
1965	*Gale Sayers, Chicago, NFL	22	0	0	132
	Gino Cappelletti, Boston, AFL	9	17	27	132
1964	Gino Cappelletti, Boston, AFL	7	25	36	#155
	Lenny Moore, Baltimore, NFL	20	0	0	120
1963	Gino Cappelletti, Boston, AFL	2	22	35	113
	Don Chandler, N.Y. Giants, NFL	0	18	52	106
1962	Gene Mingo, Denver, AFL	4	27	32	137
	Jim Taylor, Green Bay, NFL	19	0	0	114
1961	Gino Cappelletti, Boston, AFL	8	17	48	147
	Paul Hornung, Green Bay, NFL	10	15	41	146
1960	Paul Hornung, Green Bay, NFL	15	15	41	176
	*Gene Mingo, Denver, AFL	6	18	33	123
1959	Paul Hornung, Green Bay	7	7	31	94
1958	Jim Brown, Cleveland	18	0	0	108
1957	Sam Baker, Washington	1	14	29	77
	Lou Groza, Cleveland	0	15	32	77
1956	Bobby Layne, Detroit	5	12	33	99
1955	Doak Walker, Detroit	7	9	27	96
1954	Bobby Walston, Philadelphia	11	4	36	114
1953	Gordy Soltau, San Francisco	6	10	48	114
1952	Gordy Soltau, San Francisco	7	6	34	94
1951	Elroy (Crazylegs) Hirsch, Los Angeles	17	0	0	102
1950	*Doak Walker, Detroit	11	8	38	128
1949	Pat Harder, Chi. Cardinals	8	3	45	102
	Gene Roberts, N.Y. Giants	17	0	0	102
1948	Pat Harder, Chi. Cardinals	6	7	53	110
1947	Pat Harder, Chi. Cardinals	7	7	39	102
1946	Ted Fritsch, Green Bay	10	9	13	100
1945	Steve Van Buren, Philadelphia	18	0	2	110
1944	Don Hutson, Green Bay	9	0	31	85
1943	Don Hutson, Green Bay	12	3	36	117
1942	Don Hutson, Green Bay	17	1	33	138
1941	Don Hutson, Green Bay	12	1	20	95
1940	Don Hutson, Green Bay	7	0	15	57
1939	Andy Farkas, Washington	11	0	2	68
1938	Clarke Hinkle, Green Bay	7	3	7	58
1937	Jack Manders, Chi. Bears	5	8	15	69
1936	Earl (Dutch) Clark, Detroit	7	4	19	73
1935	Earl (Dutch) Clark, Detroit	6	1	16	55
1934	Jack Manders, Chi. Bears	3	10	31	79
1933	Ken Strong, N.Y. Giants	6	5	13	64
	Glenn Presnell, Portsmouth	6	6	10	64
1932	Earl (Dutch) Clark, Portsmouth	6	3	10	55

*First year in the league.
#Cappelletti's total includes a two-point conversion.

ANNUAL LEADERS—MOST FIELD GOALS MADE

Year	Player, Team	Att.	Made	Pct.
1985	Gary Anderson, Pittsburgh, AFC	42	33	78.6
	Morten Andersen, New Orleans, NFC	35	31	88.6
	*Kevin Butler, Chicago, NFC	37	31	83.8
1984	*Paul McFadden, Philadelphia, NFC	37	30	81.1
	Gary Anderson, Pittsburgh, AFC	32	24	75.0
	Matt Bahr, Cleveland, AFC	32	24	75.0
1983	*Ali Haji-Sheikh, N.Y. Giants, NFC	42	35	83.3
	*Raul Allegre, Baltimore, AFC	35	30	85.7
1982	Mark Moseley, Washington, NFC	21	20	95.2
	Nick Lowery, Kansas City, AFC	24	19	79.2
1981	Rafael Septien, Dallas, NFC	35	27	77.1
	Nick Lowery, Kansas City, AFC	36	26	72.2
1980	*Ed Murray, Detroit, NFC	42	27	64.3
	John Smith, New England, AFC	34	26	76.5
	Fred Steinfort, Denver, AFC	34	26	76.5
1979	Mark Moseley, Washington, NFC	33	25	75.8
	John Smith, New England, AFC	33	23	69.7
1978	*Frank Corral, Los Angeles, NFC	43	29	67.4
	Pat Leahy, N.Y. Jets, AFC	30	22	73.3
1977	Mark Moseley, Washington, NFC	37	21	56.8
	Errol Mann, Oakland, AFC	28	20	71.4
1976	Mark Moseley, Washington, NFC	34	22	64.7
	Jan Stenerud, Kansas City, AFC	38	21	55.3
1975	Jan Stenerud, Kansas City, AFC	32	22	68.8
	Toni Fritsch, Dallas, NFC	35	22	62.9
1974	Chester Marcol, Green Bay, NFC	39	25	64.1
	Roy Gerela, Pittsburgh, AFC	29	20	69.0
1973	David Ray, Los Angeles, NFC	47	30	63.8
	Roy Gerela, Pittsburgh, AFC	43	29	67.4
1972	*Chester Marcol, Green Bay, NFC	48	33	68.8
	Roy Gerela, Pittsburgh, AFC	41	28	68.3
1971	Curt Knight, Washington, NFC	49	29	59.2
	Garo Yepremian, Miami, AFC	40	28	70.0
1970	Jan Stenerud, Kansas City, AFC	42	30	71.4
	Fred Cox, Minnesota, NFC	46	30	65.2
1969	Jim Turner, N.Y. Jets, AFL	47	32	68.1
	Fred Cox, Minnesota, NFL	37	26	70.3
1968	Jim Turner, N.Y. Jets, AFL	46	34	73.9
	Mac Percival, Chicago, NFL	36	25	69.4
1967	Jim Bakken, St. Louis, NFL	39	27	69.2
	Jan Stenerud, Kansas City, AFL	36	21	58.3
1966	Bruce Gossett, Los Angeles, NFL	49	28	57.1
	Mike Mercer, Oakland-Kansas City, AFL	30	21	70.0
1965	Pete Gogolak, Buffalo, AFL	46	28	60.9
	Fred Cox, Minnesota, NFL	35	23	65.7
1964	Jim Bakken, St. Louis, NFL	38	25	65.8
	Gino Cappelletti, Boston, AFL	39	25	64.1
1963	Jim Martin, Baltimore, NFL	39	24	61.5
	Gino Cappelletti, Boston, AFL	38	22	57.9
1962	Gene Mingo, Denver, AFL	39	27	69.2
	Lou Michaels, Pittsburgh, NFL	42	26	61.9
1961	Steve Myhra, Baltimore, NFL	39	21	53.8
	Gino Cappelletti, Boston, AFL	32	17	53.1
1960	Tommy Davis, San Francisco, NFL	32	19	59.4
	*Gene Mingo, Denver, AFL	28	18	64.3
1959	Pat Summerall, New York Giants	29	20	69.0
1958	Paige Cothren, Los Angeles	25	14	56.0
	*Tom Miner, Pittsburgh	28	14	50.0
1957	Lou Groza, Cleveland	22	15	68.2
1956	Sam Baker, Washington	25	17	68.0
1955	Fred Cone, Green Bay	24	16	66.7
1954	Lou Groza, Cleveland	24	16	66.7
1953	Lou Groza, Cleveland	26	23	88.5
1952	Lou Groza, Cleveland	33	19	57.6
1951	Bob Waterfield, Los Angeles	23	13	56.5
1950	*Lou Groza, Cleveland	19	13	68.4
1949	Cliff Patton, Philadelphia	18	9	50.0
	Bob Waterfield, Los Angeles	16	9	56.3
1948	Cliff Patton, Philadelphia	12	8	66.7
1947	Ward Cuff, Green Bay	16	7	43.8
	Pat Harder, Chi. Cardinals	10	7	70.0
	Bob Waterfield, Los Angeles	16	7	43.8
1946	Ted Fritsch, Green Bay	17	9	52.9
1945	Joe Aguirre, Washington	13	7	53.8
1944	Ken Strong, N.Y. Giants	12	6	50.0
1943	Ward Cuff, N.Y. Giants	9	3	33.3
	Don Hutson, Green Bay	5	3	60.0
1942	Bill Daddio, Chi. Cardinals	10	5	50.0
1941	Clarke Hinkle, Green Bay	14	6	42.9
1940	Clarke Hinkle, Green Bay	14	9	64.3
1939	Ward Cuff, N.Y. Giants	16	7	43.8
1938	Ward Cuff, N.Y. Giants	9	5	55.6
	Ralph Kercheval, Brooklyn	13	5	38.5
1937	Jack Manders, Chi. Bears		8	
1936	Jack Manders, Chi. Bears		7	
	Armand Niccolai, Pittsburgh		7	
1935	Armand Niccolai, Pittsburgh		6	
	Bill Smith, Chi. Cardinals		6	
1934	Jack Manders, Chi. Bears		10	
1933	*Jack Manders, Chi. Bears		6	
	Glenn Presnell, Portsmouth		6	
1932	Earl (Dutch) Clark, Portsmouth		3	

*First year in the league.

ANNUAL RUSHING LEADERS

Year	Player, Team	Att.	Yards	Avg.	TD
1985	Marcus Allen, L.A. Raiders, AFC	380	1,759	4.6	11
	Gerald Riggs, Atlanta, NFC	397	1,719	4.3	10
1984	Eric Dickerson, L.A. Rams, NFC	379	2,105	5.6	14
	Earnest Jackson, San Diego, AFC	296	1,179	4.0	8
1983	*Eric Dickerson, L.A. Rams, NFC	390	1,808	4.6	18
	*Curt Warner, Seattle, AFC	335	1,449	4.3	13
1982	Freeman McNeil, N.Y. Jets, AFC	151	786	5.2	6
	Tony Dorsett, Dallas, NFC	177	745	4.2	5

1981	*George Rogers, New Orleans, NFC	378	1,674	4.4	13
	Earl Campbell, Houston, AFC	361	1,376	3.8	10
1980	Earl Campbell, Houston, AFC	373	1,934	5.2	13
	Walter Payton, Chicago, NFC	317	1,460	4.6	6
1979	Earl Campbell, Houston, AFC	368	1,697	4.6	19
	Walter Payton, Chicago, NFC	369	1,610	4.4	14
1978	*Earl Campbell, Houston, AFC	302	1,450	4.8	13
	Walter Payton, Chicago, NFC	333	1,395	4.2	11
1977	Walter Payton, Chicago, NFC	339	1,852	5.5	14
	Mark van Eeghen, Oakland, AFC	324	1,273	3.9	7
1976	O.J. Simpson, Buffalo, AFC	290	1,503	5.2	8
	Walter Payton, Chicago, NFC	311	1,390	4.5	13
1975	O.J. Simpson, Buffalo, AFC	329	1,817	5.5	16
	Jim Otis, St. Louis, NFC	269	1,076	4.0	5
1974	Otis Armstrong, Denver, AFC	263	1,407	5.3	9
	Lawrence McCutcheon, Los Angeles, NFC	236	1,109	4.7	3
1973	O.J. Simpson, Buffalo, AFC	332	2,003	6.0	12
	John Brockington, Green Bay, NFC	265	1,144	4.3	3
1972	O.J. Simpson, Buffalo, AFC	292	1,251	4.3	6
	Larry Brown, Washington, NFC	285	1,216	4.3	8
1971	Floyd Little, Denver, AFC	284	1,133	4.0	6
	*John Brockington, Green Bay, NFC	216	1,105	5.1	4
1970	Larry Brown, Washington, NFC	237	1,125	4.7	5
	Floyd Little, Denver, AFC	209	901	4.3	3
1969	Gale Sayers, Chicago, NFL	236	1,032	4.4	8
	Dickie Post, San Diego, AFL	182	873	4.8	6
1968	Leroy Kelly, Cleveland, NFL	248	1,239	5.0	16
	*Paul Robinson, Cincinnati, AFL	238	1,023	4.3	8
1967	Jim Nance, Boston, AFL	269	1,216	4.5	7
	Leroy Kelly, Cleveland, NFL	235	1,205	5.1	11
1966	Jim Nance, Boston, AFL	299	1,458	4.9	11
	Gale Sayers, Chicago, NFL	229	1,231	5.4	8
1965	Jim Brown, Cleveland, NFL	289	1,544	5.3	17
	Paul Lowe, San Diego, AFL	222	1,121	5.0	7
1964	Jim Brown, Cleveland, NFL	280	1,446	5.2	7
	Cookie Gilchrist, Buffalo, AFL	230	981	4.3	6
1963	Jim Brown, Cleveland, NFL	291	1,863	6.4	12
	Clem Daniels, Oakland, AFL	215	1,099	5.1	3
1962	Jim Taylor, Green Bay, NFL	272	1,474	5.4	19
	*Cookie Gilchrist, Buffalo, AFL	214	1,096	5.1	13
1961	Jim Brown, Cleveland, NFL	305	1,408	4.6	8
	Billy Cannon, Houston, AFL	200	948	4.7	6
1960	Jim Brown, Cleveland, NFL	215	1,257	5.8	9
	*Abner Haynes, Dall. Texans, AFL	156	875	5.6	9
1959	Jim Brown, Cleveland	290	1,329	4.6	14
1958	Jim Brown, Cleveland	257	1,527	5.9	17
1957	*Jim Brown, Cleveland	202	942	4.7	9
1956	Rick Casares, Chi. Bears	234	1,126	4.8	12
1955	*Alan Ameche, Baltimore	213	961	4.5	9
1954	Joe Perry, San Francisco	173	1,049	6.1	8
1953	Joe Perry, San Francisco	192	1,018	5.3	10
1952	Dan Towler, Los Angeles	156	894	5.7	10
1951	Eddie Price, N.Y. Giants	271	971	3.6	7
1950	*Marion Motley, Cleveland	140	810	5.8	3
1949	Steve Van Buren, Philadelphia	263	1,146	4.4	11
1948	Steve Van Buren, Philadelphia	201	945	4.7	10
1947	Steve Van Buren, Philadelphia	217	1,008	4.6	13
1946	Bill Dudley, Pittsburgh	146	604	4.1	3
1945	Steve Van Buren, Philadelphia	143	832	5.8	15
1944	Bill Paschal, N.Y. Giants	196	737	3.8	9
1943	*Bill Paschal, N.Y. Giants	147	572	3.9	10
1942	*Bill Dudley, Pittsburgh	162	696	4.3	5
1941	Clarence (Pug) Manders, Brooklyn	111	486	4.4	5
1940	Byron (Whizzer) White, Detroit	146	514	3.5	5
1939	*Bill Osmanski, Chicago	121	699	5.8	7
1938	*Byron (Whizzer) White, Pittsburgh	152	567	3.7	4
1937	Cliff Battles, Washington	216	874	4.0	5
1936	*Alphonse (Tuffy) Leemans, N.Y. Giants	206	830	4.0	2
1935	Doug Russell, Chi. Cardinals	140	499	3.6	0
1934	*Beattie Feathers, Chi. Bears	101	1,004	9.9	8
1933	Jim Musick, Boston	173	809	4.7	5
1932	*Cliff Battles, Boston	148	576	3.9	3

**First year in the league.*

ANNUAL PASSING LEADERS

Year	Player, Team	Att.	Comp.	Yards	TD	Int.
1985	Ken O'Brien, N.Y. Jets, AFC	488	297	3,888	25	8
	Joe Montana, San Francisco, NFC	494	303	3,653	27	13
1984	Dan Marino, Miami, AFC	564	362	5,084	48	17
	Joe Montana, San Francisco, NFC	432	279	3,630	28	10
1983	Steve Bartkowski, Atlanta, NFC	432	274	3,167	22	5
	*Dan Marino, Miami, AFC	296	173	2,210	20	6
1982	Ken Anderson, Cincinnati, AFC	309	218	2,495	12	9
	Joe Theismann, Washington, NFC	252	161	2,033	13	9
1981	Ken Anderson, Cincinnati, AFC	479	300	3,754	29	10
	Joe Montana, San Francisco, NFC	488	311	3,565	19	12
1980	Brian Sipe, Cleveland, AFC	554	337	4,132	30	14
	Ron Jaworski, Philadelphia, NFC	451	257	3,529	27	12
1979	Roger Staubach, Dallas, NFC	461	267	3,586	27	11
	Dan Fouts, San Diego, AFC	530	332	4,082	24	24
1978	Roger Staubach, Dallas, NFC	413	231	3,190	25	16
	Terry Bradshaw, Pittsburgh, AFC	368	207	2,915	28	20
1977	Bob Griese, Miami, AFC	307	180	2,252	22	13
	Roger Staubach, Dallas, NFC	361	210	2,620	18	9
1976	Ken Stabler, Oakland, AFC	291	194	2,737	27	17
	James Harris, Los Angeles, NFC	158	91	1,460	8	6
1975	Ken Anderson, Cincinnati, AFC	377	228	3,169	21	11
	Fran Tarkenton, Minnesota, NFC	425	273	2,994	25	13
1974	Ken Anderson, Cincinnati, AFC	328	213	2,667	18	10
	Sonny Jurgensen, Washington, NFC	167	107	1,185	11	5
1973	Roger Staubach, Dallas, NFC	286	179	2,428	23	15
	Ken Stabler, Oakland, AFC	260	163	1,997	14	10
1972	Norm Snead, N.Y. Giants, NFC	325	196	2,307	17	12
	Earl Morrall, Miami, AFC	150	83	1,360	11	7
1971	Roger Staubach, Dallas, NFC	211	126	1,882	15	4
	Bob Griese, Miami, AFC	263	145	2,089	19	9
1970	John Brodie, San Francisco, NFC	378	223	2,941	24	10
	Daryle Lamonica, Oakland, AFC	356	179	2,516	22	15
1969	Sonny Jurgensen, Washington, NFL	442	274	3,102	22	15
	*Greg Cook, Cincinnati, AFL	197	106	1,854	15	11
1968	Len Dawson, Kansas City, AFL	224	131	2,109	17	9
	Earl Morrall, Baltimore, NFL	317	182	2,909	26	17
1967	Sonny Jurgensen, Washington, NFL	508	288	3,747	31	16
	Daryle Lamonica, Oakland, AFL	425	220	3,228	30	20
1966	Bart Starr, Green Bay, NFL	251	156	2,257	14	3
	Len Dawson, Kansas City, AFL	284	159	2,527	26	10
1965	Rudy Bukich, Chicago, NFL	312	176	2,641	20	9
	John Hadl, San Diego, AFL	348	174	2,798	20	21
1964	Len Dawson, Kansas City, AFL	354	199	2,879	30	18
	Bart Starr, Green Bay, NFL	272	163	2,144	15	4
1963	Y.A. Tittle, N.Y. Giants, NFL	367	221	3,145	36	14
	Tobin Rote, San Diego, AFL	286	170	2,510	20	17
1962	Len Dawson, Dall. Texans, AFL	310	189	2,759	29	17
	Bart Starr, Green Bay, NFL	285	178	2,438	12	9
1961	George Blanda, Houston, AFL	362	187	3,330	36	22
	Milt Plum, Cleveland, NFL	302	177	2,416	18	10
1960	Milt Plum, Cleveland, NFL	250	151	2,297	21	5
	Jack Kemp, L.A. Chargers, AFL	406	211	3,018	20	25
1959	Charlie Conerly, N.Y. Giants	194	113	1,706	14	4
1958	Eddie LeBaron, Washington	145	79	1,365	11	10
1957	Tommy O'Connell, Cleveland	110	63	1,229	9	8
1956	Ed Brown, Chi. Bears	168	96	1,667	11	12
1955	Otto Graham, Cleveland	185	98	1,721	15	8
1954	Norm Van Brocklin, Los Angeles	260	139	2,637	13	21
1953	Otto Graham, Cleveland	258	167	2,722	11	9
1952	Norm Van Brocklin, Los Angeles	205	113	1,736	14	17
1951	Bob Waterfield, Los Angeles	176	88	1,566	13	10
1950	Norm Van Brocklin, Los Angeles	233	127	2,061	18	14
1949	Sammy Baugh, Washington	255	145	1,903	18	14
1948	Tommy Thompson, Philadelphia	246	141	1,965	25	11
1947	Sammy Baugh, Washington	354	210	2,938	25	15
1946	Bob Waterfield, Los Angeles	251	127	1,747	18	17
1945	Sammy Baugh, Washington	182	128	1,669	11	4
	Sid Luckman, Chi. Bears	217	117	1,725	14	10
1944	Frank Filchock, Washington	147	84	1,139	13	9
1943	Sammy Baugh, Washington	239	133	1,754	23	19
1942	Cecil Isbell, Green Bay	268	146	2,021	24	14
1941	Cecil Isbell, Green Bay	206	117	1,479	15	11
1940	Sammy Baugh, Washington	177	111	1,367	12	10
1939	*Parker Hall, Cleveland	208	106	1,227	9	13
1938	Ed Danowski, N.Y. Giants	129	70	848	7	8
1937	*Sammy Baugh, Washington	171	81	1,127	8	14
1936	Arnie Herber, Green Bay	173	77	1,239	11	13
1935	Ed Danowski, N.Y. Giants	113	57	794	10	9
1934	Arnie Herber, Green Bay	115	42	799	8	12
1933	*Harry Newman, N.Y. Giants	136	53	973	11	17
1932	Arnie Herber, Green Bay	101	37	639	9	9

**First year in the league.*

ANNUAL PASS RECEIVING LEADERS

Year	Player, Team	No.	Yards	Avg.	TD
1985	Roger Craig, San Francisco, NFC	92	1,016	11.0	6
	Lionel James, San Diego, AFC	86	1,027	11.9	6
1984	Art Monk, Washington, NFC	106	1,372	12.9	7
	Ozzie Newsome, Cleveland, AFC	89	1,001	11.2	5
1983	Todd Christensen, L.A. Raiders, AFC	92	1,247	13.6	12
	Roy Green, St. Louis, NFC	78	1,227	15.7	14
	Charlie Brown, Washington, NFC	78	1,225	15.7	8
	Earnest Gray, N.Y. Giants, NFC	78	1,139	14.6	5
1982	Dwight Clark, San Francisco, NFC	60	913	15.2	5
	Kellen Winslow, San Diego, AFC	54	721	13.4	6
1981	Kellen Winslow, San Diego, AFC	88	1,075	12.2	10
	Dwight Clark, San Francisco, NFC	85	1,105	13.0	4
1980	Kellen Winslow, San Diego, AFC	89	1,290	14.5	9
	*Earl Cooper, San Francisco, NFC	83	567	6.8	4
1979	Joe Washington, Baltimore, AFC	82	750	9.1	3
	Ahmad Rashad, Minnesota, NFC	80	1,156	14.5	9
1978	Rickey Young, Minnesota, NFC	88	704	8.0	5
	Steve Largent, Seattle, AFC	71	1,168	16.5	8
1977	Lydell Mitchell, Baltimore, AFC	71	620	8.7	4
	Ahmad Rashad, Minnesota, NFC	51	681	13.4	2
1976	MacArthur Lane, Kansas City, AFC	66	686	10.4	1
	Drew Pearson, Dallas, NFC	58	806	13.9	6
1975	Chuck Foreman, Minnesota, NFC	73	691	9.5	9
	Reggie Rucker, Cleveland, AFC	60	770	12.8	3
	Lydell Mitchell, Baltimore, AFC	60	544	9.1	4
1974	Lydell Mitchell, Baltimore, AFC	72	544	7.6	2
	Charles Young, Philadelphia, NFC	63	696	11.0	3
1973	Harold Carmichael, Philadelphia, NFC	67	1,116	16.7	9
	Fred Willis, Houston, AFC	57	371	6.5	1
1972	Harold Jackson, Philadelphia, NFC	62	1,048	16.9	4
	Fred Biletnikoff, Oakland, AFC	58	802	13.8	7
1971	Fred Biletnikoff, Oakland, AFC	61	929	15.2	9
	Bob Tucker, N.Y. Giants, NFC	59	791	13.4	4
1970	Dick Gordon, Chicago, NFC	71	1,026	14.5	13
	Marlin Briscoe, Buffalo, AFC	57	1,036	18.2	8
1969	Dan Abramowicz, New Orleans, NFL	73	1,015	13.9	7
	Lance Alworth, San Diego, AFL	64	1,003	15.7	4
1968	Clifton McNeil, San Francisco, NFL	71	994	14.0	7
	Lance Alworth, San Diego, AFL	68	1,312	19.3	10
1967	George Sauer, N.Y. Jets, AFL	75	1,189	15.9	6
	Charley Taylor, Washington, NFL	70	990	14.1	9
1966	Lance Alworth, San Diego, AFL	73	1,383	18.9	13
	Charley Taylor, Washington, NFL	72	1,119	15.5	12
1965	Lionel Taylor, Denver, AFL	85	1,131	13.3	6
	Dave Parks, San Francisco, NFL	80	1,344	16.8	12

Year	Player, Team	No.	Yards	Avg.	TD
1964	Charley Hennigan, Houston, AFL	101	1,546	15.3	8
	Johnny Morris, Chicago, NFL	93	1,200	12.9	10
1963	Lionel Taylor, Denver, AFL	78	1,101	14.1	10
	Bobby Joe Conrad, St. Louis, NFL	73	967	13.2	10
1962	Lionel Taylor, Denver, AFL	77	908	11.8	4
	Bobby Mitchell, Washington, NFL	72	1,384	19.2	11
1961	Lionel Taylor, Denver, AFL	100	1,176	11.8	4
	Jim (Red) Phillips, Los Angeles, NFL	78	1,092	14.0	5
1960	Lionel Taylor, Denver, AFL	92	1,235	13.4	12
	Raymond Berry, Baltimore, NFL	74	1,298	17.5	10
1959	Raymond Berry, Baltimore	66	959	14.5	14
1958	Raymond Berry, Baltimore	56	794	14.2	9
	Pete Retzlaff, Philadelphia	56	766	13.7	2
1957	Billy Wilson, San Francisco	52	757	14.6	6
1956	Billy Wilson, San Francisco	60	889	14.8	5
1955	Pete Pihos, Philadelphia	62	864	13.9	7
1954	Pete Pihos, Philadelphia	60	872	14.5	10
	Billy Wilson, San Francisco	60	830	13.8	5
1953	Pete Pihos, Philadelphia	63	1,049	16.7	10
1952	Mac Speedie, Cleveland	62	911	14.7	5
1951	Elroy (Crazylegs) Hirsch, Los Angeles	66	1,495	22.7	17
1950	Tom Fears, Los Angeles	84	1,116	13.3	7
1949	Tom Fears, Los Angeles	77	1,013	13.2	9
1948	*Tom Fears, Los Angeles	51	698	13.7	4
1947	Jim Keane, Chi. Bears	64	910	14.2	10
1946	Jim Benton, Los Angeles	63	981	15.6	6
1945	Don Hutson, Green Bay	47	834	17.7	9
1944	Don Hutson, Green Bay	58	866	14.9	9
1943	Don Hutson, Green Bay	47	776	16.5	11
1942	Don Hutson, Green Bay	74	1,211	16.4	17
1941	Don Hutson, Green Bay	58	738	12.7	10
1940	*Don Looney, Philadelphia	58	707	12.2	4
1939	Don Hutson, Green Bay	34	846	24.9	6
1938	Gaynell Tinsley, Chi. Cardinals	41	516	12.6	1
1937	Don Hutson, Green Bay	41	552	13.5	7
1936	Don Hutson, Green Bay	34	536	15.8	8
1935	*Tod Goodwin, N.Y. Giants	26	432	16.6	4
1934	Joe Carter, Philadelphia	16	238	14.9	4
	Morris (Red) Badgro, N.Y. Giants	16	206	12.9	1
1933	John (Shipwreck) Kelly, Brooklyn	22	246	11.2	3
1932	Ray Flaherty, N.Y. Giants	21	350	16.7	3

*First year in the league.

ANNUAL INTERCEPTION LEADERS

Year	Player, Team	No.	Yards	TD
1985	Everson Walls, Dallas, NFC	9	31	0
	Albert Lewis, Kansas City, AFC	8	59	0
	Eugene Daniel, Indianapolis, AFC	8	53	0
1984	Ken Easley, Seattle, AFC	10	126	2
	*Tom Flynn, Green Bay, NFC	9	106	0
1983	Mark Murphy, Washington, NFC	9	127	0
	Ken Riley, Cincinnati, AFC	8	89	2
	Vann McElroy, L.A. Raiders, AFC	8	68	0
1982	Everson Walls, Dallas, NFC	7	61	0
	Ken Riley, Cincinnati, AFC	5	88	1
	Bobby Jackson, N.Y. Jets, AFC	5	84	1
	Dwayne Woodruff, Pittsburgh, AFC	5	53	0
	Donnie Shell, Pittsburgh, AFC	5	27	0
1981	*Everson Walls, Dallas, NFC	11	133	0
	John Harris, Seattle, AFC	10	155	2
1980	Lester Hayes, Oakland, AFC	13	273	1
	Nolan Cromwell, Los Angeles, NFC	8	140	1
1979	Mike Reinfeldt, Houston, AFC	12	205	0
	Lemar Parrish, Washington, NFC	9	65	0
1978	Thom Darden, Cleveland, AFC	10	200	0
	Ken Stone, St. Louis, NFC	9	139	0
	Willie Buchanon, Green Bay, NFC	9	93	1
1977	Lyle Blackwood, Baltimore, AFC	10	163	0
	Rolland Lawrence, Atlanta, NFC	7	138	0
1976	Monte Jackson, Los Angeles, NFC	10	173	3
	Ken Riley, Cincinnati, AFC	9	141	1
1975	Mel Blount, Pittsburgh, AFC	11	121	0
	Paul Krause, Minnesota, NFC	10	201	0
1974	Emmitt Thomas, Kansas City, AFC	12	214	2
	Ray Brown, Atlanta, NFC	8	164	1
1973	Dick Anderson, Miami, AFC	8	163	2
	Mike Wagner, Pittsburgh, AFC	8	134	0
	Bobby Bryant, Minnesota, NFC	7	105	1
1972	Bill Bradley, Philadelphia, NFC	9	73	0
	Mike Sensibaugh, Kansas City, AFC	8	65	0
1971	Bill Bradley, Philadelphia, NFC	11	248	0
	Ken Houston, Houston, AFC	9	220	4
1970	Johnny Robinson, Kansas City, AFC	10	155	0
	Dick LeBeau, Detroit, NFC	9	96	0
1969	Mel Renfro, Dallas, NFL	10	118	0
	Emmitt Thomas, Kansas City, AFL	9	146	1
1968	Dave Grayson, Oakland, AFL	10	195	1
	Willie Williams, N.Y. Giants, NFL	10	103	0
1967	Miller Farr, Houston, AFL	10	264	3
	*Lem Barney, Detroit, NFL	10	232	3
	Tom Janik, Buffalo, AFL	10	222	2
	Dave Whitsell, New Orleans, NFL	10	178	2
	Dick Westmoreland, Miami, AFL	10	127	1
1966	Larry Wilson, St. Louis, NFL	10	180	2
	Johnny Robinson, Kansas City, AFL	10	136	1
	Bobby Hunt, Kansas City, AFL	10	113	0
1965	W.K. Hicks, Houston, AFL	9	156	0
	Bobby Boyd, Baltimore, NFL	9	78	1
1964	Dainard Paulson, N.Y. Jets, AFL	12	157	1
	*Paul Krause, Washington, NFL	12	140	1
1963	Fred Glick, Houston, AFL	12	180	1
	Dick Lynch, N.Y. Giants, NFL	9	251	3
	Roosevelt Taylor, Chicago, NFL	9	172	1
1962	Lee Riley, N.Y. Titans, AFL	11	122	0
	Willie Wood, Green Bay, NFL	9	132	0
1961	Billy Atkins, Buffalo, AFL	10	158	0
	Dick Lynch, N.Y. Giants, NFL	9	60	0
1960	*Austin (Goose) Gonsoulin, Denver, AFL	11	98	0
	Dave Baker, San Francisco, NFL	10	96	0
	Jerry Norton, St. Louis, NFL	10	96	0
1959	Dean Derby, Pittsburgh	7	127	0
	Milt Davis, Baltimore	7	119	1
	Don Shinnick, Baltimore	7	70	0
1958	Jim Patton, N.Y. Giants	11	183	0
1957	*Milt Davis, Baltimore	10	219	2
	Jack Christiansen, Detroit	10	137	1
	Jack Butler, Pittsburgh	10	85	0
1956	Lindon Crow, Chi. Cardinals	11	170	0
1955	Will Sherman, Los Angeles	11	101	0
1954	Dick (Night Train) Lane, Chi. Cardinals	10	181	0
1953	Jack Christiansen, Detroit	12	238	1
1952	*Dick (Night Train) Lane, Los Angeles	14	298	2
1951	Otto Schnellbacher, N.Y. Giants	11	194	2
1950	*Orban (Spec) Sanders, N.Y. Yanks	13	199	0
1949	Bob Nussbaumer, Chi. Cardinals	12	157	0
1948	*Dan Sandifer, Washington	13	258	2
1947	Frank Reagan, N.Y. Giants	10	203	0
	Frank Seno, Boston	10	100	0
1946	Bill Dudley, Pittsburgh	10	242	1
1945	Roy Zimmerman, Philadelphia	7	90	0
1944	*Howard Livingston, N.Y. Giants	9	172	1
1943	Sammy Baugh, Washington	11	112	0
1942	Clyde (Bulldog) Turner, Chi. Bears	8	96	1
1941	Marshall Goldberg, Chi. Cardinals	7	54	0
	*Art Jones, Pittsburgh	7	35	0
1940	Clarence (Ace) Parker, Brooklyn	6	146	1
	Kent Ryan, Detroit	6	65	0
	Don Hutson, Green Bay	6	24	0

*First year in the league.

ANNUAL PUNTING LEADERS

Year	Player, Team	No.	Avg.	Long
1985	Rohn Stark, Indianapolis, AFC	78	45.9	68
	*Rick Donnelly, Atlanta, NFC	59	43.6	68
1984	Jim Arnold, Kansas City, AFC	98	44.9	63
	*Brian Hansen, New Orleans, NFC	69	43.8	66
1983	Rohn Stark, Baltimore, AFC	91	45.3	68
	*Frank Garcia, Tampa Bay, NFC	95	42.2	64
1982	Luke Prestridge, Denver, AFC	45	45.0	65
	Carl Birdsong, St. Louis, NFC	54	43.8	65
1981	Pat McInally, Cincinnati, AFC	72	45.4	62
	Tom Skladany, Detroit, NFC	64	43.5	74
1980	Dave Jennings, N.Y. Giants, NFC	94	44.8	63
	Luke Prestridge, Denver, AFC	70	43.9	57
1979	*Bob Grupp, Kansas City, AFC	89	43.6	74
	Dave Jennings, N.Y. Giants, NFC	104	42.7	72
1978	Pat McInally, Cincinnati, AFC	91	43.1	65
	*Tom Skladany, Detroit, NFC	86	42.5	63
1977	Ray Guy, Oakland, AFC	59	43.3	74
	Tom Blanchard, New Orleans, NFC	82	42.4	66
1976	Marv Bateman, Buffalo, AFC	86	42.8	78
	John James, Atlanta, NFC	101	42.1	67
1975	Ray Guy, Oakland, AFC	68	43.8	64
	Herman Weaver, Detroit, NFC	80	42.0	61
1974	Ray Guy, Oakland, AFC	74	42.2	66
	Tom Blanchard, New Orleans, NFC	88	42.1	71
1973	Jerrel Wilson, Kansas City, AFC	80	45.5	68
	*Tom Wittum, San Francisco, NFC	79	43.7	62
1972	Jerrel Wilson, Kansas City, AFC	66	44.8	69
	Dave Chapple, Los Angeles, NFC	53	44.2	70
1971	Dave Lewis, Cincinnati, AFC	72	44.8	56
	Tom McNeill, Philadelphia, NFC	73	42.0	64
1970	*Dave Lewis, Cincinnati, AFC	79	46.2	63
	*Julian Fagan, New Orleans, NFC	77	42.5	64
1969	David Lee, Baltimore, NFL	57	45.3	66
	Dennis Partee, San Diego, AFL	71	44.6	62
1968	Jerrel Wilson, Kansas City, AFL	63	45.1	70
	Billy Lothridge, Atlanta, NFL	75	44.3	70
1967	Bob Scarpitto, Denver, AFL	105	44.9	73
	Billy Lothridge, Atlanta, NFL	87	43.7	62
1966	Bob Scarpitto, Denver, AFL	76	45.8	70
	*David Lee, Baltimore, NFL	49	45.6	64
1965	Gary Collins, Cleveland, NFL	65	46.7	71
	Jerrel Wilson, Kansas City, AFL	69	45.4	64
1964	*Bobby Walden, Minnesota, NFL	72	46.4	73
	Jim Fraser, Denver, AFL	73	44.2	67
1963	Yale Lary, Detroit, NFL	35	48.9	73
	Jim Fraser, Denver, AFL	81	44.4	66
1962	Tommy Davis, San Francisco, NFL	48	45.6	82
	Jim Fraser, Denver, AFL	55	43.6	75
1961	Yale Lary, Detroit, NFL	52	48.4	71
	Billy Atkins, Buffalo, AFL	85	44.5	70
1960	Jerry Norton, St. Louis, NFL	39	45.6	62
	*Paul Maguire, L.A. Chargers, AFL	43	40.5	61
1959	Yale Lary, Detroit	45	47.1	67
1958	Sam Baker, Washington	48	45.4	64
1957	Don Chandler, N.Y. Giants	60	44.6	61
1956	Norm Van Brocklin, Los Angeles	48	43.1	72
1955	Norm Van Brocklin, Los Angeles	60	44.6	61
1954	Pat Brady, Pittsburgh	66	43.2	72
1953	Pat Brady, Pittsburgh	80	46.9	64
1952	Horace Gillom, Cleveland	61	45.7	73
1951	Horace Gillom, Cleveland	73	45.5	66
1950	*Fred (Curly) Morrison, Chi. Bears	57	43.3	65
1949	*Mike Boyda, N.Y. Bulldogs	56	44.2	61
1948	Joe Muha, Philadelphia	57	47.3	82

1947	Jack Jacobs, Green Bay	57	43.5	74
1946	Roy McKay, Green Bay	64	42.7	64
1945	Roy McKay, Green Bay	44	41.2	73
1944	Frank Sinkwich, Detroit	45	41.0	73
1943	Sammy Baugh, Washington	50	45.9	81
1942	Sammy Baugh, Washington	37	48.2	74
1941	Sammy Baugh, Washington	30	48.7	75
1940	Sammy Baugh, Washington	35	51.4	85
1939	*Parker Hall, Cleveland	58	40.8	80

First year in the league.

ANNUAL PUNT RETURN LEADERS

Year	Player, Team	No.	Yards	Avg.	Long	TD
1985	Irving Fryar, New England, AFC	37	520	14.1	85	2
	Henry Ellard, L.A. Rams, NFC	37	501	13.5	80	1
1984	Mike Martin, Cincinnati, AFC	24	376	15.7	55	0
	Henry Ellard, L.A. Rams, NFC	30	403	13.4	83	2
1983	*Henry Ellard, L.A. Rams, NFC	16	217	13.6	72	1
	Kirk Springs, N.Y. Jets, AFC	23	287	12.5	76	1
1982	Rick Upchurch, Denver, AFC	15	242	16.1	78	2
	Billy Johnson, Atlanta, NFC	24	273	11.4	71	0
1981	LeRoy Irvin, Los Angeles, NFC	46	615	13.4	84	3
	*James Brooks, San Diego, AFC	22	290	13.2	42	0
1980	J. T. Smith, Kansas City, AFC	40	581	14.5	75	2
	*Kenny Johnson, Atlanta, NFC	23	281	12.2	56	0
1979	John Sciarra, Philadelphia, NFC	16	182	11.4	38	0
	*Tony Nathan, Miami, AFC	28	306	10.9	86	1
1978	Rick Upchurch, Denver, AFC	36	493	13.7	75	1
	Jackie Wallace, Los Angeles, NFC	52	618	11.9	58	0
1977	Billy Johnson, Houston, AFC	35	539	15.4	87	2
	Larry Marshall, Philadelphia, NFC	46	489	10.6	48	0
1976	Rick Upchurch, Denver, AFC	39	536	13.7	92	4
	Eddie Brown, Washington, NFC	48	646	13.5	71	1
1975	Billy Johnson, Houston, AFC	40	612	15.3	83	3
	Terry Metcalf, St. Louis, NFC	23	285	12.4	69	1
1974	Lemar Parrish, Cincinnati, AFC	18	338	18.8	90	2
	Dick Jauron, Detroit, NFC	17	286	16.8	58	0
1973	Bruce Taylor, San Francisco, NFC	15	207	13.8	61	0
	Ron Smith, San Diego, AFC	27	352	13.0	84	2
1972	*Ken Ellis, Green Bay, NFC	14	215	15.4	80	1
	Chris Farasopoulos, N.Y. Jets, AFC	17	179	10.5	65	1
1971	Les (Speedy) Duncan, Washington, NFC	22	233	10.6	33	0
	Leroy Kelly, Cleveland, AFC	30	292	9.7	74	0
1970	Ed Podolak, Kansas City, AFC	23	311	13.5	60	0
	*Bruce Taylor, San Francisco, NFC	43	516	12.0	76	0
1969	Alvin Haymond, Los Angeles, NFL	33	435	13.2	52	0
	*Bill Thompson, Denver, AFL	25	288	11.5	40	0
1968	Bob Hayes, Dallas, NFL	15	312	20.8	90	2
	Noland Smith, Kansas City, AFL	18	270	15.0	80	1
1967	Floyd Little, Denver, AFL	16	270	16.9	72	1
	Ben Davis, Cleveland, NFL	18	229	12.7	52	1
1966	Les (Speedy) Duncan, San Diego, AFL	18	238	13.2	81	1
	Johnny Roland, St. Louis, NFL	20	221	11.1	86	1
1965	Leroy Kelly, Cleveland, NFL	17	265	15.6	67	2
	Les (Speedy) Duncan, San Diego, AFL	30	464	15.5	66	2
1964	Bobby Jancik, Houston, AFL	12	220	18.3	82	1
	Tommy Watkins, Detroit, NFL	16	238	14.9	68	2
1963	Dick James, Washington, NFL	16	214	13.4	39	0
	Claude (Hoot) Gibson, Oakland, AFL	26	307	11.8	85	2
1962	Dick Christy, N.Y. Titans, AFL	15	250	16.7	73	2
	Pat Studstill, Detroit, NFL	29	457	15.8	44	0
1961	Dick Christy, N.Y. Titans, AFL	18	383	21.3	70	2
	Willie Wood, Green Bay, NFL	14	225	16.1	72	2
1960	*Abner Haynes, Dall. Texans, AFL	14	215	15.4	46	0
	Abe Woodson, San Francisco, NFL	13	174	13.4	48	0
1959	Johnny Morris, Chi. Bears	14	171	12.2	78	1
1958	Jon Arnett, Los Angeles	18	223	12.4	58	0
1957	Bert Zagers, Washington	14	217	15.5	76	2
1956	Ken Konz, Cleveland	13	187	14.4	65	1
1955	Ollie Matson, Chi. Cardinals	13	245	18.8	78	2
1954	*Veryl Switzer, Green Bay	24	306	12.8	93	1
1953	Charley Trippi, Chi. Cardinals	21	239	11.4	38	0
1952	Jack Christiansen, Detroit	15	322	21.5	79	2
1951	Claude (Buddy) Young, N.Y. Yanks	12	231	19.3	79	1
1950	*Herb Rich, Baltimore	12	276	23.0	86	1
1949	Verda (Vitamin T) Smith, Los Angeles	27	427	15.8	85	1
1948	George McAfee, Chi. Bears	30	417	13.9	60	1
1947	*Walt Slater, Pittsburgh	28	435	15.5	33	0
1946	Bill Dudley, Pittsburgh	27	385	14.3	52	0
1945	*Dave Ryan, Detroit	15	220	14.7	56	0
1944	*Steve Van Buren, Philadelphia	15	230	15.3	55	1
1943	Andy Farkas, Washington	15	168	11.2	33	0
1942	Merlyn Condit, Brooklyn	21	210	10.0	23	0
1941	Byron (Whizzer) White, Detroit	19	262	13.8	64	0

First year in the league.

ANNUAL KICKOFF RETURN LEADERS

Year	Player, Team	No.	Yards	Avg.	Long	TD
1985	Ron Brown, L.A. Rams, NFC	28	918	32.8	98	3
	Glen Young, Cleveland, AFC	35	898	25.7	63	0
1984	*Bobby Humphery, N.Y. Jets, AFC	22	675	30.7	97	1
	Barry Redden, L.A. Rams, NFC	23	530	23.0	40	0
1983	Fulton Walker, Miami, AFC	36	962	26.7	78	0
	Darrin Nelson, Minnesota, NFC	18	445	24.7	50	0
1982	*Mike Mosley, Buffalo, AFC	18	487	27.1	66	0
	Alvin Hall, Detroit, NFC	16	426	26.6	96	1
1981	Mike Nelms, Washington, NFC	37	1,099	29.7	84	0
	Carl Roaches, Houston, AFC	28	769	27.5	96	1
1980	Horace Ivory, New England, AFC	36	992	27.6	98	1
	Rich Mauti, New Orleans, NFC	31	798	25.7	52	0
1979	Larry Brunson, Oakland, AFC	17	441	25.9	89	0
	*Jimmy Edwards, Minnesota, NFC	44	1,103	25.1	83	0
1978	Steve Odom, Green Bay, NFC	25	677	27.1	95	1
	*Keith Wright, Cleveland, AFC	30	789	26.3	86	0
1977	*Raymond Clayborn, New England, AFC	28	869	31.0	101	3
	*Wilbert Montgomery, Philadelphia, NFC	23	619	26.9	99	1
1976	*Duriel Harris, Miami, AFC	17	559	32.9	69	0
	Cullen Bryant, Los Angeles, NFC	16	459	28.7	90	1
1975	*Walter Payton, Chicago, NFC	14	444	31.7	70	0
	Harold Hart, Oakland, AFC	17	518	30.5	102	1
1974	Terry Metcalf, St. Louis, NFC	20	623	31.2	94	1
	Greg Pruitt, Cleveland, AFC	22	606	27.5	88	1
1973	Carl Garrett, Chicago, NFC	16	486	30.4	67	0
	*Wallace Francis, Buffalo, AFC	23	687	29.9	101	2
1972	Ron Smith, Chicago, NFC	30	924	30.8	94	1
	*Bruce Laird, Baltimore, AFC	29	843	29.1	73	0
1971	Travis Williams, Los Angeles, NFC	25	743	29.7	105	1
	Eugene (Mercury) Morris, Miami, AFC	15	423	28.2	94	1
1970	Jim Duncan, Baltimore, AFC	20	707	35.4	99	1
	Cecil Turner, Chicago, NFC	23	752	32.7	96	4
1969	Bobby Williams, Detroit, NFL	17	563	33.1	96	1
	*Bill Thompson, Denver, AFL	18	513	28.5	63	0
1968	Preston Pearson, Baltimore, NFL	15	527	35.1	102	2
	*George Atkinson, Oakland, AFL	32	802	25.1	60	0
1967	*Travis Williams, Green Bay, NFL	18	739	41.1	104	4
	*Zeke Moore, Houston, AFL	14	405	28.9	92	1
1966	Gale Sayers, Chicago, NFL	23	718	31.2	93	2
	*Goldie Sellers, Denver, AFL	19	541	28.5	100	2
1965	Tommy Watkins, Detroit, NFL	17	584	34.4	94	0
	Abner Haynes, Denver, AFL	34	901	26.5	60	0
1964	*Clarence Childs, N.Y. Giants, NFL	34	987	29.0	100	1
	Bo Roberson, Oakland, AFL	36	975	27.1	59	0
1963	Abe Woodson, San Francisco, NFL	29	935	32.2	103	3
	Bobby Jancik, Houston, AFL	45	1,317	29.3	53	0
1962	Abe Woodson, San Francisco, NFL	37	1,157	31.3	79	0
	*Bobby Jancik, Houston, AFL	24	826	30.3	61	0
1961	Dick Bass, Los Angeles, NFL	23	698	30.3	64	0
	*Dave Grayson, Dall. Texans, AFL	16	453	28.3	73	0
1960	*Tom Moore, Green Bay, NFL	12	397	33.1	84	0
	Ken Hall, Houston, AFL	19	594	31.3	104	1
1959	Abe Woodson, San Francisco	13	382	29.4	105	1
1958	Ollie Matson, Chi. Cardinals	14	497	35.5	101	2
1957	*Jon Arnett, Los Angeles	18	504	28.0	98	1
1956	*Tom Wilson, Los Angeles	15	477	31.8	103	1
1955	Al Carmichael, Green Bay	14	418	29.9	100	1
1954	Billy Reynolds, Cleveland	14	413	29.5	51	0
1953	Joe Arenas, San Francisco	16	551	34.4	82	0
1952	Lynn Chandnois, Pittsburgh	17	599	35.2	93	2
1951	Lynn Chandnois, Pittsburgh	12	390	32.5	55	0
1950	Verda (Vitamin T) Smith, Los Angeles	22	742	33.7	97	3
1949	*Don Doll, Detroit	21	536	25.5	56	0
1948	*Joe Scott, N.Y. Giants	20	569	28.5	99	1
1947	Eddie Saenz, Washington	29	797	27.5	94	2
1946	Abe Karnofsky, Boston	21	599	28.5	97	1
1945	Steve Van Buren, Philadelphia	13	373	28.7	98	1
1944	Bob Thurbon, Card-Pitt.	12	291	24.3	55	0
1943	Ken Heineman, Brooklyn	16	444	27.8	69	0
1942	Marshall Goldberg, Chi. Cardinals	15	393	26.2	95	1
1941	Marshall Goldberg, Chi. Cardinals	12	290	24.2	41	0

First year in the league.

POINTS SCORED

Year	Team	Points
1985	San Diego, AFC	467
	Chicago, NFC	456
1984	Miami, AFC	513
	San Francisco, NFC	475
1983	Washington, NFC	541
	L.A. Raiders, AFC	442
1982	San Diego, AFC	288
	Dallas, NFC	226
	Green Bay, NFC	226
1981	San Diego, AFC	478
	Atlanta, NFC	426
1980	Dallas, NFC	454
	New England, AFC	441
1979	Pittsburgh, AFC	416
	Dallas, NFC	371
1978	Dallas, NFC	384
	Miami, AFC	372
1977	Oakland, AFC	351
	Dallas, NFC	345
1976	Baltimore, AFC	417
	Los Angeles, NFC	351
1975	Buffalo, AFC	420
	Minnesota, NFC	377
1974	Oakland, AFC	355
	Washington, NFC	320
1973	Los Angeles, NFC	388
	Denver, AFC	354
1972	Miami, AFC	385
	San Francisco, NFC	353
1971	Dallas, NFC	406
	Oakland, AFC	344
1970	San Francisco, NFC	352
	Baltimore, AFC	321
1969	Minnesota, NFL	379
	Oakland, AFL	377
1968	Oakland, AFL	453
	Dallas, NFL	431
1967	Oakland, AFL	468
	Los Angeles, NFL	398
1966	Kansas City, AFL	448
	Dallas, NFL	445
1965	San Francisco, NFL	421
	San Diego, AFL	340
1964	Baltimore, NFL	428
	Buffalo, AFL	400
1963	N.Y. Giants, NFL	448
	San Diego, AFL	399
1962	Green Bay, NFL	415
	Dall. Texans, AFL	389
1961	Houston, AFL	513
	Green Bay, NFL	391
1960	N.Y. Titans, AFL	382
	Cleveland, NFL	362
1959	Baltimore	374
1958	Baltimore	381
1957	Los Angeles	307
1956	Chi. Bears	363
1955	Cleveland	349
1954	Detroit	337
1953	San Francisco	372
1952	Los Angeles	349
1951	Los Angeles	392
1950	Los Angeles	466
1949	Philadelphia	364
1948	Chi. Cardinals	395
1947	Chi. Bears	363
1946	Chi. Bears	289
1945	Philadelphia	272
1944	Philadelphia	267
1943	Chi. Bears	303
1942	Chi. Bears	376
1941	Chi. Bears	396
1940	Washington	245
1939	Chi. Bears	298
1938	Green Bay	223
1937	Green Bay	220
1936	Green Bay	248
1935	Chi. Bears	192
1934	Chi. Bears	286
1933	N.Y. Giants	244
1932	Green Bay	152

TOTAL YARDS GAINED

Year	Team	Yards
1985	San Diego, AFC	6,535
	San Francisco, NFC	5,920
1984	Miami, AFC	6,936
	San Francisco, NFC	6,366

1983	San Diego, AFC	6,197
	Green Bay, NFC	6,172
1982	San Diego, AFC	4,048
	San Francisco, NFC	3,242
1981	San Diego, AFC	6,744
	Detroit, NFC	5,933
1980	San Diego, AFC	6,410
	Los Angeles, NFC	6,006
1979	Pittsburgh, AFC	6,258
	Dallas, NFC	5,968
1978	New England, AFC	5,965
	Dallas, NFC	5,959
1977	Dallas, NFC	4,812
	Oakland, AFC	4,736
1976	Baltimore, AFC	5,236
	St. Louis, NFC	5,136
1975	Buffalo, AFC	5,467
	Dallas, NFC	5,025
1974	Dallas, NFC	4,983
	Oakland, AFC	4,718
1973	Los Angeles, NFC	4,906
	Oakland, AFC	4,773
1972	Miami, AFC	5,036
	N.Y. Giants, NFC	4,483
1971	Dallas, NFC	5,035
	San Diego, AFC	4,738
1970	Oakland, AFC	4,829
	San Francisco, NFC	4,503
1969	Dallas, NFL	5,122
	Oakland, AFL	5,036
1968	Oakland, AFL	5,696
	Dallas, NFL	5,117
1967	N.Y. Jets, AFL	5,152
	Baltimore, NFL	5,008
1966	Dallas, NFL	5,145
	Kansas City, AFL	5,114
1965	San Francisco, NFL	5,270
	San Diego, AFL	5,188
1964	Buffalo, AFL	5,206
	Baltimore, NFL	4,779
1963	San Diego, AFL	5,153
	N.Y. Giants, NFL	5,024
1962	N.Y. Giants, NFL	5,005
	Houston, AFL	4,971
1961	Houston, AFL	6,288
	Philadelphia, NFL	5,112
1960	Houston, AFL	4,936
	Baltimore, NFL	4,245
1959	Baltimore	4,458
1958	Baltimore	4,539
1957	Los Angeles	4,143
1956	Chi. Bears	4,537
1955	Chi. Bears	4,316
1954	Los Angeles	5,187
1953	Philadelphia	4,811
1952	Cleveland	4,352
1951	Los Angeles	5,506
1950	Los Angeles	5,420
1949	Chi. Bears	4,873
1948	Chi. Cardinals	4,705
1947	Chi. Bears	5,053
1946	Los Angeles	3,793
1945	Washington	3,549
1944	Chi. Bears	3,239
1943	Chi. Bears	4,045
1942	Chi. Bears	3,900
1941	Chi. Bears	4,265
1940	Green Bay	3,400
1939	Chi. Bears	3,988
1938	Green Bay	3,037
1937	Green Bay	3,201
1936	Detroit	3,703
1935	Chi. Bears	3,454
1934	Chi. Bears	3,900
1933	N.Y. Giants	2,973
1932	Chi. Bears	2,755

YARDS RUSHING

Year	Team	Yards
1985	Chicago, NFC	2,761
	Indianapolis, AFC	2,439
1984	Chicago, NFC	2,974
	N.Y. Jets, AFC	2,189
1983	Chicago, NFC	2,727
	Baltimore, AFC	2,695
1982	Buffalo, AFC	1,371
	Dallas, NFC	1,313
1981	Detroit, NFC	2,795
	Kansas City, AFC	2,633
1980	Los Angeles, NFC	2,799
	Houston, AFC	2,635
1979	N.Y. Jets, AFC	2,646
	St. Louis, NFC	2,582
1978	New England, AFC	3,165
	Dallas, NFC	2,783
1977	Chicago, NFC	2,811
	Oakland, AFC	2,627
1976	Pittsburgh, AFC	2,971
	Los Angeles, NFC	2,528
1975	Buffalo, AFC	2,974
	Dallas, NFC	2,432
1974	Dallas, NFC	2,454
	Pittsburgh, AFC	2,417
1973	Buffalo, AFC	3,088
	Los Angeles, NFC	2,925
1972	Miami, AFC	2,960
	Chicago, NFC	2,360
1971	Miami, AFC	2,429
	Detroit, NFC	2,376
1970	Dallas, NFC	2,300
	Miami, AFC	2,082
1969	Dallas, NFL	2,276
	Kansas City, AFL	2,220
1968	Chicago, NFL	2,377
	Kansas City, AFL	2,227
1967	Cleveland, NFL	2,139
	Houston, AFL	2,122
1966	Kansas City, AFL	2,274
	Cleveland, NFL	2,166
1965	Cleveland, NFL	2,331
	San Diego, AFL	2,085
1964	Green Bay, NFL	2,276
	Buffalo, AFL	2,040
1963	Cleveland, NFL	2,639
	San Diego, AFL	2,203
1962	Buffalo, AFL	2,480
	Green Bay, NFL	2,460
1961	Green Bay, NFL	2,350
	Dall. Texans, AFL	2,189
1960	St. Louis, NFL	2,356
	Oakland, AFL	2,056
1959	Cleveland	2,149
1958	Cleveland	2,526
1957	Los Angeles	2,142
1956	Chi. Bears	2,468
1955	Chi. Bears	2,388
1954	San Francisco	2,498
1953	San Francisco	2,230
1952	San Francisco	1,905
1951	Chi. Bears	2,408
1950	N.Y. Giants	2,336
1949	Philadelphia	2,607
1948	Chi. Cardinals	2,560
1947	Los Angeles	2,171
1946	Green Bay	1,765
1945	Cleveland	1,714
1944	Philadelphia	1,661
1943	Phil-Pitt	1,730
1942	Chi. Bears	1,881
1941	Chi. Bears	2,263
1940	Chi. Bears	1,818
1939	Chi. Bears	2,043
1938	Detroit	1,893
1937	Detroit	2,074
1936	Detroit	2,885
1935	Chi. Bears	2,096
1934	Chi. Bears	2,847
1933	Boston	2,260
1932	Chi. Bears	1,770

YARDS PASSING

Leadership in this category has been based on net yards since 1952.

Year	Team	Yards
1985	San Diego, AFC	4,870
	Dallas, NFC	3,861
1984	Miami, AFC	5,018
	St. Louis, NFC	4,257
1983	San Diego, AFC	4,661
	Green Bay, NFC	4,365
1982	San Diego, AFC	2,927
	San Francisco, NFC	2,502
1981	San Diego, AFC	4,739
	Minnesota, NFC	4,333
1980	San Diego, AFC	4,531
	Minnesota, NFC	3,688
1979	San Diego, AFC	3,915
	San Francisco, NFC	3,641
1978	San Diego, AFC	3,375
	Minnesota, NFC	3,243
1977	Buffalo, AFC	2,530
	St. Louis, NFC	2,499
1976	Baltimore, AFC	2,933
	Minnesota, NFC	2,855
1975	Cincinnati, AFC	3,241
	Washington, NFC	2,917
1974	Washington, NFC	2,978
	Cincinnati, AFC	2,804
1973	Philadelphia, NFC	2,998
	Denver, AFC	2,519
1972	N.Y. Jets, AFC	2,777
	San Francisco, NFC	2,735
1971	San Diego, AFC	3,134
	Dallas, NFC	2,786
1970	San Francisco, NFC	2,923
	Oakland, AFC	2,865
1969	Oakland, AFL	3,271
	San Francisco, NFL	3,158
1968	San Diego, AFL	3,623
	Dallas, NFL	3,026
1967	N.Y. Jets, AFL	3,845
	Washington, NFL	3,730
1966	N.Y. Jets, AFL	3,464
	Dallas, NFL	3,023
1965	San Francisco, NFL	3,487
	San Diego, AFL	3,103
1964	Houston, AFL	3,527
	Chicago, NFL	2,841
1963	Baltimore, NFL	3,296
	Houston, AFL	3,222
1962	Denver, AFL	3,404
	Philadelphia, NFL	3,385
1961	Houston, AFL	4,392
	Philadelphia, NFL	3,605
1960	Houston, AFL	3,203
	Baltimore, NFL	2,956
1959	Baltimore	2,753
1958	Pittsburgh	2,752
1957	Baltimore	2,388
1956	Los Angeles	2,419
1955	Philadelphia	2,472
1954	Chi. Bears	3,104
1953	Philadelphia	3,089
1952	Cleveland	2,566
1951	Los Angeles	3,296
1950	Los Angeles	3,709
1949	Chi. Bears	3,055
1948	Washington	2,861
1947	Washington	3,336
1946	Los Angeles	2,080
1945	Chi. Bears	1,857
1944	Washington	2,021
1943	Chi. Bears	2,310
1942	Green Bay	2,407
1941	Chi. Bears	2,002
1940	Washington	1,887
1939	Chi. Bears	1,965
1938	Washington	1,536
1937	Green Bay	1,398
1936	Green Bay	1,629
1935	Green Bay	1,449
1934	Green Bay	1,165
1933	N.Y. Giants	1,348
1932	Chi. Bears	1,013

FEWEST POINTS ALLOWED

Year	Team	Points
1985	Chicago, NFC	198
	N.Y. Jets, AFC	264
1984	San Francisco, NFC	227
	Denver, AFC	241
1983	Miami, AFC	250
	Detroit, NFC	286
1982	Washington, NFC	128
	Miami, AFC	131
1981	Philadelphia, NFC	221
	Miami, AFC	275
1980	Philadelphia, NFC	222
	Houston, AFC	251
1979	Tampa Bay, NFC	237
	San Diego, AFC	246
1978	Pittsburgh, AFC	195
	Dallas, NFC	208
1977	Atlanta, NFC	129
	Denver, AFC	148
1976	Pittsburgh, AFC	138
	Minnesota, NFC	176
1975	Los Angeles, NFC	135
	Pittsburgh, AFC	162
1974	Los Angeles, NFC	181
	Pittsburgh, AFC	189
1973	Miami, AFC	150
	Minnesota, NFC	168
1972	Miami, AFC	171
	Washington, NFC	218
1971	Minnesota, NFC	139
	Baltimore, AFC	140
1970	Minnesota, NFC	143
	Miami, AFC	228
1969	Minnesota, NFL	133
	Kansas City, AFL	177
1968	Baltimore, NFL	144
	Kansas City, AFL	170
1967	Los Angeles, NFL	196
	Houston, AFL	199
1966	Green Bay, NFL	163
	Buffalo, AFL	255
1965	Green Bay, NFL	224
	Buffalo, AFL	226
1964	Baltimore, NFL	225
	Buffalo, AFL	242
1963	Chicago, NFL	144
	San Diego, AFL	255
1962	Green Bay, NFL	148
	Dall. Texans, AFL	233
1961	San Diego, AFL	219
	N.Y. Giants, NFL	220
1960	San Francisco, NFL	205
	Dall. Texans, AFL	253
1959	N.Y. Giants	170
1958	N.Y. Giants	183
1957	Cleveland	172
1956	Cleveland	177
1955	Cleveland	218
1954	Cleveland	162
1953	Cleveland	162
1952	Detroit	192
1951	Cleveland	152
1950	Philadelphia	141
1949	Philadelphia	134
1948	Chi. Bears	151
1947	Green Bay	210
1946	Pittsburgh	117
1945	Washington	121
1944	N.Y. Giants	75
1943	Washington	137
1942	Chi. Bears	84
1941	N.Y. Giants	114
1940	Brooklyn	120
1939	N.Y. Giants	85
1938	N.Y. Giants	79
1937	Chi. Bears	100
1936	Chi. Bears	94
1935	Green Bay	96
	N.Y. Giants	96
1934	Detroit	59
1933	Brooklyn	54
1932	Chi. Bears	44

FEWEST TOTAL YARDS ALLOWED

Year	Team	Yards
1985	Chicago, NFC	4,135
	L.A. Raiders, AFC	4,603
1984	Chicago, NFC	3,863
	Cleveland, AFC	4,641
1983	Cincinnati, AFC	4,327
	New Orleans, NFC	4,691
1982	Miami, AFC	2,312
	Tampa Bay, NFC	2,442
1981	Philadelphia, NFC	4,447
	N.Y. Jets, AFC	4,871
1980	Buffalo, AFC	4,101
	Philadelphia, NFC	4,443
1979	Tampa Bay, NFC	3,949
	Pittsburgh, AFC	4,270
1978	Los Angeles, NFC	3,893
	Pittsburgh, AFC	4,168
1977	Dallas, NFC	3,213
	New England, AFC	3,638
1976	Pittsburgh, AFC	3,323
	San Francisco, NFC	3,562
1975	Minnesota, NFC	3,153
	Oakland, AFC	3,629
1974	Pittsburgh, AFC	3,074
	Washington, NFC	3,285
1973	Los Angeles, NFC	2,951
	Oakland, AFC	3,160
1972	Miami, AFC	3,297
	Green Bay, NFC	3,474
1971	Baltimore, AFC	2,852
	Minnesota, NFC	3,406
1970	Minnesota, NFC	2,803
	N.Y. Jets, AFC	3,655
1969	Minnesota, NFL	2,720
	Kansas City, AFL	3,163
1968	Los Angeles, NFL	3,118
	N.Y. Jets, AFL	3,363
1967	Oakland, AFL	3,294
	Green Bay, NFL	3,300
1966	St. Louis, NFL	3,492
	Oakland, AFL	3,910
1965	San Diego, AFL	3,262
	Detroit, NFL	3,557
1964	Green Bay, NFL	3,179
	Buffalo, AFL	3,878
1963	Chicago, NFL	3,176
	Boston, AFL	3,834
1962	Detroit, NFL	3,217
	Dall. Texans, AFL	3,951
1961	San Diego, AFL	3,726
	Baltimore, NFL	3,782
1960	St. Louis, NFL	3,029
	Buffalo, AFL	3,866
1959	N.Y. Giants	2,843
1958	Chi. Bears	3,066
1957	Pittsburgh	2,791
1956	N.Y. Giants	3,081
1955	Cleveland	2,841
1954	Cleveland	2,658
1953	Philadelphia	2,998
1952	Cleveland	3,075
1951	N.Y. Giants	3,250
1950	Cleveland	3,154
1949	Philadelphia	2,831
1948	Chi. Bears	2,931
1947	Green Bay	3,396
1946	Washington	2,451
1945	Philadelphia	2,073
1944	Philadelphia	1,943
1943	Chi. Bears	2,262
1942	Chi. Bears	1,703
1941	N.Y. Giants	2,368
1940	N.Y. Giants	2,219
1939	Washington	2,116
1938	N.Y. Giants	2,029
1937	Washington	2,123
1936	Boston	2,181
1935	Boston	1,996
1934	Chi. Cardinals	1,539
1933	Brooklyn	1,789

FEWEST YARDS RUSHING ALLOWED

Year	Team	Yards
1985	Chicago, NFC	1,319
	N.Y. Jets, AFC	1,516
1984	Chicago, NFC	1,377
	Pittsburgh, AFC	1,617
1983	Washington, NFC	1,289
	Cincinnati, AFC	1,499
1982	Pittsburgh, AFC	762
	Detroit, NFC	854
1981	Detroit, NFC	1,623
	Kansas City, AFC	1,747
1980	Detroit, NFC	1,599
	Cincinnati, AFC	1,680
1979	Denver, AFC	1,693
	Tampa Bay, NFC	1,873
1978	Dallas, NFC	1,721
	Pittsburgh, AFC	1,774
1977	Denver, AFC	1,531
	Dallas, NFC	1,651
1976	Pittsburgh, AFC	1,457
	Los Angeles, NFC	1,564
1975	Minnesota, NFC	1,532
	Houston, AFC	1,680
1974	Los Angeles, NFC	1,302
	New England, AFC	1,587
1973	Los Angeles, NFC	1,270
	Oakland, AFC	1,470
1972	Dallas, NFC	1,515
	Miami, AFC	1,548
1971	Baltimore, AFC	1,113
	Dallas, NFC	1,144
1970	Detroit, NFC	1,152
	N.Y. Jets, AFC	1,283
1969	Dallas, NFL	1,050
	Kansas City, AFL	1,091
1968	Dallas, NFL	1,195
	N.Y. Jets, AFL	1,195
1967	Dallas, NFL	1,081
	Oakland, AFL	1,129
1966	Buffalo, AFL	1,051
	Dallas, NFL	1,176
1965	San Diego, AFL	1,094
	Los Angeles, NFL	1,409
1964	Buffalo, AFL	913
	Los Angeles, NFL	1,501
1963	Boston, AFL	1,107
	Chicago, NFL	1,442
1962	Detroit, NFL	1,231
	Dall. Texans, AFL	1,250
1961	Boston, AFL	1,041
	Pittsburgh, NFL	1,463
1960	St. Louis, NFL	1,212
	Dall. Texans, AFL	1,338
1959	N.Y. Giants	1,261
1958	Baltimore	1,291
1957	Baltimore	1,174
1956	N.Y. Giants	1,443
1955	Cleveland	1,189
1954	Cleveland	1,050
1953	Philadelphia	1,117
1952	Detroit	1,145
1951	N.Y. Giants	913
1950	Detroit	1,367
1949	Chi. Bears	1,196
1948	Philadelphia	1,209
1947	Philadelphia	1,329
1946	Chi. Bears	1,060
1945	Philadelphia	817
1944	Philadelphia	558
1943	Phil-Pitt	793
1942	Chi. Bears	519
1941	Washington	1,042
1940	N.Y. Giants	977
1939	Chi. Bears	812
1938	Detroit	1,081
1937	Chi. Bears	933
1936	Boston	1,148
1935	Boston	998
1934	Chi. Cardinals	954
1933	Brooklyn	964
1978	Buffalo, AFC	1,960
	Los Angeles, NFC	2,048
1977	Atlanta, NFC	1,384
	San Diego, AFC	1,725
1976	Minnesota, NFC	1,575
	Cincinnati, AFC	1,758
1975	Minnesota, NFC	1,621
	Cincinnati, AFC	1,729
1974	Pittsburgh, AFC	1,466
	Atlanta, NFC	1,572
1973	Miami, AFC	1,290
	Atlanta, NFC	1,430
1972	Minnesota, NFC	1,699
	Cleveland, AFC	1,736
1971	Atlanta, NFC	1,638
	Baltimore, AFC	1,739
1970	Minnesota, NFC	1,438
	Kansas City, AFC	2,010
1969	Minnesota, NFL	1,631
	Kansas City, AFL	2,072
1968	Houston, AFL	1,671
	Green Bay, NFL	1,796
1967	Green Bay, NFL	1,377
	Buffalo, AFL	1,825
1966	Green Bay, NFL	1,959
	Oakland, AFL	2,118
1965	Green Bay, NFL	1,981
	San Diego, AFL	2,168
1964	Green Bay, NFL	1,647
	San Diego, AFL	2,518
1963	Chicago, NFL	1,734
	Oakland, AFL	2,589
1962	Green Bay, NFL	1,746
	Oakland, AFL	2,306
1961	Baltimore, NFL	1,913
	San Diego, AFL	2,363
1960	Chicago, NFL	1,388
	Buffalo, AFL	2,124
1959	N.Y. Giants	1,582
1958	Chi. Bears	1,769
1957	Cleveland	1,300
1956	Cleveland	1,103
1955	Pittsburgh	1,295
1954	Cleveland	1,608
1953	Washington	1,751
1952	Washington	1,580
1951	Pittsburgh	1,687
1950	Cleveland	1,581
1949	Philadelphia	1,607
1948	Green Bay	1,626
1947	Green Bay	1,790
1946	Pittsburgh	939
1945	Washington	1,121
1944	Chi. Bears	1,052
1943	Chi. Bears	980
1942	Washington	1,093
1941	Pittsburgh	1,168
1940	Philadelphia	1,012
1939	Washington	1,116
1938	Chi. Bears	897
1937	Detroit	804
1936	Philadelphia	853
1935	Chi. Cardinals	793
1934	Philadelphia	545
1933	Portsmouth	558

FEWEST YARDS PASSING ALLOWED

Leadership in this category has been based on net yards since 1952.

Year	Team	Yards
1985	Washington, NFC	2,746
	Pittsburgh, AFC	2,783
1984	New Orleans, NFC	2,453
	Cleveland, AFC	2,696
1983	New Orleans, NFC	2,691
	Cincinnati, AFC	2,828
1982	Miami, AFC	1,027
	Tampa Bay, NFC	1,384
1981	Philadelphia, NFC	2,696
	Buffalo, AFC	2,870
1980	Washington, NFC	2,171
	Buffalo, AFC	2,282
1979	Tampa Bay, NFC	2,076
	Buffalo, AFC	2,530

Index